Spatial Sector Programming Models in Agriculture

Spatial Sector Programming Models in Agriculture

EARL O. HEADY
DISTINGUISHED PROFESSOR OF AGRICULTURE, PROFESSOR OF ECONOMICS, AND DIRECTOR OF THE CENTER FOR AGRICULTURAL AND RURAL DEVELOPMENT, IOWA STATE UNIVERSITY

UMA K. SRIVASTAVA
ASSISTANT PROFESSOR, INDIAN INSTITUTE OF MANAGEMENT, VASTRAPUR, INDIA

IOWA STATE UNIVERSITY PRESS / AMES

Library of Congress Cataloging in Publication Data
Heady, Earl Orel, 1916–
  Spatial sector programming models in agriculture.

  Includes bibliographical references and index.
  1. Agriculture and state—Mathematical models—
Addresses, essays, lectures. I. Srivastava, Uma K.,
joint author. II. Title.
HD1415.H34   338.1'8'0184   74-20873
ISBN 0-8138-1575-4

CONTRIBUTORS

RAY F. BROKKEN is Agricultural Economist, Economic Research Service of the U.S. Department of Agriculture; and Collaborator, Agricultural Economics Department, Oregon State University.

ALVIN C. EGBERT is Senior Economist, The World Bank.

ROGER K. EYVIDSON is Economist, The Canadian Department of Agriculture.

JERRY A. FEDELER is Staff Economist, The Center for Agricultural and Rural Development, Iowa State University.

HARRY H. HALL is Associate Professor of Agricultural Economics and Statistics, University of Kentucky.

STANLEY H. HARGROVE is Project Officer, Management Science Systems, Inc.

WON W. KOO is Graduate Research Assistant, The Center for Agricultural and Rural Development, Iowa State University.

HOWARD C. MADSEN is Staff Economist, The Center for Agricultural and Rural Development, Iowa State University.

KENNETH J. NICOL is Staff Economist, The Center for Agricultural and Rural Development, Iowa State University.

MELVIN D. SKOLD is Deputy Director, Livestock Section, Economic Research Service, U.S. Department of Agriculture.

STEVEN T. SONKA is Research Economist, The Center for Agricultural and Rural Development, Iowa State University.

VINCENT A. SPOSITO is Associate Professor of Statistics, Iowa State University.

ARTHUR L. STOECKER is Staff Economist, The Center for Agricultural and Rural Development, Iowa State University, deputized to the Division of Agricultural Economics, Ministry of Agriculture, Government of Thailand.

NORMAN K. WHITTLESEY is Associate Professor, Washington State University.

CONTENTS

TABLES Appearing
in
Microfiche

PREFACE

SYSTEMATIC agricultural planning on a large and detailed basis has become possible by means of data generally available through use of modern computers and linear economic models that are manageable. Hence, the time in history has arrived when the computer and theoretical bases for large-scale and detailed national plans typically exceed the data that can be provided for these planning tools. This situation contrasts with several previous decades when available data, scanty as they were, exceeded computational ability and theoretical constructs for applying national and interregional planning models in detail.

Prospects for the next two decades are for organizing data collection, generation, storage, and retrieval systems that will allow capitalization, for planning purposes, on computer and theoretical facilities now in existence. In many countries, data systems now are in preparation so that these sector planning models can be applied. In the future it is likely that the majority of countries will be applying agricultural or sector planning models of the type developed and illustrated in this monograph, or those closely related to them. The initial start will need to be made with relatively simple models, with progression to more detailed and sophisticated ones as additional data and model bases are accumulated.

The application of mathematical programming models to agricultural planning, policy, resource use, and spatial analysis reported in this book was initiated in 1955. The progression was from less complex models to extended, more detailed, and more sophisticated ones as data and modeling capabilities proceeded. Certain of the models reported, as well as others under development, incorporate as many as 10,000 equations and 75,000 variables. They include every major commodity and resource area of U. S. agriculture. Models developed in other countries similarly will need to follow a path from the less complex to the more detailed as data and investigational resources allow. The progression of models reported here provides an example of how these developments may take place with time.

The initial models reported in this book were the first ones developed on a detailed, interregional basis for the agriculture of any nation. The modeling was initiated in 1954 and applications began in 1956 as soon as data from the 1955 census became available. While a progression of models has been developed and applied, with some incorporating demand functions and water use as well as land use, even the first ones (or modifications of them) are still in application for specific agricultural policy analysis. The various models, ranging in size and scope of commodities and resources included, can have continuous use in agricultural policy and resource evaluations. Hence, the development and application of detailed spatial programming models for agricultural sector and policy analysis are not discrete tasks. Instead, the models provide continuous activities which can be used as building blocks and for continued use over time. This, in fact, has been the rule for the models reported.

Numerous types of quantitative models can be applied in the analysis of the agricultural sector and its resources, and each one has its advantages for particular types of analyses. However, only programming models allow the detail in analysis reported in this book wherein interest is in specific land and water regions and the individual commodities and technologies specific to these regions. It is for this reason that programming models allow examination of commodity and resource relationships for each one of several hundred producing regions and can be aggregated to reflect national and interregional relationships. Application of these models is beginning in numerous countries and further development can be expected in the future. While the family of programming models summarized in this book was initiated in 1954, several somewhat similar but less detailed models have been initiated in developed countries. The majority of these models are summarized in Chapter 1. Current interest in developing countries is expanding and the authors are in the process of developing and applying similar models in Thailand. Other countries have requested help. The U. S. Agency for International Development is now in the process of providing facilities to help developing countries in applying these models so that their planners will be able to answer the questions of how much, where, and what for as they gauge alternative investment opportunities.

The models and interpretations of their results in the chapters of this book can help the process of model development in other countries and the extension of their use in the United States. The persons listed as authors of the numerous chapters should be looked upon as coauthors of this book. We thus serve largely as editors of the complete volume.

EARL O. HEADY
UMA K. SRIVASTAVA

Spatial Sector Programming Models in Agriculture

Introduction

EARL O. HEADY and UMA K. SRIVASTAVA

Progress in economic modeling and computer capacity now provides powerful and practical means for analysis of and choice among alternatives for agriculture and other sectors. Current modeling capabilities thus allow the construction and operational use of models which encompass and capture both relationships at the national level and detail at area or regional levels. Available models also can incorporate project evaluation and time dimensions with impacts of policies, technologies, market changes, and institutional considerations at national and regional levels.

Extension and refinement of economic models and computer capabilities generally have progressed beyond data availability in the application in sector analysis. These are not, however, phenomena of recent origin. Even in earlier days of digital computers, data typically served as a major restraint in the application of models which allowed simultaneous analysis of national, regional, and project outcomes. This restraint is being relaxed as data banks, budget generators, and statistical collection are being developed, improved, and extended. Also, modeling capabilities now provide incentives and goals for systematic data collection and summary at national, regional, and state levels. While the optimum information system for the agricultural sector is not yet available in any country, data available and being used in informal planning methods and for important policy decisions are generally adaptable to more systematically specified models. Knowledge and decisions typically can be improved if data at any level of completeness and perfection and now being used for planning and policy purposes are integrated into models which are logical in terms of the real world and capable of computer application. Improvements in models and their capacities in allowing analysis of alternatives of the real world then can parallel improvements in the data base. This book reports a sequence of models developed for the U.S. agriculture under these conditions of data availability. Starting from a relatively simple spatial model, subsequent generations of models have been developed and applied as allowed by data availability, research funds, and the need to interpret and use each major set of solutions. The process is still in progress and implied are extensions incorporating dynamic, recursive, nonlinear, stochastic, integer, employment, and equity characteristics. Model development and use in the dimensions of those illustrated are not discrete operations but must progress as restraints in time, data, resources, and experience are lifted.

The models and analyses reported are a selection of those developed and applied by the senior author and his associates over a period of 20 years. A particular sequence is selected for reporting, since parallel steps in progression through generations of models are necessary in many countries where the data base and

3

facilities are now inadequate and models which may be applied currently will serve as infants relative to more mature ones attained over time as environments of agricultural statistics, research personnel, computer facilities, and administrative interests allow.

The family of models reported is mainly of linear programming nature. These models are only one type of a general family being applied at Iowa State University to the micro and macro characteristics of the agricultural sector. Others include various adaptations of regression or econometric and simulation models based on time series, cross sectional, and synthesized data at national, regional, and farm levels. The linear programming models have been employed by every major national commission concerned with agricultural and resource policy over the last dozen years. They have been used especially where the need is to determine impacts of different policy alternatives at both national and regional levels; to evaluate the productivity potentials of the agricultural sector and the nation's land and water resources; to indicate generally "the what and where" as variables at the national level and in international trade have impacts which thread back to individual producing and resource areas; and to reflect interdependencies among regions, technologies, resources, commodities, and policies. These generally are their potentials in application to the agricultural sector composed as it is of complex spatial entities and substitute resources, commodities, structures, and technologies.

The sequence of models reported was initiated in 1955 at the time of the U.S. Census of Agriculture for that year. Due to pressures to complete and report the research, the lack of available data, and limited research funds, the initial model applied only to a few crops and did not incorporate transportation and markets. Subsequent models were extended to incorporate other major crops, livestock products, transportation, domestic and export markets, alternatives in policy, and other characteristics of the nation's agriculture. One generation of models incorporated individual farm and soil groups within regions as well as endogenous determination of resource allocation to both crops and livestock. Another generation was extended to water resources and their reallocation among competing agricultural, industrial, and urban uses. Those currently under development incorporate conservation and environmental possibilities and nonlinear market relationships as well as the more general spatial, interregional, land-use, water allocation, commodity interaction, technological, and policy aspects of agricultural structure and problems.

Since the initiation of these several generations of programming models at Iowa State University, parallel work has been implemented in a number of countries. We review those available to date as a means of placing an inventory of experience and methods before the reader. Only programming models are reviewed since a complete summary of all alternatives in econometric and quantitative methods is not the purpose here. The method selected needs to conform with time and resource pressures, the nature and extent of data available, and the types of problems to be analyzed. Concern here is with models designed to supply both national and regional detail of potentials and policies of agriculture.

BASIS OF SPATIAL PROGRAMMING MODELS

An increasing number of countries have begun application of interregional programming models for agricultural policy formulation and evaluation over the last decade.[1] Interregional relationships in agriculture are important because producing units are spatially distributed. There are regional differences in soil fertility, water resource development, capital availability, and labor supply constraints. Furthermore, there is a lack of resource mobility among regions. These factors cause a differential comparative advantage among regions in production of certain crop and livestock commodities. The comparative advantage, production possibilities, policy alternatives, and resource development needs of a region are not static over time. Technological progress in agriculture continually causes development possibilities and comparative advantage to change. Therefore, an efficient spatial allocation of production and resources in agriculture requires continuous consideration of new regional possibilities and interregional relationships.

Although resource endowments, rate of technological change, and demand conditions differ considerably, interregional relationships are important both in developed and developing countries. In developed countries, those which face the problem of excess capacity, the analysis of interregional relationships helps locate production and resource use in most efficient areas and minimizes the cost of supply control programs. In developing countries, the analysis of interregional relationships can help to readjust the spatial distribution of crop and livestock production on the basis of comparative advantage. Such a readjustment allows output to be increased from a given collection of resources. Interregional analysis with incorporation of project possibilities also provides a basis for distribution of new investment funds among various regions.

PREREQUISITES FOR BUILDING AN INTERREGIONAL
PROGRAMMING MODEL

There are three basic prerequisites for building an interregional programming model of agriculture in a particular country: (1) the existence of a mathematical tool to formulate and solve the problem, (2) availability of computing facilities of the required magnitude, and (3) availability of the vast amount of basic data for various homogeneous regions.

Linear programming has now advanced to such a stage that theoretically there is no limit on the size and complexity of models.[2] A limited number of nonlinear

---

1. For an idea of work in process in various countries, see OECD, "Economic Planning Research in Agriculture—Optimal Location Models in OECD," Member countries, OECD, Directorate for Agriculture and Food Division for Technical Action (AGR/T(67)2), Paris, 1967; Earl O. Heady (ed.). *Economic Models and Quantitative Methods for Decisions and Planning in Agriculture*, Proceedings of East-West Seminar, Iowa State Univ. Press, Ames, 1971.

2. For most comprehensive presentation of theoretical advances in spatial programming, see J. L. Guigou. *Théorie Économique et Transformation de L'Espace Agricole, 1. Théorie Spatiale et Localisation Agricole, II. Méthodologie et analyse*, Serie Espace Economique 14, Gauthier-Villars, Paris, 1972.

models are also available which satisfy accepted theoretical requirements for global optimality.[3] Development of large computers has made it possible to solve very complicated problems. However, the most difficult, and most costly, part in building an interregional programming model in any country is the compilation of statistics. The usefulness of the model depends to a large extent on how close its numerical coefficients are to reality. The state of existing data sources and availability of funds for collections of additional data are by far the most important conditioning factors in determining the prospects of building an interregional programming model in a particular country.

The main coefficients to be gathered for building an interregional programming model are yields and production costs. Often various micro studies use different definitions of yield and production cost measurements. It is necessary, therefore, to adjust existing data to make them comparable. Such adjustments are easier to make if an extensive statistical documentation is available by small geographical units. Some countries have the advantage of possessing such an extensive statistical documentation, as, for example, that which is available by counties (districts) in the United States.

The volume of work required in collecting and adapting data depends on the complexity of the model used. For example, if the heterogenity of farms is to be integrated into the model, production and yield coefficients must be derived for each farm size group included. This multiplies the work considerably. Similarly, if constraints, in addition to land, are to be included in the model, additional data must be collected.

Collection of data is only the first step in developing the required coefficients. It is necessary to develop checks and cross-checks to ensure the compatibility of figures. For example, it is necessary to check if the figures of cost correspond with those adopted for yields (i.e., quantities of fertilizers needed to obtain the assumed yields). Most importantly, it is necessary to check the comparability of data collected in different regions.

The enormous effort required to collect data, and the near impossibility of making the figures gathered in different regions compatible, suggest initial building of simple models. While less complex models may not provide specific guidance for policymaking, initial work with these models is useful if serious mistakes are to be avoided in those adapted to decision processes. Moreover, relatively simple models can prove useful if the results are interpreted as general policy guidelines. More complex models should be specified and built to approximate the real conditions as more data and experience are available.

STUDIES IN DEVELOPED COUNTRIES

Most developed countries possess the prerequisites for building interregional programming models. Availability of prerequisites, combined with the interest of

3. See T. Takayama and G. C. Judge, "Spatial Equilibrium and Quadratic Programming," *J. Farm Econ.* 46 (Feb. 1964): 67–93; Yakir Plessner and Earl O. Heady, "Competitive Equilibrium Solutions with Quadratic Programming," *Metroeconomica* 17 (Sept.–Dec. 1965): 117–30; Yakir Plessner, "Quadratic Programming, Activity Analysis and Market Equilibrium," *Intern. Econ. Rev.* 8 (June 1967): 168–79.

policymakers in distributing the specified level of national demand for agricultural products among various regions on the basis of relative efficiency, has led to several empirical studies in the last decade. Some of the initial studies in this area were conducted in the United States. In a pioneering study, Fox reported an application of a spatial programming model to the U.S. livestock-feed economy.[4] This model was basically an application of a transportation technique with production, prices, and demands given for each region. Since then, the transport programming model has been extensively applied to various livestock products at the national level as well as at the regional level.[5]

To make realistic models for agricultural policy decision, it was necessary to consider production and demand requirements for all major crops and livestock commodities simultaneously. This required application of multiproduct spatial models. The first attempt to apply multiproduct linear programming models to U.S. agriculture was made by the senior author of this book and his associates. Subsequent models have been more refined and a wide range of policy alternatives has been analyzed by them. A range of these applications is presented in this book. Besides the studies reported later in this book, multiproduct interregional models have been extensively applied to various crop and livestock products in the United States.[6]

Some of the initial models reported later in this book were adapted to Swedish agriculture in 1963.[7] Swedish models included several categories of farms in each region and they also considered the distribution of man-hours over the year. However, the initial Swedish models did not include crop rotation possibilities and transportation costs. To make them more realistic, the initial models were extended and refined in subsequent studies.[8]

Langvatn built an interregional model incorporating 26 typical farm size groups, and 1 reserve group, spread over 8 regions to provide a basis for inter-

4. K. A. Fox, "A Spatial Equilibrium Model of the Livestock-Feed Economy in the United States," *Econometrica* 21 (1953): 547–66.

5. See, for example, W. R. Henry and C. E. Bishop, *North Carolina Broiler in Interregional Competition*, N. C. State College, Raleigh, Agr. Exp. Info. Serv. Report 56, 1957; G. C. Judge and T. D. Wallace, *Spatial Price Equilibrium Analysis of the Livestock Economy: 1. Methodological Development and Annual Spatial Analysis of Beef Marketing Sector*, Tech. Bull. T-5, Okla. Agr. Exp. Sta., Stillwater, 1958; L. F. Schrader and G. A. King, "Regional Location of Beef Cattle Feeding," *J. Farm Econ.* 44:64–81; M. M. Snodgrass and C. E. French, *Linear Programming Approach to Interregional Competition in Dairying*, Stat. Bull. 637, Purdue Univ. Agr. Exp. Sta., Lafayette, 1958; J. F. Stollsteimer, "A Working Model for Plant Numbers and Locations," *J. Farm Econ.* 45 (1963): 631–45.

6. See Raymond M. Lenthold and D. Lee Bawden, "Annotated Bibliography of Spatial Studies," Wis. Agr. Exp. Sta. Res. Rep. 25, Aug. 1966.

7. A. T. Birowo, "Programming Models for Regional Planning: An Approach to the Problems of Regional Specialization in Swedish Agriculture," Agr. College of Sweden, Dept. Agr. Econ., Uppsala. (Mimeo.)

8. See A. T. Birowo, "Interregional Competition in Agricultural Production in Sweden—A Methodological Study with an Interregional Programming Model," *Lantbrukshogskolans Annaler.* 31 (1965):367–404; A. T. Birowo and Ulf Renborg, "Interregional Planning for Agricultural Production in Sweden," in OECD, *Interregional Competition in Agriculture: Problems of Methodology*, OECD Directorate of Agriculture and Food, Division of Technical Action, Paris, 1965; Lars Folkesson, "A Linear Programming Analysis of the Agricultural Sector in Sweden," *Lantbrukshogskolans Annaler.* 34 (1968):391–435.

regional adjustment of production in Norwegian agriculture.[9]   Although the size
of the model was small (consisting of 120 restrictions and 255 variables), the results showed that the optimum plan would employ only 67 percent of the land
and about half the labor force. The study also showed a comparative advantage of
large farms over small farms.

Recently, a comprehensive interregional programming model was built for the
Niedersachsen area in Germany.[10]   This model includes 8 producing regions, and
all farms in a region were aggregated into 5 farm size groups. Land, labor, and
capital constraints were incorporated. The models also simulate various technologies and rotation possibilities. The results provide an assessment of interregional and interfarm adjustment problems in the area studied.

Ross applied an interregional programming model to Irish agriculture in
1966.[11]   This model divided Ireland into 7 homogeneous producing regions.
Region 1 was not included in the analysis. The model included milk, cattle,
sheep, pigs, and cereals as commodities produced. All holdings under 15 acres
were excluded and other holdings were aggregated into 6 groups of representative
farms. The objective of the programming model was to maximize family farm income subject to the goals of the Second Program of Economic Expansion and the
resources available to each representative farm.

Inadequacies of existing data made it difficult to construct an interregional
programming model for French agriculture in 1963. Furthermore, data collection
possibilities were limited.   Under such circumstances, Klatzmann developed a
more simplified model which used graphic methods to analyze the interregional
relationships.[12]   The "potentiality curves" were derived for each of the 21 producing regions. These curves were designed to indicate the optimal level of inputs
and outputs. To derive the allocation pattern at the national level, the potentiality curves of all the regions were synthesized. The model gave useful results for
the objectives of maximizing average labor productivity and equalization of product per worker among regions. In recent years, a systematic effort has been made
by the Ministry of Agriculture and CERMAP (Centre d'Etudes et de Recherches
mathematiques pour la planification) to collect the data required for building a
production-allocation linear programming model.

Interregional programming models for various countries have revealed numerous deficiencies or difficulties in data collection and coefficient derivation. They
have also generated interest in collecting the missing data and in maintaining comparability in data collection procedures in various regions. The improvements
under way in statistical documentation will facilitate formulation of more complex models in the future.

9. Harry Langvatn, *Allocation of Production in Norwegian Agriculture: An Attempt of
Industrial-Economic Programming,* Norwegian Inst. Agr. Econ., Res. Bull. 27, Oslo, 1962.
10. Von Dr. Dieter Sauer, *Regionales Modell Der Landwirtschaftlichen Produktion in
Niedersachsen,* Alfred Strothe Verlag, Hannover, 1970.
11. Miceal Ross, *Regional Allocation in Irish Agriculture: An Application of Operations
Research,* Univ. College, Dublin, 1966.
12. J. Klatzmann, "Interregional Competition in Agricultural Research in France," in
OECD, *Interregional Competition in Agriculture: Problems of Methodology,* Final Report,
OECD Directorate of Agriculture and Food, Division of Technical Action, Paris 1965.

An ambitious recent model has been initiated by John Dillon and John Kennedy for Australia.[13] This model will be representative of individual farms which can be aggregated to region, state, and national levels or on a commodity basis. The objective is to determine and assess aggregative effects of individual farm decisions on more macro impacts and vice versa. This model generally parallels those developed by agricultural economists in the United States during the 1960s.[14]

STUDIES IN DEVELOPING COUNTRIES

Developing countries have not widely used interregional models for agricultural policymaking because they have been unable to fulfill the prerequisites for model building.[15] Since the objectives of agricultural development and constraint types are quite different in these countries, spatial agricultural planning models need to be adapted to the main characteristics of their agricultures. Further, spatial models for agriculture need to be related to the national planning framework in these countries. There are, however, great opportunities and needs in these countries since orderly development requires answers to the specific questions of "what, where, and how."

In the past, modern computer facilities were limited in developing countries. But the most important limiting factor has been a lack of data required for smaller geographic units in these countries. Data costs prevented collection of the necessary statistics. Even in the case of India where systematic farm management surveys have been conducted over the last two decades, data on production costs and input use are available only for selected regions.[16] There are hazards in using the available farm management data in spatial agricultural planning models.[17]

In recent years, efforts have been under way which would create the prerequisites for building spatial models. Bishay has adapted the spatial models to include various objectives of agricultural development, actual constraints on production, and transportation costs in developing countries.[18] These models account for short-run and long-run changes in constraining factors of production.

13. J. Kennedy, "J. O. S. Progress Report on a Programming Model for Australian Agriculture," Report No. 3, Univ. of New England, Armidale, 1974. (Mimeographed.)

14. See R. D. Krenz and Earl O. Heady, *Profit Maximizing Plans and Static Supply Schedules in Fluid Milk*, Iowa Agr. Exp. Sta. Bull. 486. Iowa State Univ., Ames, 1960; and North Central Regional Farm Management Research Committee, *Equilibrium Analyses of Income Improving Adjustments on Dairy Farms, 1965*, Univ. of Minn. Agr. Exp. Sta. Tech. Bull. 246, St. Paul, 1963.

15. Some methodological studies on the applications of interregional models are available. See D. K. Desai, *Increasing Income and Production in Indian Farming*, Vora, Bombay, 1963; N. S. Randhawa and Earl O. Heady, "Interregional Programming Models for Land Use Planning under Agricultural Development," *J. Farm Econ.* 46 (Feb. 1964):137–49.

16. See Uma K. Srivastava and Thomas L. Mann, "An Interregional Programming Model for Crop Production, Problems and Prospects," *Economics and Political Weekly* (Quarterly Review of Agriculture) 7:A181–184, Dec. 30, 1972.

17. See W. P. Falcon, "Programming Models for the Planning of the Agricultural Sector—A Comment," in I. Adelman and E. Thorbecke (eds.), *Theory and Design of Economic Development*, Johns Hopkins Press, 1969.

18. Fahmi K. Bishay, *Models for Spatial Agricultural Development Planning*, Center for Development Planning, Netherlands School of Economics, Rotterdam, 1973.

Bishay has also discussed the advantages and disadvantages of various criteria for delineation of regions in the context of developing countries. He has emphasized the problems in dealing with a large number of regions at once. He has suggested a stepwise analysis beginning with a small number of regions. Second, availability of modern computing facilities is increasing in developing countries, making it possible to solve reasonable size models. Third, agricultural data-collecting machinery is geared to gather comparable information on the district basis. These developments will facilitate construction and use of spatial models for policy purposes in coming years.

Models in progress suggest great potential as illustrated by a model of Portugal agriculture by A. C. Egbert, a model of Mexican agriculture by Roger Norton, and several others. A model being developed particularly for policy and development purposes is the Thai model family being developed under Somnuk Sriplung of the Division of Agricultural Economics, Ministry of Agriculture and Cooperatives, and Earl O. Heady of the Center for Agricultural and Rural Development (CARD) of Iowa State University. Initially, 19 separate zone or regional models were developed and solved which incorporate resource restraints and crop production possibilities by months, subsistence demand, and other characteristics important in the agriculture of Thailand. These were then linked together in a national model capable of generating the third 5-year plan and for evaluation of policy and developmental alternatives. The programming of subsequent model generations includes a mixed integer formulation to represent discrete project alternatives, separable demand relationships, recursive submodels of individual regions, and conformable individual farm simulators.

CARD MODELS

Following chapters review the development, application, and interpretation of models applied to U.S. agriculture in the Center for Agricultural and Rural Development at Iowa State University by Earl O. Heady and associates. These CARD models progress from pioneer programming models applied among regions on a national basis to those more complete in the inclusion of resource supplies, commodity possibilities, environmental impacts, transportation and agricultural technologies, policy alternatives, and domestic and export demand relationships. As in the case of the model sequence reported, future developments will result in advanced generations incorporating added dimensions as time and resources allow.

Chapter 1: Prototype Model of Regional Production Adjustment

ALVIN C. EGBERT and EARL O. HEADY

The chapter reports the development of spatial programming models in the first phase of a larger and on-going research program dealing with the interregional structure of the farm industry in the United States. The first study was initiated in 1955 as soon as data from the 1954 farm census became available. Hence, 1954 was used as the "point of departure" for all the subsequent analyses.

Under ideal conditions, an interregional programming model for U.S. agriculture should consider all major crops and livestock products and account for regional demands, resource restraints, transportation costs, and substitution possibilities. But the availability of computational facilities and funds at that time permitted only the consideration of grain production with the minimum necessary restraints. The restraints were the acreage of land considered to be available for production of grains in each region and the quantities of wheat and feed grain required for consumption in 1954.[1] Given the chosen level of production restraints, product prices, and production costs, the optimal region location of production was determined by those areas that produce the specific grain requirements at either minimum cost or maximum profit, depending on the assumptions of the specific models. The models and solutions provided a stepping stone for the more refined studies that are reported in later chapters.

ANALYSIS OBJECTIVES

The general objective of the studies was to determine the most efficient pattern of grain production to meet annual requirements at least cost relative to the

NOTE: For further details on data used and regions covered by the studies summarized in this chapter, see Alvin C. Egbert and Earl O. Heady, *Regional Adjustment in Grain Production: A Linear Programming Analysis*, USDA Tech. Bull. 1241; Supplement to Technical Bulletin No. 1241, June 1961; Alvin C. Egbert, Earl O. Heady, and Ray F. Brokken, *Regional Changes in Grain Production: An Application of Spatial Linear Programming*, Agr. and Home Econ. Exp. Sta., Res. Bull. 521, Iowa State Univ., Ames, Jan. 1954; Alvin C. Egbert and Earl O. Heady, *Regional Analysis of Production Adjustment in the Major Field Crops: Historical and Prospective*, USDA Tech. Bull. 1294, Nov. 1963.

1. Some extensions of the prototype model are reported later in this chapter. These extensions also project the optimal production pattern for the year 1965.

comparative advantage of various regions in producing grain. Several exploratory models were used to determine which regions might shift from grain production if these objectives were attained. The more specific objectives of the analysis were

1. To formulate several programming models with special characteristics for analyzing particular facets of the grain-surplus problem.
2. To obtain empirical solutions to the analytical models that will indicate comparative regional efficiencies of resource use in production of wheat and feed grain.
3. To use the empirical solutions to suggest optimum spatial production and land-use patterns for wheat and feed grain.
4. To estimate competitive rents for grainland, and prices of wheat and feed grain.
5. To analyze the weaknesses in the basic assumptions of the analyses and suggest ways of improving similar investigations.
6. To describe the problems encountered in collecting and processing data for the study, and to suggest means of acquiring improved data.

ECONOMIC MODELS

Several linear programming models were used in this analysis. By using the simplex linear programming routine, it is possible to derive a competitive equilibrium solution. This equilibrium solution includes the specification of regional product levels and factor and product prices. The basic model and various analytical models underlying the study reported are presented below after stating the basic assumptions used.

BASIC ASSUMPTIONS

To reduce the analysis of the wheat and feed-grain economy to a manageable size, certain simplifying assumptions were necessary. Although these assumptions may not describe exactly the economic structures within regions, they permitted the use of programming models that were sufficiently comprehensive and detailed to be consistent with the general objectives of analysis. These formal basic assumptions for the structure of the grain economy were made:

1. There are N unique, spatially separated but interdependent production regions, with many producers of wheat and feed grain.
2. All producers in a specific production region have only the choice of producing the same (homogeneous) products or product mixes, and quality is uniform between regions.
3. All producers in a specific production region have identical input-output coefficients and use the same production.
4. Input-output coefficients are constant within the relevant range, i.e., constant returns to scale exist.
5. An acre of feed-grain land (or wheatland) can be substituted for an acre of wheatland (or feed-grain land) at a constant rate within each region.

6. Total production in each region is limited only by fixed quantities of land suitable for grain production.
7. The economic objective of each producer is profit maximization.
8. The system is static in that consumption must be met from current production; the production period is crop year.
9. Total grain-consumption requirements are exogenous, determined by annual per-unit requirements of the human and livestock populations at a point in time.

THE MATHEMATICAL MODEL

The interrelations of the activities and restraints are formally identified in the mathematical model presented below. To simplify the notations, the producing regions are assumed to be consecutively numbered beginning with one. The notations used are as follows:

Let q be a subscript denoting the type of grain-producing activity

$$q = 1 \text{ for food wheat}$$
$$q = 2 \text{ for feed wheat}$$
$$q = 3 \text{ for feed grains}$$

k a subscript denoting the grain-producing regions ($k = 1, \ldots, \ldots 104$)
Z total production cost
C_{kq} acres of crop activity q
c_{kq} cost of producing one acre of crop activity q in region k
b_{kq} per-acre yield of crop activity q in region k
R_n national requirements for product n ($n = 1$ for food wheat, 2 for feed grains)
A_k total grain acreage available for production of included crops (includes area under summer fallow)

OBJECTIVE FUNCTION

$$\min Z = \sum_{k=1}^{104} \sum_{q=1}^{3} c_{kq} \, C_{kq} \qquad (1.1)$$

subject to the following restraints:

1. land restraints

$$\sum_{q=1}^{3} C_{kq} \leqslant A_k \qquad (1.2)$$

2. requirement restraints

$$\sum_{k=1}^{104} b_{k1} \, C_{k1} = R_1 \qquad (1.3)$$

$$\sum_{k=1}^{104} \sum_{q=2}^{3} b_{kq} \, C_{kq} = R_2 \tag{1.4}$$

3. nonnegativity restraint

$$C_{kq} \geq 0 \tag{1.5}$$

ANALYTICAL MODELS

Five analytical models were formulated as steps in attaining the objectives outlined. The structural changes made from model to model were attempts to add greater realism to the analysis or to investigate some particular facet of the grain problem. Only the structure and objectives of the models are described here. The methods used in obtaining the data needed in each of these models are briefly outlined in the following section.

MODEL A

Model A corresponds exactly to the mathematical model described in Equations 1.1 to 1.5. For each of the homogeneous grain-producing regions ($k = 104$), three types of grain-producing activities were considered: food wheat, feed wheat, and a feed-grain rotation. The quantity of grain produced by these three activities, individually or in combination, is limited by the maximum acreage available within each region for production of grain. The production costs associated with each of these activities include labor, power, machinery, seed, chemicals, and certain miscellaneous items. A central market was assumed for wheat and feed grain, and the cost of transporting these grains from the producing regions to the market was set at zero. There are two national demand restraints, one for food wheat and one for feed grain.

The objective of model A was to determine the spatial pattern of grain production that would provide the nation's annual requirements of wheat and feed grain at minimum total cost, under the cost conditions specified.

MODEL B

Model A assumed that land has no alternative use or that its opportunity cost in the next best enterprise is not significant (for example, grass in the western plains). In some areas, however, alternative enterprises provide opportunity costs of some importance. Therefore, model B was formulated to determine how consideration of certain opportunity costs, represented by specified land rents, would affect the optimum grain-production pattern. Thus the sole difference between model A and model B is in the cost coefficients (c_{kq}'s), which, in addition to the costs enumerated, include an estimated land rent.

MODEL C

The basic assumption, stated earlier, that an acre of land in each region could be used for production of either wheat or a feed-grain rotation was relaxed for model C. In model C the acreage of grain in each region was divided into two components: a maximum wheat acreage and a maximum feed-grain acreage. Thus in model C there are 208 land restraints or restrictions instead of 104 as in the models A and B. All other variables in model C are the same as those in model A.

MODEL D

Agronomists have posed the possibility of establishing a meadow crop in a rotation without using a nurse crop such as oats. The feed value produced from an acre of oats is less than that produced from corn. Hence, if oats could be eliminated from the customary rotation, a large potential increase in the feed supply would result. Model D was designed to investigate the possible impact of this innovation on the optimum grain-production pattern. This model used six grain activities: food wheat, feed wheat, corn, oats, barley, and sorghum. Production costs and production and consumption restraints are the same as those in model A. Again, the objective is that of minimizing total production cost.

MODEL E

Preceding models assumed that production regions, although spatially separated, are interdependent in a central market, but that transportation costs are zero. The unrealistic assumption of one market and a transportation cost of zero was withdrawn for model E and replaced by these assumptions: (1) farm prices of wheat and feed grain at all points are equal to the prices at a central market minus transportation costs; and (2) the differences between historic prices for different locations are due solely to differences in transportation costs. If these assumptions are approximated, a net profit solution of a combination production-transportation problem, provided the markets absorb the programmed quantities at the assumed prices, should result in a similar solution and production pattern. The objective of model E then is to maximize total net profit, given the production and consumption restraints. These restraints are the same as those in model A. The input-output coefficients, also, are the same for the two models. The objective function can be formally expressed as

$$\max f(r) = \sum_{k=1}^{104} \sum_{q=1}^{3} C_{kq}\, r_{kq} \tag{1.6}$$

when r_{kq} = the net return per bushel of qth product in kth region.

BASIC DATA AND COEFFICIENT DERIVATION

This section describes the methods and problems involved in estimating for each region maximum acreages, normal yields, production costs, demand restraints, and corn and wheat prices. The general procedures used in converting these data into coefficients for the analytical models are also described. Because of the many data assembled in the 1954 *Census of Agriculture* and the publications that summarize and supplement the census, most of the basic data used in the analysis are for 1954. Maximum grain acreages in each region are the only exception—they are from 1953 data.

DELINEATION OF GRAIN-PRODUCING REGIONS

In many parts of the United States, grain production is only a small part of the total agricultural production and an insignificant part of the total grain economy. Also, the data were very scarce for these sparse grain areas. For these reasons, only major grain-producing areas of the country were used for the analysis reported here. Areas in which wheat and feed grain were harvested from 22 percent or more of the total cropland in 1954 were defined as major grain-producing areas. To some extent, this demarcating percentage was arbitrary. But the major grain-producing areas thus defined represented 90 percent of the total wheat and feed-grain acreages in 1953. Furthermore, in 1954 the percentages of wheat, corn, oats, barley, and sorghum produced in these major grain areas were estimated to be 93.1, 93.4, 86.9, 72.7, and 91.0, respectively, of the total production. Thus the defined major grain-producing areas are the source of most of the wheat and feed grain produced in the United States.

All the major grain-producing areas were divided into 104 "homogeneous" grain-producing regions. The geographical outlines of these regions, together with their assigned numbers, are shown in Figure 1.1. Henceforth, they are referred to as "producing areas" or simply "areas." The producing areas were based pri-

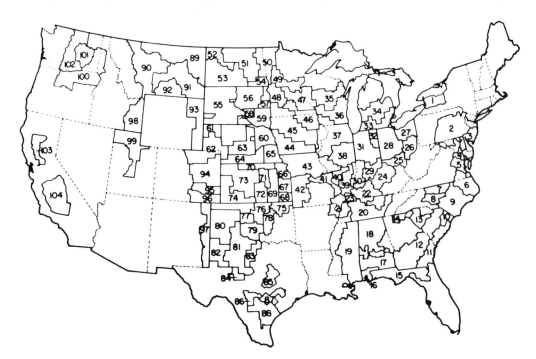

Fig. 1.1. Location of wheat-producing and feed-grain–producing areas.

marily on state economic areas.[2] To demarcate producing areas that were relatively homogeneous for grain production and to keep the computational work at
a minimum, the following procedure was used. First, four classes of economic
areas were defined:

1. Areas with grain production uniformly distributed, i.e., the concentration of
   grain acreage within each county was approximately the same for all counties
   in the economic area.
   a. Areas with total harvested acreage of wheat and feed grain combined
      equal to or greater than 25 percent of total cropland.
   b. Areas with total harvested acreage of wheat and feed grain combined less
      than 25 per cent of total cropland.
2. Areas with grain production not uniformly distributed.
   a. Areas with total harvested acreage of wheat and feed grain combined
      equal to or greater than 25 percent of total cropland.
   b. Areas with total harvested acreage of wheat and feed grain combines less
      than 25 percent of total cropland.

By using dot maps, showing the geographic distributions and concentrations of
the harvested acreages of wheat and feed grain in 1954, state economic areas were
placed in either group 1 or group 2. Group 1 was divided into classes 1a and 1b
by computing the required percentages, a and b above, from state economic area
acreages.   County acreages were used to divide group 2 into classes 2a and 2b.
Thus classes 1a and 1b are state economic areas and classes 2a and 2b are counties.

Finally, classes 1a and 2a were aggregated to form the 104 producing areas.
Criteria used to guide aggregation were as follows: state economic areas and
counties within each region were required to be contiguous and to have similar
grain yields, similar proportions of the crops considered, and similar numbers of
combines, corn pickers, and tractors per 1,000 acres of cropland. On the basis of
these criteria, two or more state economic areas often could not be aggregated.
Hence, some producing areas consist of only one state economic area. In other
instances, it was possible only to aggregate one economic area and a group of
counties. A few areas are made up of counties only.

The 104 producing areas shown in Figure 1.1 provided the basic units for
making estimates of acreage, yield, and cost. But when the necessary data were
not available for these areas for estimating input coefficients, state data were adjusted by other related data to compensate for within-state differences. In a few
instances, state data were used without adjustment when a logical means of adjustment was not apparent.

The concept of "normal" is basic to the methods used in estimating the maximum area grain acreages and area yields. The word "normal" is used here to
mean expected or average. The objective for yields was to obtain estimates that
would reflect accurately the average quantity of inputs used per acre for production of wheat and feed grain in 1954. The general objective for all estimates was

2. State economic areas were used because (1) types of farming and land productivity are
similar within these areas; and (2) many of the data required for the study are summarized in
the census by state economic areas.

the obtaining of data that would reflect the relative competitive positions of the regions in production of wheat and feed grain.

PRODUCING AREA ACREAGES

Grain acreages of 1953 were used as estimates of the maximum area restraints. In this year, more grain was planted than in any year of history. Acreage control programs were not in effect and the large 1953 grain acreages perhaps represent maximum area adapted to these crops under peacetime economic conditions. Thus later figures on production adjustment suggest the quantity of land that might need to be withdrawn, relative to the 1953 base acreage, if production of feed grain and wheat were balanced with annual use. Acreages planted to grain and summer-fallowed are the components of the area acreage restraints. Acreages planted to grain were not easily estimated for many areas because (1) estimates of planted acres were not available, or (2) when planted acre estimates were available, they included plants for hay, pasture, silage, cover crops, etc. These difficulties existed mainly for small grains. The total number of acres harvested for the various uses of corn are estimated by federal-state agencies. Due to the nature of the data available, a different method was used to estimate acreages of corn and small grains. The acreages of corn planted for grain were estimated by the following formula:

$$
\begin{array}{c}
\text{estimated acres of} \\
\text{corn planted for grain} = \\
\text{in } k\text{th producing area}
\end{array}
\quad
\begin{array}{c}
\text{acres of corn planted} \\
\text{for all purposes in} \\
\text{the } k\text{th producing area}
\end{array}
\quad - \quad
\begin{array}{c}
\text{estimated acres of corn} \\
\text{planted for silage in} \\
k\text{th producing area}
\end{array}
$$

$$(k = 1, \ldots, \ldots 104)$$

The acres of wheat, oats, barley, and grain sorghums planted for grain were estimated by the following relationship:

$$
\begin{array}{c}
\text{estimated acres of } n\text{th} \\
\text{grain planted for grain} = \\
\text{in } k\text{th area}
\end{array}
\quad
\frac{\text{acres of the } n\text{th grain harvested for}}{\text{grain in the } k\text{th producing area}}{1\text{-average abandonment rate of the } n\text{th}}
$$

$$(n = 1, \ldots, \ldots 5)$$

The number of cultivated summer-fallow acres was included as a component of the area acreage restraints because fallowed acreages are a necessary land input in semiarid wheat areas. Machinery and labor costs associated with fallowed land are a necessary part of the total per-acre cost of production. Also, historic yields are based on production resulting from the use of cultivated summer fallow in rotation. Thus the inclusion of cultivated summer fallow places estimates of acreage, yield, and cost in their proper relationship. Estimates of cultivated summer-fallow acreages were obtained from the census and from unpublished data of the Crop Estimates Division, Agricultural Marketing Service. It was assumed that fallowed acreages did not change significantly from 1953 to 1954.

REGIONAL YIELDS

Normal area yields, as defined previously, were estimated in two steps. First, the 1945–54 average yields were computed. These yields were then adjusted by a factor representing the average increase in yield between the midpoint of the period 1945–54 and the year 1954. Regression trends were computed from data for the period 1937–54 to accomplish this end. When annual data were available, yields were computed by this method. When the annual data were not available for the period 1945–54, harvested yields per acre were estimated from state data and census economic area and country data. These yields per harvested acre were then adjusted by a factor representing the average percentage of the total acreage harvested, with total acreage equaling harvested acreage plus abandonment plus fallow.

PRODUCTION COSTS

The methods used in estimating per-acre costs of grain production are described in this section. The basic items making up per-acre cost are land, labor, machinery and power, seed, chemicals, and miscellaneous inputs. A charge for annual land services was included for model B only. Indirect or overhead costs, such as management, purchasing, selling, housing, and so on, were not estimated because a satisfactory method and data for estimation were lacking. Some detailed unit cost studies have used 10 percent of the direct cost as an estimate of the indirect cost, but use of this method would not change the relative values of the activity costs. Hence, the inclusion of a proportional indirect cost would not affect the programming solutions in this study.

COMPOSITE ACRE

Uniform and complete data on average production costs for wheat and feed grain in each programming region were lacking. Hence, these costs had to be synthesized. To make realistic estimates of per-acre cost, a composite acre was devised for each producing area. This composite acre was made up of 12 possible elements, each of which represents a unique production operation. These 12 acre elements, or types of production situations, used for production-cost estimates are

1. Mechanical, planted and harvested, not irrigated.
2. Mechanical, planted and harvested, irrigated.
3. Mechanical, planted but not harvested (abandoned).
4. Mechanical, cultivated summer fallow.
5. Semimechanical, planted and harvested, not irrigated.
6. Semimechanical, planted but not harvested, irrigated.
7. Semimechanical, planted but not harvested (abandoned).
8. Semimechanical, cultivated summer fallow.
9. Nonmechanical, planted and harvested, not irrigated.
10. Nonmechanical, planted and harvested, irrigated.

11. Nonmechanical, planted but not harvested (abandoned).
12. Nonmechanical, cultivated summer fallow.

Except for the mechanical items, these acre elements are self-explanatory. They are defined as follows: mechanical—tractor power is used for all tillage operations and harvesting is done by combine or corn picker; semimechanical—tractor power is used for all tillage operations and harvesting is done by hand (for corn) or with binder and thresher (for small grain); and nonmechanical—animal power is used for all tillage operations and harvesting is done by hand (as for corn) or with binder and thresher (as for small grain). Also, acre elements 2, 6, and 10 imply that no abandonment is assumed on irrigated acres.

The list of 12 acre elements is not exhaustive. On the basis of regional data, however, they seemed to be complete enough to provide reasonable estimates of average production costs and at the same time to facilitate computations for planned further investigations.

An example will help to explain the method used in deriving costs for each of 12 possible elements, each of which represents (1) a unique production by mechanical techniques, (2) no irrigation, (3) no harvesting from land in cultivated summer fallow the preceding year, and (4) an average of 1 percent abandonment of the planted acres. Attached to each corn acre in area 1, therefore, were two types of acre-element costs—mechanical, planted and harvested but not irrigated; and mechanical, planted but not harvested. The weights, which are computed elsewhere on an acreage basis, are 0.99 for mechanical, planted and harvested but not irrigated; and 0.01 for mechanical, planted but not harvested. Furthermore, given per-acre costs of $42.20 for the mechanical, planted and harvested acre, and $34.50 for the mechanical, planted but not harvested acre, the estimated average per-acre production cost for corn in area 1 is $42.12 (42.20 × 0.99 + 34.50 × 0.01).

Estimates of costs of labor, machinery, and power provided the greatest conceptual and empirical difficulties. Aggregate estimates of machinery and labor inputs exist for U.S. farms, but they were not broken down among individual farm enterprises. Hence, these costs were derived by estimating the average physical inputs per acre by type of operation (plowing, disking, harrowing, and so on) and then weighting physical inputs by the estimated per-unit cost of the inputs involved. Because many of the published data on labor and machinery costs were either incomplete or out of date, supplementary data on these inputs were obtained from 25 state agricultural experiment stations or colleges.

LAND

The annual value of land for grain production was used only in model B. The per-acre value of land on cash-grain farms was assumed to be the best available basis for estimating the annual value of land services for grain production. The sum of the interest rate and tax rate was multiplied by the per-acre value to obtain the annual input value of land. In area 1, for example, the interest and tax rates were 0.049 and 0.0184, respectively, per dollar of value, and the land value was $111 per acre.

LABOR

Inputs of physical labor were estimated for each production operation. The method is illustrated in the tabulation below for wheat production in area 1, which is based on the mechanical, planted and harvested, not irrigated acre element.

Operation	Hours Required per Acre
Plowing	1.46
Disking	1.15
Harrowing	.69
Drilling	.82
Harvesting	1.54
Hauling	1.03
Total	6.69

The data on labor hours required for harvesting and hauling omit the portion of an "average" acre not harvested.

Data on the number of man-hours of labor required for each production operation were obtained from several publications and from the survey data. When possible, modal coefficients were used. When a modal production operation was not evident in the data, simple averages or single estimates were used. The per-acre labor cost for each acre element was obtained by multiplying the estimated number of man-hours required per acre by an estimate of the hourly wage rates on cash-grain farms. The per-acre labor costs for each grain and each area were computed by weighting each acre-element labor cost by the proper coefficient.

POWER AND MACHINERY

The method used in estimating the power and machinery cost was similar to that used in estimating labor. The estimating problem was more complex, however, because of the multitude of items that compose machinery costs. Instead of one coefficient (hours per acre) and one price (wages), coefficients and prices for each implement required to produce each grain in each area were estimated. The tabulation that follows illustrates the procedure used in estimating this cost for an acre of corn in area 28 in Ohio. The example is for the mechanical, planted and harvested, not irrigated acre element.

Implement	Size	Hours of Use Required per Acre	X	Cost per Hour	=	Cost for Implement per Acre
Tractor	19 hp	10.45		$0.81		$8.46
Plow	2-14"	1.30		0.71		0.92
Disk	7' T	1.00		0.67		0.67
Harrow	10'	0.50		0.22		0.11
Drag	9'	0.35		0.26		0.09

Implement	Size	Hours of Use Required per Acre	X	Cost per Hour	=	Cost for Implement per Acre
Cultipactor	10′	0.40		0.60		0.24
Planter	2-R	0.60		0.65		0.39
Cultivator	2-R	1.50		0.80		1.20
Picker	1-R	1.80		1.71		3.08
Wagon	Std	1.00		0.08		0.08
Total						15.24

The machinery sizes and number of hours required per acre used in estimating machinery cost were modal values when these values could be determined. When a modal value was not apparent, simple acreages or single observations were used. Machinery sizes and hours of use required per acre were obtained from USDA data and from survey data. Extensive searching and many computations were necessary to estimate the per-hour cost of each implement. Information was obtained or estimated for this purpose as to size, price, annual use; total life; interest, tax, and insurance rates; grease and repair rates; and fuel and oil consumption rates. With these basic data, the items that make up the per-hour cost of each implement—depreciation, insurance, interest, taxes, fuel, oil, grease, and repairs—could be computed.

SEED

The cost of seed was not included as a part of the total per-acre production cost. Instead, the estimated quantity of seed required per acre was subtracted from the estimated yield. This method was used because total demand for seed is a function of the acreage grown in each area. But these acreages are variables to be determined within the system (i.e., the model). Hence, the simplest way of allowing seed cost and demand for seed to be variables determined by the system is to deduct the seeding rate from the yield. To use this method, it is necessary that grain seed be planted in the region in which it is produced, and that planted acreages within each region be constants between years. Only state seeding rates were available. Therefore, adjustments were made in state rates to compensate for variations within the states.

CHEMICALS

Area fertilizer costs for each of the five grains were calculated mainly from the *United States Census of Agriculture*. Specific data for only the "more important" crops are recorded in the census. When fertilizer applications were not tabulated for a grain crop in the census, this cost was estimated with the aid of unpublished data of the Farm Economics Research Division, ARS. The per-acre cost of lime for each grain was estimated by dividing the total cost of lime applied in an area in 1954 by the total cropland.

Data were not available to show expenditures by regions for insecticides, fungicides, and herbicides for wheat and feed grain. Hence, these costs were first estimated for each state. The state estimates were then used to estimate chemical costs for producing areas within states. The basic data used for insect, pest, and chemical weed control expenditures were those compiled by USDA workers.

MISCELLANEOUS

Miscellaneous costs include those involved in the spreading of manure, fertilizer, and lime, and those of water for acreages produced by irrigation. No attempt was made to estimate the value of manure applied to wheat and feed grain. The spreading cost alone was charged to crop enterprises. Costs of spreading manure were estimated only for the producing areas in the Northeast, Appalachian, Corn Belt, and Lake states regions and the corn-producing areas of the Northern Plains. For some of the fertilizer applied to grains, the cost of application was accounted for in the method used to compute machinery and labor cost. This accounting method was used for fertilizer applied by attachments on planters, drills, and cultivators. For fertilizer spread by other methods, an additional application cost, which included charges for labor, power, and machinery, was computed. Costs of lime spreading by custom operators were assumed to have been included in the lime expenditures reported by farmers. An additional spreading cost was computed for lime spread by farmers. In areas in which less than 0.5 percent of the grains were produced by irrigation methods, irrigation costs were not estimated.

DEMAND RESTRAINTS

Separate demand restraints were considered for food wheat and feed grain in aggregate for 1954. Hence, the calculations provided later show regional production patterns designed to meet aggregate demand at the 1954 level. Techniques of production also represent 1954 as a point in time. The year 1954 was used because more complete production data for it were available. These demand restraints, which are assumed to be fixed or constant, were based on the normal per-unit requirements of the human or livestock populations, or both, and the actual net exports in the base year 1954.

Because it was believed that grain stocks put an "abnormal pressure" on grain disappearance in 1954, an attempt was made to estimate a normal domestic disappearance for each grain. No attempt was made, however, to estimate normal net exports, because of the many unmeasurable factors in the world market.

The total (domestic and foreign) estimated demand levels were approximately 758 million bushels of wheat and 3.9 billion corn-equivalent bushels of feed grain. Although these estimates were derived by simple techniques, they seem quite reasonable and do not differ greatly from actual disappearances of wheat and feed grain in 1954. Seed requirements and grain for forage were not included in the estimates, as seed requirements were subtracted from yields and the study reported is concerned with grain production alone.

Since not all the land area in the United States was included in the programming regions, it was necessary to estimate the normal production of wheat and feed grain in these nonprogrammed areas to determine how much of the estimated total demand or requirements would need to be produced in the programming regions. Production from the nonprogrammed areas was subtracted from the total demand requirements mentioned above. This remainder formed the demand restraints that had to be met from production in the programmed regions.

The normal production in the nonprogrammed areas was estimated by a residual method. First, for each state and each grain, the total planted acreage in the producing areas within a state was subtracted from the 1953 acreage planted for grain in the state. When these residual acreages were multiplied by the estimated 1954 normal yields for the state, the total production in the nonprogrammed areas was obtained. With corn, oats, barley, and grain sorghums converted to corn equivalents, these quantities were 80 and 338 million bushels of wheat and feed grain, respectively. Subtracting these quantities from total requirements gave 678 million and 3.5 billion bushels of wheat and feed grain, respectively, as the demand or requirement quantities to be provided from the programmed regions.

PRICES USED

Model E is based on the criterion of maximum profit. Hence, it was necessary, for this model, to estimate the regional grain prices. Estimating grain prices consistent with the fundamental concepts underlying model E was not simple. First, the differences in regional prices should be a measure of the relevant transportation cost between regions. Second, the regional prices should represent the relative values of each grain in a competitive market.

Briefly, regional grain prices were estimated as follows: the average wheat-corn price relative for the period 1932-41 provided the basis for estimating the price of wheat.[3] First, the 1945-54 U.S. average price of corn was multiplied by the 1932-41 U.S. wheat-corn price relative. This product was then subtracted from the actual U.S. average price of wheat for the period 1945-54. Next, this difference was subtracted from each average state wheat price for the period 1945-54. Finally, regional wheat prices were estimated by adjusting the calculated state average prices by the price gradients indicated on a wheat isoprice map. It was assumed that prices within each state were a linear function of distance. Regional corn prices were estimated, with the aid of a corn isoprice map, by adjusting 1945-54 average state corn prices in a way similar to that used in adjusting state wheat prices. Individual prices for oats, barley, and sorghum were not estimated—these grains are converted to corn equivalents for programming. Thus in essence the prices used for these three grains were the corn prices weighted by their respective feed values in terms of corn.

---

3. For more recent periods, the market wheat price has been maintained above the competitive level; for example, the price of wheat relative to corn increased from 122 for the period 1931-42 to 131 for the period 1945-54.

STRUCTURE OF COEFFICIENT MATRICES AND WEIGHTING METHODS

To illustrate more clearly the nature of the programming models, the coefficient matrix for model A is outlined below, followed by a summary of the weighting methods used to form aggregate coefficients and restraints. In the tableau below, P_{kq} is a vector of requirements for the qth crop activity for the kth restraint, while A is the vector of restraints. Using an acre as the unit of output, all activities have a land input requirement of 1, where they are relevant for the area. Considering a unit of output to be the product of an acre, the y_{kq} simply represent the per-acre yield of the qth crop activity in the kth producing area. The first $m = 104$ equations are for the land restraints while the last two are demand restraints. The y_{kq} or per-acre yields of grain crops are defined later in respect to method of computation. The number of P_{kq} is $mr = 312$ for model A (without vectors of identity matrix).

P_{11}	P_{12}	P_{13}	P_{21}	P_{22}	P_{23}	$\cdots$	P_{m1}	P_{m2}	P_{m3}		A
1	1	1	0	0	0	$\cdots$	0	0	0	$\leqslant$	A_1
0	0	0	1	1	1	$\cdots$	0	0	0	$\leqslant$	A_2
0	0	0	0	0	0	$\cdots$	0	0	0	$\leqslant$	A_3
.	.	.	.	.	.		.	.	.		.
.	.	.	.	.	.		.	.	.		.
.	.	.	.	.	.		.	.	.		.
0	0	0	0	0	0	$\cdots$	1	1	1	$\leqslant$	A_{104}
y_{11}	0	0	y_{21}	0	0	$\cdots$	y_{m1}	0	0	$=$	R_1
0	y_{12}	y_{13}	0	y_{22}	y_{23}	$\cdots$	0	y_{m2}	y_{m3}	$=$	R_2

RESTRAINTS AND OUTPUTS

The land restraints based on 1953 acreages are defined as follows:

$$A_k = \sum_{n=1}^{5} Q A_{kn} + \sum_{n=2}^{5} F_{kn} \tag{1.7}$$

$$k = 1, \ldots, \ldots, 104$$

when $Q A_{kn}$ denotes planted acreage in the kth area of the nth grain, and F_{kn} acreage of nth grain planted on summer fallow in the kth area.

The y_{kq} or per-acre yields have been computed on this basis:

$$y_{k1} = (Q_{k1} \, T_{k1})/(H_{k1} + A_{k1} + F_{k1}) \tag{1.8}$$

$$y_{k2} = (Q_{k1} \, T_{k1} \, K_1)/(H_{k1} + A_{k1} + F_{k1}) \tag{1.9}$$

$$y_{k3} = \sum_{n=2}^{5} g_{kn} \, (Q_{kn} \, T_{kn} \, K_n)/(H_{kn} + A_{kn} + F_{kn}) \qquad (1.10)$$

$$\sum_{n=2}^{5} g_{kn} = 1$$

where y_{k1} = estimated 1954 normal per-acre yield of wheat in kth area

y_{k2} = estimated 1954 normal per-acre yield of wheat in corn-equivalent bushels in kth area

y_{k3} = estimated 1954 weighted normal per-acre yield of feed grain in kth area

Q_{kn} = 1945–54 trend adjustment factor for nth crop in kth area

H_{kn} = 1945–54 harvested acreage of nth crop in kth area

A_{kn} = estimated 1945–54 abandoned acreage (acreage seeded for grain minus harvested acreage) of nth crop in kth area

F_{kn} = estimated 1954 acreage of nth crop in kth region planted on fallowed land multiplied by the factor 10

K_n = corn-equivalent bushel conversion factor of nth grain

g_{kn} = proportion nth crop acreage is of total corn, barley, and grain sorghums acreage, 1953

T_{kn} = 1945–54 total production of the nth crop in kth area

The demand restraints at the national level are the following for food wheat and feed grain:

$$R_1 = Nb_1 + E_w - R_w \qquad (1.11)$$

$$R_2 = Nb_2 + Lb_3 + E_f - R_f \qquad (1.12)$$

where N = U.S. population, January 1955

b_1 = estimated 1954 normal per capita consumption in bushels

E_w = net exports of wheat, 1954

R_w = residual wheat production in nonprogrammed areas

b_2 = estimated 1954 normal per capita use of feed grain in direct consumption

L = number of grain-consuming livestock units, 1954–55

b_3 = normal feed production per livestock unit

E_f = net exports of feed grain, 1954

R_f = residual feed grain in nonprogrammed areas

ACTIVITY COSTS

The activity of per-acre costs are defined as follows:

$$C_{kq} = \sum_{h=1}^{3} \sum_{l=1}^{4} g_{kn}^{\prime hl} \, e_{kn}^{hl} \qquad (q = 1, n = 1) \qquad (1.13)$$

$$C_{k3} = \sum_{n=2}^{5} \sum_{h=1}^{3} \sum_{l=1}^{4} g_{kn}^{hl} e_{kn}^{hl} \quad (q = 3) \tag{1.14}$$

$k = 1, \ldots, \ldots 104$

$l = 1$ for crop-acre component with planted and harvested acre, not irrigated; 2 for planted, but not harvested acre (abandoned); 3 for planted and harvested acres, irrigated; 4 for cultivated summer-fallow acre

$h = 1$ for production technique with mechanical production; 2 for semimechanical production; 3 for nonmechanical production

where

$$\sum_{h=1}^{3} \sum_{l=1}^{4} g_{kn}^{'hl} = 1, \sum_{n=2}^{5} \sum_{n=1}^{3} \sum_{l=1}^{4} g_{kn}^{hl} = 1, g_{kn} g_{kn}^{'hl} = g_{kn}^{hl}$$

C_{kq} = estimated cost of producing a composite wheat acre for food or feed $(q = 1, 2)$ in the kth producing area, 1954 $(C_{k1} = C_{k2})$

C_{k3} = estimated cost of producing a composite feed-grain acre in the kth area, 1954

e_{kn}^{hl} = estimated per-acre cost of the lth crop-acre component by the hth production technique for the nth crop in kth region

$g_{kn}^{'hl}$ = estimated proportion of per-acre production cost of nth crop due to the hth technique on the lth crop-acre component in the kth region.

The estimates of per-acre cost of lth crop-acre component by hth production technique for the nth crop in kth region were made as follows:

$$e_{kn}^{hl} = w_{kn}^{hl} + v_{kn}^{hl} + o_{kn}^{hl} + m_{kn}^{hl} \tag{1.15}$$

where　w = estimated per-acre labor cost
　　　　v = estimated per-acre power and machinery cost
　　　　o = estimated per-acre chemical cost
　　　　m = estimated per-acre miscellaneous cost

OTHER MODELS

The structure of the coefficients and model for B is the same as described above for A, except the e_{kn}^{hl} is redefined. Equation 1.15 becomes

$$e_{kn}^{'hl} = (a + w + v + o + m)_{kn}^{hl} \tag{1.16}$$

where a is estimated per-acre land rent. All other symbols have the same meaning as before. The land restraints are partitioned for model C into a wheatland maximum and a feed-grain land maximum as follows:

$$A_{kw} = Q A_{k1} + F_{k1} \tag{1.17}$$

$$A_{kf} = \sum_{n=2}^{5} Q A_{kn} + F_{kn} \tag{1.18}$$

where A_{kw} = wheat restraint in kth production area

A_{kf} = feed-grain restraint in kth producing area

The cost and yield coefficients for the wheat activities in model D are the same as in model A. Since corn, oats, barley, and sorghum are independent activities in model D, the following equations define the weighting method used for the y_{kq}'s and c_{kq}'s of these activities:

$$y_{kq} = (Q_{kn} \ T_{kn} \ K_{kn})/(H_{kn} + A_{kn} + F_{kn}) \tag{1.19}$$

$$C_{kq} = \sum_{n=1}^{3} \sum_{l=1}^{4} g_{kn}^{'hl} \ e_{kn}^{hl} \tag{1.20}$$

where notations have the same meaning as in Equations 1.8 through 1.10 and 1.13 to 1.14, and

$$\sum_{h=1}^{3} \sum_{l=1}^{4} g_{kn}^{'hl} = 1$$

EMPIRICAL RESULTS

Since this study was initiated, the American public has put into effect a national land withdrawal program. The program attempts to withdraw land in all producing areas which is often inconsistent with the optimal pattern. Hence, our major interest is in specifying the amount of land needed for crops and available for withdrawal and shift to other crops, to serve as a benchmark for comparison with more recent models.

We summarize the aggregate results in Table 1.1 where it is assumed that land not required for grain production would be shifted to "lower uses" such as grass and forestry. The acreage specified for food wheat and feed grain in Table 1.1 would allow attainment of the "discrete demand restraints" of 758 million bushels of food wheat and 3.9 billion bushels of feed grain (in corn equivalent). Three models—A, B, and E—provide somewhat similar results. Model D, including a new crop technique not in use by farmers, specifies a much smaller feed-grain acreage and a higher wheat acreage because the latter crop would be grown more on land of lower yield and not so well adapted to the new rotational technique for feed grain. The results of model D are not applicable unless there is a widespread use of the new technique by the farmers. Model C, which is somewhat unrealistic since it does not allow wheat and feed grain to compete for land, indicates the smallest surplus acreage and the largest amount of land required for feed grain. Since the models A, B, and E are most realistic, detailed description which follows will relate only to these three.

REGIONAL PATTERN OF WITHDRAWAL AND PRODUCTION

There is a large degree of similarity among some of the programming models in the production patterns specified. The total acreages specified to remain in grain production and the bushel production of wheat and feed grain for each area are specified in Tables 1.2 through 1.6. Where an area is not indicated in these tables, it is not specified to produce wheat or feed grain, given the objective function of the particular model.

To summarize more clearly the geographic production pattern specified by models A, B, and E, we include Figures 1.2, 1.3, and 1.4 to indicate the areas in which feed grain and wheat would be located if average annual production were to equal requirements under the conditions assumed and if the geographic pattern of production were consistent with certain restricted comparative advantage of various producing areas. Figure 1.5 indicates the extent of agreement in number of times a particular area is specified for a particular use by the three models. The nonshaded areas include feed-grain and wheat production at the same levels as in the base year.

Under the assumptions of model A, areas would be withdrawn from production of all grain in southeastern Colorado, eastern New Mexico, northern Utah, and eastern Wyoming and Montana. Areas scattered among Texas, Nebraska, Wisconsin, Michigan, Oklahoma, Missouri, Kansas, and New York also would be withdrawn. In the Southeast, regions representing a large acreage would be withdrawn from production of grains. It is interesting to note that the major wheat and feed-grain areas would remain entirely in production under the construction and assumptions of the models. Southwestern Kansas and western Texas would shift to sorghums for feed.

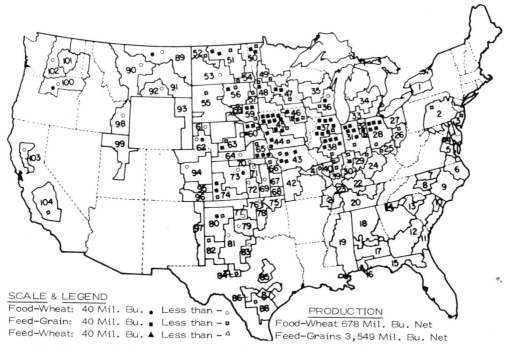

SCALE & LEGEND

Food-Wheat: 40 Mil. Bu. ● Less than – ○
Feed-Grain: 40 Mil. Bu. ■ Less than – □
Feed-Wheat: 40 Mil. Bu. ▲ Less than – △

PRODUCTION
Food-Wheat 678 Mil. Bu. Net
Feed-Grains 3,549 Mil. Bu. Net

Fig. 1.2. Specified locations of wheat and feed-grain production: model A solution.

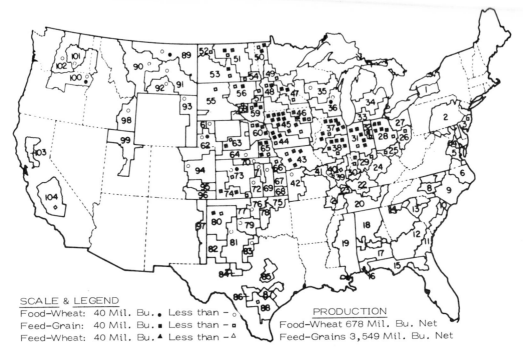

Fig. 1.3. Specified locations of wheat and feed-grain production: model B solution.

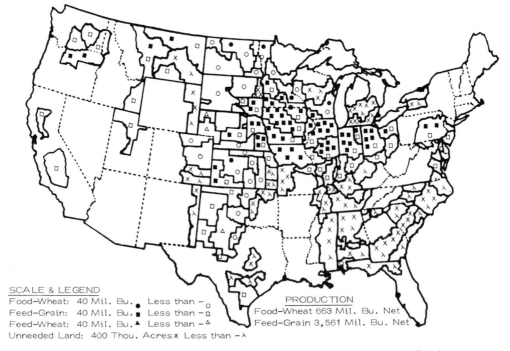

Fig. 1.4. Specified locations for wheat and feed-grain production: model E solution.

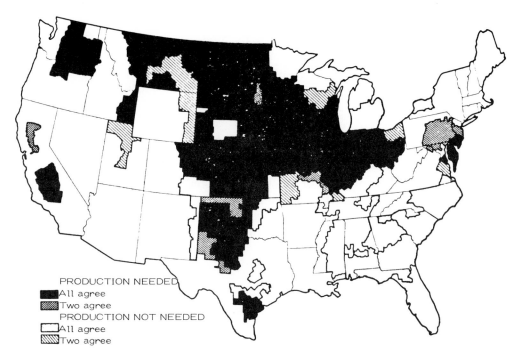

Fig. 1.5. Agreement of models A, B, and E in location of production of wheat and feed grain.

Model B (Figure 1.3) provides a spatial production pattern differing some-what from both A and E. The main differences under B are: all of Montana would be devoted to wheat for food, the Oklahoma panhandle and Pennsylvania would be shifted out of grains, and the region in southwestern Missouri would be used for food wheat. Also, a large portion of Kansas would be used for both wheat and feed grain.

Under model C, as compared to model A, large parts of Montana, Washington, Oregon, Idaho, and Nebraska would be devoted to wheat for feed only. In parts of Nebraska and Colorado, wheat would be grown for both feed and food. In the upper plains, North Dakota and South Dakota, along with parts of Minnesota and Wisconsin, would be devoted to wheat for food. Also, slightly more feed grain would be produced along the Atlantic seaboard and the Gulf of Mexico. Under this profit-maximizing model, it is the relatively high wheat prices, because of lo-cation near larger milling and consuming centers, and because of prices paid for hard red spring and durum wheats, that cause wheat for food to be specified in Minnesota and Wisconsin, as well as the Dakotas. While there is considerable dif-ference in the food-wheat and feed-grain patterns specified by models A and E, they largely agree regarding areas specified to remain in grain production. Only five areas specified for production of some grain by model E are not specified by model A. Conversely, only one area specified to remain in grain production by model A is not specified by model E. Hence, only 4 more of the 104 areas would be needed to meet feed-grain and food-wheat requirements in model E than in A. The 5 additional areas for fulfilling feed or food requirements under E include areas in eastern Virginia, northeastern Ohio, western Kansas, southern Alabama, and northern Utah. The area specified by model A, but not by C, is in northeastern South Dakota. Thirty-five entire areas and part of a small area in western Kentucky would not be required for grain production in model E. These 36 areas represent the 28.8 million acres which could be shifted to nongrain uses. The pattern is the same, except for the 6 areas noted above, for model A (Figure 1.4).

Consistency or lack of consistency in the three models is indicated by Figure 1.5. The major corn and winter and spring wheat areas are specified to remain in production of grain in all three models. In a similar manner, all three models specify withdrawal from grain production of eastern Colorado and New Mexico, parts of Kansas, Oklahoma, Texas, Michigan, and New York, and practically all of the Southeast—from Arkansas, Tennessee, and southeastern Virginia to the coasts. Only one model, B, specified grain production in eastern Wyoming, southeastern Montana, western Missouri, and a few other scattered areas.

All three models are consistent for 88 of the 104 areas in the sense that they specify 88 areas (those indicated in Figure 1.5 as "all agree") that should remain in grain production or shift completely out of grains. Hence, disagreement among the three models existed for 16 areas. However, disagreement between models A and E, the two models deemed most appropriate by the writers, existed for only 6 areas.

SOME EXTENSIONS OF ABOVE MODELS

This section presents the results of two studies[4] which were extensions of the above models. These studies will be referred to as extensions I and II. The extensions attempted to project the analysis into the future as means of specifying regional production patterns and suggesting agricultural policies relating to prospects in food demand and agricultural production possibilities.

EXTENSION I

The grain economy was further explored mainly by comparative statics or comparisons of particular partial equilibrium situations. First, the grain economy was analyzed with no changes in production efficiency but with projected population growth. This is called the ex post model. Then we looked at this economy under increased production efficiency generated by optimum fertilizer use and fully mechanized production methods using the same projections of population growth. This is called the ex ante model. Finally, we used the production data of the ex post model, plus transportation data, to answer the methodological question: How well have we been able to simulate a general spatial equilibrium system? This is called the production-distribution model.

In the ex post model, net returns from wheat and feed grain were maximized

4. See Egbert, Heady, and Brokken, *Regional Changes in Grain Production*; Egbert and Heady, *Regional Analysis of Production Adjustment*.

for farmers as a group for a range of outputs given (1) production techniques, (2) price relations of 1954, and (3) various demand combinations. In the ex ante model, net returns from wheat and feed grain were maximized for farmers as a group and for a range of outputs given (1) improved production practices, (2) price relations of 1954, and (3) various demand combinations. In the production-distribution model, total production and distribution costs for wheat and feed grain were minimized for the industry as a whole given (1) crop production techniques, (2) distribution costs, (3) factor prices of 1954, and (4) wheat and feed-grain requirements of 1954.

MATHEMATICAL STRUCTURE OF THE MODELS

The mathematical structure of the ex post and ex ante models is exactly the same as that of model E presented above. The requirement levels and some coefficients have been changed. These changes will be presented in the next section.

The structure of the production-distribution model can be summarized as follows:

Let C_{kjq} = quantity of the qth crop produced in kth area and shipped to jth consuming region

c_{kjq} = cost of producing the qth crop in the kth area and shipping it to the jth consuming region

A_k = as defined for Equations 1.1 through 1.5

R_{jq} = consumption requirement of the qth production in the jth consuming region

The programming objective is to

$$\min f(z) = \sum_{k=1}^{104} \sum_{j=1}^{10} \sum_{q=1}^{3} c_{kjq} \, C_{kjq} \qquad (1.21)$$

Subject to these restraints

$$\sum_{j=1}^{10} \sum_{q=1}^{3} C_{kjq} \leqslant A_k \qquad (1.22)$$

$$\sum_{k \in j} C_{kjq} = R_{jq} \qquad (1.23)$$

$$C_{kjq} \geqslant 0 \qquad (1.24)$$

It can be seen from Equations 1.21 through 1.24 that the transportation costs, plus production costs, were used to construct activities to represent shipments of grain from the 104 production areas shown in Figure 1.1 to centers of 10 consuming regions shown in Figure 1.6. The consuming centers represent the mean transportation cost locations of the regions.

Domestic wheat and feed-grain requirements for the base period of 1954 were

Fig. 1.6. Consuming regions.

established as a production of "normalized"[5] per capita consumption of each grain and U.S. population of 1954. All feed-grain quantities except those used for food were converted to corn-equivalent feed units. National requirements, so estimated, were allocated to the 10 consuming regions on the basis of relative population for the production-distribution model. Actual net exports were taken as the best estimate of export needs. These exports were allocated to the 10 consuming regions on the basis of the actual port from which they were shipped. For example, the net overseas shipment of wheat, corn, oats, and barley from the ports of Boston, New York, Baltimore, and other cities in the Northeast area made up part of the requirement or demand for wheat and feed grain in the Northeast.

DATA USED IN THE ABOVE MODELS

The data on yields and cost were based on production practices in 1954. The methods of estimating particular data are exactly the same as that of model E above. The methods of estimating data for the ex ante model and the production-distribution model are described in the next few paragraphs.

EX ANTE MODEL

The yields of the ex ante model are those expected when fertilizer is applied at optimum rates. Fertilizer use and optimum yields were determined by fitting

5. This term has been defined in a previous section: Basic Data and Coefficient Derivation.

functions to fertilizer response data represented in USDA Handbook 68.[6] The response data given in this publication are for each of the major plant nutrients—N, P_2O_5, and K_2O—when it is assumed that each of the other two is used at unlimiting rates. Because the data were presented in this way, simple quadratic functions of the form $Y = a + bN + cN^2$ (in which Y is the estimated yield, N stands for nitrogen, and a, b, and c are estimates of parameters) were fitted to the nitrogen response data in most cases. In some areas, where little response to nitrogen was evident in the data, a P_2O_5 or K_2O production function was fitted and used if it showed evident response because of the nature of the data. These fitted functions were considered as reduced form functions in which the response to the other nutrients is accounted for in the estimated parameters a, b, and c.

If the explicit relationship between N and nutrients were known, the optimum rate for N would be $dY/dN = [P_n + P_b \, g(N) + P_k \, h(N)] P_y$. Given N, then P_2O_5 and K_2O would be given by $g(N)$ and $h(N)$ which represent phosphorus and potash, respectively, as the function of nitrogen. In the absence of these explicit functions, optimum rates were found by successive approximations as follows:

1. An optimum yield (Y') was estimated.
2. For this yield ΔN, ΔP_2O_5, and ΔK_2O (where Δ represents a small change in the specific nutrient) were computed.
3. A price was computed by the following linear combinations:

$$P'_f = (\Delta N/\Delta N) P_n + (\Delta P_2O_5/\Delta N) P_p + (\Delta K_2O/\Delta N) P_k,$$

in which P'_f is the aggregate price of fertilizer inputs, P_n is the price of nitrogen, etc.
4. P'_f was set equal to $(dY/dN) P_y$ and N was solved for; $\hat{Y}$ was then derived.
5. $\hat{Y}$ was compared with Y'.
6. If $\hat{Y}$ was nearly equal to Y', then N was taken to be the optimum nitrogen application, and P_2O_5 and K_2O were found by linear interpolation from the data given in *Handbook 68*.
7. If $\hat{Y}$ was not nearly equal to Y', steps (1) through (4) were repeated until $\hat{Y}$ was nearly equal to Y'.

This procedure gave the optimum yields by states. These yields were compared with economic optimum yields estimated by USDA agronomists at Beltsville, Maryland.[7] In about 50 percent of the cases, the separate estimates were very close. When they differed by as much as 2 bushels, the new optimum yield was estimated by averaging the two independent estimates. Finally, the intercept value of the fitted fertilizer response functions was adjusted so that $\hat{Y}$ was equal to this average. Hence, fertilization rates did not change because of yield adjustments. To estimate regional yields, a further assumption was made. We assumed that the response curves of fertilizer use within states were the same and that yield differences observed for the same application of fertilizer in separate areas were due to different levels of nutrients in the soil. Therefore, optimum yields for producing areas differed only because of differences in the grain and

---

6. USDA, *Fertilizer Use and Crop Yields in the United States*, USDA Handbook 68, 1954.
7. Unpublished data of the Farm Economics Division, USDA.

fertilizer prices. There was, of course, a wide range in fertilizer application rates within states.

Labor costs in the ex ante model were made up of the labor inputs of the fully mechanized production activities used in the ex post model plus additional labor costs associated with the increased yields.

Machinery costs, as for labor, include those associated with mechanized methods of model E (and ex post model) plus costs associated with increased yields. The seed and lime inputs were the same as those used in the ex post model.

Given the regional yields, the steps used to calculate fertilizer costs by crops and by producing areas were as follows:

1. With regional yields of 1954, and the particular fertilizer production function, N' (nitrogen associated with 1954 yield) was derived from the functions of the type $Y = a + bN + cN^2$.
2. This N' was subtracted from N (nitrogen associated with $\hat{Y}$) to obtain the additional nitrogen required to produce optimum yield.
3. Additional quantities of P_2O_5 and K_2O associated with the increment in N were obtained by interpolation from data given in *Handbook 68*.
4. Total fertilizer costs for each crop were finally computed by weighting the additional quantities of N, P_2O_5, and K_2O by their respective regional prices and then summing these costs and adding the sum of 1954 estimates of fertilizer costs. Miscellaneous costs were adjusted to include the cost of applying additional fertilizer.

PRODUCTION-DISTRIBUTION MODEL

The production costs used in the production-distribution model were the same as those used in the ex post model. Freight costs or shipping charges for each programming activity were derived from tariffs furnished by the Transportation and Storage Division of the Commodity Stabilization Service. Commodity tariffs are available only for routes and commodities for which the volume usually shipped warrants the setting of a special rate. If this is not the case, class I rates prevail. The class I rates are higher than commodity rates in nearly all cases. The activity cost of the production-distribution model was computed by adding the approximate production cost and shipping charges as given in Equation 1.25,

$$C_{kjq} = C_{kj} + t_{kjq} \tag{1.25}$$

where t_{kjq} is the estimated cost of shipping the qth commodity from the kth production region to the jth consumption region.

The acreage constraints, function 1.21, were the same as those in the ex post model. Regional consumption requirements (a_{jq}) were calculated by allocating national requirements of 1954 to regions on the basis of normal consumption rates and population and livestock numbers. Actual net exports were allocated to consumption regions by the port of exit.

QUANTITATIVE RESULTS

Results of the ex post and ex ante models will be presented first. Charts or maps will be used for presentation of most quantitative results. Then, comparisons will be made of regional production patterns specified by solutions to these two models to show how production location might change with (1) change in regional production techniques and (2) change in national requirements or needs. Following this, the results derived by the production-distribution model will be presented. Finally, this result will be compared with the result of the ex post model for comparable output mix and national requirement levels.

As stated earlier, optimum regional patterns of production for the ex post and ex ante models were defined for several levels of wheat and feed-grain requirements. These locational patterns were derived by the technique of variable resource of parametric programming. By this technique, a unique program (or, in technical terms, a unique basis) is obtained for each level of a particular resource or combination of resources. In the analysis of wheat and feed grain, a program (or regional production pattern) was obtained for numerous combinations of wheat and feed-grain outputs or demand levels. Although a large number of programs (i.e., the specific grains and quantities to be produced in each region) were available for presentation within certain ranges of the requirement variables, only a few of the possible programs will be presented. These should provide a general picture of how regional adjustments in production might occur under demand expansion and technological change.

REGIONAL PRODUCTION PATTERN, EX POST MODEL

The ex post model used data related to the year 1954. The objective was to define a regional production pattern that would give farmers, as a group, the greatest net return, while at the same time keeping output in balance with particular wheat and feed-grain requirements or consumption mixes at the national level.

Figure 1.7 shows the regional production pattern to produce 800 million bushels of food wheat and 4 billion bushels of feed grain. In other words, the "discrete" demands or requirements were increased over those upon which the results in Figure 1.4 were based. Figure 1.4 is used as a benchmark with which to compare results. Compared with Figure 1.4, grain production has moved into marginal areas 33 (southern Michigan), 20 and 21 (which include parts of Tennessee, Missouri, and Arkansas), 85, 87, and 88 (Texas). The additional wheat required is supplied by area 86 (Texas), areas 17 and 18 (Alabama), area 10 (South Carolina), and area 68 (Kansas). If demand or requirements had been raised even higher, areas in addition to those shown in Figure 1.7 would have been drawn into production.

REGIONAL PRODUCTION PATTERN, EX ANTE MODEL

In developing the data used in the analysis, it was assumed that (1) farmers applied fertilizer at maximum profit rates and (2) only mechanized production

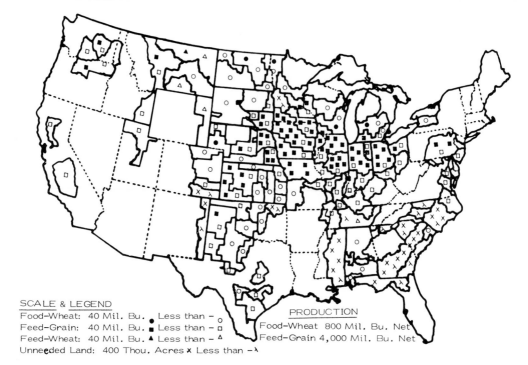

SCALE & LEGEND
Food–Wheat: 40 Mil. Bu. ● Less than – ○
Feed–Grain: 40 Mil. Bu. ■ Less than – □
Feed–Wheat: 40 Mil. Bu. ▲ Less than – △
Unneeded Land: 400 Thou. Acres ✕ Less than – ⅄

PRODUCTION
Food–Wheat 800 Mil. Bu. Net
Feed–Grain 4,000 Mil. Bu. Net

Fig. 1.7. Economic optimum pattern of regional grain production for specified production levels, ex post model.

techniques were used to produce wheat and feed grain. These changes in production technique are perhaps those that have had and promise to have the greatest impact on output and shifts in comparative advantage over time. Again regional production patterns are presented for several combinations of wheat and feed-grain outputs or national requirements level.

Figure 1.8 presents the optimum pattern of grain production under the ex ante model to meet food-wheat requirements of 678 million bushels and feed-grain requirements of 3.6 billion bushels. If we compare Figure 1.8 with Figure 1.4—the figure, showing the pattern of the ex post model at a comparable requirements level—we see that these two figures differ significantly. The acreages in the Corn Belt fringes have shrunk considerably. The same is true, but to a lesser degree, for the acreages of wheat in the Great Plains. Part of the contraction in the Corn Belt results from increased per-acre yields because of much higher rates of commercial fertilizer use in the more productive parts of this area. Part of the contraction is due to a substitution of grain acreage in the Delta, the eastern and western Appalachian area, and the Southwest. This later result indicates that these southern areas could increase their competitive positions in grain production if more intensive cultivation methods were used to produce corn and other feed grain. The changes in cultural practices implied in the production coefficients underlying the yields of the ex ante model are greatly different from those of the present. Fertilization rates are assumed to be much higher than those currently

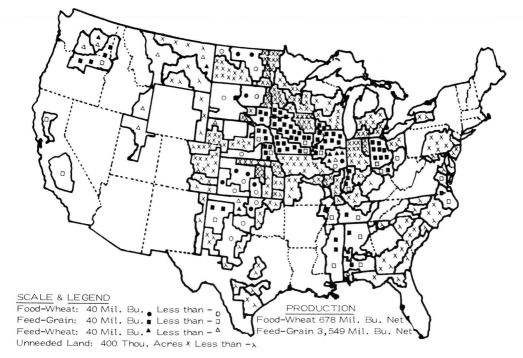

Fig. 1.8. Economic optimum pattern of regional grain production for specified production levels, ex ante model.

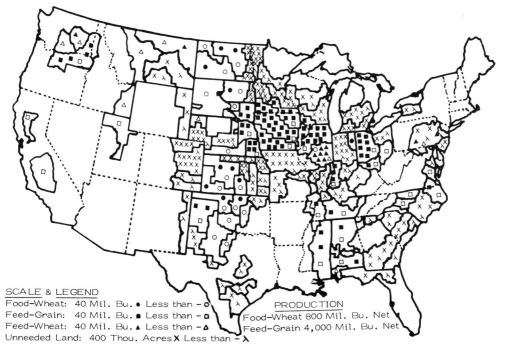

Fig. 1.9. Economic optimum pattern of regional grain production for specified production levels, ex ante model.

being used, and this change requires that (1) farmers be aware of the output-increasing effects of fertilizer use and (2) they have the money to buy it. The latter perhaps is a significant obstacle to raising the competitive advantage of the Southeast in grain production. But the use of mechanized production methods in many areas not only means sizable investments in machinery but also may mean farm consolidation sufficient to cause the necessary machinery inputs and outputs to be economically attainable. Such changes may take time and involve considerable adjustments in the economic and social structure of an area. Nonetheless, these results suggest that improvements in the relative competitive positions of these areas are possible, if not probable.

Figure 1.9 shows the changes in regional production pattern when wheat production was raised from 678 to 800 million bushels and feed-grain production was increased from 3.6 billion to 4 billion bushels. The increased requirements of wheat and feed grain (over the requirements specified for Figure 1.8) are met as production is extended to area 53 (North Dakota), area 46 (Minnesota and Iowa), areas 7 and 8 (North Carolina), and area 32 (Indiana). A shift in production from wheat to all feed grain takes place in area 38 (Illinois). Area 2 is brought into production of feed wheat as compared to Figure 1.8.

REGIONAL PRODUCTION PATTERN, PRODUCTION-DISTRIBUTION MODEL

The production-distribution model specifies not only where wheat and feed grains would be produced under economic efficiency criteria but also to which destination they would flow. It specifies the areas (given in Figure 1.1) where each grain is to be produced as well as the centers or regions (shown in Figure 1.6) to which this grain flows for consumption. Both primary production costs and distribution costs make up the objective to be minimized in the model. The national requirements of food wheat and feed grain are distributed among the 10 consuming regions (Figure 1.6) as shown in Table 1.7. This distribution was made on the basis of the January 1955 population in each of the 10 regions, U.S. average per capita consumption rates, and actual net exports shipped from each of these 10 regions.

Figure 1.10 presents the location of the areas where production is to take place under the formulation of the production-distribution model. Before turning to the distribution pattern of this specified production, we shall compare Figure 1.10 with Figure 1.4. Figure 1.4 used the same production coefficients and output specifications.

First of all, we see that more areas are specified to produce two products in Figure 1.10 than in Figure 1.4. This phenomenon is simply the function of the number of demand restraints in the system and the number of activities available per region.[8]

8. If the number of demand constraints is equal to or greater than the number of activities per region, all activities of any one region could be specified by a production plan. While such is the case for one region, it cannot be true for all, because the number of nonzero activity levels cannot be greater than the number of constraints. For example, we could not have two nonzero activities for each of 100 regions if there are but 199 constraints. One significant point here is that regional diversification is not precluded because linear input-output coefficients are used. Furthermore, we could say the same would be true for individual firms if they were large enough to experience price changes with changes in output. However, a direct awareness of

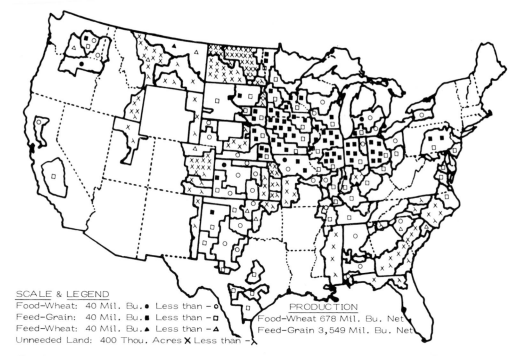

SCALE & LEGEND
Food-Wheat: 40 Mil. Bu. ● Less than – o
Feed-Grain: 40 Mil. Bu. ■ Less than – □
Feed-Wheat: 40 Mil. Bu. ▲ Less than – △
Unneeded Land: 400 Thou. Acres ✗ Less than – ⅄

PRODUCTION
Food-Wheat 678 Mil. Bu. Net
Feed-Grain 3,549 Mil. Bu. Net

Fig. 1.10. Economic optimum pattern of regional grain production for specified production levels, production-distribution model.

Figure 1.10 shows that the location of food wheat has moved eastward as compared with that shown in Figure 1.4. For example, in Figure 1.4, wheat production is specified in only three areas east of Mississippi. These are in southern Wisconsin, east central Wisconsin, and southern Alabama. On the other hand, Figure 1.10 shows that either all or part of 13 areas are designated for food-wheat production by the solution to the production-distribution model. Likewise, in the Pacific states, Figure 1.4 designates areas 100, 101, 102, and 103 for wheat production earmarked for feed. But Figure 1.10 shows all or part of three areas— 100, 101, and 103—earmarked for food wheat.

Figure 1.10 implies that wheat for food would be shipped to the West Coast from areas east of the Rocky Mountains, presumably from the Northern Plains states. The production-distribution model (Figure 1.10) indicates, on the other hand, that such a production allocation is not the most economical spatial production pattern. This model indicates that it would be cheaper to produce all the food wheat locally and to import some feed grain instead of producing, as implied by the ex post model (Figure 1.10), all required feed locally (as wheat) plus some for outshipment.

The two models also differ concerning the production of feed grain in the Mountain states. Inasmuch as the feed wheat produced by areas 89 and 90 (Montana, Figure 1.10) is equal to the feed-grain needs of the Mountain states, produc-

price changes would not be necessary for firms to practice diversification because of adjustment to price. See the Supplement to USDA Tech. Bull. 1241 (pp. 2–3) for an elaboration on this point.

tion specified for areas 89, 90, 93, and 99 by the ex post model exceeds the needs of the Mountain states. Hence, the ex post model implicitly specifies exports of feed from this area.

There are also differences between the results of the two models with respect to food-wheat production in the Northern Plains. The ex post model specifies food-wheat production for areas 55 and 56 (South Dakota). The production-distribution model, in contrast, specifies feed grain for these areas. Another example is that the ex post model specifies food wheat for areas 51, 52, and 53 (North Dakota) and area 69 (Kansas), whereas the production-distribution model specifies no production of grains for these areas.

The foregoing comparisons simply mean that, when distance and shipping charges are taken into account, the Northern Plains loses its relatively prime competitive position in grain production. However, countervailing factors other than shipping charges appear to be important in establishing the actual competitive status of any one area. Some of these factors will be discussed later.

The food-wheat and feed-grain requirements of all 10 consuming regions (Table 1.7) are not satisfied by the production region pattern shown by Figure 1.10. By this we mean that the specified aggregate output of all the production regions contained in the outlines of the 10 consuming regions, group by group, does not match these consumption requirements, and hence surpluses and deficits exist. Production surpluses of certain consuming regions, of course, must

Fig. 1.11. Regional shipment of food wheat to minimize production and distribution cost of both wheat and feed grain.

Fig. 1.12. Regional shipment of feed grain to minimize production and distribution cost of both feed grain and food wheat.

be distributed to consuming regions with deficits. The analytical model used solves the production and distribution problems simultaneously. Figures 1.11 and 1.12 show the regional shipments of food wheat and feed grain, respectively, which balance the implied surpluses and deficits as designated by the model solution.

Figure 1.11 shows that most of the food-wheat shipments specified by the solution are to the Northeast. Of a total of 211 million bushels of food wheat going to the Northeast, 27.7 million are from Ohio, 26.8 million from Indiana, 69.7 million from Michigan, 4.5 million from Illinois, and 82.5 million from Kansas. Kansas also is designated to ship 37.2 million bushels of wheat for food to the Appalachian area and 29.1 million to the Delta states.

Again, Figure 1.12 shows that most feed-grain shipments are to the Northeast under the production-distribution model. Of the 296 million bushels to be shipped to this area, 278.9 million are to be supplied by Ohio and 17.5 million by Indiana. Indiana also ships 118.4 million bushels to the Appalachian area and 159.9 million to the Southeast. Illinois ships 39 million bushels to the Southeast, also. Nebraska ships 129.2 million bushels of feed grain to the Delta states and also 21 million bushels to the Southern Plains. Finally, Kansas is designated to ship 74.3 million bushels to the Pacific states. Other shipments within consuming regions can and are expected to take place, of course, but are not specifeid. For example, feed grain can flow from Iowa to Illinois or Missouri, or wheat, from Colorado to Arizona.

EXTENSION II

The above analysis was further extended by (1) including soybeans and cotton, in addition to wheat and feed grain; (2) delineating 122 producing areas (as compared to 104 areas in earlier analysis) to serve as basic producing units; and (3) projecting the optimal production locations for 1965.

Again the general objective of the analysis was to define an economically efficient pattern of regional production of the major field crops that would bring production into balance with consumption and prevent continued buildup of stocks. Regional production efficiency is defined in the analysis as a spatial distribution of production that would provide only our annual needs—both domestic and foreign—at minimum total cost. The specific objectives were (1) to construct regional programming models with production activities for wheat, corn, oats, barley, sorghum, soybeans, and cotton for two points of time—1954 and 1965; and (2) to use the programming models to define the economic optimum regional distribution of production of these major field crops given output requirements, production restraints, and technical coefficients of 1954 and as projected for 1965.

MATHEMATICAL STRUCTURE OF THE MODELS

Several linear programming models were constructed to achieve the analysis objectives. Four of these models are reported here. The distinguishing characteristics of these models are summarized in Table 1.8. The A models relate to the 1954 data and the B's to 1965 projections. The general objective for each of the models listed in Table 1.8 was that of determining optimum regional economic efficiency within the structure of each model. The actual programming objective of A models differed from B models (Table 1.8). In the A models, the formal empirical objective was to maximize aggregate net returns, given product prices, for the overall or national farm sector incorporated in the programming analysis. The objective for the B models was to minimize supply costs, given regional price differences for this national farm aggregate. The solutions, however, are comparable.

MODELS A.1 AND A.2

The objective of model A.1 is to

$$\max f(r) = \sum_{k=1}^{122} \sum_{q=1}^{5} C_{kq}\, r_{kq} \tag{1.26}$$

subject to
regional land restraints

$$\sum_{q=1}^{5} C_{kq} \leqslant A_k \tag{1.27}$$

national demand restraints

$$\sum_{k=1}^{122} b_{k1} \, C_{k1} = R_1 \tag{1.28}$$

$$\sum_{k=1}^{122} \sum_{q=2}^{4} b_{kq} \, C_{kq} = R_2 \tag{1.29}$$

$$\sum_{k=1}^{122} \sum_{q=4}^{5} b'_{kq} \, C_{kq} = R_3 \tag{1.30}$$

$$\sum_{k=1}^{122} b_{k5} \, C_{k5} = R_4 \tag{1.31}$$

$k = 1, \ldots, \ldots 122$

$q = 1$ for food wheat, 2 for feed wheat, 3 for feed grains, 4 for feed grain–soybeans, 5 for cotton-cottonseed

$n = 1$ for food wheat, 2 for feed grain, 3 for oil meal, and 4 for cotton lint

when all the terms are as defined for Equations 1.21 through 1.24. Model A.2 is similar to model A.1 in all respects except for the demand restraints in Equations 1.29 through 1.31 which become

$$\sum_{k=1}^{122} \sum_{q=2}^{4} b_{kq} \, C_{kq} \leqslant R'_2 \tag{1.32}$$

$$\sum_{k=1}^{122} \sum_{q=4}^{5} b'_{kq} \, C_{kq} \geqslant R_3 \tag{1.33}$$

$$\sum_{k=1}^{122} b_{k5} \, C_{k5} = R_4 \tag{1.34}$$

$$\left[R'_2 - \sum_{k=1}^{122} \sum_{q=2}^{4} b_{kq} \, C_{kq} \right] + \lambda \left[R_3 - \sum_{k=1}^{122} \sum_{q=4}^{5} b'_{kq} \, C_{kq} \right] = 0 \tag{1.35}$$

where R'_2 is the upper bound or feed-grain requirements, R_3 is the lower bound or oil meal requirements, R_4 is the requirements for cotton, and λ is a constant equal to the marginal rate of substitution of oil meal for feed grain.

MODELS B.1 AND B.2

Models B.1 and B.2 are similar to models A.1 and A.2, respectively, except for the objective function. The objective function of models B.1 and B.2 is the same as presented in Equation 1.1 (except for increased number of regions and crops).

Fig. 1.13. Location of crop-producing areas.

ASSEMBLY OF BASIC DATA

Basic data were assembled on the basis of 122 separate producing areas used for the analysis. Producing areas 1 through 104 were the same as delineated for the earlier analysis dealing with wheat and feed grain (Figure 1.1). The additional 18 producing areas were delineated in order to include cotton and soybeans. These later regions aggregated on the county basis included counties in which 10 percent or more of the total cropland was planted to either cotton or soybeans in 1954, or in which at least 15 percent of the total cropland was planted to soybeans and cotton if both were grown. Under this criterion, a few additional counties were added to the 104 wheat and feed-grain–producing areas delineated previously to form those indicated by the boundary outlines shown in Figure 1.13. Rules for aggregation of state economic areas and counties into the 18 additional areas were the same as those used for the primary 104 areas. A brief summary of data assembly procedures is presented below.

OUTPUT DATA

Crop yields were estimated by producing areas for the years 1954 and 1965. The method used for estimating crop yields for 1954 was described above. Projected crop yields for 1965 were estimated by areas in a similar way. Again, 1945-54 average yields were used as the basic data. However, the annual linear trend for the period 1940-59, instead of the 1937-54 trend, was used to project

1945-54 average yields to 1965. This method of projecting yields assumed that technological advancement in production of crops involved will be at about the same rate as it was from 1940 to 1959, and that the output-increasing effect of this added technology also will be similar to this period.

INPUT DATA

Input data or production costs for 1954 were similar in structure to those used in previous analyses involving wheat and feed grain only. Cost of production included those for labor, machinery, seed, chemicals, and miscellaneous items. Estimated production costs were weighted averages of several production methods used within each area. Production costs for cotton included two additional cost components: costs of hauling cotton to the gin and costs of the ginning.

Production costs for 1965 were estimated primarily by adjusting 1954 data to the later point in time. Adjustments were made in estimates of fertilizer use and resource prices. Estimates of new levels of fertilizer use were made by fitting linear regression to the use of nitrogen, phosphorus, and potassium individually, by states. These trends were then used to adjust the fertilizer use of 1954 to estimated 1965 levels. Estimated changes in fertilizer use were compared with the estimated yield increases. For crops, if the ratio of the estimated marginal value product of fertilizer to its marginal cost was less than two or greater than four, adjustments were made in the fertilizer input to bring the ratio within these bounds.[9]

Simple linear projections of trends in price indices of particular input categories were used to adjust factor costs after adjustments in physical quantities had been made. For all inputs, except labor, national trends were used to make factor price adjustments. Labor costs, on the other hand, were adjusted by state trends in wage rates to account for regional variations in wages.

These methods used to estimate 1965 production costs are somewhat arbitrary and involve judgment of trends in the direction of major economic variables. However, in light of the degree of uncertainty involved in such projections even where they are made with a greater degree of refinement, and of inexactness in empirical tools, the method used was judged to be adequate for achieving the following important objectives: (1) to estimate input levels of wheat, feed grain, soybean, and cotton prices in 1965, and (2) to describe an efficient regional production pattern when production is in balance with needs.

PRODUCTION REQUIREMENTS AND RESTRAINTS

Two types of restraints were used in this analysis: (1) national restraints or requirements specifying the amounts of crops necessary for human consumption and livestock feed, and (2) regional production restraints representing the maximum acreage of crops for each producing region. In general, national consumption restraints or requirements were entered into the programming models as

9. These limits were set after consulting with Iowa State agronomists and reviewing fertilizer response functions and recommended application rates.

equalities so the amounts to be produced would exactly meet the requirements. For regional crop activities, restraints were defined so that acreage was equal to or less than the amounts explained below.

Requirements of wheat and feed grain for 1954 were based on average per capita consumption adjusted for long-term trends and the population at that time. The exact procedures were described earlier. Cotton lint requirements were estimated by a procedure similar to that used for wheat and feed grain. However, soybean and cottonseed requirements were estimated by slightly different methods. As for the four feed grains, all oilseeds were assumed to be perfect substitutes in the sense of constant rate of substitution based on their feeding value. It was also assumed that primary demand for these crops was in terms of oil meal, and the associated oil produced was a by-product. Consequently, the demand for vegetable oil was not estimated explicitly. The method assumes that if oil meal requirements were met, vegetable oil supply would be adequate.

Given these assumptions, the first step involved in estimating soybean and cottonseed requirements was to fit a time series regression to the average oil meal consumption per high protein-consuming livestock unit for the period 1940-54. The per-unit consumption of oil meal estimated by the regression equation was then multiplied by the number of high protein-consuming livestock units on farms in 1954 to obtain an estimate of total oil meal requirements for that year. In estimating the part of total oil-meal consumption derived from soybeans and cottonseed, it was assumed that the proportion of SBOM (soybean oil meal) and CSOM (cottonseed oil meal) making up total oil-meal consumption was relatively constant. Total requirements of SBOM and CSOM were then estimated by multiplying estimated total oil-meal requirements by a factor representing the average proportion of total oil-meal consumption represented by SBOM and CSOM in the period 1950-59. The other components of domestic demand, i.e., seed, oilseeds fed as such, and fertilizer, were taken as the actual disappearances in these forms in 1954. Export demand for soybeans and cottonseed was taken as the actual net exports of 1954. As with other commodities, actual exports were used because of the great fluctuations of agricultural exports, primarily because of changes in public export policy and the uncertain world food situation.

Projected requirements for 1965 were estimated by a more complex method than that used to estimate 1954 requirements. A more complex method was used because the objective was to define a regional production pattern and output mix that would be consistent with long-run price equilibrium or nearly so.

The model used to estimate the requirements of wheat, feed grain, oil meal, and cotton considered the demand for each commodity to be a function of its own price, the price of those substitutes, per capita income, and population. Because per capita income and population are exogenous variables with respect to the production or programming problem, their values could be derived independently and were obtained from other independent projections. On the other hand, commodity prices were endogenous with respect to the programming problem. Hence, to estimate the demand requirements for programming, it was necessary to estimate what the equilibrium market prices might be under the optimal production pattern. The estimated equilibrium prices were wheat, $1.30 per bushel; corn, $1.00 per bushel; soybeans, $1.85 per bushel; and cotton, $0.25 per pound.[10]   Given these prices, total requirements of each commodity were estimated on the basis of a national demand model.[11]

Acreage constraints or maximum total acreage that could be planted to the seven crops in the analysis for 1954 were the actual acreages of these crops planted in 1953. Production was limited in this way because acreage controls were not in effect that year. Hence, these acreages perhaps best represent maximums that would have been planted in 1954 under a free market.

Acreage constraints for 1965 were estimates designed to reflect the changing regional land-use pattern of agriculture. Two objectives in making these adjustments were (1) to establish a realistic upper bound on plantings of wheat, feed grain, soybeans, or cotton; and (2) to establish new weights for feed-grain rotations that reflect trends evident in a number of sections in the country.

QUANTITATIVE RESULTS

The results presented in the following paragraphs show the crops which would probably be produced in each area if the criterion of the most efficient production pattern to exactly meet specified national requirements was attained for each model. Hence the results also suggest the location and extent of surplus acreage devoted to the specified field crops in meeting national requirements. In this sense, they suggest under each model the land area which might be withdrawn from these particular crops (1) if buildup of surpluses were stopped, (2) if certain demand requirements and price levels were attained, and (3) if the technology and other conditions of the particular models prevailed. It is recognized, of course, that parts of some regions indicated for crop production would not be so used. Also, parts of some regions not included for crop production would actually be used for these purposes. The level of original aggregation in the several models requires that these qualifications be mentioned.

MODEL A.1

Five programming activities included in this analysis were food wheat, feed wheat, feed-grain rotation, feed-grain–soybean rotation, and cotton. Thus one difference between model A.1 and earlier models is that feed-grain–soybean and cotton activities have been added to the regional production possibilities. With the addition of soybeans and cotton, the regional acreage restraints are larger for

10. In the programming models, other feed grains—oats, barley, and sorghum—were converted to corn-equivalent feed units and cottonseed converted to soybean-oilmeal—equivalent feed units. Therefore, the prices of other feed grains are related to corn price as they are related in feed value. Likewise the price of cottonseed is related to the price of soybeans as it is related in terms of feed value, but also, the price of cottonseed included a differential to reflect that the yield of oil per soybean-oilmeal—equivalent unit is higher for cottonseed and also to reflect the value of linters and hulls.

11. For details of the national demand model, see Egbert and Heady, *Regional Analysis of Production Adjustment*.

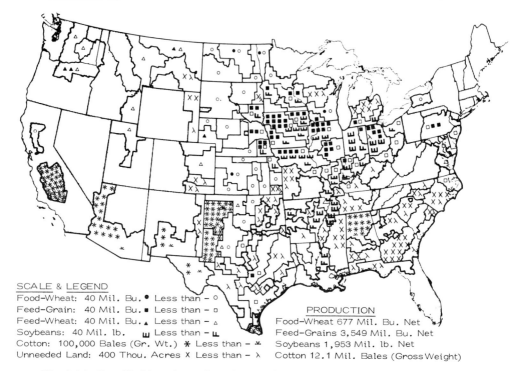

SCALE & LEGEND
Food–Wheat: 40 Mil. Bu. • Less than – ○
Feed–Grain: 40 Mil. Bu. ■ Less than – □
Feed–Wheat: 40 Mil. Bu. ▲ Less than – △
Soybeans: 40 Mil. lb.   ⊔ Less than – ⊔
Cotton: 100,000 Bales (Gr. Wt.) ✳ Less than – ✻
Unneeded Land: 400 Thou. Acres X Less than – λ

PRODUCTION
Food–Wheat 677 Mil. Bu. Net
Feed–Grains 3,549 Mil. Bu. Net
Soybeans 1,953 Mil. lb. Net
Cotton 12.1 Mil. Bales (Gross Weight)

Fig. 1.14. Specified locations of production for major field crops: model Al solution.

model A.1 than earlier models by the number of acres planted to soybeans and cotton in 1953.

A comparison of Figures 1.14 and 1.4 shows, for crops common to both models, few differences in the specified regional patterns of production. Feed grains are specified virtually for the same producing areas under model A.1 as under model E (Figure 1.4). However, soybeans generally are indicated in the same areas as feed grain under model A.1. Because maximum regional acreages are greater for model A.1, the indicated presence of soybeans in feed-grain–producing areas does not require that feed-grain production be expanded greatly in other areas.[12]   In areas where sizable acreages of wheat have been grown, such as the eastern Corn Belt, feed-grain production for model A.1 is less than that specified under model E (Figure 1.4). This occurs because the soybean acreage in the rotation at that maximum level is greater than the additional acreage added to the regional base by soybeans.

The most significant differences in the results of model A.1 and model E (Figure 1.4) are in the production pattern specified for the High Plains of Texas and the lower Central Valley of California. In these areas, cotton production replaces the feed-grain production specified by model E.

Other results of particular importance are these: for model A.2, most of the

12. The results of model A.1 essentially reproduce or reflect the historical pattern of crop production in many parts of the Corn Belt where little or no wheat is now grown.

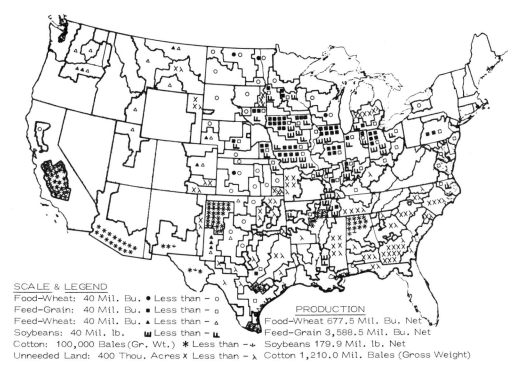

SCALE & LEGEND
Food–Wheat: 40 Mil. Bu. ● Less than – o
Feed–Grain: 40 Mil. Bu. ■ Less than – ▫
Feed–Wheat: 40 Mil. Bu. ▲ Less than – ▵
Soybeans: 40 Mil. lb.   ш Less than – ш
Cotton: 100,000 Bales (Gr. Wt.) ✳ Less than – ⩊
Unneeded Land: 400 Thou. Acres x Less than – ⋋

PRODUCTION
Food–Wheat 677.5 Mil. Bu. Net
Feed–Grain 3,588.5 Mil. Bu. Net
Soybeans 179.9 Mil. lb. Net
Cotton 1,210.0 Mil. Bales (Gross Weight)

Fig. 1.15. Specified locations of production for major field crops allowing feed-grain–soybean substitution: model A2 solution.

cotton production is specified for the Southwest. On the basis of the models and data used, only the Mississippi Delta and northern Alabama appear to be serious competitors of the Southwest in meeting national and foreign needs for cotton. Soybeans also appear to be a competitive crop in the Delta where increased production of this crop has taken place since the 1950s. However, as will be shown later, this position could be threatened by changes in production patterns in the Corn Belt.

We now turn to regional changes that occur when such a model is used to allow the most economical source of feed, either feed grain or oil meal, to be substituted in meeting total feed requirements.

MODEL A.2

Figure 1.15, the regional production patterns specified by model A.2, shows only minor differences when compared with Figure 1.14. These differences result mainly from the relative small substitution of feed grain for oil meal that occurs in the solution of A.2. The changes for model A.2 are these: area 39 (southern Illinois) produces only feed grain in place of feed grain and soybeans. Area 81 (central Texas) is specified to increase its feed-wheat production and consequently to contract food-wheat production i.e., substitute feed wheat for food wheat. This deficit in food wheat is suggested by model A.2, to be made up by

wheat production in area 35 (north central Wisconsin). Additional feed-grain production in areas 39 and 81 replaces soybean production in area 108 (Mississippi
and Arkansas). These are minor changes when the total or national production
area is considered. Given the structure of the model, the solution implies the extent to which it would be profitable for the industry to substitute feed grain for
oil meal in meeting total feed requirements.

MODEL B.1

Structurally, model B.1 is similar to model A.1, i.e., it has the same activities,
and the requirement levels to be met are fixed for feed grain and oil meal, as well
as for food wheat and cotton, only the programming coefficients differ. Figure
1.16 shows the specified regional pattern of production from this model.

Since the 1965 requirements, as compared to 1954, express a greatly increased
output, ranging from 33 percent for cotton to 55 percent for soybeans, a greater
proportion of the acreage base is used. Compared to Figure 1.14—the 1954
counterpart of Figure 1.16—Figure 1.16 shows some wheat production moving
into the Southeast and some feed grain moving into the eastern seaboard of the
Appalachian area. The specification of wheat production in the Southeast may be
due to inappropriateness of production coefficients and prices. First, production
coefficients were based on only a few observations and were from the limited area

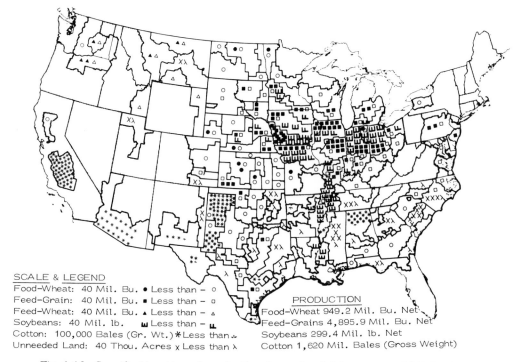

SCALE & LEGEND
Food–Wheat: 40 Mil. Bu. • Less than – o
Feed–Grain: 40 Mil. Bu. ▪ Less than – ▫
Feed–Wheat: 40 Mil. Bu. ▲ Less than – △
Soybeans: 40 Mil. lb.   ⨄ Less than – ⨄
Cotton: 100,000 Bales (Gr. Wt.) ✳ Less than ⨄
Unneeded Land: 40 Thou. Acres x Less than λ

PRODUCTION
Food–Wheat 949.2 Mil. Bu. Net
Feed–Grains 4,895.9 Mil. Bu. Net
Soybeans 299.4 Mil. lb. Net
Cotton 1,620 Mil. Bales (Gross Weight)

Fig. 1.16. Specified location of production for major field crops: model B.1 solution.

in the region where wheat is grown. Therefore, they may not adequately represent an entire region which might move into wheat production. Second, regional price differentials may be "in the wrong direction" for this area. Specifically, this area has a history for garlicky wheat which is heavily discounted at the mills. In the analysis, however, U.S. prices for average grade wheat were used to construct price differentials. If these prices were too high in terms of quality of the crop produced in the area, wheat would be included for the Southeast in the programming results, when actually it would be produced more efficiently elsewhere. The indicated shift of wheat production to the Southeast is perhaps forced there by an obvious pattern of production which emerges under the model. If Figures 1.14 and 1.16 are compared, it can be seen that model B.1 causes feed-grain production to replace wheat production in most of South Dakota.

Fewer regions produce soybeans in the solution of model B.1 as compared with that of model A.1. This result can be explained because soybean yields are assumed to increase more rapidly than demand from 1954 to 1965, and because soybeans make up a larger proportion of the rotation acre under the 1965 assumptions as compared with the 1954 assumptions.

The results presented in Figure 1.16 suggest a smaller potential surplus acreage than do previous models. More specifically, the results for model B.1 have this meaning: given the production coefficients as measured and the regional price structure assumed, the production pattern shown is the most economically efficient one for producing the specified output mix. However, this would not be the equilibrium output mix. This occurs because the derived supply prices, except for cotton, are higher than the demand prices assumed for estimating demand requirements. For output to be maintained at the specified levels, resources employed would have to accept earnings below those reflected by the factor or resource prices used to estimate production costs.

MODEL B.2

Model B.2 permitted either feed-grain or oil-meal production to expand beyond the levels of model B.1. As with model A.2, the comparable model of 1954, minimum cost feed production is achieved by substituting feed grain for soybeans. The regional production pattern arising from model B.2 is shown in Figure 1.17. Some minor changes do occur in the regional pattern from model B.2 as compared with model B.1. Feed-grain production is increased in area 31 (Indiana) to replace soybean production in this region. Feed-grain production decreases in area 55 (South Dakota) and area 36 (Wisconsin). Wheat output increases in these two areas because the supply price of feed grain declines slightly as compared with model B.1.[13]

The supply price for feed is lower under this model than under B.1 because the marginal units of feed are produced at lower costs. Model B.1 forced a specific proportion of oil meal into the production requirements and the resulting

---

13. The term "programmed price" refers to the marginal supply price obtained by the dual programming solution. These prices determine if a region will be "selected" to produce and which activity within the region will be selected.

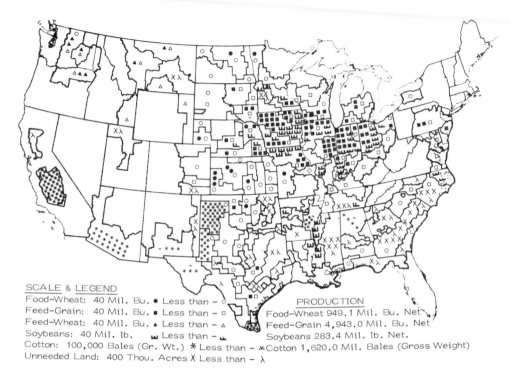

SCALE & LEGEND
Food–Wheat: 40 Mil. Bu. ● Less than – ○
Feed–Grain: 40 Mil. Bu. ■ Less than – □
Feed–Wheat: 40 Mil. Bu. ▲ Less than – △
Soybeans: 40 Mil. lb.   ⊔ Less than – ⊔
Cotton: 100,000 Bales (Gr. Wt.) ✶ Less than – ✶
Unneeded Land: 400 Thou. Acres X Less than – λ

PRODUCTION
Food–Wheat 949.1 Mil. Bu. Net
Feed–Grain 4,943.0 Mil. Bu. Net
Soybeans 283.4 Mil. lb. Net.
Cotton 1,620.0 Mil. Bales (Gross Weight)

Fig. 1.17. Specified location of production for major field crops allowing feed-grain–soybean substitution: model B.2 solution.

oil-meal component of total feed production was greater. Both models allow the production of soybeans only as a part of a feed-grain rotation. Given this fact, some region may be able to produce soybeans at a relatively low cost, but the cost of feed-grain production included in the "fixed" rotation may be relatively high. Therefore, if the total requirement of oil meal is so high that this region must be selected to produce soybeans, the marginal quantities of feed grain, which are tied to the soybean production by the rotation, will have relatively high unit costs.

SIGNIFICANCE AND LIMITATIONS OF RESULTS

The models used in the studies reported above represented some refinement over similar calculations made in the previous studies. But the studies were somewhat methodological in nature—to establish the steps necessary leading to data and models realistic for the policymaking in agriculture. The empirical results are conditioned by the data deficiencies and simplifying assumptions. Various simplifying assumptions were made because of computational necessity at the time these studies were conducted.

More realistic models would not only have included more crop activities but also more crops, such as flax and rice, as well as livestock activities which produced feeder stocks and slaughter animals. These models would have allowed shipping grain and livestock from one area to another to take account of regional comparative advantages and market demands. An effort was made to include transportation costs from one region center to another in the production-distribution model. The empirical results indicated a geographic distribution pattern of the specified production which included more areas than the other models. But the production-distribution model also has its limitations. The consuming regions are much too broad. These broad regions obviously cannot generate a completely satisfactory regional price structure, and they can distort the regional production patterns given by the programming solution. The model also assumes that consumption occurs near production, except for interregional shipments. This assumption, too, probably has had considerable effect on the programming solution.

Further, the producers do not have identical input-output coefficients. The quality of management varies. The quality of land used for grain, soybean, and cotton production varies not only between but also within farms. Classification of land within regions by productive capacity for crops and the use of several classes of land for regional land restraints would have been more realistic. If several land classes were used, however, the size of the problem (matrix) would have been greatly expanded. Some of the above limitations have been removed in the models reported in subsequent chapters.

Chapter 2: Land Qualities and Crop Production Capacity

EARL O. HEADY and NORMAN K. WHITTLESEY

The major purpose of this study was to define efficient interregional allocation of food and fiber production over the United States and to designate the possible effect of alternative market equilibriums or farm policies in attaining or restraining these patterns. While prior studies dealt mainly with benchmark solutions in 1954, this study emphasized interregional competition and surplus agricultural capacity estimated to have existed in 1965. The emphasis was on interregional allocations of production for wheat, feed grain, soybeans, and cotton and on the flow of products among consuming regions in a manner to provide an optimal U.S. use of resources and to mesh production exactly with consumption and export requirements.

The analysis was made by several linear programming models and solutions which included up to 962 equations and 2,682 real variables. An effort was made to delineate more homogeneous producing areas and consuming regions, and to include transfer and transportation activities. The models included 144 spatially separated producing areas. About 96 percent of the national output of wheat, feed grain, cotton, and soybeans was covered by the 144 producing areas. The individual areas were sufficiently homogeneous with respect to soil types, climate, historic yields, and production costs to serve as a producing entity. The models also contained 31 spatially separated consuming regions, defined by state boundaries of 48 states, to reflect the projected demand requirements of wheat, feed grain, and oil meal (a single national demand was specified for cotton lint). The discrete demand quantities were composites of industrial (for both food and nonfood uses), livestock, and export needs for each region. The 1,400 transportation activities provide for movement of wheat, feed grain, and oil meal among the consuming regions. Transportation activities are defined only between groups of producing areas aggregated to the level of consuming regions rather than from individual producing areas to consuming regions. A transfer activity in each consuming region allows wheat to be used for livestock feed at a "transformation" cost varying upward from zero. This activity and the "transformation" costs attached to it provide the possibility of considering single-price or multiple-price plans for wheat.

Acreage restraints, provided individually for wheat, feed grain, and cotton in each producing area, were based upon the historical acreage of each crop within

NOTE: For further details, see Earl O. Heady and Norman K. Whittlesey, *A Programming Analysis of Interregional Competition and Surplus Capacity of American Agriculture*, Agr. and Home Econ. Exp. Sta., Iowa State Univ., Ames, Res. Bull. 538, July 1965.

the area. Acreage restraints for individual crops were varied, however, for models representing different assumptions regarding agricultural programs. The upper limit on soybean production was set at 40 percent of total cropland acreage in each producing area. Minimum production was not required of any crop in any area.

SPECIFIC OBJECTIVES OF THE ANALYSIS

The specific objectives of this analysis were

1. To indicate the amount and location of land that should be withdrawn from wheat, feed grain, and cotton production if surplus production were eliminated in 1965.
2. To reflect an efficient allocation of production and land use under a minimum cost objective function for alternative adjustment or supply control programs.
3. To specify the impact of programs aimed directly at wheat or feed grain upon the production allocation of nonprogram crops.
4. To analyze the effect of changes in final demand upon the allocation of production and land disposal.
5. To formulate optimal land-use patterns when marginal land within, as well as between, regions is removed from production.
   Other objectives of the study were
6. To estimate the regional and national derived equilibrium product prices under each of the program alternatives.
7. To estimate the regional rental value of cropland and acreage quotas under optimal land-use patterns.
8. To determine the net interregional flows of final products under the production patterns of each program alternative.

The analysis relating to objectives (6) and (7) will, however, be presented in detail in a subsequent chapter.

BASIC MODEL

Since construction of the three models was similar, we include a mathematical summary of a "basic model" whose characteristics are common to all programming models used. The objective function, indicated in Equation 2.1, relates to minimizing national costs of production and interregional transportation of the bill of goods represented by demand of the 31 consuming regions for wheat, feed grain, cotton, and oil meal.

$$\min f(C) = cC \tag{2.1}$$

In Equation 2.1, c is a $(kq + t)$ row vector including production, transfer, and transportation costs corresponding to q crop activities, k producing areas, and t transfer and transportation activities; C is a $(kq + t)$ column vector representing levels of crop production, transfer, and transportation activities. Equation 2.1 is minimized subject to the conventional restraints $AC \geqslant b$ and $C \geqslant 0$, where A is a coefficient matrix of $(n + jd) \times (kq + t)$ order (conforming to the n land restraints for each producing area, j demand regions, and d regional demand restraints) and b is a $(n + jd)$ column vector reflecting maximum acreage restraints in each producing area and minimum demand requirements in each consuming region. More specifically, the objective function is

$$\min Z = \sum_{k=1}^{144} \sum_{q=1}^{4} c_{kq}^1 C_{kq} + \sum_{j=1}^{31} c_j^2 Y_j + \sum_{n=1}^{3} \sum_{\substack{j=1 \\ j \neq j'}}^{31} c_{njj'}^3 z_{njj'} \tag{2.2}$$

where Z = total cost of production, transfer, and transportation

c_{kq}^1 = cost of producing one acre of crop activity q in the kth producing area

c_j^2 = cost (artificial price differential) of using one unit of wheat as a feed grain in jth consuming region

$c_{njj'}^3$ = cost of transporting one unit of nth commodity to (from) the jth consuming region from (to) j'th region

C_{kq} = level (in acres) of the qth producing activities in the kth producing area (q = 1, 2, 3, and 4 for wheat, feed grain, soybeans, and cotton respectively

Y_j = level of activity transferring wheat into a feed grain in the jth consuming region

$z_{njj'}$ = level of transportation of the nth commodity to (from) the jth consuming region from (to) the jth consuming region (n = 1, 2, 3 for wheat, feed grain, and oil meal, respectively).

The Equation 2.2 is minimized subject to the following restraints:
    requirement restraints

(1)
$$\sum_{k=1}^{v^j} b_{1k} C_{1k} - h_j Y_j \pm \sum_{\substack{j=1 \\ j \neq j'}}^{31} t_{1jj'} z_{1jj'} = R_{1j} \tag{2.3}$$

(2)
$$\sum_{k=1}^{v^j} b_{2k} C_{2k} + h_j Y_j \pm \sum_{\substack{j=1 \\ j \neq j'}}^{31} t_{2jj'} z_{1jj'} = R_{2j} \tag{2.4}$$

(3)
$$\sum_{k=1}^{v^j} b_{3k} C_{3k} + \sum_{k=1}^{v^j} b'_{4k} C_{4k} \pm \sum_{\substack{j=1 \\ j \neq j'}}^{31} t_{3jj'} z_{3jj'} = R_{3j} \tag{2.5}$$

(4)
$$\sum_{k=1}^{144} b_{4k} C_{4k} = Q \tag{2.6}$$

land restraints

(5) $$\sum_{q=1}^{4} C_{qk} \leqslant A_k \tag{2.7}$$

(6) $$C_{kq} \leqslant A_{kq} \tag{2.8}$$

and nonnegativity restraints

(7) $$C_{kq} \geqslant 0, Y_j \geqslant 0, Z_{njj'} \geqslant 0 \tag{2.9}$$

where R_{nj} = demand for nth commodity, expressed in feed units[1] in jth consuming region where n is defined as above

Q = national demand for cotton lint expressed in pounds

h_j = amount of wheat transferred from the jth wheat demand restraint to jth feed-grain demand restraints by one unit of transfer activity

$t_{njj'}$ = amount of the nth commodity transferred to (from) the jth consuming region from (to) the j'th consuming region by the njj'th transportation activity (n equals 1, 2, 3, respectively, for wheat, feed grain, and oil meal (oil meal includes soybean and cottonseed)

v^j = number of producing areas in consuming region j

b_{qk} = per-acre yield of qth activity in the kth producing area, expressed in feed units for all products except cotton lint, which is expressed in pounds (q = 1 for wheat, 2 for feed grain, 3 for soybeans, and 4 for cotton)

b'_{4k} = oil-meal output, in feed units, of the cotton activity in the kth producing area

The "basic model" just summarized is the same as models I and II applied later. The basic models are from a matrix of the order 674 × 1,814 without slack vectors (as shown in tabular form in Table 2.1). Model III differs slightly and will be explained later. It has 962 restraints and 2,682 real activities.

SPECIFIC MODELS

Potentially, four individual producing activities were available in each of the 144 producing areas. However, activities were included in an individual area only if it had a historical record in producing the crop. There were 144, 134, 99, and 58 areas having previously produced feed grain, wheat, soybeans, and cotton, respectively. Although cotton contributes lint for the single national demand, oil meal from cottonseed contributes to individual regional demands. The output of each crop activity is considered to contribute directly to demand at zero transport cost in the consuming region where it is produced.

All models have producing area acreage restraints for each of the major crop activities. Regional restraints also exist for acreage of total cropland. Individual

1. All crop-activity outputs, except cotton lint, were converted to equivalent feed units for use in computations and for comparing the output of various activities with final demands. Since each consuming region had feed-grain demands for which all feed-grain activities and wheat activities competed, the output of the four feed grains and the wheat was most conveniently expressed in similar units. The output of soybeans and cottonseed was similarly expressed in equivalent feed units.

area crop-acreage restraints need not sum to total cropland acreage in each area, since the former reflects the maximum allowable production of each crop in the area to simulate various supply-control programs.

Regional production requirements were estimated for wheat, feed grain, and oil meal and include quantities for human food, livestock feed, and foreign export. A single national demand was specified for cotton lint. Except for two solutions of model I, demand restraints were similar for all solutions in the sense that they require the same total production and the same final product distribution. The two exceptions are solutions of model I to examine the effects of different levels of demand and price on interregional production patterns.

Transportation activities (459, 459, and 430 activities for wheat, feed grain, and oil meal, respectively) were included for all rational possibilities of commodity movements among consuming regions. Movement was assumed to originate and terminate at the geographic center of consuming regions. A transfer activity in each consuming region allowed the use of wheat for feed in cases where the farm crop serves as an efficient source of livestock feed.

MODEL I

Model I is basically the one previously outlined in mathematical form. Its solutions serve as the basis for comparison with those from other models. It has cost coefficients of the wheat–feed-grain transfer activities equal to zero, implying a multiple-price plan for wheat. Wheat can be used for livestock, at a price equal to its equilibrium feed value, as long as wheat requirements used for food and export purposes are first attained (at a price level corresponding to these uses).

MODEL II

Model II is the same as model I except that wheat–feed-grain transfer activities have nonzero costs. The cost is assumed equivalent to the differential between a supported price of wheat at $1.95 per bushel and the price of corn at $1.10 per bushel. The cost differential varies, however, depending upon the actual historical ratio of wheat and corn prices in each consuming region. Hence, this solution examines the regional production distribution when all wheat is priced at a higher support level, but with the possibility that it can be used as feed grain if this "excess price" is considered for its usage as feed grain. This cost is assumed representative of the difference between the equilibrium value and the supported price of wheat. In this model, wheat and feed-grain production patterns are analyzed under the assumption of a single-price level (supported at its historic "food" level) for wheat.

MODEL III

Model III differs from model I with respect to the structure of cropland restraints. Cropland in each producing area is divided into three production or soil categories on the basis of the estimated differences in crop yield and permissible cropping intensity. This change has the effect of multiplying total cropland restraints and producing activities by three, resulting in a coefficient matrix with 962 restraints and 2,682 real activities. This condition adds realism in the sense that it is no longer necessary to have complete retirement of an area from production of a particular crop activity.

BASIC DATA AND COEFFICIENT DERIVATION

Data for the previous studies[2] served as the initial base from which certain coefficients for the current study were projected. The early models were representative of the year 1954, except that acreage serving as maximum production restraints were for 1953. The year 1953 was the last one in which major farm programs did not restrict acreages of wheat, feed grain, or cotton. In general, the methods of the earlier studies were used with yields and costs by producing areas projected to 1965, the year to which this study refers. However, modifications were made, where possible or necessary, to improve coefficients and provide data unique to particular models.

DELINEATION OF PRODUCING AREAS AND CONSUMING REGIONS

The producing areas from the earlier studies formed the basis for those used in this analysis. The producing areas, circumscribed by political boundaries, were based primarily on state economic areas or groups of counties. These areas were assumed internally homogeneous with respect to type of farming and resource productivity. However, they were used mainly because most production information is reported on the basis of counties or economic areas. The criteria for demarcation of the 122 producing areas were described earlier by Egbert and Heady (Chapter 1). Basically, the same criteria were used for this study. But it was necessary to make some adjustments in the producing areas delineated by Egbert and Heady. These changes primarily involved the splitting of an Egbert area into 2 or more areas so they would coincide more closely with the consuming regions of this study. No previously segregated areas were aggregated together, with the result that 144 producing areas were established. These are shown in Figure 2.1 and, henceforth, will be referred to by appropriate number.

All production cost and yield coefficients used in this study were established on the basis of these producing areas. These input-output data were assumed to be comparable to one another and are reflective of those expected for 1965 under normal production practices. A single cost and yield coefficient was assumed to be applicable for each crop over all relevant acreage in a given area. These data, then, provided for investigating regional productional response to various acreage control programs.

One of the major refinements of this study, when compared to previous studies, was the delineation of individual consuming regions. Instead of having single demands representing total U.S. consumption for each product, specifica-

2. The studies reported in Chapter 1.

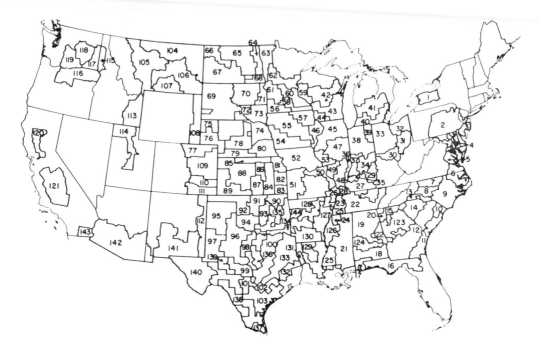

Fig. 2.1. Spatial location of producing areas.

tion of regional product demands was possible in the models of this study. For this purpose, 31 consuming regions, containing all of the coterminous 48 states, were defined.

Spatially separated markets simulating actual consuming patterns were necessary to derive the optimum pattern of commodity production while maintaining the principle of spatially separated markets; the number of consuming regions was restrained to limit the model size for computing purposes. The consuming regions, shown in Figure 2.2, were each defined on the basis of state boundaries. Generally, each consuming region was a single state. For regions including coastal states, it was considered desirable to have a single consuming region encompass as few ports of export or import as possible. In the less populated areas of the West and in the smaller states of the East, more than one state was sometimes included in a single region.

PRODUCTION RESTRAINTS

CROPLAND: MODELS I AND II

Models I and II have a single upper restraint to limit acreage of each crop in in each area. In general, 1953 acreages were used for these regional cropland restraints, because acreage controls were not used to limit the production of crops in that year.[3] Both intraregional and interregional adjustments in crop production

3. Nationally, the total acreage of wheat, feed grain, cotton, and soybeans was greater in 1953 than in any previous or subsequent year.

Fig. 2.2. Spatial location of consuming regions.

are allowed within the boundaries of the regional production capacity reflected by 1953 acreages. In addition, a total cropland restraint, A_k, in each producing area is defined as

$$\sum_{p=1}^{7} C_{kp} = A_k \qquad (2.10)$$

$k = 1, \ldots, \ldots 144$
$p = 1$ for wheat, 2 for corn, 3 for oats, 4 for barley, 5 for grain sorghum, 6 for soybeans, and 7 for cotton

where C_{kp} is the harvested acreage of the pth crop in kth region in 1953.

It can be seen that the Equation 2.10 is equivalent to the Equation 2.7 because corn, oats, barley, and feed-grain sorghum were combined to set up the crop activity for feed grain ($q = 2$ for feed grain). Where 1953 data were not available, 1954 census data were used to establish this restraint. Also, in any case where 1954 acreage was greater than 1953 acreage, the larger of the two totals was used. In Equation 2.10, the C_{kp} for wheat includes summer fallow acreage for areas where this practice is used.

Acreage quotas. The individual restraints indicated in Equation 2.8 were used to simulate production control programs in models testing various policies. They are referred to as acreage quotas at later points in this chapter. As a basis of these individual crop restraints, it was necessary to establish an area base acreage for each crop activity. These base acreages, consistent with procedures used in administering production control programs, represent historical production patterns for each producing area computed as 1951–60 average acreages. The 10-year average acreage, $\bar{C}_{kp}$, first was computed for each crop as

$$\bar{C}_{kp} = \frac{\sum\limits_{t=1}^{10} C_{kpt}}{10} \tag{2.11}$$

$$k = 1, \ldots, \ldots 144$$
$$p = 1, \ldots, \ldots 7$$

where C_{kpt} is the acreage of pth crop in kth producing area during year t.

The base acres of several crops were summed. The proportion of each was then computed as

$$P_{kp} = C_{kp} \left[\sum_{p=1}^{7} \bar{C}_{kp} \right]^{-1} \tag{2.12}$$

$$k = 1, \ldots, \ldots 144$$
$$p = 1, \ldots, \ldots 7$$

where P_{kp} is the 10-year average proportion of acreage devoted to the pth crop in the kth producing area.

This proportion then is used to establish the base acreage of the pth crop in the kth area. For example, the base acreage of wheat, C_{k1} in the kth area is

$$C_{k1} = P_{k1} A_k \tag{2.13}$$

$$k = 1, \ldots, \ldots 144$$

where A_k is the total acreage restraint for the kth producing area and P_{k1} is the 10-year average proportion of acreage devoted to wheat.

A similar base acreage was established for feed grain and cotton in each area. The upper limit on soybean acreage in each area was set up as

$$C_{k6} = A_k \, (0.4) \tag{2.14}$$

$$k = 1, \ldots, \ldots 144$$

Hence, for many areas, we assumed that soybeans cannot be grown on more than 40 percent of existing cropland without a significant effect on yield or soil erosion. However, in areas where the historic percentage of soybeans, P_{k6}, was greater than 40 percent, the larger actual percentage was used. In instances where $P_{k6} = 0$, the pth crop was assumed not adaptable in the kth area.

The base acreages of each crop were used in five solutions of the programming models. The remaining solutions were derived while using variations of the wheat, feed grain, and cotton base acreages to simulate various government-controlled programs. Hence, if we set $C_{k1} = A_k$, while feed grain and cotton are held at their base acreage, a policy of no acreage restriction on wheat production is simulated.

Likewise, if regional acreage restrictions are set at $C_{k1} = 0.9\ A_k$, the wheat production is simulated, since it allowed wheat acreage to be only 90 percent of the base acreage.

CROPLAND: MODEL III

Model III allows three qualities of land in each producing area. Basic assumptions used in this model were (1) that land of one quality can be farmed independently of land of a different quality, (2) that the overall costs of producing a crop are equal for the three land qualities, and (3) that land of different qualities differs in the yield per acre and in possible cropping intensity. For example, the best quality of land may be used for continuous corn, while erosion problems allow corn in only 3 out of 5 years on land of another quality. Henceforth, the three qualities or groups of land will be referred to as class 1 (the best land), class 2, and class 3 (the poorest land).

Model III requires a uniform method of classifying soils among regions. Shrader and Langren[4] indicate that the Conservation Needs Inventory (CNI) of the USDA[5] is the only consistent set of soil groupings throughout the United States. Although this classification scheme was designed to indicate erosion susceptibility and to guide intensiveness of land use, it is the best available method for classifying soil according to productivity and is used in the current study.

The CNI study defined eight (I–VIII) classes of land and subdivided these into subclasses (a–h) according to particular problems regarding erosion and cropping intensity. The risks of soil damage or limitations in use become increasingly greater from class I to class VIII. Soils in the first four classes are capable, under good management, of producing adapted cultivated field crops. Classes V–VII are capable of producing some crops under highly intensive management practices but are better left in their natural vegetation. Class VIII soils do not return on-site benefits for inputs of management of crops, grasses, or trees. However, areas classified as cropland in nearly every county of the United States include land of one or more of the soil classes V–VIII.

For the current study, a sample of counties was drawn from records of the CNI study for each of the 144 producing areas.[6] Three soil classes were determined accordingly. For purposes of the current study, identification of soil groups by producing areas is this:

1. Class 1 of this study equals the CNI classes I and II.
2. Class 2 of this study equals CNI class III.
3. Class 3 of this study equals CNI classes IV–VIII.

A cropland restraint was established for each of the regional soil classes of this

4. William D. Shrader and Norman E. Landgren, "Land Use Implications of Agricultural Production Potentials, Dept. Econ. and Sociol., Iowa State Univ., Ames, unpublished paper, 1962.

5. USDA, *Basic Statistics of the National Inventory of Soil and Water Conservation Needs,* NIC, USDA Stat. Bull. 317, 1962.

6. The county data from the CNI were acquired from records at Iowa State University and various state Soil Conservation Service offices.

study. Since all crops of this study are fairly intensive, it was deemed necessary to adjust the sample distributions of cropland in the various classes for the potential erosion hazard involved. This adjustment made the sample distribution of soil classes consistent with the total cropland restraints used in each area. To clarify this requirement, assume that an area has only two classes of cropland, class I and class IVe, in equal proportions of 100 acres each, and that corn is the only grain crop grown in the region.[7] Class I land could be in continuous corn and class IVe land could be in corn only 3 out of 5 years. This structure would need to be reflected in the regional historical acreage of corn in the area. The base acreage of corn for this area would be 100 + 100 (0.6) = 160 acres, and this figure would be used as the cropland restraint in the context of this study. Notice, however, that only 37.5 percent of this acreage would be on class IVe land, as compared with 50 percent of class IVe land in all cropland of the area.

To make the adjustment just described, it was necessary to use state totals for the complete breakdown of cropland by class and subclass. The estimated acres of cropland, available after considering the intensity with which land could be used, in each of the three productivity classes by region were substituted for the total cropland used for models I and II. Crop yields also had to be estimated for each of these three soil classes. The process used in making these yield estimates is explained for Equations 2.15 and 2.16.

CROP YIELDS

All input-output coefficients, including crop yields, were estimated for 1965. Crop yields and per-acre costs were estimated for each of the 144 producing areas.

MODELS I AND II

Crop yields first were projected to 1965 for each state. Average state yields per harvested acre for the years 1944-62 formed the basis for the projections. The state yield for each crop was estimated by the linear regression

$$\hat{Y}_{pj} = a + bt \tag{2.15}$$

where $\hat{Y}_{pj}$ refers to the 1965 estimated yield of the kth crop in the jth state and t refers to the year. Where b was negative, the mean for the series was used as $\hat{Y}_{pj}$. The projected figures were used for the 1965 state yields, except for certain "boundary conditions" used to insure against unreasonable or unattainable yields. In no case was a state yield projected beyond the highest level attained during the base period.

To complete the estimation process, it was necessary to compute relative mean yields for each state $\overline{Y}_{pj}$, and areas within the states, $\overline{Y}_{pjk}$. These estimates were made from data of the period 1950-60. Some cases were encountered in which area data for the 11-year period were not available. In these instances, census data

---

7. The subclassification "e" denotes a potential erosion hazard in the CNI classification. USDA, *Basic Statistics.*

for the years 1949, 1954, and 1959 were used to compute the mean estimates. These mean yields were assumed comparable to one another and were used in predicting producing area crop yields for 1965. The following relationship was assumed in estimating the 1965 yields by producing areas:

$$\hat{y}_{pjk} = \overline{Y}_{pjk} \, \hat{Y}_{pj}/\overline{Y}_{pj} \qquad (2.16)$$

In Equation 2.16, $\hat{y}_{pjk}$ refers to the 1965 projected yield of the pth crop in the kth producing area and jth state.

MODEL III

As described, the cropland restraints of each area were divided into three production categories in model III. It was necessary to estimate crop yields for each of the three land classes in each producing area. Total variable costs of production were assumed generally the same for all classes of land within an area, an assumption substantiated by budget studies for the various CNI land classes in Texas and Oklahoma.[8] The only differences assumed in crop production on the three land classes within an area were reflected by crop yields.

The procedure for estimating crop yields by land class incorporated the concepts discussed in the previous paragraph. Yield data based upon the CNI soil class were scarce, but some observations were available and useful for establishing estimational methods.[9] These crop-yield estimates by soil class were assumed representative of the relative within-area yield responses for all areas. It was recognized that class 2 land in Iowa is not the same as class 2 land in New Mexico. However, the land classes were established by soil scientists such that class 2 land relative to class 1 land in Iowa is about the same as class 2 land relative to class 1 land in New Mexico. It was possible, by using the above-mentioned data, to construct yield response equations, relative to the regional mean yield, that gave consistent estimates by land class for all areas. The estimated yields were weighted by the CNI soil-class acreages to provide yield estimates for the soil classes used in this study.

8. Larry J. Connor, William F. Lagrone, and James S. Plaxico, *Resource Requirements, Costs and Expected Returns; Alternative Crop and Livestock Enterprises; Loam Soils of the Rolling Plains of Southwestern Oklahoma*, Okla. Agr. Exp. Sta. Processed Series P-368, 1961.

J. W. Goodwin, J. S. Plaxico, and William F. Lagrone, *Resource Requirements, . . . Clay Soils of the Rolling Plains of Southwestern Oklahoma*, Okla. Agr. Exp. Sta. Processed Series P-357, 1960.

William F. Lagrone, P. L. Strickland, and J. S. Plaxico, *Resource requirements, . . . Sandy Soils of the Rolling Plains of Southwestern Oklahoma*, Okla. Agr. Exp. Sta. Processed Series P-369, 1961.

D. S. Moore, K. R. Tefertiller, W. F. Hughes, and R. H. Rogers, *Production Requirements, Costs and Expected Returns; Alternative Crop and Livestock Enterprises; Clay Soils in the Northern Portion of the Rolling Plains of Texas*, Tex. Agr. Exp. Sta. Misc. Publ. Mp-445, 1960.

9. T. E. Corely, C. M. Stokes, and F. A. Kummer, *Mechanized Cotton Production in Alabama*, Ala. Agr. Exp. Sta. Circ. 127, 1959; Goodwin, Plaxico, and Lagrone, *Resource Requirements;* Lagrone, Strickland, and Plaxico, *Resource Requirements;* Moore, Tefertiller, Hughes, and Rogers, *Production Requirements, . . . Harland soils—High Plains of Texas*, Tex. Agr. Exp. Sta. Misc. Publ. MP-601, 1962; Ibid.

PRODUCTION COSTS

Cost coefficients, estimated for each crop in each region, were brought up to date from the 1954 data by use of indexes of costs and technological trends. The cost figures estimated for 1965 include expenditures for labor, machinery and power, chemicals, and miscellaneous inputs. Charges for land and overhead costs, including management, housing, purchasing, and selling, were not included. These costs usually represent 10 percent or more of total production costs but, for lack of data, were not included in estimates.

Individual feed-grain crops were not included as distinct activities in the programming models. Instead, the corn, oats, barley, and grain-sorghum crops were aggregated into a single producing activity for each producing area. The output of this activity, and therefore the costs, consisted of a weighted average of each of the regional feed-grain crops. The weights used were the same as those employed in computing producing area acreage restraints for individual crops. In other words, the weight of each crop included in the feed-grain activity was based upon the historical acreage of that crop.

DEMAND DATA AND RESTRAINTS

Demand restraints for wheat, feed grain, and oil meal were computed for each of the 31 consuming regions. The regional demand restraints, reflecting expected consumption patterns for 1965, are based on projected livestock production patterns, historical industrial uses, average patterns of export, population, per capita consumption, and normal price levels. The 1965 U.S. population was estimated to be 193.6 million persons.[10] Exports for commodities were assumed equal to average levels of the years 1957-61. Data[11] for every major port were used to compute the normal export levels, which then became a portion of the total demand for the respective consuming regions.

WHEAT

The total demand for wheat was computed to include both domestic and export requirements. Wheat for domestic purposes was broken into five categories: (1) flour and cereal consumption, (2) industrial uses, (3) military procurements, (4) net exports of flour, and (5) wheat commonly used for feed. The average percentage of U.S. flour production by states was used to distribute the estimated total domestic wheat demand among consuming regions. Regional flour production during the 1950–60 decade was expressed as a percentage of total flour production. These percentages were then multiplied by the aggregate domestic wheat demand to make the regional allocations. This procedure accurately accounts for about 97 percent of wheat consumption at the level of domestic processing.

10. U.S. Dept. Commerce, U.S. Bureau of Census, *Current Population Reports, Population Estimates*, Series P-25, No. 180, 1957; ibid., No. 187, 1958.
11. USDA, *Grain Market News*, 1956–61.

FEED GRAIN

Regional feed-grain demands are a composite of requirements for corn, oats, barley, grain sorghums, and wheat used for feed. The total regional demand for feed grain also includes exports and domestic consumption. Domestic consumption of feed grain, while dominated by livestock needs, also includes some disappearance for processed cereals and industrial uses.

The 1965 total food-demand restraint of each feed grain was estimated by projecting per capita consumption rates and multiplying them by the estimated 1965 population. Demand restraints were then distributed to consuming regions by *Census of Manufacturers* records of processing and value of shipments for these grains.[12] Aggregate 1965 livestock needs for feed grain were estimated by projecting the 1956–62 trend in total feed-unit consumption of the four major crops. The distribution over consuming regions was accomplished on the basis of estimated grain consumption in each region.

OIL MEAL

The domestic soybean consumption has increased steadily for many years. Therefore, the 1951–61 trend in consumption of soybean meal was linearly projected for the 1965 consumption. A similar procedure was used for projecting annual domestic consumption of cottonseed meal. The distribution of domestic oil-meal demand among consuming regions was accomplished on the basis of estimated regional livestock consumption. Jennings's estimates of cottonseed-meal and soybean-meal consumption by states for 1949 were used to compute the percentage of U.S. total consumption for each consuming region.[13] The percentages were then adjusted for the trend in grain-consuming animal units within each region.

COTTON

The 1950–61 trend in per capita consumption of cotton fibers was projected to 1965. Regional demand restraints for cotton lint were not used, since transportation costs of fiber are low relative to the specific value of the fiber and are unimportant in determining the regional allocation of production. Thus a single national demand was specified for cotton, which included both export and domestic needs. Cotton was considered to be a homogeneous product and cotton from regions was considered to be equivalent (the same commodity) in consumption.

PRICE AND DEMAND LEVELS

The domestic demand restraints were based on domestic demand at the "normal" price level (Table 2.2). To test the effect of various domestic demands at

12. USDA, *Cotton Situation*, CS-202, 1962.
13. R. D. Jennings, *Animal Units of Livestock Fed Annually, 1909 to 1955*, USDA Stat. Bull. 194, 1956.

other price levels upon resource use, prices were assumed to change to the other levels. The effect of the price changes upon the total demand quantity of each product was then evaluated, and the various demand levels were used as restraints, under a constant set of acreage restraints, for indication of optimum regional production patterns.

In computing the demand restraints associated with each price level, a constant price elasticity of demand was assumed for each major commodity, based upon Brandow's estimates of demand and supply relationships.[14] These were -0.23 for feed grain and oil meal, -0.02 for wheat, and -0.40 for cotton lint. Exports were considered constant, because the overall level of exports depends more upon government policies and other nonquantitative factors than upon price. The various total demands (Table 2.2) were allocated to regions in the manner described for the "normal" demands. The several demand levels were used only in model I, to compare the effects of changes in the relative level of farm prices upon patterns of production and cropland requirements.

WHEAT-FEED-GRAIN TRANSFER COSTS

Models I and III have zero costs on the intraregional transfer of wheat into feed grain. In these models, the only criterion to determine the use of the transfer activities was the relative production costs of wheat and feed grain. The assumption in these models is that a two-price plan for wheat is in effect (i.e., if the food demand for wheat is met, other wheat can be used for feed grain if its production costs are sufficiently low). However, a one-price plan for wheat is assumed in effect for model II. In this model, wheat would be supported at a price above its normal equilibrium level. Wheat could still be used as a feed grain, but only if its value of food wheat were paid in its transfer to feed grain. The support price creates an artificial opportunity cost for wheat used for feed. The transfer activities thus are charged a "cost," in general equal to the difference between the projected prices of wheat and corn within the respective consuming regions. To estimate the prices of corn and wheat in each consuming region, the average product price in each state, based on the national average for 1965, was converted to a regional basis.

TRANSPORTATION DATA

Approximately 1,400 transportation activities are included in the programming model to allow commodity distribution possibilities and an optimum spatial allocation of production processes while satisfying regional demands for each major commodity. Transportation costs are involved only if commodities move between consuming regions. Transportation activities were specified for each of the regional demand aggregates (wheat, feed grain, and oil meal).

Rail rates were assumed to accurately reflect the costs of transporting wheat, feed grain, and oil meal among the various consuming regions. The lack of data

14. G. E. Brandow, *Interrelations among Demands for Farm Products and Implication for Control of Market Supply*, Pa. Agr. Exp. Sta. Bull. 680, 1961.

for truck transportation and the difficulty of including combinations of rail and barge rates or barge and truck rates excluded the use of these rates. For this study, actual flat rail rates were computed from the 1962 Interstate Commerce Commission tariff schedule. Transportation rates were the only items included in the programming models not projected to 1965. The construction of these rates is complex and is dependent upon government policies. All rates used in this study were for transportation of grain and oil meal for domestic consumption.[15]

A city was designated within each consuming region to act as the location for export (import) from (to) that region to (from) all other regions. These points were selected with the objective of having them approximately centered with respect to the consumption distribution of the region. Since rail rates were used as transportation costs, it was necessary that each of these selected cities have access to railroad transportation. In most regions, these cities coincided approximately with the geographical center of the region. Several compromises among these criteria were necessary in making the final selection of cities shown in Table 2.3.

Transportation activities were included in the models only if there was opportunity for them to be used. It was reasonable to include activities for the movement of feed grain from the Corn Belt into the New England states, but the opposite would not be reasonable. Likewise, we would not expect wheat to be shipped into Kansas or Montana from the Corn Belt or the Southeast. Hence, the final number of transportation activities was 459 each for wheat and feed grain and 430 for oil meal, giving a total of 1,348 transportation activities.

EMPIRICAL RESULTS

The three linear-programming models were used to generate 17 solutions. Code numbers (Table 2.4) were used to identify each of the solutions. Solution 43 was considered a benchmark solution, since normal prices were used and no crop-control program was assumed. It was used as a comparison for most other solutions of model I and for several solutions of models II and III. Solutions 40 and 47 were a study of the possibilities of land-retirement programs for wheat. Solutions 51 and 54 were designed to observe methods of controlling feed-grain supplies. The effects of changes in the price level of farm products are evident in the results of solutions 41 (low price level and large demand quantity), 43 (normal price level and demand quantity), and 45 (high price level and small demand quantity). A simulated two-price plan for wheat was used throughout the solutions of model I.

15. For use in the programming models, transportation rates were expressed in costs per hundred feed units. This procedure offered no difficulty in the transportation of wheat and oil-meal. However, the costs of transporting corn, oats, barley, or grain sorghums were not necessarily the same either in weight or in feed units. Adjustments for the composite of the feed grain being transported were thus required. Since it was difficult to predict which producing regions within a consuming region would produce feed grain, it was equally difficult to predict the actual mix of feed grain being transported from a consuming region. As a compromise, the 1950–59 average production, by weight of the four feed grains, was used to estimate the feed units per pound of feed grain produced in each state. Likewise, if different rates existed for each of the crops, it was possible to weigh the rates by the percentage of each crop grown.

Solution 36, from model I, was aimed at no particular crop. Production restraints for this solution were assumed to be physical rather than institutional.
Soybeans, again, were limited to 40 percent of total cropland, and cotton was
limited to 200 percent of its base acreage. Wheat and feed grain were limited only
by cropland availability. The results of this solution estimate the expected long-
run equilibrium effects of having a minimum of government influence in agricultural production decisions (i.e., the production result if free markets were used as
a policy).

Model II simulated a one-price plan for wheat, as compared with a two-price
plan for model I. The acreage restraints for solutions 402 and 432 under model II
were the same as for their counterpart solutions 40 and 43 under model I. Thus
the effects of the price assumption for wheat can be isolated by comparing these
two sets of results.

Model III emphasized different land qualities within a producing area. The
total land restraint for each area was divided into three parts, depicting the three
land qualities. The demand and resource constraints of solutions in this model
correspond exactly to solutions of model I. (Solution 403 corresponds to solution
40 in model I, while solution 513 corresponds to 51, etc.)

A specific price level and the resulting demand have been specified in every
model solution. Each solution is a simulated expression of a particular land-retirement program (except solution 36 as just explained). Both mandatory and voluntary land-retirement methods, sometimes in combination, are considered in the
simulated program. For example, solution 47 forces the retirement of 10 percent
of the wheat base in every producing area. Further restriction of wheat production was necessary in some producing areas to cause aggregate production to equal
aggregate demand. This additional retirement of wheatland can be termed voluntary. It could be brought about by incentive payments to farmers in the short run
or by normal adjustments to equilibrium prices in the long run.

The discussion that follows explains and interprets the results of the various
programming solutions indicated in Table 2.4. Only the more relevant and important aspects of each solution and their implications are discussed in this chapter. The discussion relates especially to regional patterns of land use and interregional product flows resulting from each major program alternative. Some of
the basic solutions are presented and discussed in detail. Others are described only
as they differ from the basic solutions. The programmed equilibrium prices of
products and factors (shadow prices) are presented in the next chapter along with
an assessment of cost and benefits of various supply control programs.

RESULTS OF MODEL I

MODEL I: BENCHMARK SOLUTION 43

Solution 43 has been designated as a benchmark situation and will be used as a
basis for comparison with results of several other simulated production programs
or policies. The results under solution 43 simulate those that might be approximated under the long-run equilibrium adjustment of agriculture to a competitive
market, or to a voluntary farm program resulting in land withdrawal at lowest

public cost (with production just equal to national requirements at the "normal" price level in both cases). No crop of the study in any area could exceed 100 percent of its historic maximum (base) acreage. Soybeans, as in all model solutions, were restricted to not more than 40 percent of available cropland in each area, except as noted earlier.

Model I, as well as others, assumes that demand is exactly satisfied from current production, although normal stocks also could be carried at the price level specified in Table 2.4. The area crop acreages indicated, including the land withdrawn from production, could result from market equilibrium forces or voluntary reductions in crop production through incentive payments in the most efficient national pattern. However, the model also could be consistent with other assumptions: it could be assumed that total demand is greater than production generated within the model and that the difference is supplied by changes in stocks of farm products. Similarly, it might be assumed that the regional production quotas are restraints on actual units of production rather than on acreage. Since fixed coefficients of production were used in the programming model, this assumption would not affect producing patterns. Wheat, beyond that required for food and exports, can be used for livestock feed at no expense above the normal production costs.

The regional pattern of land use under solution 43 is shown in Figure 2.3. Most producing areas produce at least one crop under this benchmark solution.

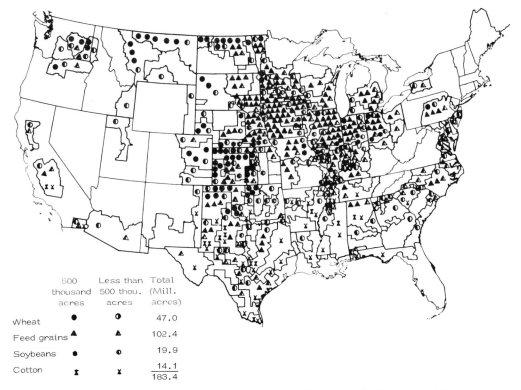

	500 thousand acres	Less than 500 thou. acres	Total (Mill. acres)
Wheat	●	◐	47.0
Feed grains	▲	▲	102.4
Soybeans	●	◐	19.9
Cotton	x	x	14.1
			183.4

Fig. 2.3. Model I—Regional location and acreage of crop production for solution 43.

Although crops were limited to 100 percent of their base acreages, adjustment of crop production within and among producing areas could still occur. Only 80 percent of the total base acreages of wheat and feed grain was necessary to meet the specified demand requirements for 1965, given the "normal" level of prices. About 76 percent of the total cotton base was required. Soybeans, with an upward trend in demand over recent years, required more than the historical base acreage for 1965. Approximately 82 percent of the 223.9 million base acres of cropland for wheat, feed grain, cotton, and soybeans was needed to satisfy all demands.

In comparison with the base acreage, 40.5 million acres were not needed to meet the projected national demands for 1965. Hence, 40.5 million acres of surplus land could be considered as surplus, for the stated price level, and could be shifted to other uses. This amount of land was surplus for the specified crops if crops were allocated among producing areas with production to "just match demand." The allocation would have been most efficient in terms of the objective function used in the study. Of course, the amount of surplus land did not exceed by 40.5 million acres the acreage used for production at the time of the study. Some land had already been diverted through the feed-grain program, the Conservation Reserve, and wheat and cotton allotment programs. However, the 40.5 million acres is one expression or measurement of the extent of excess capacity in the U.S. field-crop economy for 1965.

A comparison of actual crop production in 1962 with the pattern of crop production suggested by benchmark solution 43 is provided in Table 2.5. Where differences between derived production patterns and the actual 1962 production patterns occur, the time trend mainly is toward the location of production suggested by the model. Given time and the removal of artificial barriers to shifts of production, such as quotas on wheat and feed grain holding them to their historic locations, the actual production patterns will approach those of solution 43.

The largest discrepencies between the model solution and the actual 1962 acreage occur for soybeans. This difference may have occurred because the demand specified for soybeans in the model was relatively low and because soybeans are responsive in yield to acreage changes within an area (a fact not sufficiently recognized by the fixed regional coefficients). However, the time trend is toward movement of soybeans to the areas that have model solutions exceeding the 1962 acreage by the greatest amount. In model III, with soil quality differences recognized, the soybean acreage is greater than in model I.

Solution 43, with crop production located in conformity with greater comparative advantage of each producing area, has feed-grain acreages which shift toward the Corn Belt, with smaller acreages elsewhere when compared with the 1962 actual figures. Areas of the northern Great Plains (North Dakota and Montana) are indicated to have the greatest reduction in feed-grain acreage.

Wheat-production patterns from solution 43, while showing no drastic changes from the current location, indicate a smaller acreage in the Corn Belt and the South, with an increased acreage in the major areas of the Great Plains and the West. In addition to the 50 million bushels of wheat normally used for feed and included in the total demand restraint for wheat, an additional 310 million bushels are specified for feed use in solution 43. The bulk of this increment would be grown in Wisconsin, Kansas, Colorado, and the four northwestern states of Montana, Idaho, Oregon, and Washington.

The location of cotton production, in solution 43, would shift slightly from the Southeast into Texas and Oklahoma. South Carolina and Georgia would have the greatest loss in acreage. Little cotton acreage was located in New Mexico and Arizona under solution 43.[16]

Interregional product flows. For solution 43, wheat is generally in surplus in the Great Plains states and Montana and in deficit supply elsewhere (Fig. 2.4). North

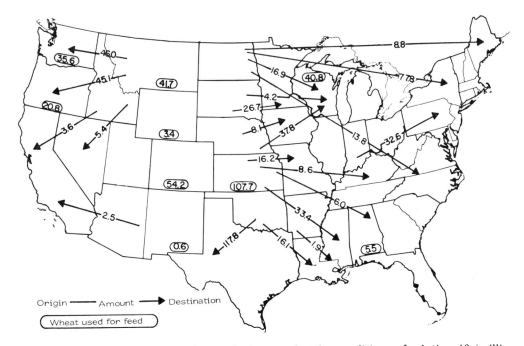

Fig. 2.4. Model I—Interregional flows of wheat under the conditions of solution 43 (million bushels).

and South Dakota, Nebraska, Kansas, and Oklahoma supply most of the excess demand for the eastern half of the United States. Likewise, Montana exports wheat to the Pacific coast regions. The general movement of feed grain (Fig. 2.5) is from the Corn Belt into the southern and eastern states, with Illinois and Indiana being the largest exporters. Kansas and Montana export wheat for livestock feed.

16. The linear-programming model did not recognize the quality advantage for western-grown cotton. Also, a review of the coefficients of production used for cotton in model I indicated that perhaps a slight revision of cotton yields was needed. Thus, the cotton yields for producing regions 121, 141, 142, and 143 were raised slightly, and the yield for region 140 was lowered slightly in models II and III.

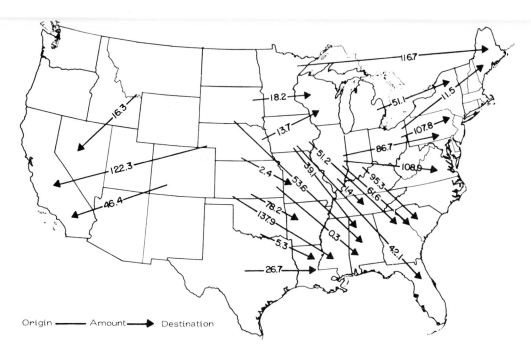

Fig. 2.5. Model I—Interregional flows of feed grain under the conditions of solution 43 (million bushels of corn).

Model I is sensitive with respect to the locational pattern of potential soybean production. Nebraska, because of combined advantages in production and location, serves as a main producer (Fig. 2.3) and the main exporter (Fig. 2.6) of oil meal to the Pacific states. Nebraska regions also are indicated to export some oil meal to the Southeast. Otherwise, the central Corn Belt serves as the main source of oil-meal imports by other regions, with Illinois as the largest producer and exporter of soybeans. Cottonseed meal, when available, is specified to satisfy oil-meal demands. However, none of the cotton-producing states exports oil meal, and only soybean meal is indicated to move among consuming regions.

Figure 2.7 indicates the amount and location, given the price level specified, of surplus land under benchmark solution 43. It is highly concentrated in the Southeast and in the Great Plains areas. Concentration also is fairly great in the Lake states and along the Atlantic Seaboard. Under the demand and technology conditions used in the study, some far-reaching impacts were indicated from a market equilibrium or government program that resulted in an optimal interregional allocation of production in the context of solution 43 and its specified restraints. Alternative land uses implied are grazing, forestry, and recreation. Obviously, the magnitude of regional adjustments implied would cause some sharp reductions in farm incomes and resource values. Too, a large amount of capital would be required to facilitate the shift from existing production patterns to less intensive land use. Finally, entire communities would bear the impact of the adjustments, since the less intensive agriculture so resulting would mean smaller farm populations and a reduced demand for nonfarm goods and services in the specified re-

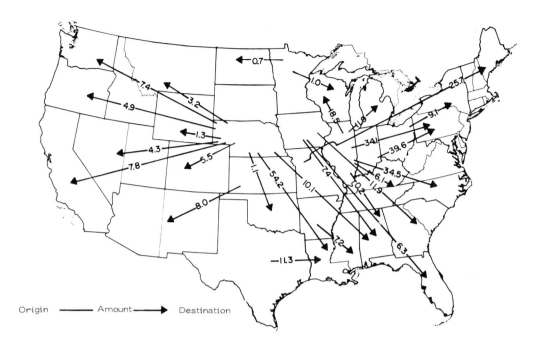

Origin ———— Amount ——→ Destination

Fig. 2.6. Model I—Interregional flows of oil meal under the conditions of solution 43 (million bushels of soybeans).

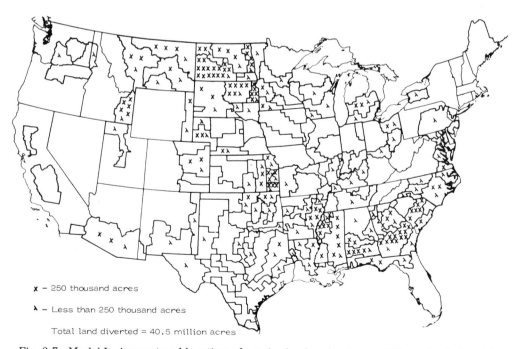

x – 250 thousand acres

⋏ – Less than 250 thousand acres

Total land diverted = 40.5 million acres

Fig. 2.7. Model I—Amount and location of surplus land under the conditions of solution 43.

gions. It was not the purpose of this study to explore these second-round effects or to suggest policies that would alleviate them. However, the consequences of the shifts suggested are both obvious and important.

MODEL I: WHEAT PROGRAMS REFLECTED IN SOLUTIONS 40 AND 47

Two solutions from model I were used to simulate production-control programs directed at wheat.[17] Among others, two departures were made from the mildly restrictive program simulated by solution 43:

1. A mandatory program was selected which is even more restrictive. It would force the retirement of a fixed portion of the base acreage in every area, leaving the remaining surplus wheatland to be retired voluntarily through monetary incentives from the government.
2. A voluntary program was selected with no quotas for wheat and with government payments used to enlist participation.

These two alternatives are simulated by solutions 47 and 40, respectively.

Mandatory retirement of wheat quotas. Ten percent of the wheat base acreage, uniformly over all producing areas, is forced out of production in solution 47. It is assumed that additional surplus-producing capacity will be voluntarily restricted so that production will exactly meet demand at the assumed price level (level three or normal prices). The voluntary portion of the wheatland retirement would be brought about by incentive payments from the government.

Under the plan suggested by solution 47, 44.3 million acres are used for wheat production, 105.1 million acres for feed grain, and 19.9 million acres for soybeans (Table 2.6). Cotton acreage is unchanged from solution 43. The production patterns suggested by this solution are illustrated in Figure 2.8. Figures for interregional movements of products are not shown, since the patterns are changed only slightly as compared with solution 48.

Since solution 47 requires that all areas reduce wheat acreage by 10 percent from their base, with a national wheat base acreage of 58.5 million acres, wheat must be reduced by at least the mandatory requirement of 5.9 million acres. But since the remaining 52.6 acres would, if planted to wheat, exceed the demands for domestic and export constraints, additional land must be withheld from wheat. The model allows the additional acreage to be withdrawn at the most efficient locations, namely, in areas distributed such that the national costs of producing the indicated bill of goods is at a minimum—subject to the requirement that all regions reduce wheat acreage by a minimum of 10 percent.

Since 10 percent of wheatland in every area is forcibly retired by solution 47, national production costs are minimized by use of 2.7 million fewer total acres for wheat production than under solution 43 (compare Table 2.6 with Table 2.5). This is a 5.7 percent reduction in the acres of wheat grown, or a 6.4 percent reduction in amount of wheat produced. The same amount of wheat is used for food,

17. In discussion of solutions 40 and 47, output comparisons will be made with solution 43 unless otherwise stated.

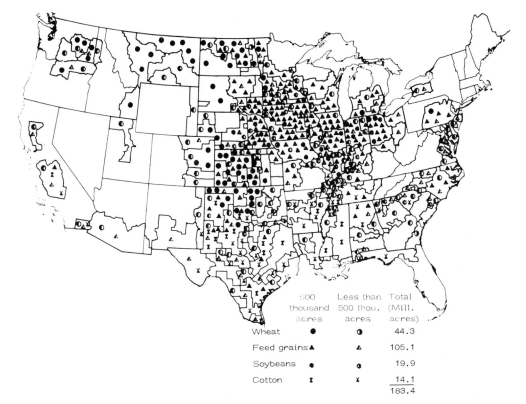

	500 thousand acres	Less than 500 thou. acres	Total (Mill. acres)
Wheat	●	◐	44.3
Feed grains	▲	▲	105.1
Soybeans	●	◐	19.9
Cotton	I	x	14.1
			183.4

Fig. 2.8. Model I—Regional location and acreage of crop production for solution 47.

but less is used for feed. Feed-grain acreage increases by exactly 2.7 million acres under solution 47. Most of the increased feed-grain acreage occurs in Nebraska, Kansas, and North Dakota.

Soybean production is not greatly affected by the regionally forced reduction plan for wheat. While about 28.5 thousand fewer acres are needed for soybean production, Nebraska has a substantial decrease. A decline is required in Nebraska so that feed grain can be produced most efficiently within the context of a 10 percent wheat acreage reduction in all producing areas. The total surplus land indicated by solution 47 (40.6 million acres) is practically the same as that indicated by solution 43. The distribution of unused land for solution 47 also is quite similar to that for solution 43. However, as Figure 2.9 shows, unused land would decline in such regions as northeastern Colorado and southern Nebraska but would increase in Washington, Oregon, northern Montana, northern Oklahoma, western Missouri, and other scattered regions.

Unlimited wheat acreage under solution 40. Solution 43, the benchmark situation, requires all areas to restrain wheat acreage to the 1953 base level. Solution 47 requires that all 144 areas reduce their wheat acreage by 10 percent or more, relative to solution 43. In contrast, solution 40 allows all acreage restrictions to be lifted on wheat in all areas. This crop can be extended to the limit of all crop-

X – 250 thousand acres

λ – Less than 250 thousand acres

Total land diverted – 40.6 million acres

Fig. 2.9. Model I—Amount and location of surplus land under the conditions of solution 47.

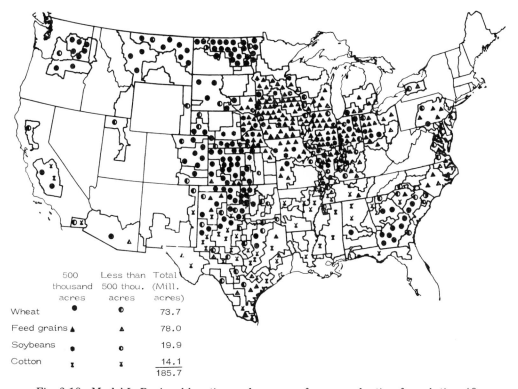

	500 thousand acres	Less than 500 thou. acres	Total (Mill. acres)
Wheat	●	◐	73.7
Feed grains	▲	▲	78.0
Soybeans	●	○	19.9
Cotton	x	x	14.1
			185.7

Fig. 2.10. Model I—Regional location and acreage of crop production for solution 40.

land in any areas, although other feed grain and cotton cannot exceed the 1953, or base, level and soybean acreage cannot exceed 40 percent of the land in any area. Total national wheat production in solution 40 is limited to the same domestic and export demand levels as solutions 43 and 47. Hence, wheat is produced, in competition with other crops for solution 40, so that national crop requirements are met at the lowest possible production and transportation costs.

Considerable changes in crop production patterns and unused land result with relaxation of wheat acreage restraints in solution 40 (Figure 2.10). Compared with benchmark solution 43, the use of wheat for feed increases greatly, and the interregional flows of products are altered accordingly, as evidenced in comparison of Figures 2.11, 2.12, and 2.13 with Figures 2.4, 2.5, and 2.6. Total acreage of wheat increases to 73.7 million, 26.7 million acres more than for solution 43. Feed-grain acreage decreases to 78.0 million acres, 24.5 million acres less than for solution 43. Lifting the restraints on wheat acreage has little effect on soybean production. Cotton production is left unchanged.

Of eastern states, South Carolina and Georgia have the largest increase in wheat acreage as land is shifted to wheat for feed. A substantial increase in wheat acreage, also for feed purposes, occurs in all Great Plains and western states except Wyoming and Montana. Nearly a billion bushels of wheat are used for feed under solution 40, an increase of 700,000 bushels over solution 43.

The large increase in wheat production is offset by an equivalent decrease in feed-grain production (Figure 2.10). The Great Plains states, from North Dakota through Texas, have the largest reductions in feed-grain production. Although

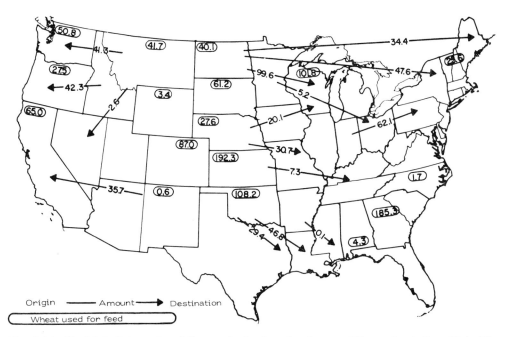

Fig. 2.11. Model I—Interregional flows of wheat under the conditions of solution 40 (million bushels).

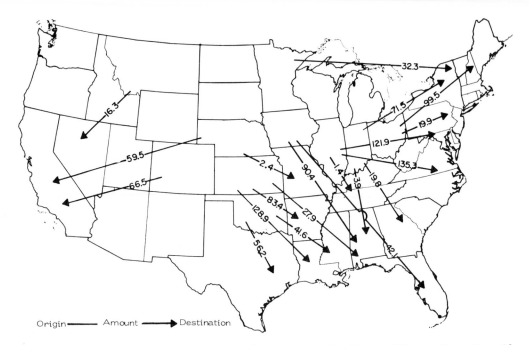

Origin———— Amount ————▶ Destination

Fig. 2.12. Model I—Interregional flows of feed grain under the conditions of solution 40 (million bushels of corn).

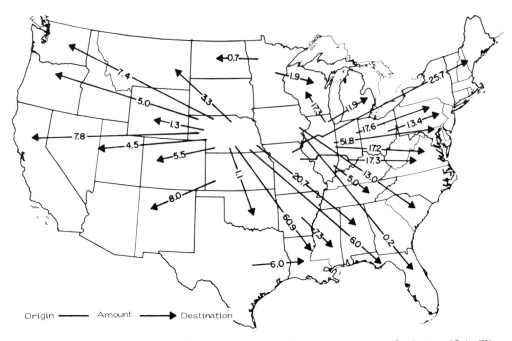

Origin ———— Amount ————▶ Destination

Fig. 2.13. Model I—Interregional flows of oil meal under the conditions of solution 40 (million bushels of soybeans).

these states generally have an offsetting increase in wheat acreage, South Dakota and Kansas have net losses in total land used for crops. Areas of the Lake states and the Southeast also suffer decreases in feed-grain production, but the major producing areas of the Corn Belt maintain feed grain at the same level as in solution 43. Wheat mainly is substituted for barley and grain sorghums under solution 40, while corn production remains relatively constant.

Total soybean acreage is relatively unaffected by the change in wheat acreage. Missouri and Nebraska, however, have substantial increases in acres of soybeans (mainly at the expense of Ohio, Illinois, and Kansas) as land is released from feed grain in Nebraska and from wheat in Missouri.

Under solution 40, with no specific producing area restrictions on wheat acreage, surplus land for crops is indicated to be 38.2 million acres. Surplus acreage drops slightly from solution 43 because more wheatland is used to produce feed. While the land so used has a locational advantage in transportation costs, its lower yields cause more land to be absorbed in meeting the nation's requirements. Surplus or unused land would decline (Figure 2.14) considerably in the Southeast under solution 40 (as compared with solution 43 in Figure 2.7). It also would be eliminated in Arizona, eastern Colorado, and most of Oklahoma and Texas.

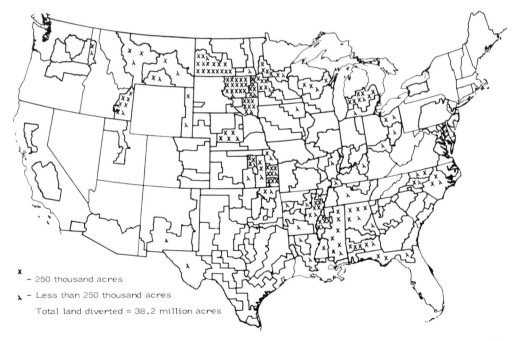

x — 250 thousand acres

⅄ — Less than 250 thousand acres

Total land diverted = 38.2 million acres

Fig. 2.14. Model I—Amount and location of surplus land under the conditions of solution 40.

MODEL I: FEED-GRAIN PROGRAMS REFLECTED IN SOLUTIONS 51-54

Solutions 51-54 involve various simulated production controls for feed grain. Benchmark solution 43 required that no crop exceed its base acreage. Solutions

52, 53, and 54 allow other crops to remain at this level but cause feed grain to be restrained below this base acreage of benchmark solution 43. Solution 51, similar to solution 40 of the wheat series, allows feed-grain acreage restraints to be abolished (feed-grain acreage cannot, of course, exceed total cropland acreage). In all solutions emphasizing feed grain, the quotas or acreage restraints of wheat and cotton are constant at 100 percent (see Table 2.4) of their base level. Likewise, soybeans were restricted to 40 percent of total cropland in each area.

Feed-grain quotas reduced. Solutions 52–54 will be analyzed as a group because of their similarity. The feed-grain base was reduced by increments of 2.5 percent in going from solution 43 to solution 54 (i.e., from 100 in solution 43 to 92.5 percent in solution 54). A 25 percent reduction of the feed-grain base in each area represents a total reduction of about 3.2 million acres. Thus in solution 54 approximately 9.6 million acres of feed grain are considered to be retired by mandatory means.

As compared with solution 43, the major change under solution 52 is a 2.2-million–acre increase in wheat to serve as a means of meeting national feed requirements. North Dakota increases wheat acreage by 1.5 million acres. The changes are progressive, up to those represented by solution 54 (see Table 2.7 and Figure 2.15) where wheat acreage also is expanded greatly in the eastern Corn Belt and

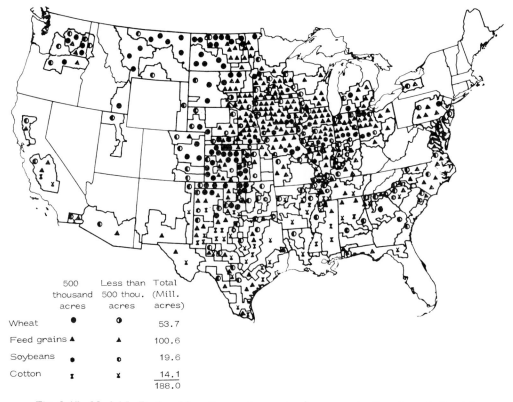

	500 thousand acres	Less than 500 thou. acres	Total (Mill. acres)
Wheat	●	◐	53.7
Feed grains	▲	▲	100.6
Soybeans	●	◐	19.6
Cotton	x	x	14.1
			188.0

Fig. 2.15. Model I—Regional location and acreage of crop production for solution 54.

throughout the Great Plains. Soybeans shift toward the Corn Belt as an efficient replacement for feed grain. Approximately 470 million bushels of wheat are used as feed under solution 54, an increase of 160 million over solution 43. The total acreage of surplus or unused land is 36.1 million acres under solution 54.

Feed-grain quotas absent as represented in solution 51. Solution 51 simulates conditions in which no production restraints apply to feed grain, and its acreage is restrained only by available cropland. Wheat and cotton production are held at their respective base acreages in each area, and soybeans are restricted to no more than 40 percent of total cropland (see Table 2.4). Wheat production, after meeting food demand and where competitive, can be raised up to limits of the base wheat acreage in each area. Feed grain then is produced in competition with feed wheat, in sufficient quantity to satisfy the feed-grain demand.

Removing the base acreage restriction allows feed grain to be distributed more efficiently among producing areas (Figure 2.16 and Table 2.8) than in the bench-

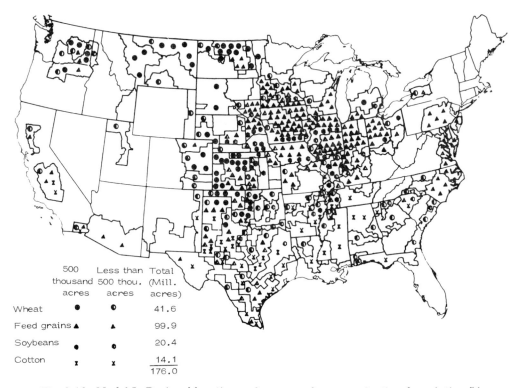

	500 thousand acres	Less than 500 thou. acres	Total (Mill. acres)
Wheat	●	◐	41.6
Feed grains	▲	▲	99.9
Soybeans	●	●	20.4
Cotton	x	x	14.1
			176.0

Fig. 2.16. Model I—Regional location and acreage of crop production for solution 51.

mark solution (Figure 2.3). Consequently, only 176.0 million acres of cropland are required to produce the national requirements of wheat, feed grain, cotton, and oilmeal, leaving 47.9 million acres of cropland unused. Hence, the total surplus acreage represented by solution 51 is 7.4 million acres more than for solution 43.

Wheat acreage is reduced by 5.4 million acres from solution 43. With only 41.6 million acres of wheat grown, wheat used for feed declines to 141 million bushels. Eastern and Corn Belt states have the biggest losses in wheat production. Kansas has a substantial drop in wheat production, but feed grain and soybeans increase by an even greater acreage in this state. Illinois and Nebraska are the only states with an increase in wheat acreage.

Feed-grain acreage, though unrestricted, actually decreases by 2.5 million acres. A smaller acreage is possible because the improved interregional distribution of feed grain allows the national per-acre yield to rise. Feed grain becomes specialized in producing areas having an advantage in its production. The increase in feed-grain acreage in the Corn Belt forces soybeans into areas of lower per-acre yields. Hence, solution 51 requires about 0.5 million more soybean acres than does solution 43. Producing regions in Nebraska, Kansas, and Arkansas have the greatest increase in soybean acreage. Indiana has the largest loss. Cotton acreage shifts slightly in solution 51 compared with benchmark solution 43. A slight increase in acreage occurs in Alabama, and a slight decrease takes place in Kentucky. The interregional commodity flows are shown in Figures 2.17, 2.18, and 2.19.

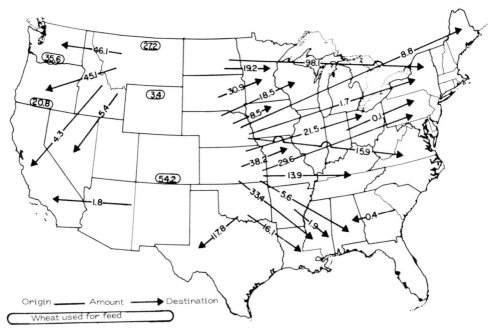

Fig. 2.17. Model I—Interregional flows of wheat under the conditions of solution 51 (million bushels).

MODEL I: MARKET EQUILIBRIUM OF QUOTAS OR OPTIMAL INTERREGIONAL PATTERNS UNDER SOLUTION 36

Solution 36 was designed to approximate the long-run conditions approached under a competitive market (both with production restrained to the given demand

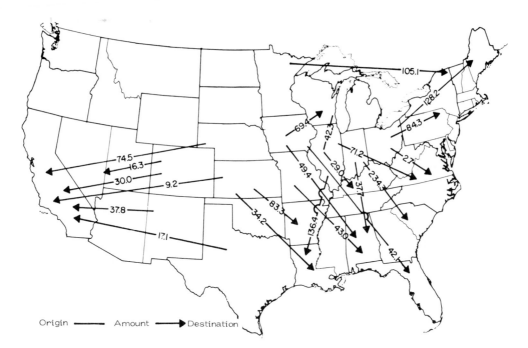

Fig. 2.18. Model I—Interregional flows of feed grain under the conditions of solution 51 (million bushels of corn).

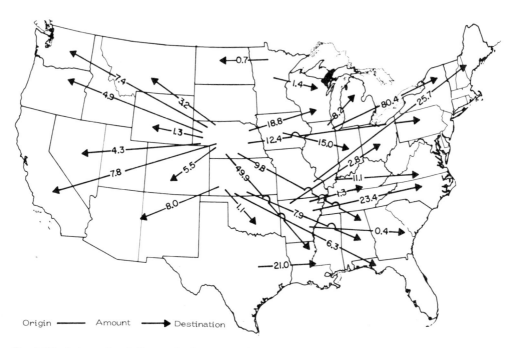

Fig. 2.19. Interregional flows of oil meal under the conditions of solution 51 (million bushels of soybeans).

levels and the prices indicated in Table 2.4) or under government programs that result in an optimal interregional allocation of crop production and land use.

Negotiable marketing quotas are another possible means of deriving a production pattern corresponding to solution 36. Production quotas, equaling the previously specified total national demand for each product, would be issued to farmers of the nation. Initially, these quotas would be allocated on the basis of historical crop production on each farm. Quotas would then be traded among farmers until they were held by the most efficient producers. The farmers capable of getting the highest net return per unit of production would eventually bid the production quotas from less efficient producers.

To simulate the conditions of markets or government programs just outlined for solution 36, separate acreage restrictions for wheat and feed grain were removed. Physical characteristics of the producing areas were assumed to limit soybean production to 40 percent of available cropland. Total cropland restrictions by regions were retained.

Production patterns. Compared with solution 43, very large changes in crop production prevail under the conditions of solution 36. Total acreage for the crops declines to 176.9 million acres. Surplus acreage, land not needed to satisfy 1965 demand at price level 3, increases to 47.1 million acres. Considering all models and solutions analyzed, we consider this quantity to best characterize surplus capacity (for wheat, feed grain, cotton, and soybeans) in 1965, given the "normal" level of prices.

Wheat production is increased to 55.0 million acres (Table 2.9). Approximately 487 million bushels of wheat are used for feed, an increase of 177 million bushels over solution 43. Wheat production shifts from the Corn Belt into the Great Plains and western states (Figure 2.20). Kansas is the only Great Plains state with a decrease in wheat acreage, but the decrease is offset by an increase in feed-grain production. Producing areas in North Dakota, Colorado, and South Dakota have the largest increases in wheat acreage.

Feed-grain acreage, because of increased efficiency arising from an improved interregional allocation of production and the use of more feed wheat, is sharply reduced under solution 36. The 89.4 million acres used for feed grain are 13 million fewer than under solution 43. Feed-grain production is nearly eliminated in producing areas from Colorado on west (Figure 2.20) where both food and feed wheat becomes concentrated. Feed-grain production is concentrated in the Corn Belt, Texas, Kansas, Nebraska, and South Dakota. However, a substantial amount is produced in Pennsylvania and North Carolina, mainly because of locational advantages. The patterns of wheat and feed-grain transfers under solution 36 are those shown in Figures 2.21 and 2.22.

Soybean production shifts slightly among producing areas, although total acreage is not greatly changed under solution 36, which approximates long-run adjustments to certain market conditions or to government programs aimed at retaining interregional equilibrium. Soybean production is decreased in Nebraska, Arkansas, and Missouri. Soybeans remain concentrated in the Corn Belt, with

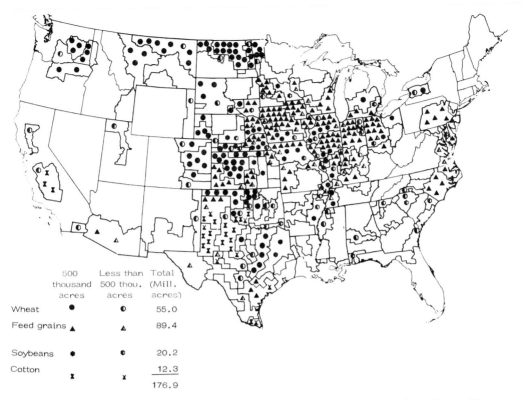

	500 thousand acres	Less than 500 thou. acres	Total (Mill. acres)
Wheat	●	◑	55.0
Feed grains	▲	△	89.4
Soybeans	●	◑	20.2
Cotton	✗	✗	12.3
			176.9

Fig. 2.20. Model I—Regional location and acreage of crop production for solution 36.

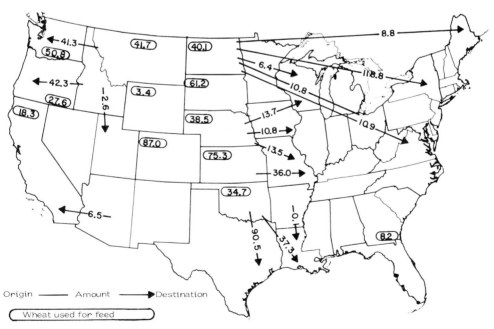

Origin ——— Amount ———▶ Destination

Wheat used for feed

Fig. 2.21. Model I—Interregional flows of wheat under the conditions of solution 36 (million bushels).

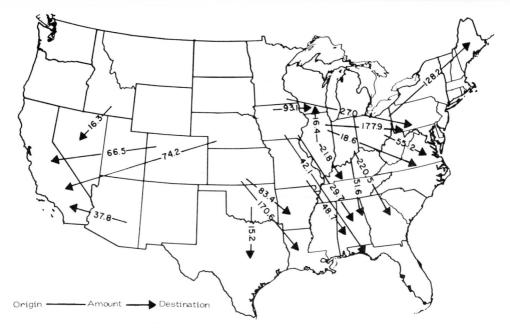

Origin ——————— Amount ——————▶ Destination

Fig. 2.22. Model I—Interregional flows of feed grain under the conditions of solution 36 (million bushels of corn).

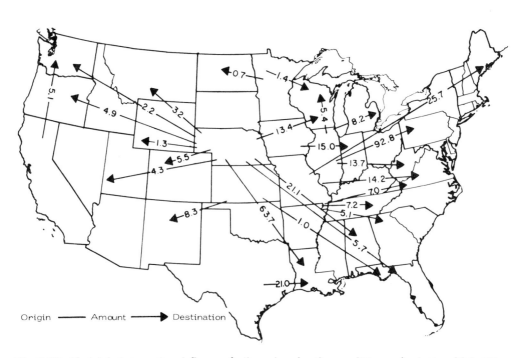

Origin ——————— Amount ——————▶ Destination

Fig. 2.23. Model I—Interregional flows of oil meal under the conditions of solution 36 (million bushels of soybeans).

Illinois having the greatest production. Nebraska, with an advantage in production and location, supplies most western states with oil meal (Figure 2.23).

Under the interregional equilibrium conditions suggested by solution 36, cotton is eliminated from all states except Texas, Oklahoma, and California. Arizona has no cotton, because its cropland is completely utilized for feed grain. Later solutions result in cotton production in consuming region 27.

The interregional allocation of crop production under solution 36 has the greatest effect on producing areas in the South. As evident in Table 2.9, consuming regions 4, 5, 6, 7, 16, and 17 have a sharp reduction in agricultural production. About 20 percent of the cropland in these regions, compared with solution 43, is shifted from crop production (Figure 2.24). Only 30 percent of the total cropland in these regions remains in production of the specified crops, as compared with 79 percent for the United States. Of the 47.1 million acres of cropland indicated as surplus for the study crops under solution 36, approximately 38 percent is located in these six regions. Other producing areas indicated to have land not used for the grains or cotton under the equilibrium conditions are concentrated in Nebraska, the Dakotas, Kansas, Oklahoma, Wyoming, Montana, and Idaho.

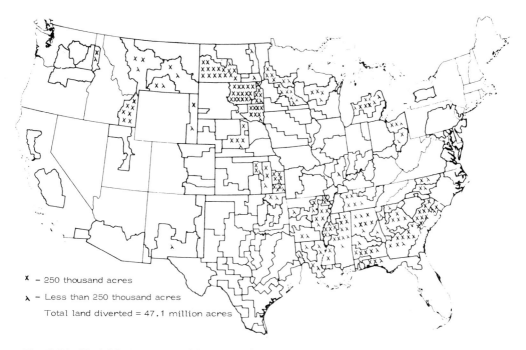

x – 250 thousand acres

λ – Less than 250 thousand acres

Total land diverted = 47.1 million acres

Fig. 2.24. Model I—Amount and location of surplus land under the conditions of solution 36.

MODEL I: DEMAND CHANGES UNDER SOLUTIONS 41 AND 45

The level of prices is an essential consideration in establishing the amount of land which must be diverted from production by public programs. If the price level is raised, the demand quantity of farm products should be lowered, and less total production will be required.   If the price level is lowered, the opposite should occur.

In considering the effect of price changes on cropland requirements, all variables except demand were held constant.   Area total cropland and acreage or quota restraints for individual crops were held at the same level as for solution 43 (Table 2.10).   Demand quantities were then increased, and prices were decreased, for solution 41 relative to solution 43 (Tables 2.2 and 2.4).   For solution 45, demand quantities were decreased, and prices were increased, relative to solution 43.   The assumed corn price was $0.80 per bushel for solution 41 and $1.40 per bushel for solution 45, with the prices of all other products varied proportionately from the levels of solution 43.   For solution 43 and all other solutions, the price level is that corresponding to a corn price of $1.10 in Tables 2.2 and 2.4.   Domestic demand levels alone were assumed to be affected by the change in prices. Some regions have a greater portion of export demand than others.   Hence, regional demands are not all affected equally by the demand and price changes.

While areas of specialization are not changed greatly for any one crop under the different solutions, the residual effects expressed in unused cropland are quite important.   Under the lower set of prices and larger demand quantities, surplus capacity as represented by unused land declines to 24.6 million acres.   Under the higher prices and smaller quantities of solution 45, surplus capacity increases to 51.4 million acres.

Under solution 41 (lower prices and larger quantities), wheat acreage would expand mainly (over solution 43) in the Dakotas, Ohio, Michigan, North Carolina, and Montana.   Feed-grain acreage would expand most (Table 2.11) in Nebraska, North Dakota, Mississippi, Kansas, Florida, and Oklahoma.   Soybean acreage would decrease in Nebraska in response to the greater feed-grain acreage but would expand in most other states where soybeans are grown.   Cotton, with a total increase of 1.4 million acres, would expand largely in South Carolina, North Carolina, Georgia, and Alabama.

With the 10.8-million-acre decline in cropland requirements under solution 45, the greatest change would be in feed grain and cotton.   Large reductions in feed-grain production, as compared with the price level under solution 43, would occur in South Dakota, Michigan, Minnesota, and Alabama.   The central Corn Belt would have little change in feed grain (Table 2.12).

Because of the very low price elasticities of demand for the commodities in question, the quantities involved in solutions 41 and 45 (low and high prices, respectively) change from those of solution 43 by a smaller percentage than price. With the lower prices under solution 41, for example, prices average about 27 percent lower than under solution 43, but increases in quantities are only 7.2 percent for feed grain, 8.0 percent for cotton, 5.9 percent for oil meal, and 0.4 percent for wheat.   Under solution 45, changes in quantities were only 5.3, 4.3, 5.8, and 0.4 percent, respectively, for feed grain, oil meal, cotton, and wheat.   Of course, solution 41 requires an increase in crop acreage to supply the greater demand quantities at the lower prices, while the opposite is true for the higher prices of solution 45.   Table 2.10 summarizes land use at the national level for solutions 41, 43, and 45 corresponding to the low, medium, and high price levels, respectively, of Tables 2.2 and 2.4.   Illinois and Iowa both would have relatively large reductions in soybean production.   For cotton, the large reduction in acreage and production would be in Alabama, Kentucky, and Tennessee.

MODEL II: ONE-PRICE PLAN FOR WHEAT

In contrast to model I, model II implies a one-price plan for wheat. All wheat produced under model II would receive a relative price representing its historic food value.   However, wheat also could be used for feed.   As feed wheat, it would need to be priced in terms of its relative nutritive value as a feed grain. Thus there would be a transfer cost involved in shifting wheat to feed.   This transfer cost would be equal to the differences in prices for wheat in food and feed uses.   This cost, added to the production costs of wheat in its use as feed, would also be included in the objective function.   Hence, under model I as compared with other models, wheat must bear a penalty in the transfer cost attaching to its feed use. The charge placed on the use of feed wheat was different for each region and was based upon historic regional differences between prices received for wheat and prices received for corn.   The charge averaged 85 cents per bushel for the United States.

Two solutions from model II assess the effect of a one-price plan for wheat. The production and demand constraints for these two solutions, 402 and 432, are identical to solutions 40 and 43, respectively, under model I and allow comparison of parallel outcomes under a one-price and a two-price plan for wheat.

A summary of the aggregate effects of applying the one-price wheat plan is given in Table 2.13.   Wheat acreage and production are considerably smaller under the two one-price plans for wheat where a transfer cost, perhaps paid through treasury outlays, is involved in using wheat for feed.   Both solution 40 (a two-price plan) and solution 402 (a one-price plan) leave wheat unrestricted in its competition for cropland, although other crops are restrained to their historic maximum acreage.   The one-price plan (solution 402) would cause wheat acreage to decrease by 32.5 million acres.   Simultaneously, acreage would be increased by 29.4 million for feed grain, 1.4 million for soybeans, and 4.9 million for unused or surplus land.   Indicated feed use of wheat declines by more than 0.8 million bushels.   Under solution 43 (a two-price plan) and solution 432 (a one-price plan), wheat is restricted to its historic maximum acreage in each of the 144 producing areas.   Again, however, the acreages of wheat and cotton are less under the one-price plan, and the acreages of feed grain and soybeans are greater, than under the two-price plan.   The penalty represented by the transfer cost of wheat to feed under the one-price plan causes the national pattern of production to be less efficient in a cost sense, but it reduces acreage required for crops, because land used for feed grain has a higher yield per acre than that otherwise used for wheat.

Most of the change in wheat production, under solution 432 as compared with 43, comes about in the eastern half of the United States where nearly every state shows a loss in wheat production (Figure 2.25).   Kansas is the only western state showing a significant drop in wheat production under solution 432, although it continues to be the greatest wheat-producing state. Producing areas in Montana, Oklahoma, and Colorado have reductions in wheat production but show increases in feed-grain production.   Feed grain also is substituted for wheat in Louisiana

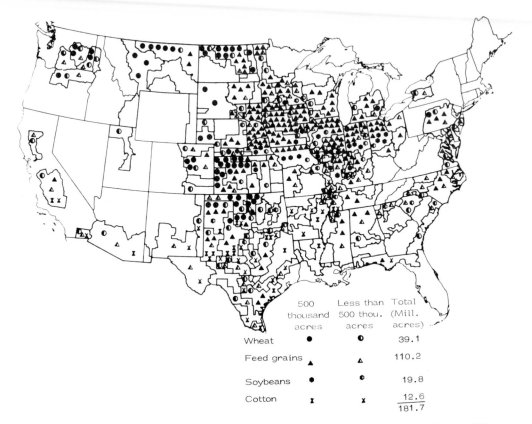

	500 thousand acres	Less than 500 thou. acres	Total (Mill. acres)
Wheat	●	◗	39.1
Feed grains	▲	△	110.2
Soybeans	●	◐	19.8
Cotton	x	x	12.6
			181.7

Fig. 2.25. Model II—Regional location and acreage of crop production for solution 432.

and Mississippi. Most of the Corn Belt and eastern states are indicated to produce to the limit of their feed-grain quota or acreage restraints under solution 43 and cannot expand acreage under solution 432. However, Mississippi and Louisiana increase feed-grain production by about 1.4 million acres. The remainder of the change in feed-grain production occurs in the Great Plains and western states where nearly every producing area has more feed grain under solution 432 than under 43. The spatial location of soybean production is appreciably affected by the application of the one-price plan on wheat. However, the total acreage of soybeans is affected very little. A general shift of soybean production from Kansas and Nebraska into Missouri and the eastern part of the Corn Belt is indicated in Figure 2.25. The shift eastward results partly from a decrease in cotton production over the Southeast. Mainly, however, the increased need for feed grain in the West caused soybeans to shift out of these areas and into the regions of the East.

Results of model III. The major objective of model III is to analyze the realism and usefulness of programming models that incorporate intraregional soil-quality differences. Even areas with least productive soils have some good cropland, and the most productive areas have some poor cropland. Model III allows the intraregional selection and use of cropland, based on potential soil productivity as well as interregional allocations of production for optimal attainment of the national objective.

Solution 403 of model III is the counterpart of solution 40 for model I where only one class of land is considered per producing area. Likewise, solution 433 is the counterpart of solution 43 under model I. A corresponding relationship holds for the remaining solutions of model III. (Solution 433 is the counterpart of 43, 473 is the counterpart of 47, etc.) The production and transportation patterns resulting from solutions of model III are similar to corresponding solutions of model I. The results often must be examined in detail to recognize broad differences among consuming regions. Most of the changes brought about by this model were small for any single region. However, several aggregate changes were evident among producing regions. Results from model III and from similar solutions of model I are summarized in Table 2.14. Total cropland used is much less in model III than in model I. Wheat, feed grain, and cotton acreages are generally reduced, while soybean acreage is increased.

MODEL III: BENCHMARK SOLUTION 433

Solution 433 under model III is the counterpart of benchmark solution 43 under model I. In both solutions, restraints for acreage quotas of wheat, feed grain, and cotton are set at 100 percent of their respective base levels of historic maxima. Prices and demand quantities are at the "normal" level. Soybeans are restrained to 40 percent of total cropland.

Approximately 8.2 million fewer acres are specified to attain the national bill of goods when intraregional differences in soil productivity are incorporated in the programming model (model III compared with model I in Table 2.14). Thus 48.7 million acres of cropland could be diverted from wheat, feed grain, soybeans, and cotton under solution 433 of model III. Most of the increase in land diversion is indicated for the eastern half of the United States and in the Great Plains states (Table 2.15).

Wheat shifts westward under model III, both in terms of acres and bushels (compare Figures 2.26 and 2.3). Nearly every state west of the Missouri River has an increase in wheat production; the opposite is true in regions east of the Missouri River. Consideration of land-quality differentials allows western states to more fully exploit their comparative advantage in wheat production. In total, however, wheat acreage is reduced by 1.2 million acres (Table 2.14). Consequently, as a result of the relocation of wheat production, a somewhat different pattern of transportation is required to attain demand for wheat in consuming regions (Figure 2.27 as compared with Figure 2.4).

Wheat used for feed is reduced to 280 million bushels under model III. Wisconsin has the largest decrease, 40.8 million bushels, in use of feed wheat. Kansas has a small decrease, while Colorado, Arizona, New Mexico, Washington, and Oregon use greater amounts of wheat for feed. The construction of model III better reflects comparative advantage of wheat production relative to feed-grain production in the West and Great Plains.

Feed-grain production is increased slightly to offset the lower utilization of

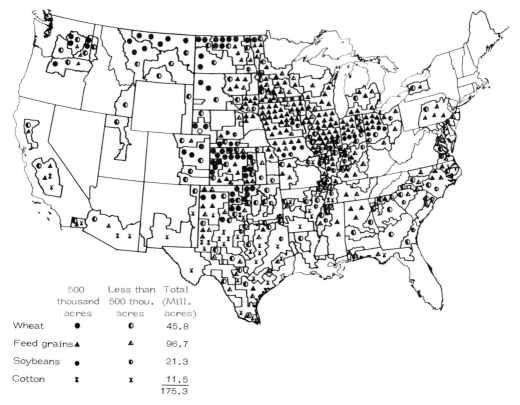

	500 thousand acres	Less than 500 thou. acres	Total (Mill. acres)
Wheat	●	◐	45.8
Feed grains	▲	▲	96.7
Soybeans	●	◐	21.3
Cotton	✗	✗	11.5
			175.3

Fig. 2.26. Model III—Regional location and acreage of crop production for solution 433.

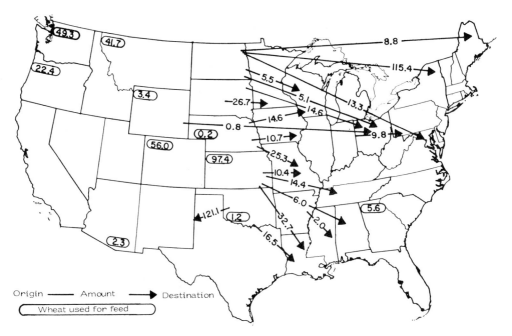

Fig. 2.27. Model III—Interregional flows of wheat under the conditions of solution 433 (million bushels).

feed wheat, under model III, even though the acreage of feed grain is decreased by nearly 5.8 million acres. Corn Belt states, with their comparative advantage in these crops, replace feed-grain production in other regions. Feed grain moves onto the more productive soils of the Corn Belt, while some less productive land which otherwise would shift to other crops or be diverted to noncrop use is withdrawn from feed grain. Higher average yields result, and total feed-grain production is greater than previously. As in the case of wheat, total interregional shipments of feed grain were increased in solution 433 of model III over that of solution 43 of model I (Figure 2.28).

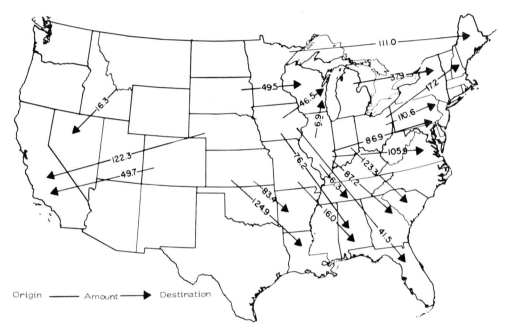

Fig. 2.28. Model III—Interregional flows of feed grain under the conditions of solution 433 (million bushels of corn).

Since feed grain utilizes a majority of the best land in the Corn Belt under model III, the efficiency of soybean production is reduced in these regions. Accordingly, total acreage of soybeans increases to 21.3 million acres, the highest level of any solution in the study. Soybean acreage in Iowa is indicated to decrease by 1.2 million acres. Producing areas in Illinois also experience a decrease in soybeans, while acreage in Ohio increases by 0.9 million acres. Such southern states as Arkansas, Missouri, Mississippi, Louisiana, and Texas also have an expanded soybean acreage (Figure 2.26, as compared with Figure 2.3). Soybean oil meal flows between regions as presented in Figure 2.29.

Cotton acreage is reduced by 2.7 million under model III. A portion of this decrease, however, is attributable to the movement of cotton into New Mexico and Arizona as a result of different technical coefficients for cotton.[18] All other

18. From the results of model II, cotton acreage was reduced by 1.5 million acres as a result of the new production coefficients. The remaining 1.2-million-acre drop in this solution is attributable to the characteristics of model III.

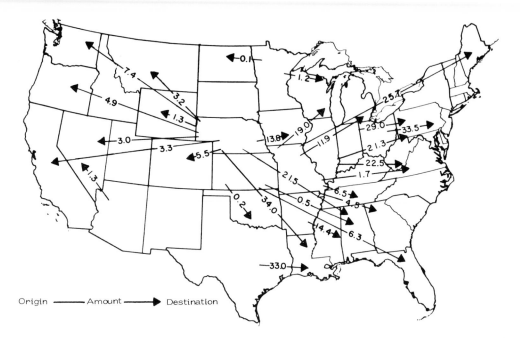

Fig. 2.29. Model III—Interregional flows of oil meal under the conditions of solution 433 (million bushels of soybeans).

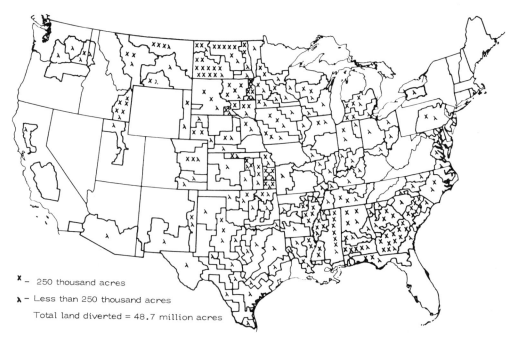

Fig. 2.30. Model III—Amount and location of surplus land under the conditions of solution 433.

states have a reduction in cotton acreage. Since cotton utilizes the majority of class I land wherever cotton is produced, increased yield and efficiency of cotton production cause a big drop in cotton acreage.

Under model III, with land differentiated by classes within producing areas, the surplus land is spread much more evenly over the nation. For example, solution 433 under model III (Figure 2.30) provides a picture that is different from its counterpart solution 43 under model I (Figure 2.7). Few areas fail to have some land that would be shifted from cotton, wheat, feed grain, or soybeans under the conditions of model III. Thus, while the impact would not be as deep on some communities as suggested under the pattern of solution 43 for model I in Figure 2.7, it would touch upon more communities over the nation.

SUMMARY AND CONCLUSIONS

This study was made to analyze certain facets of interregional competition in agriculture and to appraise the extent of surplus capacity as represented by cropland that can be shifted from wheat, feed grain, cotton, and soybeans in meeting domestic and export demands in 1965. Another purpose of the study was to determine the interregional shifts in agricultural production that might be expected if the nation's "bill of goods" in required wheat, feed grain, cotton, and soybeans were produced most efficiently under current technologies and farming practices. Finally, we attempted to identify individual producing areas that would need to shift from crop production to less intensive uses of land, such as grazing, forestry, or recreation.

Linear-programming models, including 962 equations and 2,682 real variables, and based on 144 spatially separated producing areas, were constructed to analyze the needed adjustments in resource use. These areas were defined to recognize the variations in technology, soil productivity, and climatic conditions existing across the United States. Each producing area has four potential producing activities (wheat, feed grain, soybeans, and cotton) from which projected demand requirements are met. The inclusion of potential activities in an area rests solely on the cropping history of the area. The producing areas used account for about 95 percent of the U.S. production of the four crops.

Also, 31 spatially separated demand regions, encompassing 48 states, were delineated and used in the analysis. Demands for wheat, feed grain, and oil meal were specified to reflect the projected trend in commodity requirements for each consuming region. A single national demand was used for cotton lint. Transportation activities allowed the designation of commodity movement among consuming regions and were used to insure an optimum allocation of production in meeting the regional demand requirements. The objective function of each programming model includes minimization of the total costs of producing and transporting commodities. A transfer activity in each consuming region allows wheat to be used for livestock feed at a cost varying upward from zero. This activity also provides the possibility of considering single-price or multiple-price plans for wheat as alternative policy programs.

Cropland is considered the limiting factor of crop production in each producing region. Regional acreage quotas (historic maximum acreages) for specific crops are used to simulate different land-retirement or supply-control schemes. Soybeans, in all solutions, are limited to the use of 40 percent of available cropland in each producing area.

Models I and II each were constructed under the assumption of homogeneous land within the producing areas. Regional productivity of each crop thus is reflected by a fixed coefficient of production. The two models differ in the pricing scheme employed for wheat. Model I uses a multiple-price plan for wheat. The food-wheat demand can be satisfied at a price above the equilibrium value of wheat, while feed wheat is utilized at its value as feed. Model II supposes all wheat to be supported at a price above the equilibrium value of wheat. Model III relaxes the assumption, used in model I and model II, of cropland homogeneity within producing areas. Regional cropland constraints for model III are divided into three categories on the basis of the estimated potential productivity of each.

In the programming models, 223.9 million acres of cropland are available for the production of feed grain, wheat, cotton, and soybeans. Excess capacity is measured in terms of unused cropland (i.e., land formerly devoted to the four crops but not needed to meet 1965 demand requirements and which could be shifted to other crops). Surplus capacity so measured ranges from 24.6 million acres, for a mildly restrictive program on all crops and a very high product-demand level, to 52.3 million acres, for an unrestrictive feed-grain program and a normal demand level. Typically, the benchmark solution with single soil classes in each area indicates a national surplus capacity of 40.5 million acres for 1965. If soil differences within areas are recognized through use of model III, this surplus capacity extends to 48.7 million acres.

If production were restrained to mesh exactly with demand levels at normal prices for 1965 and if production were allocated optimally among producing areas, many individual areas would need to shift almost entirely from the specified crops. These areas would be located mainly in the South and marginal areas of the Great Plains. Some land also would need to be diverted in fringe areas of the Corn Belt and other scattered regions of the nation. However, when intraregional soil differences are recognized, almost every producing region has some land that would need to be shifted from field crops. The amount would vary, of course, with the level of prices and the demand quantities to be attained. Under three solutions based on corn prices of $0.85, $1.10, and $1.40 per bushel, with corresponding prices of other commodities, the amount of surplus land was indicated to be 24.6 million, 40.5 million, and 51.4 million acres, respectively.

It must be concluded that conditions affecting the spatial allocation and amount of production of either wheat or feed grain may also substantially affect the other crop. There is considerable interaction of the two major commodities both in their competition for land use and in their substitution in consumption.

The spatial allocation of production appreciably affects the needed transportation of products. On the other hand, transportation charges had little effect on production allocation. Model III, with the advantage of using only the best land in each area, allows the greatest opportunities for adjusting the location of production. However, there is very little difference in transportation requirements of comparable solutions from models I and III. Hence, comparative advantages in production seem to outweigh the influence of transportation costs. Using shadow prices as the criterion, transportation charges added an average of about $0.28 to $0.31 per bushel to derived wheat equilibrium prices, $0.09 to $0.10 per bushel to feed-grain prices, and $0.13 to $0.15 per bushel to soybean prices. The solutions to specific programming models also yielded results which can be used to compare government cost of supply control under various policies. These results are presented in the next chapter.

Chapter 3: Aggregate Effects of Government Policies

NORMAN K. WHITTLESEY and EARL O. HEADY

The previous analysis clearly indicated excess capacity in agriculture for the projected levels of commodity demand, production coefficients, and crop acreages. This study presents the relative costs of simulated land-retirement programs represented by the several model solutions (as formulated in Chapter 2). Each of these solutions assumed that production is restrained to the demand levels mentioned earlier, with resulting prices which are above market equilibrium levels. All solutions and programs analyzed assumed the same demand and price levels. Hence, for each solution or land diversion program it represents, the cost to the government for shifting the specified amount of unused land from crops was estimated. In estimating these costs, we assumed

1. The government supports crop prices at the same level for all programs, a level commensurate with the demand levels used in the models.
2. Soybeans are not in excess supply and government expenditures are not necessary to establish appropriate output levels for this crop.
3. Wheat, feed grain, and cotton can be limited to their individual regional base acreages without government expenditures for land diversion.
4. Government expenditures are necessary for reducing the production of any crop below its regional base acreage or retiring land not under a specific acreage quota.
5. The government cost of withdrawing land from production of any crop is equal to or greater than the potential net revenue from producing that crop at the supported price level.
6. The production patterns resulting from the model solutions are those desired by the government for each programming alternative of the land-diversion program represented by it.

In calculating government program costs, a distinction was made between a

NOTE: For further details, see Norman K. Whittlesey and Earl O. Heady, *Alternative Economic Effects of Alternative Land Retirement Programs: A Linear Programming Analysis,* USDA Tech. Bull. 1351, Aug. 1966; and Norman K. Whittlesey and Melvin D. Skold, "Production Quotas and Land Values: Importance of the Dual in a Spatial Linear Programming Problem," *J. Farm Econ.* 46: 993–98, Dec. 1964.

proportional reduction of production in all areas and diversion occurring by dis-proportionate amounts in submarginal areas. Proportional reduction of area production is termed "mandatory diversion."[1] Nonproportionate diversion of land, where producing areas need not shift the same percentage of land from crops, is termed "voluntary diversion." All models had some solutions represent-ing voluntary diversion.

Government outlays for either the mandatory or voluntary diversion were assumed to compensate farmers for net income that could have been realized at the specified price levels.[2] Total outlays differ between the two programs since the mandatory program requires the same percentage reduction of crops in all producing areas. Income per acre is higher for land in high-yield areas. Govern-ment payments are consequently larger under the mandatory program even though fewer acres must be diverted than under voluntary programs where the lower-yielding land can be shifted in concentrated regions. In the voluntary programs, more land is retired from crops, and although the number of acres diverted is generally large, the diversion cost per acre is small. (Because of fixed costs, and lower per-acre yields, the net income which must be offset by pay-ments results in a lower diversion cost per bushel.)

An additional factor which increases costs under the mandatory programs is the requirement, in this study, that payments must include, in addition to the expected return to land, the returns to labor foregone from the diverted land. Labor costs were added to government outlay because a mandatory program that diverts a small proportion of the land from each farm and region provides little opportunity for reemployment of labor in nonagricultural pursuits.[3] Under the voluntary diversion program, we assumed that entire farms and regions could be shifted from crops and that the labor so released could find employment in other pursuits. Hence, labor returns foregone (i.e., the value of labor used in crop production) are not included in required government costs for land diversion.

Certain administrative and other government costs for agriculture are assumed to be fixed and unrelated to land diversion. These fixed costs are listed in Table 3.1 and are assumed to be the same regardless of the type of land-diversion pro-gram which might be put into effect. Under all programs, we assume the con-tinuation of agricultural exports for "food for peace" and foreign development programs. Hence, costs are included to cover the storage and public deficits related to these exports. The government costs related to land-diversion costs and

1. It is true that a program that was, strictly speaking, voluntary might achieve an evenly distributed pattern of diversion over all areas. However, this pattern would most likely occur if the program allowed only one proportionate rate of participation and provided such high pay-ments that all farmers in every producing area had no economic choice other than to participate.

2. The U.S. average prices for the relevant products, given the demand levels used, are $33.87 per hundredweight for cotton, $1.10 per bushel for corn, and $1.16 per bushel for wheat. The prices for the remaining feed grains are $0.67, $0.96, and $0.96 per bushel for oats, barley, and grain sorghums, respectively. This price for wheat assumes its value for feeding purposes.

3. The national weighted average labor costs are $5.59 per acre for feed grain and $2.17 for wheat. These costs are based upon those used to compute the total variable costs of each pro-ducing activity.

detailed later are in addition to the fixed costs for agriculture shown in Table 3.1. Total costs, including fixed costs, will differ only by the amounts shown later for the various diversion programs.

The relative cost estimates for various models were derived from dual solutions. The dual solutions of specific models provide equilibrium product prices and imputed values to the limiting resources (shadow prices). These prices are an indication of the relative value of factors in the production of crops under consideration. In the case of mobile factors, the differences between shadow prices for factors in different areas are an indication of the misallocation of resources. Acreage or production quotas are the only factors directly considered in this study which may be termed as mobile. The major factor of production in this study is land, an immobile resource. Shadow prices of land in the models (presented in previous chapters) are estimates of land rental value for the production of a given crop or a combination of crops. These values depend upon the efficiency of the region in production, the demand for products in that region, or in the latter case, the relative abundance of the resource. Land rental values are an indication of the annual return from the production of a particular crop or group of crops and may in real life be capitalized into the land market values.

In this study, individual land restraints were employed for each major crop-producing activity. These individual land restraints were an artificial restriction on production. They were similar to the acreage quota restrictions used in the administration of present farm programs. The soybean acreage restraint was an exception in that it was employed as an actual physical limitation within the producing areas. In any case, individual crop acreages that became binding in the models resulted in having a nonzero shadow price.[4] These shadow prices are an estimate of the marginal value of the acreage quota in each area. They would indicate the direction of movement of such quota in case a negotiable marketing quota program were used. Also, these quota shadow prices may be capitalized into cropland market value, if they are considered to be fixed to the land (i.e., nontransferable).

PRODUCTION QUOTAS AND LAND VALUES: DERIVATION OF THE DUAL SOLUTION

To demonstrate the derivation of the dual solution, we will initially employ an interregional competition model with k producing areas and m consuming regions. The producing areas are more numerous $(k > m)$ so that a given consuming region may contain more than one producing area. We assume, initially, that a single commodity A is being produced. Regional production costs, crop yields, transportation costs, and minimum commodity demands are determined outside the model.

The land rents LR in a particular producing area are determined by the imputed price P of the final product in the consuming region containing the pro-

---

4. This statement applies to any unused factor of production, including cropland. For a proof of the dual see Robert Dorfman, Paul A. Samuelson, and Robert M. Solow, *Linear Programming and Economic Analysis*, McGraw Hill, New York, 1958.

ducing area, the per-acre yield Y of the crop using the last unit of land, and the per-acre cost c_A of producing commodity A. Land rent may be defined as in Equation 3.1:

$$LR = Y \cdot P - c_A \tag{3.1}$$

The imputed values of production quotas QR are determined in the same manner as land rents. If a production quota (e.g., a wheat acreage allotment) becomes limiting before total cropland is exhausted, the production quota takes on a value as shown in equation 3.2:

$$QR = Y \cdot P - c_A \tag{3.2}$$

With a single production alternative and production quotas restricting regional output, the regional land rent LR would be zero. The total value of the agricultural output is imputed to the quota. It will be demonstrated later that if there are several production alternatives, both land rents and quota rents may be greater than zero.

A product equilibrium price is determined for each regional demand constraint. These imputed product prices reflect the per-unit costs of production in the least efficient producing region that is being used to satisfy the final product demand of a given consuming region. If the variables are defined as in Equations 3.1 and 3.2 and no inshipments of products are involved, the product shadow price P is determined as in Equation 3.3.

$$P = (c_A + LR + QR)/Y \tag{3.3}$$

In this case, the cost, land rent, quota rent, and yield are those of the highest-cost producing region employed within that consuming region. The land rent LR and the quota value QR of this producing area may not both be greater than zero since only one crop is competing for the cropland. If inshipments are necessary or desirable to satisfy the demand in question, transportation cost c_t must be added to the price shown in 3.3. Thus

$$P = [(c_A + LR + QR)/Y] + c_t \tag{3.4}$$

where c_A, LR, QR, and Y are values for the highest-cost producing area supplying the demand in question—a producing area which is not within the consuming region whose product price is being determined. The necessary condition for this product transport to occur is that the supply cost plus transportation cost from the foreign producing area is less than supply cost in an internal producing area. Product movement also must occur if a regional demand is greater than the internal production capacity.

The product and factor prices, as illustrated in Equations 3.1 through 3.4 are determined simultaneously in the model while satisfying the demand requirements at the least possible cost. Figure 3.1 is an illustration of the product supply curve SS within the jth consuming region of our theoretical model.[5] The horizontal segments OX_1, X_1X_2, and X_2X_3 are the possible product outputs from three

5. There are 31 consuming areas in the actual models.

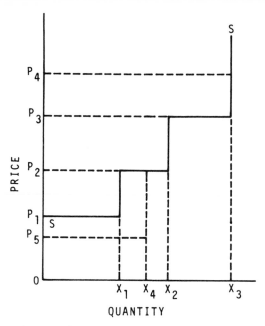

Fig. 3.1. Product supply curve for a consuming region containing three producing areas.

producing areas within the consuming region. The product supply prices for the three producing areas are defined as

$$P_1 = c_{A1}/Y_1 \tag{3.5}$$

$$P_2 = c_{A2}/Y_2 \tag{3.6}$$

$$P_3 = c_{A3}/Y_3 \tag{3.7}$$

The first producing area is the most efficient and the two remaining areas have higher per-unit costs, respectively. Land is the limiting resource in each producing area. Assume that the jth consuming region neither exports nor imports the product, and that the product demand in this consuming region is equal to OX_4. The regional product price is determined by the cost of production in the highest-cost producing area contributing to the product demand—producing area two. The product price (supply cost) is P_2 and the land rents for the second and third producing areas are zero, since the lands in these areas are not exhausted. Land rent for the first producing area is determined by P_2 in the manner of Equation 3.1. The land rent in this area is $(P_2 - P_1) \cdot Y_1$ or $P_2 \cdot Y_1 - c_{A1}$ where the prices are defined as in Equations 3.5, 3.6, and 3.7.

When interregional transport of the product occurs, the regional product equilibrium price may be defined differently. If regional exports are equal to $X_4 X_3$, the product price must be greater than or equal to P_3. Suppose that the product price in the importing region j' is P_4 plus the transportation costs from the exporting region j to the importing region j'. The price P_4 is determined by a producing area outside the exporting consuming region. The product price in the

jth consuming region is P_4 and land rent in the third producing area is $(P_4 - P_3) \cdot Y_3$. Likewise, the land rent in the second producing area is $(P_4 - P_2) \cdot Y_2$, and for the first producing area the land rent is $(P_4 - P_1) \cdot Y_1$. If no other regions are supplying region j', the product price in region j will be P_3. It is also possible that another producing area outside the jth consuming region could produce the commodity and ship it into this region at a total cost of P_5. The product price would be P_5, and all land rents in this consuming region would be zero. The quantity OX_4 would be imported and no internal production would occur.

Assume now that production quotas are the limitation on output and that land is not restricting in each producing area. If a single product is being produced, as in the above examples, the differences in total revenues and production costs are imputed to the production quotas. Land rents are zero and we have positive quota rents. If two commodities, A and B, are produced, it is possible to have both land rents and quota rents greater than zero. Suppose that an external demand exists for the amount $X_4 X_3$ of commodity A. Suppose further that commodity A is the most profitable crop in each area and that its production is limited by quotas in all three producing areas. Assume that commodity B is produced in the first and third producing areas, exhausting the remainder of the land resource therein. The imputed price for commodity A is P_4, but the value imputed to quotas in areas one and three is less than before. The land rent in these two areas (areas one and three) is equal to the net revenue per acre from producing commodity B. The amount by which the net revenue from producing commodity A exceeds that for commodity B is imputed to the production quota of commodity A in producing area three, as

$$LR_3 = P_B Y_{B3} - c_{B3} \tag{3.8}$$

$$QR_{A3} = P_{A4} Y_{A3} - c_{A3} - LR_3 \tag{3.9}$$

$$P_{A4} = (c_{A3} + LR_3 + QR_{A3})/Y_{A3} \tag{3.10}$$

P_{A4} (equals P_4 in Figure 3.1) and P_B refer to the prices of A and B, respectively; Y_{A3} and Y_{B3} are the yields of A and B, respectively; and QR_{A3} is the quota rent of commodity A in the third producing area. Costs are defined similarly. A similar set of equations could be developed for the first producing area. However, in the second producing area, the entire net revenue from commodity A is imputed to the quota rent since land is not restricting. We have now demonstrated how production alternatives affect land and quota values in a supply control program.

The importance of distinguishing between land rents and quota rents is now evident. The method in which quotas are used affects, to a large extent, land values. If quotas are fixed to the land, the value of the quota is imputed to land. If quotas are not attached to the land (i.e., they are of a negotiable type or are output quotas), land values may be much smaller, with the majority of the land rent then attributed to the production quota. Also production quotas attached to the land take on a smaller value if alternative uses for the land are available than if no alternative uses are existent. These factors are all quite important when evaluating alternative agricultural policies.

SPECIFIC MODELS AND PROGRAM ALTERNATIVES

The relative cost estimates in this study are derived on the basis of various specific models presented in Chapter 2.[6] As an aid to the reader, a summary of base acreages for specific crops used as limits in simulated land-retirement programs is presented in Table 3.2. In Table 3.2 the model solutions are explicitly linked with a particular type of land-retirement program. For example, the solution of model I in which wheat acreage quotas are removed while acreage for other crops is at the base acreage level is labeled IWU (I for model I, W for wheat, and U for unlimited acreage of wheat). Program IBN is a benchmark solution since regional crop acreage restraints for wheat, feed grain, and cotton are held at 100 percent of their respective base acreages. The benchmark solution does not focus on any particular crop.

The regional soybean acreage restraint was set at a maximum of 40 percent of available cropland (because of possible diminishing soil productivity or potential erosion hazards), or at the historical acreage in regions where this exceeded 40 percent of available cropland. The regional soybean acreage restraints were the same for all situations of each model. The regional acreages for wheat, feed grain, and cotton are based on historical production of each crop from 1951 to 1960 (as explained in Chapter 2). The base acreage of each regional crop activity is shown in Table 3.3.

LAND, QUOTA, AND EQUILIBRIUM PRICES

SOLUTIONS IBN, IWU, AND IWL

The shadow prices of land and crop quotas, shown in Table 3.4, are termed as "rental values" in the discussion that follows.

Under the benchmark solution, derived prices for wheat are highest in the eastern states because of their relatively large demand constraints and the locational disadvantage in meeting them (Table 3.5). The derived prices of wheat generally diminish westward and are lowest in the large wheat-producing areas of the Great Plains. Location and transportation charges mainly account for differences in wheat prices between areas of the West and the highly populated areas of the East.

Derived feed-grain prices also diminish from east to west. However, the lowest derived feed-grain prices of the West are determined by wheat, and not by feed grain, where wheat is used as a feed grain. The derived or programmed equilibrium price of feed grain, expressed as corn equivalent, is about $0.80 per bushel in the large producing states of Iowa and Illinois. (As mentioned previously, a few fixed costs are excluded in these derivations.)

Derived oil-meal prices are expressed as soybean-equivalent prices in Table 3.5 and include only the oil-meal values of soybeans, with the oil value excluded.

---

6. For details of each model, see Chapter 2.

These prices are lowest in Corn Belt areas where production of soybeans mainly is concentrated (Figure 2.3). West Coast states, supplied by Nebraska, all have about the same derived prices of soybeans. The programmed prices vary among states, mainly according to transportation costs from the Corn Belt source.

Since the costs of production used in programming did not include items for marketing, housing, management, and other overhead items, the derived prices may be around 10 percent lower than they would otherwise be. Nevertheless, their relative magnitudes among regions still reflect programmed equilibrium conditions and the relative advantage of different regions.

Derived product prices are not greatly changed by the regional wheat quotas used as restraints in solution 47 (IWL). Derived wheat prices are increased compared with the benchmark solution by $0.01 or $0.02 per bushel in the eastern half of the United States and by about $0.06 in the western states. Feed-grain prices, expressed in corn-equivalent prices, are changed even less—$0.02 per bushel being maximum change in any region. Derived regional soybean prices are increased by about the same amount as the feed-grain prices. Derived soybean prices decrease, however, in Kansas, Oklahoma, New Mexico, and Arizona because of the forced shift in wheat acreages. Kansas, substituting soybeans for wheat, is able to export oil meal to the states just mentioned and to lower the programmed equilibrium price for soybeans in these consuming regions.

Compared with the benchmark solution, the programmed equilibrium prices change considerably under solution IWU. Derived wheat prices decrease by an average of about $0.15 per bushel, thus suggesting a more efficient pattern of production under that solution. Imputed feed-grain prices also decrease, but relatively less so than for wheat. Derived feed-grain prices decline because wheat for feed can be produced more efficiently than other grains. Feed-grain prices drop by about $0.10 per bushel of corn-equivalent grain in most producing areas.

SOLUTIONS IFL AND IFU

As compared with the benchmark solution, the major change under solution IFL is increase in wheat production, to serve as a means of meeting national feed requirements. The wheat acreage also is expanded greatly in the eastern Corn Belt and throughout the Great Plains. Soybeans shift toward the Corn Belt as an efficient replacement for feed grain. Approximately 470 million bushels of wheat are used as feed under solution IFL, an increase of 160 million over the benchmark solution. Typically, the derived equilibrium prices for wheat and feed grain increase by $0.06 to $0.07 as feed grain is restrained to more efficient producing areas and as wheat on lower-yielding land is substituted for livestock feed (Table 3.6). The total acreage of surplus or unused land is 36.1 million acres under solution IFL.

Under solution IFU, programmed equilibrium prices for feed grain are lowered substantially by relaxation of base-acreage restraint on feed grain. The reduction ranges from $0.09 to $0.20 per bushel in the eastern half of the United States because of the greater concentration of production in these regions (Table 3.7). Derived feed-grain prices were changed by smaller amounts in western states since regions here continue to use substantial amounts of wheat for feed. Changes in derived wheat prices range from a decrease of $0.22 in Florida to an increase of $0.08 in Illinois.

SOLUTION IUU

Derived equilibrium prices for wheat and feed grain are reduced considerably under solution IUU as compared with the benchmark solution. Derived soybean prices increase in most regions (Table 3.8). The decline comes about since the model represented by solution IUU allows an improved interregional allocation of the nation's bill of goods represented by wheat, feed grain, cotton, and soybeans. Crops are unrestrained in being produced where they have the greatest comparative advantage. In contrast to solution IWU, with quotas or regional total cropland restraints, the conditions of IUU cause a widespread increase in the value of cropland. Cotton quota values are reduced to zero in all regions except Texas, Oklahoma, and California. Even in these states the price of cotton quotas is reduced because of the lower equilibrium price of cotton lint ($19.32 per cwt).

SOLUTION IIIBN

Derived equilibrium prices for wheat are not greatly affected by model III (Table 3.9). Since Ohio reduces wheat production and increases imports by about 21 million bushels, its derived wheat price increases by $0.09 per bushel. Illinois, with wheat pushed onto lower quality land under model III, has a $0.10 increase in its derived equilibrium price for wheat. Since feed grain accounts for more than 50 percent of total cropland acreage included in the model, and since it utilizes the better quality land at the expense of wheat and soybeans, the derived equilibrium prices are significantly reduced under model III as compared to model I. Nearly all Corn Belt states and states importing feed grain from the Corn Belt experience a drop of about $0.05 per bushel. Texas, Oklahoma, New Mexico, and Arizona, each allowing cotton to utilize class 1 land, have increases in derived feed-grain prices. North Dakota, because of a large increase in wheat production, has a slight increase in derived feed-grain prices.

Derived oil-meal prices increase in all regions except one under model III, because lower yields and higher acreages are required as soybeans are pushed onto the less productive land in most producing areas. Soybeans, when grown, compete quite closely with feed grain for cropland. Total cottonseed production is not changed under model III, but the large percentage is concentrated in the western states. Consequently, oil-meal prices are subsequently reduced in these states.

Rental values imputed to cropland and acreage quotas are changed significantly by model III. Cropland restraints are tripled under model III, while acreage quota restraints are unchanged. This ratio, of land qualities relative to acreage quotas, is probably more realistic than that represented by previous models. As a result, cropland restraints become limiting much more frequently and acreage quotas less frequently than in the previous models. Consequently, the rental values imputed to production quotas or acreage restraints for individual crops were reduced, and the imputed values of cropland generally increased. The magnitudes of these changes are reflected in Table 3.10. These differences may be compared with original values for solution 43, model I, shown in Table 3.4.

NATIONAL AVERAGE EQUILIBRIUM PRICES

The average equilibrium prices of products derived for each program are presented in Table 3.11. Average farm prices and average consumer prices for each product, as reflected in the programming solutions, are listed separately. The difference between these two sets of prices is represented by transportation costs. Prices received are estimated by weighting the regional equilibrium price of each product by its corresponding regional production. Prices paid were similarly weighted by regional product demands.

Transportation charges added an average of about $0.30 per bushel to wheat prices, $0.10 per bushel to feed-grain prices, and $0.14 per bushel to soybean prices (Table 3.11). The spread between prices paid and prices received for wheat is reduced when wheat acreage quotas are lifted, allowing more freedom to adjust production (programs IWU and IIIWU). However, the effect of transportation charges on equilibrium prices of feed grain and oil meal is relatively constant over all solutions. This fact is further evidence of the small influence which transportation requirements have on production allocation.

There are considerable differences in equilibrium product prices among solutions. Programs allowing freedom to adjust production patterns (IWU, IFU, IUU, IIIWU, and IIIFU) result in much lower equilibrium prices of wheat and feed grain than programs which partially dictate the spatial allocation of production (IWL, IFL, IIIWL, and IIIBN). The variation in programmed oil-meal prices is less than for wheat or feed grain. However, the competition of soybeans and feed grain for cropland is emphasized by Table 3.11. Programs which allow full adjustment of feed-grain production result in lower feed-grain prices but higher oil-meal prices (program IFU). Conversely, a program which restricts the location adjustments of feed-grain production results in higher feed-grain prices but lower oil-meal prices (program IFL).

Cotton prices are very responsive to adjustments in production location. Program IUU, allowing regional cotton acreage quotas to be increased by 100 percent over that of other solutions, reduces cotton prices by 40 percent. Solutions from model II result in slightly lower cotton prices than corresponding solutions of model I because of an adjustment of cotton yields in Texas, New Mexico, and Arizona. Recognition of intraregional differentials in land quality through model III further reduced cotton prices by about 25 percent below those of model I.

Government programs, therefore, can influence the efficiency of agricultural production. Programs which prescribe the location of crop production and resource use in agriculture may result in higher costs of production than programs which allow more freedom of action. However, the type or program employed probably will not affect the total costs of transportation or marketing.

Net farm income can be maintained at a given level, above that specified by market price equilibrium, either through restrictions on output which cause an income transfer from consumers through the market or through unrestricted production with direct payments made from the taxpayer, through the treasury, to the farmer. It is sometimes contended that the two methods have about the same net social costs. However, this argument overlooks the rather large differences in production efficiency that may exist under alternative supply control programs. These differences in efficiency, as indicated by the relative equilibrium product prices shown in Table 3.11, could be quite significant if the program alternatives were unconstrained production adjustment (IUU) and a restrictive feed-grain program (IFL).

ESTIMATED PROGRAM COSTS

Under the assumptions of this study, total potential production capacity and national product demands are the same for all model solutions or simulated programs. Thus differences in estimated government outlays under the alternative programs are one indication of the relative efficiency of these programs. Estimated government costs for land diversion to meet specified national demands and maintain farm prices at the specified levels are lowest for programs allowing all land diversion to be voluntary. Programs requiring a proportionate output reduction in all areas (mandatory diversion) resulted in the highest estimated government costs for supply control under the conditions of this study.

MODEL I: CROPLAND DIVERSION AND PROGRAM COSTS

Detailed analyses of costs of land diversion are provided in this section. Only the solutions of model I are used to estimate government costs of land diversion. The relative differences in diversion costs among solutions for model I parallel those expected for model II and model III, although the absolute level of costs may differ considerably among models.

BENCHMARK PROGRAM

The results of benchmark solution IBN have been described in considerable detail. This program is not directed toward controlling the supply of any particular crop. Instead, the regional acreage quotas of wheat, feed grain, and cotton are limited to the base acreage of each crop. Soybeans, as in all programs, are physically limited to the use of 40 percent of available cropland. All land diverted from agricultural production under this program is a voluntary reduction below regional acreage quotas. Land diversion can be concentrated in entire areas, depending on the relative costs of obtaining a shift of land from crops. Entire farms can be diverted so that labor can move into other employment. This voluntary land diversion may, in the short run, result from an incentive such as direct government payments to farmers. The same pattern of land diversion would be expected in the long run under the free play of market variables. Equilibrium market price would force out land with highest production costs (i.e., the land which has lowest comparative advantage under the programming models).

The pattern of land diversion, 40.5 million acres, under the benchmark program was shown in Figure 2.7. Unused acreage quotas for wheat, feed grain, and cotton amount to 42.8 million acres for the benchmark solution (Table 3.12). However, 2.3 million acres of feed-grain land in the Corn Belt are used for soybeans, leaving 40.5 million acres of cropland to be diverted from production. Feed grain is voluntarily diverted from 24.5 million acres of cropland in submarginal producing areas. Concentrations of retired land appear in producing areas in North Dakota, South Dakota, Kansas, Arkansas, Mississippi, South Carolina, and Georgia. These areas account for about 62 percent of the total land diversion. The remaining 38 percent is rather uniformly distributed throughout the other states. Only Corn Belt regions have land which remains fully devoted to the study crops.

The diversion cost for feed grain is $188.4 million, or an average of only $7.69 per acre. This is the estimated amount necessary to compensate farmers for income losses, at the previously specified price levels, in diverting their land from feed grain. This average payment rate is low in comparison with that under the present feed-grain program. However, only the low-productivity areas are indicated for diversion under program IBN, while land of average (or slightly below average) productivity is diverted in all regions under the feed-grain program.

Diverted wheatland amounts to 11.5 million acres under program IBN and would require total payments of $80.5 million or $7 per acre. Cotton, a more intensive crop, has a higher per-acre diversion cost. Under program IBN, 4.5 million acres of cotton land is indicated for diversion. The average cost per acre is $26.20. Land diversion in the pattern allowed by the benchmark program (IBN), allowing land diversion to be concentrated entirely in areas of lowest comparative advantage except for historic base acreages, would require a total government cost of $386.6 million. The costs of other government programs for agriculture indicated in Table 3.1 would be in addition to the $386.6 million. The 40.5 million acres diverted from wheat, feed grain, and cotton represent 18.1 percent of the nation's total cropland considered in this study. The average diversion cost per acre for the 40.5 million acres is $9.55 per acre. Within the confines of the assumptions employed in this study, this program is less costly than any other program alternative analyzed. To shift land from production voluntarily through incentive payments to farmers in submarginal areas appears, therefore, to be a relatively efficient method of land diversion under a criterion of treasury costs.

MANDATORY DIVERSION OF WHEATLAND

Program IWL simulates a mandatory wheat program. It requires a proportionate 10 percent diversion of wheatland in each producing area and in addition 8.4 million acres of wheatland are retired voluntarily (Table 3.13). Aside from this "proportionate restriction" on wheat, reduction of acreage for other crops is the same as that allowed for the benchmark program (i.e., diversion in entire regions where comparative advantage is lowest and diversion payments are minimized). Total land indicated for mandatory diversion under this program is 40.6 million acres, about the same as for the benchmark program. However, program IWL results in a somewhat less efficient agriculture and higher indicated government costs for diversion to attain the same demand quantities and farm price levels. Land diversion (Figure 2.9) is less concentrated than under the benchmark program since all areas producing wheat are required to reduce acreage diversion of this crop. Consequently, the amount of unused land in the northern Great Plains is much smaller than under the benchmark program. These states are required to increase wheat and feed-grain production to compensate for reduced production in other regions of the nation.

Approximately 21.8 million acres of land are voluntarily diverted from feed grain and 4.5 million acres from cotton under this program, which requires a 10 percent reduction of wheat acreage in all producing areas but allows other land to be diverted voluntarily. The voluntary diversion allows, aside from the 5.9 million acres of wheatland, concentration of land withdrawal in areas of lowest comparative advantage in production and lowest government costs. Costs of mandatory diversion of wheatland under program IWL are higher than for voluntary diversion under the benchmark program (and also for the voluntary portion of wheatland diversion allowed under IWL). Costs, including a charge for labor, for the land being forcibly retired average $17.51 per acre. The per-acre cost for the remaining wheat acreage diverted on a voluntary basis is only $6.44. It is much less costly to attain a given output reduction if diversion is in submarginal areas.

Costs of diverting 4.5 million acres of cotton land under program IWL are the same as for the benchmark solution, $26.20 per acre. Fewer acres are diverted from feed grain under program IWL than under program IBN. Hence, per-acre costs for diverting feed grain decline by about 12 percent to $6.71 per acre.

The total estimated government cost for program IWL is $421.6 million, to divert 40.6 million acres at an average cost of $10.38 per acre. This program has a total cost amounting to $34.8 million more than for the benchmark program. IWL would probably result in payments to a greater number of farmers than the benchmark program since it forces some diversion into all producing areas. Thus the higher costs of supply control under this program might be justified to benefit a greater number of persons through direct payments.

UNRESTRICTED WHEAT PRODUCTION

An unrestricted wheat program is represented by IWU. Wheat is limited only by total cropland in each area while feed grain and cotton are restricted to their regional historic base acreages. Land diversion under program IWU utilizes a large part of the cropland in producing areas of several states (Figure 2.14). Nearly 44 percent of available cropland in North Dakota and South Dakota is indicated for diversion and 67 percent is indicated for Alabama, Mississippi, and Louisiana. Other areas of concentrated land diversion are in Kansas, Michigan, Arkansas, Minnesota, and Idaho. Only small amounts of land are indicated for diversion in other states. Under this program, some feed-wheat production is shifted into North Carolina and South Carolina.

Land diverted from crop production is 38.2 million acres under program IWU. Approximately 22.5 million acres are diverted from feed grain, 4.5 million acres from cotton, and 11.2 million acres from wheat (Table 3.14). The net shift from wheat is less than 11.2 million acres, however, since some wheat is indicated for land previously in other crops. Estimated costs for diverting the 11.2 million acres from wheat production are $84.6 million, an average of $7.55 per acre.[7] The average cost of diverting land from feed grain under this program is $9.30 per acre, a total cost of $209.3 million for feed grain (Table 3.14). Wheat utilizes some land which is marginal for feed grain. Hence, higher program costs are indicated for the retirement of higher-yielding feed-grain land. Cotton land diversion costs are the same, $117.9 million, as under previously discussed programs. The pattern of cotton production remains the same as under the benchmark program.

MANDATORY DIVERSION OF FEED-GRAIN LAND

Program IFL requires that feed-grain acreage be reduced by 7.5 percent in all producing areas. However, additional feed-grain diversion can occur on a voluntary basis in terms of comparative advantage and lowest government costs of diversion. Wheat and cotton are restrained only to their regional base acreages. Soybeans are allowed to compete for land diverted from any other crops. The mandatory diversion of feed grain is 9.7 million acres. Voluntary diversion of feed-grain, wheat, and cotton land brings total diverted land up to 36.1 million acres, an amount less than for any other programs considered.

Program IFL results in 67 percent of available cropland diverted in producing areas of South Carolina, Georgia, Alabama, Mississippi, and Louisiana. Otherwise, this program produces a more dispersed pattern of land diversion than the programs previously discussed. Nearly all areas, except those producing soybeans in the central Corn Belt, have some excess cropland. North Dakota and South Dakota have a somewhat smaller diversion, however, because of the mandatory reduction in feed-grain production in other states.

The estimated government costs of program IFL are included in Table 3.15. If payment is required for the feed-grain land forced from production, the total estimated cost is $477.3 million when returns to labor are not included. If labor costs are included in payments for the mandatory portion, since labor is not expected to move out of agriculture, the program costs total $531.5 million. The cost of a required diversion of 9.7 million acres of cropland from feed-grain production, proportionately over all producing areas, is great, amounting to $23.66 per acre without labor charges and $29.25 with labor charges. This figure is nearly four times the average cost of $7.69 per acre for feed-grain land voluntarily diverted under the benchmark program. A program retiring average cropland in the Corn Belt is more expensive than one which reduces production by a similar amount through land diversion in less productive areas. However, programs which

---

7. Wheat was assumed to be supported at $1.16 per bushel, its feed value, for the purpose of estimating diversion costs on land other than cotton and feed grain.

reduce crop production in the major grain areas of the Corn Belt and the Great Plains winter wheat areas permit more land to be cropped in the less productive regions of the South Atlantic states and the northern Great Plains.

UNLIMITED FEED-GRAIN ACREAGE

Under program IFU, regional acreage quotas are removed entirely for feed grain. These crops are restrained only by the total cropland acreage in each producing area and national demand requirements for these products. Wheat and cotton acreages are restricted only to the regional base acreage of each crop. All land diversion is assumed to be voluntary, with compensation for this diversion computed as before. No payments are made for land diverted from wheat or cotton to the production of feed grain.

Land diversion under this program totals 47.9 million acres (Table 3.16). Approximately 7.3 million acres are diverted from wheat, 4.5 million acres from cotton, and 36.1 million acres from feed grain. Although feed-grain acreage quotas are not applied under this program, these 36.1 million acres otherwise would be in feed grain. Of the 16.9 million acres shifted from wheat, feed grain uses 9.6 million acres.

Land diversion is highly concentrated under program IFU. In South Carolina, Georgia, Alabama, Florida, Mississippi, and Louisiana, 78 percent of available cropland is diverted. Likewise, in North Dakota and South Dakota, 52 percent of the cropland is diverted. Other pockets of concentrated land diversion occur in Idaho, Michigan, Kansas, and Minnesota. The local impact of such a program thus would be great, because a less intensive agriculture and a thinning of the rural population likely would follow.

All land diversion is assumed to be voluntary and the estimated cost is $436.5 million. The 47.9 million acres are diverted at an average cost of $9.11 per acre. This cost is computed, as mentioned previously, under the assumption of feed-grain prices at a level of $1.10 per bushel for corn with comparable prices for other crops. Diversion costs for 7.3 million acres of wheatland are estimated at $66.0 million, an average of $9.04 per acre. Diversion costs for wheatland are greater only under a partially mandatory program (program IWL, Table 3.13). Costs for diverting the 36.1 million acres from feed grain, $7 per acre, were relatively low as compared to other programs. The indicated land-use pattern also could result from a program of negotiable marketing quotas on feed grain equal to the feed-grain demand requirements. If quotas were exchanged among regions in terms of comparative advantage, concentration of production would result from the eventual optimal allocation of these quotas among producing areas.

ACREAGE QUOTAS REMOVED

Program IUU is designed to simulate a condition which minimizes costs of production and transportation and government costs of land diversion to attain the given demand levels and farm product prices. Separate regional acreage restraints for wheat and feed grain are completely removed. Only total available cropland is assumed to limit these crops in each producing area. Cotton acreage is limited to 200 percent of the historical base acreage in each area and soybeans are limited to 40 percent of available cropland in each area. National production of each crop is restrained by its respective demand requirements.

The pattern represented by this solution also could result from negotiable marketing quotas, as described previously. In this case, areas of greatest comparative advantage in production would attract the quotas. Less efficient areas eventually would shift out of crop production. Also, the same pattern of production might be expected to result under long-run equilibrium of a free market. Under long-run equilibrium market prices it is possible that demand quantities would be greater than those used in the programming models of this study. In another simulated program with larger product demands assumed to result under lower prices, only 24.6 million acres of unused land were indicated for diversion.[8]

MODEL II: RETIRED CROPLAND

The constraint conditions of program IIBN are the same as those of the benchmark program IBN, except for a higher wheat price under the former (see the description of models in Chapter 2). Approximately 42.3 million acres of cropland are diverted under program IIBN, a slight increase over the benchmark program. Approximately 69 percent of the cropland in South Carolina, Georgia, Alabama, Mississippi, Louisiana, and Arkansas is diverted. North Dakota benefits from this program, since nearly 1 million more acres are devoted to crops than under program IBN. Still, 37 percent of the cropland in Montana, Idaho, North Dakota, and South Dakota is diverted, and pockets of diverted land also occur in Minnesota, Wyoming, Kansas, and Utah.

An unusual feature of program IWU under model I is the high employment of land in North Dakota, South Dakota, South Carolina, and Georgia (Figure 2.7). When the additional cost was imposed on feed wheat through program IIWU, these states again had many acres of excess land. Model II, with its one-price plan for wheat, results in higher government costs of land diversion than model I with a multiple-price plan. If land diverted from wheat production is rewarded in government payments at a rate consistent with the price of wheat assumed for model II, the cost per acre of diverted land is much higher than model I. In program IBN, 11.5 million acres of wheatland are diverted at a total cost of $80.5 million (Table 3.12) when wheat is priced at $1.16 per bushel to represent its feed value. If costs are estimated for program IBN with the assumption of wheat priced at $1.95 per bushel, the total cost of diverting the 11.5 million acres is $312.8 million. Thus commodity price levels used to compute diversion payments highly influence program costs.

---

8. This program, with larger demand requirements, was not included in the results shown in this publication. It is mentioned here because the assumed price levels were close to those acquired as equilibrium prices in program IUU. The resulting cropland requirements are, perhaps, more indicative of what would result under conditions of unrestricted production than those shown for program IUU.

MODEL III: RETIRED CROPLAND

The unique feature of model III is its recognition of intraregional land-quality differences. Model III solutions result in a more diversified crop production pattern and a more intensive land use than solutions under model I. The result is a large acreage retired under model III. The pattern of land diversion for solution IIIBN is presented in Figure 2.30. Many areas of the Corn Belt and Great Plains which employed all cropland under simulated programs from models I and II now have some idle land. However, concentrated regions of diverted land still exist in South Carolina, Georgia, and other southeastern states. The northern Great Plains states also continue to experience a rather low rate of land employment. The resulting land disposal patterns of other solutions from model III are similar in their comparisons with the solutions of model I.

The implications of model III are quite important in the formulation of agricultural policy. A program removing only submarginal land within an area will require more land diversion to accomplish the same supply control measures than a program removing land to average quality within an area. The comparative costs of such programs are probably similar if all diversion payments are governed by the productivity of land removed from production. However, if below-average land is diverted, and if the diversion payments are based on the productivity of average land, the program efficiency may be greatly reduced.

LAND-USE ALTERNATIVES

One of the major problems in land-retirement programs is determination of the proper utilization of the excess cropland. It is generally agreed that the diverted land should be devoted to grass, hay, trees, or other uses which avoid excessive erosion and growth of weeds. Establishing these cover crops involves expenses and requires incentive payments to defray establishment costs. Alternatively, farmers may be induced to establish cover crops by the expectation of future benefits. Undoubtedly the greatest short-run benefits from diverted land are derived when it is used for grazing, when considering all diverted lands collectively.

In recent farm programs, farmers have not been allowed to graze or otherwise utilize crops from diverted land during the growing season. They have been permitted to partially employ the diverted acres by grazing very late in the fall or early spring, with very little of the diverted land being fully employed. Many farmers would be willing to accept lower diversion payments if they were permitted to fully utilize the diverted acres. Bottum has estimated the difference in diversion payments between grass-used programs and grass-not-used programs.[9] When only 14.1 million acres are diverted, he estimated the costs per acre to be $1.20 and $3.00, respectively. All the retired land was considered to be marginal in production and value. However, when 80 million acres are retired, the esti-

9. USDA, *Agricultural Statistics*, 1961 and 1962.

mated costs per acre are $11.30 and $12.75, respectively. When average cropland was assumed to be retired, the costs were much higher and with less divergence between alternatives. In every instance the grass-not-used program was considered to be a more expensive land-retirement alternative to obtain a given acreage of idle land.

Estimates of land-diversion costs have not been made for a grass-used program in this study. However, the potential productivity of the diverted acres was assumed to be of interest to future researchers. Under a grass-used program, beef production seems the most likely activity to utilize the diverted acres. Other potential uses are probably of minor importance compared to beef. Therefore, using USDA data, the beef that might be produced on the diverted land under several alternative programs was estimated.[10] The impact this production might have on the supply and on the market price of beef also was estimated. Potential beef production appears to be nearly proportional to the amount and productivity of unused land (Table 3.17). Programs retiring land on the extensive margins (IWU and IUU) result in a slightly lower average production of beef per acre retired than programs retiring land on a more uniform basis (IFL).

The percentage change in total beef production, from an estimated 28.7 billion pounds of beef produced in 1960,[11] is computed for each program. Brandow's estimated demand elasticity of beef, 0.68, is used to estimate the impact of greater quantities on beef prices.[12]

Full utilization of the diverted land for beef production is estimated to produce grass-fed beef equaling 11.6 to 15.8 percent of present beef supply, inducing a reduction of 17 to 23.1 percent in the price of beef. These estimates are based upon the assumption that all diverted cropland is used for beef production. Undoubtedly, not all diverted land could or would be fully employed for beef production under a grass-used program, thus causing the beef supply and price changes to be smaller than indicated above. Also, changing structures for beef and high cross elasticities of demand with other meats would tend to cushion the price effect of any increased beef production.

10. Frank B. Morrison, *Feeds and Feeding*, the Morrison Publ. Co., Ithaca, N.Y., 1951; and USDA, *Relative Use of Feeds for Livestock including Pasture, by States*, Agr. Res. Serv., Bull. 153, 1955.

11. USDA, *Agricultural Statistics*, 1961 and 1962.

12. G.E. Brandow, *Interrelations among Demands for Farm Products and Implications of Control of Market Supply*, Pa. Agr. Exp. Res. Bull. 680, 1960.

Chapter 4: Capacity, Interregional Adjustment, and Land Use

EARL O. HEADY and MELVIN O. SKOLD

This study has been made to determine the magnitude of interregional shifts in grain production and land use implied for the future under specified conditions of technological improvement and population or demand growth. In contrast to previous studies, data of the current analysis are projected to 1975. The analysis projects conditions of interregional competition in crop production under assumptions allowing increased exports, further development of the St. Lawrence Seaway, alternative rates of technological improvement in various agricultural regions, and an advance in the technology of southern agriculture to the level of that in other regions of the nation. The crops included are wheat, corn, grain sorghums, barley, oats, soybeans, and cotton. The objectives of the study are attained through the application of several linear programming models which deal directly with crop production but incorporate feed requirements for livestock production.

NATURE OF EMPIRICAL MODELS

This study is based on 144 producing areas delineated earlier (Figure 2.1). The models also include 31 spatially separated consuming regions (Figure 2.2) for the three final product categories: wheat, feed grain and oil meal. The feed-grain product category includes corn, grain sorghums, barley, oats, and wheat used for feed. These crops were converted to a corn-equivalent basis in the analysis, rather than each being considered separately. Consuming regions follow state boundaries within the same geographic proximity. The procedure for delineation of these regions was discussed in Chapter 1.

Five production activities included in the analysis are wheat, feed-grain rotation, feed-grain and soybean rotation, soybeans, and cotton. The models include a wheat-to-feed-grain transfer activity for each consuming region, allowing for the use of wheat for feed if it is the cheapest source of livestock nutrients. The models do not restrain the amount of wheat that can be used as feed.

NOTE: For further details, see Earl O. Heady and Melvin Skold, *Projections of U.S. Agricultural Capacity and Interregional Adjustments in Production and Land Use with Spatial Programming Models*, Agr. and Home Econ. Exp. Sta., Iowa State Univ., Ames, Res. Bull. 539, Aug. 1965.

Transportation activities for each of the three demand categories allow movement of grains among consuming regions. Theoretically, $31 \times 30 = 930$ transportation activities exist for each product category, making a potential of 2,790 transportation activities for the three product categories. However, some of these activities were eliminated by physical separation of the regions. Also, for example, the possibility of shipping oil meal from consuming region 29 (Washington) to consuming region 16 (Arkansas) was eliminated since Washington has never produced soybeans or cotton, the two activities giving rise to the oil-meal product category. In final construction of the models, 1,376 transportation activities (459 each for wheat and feed grain and 428 for oil meal) were used. The transportation costs used were the 1962 "flat" railroad rates for the products in question. The points of trade (i.e., the points within each consuming region from which all importing or exporting was assumed to occur) were selected as the basis for computing these rates. The transportation rates were furnished by the Interstate Commerce Commission.

Each of the 31 consuming regions has separate demand restraints for wheat, feed grain, and oil meal. A single national demand restraint is defined for cotton lint. Wheat, feed grain, and oil meal are expressed in feed units to allow aggregation of feed-grain crops and the feed-grain and soybean rotation into a single activity, to simplify use of the wheat-to-feed-grain activities, and to allow aggregation of soybean oil meal and cottonseed oil meal into a homogeneous product.

Each of the 144 producing areas has a land restraint to reflect the total area available for use of the five crop activities. The models allow wheat and feed grain or feed grain and soybean activities to occupy all land available within an area. However, the soybean activity is restrained to not more than 50 percent of the land available; the cotton activity is restrained to the largest percentage of land used in the past for any one area.

MATHEMATICAL STRUCTURE

The mathematical structure of the models is basically the same as reported in Chapter 2 except for the addition of feed-grain–soybean rotation activity. Most of the notations are also as defined earlier (Equations 2.1 through 2.8). Only new notations will be defined here. The objective function of the models is

$$\min Z = \sum_{k=1}^{144} \sum_{q=1}^{5} c_{kq}^1 \, C_{kq} + \sum_{j=1}^{31} c^2 \, Y_j + \sum_{n=1}^{3} \sum_{\substack{j=1 \\ j \neq j'}}^{31} c_{njj'}^3 \, z_{njj'} \tag{4.1}$$

subject to the following restraints:

(1)
$$\sum_{k=1}^{v^j} b_{1k} \, C_{1k}' - h_j \, Y_j \pm \sum_{\substack{j=1 \\ j \neq j'}}^{31} t_{1jj'} \, z_{1jj'} = R_{1j} \tag{4.2}$$

(2)
$$\sum_{k=1}^{v^j} b_{2k} \, C_{2k}' - \sum_{k=1}^{v^j} b_{5k} \, C_{5k}' + h_j \, Y_j \pm \sum_{\substack{j=1 \\ j \neq j'}}^{31} t_{2jj'} \, z_{1jj'} = R_{2j} \tag{4.3}$$

$$(3) \quad \sum_{k=1}^{v^j} b_{5k} \, C'_{5k} + \sum_{k=1}^{v^j} b_{3k} \, C'_{3k} + \sum_{k=1}^{v^j} b_{4k} \, C'_{4k} \pm \sum_{\substack{j=1, \\ j \neq j'}}^{31} t_{3jj'} z_{3jj'} = R_{3j} \quad (4.4)$$

$$(4) \quad \sum_{k=1}^{144} b_{4k} \, C'_{4k} = R_c \quad (4.5)$$

land restraints

$$\sum_{q=1}^{5} C'_{qk} \leqslant A_k \quad (4.6)$$

$$C_{4k} \leqslant A_k^c \quad (4.7)$$

$$C_{3k} \leqslant A_k^s \quad (4.8)$$

nonnegativity restraints

$$C_{qk} \geqslant 0; \quad y_j \geqslant 0; \quad z_{njj'} \geqslant 0 \quad (4.9)$$

where $q = 5$ for soybean–feed-grain rotation
A_k^c = amount of land available for cotton production in kth producing area
A_k^s = amount of land available for the soybean activity in the kth producing area.

The models as outlined include a coefficient matrix of $402 \times 1{,}923$ order without slack vectors (a matrix of $402 \times 2{,}325$ order with the slack vectors). To assure against an infeasible solution in some of the empirical models with large demand restraints, 93 artificial activities were introduced (one for each of the three final demand categories in the 31 consuming regions) which enabled the demand in any consuming region to be met at a very high artificial cost if producing regions as defined were not able to satisfy the demand.[1]

VARIATIONS FOR EMPIRICAL MODELS

Several sets of assumptions were used in the various models relating to population, income, feed-livestock product conversion efficiency, and per-acre yields and costs. These alternative assumptions (i.e., different levels at which demand restraints and technical coefficients are placed) allow examination of the effect of different levels of exports, varying rates of technological advance over the nation, and similar developments in interregional competition. We now review the several empirical models used in the study. All models refer to restraints and variables for 1975.

1. Although the artificial activities were not utilized in the solutions to any of the empirical models, they had the potential of being useful for problems of the size analyzed. If results to an empirical model were obtained with the aid of these artificial activities, the least-cost real activities in the solution are meaningful economically, and some results are forthcoming from the expenditure of elapsed machine time. With the addition of these artificial activities, the matrix was of the order of $402 \times 2{,}418$ and $402 \times 2{,}016$, with and without slack vectors, respectively.

MODEL I

A United States population of 222 million is assumed for 1975. Real per capita consumption of farm products is projected to increase in accordance with the change in per capita income outlined later. Trends in per-acre yields and in feed-livestock conversion rates are predicted as a continuation of the 1940–60 trend. The trend in production cost per unit of crop output is projected from the 1949–61 trend. Exports of wheat, feed grain, and oil meal approximate the 1956–61 average export levels.

MODEL II

Model II is identical to model I except for the assumed level of real per capita income in 1975. Model II assumes an increase of 65 percent over the 1955 level, a 15 percent increase over the level in model I.

MODEL III

This model assumes a population of 230 million. Per capita consumption rates of farm products for 1975 are those estimated by Daly.[2] Feed requirements to produce a given amount of livestock product are the economic potential estimates of the USDA.[3] Exports of wheat, feed grain, and oil meal for 1975 are set at the 1956–61 level. Input-output coefficients are the same as for the first two models.

MODEL IV-A

Model IV-A is identical to model I except that the population level of 230 million is used for 1975.

MODEL IV-B

This model is the same as model IV-A except that the level of exports of feed grain and oil meal is increased to 125 percent of the 1955–61 average export levels of these commodities. Wheat exports remain as in previous models, i.e., 100 percent of the 1956–61 level.

MODEL IV-C

Wheat exports are increased to 125 percent of the 1956–61 level in model IV-C. The 25 percent increase is allocated in regions bordering the St. Lawrence Seaway (consuming regions 9, 10, 11, and 12). Feed-grain and oil-meal exports are increased to 150 percent of the 1956–61 levels, the increase being distributed

2. Rex F. Daly, "The Long-run Demand For Farm Products," *Agr. Econ. Res.* 8 (1956): 1–19.
3. Glen T. Barton, USDA, ERS, private communication, Sept. 1961.

among consuming regions in the proportion of 1956–61 exports. Other assumptions are the same as for model IV-A.

MODEL IV-D

Wheat exports are increased to 150 percent of the 1956–61 levels and are distributed among consuming regions in proportion to 1956–61 exports. Feed-grain and oil-meal exports are increased to 200 percent of their 1956–61 average levels and also are distributed among consuming regions in the 1956–61 pattern. Other assumptions are the same as for model IV-A.

MODEL IV-E

Wheat exports are at 150 percent of the 1956–61 level and are distributed among regions in the same manner as in that period. Feed-grain exports are set at 200 percent of 1956–61 levels, with 50 percent allocated equally to consuming regions 9, 10, 11, and 12 and another 50 percent allocated to the remaining regions in the same proportion as in 1956–61. Oil-meal exports, also doubled, have 20 percent of the increase allocated to Pacific Coast consuming regions, 50 percent to the St. Lawrence Seaway consuming regions (regions 9, 10, 11, and 12), and the remaining 30 percent as a residual to other consuming regions following the 1956–61 pattern. Other assumptions are the same as for model IV-A.

MODEL IV-F

Wheat exports are increased to 200 percent of 1956–61, with the distribution among regions the same as at that time. Feed-grain exports, increased to 200 percent of 1956–61, have half the increase forced through consuming regions 9, 10, 11, and 12; 20 percent allocated to consuming regions 3 and 5; and the remaining 30 percent following the 1956–61 pattern. Southeastern consuming regions 3 and 5 absorb 20 percent of the increase in oil-meal exports; Pacific Coast regions 29, 30, and 31 absorb 20 percent; and the remaining 60 percent follows the original 1956–61 regional distribution. Other assumptions are the same as for model IV-A.

MODEL V

Model V is the same as model I except that a U.S. population of 243,880,000 is assumed for 1975.

MODEL VI-A

Differences in previous models dealt only with demand restraints, or right-hand sides of the equations. We now examine alternatives concerned with differences in the technical matrix. Model VI-A assumes the 1950–62 trend in crop yields to continue until 1975. Hence, the per-acre yield estimates are higher than the projections (based on the 1940–61 trend) used for models I through V. For demand restraints, the USDA economic maximum feed-livestock conversion rates are used.[4]

MODEL VII-A

This model also utilizes a different coefficient matrix from other models just outlined. This matrix is one of "advanced technology" since the coefficients reflect conditions where states of the South and Southeast would use techniques for feed grain and soybeans equivalent to counterparts in the North Central states. Also, the coefficients for cotton in the Southeast are equivalent in technology to those of the Southwest. Labor, power and machinery, and all other crop expenses except fertilizer costs are assumed equivalent for all areas producing feed grain and soybeans in the Corn Belt and southern and eastern states. Fertilizer costs differ among producing areas, however, because of geographical dispersion and varying responses to fertilizer and related inputs among producing areas. The model assumes an equal degree of mechanization (and, hence, comparable farm size) for different crops in the various regions. The wheat activity remains unchanged from that used in models I through V. Demand levels are the same as those used for model IV-B.

MODEL VII-B

The model is identical to model VII-A except that the export demand requirements assumed are the same as those in model IV-F.

Various empirical models were created by changing the variables representing possible levels of demand for agricultural products in 1975 or by varying the coefficients representing technology. We now discuss the assumptions and conditions representing the demand restraints and technical coefficients of the various models.

DATA AND COEFFICIENTS

PER CAPITA CONSUMPTION ESTIMATES

The 1955 Household Food Consumption Survey served as the basis for estimating the per capita consumption rates of foods for 1975.[5] The technique for estimation was that suggested by Lavell,[6] who personally furnished estimates of the income distribution of the U.S. population by urbanization category and geographical area for 1975. Per capita consumption rates of food for 1975 were

4. The conversion rates of economic potential are lower than those for the economic maximum rates assumed in model VI-A.
5. USDA, *Food Consumption of Households in the United States: Household Food Consumption Survey, 1955*, Washington, D.C., 1956.
6. Robert Lavell, USDA, ERS, private communication, Oct. 1960.

established, and consuming region demand levels were estimated from the data on population distribution and the per capita consumption rates in the 1955 survey. The following equations were used for estimating the level of per capita consumption of a given food:

$$c_{kh}^{i,\,75} = \sum_{j=1}^{m} c_{jkh}^{i,\,54}\, p_{jkh}^{75} \tag{4.10}$$

$$c_{h}^{i,\,75} = \sum_{k=1}^{3} c_{kh}^{i,\,75}\, u_{kh}^{75} \tag{4.11}$$

$$c^{i,\,75} = \sum_{h=1}^{4} c_{h}^{i,\,75}\, g_{h}^{75} \tag{4.12}$$

where $c_{jkh}^{i\,54}$ = the per capita consumption of the ith food with the jth income class in the kth urbanization category and the hth geographical area in 1954

p_{jkh}^{75} = the percentage of the population falling within the jth income class in the kth urbanization category and the hth geographical area in 1975

$c_{kh}^{i,75}$ = the per capita consumption of the ith food in the kth urbanization category and the hth geographical area in 1975

u_{kh}^{75} = the percentage of the population living in the kth urbanization category in the hth geographical area in 1975

$c_{h}^{i,\,75}$ = the per capita consumption of the ith food in the hth geographical area in 1975

g_{h}^{75} = the percentage of the population living within the hth geographical area in 1975

$c^{i,\,75}$ = the per capita consumption of the ith food in 1975

Food consumption in any group is influenced by many variables such as income, sex and age distribution, occupation, and degree of urbanization. Equations 4.10 through 4.12 consider only income and degree of urbanization. A different income distribution will, of course, be reflected for each income level assumed. The national income level assumed is the same for all models but real per capita disposable income used for 1975 is 50 percent higher than in 1955. The income distributions used were generated from this level and the technique of Burk.[7] Models III-A and III-B and models VI-A and VI-B incorporate Daly's consumption estimates for 1975. Conversion of the weights of retail foods to farm weights yields the "farm level" requirements of each crop product. Multiplication of the per capita "farm level" requirements by the appropriate population figure provides the aggregate requirement for a particular crop.

7. Marguerite C. Burk, *Measures and Procedures for Analysis of U.S. Food Consumption,* USDA, Agr. Handbook 206, 1961.

POPULATION ASSUMPTIONS

The population projections incorporate varying assumptions about trends in migration, fertility, and mortality. Series I of the census projections[8] was used for most of the population estimates in this study. The 1955–70 rate of change postulated by the Bureau of the Census was assumed to continue until 1975. State estimates were aggregated into the geographical areas on which the per capita consumption estimates are based. An estimate of the percentage of total population within a given geographical area, as in Equation 4.12, was obtained by dividing the population of each geographical area by the total population.

LIVESTOCK-FEEDING EFFICIENCY

The rates of converting feed into livestock products were estimated for some models by projecting 1940–60 trends. Other models employ the economic potential or economic maximum of Barton.[9] The economic potential and attainable estimates represent the coefficients expected by 1975 from adoption of known technology at the time of the study.

From estimates of (1) livestock products required by the 1975 population and (2) projected feed-livestock conversion rates, the amount of feed necessary to meet 1975 restraints can be estimated. In making the estimates, feed requirements were first calculated in total feed units. Allocation was then made to particular classes of feed, depending on projected consumption, conversion rates, and historic trends. Equations 4.13 through 4.16 summarize the derivation of total feed units necessary to achieve the required output of livestock products.

$$Q_r^i = c^{i,75} \, n^{75} \tag{4.13}$$

$$Q_1^i = Q_r^i / f_i \tag{4.14}$$

$$FU^i = Q_1^i \, g^i \tag{4.15}$$

$$FU = \sum_{i=1}^{m} FU^i \tag{4.16}$$

$c^{i,75}$ has the same meaning as in Equation 4.12

n^{75} = population level assumed for 1975
Q_r^i = quantity of the ith food demanded expressed in retail weights
f_i = factor for converting the ith food from retail to farm level weights
g^i = feed units required to produce a unit of the ith food product
FU^i = feed units required to produce the required amounts of the ith food product
FU = feed units required to produce the required amounts of all relevant food products; m being the number of different food products

8. *Current Population Reports, Population Estimates*, U.S. Dept. Commerce, Bureau of Census, Series P-25, No. 180, 1957; ibid., No. 187, 1958.
9. Glen T. Barton, USDA, ERS, private correspondence, Sept. 1962.

REGIONAL DEMAND REQUIREMENTS

In addition to livestock feed requirements, grains of various types are used directly as human food. These cereal food requirements, based on population and income projections and the relevant demand elasticities of the products, were estimated for other grains as well as for wheat. The consumption requirements were converted to grain equivalents with feed grain expressed in feed units for purposes of aggregation. They were added to the feed grain required as livestock feed. Grain requirements for human food were expressed in feed units to enable the wheat-to-feed-grain transfer activity to be handled more easily in the programming matrix. Oil and other nonfeed products of soybeans and cottonseed are considered by-products of the meal demand.

The projection of per capita requirements for cotton lint was derived in a manner somewhat different from that for other consumption items. Changes in per capita consumption of cotton between the periods 1944–46 and 1959–61 were projected to 1975, for a national lint requirement of 18.1 pounds per person.

In initial models, we assume that 1975 exports of agricultural products will be at 1956–61 average levels. To allow increased agricultural exports and to examine their effects on the regional location of agricultural production, alternative assumptions then are posed in models IV-A through IV-F.

Tables 4.1, 4.2, and 4.3 show the 1975 demand restraints in the 31 consuming regions for wheat, feed grain, and oil meal, respectively. The demand restraint for cotton lint is on a national basis.

TRANSFER ACTIVITIES

Each consuming region has the possibility of transferring wheat into feed grain to help meet feed-grain requirements. This transfer occurs only if wheat is the cheapest source of feed in terms of per-unit production and transportation costs. Positive transfer costs are involved in converting wheat to feed grain in some models. For the programming models I through VI, zero transfer costs are assumed. In model VII, the advanced technology model, a national average price of $1.80 for wheat and $1.07 for corn was assumed in deriving the cost elements (i.e., the difference between the two prices) for the wheat-to-feed-grain transfer activity.

EMPIRICAL RESULTS

Models I through VII determine the optimal pattern of land use, agricultural production, and product shipments to meet regional demands at the least possible cost. The production and shipment patterns differ among the various models. Hence, the several models imply both the extent of surplus capacity in American agriculture in 1975 and the extent of interregional change and competition in prospect should certain conditions be realized with respect to demand and technology.

MODEL I

The regional land-use and crop-production patterns prescribed by model I are shown in Figure 4.1. This model is relatively conservative in its projection of potential yields. It, as do all other models, implies a growing surplus capacity in American agriculture. In terms of comparative advantage and interregional competition projected for 1975, the model shows the amount and location of land not needed for wheat, cotton, feed grain, and soybeans. This land is located primarily in the Southeast and Great Plains and in fringe areas of the Corn Belt. Under the conditions of the model, 74,118,600 acres of land devoted to crops in the base period 1953 are not needed for these uses in 1975. This amount is 45 million acres greater than the acreage included in the Soil Bank by 1960.

The land retirement or withdrawal indicated follows largely the pattern expected from previous studies (Chapters 1 and 2). The surplus land indicated in areas of the South Atlantic, Delta, and Appalachian states reflects the less efficient technology and structure of agriculture in these regions. With projections of per-acre production costs and yields to 1975, these areas still would be tied to their

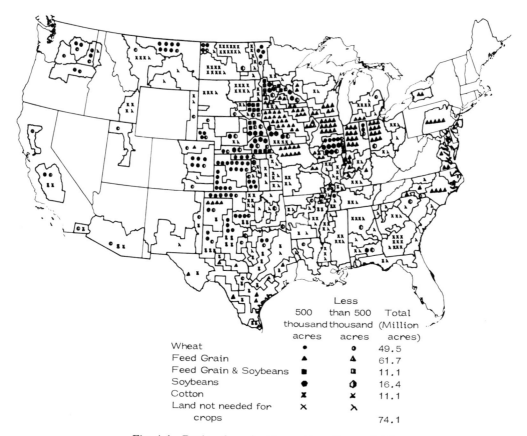

	500 thousand acres	Less than 500 thousand acres	Total (Million acres)
Wheat	•	○	49.5
Feed Grain	▲	▲	61.7
Feed Grain & Soybeans	■	▢	11.1
Soybeans	●	◐	16.4
Cotton	✗	✗	11.1
Land not needed for crops	✗	⋋	74.1

Fig. 4.1. Regional production pattern for model I.

present structure of small farms and high costs. The projections, based upon the period 1940–60, lead to an extension of relative disadvantage in crop production in these states.

Even with no change in relative yields (i.e., all areas increasing yields by the same percentage between 1960 and 1975), some areas would have surplus land by 1975, since productivity is projected to increase by a greater absolute amount than demand. Areas with lowest initial advantage and trends in technology would then have surplus land indicated.

The regional pattern of crop production conforms to the comparative advantage of the different areas under the technology and demand conditions projected to 1975. Feed-grain production is even more heavily concentrated in the Corn Belt. Soybean production is indicated in the South and in the fringes of the Corn Belt. Cotton production is allocated to the Delta states, Texas, Arizona, and California. Wheat is produced mainly in the Southern and Central Plains, northern Montana, and the Pacific Northwest. However, some wheat is indicated for producing areas in California and Arizona, while some areas in the Northern Plains produce none. Similarly, some feed grain is indicated for southern Texas, with none indicated for parts of eastern Ohio and Indiana where traditionally it has been grown. When transportation costs are included in the model, more products tend to be produced, if land is available, nearer their point of consumption. In some earlier studies (Chapter 1) of comparative advantage and interregional competition that have ignored this special aspect, greater centralization of crop production within specialized areas was indicated—as compared with the current study.

Table 4.4 includes the imputed equilibrium rents or shadow prices for all land in the 144 producing areas. The shadow prices are opportunity costs indicating the amount by which total costs could be reduced if one more acre of land were available in the specified area. For example, if area 1 had another acre of land, the national required grain production could be attained at a savings of $2.38. Similar shadow prices also are available for restraints of cotton land and soybean land but are not presented.

The composition of these equilibrium rents can be illustrated as follows: the corn-equivalent yield of feed grain in producing area 1 in New York is 53.253 bushels per acre. The price per corn-equivalent bushel in consuming region 2 (the consuming region made up of New York and Pennsylvania and which includes producing area 1) is $1.055 (the shadow price on the feed-grain demand restraint for consuming region 2). Multiplying yield times price, 53.253 × $1.055, a revenue of $56.18 is indicated for area 1 in New York. Subtracting the cost per acre of the feed-grain activity in area 1 from this revenue, $56.18 - $53.80, the land rent is $2.38 in area 1. In a similar manner, the equilibrium rent for land in area 39 (northeastern Indiana) is due to the wheat activity. The wheat yield in this area is 51.4 bushels per acre, and the equilibrium price on wheat in consuming region 8 (Indiana) is $0.982 per bushel. Multiplying 51.4 × $0.982 = $50.47 and subtracting $36.47, the cost per acre of wheat, the land rent in area 39 is $14.00. In the multiple-product programming area 47 of east central Illinois, the land rent is due to the wheat activity.[10] The wheat yield in area 47 is 48.7 bushels, and the equilibrium price in consuming region 15 (Illinois) is $0.863 per bushel. Then, 48.7 × $0.863 = $42.03, less the per-acre cost of growing wheat of $31.67, and the rent is $10.36.

The equilibrium rents, thus, are opportunity costs in the economic sense that they indicate the advantage of one alternative over the next best alternative. For a marginal producing area (such as area 40 in southern Michigan) where some of the land is used but not all is required, the rent is zero. Equilibrium land rents are provided in Appendix Table 4 A-1 (at the end of this chapter) for other models.

The demand requirements within any given consuming region can be met either by production within that region or by imports from other regions. Also, wheat from one region may be transferred into feed grain to help meet the feed-grain requirements at a lower cost either within the region or for other consuming regions. Table 4.5 indicates the sources by which demands for food wheat are satisfied in the 31 consuming regions. Tables 4.6 and 4.7 provide parallel data for feed grain and oil meal.

The last column of Table 4.5 gives the equilibrium price of the product in question. The price of $1.37 per bushel of wheat in consuming region 1 (see Figure 2.2) represents the programmed equilibrium price for wheat in this region. The equilibrium price is the supply price (cost per unit of production with certain fixed costs excluded) in the producing area of highest cost supplying the consuming region in question. Wheat demand in consuming region 1 (north-eastern United States) is met by imports from consuming region 15 (Illinois) where wheat price is $0.86 per bushel. The cost of shipping wheat from region 15 to region 1 is $0.504. Hence, $0.86 + $0.504 = $1.364 is the equilibrium price of wheat in consuming region 1. Equilibrium prices for other crops and models are included in the Appendix Tables 4 A-1 through 4 A-5.

We now examine the composition of the wheat price in several consuming regions. The equilibrium price of wheat in any consuming region may include three components: (1) the cost per unit of the highest-cost producing area contained in the consuming region, (2) the cost of transporting the product from another consuming region, and (3) the opportunity cost in sacrificing another product to produce the one in question. When demand of a consuming region is met entirely from the output of the producing regions that it contains, its equilibrium price will be made up of components (1) or of (1) and (3). When it must import wheat, the equilibrium price will include component (2). The equilibrium price of wheat in consuming region 20 (Kansas) is $0.65 per bushel. Figure 4.1 shows that producing areas 85, 87, 88, and 89, all within consuming

10. The feed-grain with soybeans activity was not restricted by the amount of land available in region 47. An equilibrium rent on soybean land also exists in region 47, since soybeans occupy all land available for this crop. The soybean activity uses both soybean land and total land. Hence, for every acre increase in soybean production in region 47, wheat production must decrease by 1 acre. Therefore, the equilibrium rent on soybean land is the difference in net returns (the value of production less cost) between soybeans and wheat.

region 20 (Kansas), produce wheat. The cost per bushel of producing wheat in these four areas is $0.58, $0.65, $0.37, and $0.28, respectively. The high-cost producing area is 87 in south central Kansas, and it provides the equilibrium price of $0.65 in consuming region 20 (Kansas). Area 87 is the only one of the four producing areas with any idle land. Hence, it is the "marginal" area in terms of supplying the wheat demand in Kansas. Since the Kansas demand is filled before all land in producing area 87 within the state is used, the land in the latter producing region has a zero opportunity cost. Thus the equilibrium price of wheat in Kansas is composed only of the "real cost" of producing wheat in producing area 87.

Consuming region 5 (Mississippi) imports all its wheat from consuming region 20 (Kansas). The equilibrium price in Mississippi is $1.40, the cost of producing wheat in producing area 87 of Kansas (or the equilibrium price of wheat in Kansas) plus the cost per bushel of transporting wheat ($0.75) from Kansas to Mississippi. Consuming region 15 (Illinois) has an equilibrium price that contains two elements of supply cost: the real cost of production and a per-bushel opportunity cost. Area 47 is the only producing region within Illinois that supplies wheat to Illinois. The cost per bushel in producing area 47 is $31.67 ÷ 48.7 = $0.65. As Figure 4.1 indicates, there is no idle land, and the imputed land rent (Table 4.4) in producing area 47 is $10.36 per acre. In other words, if there were an additional acre of land in producing area 47, it could be used to lower the total cost of producing the total product mix by $10.36. This per-acre opportunity cost results in a per-bushel opportunity cost of $0.21 ($10.36 ÷ 48.7). Thus the equilibrium price of wheat in consuming region 15 (Illinois) is a $0.65 real cost of producing a bushel of wheat in area 47 within the state, plus the opportunity cost per bushel of $0.21, or $0.86. The equilibrium price of wheat in consuming region 1 (the northeastern states) contains all three elements of supply cost: the $0.65 real cost of producing wheat in producing area 47 (within Illinois), the $0.21 opportunity cost for wheat in producing area 47, and the $0.50 cost of transporting a bushel of wheat from Illinois to consuming region 1. Hence, the sum is $0.65 + 0.21 + 0.50 = $1.36, the approximate equilibrium price of wheat in consuming region 1.

Although examples are not provided here, equilibrium prices of other crops are composed similarly from real production costs, opportunity costs, and transportation costs. In some cases, there is a "feedback" among wheat and feed grain in their opportunity and conversion costs. There also are price interdependencies among cotton, wheat for food, wheat for feed, feed grain, and soybeans. For example, the feed-grain demand in consuming region 24 (Montana and Idaho) is met by the wheat-to-feed-grain transfer activity, and the feed-grain equilibrium price is a function of the cost of producing wheat in producing area 105 of central Montana.

INTERREGIONAL FLOWS

The flows or trade among consuming regions are indicated in Figure 4.2 for wheat, Figure 4.3 for feed grain, and Figure 4.4 for oil meal. These figures

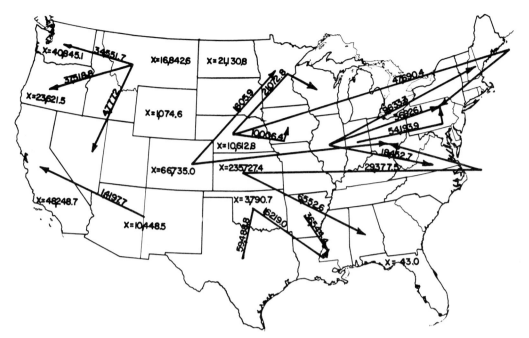

Fig. 4.2. Interregional flows (indicated by arrows and quantities) and intraregional transfers (magnitude of X) of wheat to feed grain (thousands of bushels), model I.

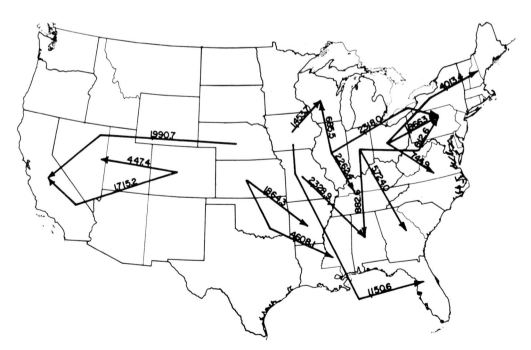

Fig. 4.3. Interregional flows (indicated by arrows and quantities) of feed grain (thousands of feed units), model I.

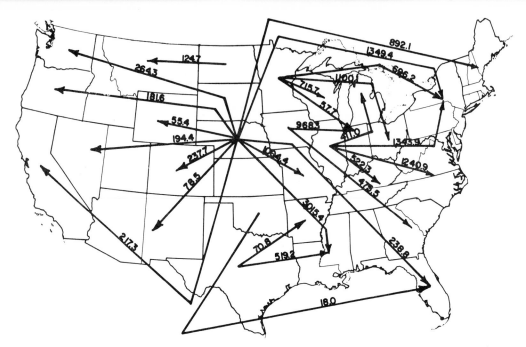

Fig. 4.4. Interregional flows (indicated by arrows and quantities) of oil meal (thousands of tons of feed units), model I.

parallel the import-export quantities indicated in Tables 4.5, 4.6, and 4.7. Wheat flows to eastern regions from producing and consuming regions in Colorado, Nebraska, and Kansas; and to Pacific states from Montana and Oklahoma. Feed grain flows eastward from the Corn Belt states and Kansas; they flow westward from Nebraska and Colorado. Oil meal shows a fairly diverse set of flows from the Corn Belt, but western regions are supplied largely by producing areas within Nebraska.

MODEL II

Model II differs from model I in only one respect: by assuming a level of consumer income 10 percent higher than in model I. The aggregate quantity of wheat required is slightly less in model II because of the negative income elasticity for wheat products. However, the demand for feed grain and oil meal is somewhat higher in model II because of positive income elasticities for livestock products. Figure 4.5 indicates the pattern of production derived under model II.

Wheat production is brought into northern South Carolina (producing area 14) and eastern Arkansas (producing area 127) under model II, but is discontinued in producing areas 13 (southern North Carolina) and 77 (northeastern Colorado). Adjustments in wheat acreages also take place in producing areas that are the programs of both models I and II. In terms of interregional transportation, consuming region 4 (Georgia and South Carolina) becomes only self-sufficient in wheat and no longer exports this product.

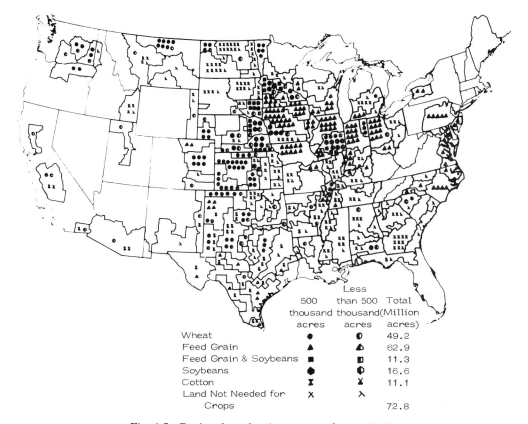

	500 thousand acres	Less than 500 thousand acres	Total (Million acres)
Wheat	●	◗	49.2
Feed Grain	▲	◭	62.9
Feed Grain & Soybeans	■	◧	11.3
Soybeans	⬟	⬠	16.6
Cotton	ⲭ	ⲭ	11.1
Land Not Needed for Crops	X	⋋	
			72.8

Fig. 4.5. Regional production pattern for model II.

An increase in income also has a small impact on the location of feed-grain production. Producing areas 30 (southeastern Ohio) and 77 (northeastern Colorado) provide most of the nation's additional requirements. Area 30 was not in feed-grain production under model I, and area 77 shifts land from wheat, as compared with model I, to feed grain. Aside from a few marginal areas, no important change occurs in the location of the feed-grain and soybean activity. The same is true for the soybean activity, acreage adjustments occurring only in the "marginal" producing areas as compared with model I.

While model II has requirements for the same amount of cotton lint, it has larger requirements for oil meal than model I. The additional oil-meal requirements are made by increases in the acreages of feed grain with soybeans and soybean activities, with no increase in the acreages of cotton.

Surplus producing capacity still is indicated for model II. Its 10 percent greater per capita income, indicating a greater consumption of livestock products and feed grain, reduces surplus land by about a million acres under that of model I. Total land not needed for the crops specified is 72,838,400 acres under model II, as compared with 74,118,600 under model I.

A comparison of the equilibrium prices for wheat in models I and II indicates that regional price differences between them are almost negligible. Also, the changes in the imputed land rents under model II are unimportant. Similarly, for feed grain and oil meal, the equilibrium prices change only very slightly under model II. The 10 percent increase in consumer income would have little aggregate effect on the nation's agriculture or the prices of its products. The income elasticity of demand for farm products is too low to cause any major change. However, the changes specified for such specific producing areas would be important for them individually.

Table 4.8 indicates the quantities and flows of interregional commodity trade under model II. While the pattern of flows remains generally the same, the quantities of wheat-to-feed-grain transfers and the movements between specific regions change in all cases. The interregional flows shown are not presented on maps because of space limitations.

MODEL III

The one-step difference between models I and II does not extend to model III. Several major variables are altered in model III: the per capita consumption rates are the 1975 estimates by Daly[11] rather than those based on the 1955 consumer's survey. The USDA estimate of the economic potential in livestock feeding efficiency is substituted for the feed-livestock conversion rates based on 1940–60 trends.

In combination, the feed-conversion rates and the per capita consumption figures upon which model III is based reduce the amount of unused land to 70,737,600 acres; an amount about 2.1 million lower than for model II and 3.4 million lower than for model I. The unused land indicated for model III would still be much greater than the amount existing in 1965, however. Hence, either major interregional shifts in land use or large production-control programs are indicated for 1975.

The land-use and production patterns for model III are indicated in Figure 4.6. Compared with model I and model II, producing areas 50 in eastern Missouri, 56 in southwestern Minnesota, and 91 in north central Oklahoma are activated for wheat production, while region 95 in northern Texas is dropped.

Feed-grain production retains the same general regional distribution as under model I and model II. Some feed-grain production shifts to the West, however, while producing areas in Kentucky (29) and southeastern Ohio (30) are dropped from feed-grain production. Areas in Minnesota (60), North Dakota (65), South Dakota (73), and western Texas (97) shift to these crops under model III. This shift results from the large increase in feed-grain requirements in the Plains states and from reduced requirements in several eastern consuming regions.

Addition of producing area 60 in Minnesota and 73 in South Dakota to feed-grain production, as a means of producing a greater proportion of feed, causes them to shift from the feed-grain and soybean rotation. Shifts in the overall distribution pattern, with an increase in oil-meal demand in consuming region 4

11. Rex F. Daly, "The Long-run Demand for Farm Products," *Agr. Econ. Res.* 8 (1956): 1–18.

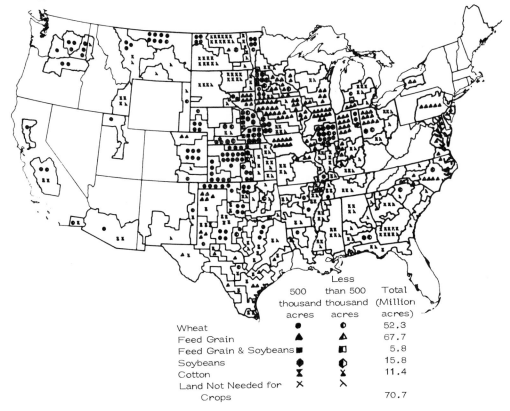

	500 thousand acres	Less than 500 thousand acres	Total (Million acres)
Wheat	●	◖	52.3
Feed Grain	▲	△	67.7
Feed Grain & Soybeans	■	◧	5.8
Soybeans	◆	◗	15.8
Cotton	✗	✗	11.4
Land Not Needed for Crops	✕	✕	70.7

Fig. 4.6. Regional production pattern for model III.

(Georgia and South Carolina) and a decrease in consuming region 5 (Mississippi), cause producing areas in eastern North Carolina (9) and in northern South Carolina (14) to be used for producing soybeans. Producing area 87 in south central Kansas also shifts to soybeans, and area 19 in northern Mississippi is retired from this use of land, the shift occurring evidently because of the greater oil-meal requirements in the Great Plains specified under model III. While a considerable increase in cotton lint demand occurs under model III, only producing area 50 in eastern Missouri shifts entirely to this crop; other slight changes take place in previously "marginal" producing areas. The interregional flows of products shown in Table 4.9 are consistent with the production and land-use pattern of Figure 4.6 and the consuming region demand restraints specified in model III.

MODEL IV-A

Model IV-A uses the same assumption as model I for per capita income, livestock feeding efficiency, and exports. However, Model IV-A (Figure 4.7) considers a population of 230 million, as compared with 222 million for model I.

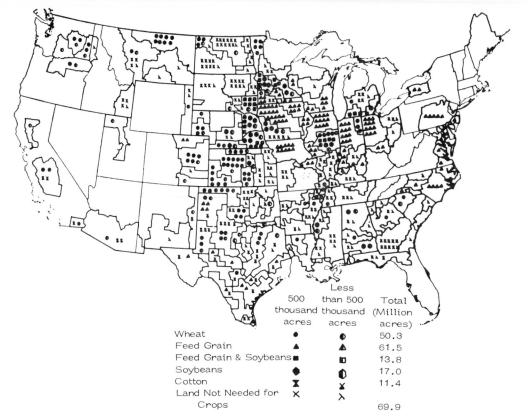

	500 thousand acres	Less than 500 thousand acres	Total (Million acres)
Wheat	•	◑	50.3
Feed Grain	▲	◮	61.5
Feed Grain & Soybeans	■	◨	13.8
Soybeans	◆	◗	17.0
Cotton	✕	⤬	11.4
Land Not Needed for Crops	✕	⤫	
			69.9

Fig. 4.7. Regional production pattern for model IV-A.

Under this change in demand, several producing areas shift entirely to wheat, as compared with model I (Figure 4.1). Three of the five areas that shift entirely to wheat are in the South, as a result of the regional increases in population assumed under model IV-A. Producing area 77 in northeastern Colorado again shifts from wheat to feed grain.

Producing area 30 in southeastern Ohio shifts to feed-grain production in model IV-A as compared with model I, while producing area 40 in southern Michigan shifts from purely feed grain to soybeans and to feed-grain and soybean rotations. Two southern producing areas, 126 in western Louisiana and 133 in eastern Texas, also shift to soybeans. Producing area 33 in northern Ohio shifts from soybean production to feed grain. Only very small changes occur in the regional production pattern of cotton.

Table 4.10 shows the interregional product flows for model IV-A. Some wheat transportation activities or flows shown in model II do not occur in model IV-A. The increase in population of 8 million, under model IV-A as compared with model I, has only a small effect in increasing equilibrium prices. Prices increase by $0.03 a bushel for both wheat and feed grain under model IV-A as compared with model I (Appendix Tables 4A-2 and 4A-3). The small increase results because a large surplus capacity of U.S. agriculture is still indicated under model IV-A. The surplus acreage for the nation is 69,878,000 under model IV-A.

MODEL IV-B

Exports of feed grain and oil meal are increased by 25 percent in model IV-B as compared with model IV-A. Demand requirements thus are increased in consuming regions, primarily in the coastal consuming regions, which historically have been exporting regions. The 25 percent increase in exports is distributed proportionately among consuming regions in the 1956–61 pattern of exports.

Figure 4.8 indicates the land-use and production patterns for model IV-B. The increased exports of feed grain have a more pronounced effect on wheat production than on feed-grain production. The increase in feed-grain requirements is attained at lowest cost by producing more wheat and converting it into feed grain. Compared with model IV-A, wheat thus is added mainly in producing areas that border on or are near exporting regions. Wheat produced in Colorado and Montana is converted to feed grain to fill the need in California for export and local livestock production.

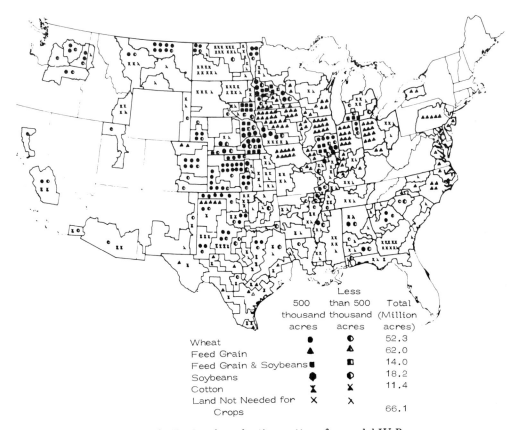

	500 thousand acres	Less than 500 thousand acres	Total (Million acres)
Wheat	●	◑	52.3
Feed Grain	▲	▲	62.0
Feed Grain & Soybeans	◼	◻	14.0
Soybeans	◆	◐	18.2
Cotton	𝗫	𝘹	11.4
Land Not Needed for Crops	𝗫	⅄	66.1

Fig. 4.8. Regional production pattern for model IV-B.

Feed-grain acreage also is increased in producing areas 56 of southwestern Minnesota and 95 of northern Texas, and the feed-grain and soybean acreage is intensified in producing areas in eastern Iowa (40) and in southeastern Illinois (47). In addition, the acreage of the soybean activity is increased in producing regions of the Corn Belt. Cotton also emerges in area 17 of southern Mississippi.

Table 4.11 indicates the interregional product movements under model IV-B and conforms to the changes in production regions as outlined. The surplus land not needed for the specified crops is 66,094,000 acres under model IV-B. In other words, the 25 percent increase in export demand reduces the surplus land by 3,784,000 acres as compared with model IV-A. Most of the reduction in surplus land comes about as more land is devoted to crops in the various producing areas but without shifting entire areas from surplus land to crop production. Producing area 123 (north central Georgia) is the only one with unused land under model IV-A that shifts entirely to crop production under model IV-B.

MODEL IV-C

Wheat exports are increased by 25 percent over model IV-B, and the entire increase is assumed to be moved through the St. Lawrence Seaway (via consuming regions represented by Ohio, Michigan, Wisconsin, and Minnesota) in model IV-C. Exports of feed grain and oil meal are increased an additional 25 percent over model IV-B (a level of 150 percent of the 1956–61 average). The increment in feed-grain and oil-meal exports is distributed proportionally to the 1956–61 patterns among regions.

Conforming with the projected 25 percent increase in wheat exports, producing regions in Georgia, South Carolina, the southern Corn Belt, and central Great Plains are brought into or increase wheat production under model IV-C (Figure 4.9). Land devoted to wheat in region 95 of northwestern Texas under model IV-B is shifted to feed grain under model IV-C. Wheat production does not concentrate near the St. Lawrence Seaway even when the 25 percent increase in exports is forced through consuming regions that border it. The effects of the increase are spread about evenly over Corn Belt and Great Plains regions having some orientation to the St. Lawrence Seaway, however.

The additional feed-grain requirements bring producing areas 81 (northeastern Kansas) and 97 (western Texas) into feed-grain production and increase the acreage of this activity in areas 50 (eastern Missouri), 56 (southwestern Minnesota), and 95 (northwestern Texas). Likewise, the feed-grain and soybean rotation is introduced into producing area 17 (southwestern Mississippi), and the activity is intensified in areas 40 (southern Michigan) and 47 (east central Illinois).

Soybean production is added in the eastern Corn Belt (producing areas 32, 34, and 48) and slightly in North Dakota (area 65) as the result of the increased oil-meal export demands. Producing areas 40 (southern Michigan) and 47 (east central Illinois) decrease in soybean acreage as a consequence of the shift to the feed-grain and rotation activity in this area. Cotton production remains the same as in model IV-B.

The interregional movement of products does not show marked departure

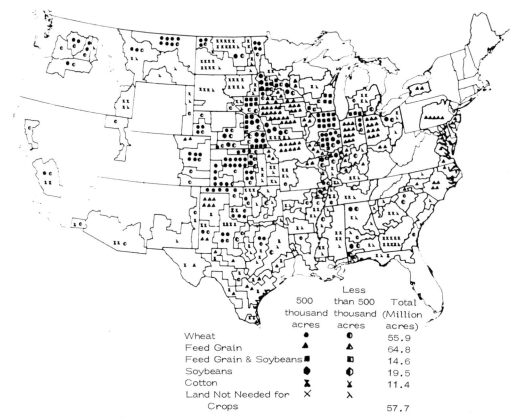

	500 thousand acres	Less than 500 thousand acres	Total (Million acres)
Wheat	●	◐	55.9
Feed Grain	▲	◮	64.8
Feed Grain & Soybeans	▮	◧	14.6
Soybeans	◆	◑	19.5
Cotton	✗	✗	11.4
Land Not Needed for Crops	✕	⋋	57.7

Fig. 4.9. Regional production pattern for model IV-C.

from the patterns established by earlier models. The volumes of interregional movements and intraregional transfers do change, however.[12] The equilibrium prices of wheat are changed slightly more than those for feed grain or oil meal between models IV-B and IV-C, a result to be expected since the increase in export demand for wheat is relatively greater than for feed grain and oil meal (Appendix Tables 4A-2 and 4A-3). Equilibrium prices under model IV-C also are only slightly greater than under model IV-B (or under model I), because surplus capacity is still indicated under the former model. Land not required for wheat, cotton, feed grain, and soybeans totals 57,709,600 acres under model IV-C— 8,384,400 less than under model IV-B and 16,409,000 less than under model I. Thus, the increased exports and demand represented by model IV-C would not eliminate surplus capacity in American agriculture, but would require a considerably larger crop acreage than under the conditions of model I. The greater acreage in crops would have great importance to the local areas concerned. Model IV-C, as compared with model I, would have more intensive agriculture (i.e., could

12. Because of space limitations, the interregional commodity flows are not presented in detail.

eliminate surplus land for crops) in producing areas of the Southeast (areas 11, 13, 17, 26, 123, and 128), in the eastern Corn Belt (areas 30, 40, 47, and 56), and in Great Plains states (areas 78, 81, 86, 87, and 110).

MODEL IV-D

Wheat exports are at 150 percent of the 1956–61 average levels, and feed-grain oil-meal exports are at 200 percent of the 1956–61 average levels in model IV-D. The distribution of each product among consuming regions follows the original, or 1956–61, export distribution pattern. Other assumptions are the same as for model IV-A.

The optimal land-use and production patterns conforming to the solution of model IV-D are shown in Figure 4.10. In comparison with model IV-C, given the further increment in export demand represented by model IV-D, producing areas in North Carolina, southeastern Idaho, western Idaho, and eastern Oklahoma (areas 7, 113, 115, and 134, respectively) are added anew to wheat production, while the acreage of wheat in other scattered areas is increased. Simultaneously, the acreage of wheat in producing areas of western South Carolina, southwestern

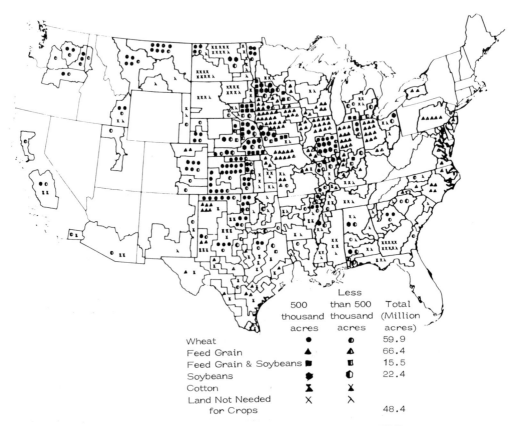

	500 thousand acres	Less than 500 thousand acres	Total (Million acres)
Wheat	•	◐	59.9
Feed Grain	▲	◮	66.4
Feed Grain & Soybeans	◼	◰	15.5
Soybeans	◆	◑	22.4
Cotton	⅄	⅄	
Land Not Needed for Crops	X	⅄	48.4

Fig. 4.10. Regional production pattern for model IV-D.

Minnesota, and western Texas (areas 41, 56, and 97, respectively) is decreased. Producing areas 28, 51, and 136 in Kentucky, Missouri, and Texas, respectively, are added to feed grain, and production is intensified in a few other areas.

Some feed grain is also produced with the feed-grain and soybean rotation introduced into producing areas 34, 54, 78, and 133, respectively, in southern Illinois, southwestern Iowa, central Nebraska, and eastern Texas. As a result of the export increase of model IV-D over model IV-C, some land is shifted from the feed-grain and soybean rotation to soybean production in central Illinois. Soybean production also is intensified in a few areas and is introduced for the first time in northern Michigan (area 41). Acreage shifts from soybeans to feed grain with soybeans and to feed-grain production, respectively, in areas 34 (southern Indiana) and 40 (southern Michigan).

The interregional flows of the three product categories show the same pattern as indicated for earlier models. There is only the difference in quantities in some cases. The surplus land indicated for model IV-D is 48,416,200 acres, an amount greater than the acreage in diversion programs in 1963. Hence, even the demand levels assumed for model IV-D do not promise to eliminate the national problem of surplus production. However, the demand conditions under this model specify about 22 million less surplus acres than model IV-A and 26 million less than model I.

MODEL IV-E

The aggregate level of exports under model IV-E remains the same as under model IV-D. The ports through which the products move are changed, however. Of the 50 percent increase in wheat exports, half is channeled through the St. Lawrence Seaway consuming regions represented by Ohio, Michigan, Wisconsin, and Minnesota. The other half is moved through the Pacific Coast consuming regions represented by Oregon, Washington, and California. Half the increase in feed-grain exports also is channeled through the St. Lawrence Seaway consuming regions (i.e., the Great Lakes states). The remaining portion of the increase in feed-grain requirements is distributed among the other consuming regions following in the proportions of the initial, or 1956-61, pattern. Oil-meal exports also are varied in direction, with 20 percent of the increase forced through the Pacific Coast consuming regions, 50 percent through consuming regions of the Great Lakes states, and the remaining 30 percent allocated on the basis of the initial pattern.

Compared with model IV-D, wheat has some acreage reallocations because of the specification of different ports for exporting the same amount of product (Figure 4.11). Producing areas 62 in central Minnesota, 95 in western Texas, and 107 in southern Montana shift to feed-grain production, and acreages of wheat in regions 41 of northern Michigan, 47 of eastern Illinois, 97 of western Texas, and 113 of southeastern Idaho are increased. Areas 7 in North Carolina, 56 in southwestern Minnesota, and 134 in southeastern Oklahoma are shifted from wheat, and a downward acreage adjustment occurs in areas 78 of central Nebraska, 86 of central Kansas, 91 of northern Oklahoma, 124 of central Alabama, and 127 of

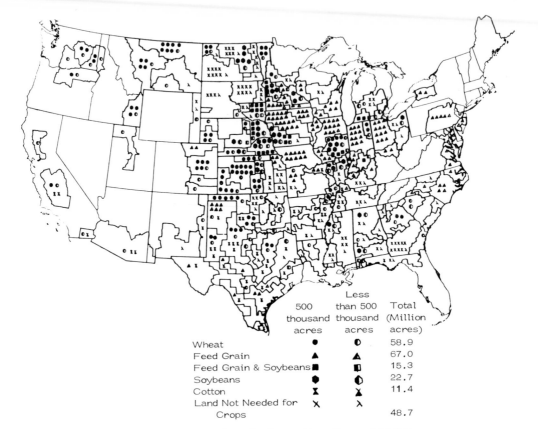

	500 thousand acres	Less than 500 thousand acres	Total (Million acres)
Wheat	●	◖	58.9
Feed Grain	▲	◮	67.0
Feed Grain & Soybeans	■	◧	15.3
Soybeans	⬟	◗	22.7
Cotton	X	⤬	11.4
Land Not Needed for Crops	X	⋋	48.7

Fig. 4.11. Regional production pattern for model IV-E.

eastern Arkansas. The shift in feed-grain and feed-grain with soybean acreage toward the consuming regions to which exports are attributed is even more obvious.

Reallocations also occur in the interregional product movements as indicated in Table 4.12. The interregional flows under model IV-E have the same general configuration as those under model I. However, the quantities moving between consuming regions are changed considerably. Also, the movement of oil meal under model IV-E differs considerably from the pattern of model I (Table 4.6). South Dakota fills more of the meal requirements of the West. Iowa supplies New York rather than South Carolina. Somewhat similar shifts take place among other regions. Surplus land of 48,689,200 acres is slightly higher under model IV-E than under model IV-D. However, the difference is so slight that differences in equilibrium prices of products are hardly noticeable.

MODEL IV-F

Model IV-F is the last of the series examining the effect of exports on the optimal interregional production and distribution patterns of crops. Wheat ex-

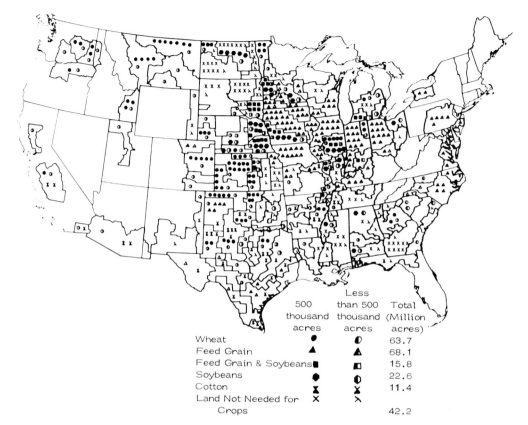

	500 thousand acres	Less than 500 thousand acres	Total (Million acres)
Wheat	●	◖	63.7
Feed Grain	▲	▲	68.1
Feed Grain & Soybeans	■	◖	15.8
Soybeans	⬢	◖	22.6
Cotton	X	X	11.4
Land Not Needed for Crops	X	⋋	42.2

Fig. 4.12. Regional production pattern for model IV-F.

ports are set at 200 percent of their 1956–61 average level in model IV-F. Feed-grain and oil-meal exports remain at the same levels (200 percent of 1956–61) assumed for models IV-D and IV-E. The increased wheat exports are allocated to the consuming regions in the initial pattern. Some alteration of this pattern is made among regions for feed grain and oil meal, however. As in model IV-E, 50 percent of the increase in feed-grain exports is channeled through the Great Lakes states (Ohio, Michigan, Wisconsin, and Minnesota), 20 percent through consuming regions 3 (West Virginia, Virginia, and North Carolina) and 5 (Mississippi), and 30 percent through other consuming regions in proportion to the initial distribution. For increases in oil-meal exports, 20 percent is forced through consuming regions 3 and 5, 20 percent through consuming regions represented by Washington, Oregon, and California, and the remaining 60 percent is allocated according to the original pattern.

As can be seen from Figure 4.12, the major change in land use occurs with regard to the wheat activity. Producing area 7 of North Carolina, 99 of south central Texas, 106 of southeastern Montana, and 134 of southeastern Oklahoma are added anew to wheat production, as compared with model IV-E. Acreages of wheat are increased in regions 23 of eastern Arkansas, 41 of northern Michigan,

47 of eastern Illinois, 62 of central Minnesota, 91 of northern Oklahoma, 95 of northern Texas, 124 of central Alabama, and 127 of eastern Arkansas. Only area 78 of central Nebraska shows a slight reduction in wheat acreage.

Except for the soybean activity introduced into area 10 of southeastern North Carolina, forcing feed-grain and oil-meal exports through consuming regions 3 and 5 has no important effect in reallocating production among areas. Most of the relocation of the feed-grain and feed-grain with soybeans activities results alone from the increased export demands for wheat. Wheat now requires land formerly used for feed-grain and feed-grain with soybeans activities. The pattern of interregional flows is indicated in Table 4.13. The total surplus land acreage indicated for model IV-F is 42,174,500—a decline of 6,514,700 acres in comparison with model IV-E. Although the change in the general pattern of crop production and product distribution does not appear great, the increase in wheat exports and the "forcing" of the feed-grain and oil-meal exports do have considerable effect on the acreage required for wheat and in causing a somewhat less efficient use of land for feed grain and soybeans. Producing areas that would be required for crop production under model IV-E, but not under model IV-F, are located in southern Ohio, Mississippi, Arkansas, Oklahoma, and Texas.

MODEL V

Model V is identical with models I and IV-A with respect to levels of per capita consumption rates, livestock feeding efficiency, export levels, crop yields, and production costs. Model V differs from the other two models in the level of population used: 244 million as compared with 230 million under model IV-A and 222 million under model I. The optimal land-use patterns for model V are shown in Figure 4.13.

Comparisons of model V (Figure 4.13) are made with model IV-A (Figure 4.7). Compared with model IV-A, new producing areas added for wheat are areas 11 of the southeastern Atlantic Coast and 110 of southeastern Colorado; the remaining additional requirements of wheat are being met by increased acreages in marginal regions scattered over most of the nation. Wheat acreage declines in a few areas as a result of the decline in need for land for other crops. Areas 26 of southern Missouri, 98 of central Texas, and 128 of northern Arkansas shift land retired from wheat to cotton.

Feed grain is introduced into two producing areas, increased in two regions, and reduced in two regions. Area 50 of eastern Missouri shifts land from feed grain to wheat, and area 99 of central Texas shifts land from feed grain to cotton. Soybeans are introduced in producing area 49 of southern Illinois in response to the increased oil-meal demands and acreage reallocations accompanying these additional requirements.

Cotton production is introduced into areas 17 of southern Alabama, 20 of northwestern Georgia, 21 of eastern Mississippi, 24 of northern Mississippi, 98 of central Texas, 99 of south central Texas, and 128 of northern Arkansas. It is increased in area 26 of south central Missouri. The addition of cotton to these producing areas requires a corresponding adjustment in the acreages of other crops.

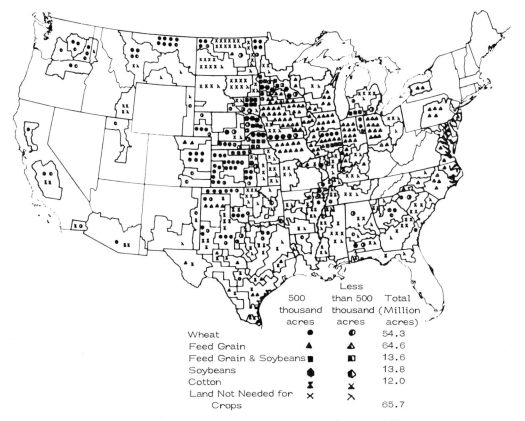

	500 thousand acres	Less than 500 thousand acres	Total (Million acres)
Wheat	●	◐	54.3
Feed Grain	▲	△	64.6
Feed Grain & Soybeans	■	▣	13.6
Soybeans	⬟	◑	13.8
Cotton	✗	✗	12.0
Land Not Needed for Crops	✗	✗	65.7

Fig. 4.13. Regional production pattern for model V.

The pattern of interregional product flows and intraregional transfers for model V is the same as indicated for model IV-A (with few exceptions). As compared with model IV-A, some of the more important interregional changes in product flows are these: under model IV-A, wheat flows from Nebraska to Pennsylvania and Virginia; under model V, it flows to Maine and New York. Feed grain flows from Colorado to Utah under model IV-A, but not under model V; from Iowa to Wisconsin under model IV-A, but to Florida under model V. Under model IV-A, oil meal flows from Illinois to Virginia, but not under model V; and from Iowa to Tennessee under model V, but not under model IV-A. Total surplus land area jumps to 65,707,900 acres under model V as compared with model IV-F, but it is less than the 69,878,000 acres under model IV-A and 74,118,600 acres under model I.

MODEL VI-A

The models discussed previously used the same matrix of input-output co-efficients for crop activities and differed only in respect to national and regional demand requirements (differences in livestock feeding efficiency were reflected in demand levels for feed grain). Models VI-A and VI-B use a different set of crop-yield coefficients and two different assumptions about demand requirements.

Yield estimates in the previous models were based upon 1940–62 yield trends but are based on 1950–62 trends for models VI-A and VI-B. Yield trends based on the period 1950–62 are considerably higher than those based on the period 1940–62. In model VI-A, the level of livestock feeding efficiency used for 1975 is the USDA economic maximum discussed previously. Hence, both crop yields and livestock efficiency are set at high levels.

The optimal land-use pattern obtained for model VI-A is presented in Figure 4.14. The resultant interregional product flows and intraregional transfers are given in Table 4.14. Land not needed for crop production jumps to the very high level of 98,946,300 acres under this model. As compared with model I, additional acreage would be shifted from crops in producing regions of New York, New Jersey, North Carolina, Arkansas, Ohio, Wisconsin, Illinois, Iowa, Minnesota, Nebraska, Kansas, Colorado, and Oklahoma. Hence, technological improvement of the rate and level used in model VI-A would mean important regional resource adjustments over the entire United States.

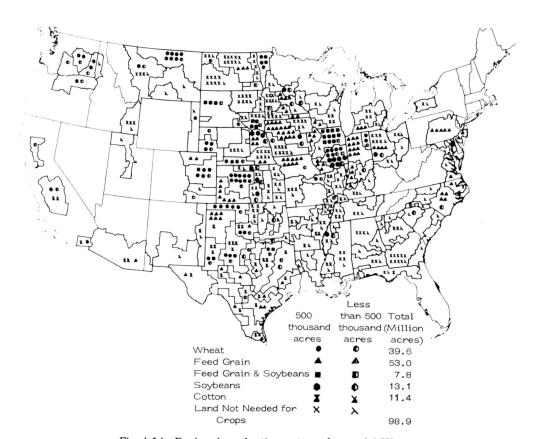

	500 thousand acres	Less than 500 thousand acres	Total (Million acres)
Wheat	●	◐	39.6
Feed Grain	▲	▲	53.0
Feed Grain & Soybeans	■	◨	7.8
Soybeans	●	◐	13.1
Cotton	✗	✗	11.4
Land Not Needed for Crops	✗	⅄	98.9

Fig. 4.14. Regional production pattern for model VI-A.

MODEL VI-B

Model VI-B employs the 1950–62 yield trends and the economic potential estimates of livestock feeding efficiency used in model IV-A, but has demand at the level of model III. Hence, the model utilizes the same demand requirements, but the input-output matrix for crops is different from that used in model III. Model VI-B uses the same coefficient matrix used in model IV-A but uses feed conversion rates and demand requirements that are different from model IV-A. (The USDA economic maximum feed conversion rates are used in model IV-A, while the economic potential rates are used in model IV-B.)

The optimal land-use pattern for model VI-B is shown in Figure 4.15. In comparison with model III, model VI-B has wheat production introduced in producing areas 23 and 25 of eastern Arkansas, while acreage is increased in regions 26 of central Arkansas, 47 of eastern Illinois, 50 of eastern Missouri, 79 of southern Nebraska, and 97 of western Texas. Wheat acreage reductions occur in some areas, while areas 41 of northern Michigan, 87 of south central Kansas, 89 of southwestern Kansas, 91 of northern Oklahoma, 112 of eastern New Mexico, 127 and 128 of Arkansas, and 142 of southern Arizona are retired from

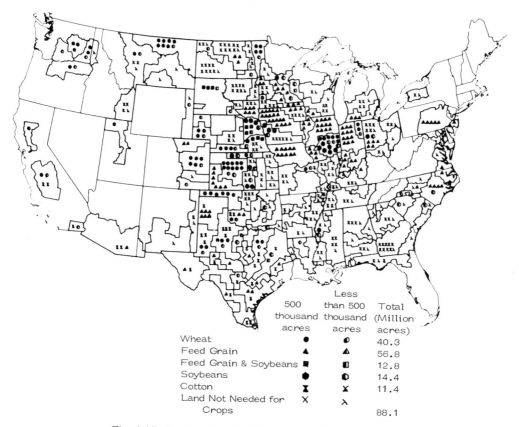

	500 thousand acres	Less than 500 thousand acres	Total (Million acres)
Wheat	●	◑	40.3
Feed Grain	▲	▲	56.8
Feed Grain & Soybeans	◼	◧	12.8
Soybeans	⬤	◐	14.4
Cotton	✖	✗	11.4
Land Not Needed for Crops	✗	⟩	88.1

Fig. 4.15. Regional production pattern for model VI-B.

wheat production under model VI-B. Areas added to feed grains under model IV-B are 34 of southern Indiana, 61 of western Minnesota, 89 of southwestern Kansas, 94 of southwestern Oklahoma, 136 of central Texas, and 142 of southern Arizona. Acreage of this activity is increased in a few areas, as compared with model III, and is eliminated in producing areas 1 of New York, 29 of central Kentucky, 36 of southeastern Illinois, 43 of eastern Wisconsin, 50 of eastern Missouri, 56 of southwestern Minnesota, 59 of northern Wisconsin, and 97 of southwestern Texas. Feed-grain acreage declines in six scattered areas.

The optimal solution for model VI-B introduces soybeans in areas 10 of eastern South Carolina, 59 and 62 of Minnesota, 85 of northern Kansas, 88 of central Kansas, 126 of western Mississippi, and 133 of eastern Texas, and increases their acreage in three other areas. Some areas also have an increase or decrease in soybean acreage; simultaneously, areas 18 of southern Alabama, 61 of western Minnesota, 65 of north central North Dakota, and 78, 79, and 80 of Nebraska discontinue production of soybeans.

Most of the change in the regional production pattern brought about by the alteration of the input-output matrix is model VI-B, as compared with model III, involves reallocations of the cropping activities among the already established group of producing areas. The new yield assumptions cause few areas to be introduced for crop production, and only a few areas are dropped from needed cropland acreage for 1975.

Model VI-B also has points of similarity and divergence with model VI-A. Both models have the high level of crop yields based on the 1950–62 trend, but the lower or economic potential level of livestock feeding efficiency is used for model IV-B, while the higher or economic maximum feeding efficiency is used in model IV-A. Thus the importance of livestock technologies on the crop sector is examined for 1975.

Comparison of Figures 4.14 and 4.15 indicates that the lower feeding and livestock efficiency of model VI-B requires the addition of producing areas 85 of northern Kansas and 114 of Utah to wheat production and increased acreage of wheat in areas 26 of southeastern Missouri and 105 of western Montana. Acreage of wheat is decreased in some areas to allow land to be shifted to feed-grain with soybeans, soybean, and feed-grain activities. Wheat production is discontinued entirely in area 52 of northern Missouri to allow for the production of more feed grain. Even though the wheat requirements are not altered greatly between models VI-A and VI-B, the changes in feed-grain and oil-meal requirements call for considerable adjustment in the regional production pattern of wheat. As compared with model VI-B, total surplus acreage (land not needed for crops in 1975) declines by about 9 million acres, to 88,079,700, under the less efficient livestock and feeding methods used in model VI-B.

MODEL VII-A

Models VII-A and VII-B employ a matrix of input-output coefficients still different from those of previous models. The coefficient matrix now used supposes that, technologically, the South catches up with the North Central

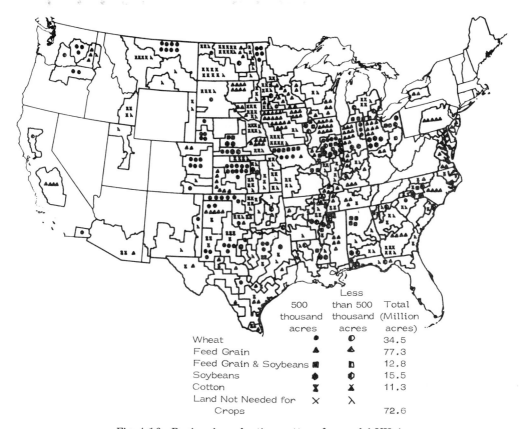

	500 thousand acres	Less than 500 thousand acres	Total (Million acres)
Wheat	●	◐	34.5
Feed Grain	▲	◮	77.3
Feed Grain & Soybeans	▰	◩	12.8
Soybeans	◆	◑	15.5
Cotton	✗	✗	11.3
Land Not Needed for Crops	✕	⋋	72.6

Fig. 4.16. Regional production pattern for model VII-A.

states in feed-grain production efficiency and with the Southwest in cotton production efficiency.

The demand requirements assumed for model VII-A are identical to those assumed under model IV-B. Comparison of Figures 4.15 and 4.16 indicates the wide difference in production patterns brought about when the South is projected to the level of technology assumed in other major farm regions. Figure 4.16, in comparison with all previous maps of crop allocation among regions, indicates a large shift of crop production to the South and to southeastern states. Somewhat surprisingly, producing areas 54 of southwestern Iowa and 74 of northeastern Nebraska are indicated as "surplus acreage" under model VII-A. The suggested retirement of these areas from crop production emphasizes the importance of space on the regional production pattern. While areas 54 and 74 have lower production costs than many other producing regions, transportation costs to the consuming regions place them at a disadvantage when advanced technology is assumed for the South. Land used for crops in the base period but indicated for retirement from crops under model VII-A totals 72,571,500 acres—nearly the same as for model II. Table 4.15 illustrates the optimum interregional commodity flows under model VII-A—a pattern differing considerably from previous models.

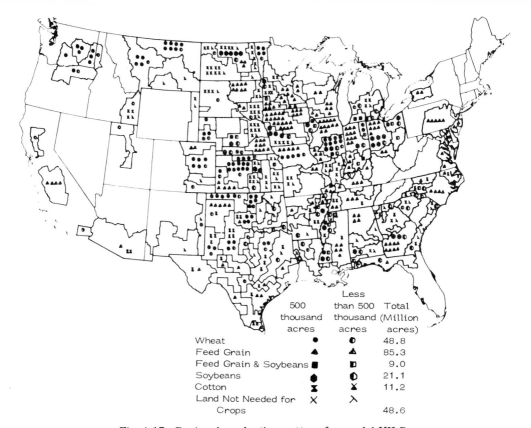

	500 thousand acres	Less than 500 thousand acres	Total (Million acres)
Wheat	●	◐	48.8
Feed Grain	▲	◭	85.3
Feed Grain & Soybeans	■	◨	9.0
Soybeans	◆	◐	21.1
Cotton	✗	✘	11.2
Land Not Needed for Crops	✕	⋏	48.6

Fig. 4.17. Regional production pattern for model VII-B.

MODEL VII-B

Model VII-B employs the same input-output matrix as model VII-A (an advanced state of technology for the South) and the same demand requirements as model IV-F. The optimum regional production patterns indicated under model VII-B are indicated in Figure 4.17. The improved position of southern agriculture is again evident under the conditions assuming a level of technology equivalent to other major producing areas. Evidently, the potential for southern agriculture is great if technology can be brought to levels comparable to the Corn Belt and Southwest. While the higher level of demand assumed under model VII-B requires a larger crop acreage (only 48,604,500 acres of surplus land for crops), the shift in production pattern gives an even greater advantage of the Southeast than model VII-A.

NATIONAL LAND-USE AND EQUILIBRIUM PRICES: A COMPARISON OF VARIOUS MODELS

Table 4.16 summarizes, at the national level, the projected land use for 1975 under the several models. Relating projected land required for cotton, wheat, soybeans, and feed grain in 1975 to the amount of land devoted to these crops in the base year 1953, it appears fairly obvious that surplus capacity of U.S. agriculture will still exist in another decade. The magnitude of this surplus capacity will depend on the level at which demand grows, the rate and distribution of technological progress, and possible changes in exports. The largest acreage of land not needed for the specified crops is 98.9 million acres indicated by model VI-A, a model assuming a low demand growth and a high level of technological improvement (i.e., extension of the 1950–62 trend). The smallest surplus of land for crops is 42.2 million acres specified by model IV-F, a model assuming a large growth in export demand and a somewhat restrained rate of technical improvement (i.e., crop-yield improvement and feeding efficiency following the 1940–62 trend).

Except for the last four models in Table 4.16, the wheat acreage is relatively larger and the feed-grain acreage is relatively smaller than contained in the historic mix of crops. This result stems from allowing wheat to be used as feed where it proves to be the most efficient, or least-cost, source of nutrients and allowing this conversion at zero cost for models I through VI-B. (For models VII-A and VII-B, a cost is charged to the wheat-to-feed-grain activity in proportion to the current wheat-corn price differential.) Thus the first 12 models represent situations in which the price support on wheat (if any) is set at a level that would reflect the feeding value of wheat. Models VII-A and VII-B, however, are similar to the existing price support operations in which the price of wheat is supported at levels in excess of its feed value relative to corn. Models IV-B and VII-A employ an identical set of demand requirements. The matrix of input-output coefficients does differ, however, and the aggregate land-use patterns under the two models reveal a marked shift from wheat to feed grain. Similar analogies exist between models IV-F and VII-B.

The aggregate acreage of feed grain is reduced in the comparison of model IV-D with model IV-E. The two models require the same amount of product at the national and export levels. However, model IV-E forces more exports through the St. Lawrence Seaway, with the result that fewer acres of feed grain are required at the national level. The shift of demand requirements, in forcing more exports through the St. Lawrence Seaway toward the higher-yielding North Central states, enables the production of the required amount of feed grain on fewer acres. A priori, one would expect the imposition of an additional restriction (i.e., specification of port of export) to require more acres for producing the necessary output.

Acreages of land indicated as surplus by the various models could be considered to include land already idled by the Soil Bank programs. In 1960 Soil Bank retirements amounted to about 29 million acres. Thus the additional land (above that already in the Soil Bank) indicated to be idled by the models varies between 13 million acres and 70 million acres.

EQUILIBRIUM PROGRAMMING PRICES

The U.S. average product equilibrium prices, as derived from the dual of the programming models, are summarized in Table 4.17. (Similar equilibrium prices by individual products and areas also are available from the programming solutions and are included in the appendix tables.) These equilibrium programming prices are functions only of variable production costs and some fixed costs. Since other fixed costs (e.g., real estate taxes, interest on land investment, and other land charges) are excluded, and since they are unrelated to governmental support prices, they are low relative to the current product prices. The absolute level of the prices should be considered with these points in mind. However, the relative levels of the average equilibrium prices for the different crops and models provide important comparisons. In comparison of model I with model IV-F, the wheat-bushel requirements (shown in the last line of Table 4.1) increase by about 53 percent. However, the wheat-supply price increases only slightly, from about $0.94 to $1.09. Feed-grain requirements increase (Table 4.2) by about 11 percent between the two models being compared, and the supply price of feed grains increases from $0.82 per bushel to $0.90 per bushel. The 13 percent increase (Table 4.3) in oil-meal requirements between models I and IV-F results in a price increase of $0.15 per bushel for soybeans and a price increase of $4.24 per ton of cottonseed. Thus the supply responses of wheat, feed grain, and oil meal are indicated, normatively, to be highly elastic.

SUMMARY AND CONCLUSIONS

This study analyzes potential adjustments necessary in the major field-crop economy of the United States in response to projected changes in technology and demand by 1975. Linear-programming models are used to specify the most efficient production and land-use patterns over 144 producing areas of the nation. Each area has the potential of five different crop activities: wheat, feed grain, feed grain with soybeans, soybeans, and cotton.

Also, 31 consuming regions, each possessing demands for wheat, feed grain, and oil meal, are delineated. Transportation activities are defined to allow transfer of the three demand entities (wheat, feed grain, and oil meal) among consuming regions. Activities are included to allow the transfer of wheat into feed use, if wheat is the cheapest source of feed nutrients. Output within each producing area is restrained only by the land resource. Alternative empirical models are used to express different assumptions regarding major variables related to growth in food demand and technological improvement. The effects of different levels of income, population, livestock feeding efficiency, exports, crop yields, and per-acre production costs on the optimal regional production and distribution of crops and land use are analyzed. Projections also are made of the surplus capacity of American agriculture in 1975 as reflected in acreage not required for specified crops. The programming models used determine the least-cost production location and product distribution patterns to satisfy regional demand requirements. The models include up to 402 equations and 2,417 variables (excluding disposal activities).

All empirical models used indicate surplus potential in American agriculture for 1975. In fact, surplus potential is projected to grow. Land not necessary to achieve projected domestic demand and export levels varies between 45 and 98 million acres. The smaller surplus acreage is specified under models assuming lower rates of technological improvement and higher rates of domestic population increase and export growth. The larger surplus acreage is specified under a model assuming a lower level of population growth, exports held at 1956–61 levels, and a rate of technological improvement paralleling 1950–60, and allowing the South to catch up with other major farm states. The empirical models are in general agreement with respect to the location of land not necessary to achieve the required levels of production. Of course, the models that suppose the greatest demand requirements specify less surplus land. Solutions to the models indicate that the major areas where land needs to be shifted to noncrop uses are in the South Atlantic states, the Delta states, the Appalachian states, the Great Plains, and fringe areas of the Corn Belt. Surplus land and projected land use are identified by a number of areas within each state.

Although a wide geographical dispersion of land withdrawal from crops is indicated, the general crop-production pattern follows existing areas of specialization, but production contracts toward the center of these. Feed-grain production becomes more concentrated in the central Corn Belt and in the North Atlantic states. Soybeans are increased importantly in the South and in the fringes of the Corn Belt. Wheat becomes more heavily concentrated in the most productive areas of the Northern Plains states and the Pacific Northwest. Cotton production shifts westward, being replaced by soybeans over part of the previous areas of specialization. From the analysis of factors affecting comparative advantage, it appears that natural conditions and technology are "stronger" than transportation costs in orienting the location of crop production.

The models that allow producing areas of the South to "catch up" with other regions in the level of farming technology result in the greatest interregional adjustment of production and land use. Producing areas stretching from the Atlantic Seaboard through Louisiana rise to a competitive position in feed production and livestock—paralleling, and surpassing in some cases, Corn Belt areas. A high level of crop technology in the South has the main effect of crowding grain production out of marginal or fringe areas of the Corn Belt and the Great Plains. Land in the Great Plains states is specified to be shifted from wheat to grazing.

By using the dual solution to the simplex programming models, equilibrium prices were determined for each product in each consuming region. Since the per-acre cost estimates used do not include fixed costs or any charges to management, these prices are somewhat low relative to the existing product prices. The equilibrium land rents also are derived from the dual solution for each of the models. These rents are the imputed values to land in each of the producing areas under the various solutions.

Chapter 5: Adjustments in Crop and Livestock Production

RAY F. BROKKEN and EARL O. HEADY

The previous studies indicate that large areas of land could be shifted to other uses if production of the major field crops were brought into balance with demand under assumptions consistent with free market equilibrium. For example, a substantial percentage of the cropland in the Appalachian areas, the Southeast, the Mississippi Delta states, the Great Plains, and fringe areas of the Corn Belt would be submarginal under the assumptions of the studies. But the possibility of interactions between the crop and livestock sectors (providing for the possibility of allocating some of this unused land to the production of forages for livestock) was not considered by studies reported in previous chapters. Also, livestock feeding accounts for a major part of the demand for feed grain and oil meal. Thus, adjustments in regional patterns of livestock production will cause shifts in regional demands for feed concentrates. In turn, shifts in regional demands for feed will affect interregional flows of feed grain and oil meal, if not the location of their production.

This study is designed to analyze crops and livestock simultaneously in a spatial equilibrium for interregional competition framework. As in the previous studies, this analysis considers wheat, feed grain, soybeans, and cotton, and in addition, land normally available for the production of harvested roughages and/or for grazing. Livestock activities considered are milk cows, beef cows-feeder calf, yearling feeders, and beef feeding.

The overall objective, as in the previous studies, is the quantitative examination of comparative advantage of the various producing areas. Emphasis is on the determination of geographic allocations of crop and livestock production and interregional commodity flows in a manner which is consistent with regional comparative advantage and meshes production exactly with domestic and export requirements at the least total resource cost. The analysis is made with several linear programming models and solutions. Each model has 891 equations and 5,131 real variables. The results and problems uncovered here are useful both for improving

NOTE: For more details about the data and results, see Ray F. Brokken and Earl O. Heady, *Interregional Adjustments in Crop and Livestock Production: A Linear Programming Analysis*, USDA Tech. Bull. 1396, July 1968.

156

methodology in further studies and for suggesting prospective trends in regional adjustments. In addition, the data assembled for the current study will contribute importantly to the more complete steps in analysis and models reported in later chapters.

SPECIFIC OBJECTIVES

Livestock and the major field crops are analyzed simultaneously in this study. The models used are designed to determine optimal patterns of production without production control and subsidy programs. The specific objectives of this study are

1. To formulate models for analyzing interregional competition and efficient resource allocation for production of wheat, feed grain, soybeans, cotton, beef, pork, and milk.
2. To determine optimal regional land use and production patterns for these commodities.
3. To determine alterations in these patterns of production resulting from (a) changes in crop and livestock production costs and technology, in output requirements, and in transportation costs in two different time periods (1954 and 1965), and rates of change in livestock production technology among the many livestock-producing regions within time periods; and (b) changes in specified output requirements within one time period.
4. To determine equilibrium returns to the various categories of land in each region.
5. To determine equilibrium prices for the commodities analyzed, and to examine possible limitations in the methodology as a basis for improving future investigations.

ECONOMIC MODELS

The mathematical structure is the same for all the linear programming models used in achieving the stated objectives. Models differ only in specified levels of technology or commodity demands. The regional framework for each model includes the 157 crop-producing areas and 20 livestock-producing, product-consuming regions shown in Figures 5.1 and 5.2, respectively. Crop-producing possibilities are defined for each of the 157 areas in Figure 5.1. Livestock-production possibilities, feed-supply equations, and demand restraints or equations are specified for each of the 20 regions shown in Figure 5.2. Each livestock-producing, product-consuming region contains one or more of the crop-producing areas as indicated in Table 5.1. This distinction between "regions" and "areas" is retained throughout this chapter.

Fig. 5.1. Geographic location of crop-producing areas.

Fig. 5.2. Geographic location of livestock-producing and livestock-consuming regions.

CROP-PRODUCING AREAS

Crop-producing areas are based on those used by Egbert.[1] However, where areas delimited by Egbert transcended the boundaries of the 20 consuming (also livestock-producing) regions, they were subdivided so that each crop-producing area was included within a single livestock-producing (or consuming) region. Thus areas 1 through 137 encompass the same land area as Egbert's 122 regions and the 144 areas used by Skold and Whittlesey.[2] Historically, areas 1 through 137 have produced approximately 95, 97, 93, 84, 99, 99, and 99 percent, respectively, of the nation's total production of wheat, corn, oats, barley, grain sorghum, soybeans, and cotton. These areas consist of contiguous counties. Each area is considered to be sufficiently homogeneous with respect to soil types, climate, historic yields, and production costs to serve as a producing entity for the purposes of the study.

Areas 138 through 157 for crops are the "white areas" not included in earlier studies. They account for a very small percentage of the nation's production of feed grain, wheat, cotton, and soybeans (the complements of the figures given for areas 1 through 137). They are of importance, however, in the production of harvested roughages and forages for grazing. Areas 138 through 157 represent the residual land and feed-grain quantities within the livestock regions not included in the earlier phases of this series of studies.

LIVESTOCK-PRODUCING, PRODUCT-CONSUMING REGIONS

Figure 5.2 delineates the 20 livestock-producing, product-consuming regions used in this study. Broad types of farming underlie the delimitation of these regions. Also, they represent subaggregates of the 10-region breakdown often used in USDA statistical series. Only 20 regions were used for livestock because of the limited funds and computing capacity of the study. Livestock and livestock products were, in the construction of the model, allowed to flow among regions to satisfy final demand restraints. Crop products were allowed to flow among regions to meet programmed demands for livestock feed, or to meet specified final consumer demands for crop products.

The model involves four types of quantitatively stated restraints. These include land restraints in each of the 157 crop-producing areas, capacity restraints for livestock in each of the 20 livestock-producing regions, supplies of concentrates and roughages from sources exogenous to the model, and consumer demand constraints in each of the 20 demand or consumption regions (the latter being identical with the livestock-producing regions).

LAND RESTRAINTS IN CROP AREAS

Land restraints were used to prevent the extension of individual crops or aggregates of crops beyond the acreage available for them. In each area, there

1. See Chapter 1.
2. See Chapters 2, 3, and 4.

are five categories of land restraints, defined as follows:

Land 1—the acreage of cotton in 1953.
Land 2—land 1 plus the 1953 acreage of wheat, corn, oats, barley, grain sorghum, soybeans, corn silage, and sorghum silage.
Land 3—land 2 plus the 1953 acreage of all tame hay.
Land 4—the 1953 acreage of wild hay.
Land 5—a pasture restraint measured in animal unit months (AUM).[3] (There is only one land-5 constraint for each of the 20 livestock regions. Hence, pasture acreages are aggregated for all of the crop-producing areas in each livestock region.) Land 5 includes cropland pasture, open permanent pasture, woodland pasture, and pasture not in farms, each weighted by its appropriate AUM coefficient; plus land 3 weighted by its appropriate AUM coefficient, then aggregated over all crop areas in each livestock region.

The structure of land restraints supposes that (1) grain crops can be grown on all the cotton land, but not vice versa, (2) hay can be grown on all the grain and cotton land, but not vice versa, and (3) pasture can be grown on all land for crops and hay, but not vice versa.

LIVESTOCK CAPACITY RESTRAINTS

The level of livestock production in any region was limited by a capacity constraint for each type of livestock. These initial capacity constraints were set at the historic high for each class of animals in each of the 20 regions. These restraints, defined as the maximum historical number of each type of livestock in each region, were computed for

1. The number of milk cows
2. The number of beef cows
3. The number of cattle placed on feed
4. The liveweight production of hogs

For different solutions, these constraints for livestock regions were varied. The variation in constraints was used to simulate different periods of time over which livestock-producing capacity might be adjusted. The nature of these variations in livestock capacity constraints is explained in a later section of this chapter.

REGIONAL DEMAND RESTRAINTS

Demand constraints for the 20 consuming regions were used for crops going into industrial uses and into direct human consumption. Regional demand restraints for these purposes were specified for wheat, feed grain, and oil meal. A single national cotton lint demand restraint was used. Regional consumption

---

3. One AUM (animal unit month) is assumed to be equivalent to 410 TDN (total digestible nutrients).

restraints also were specified for five livestock products: grade 1 beef (i.e., beef from grain-fed cattle), grade 2 beef (i.e., nongrain-fed beef), fluid milk, manufactured milk products, and pork. The regional consumption restraints (based on population, per capita income, historic trends, and regional consumption patterns) were defined for both 1954 and 1965.

Estimated export and industrial requirements for wheat were allocated among regions according to the location of flour mills and other wheat processors, past production of flour, and the relative shipments of wheat from the various seaports. Industrial and export requirements for feed grain were allocated in a similar manner. Export requirements for cottonseed and soybean meal also were allocated to regions according to relative past shipments from the various seaports.

Feed requirements for classes of livestock (sheep, goats, horses, and mules) and poultry not explicitly included in the model were estimated for each region from unpublished data secured from the USDA. These requirements were treated as negative supplies of concentrates (feed units and protein) and roughages (i.e., the feed requirements for these animals were entered as negative quantities in the appropriate cells of the restraint vector). Pasture requirements for these classes of livestock were subtracted from the pasture supply constraints in each region. National average per capita consumption requirements for livestock products were adjusted for regional variations due to differences in income and degree of urbanization. These regional estimates were then multiplied by regional population figures.

SUPPLIES OF EXOGENOUS CONCENTRATES

Concentrates are available for livestock production from sources other than the crops considered explicitly by the models. Estimates of the supplies of each of these concentrates (animal proteins, by-products from brewers, distillers, millers, and so forth) were based on unpublished data of the USDA. Activities were constructed to allow the various regions to compete for these exogenous concentrates at the observed regional prices of each type of exogenous concentrate.

ACTIVITIES

Four sets of activities were used in the basic model: crop activities for each of the 157 crop-producing areas, livestock activities for each of the livestock-producing regions, feed-transfer activities, and transportation activities to allow shipment of livestock and crops among regions. Each of these classes of activities is explained below.

CROP-PRODUCING ACTIVITIES

Each crop-producing area has potentially nine crop activities: cotton, wheat, feed-grain rotations, feed-grain–soybean rotations, feed-grain–silage rotations, feed-grain–soybean–silage rotations, hay, hay-silage rotations, and wild hay

(Table 5.2). Silage can come from either corn or sorghum. Feed-grain rotations are defined by the proportions of the land in corn, oats, barley, and grain sorghums for each area. The cropping activities and land restraints are structured so that land is available for successively less intensive uses. Thus in situations where the more intensive land uses in a particular area are precluded (under the assumptions of the model) by competition from other areas, consideration would be given to transferring cotton land to grain production, then to hay production, then pasture, before being allocated to the "surplus" category. Similarly, grain-land would be transferred first to hay production, then to pasture, before being allocated to nonuse; hay land can be allocated to pasture, then nonuse.

Output of wheat, feed grain, soybean meal, and cottonseed meal from crop activities is expressed in feed units. A feed unit is that amount of a particular concentrate feed equal in feeding value to 1 pound of corn. Feed unit factors used in this study are wheat, 1.050; oats, 0.850; barley, 0.920; grain sorghum, 0.985; soybean meal, 1.650; and cottonseed meal, 1.350. The output of the cropping activities in each area is entered into regional accounting rows with one exception: lint output from all cotton activities is channeled into one national cotton lint demand row. Accounting rows for each of the 20 regions include (1) wheat demand, (2) feed-grain accounting, (3) soybean-meal accounting, (4) cottonseed-meal accounting, and (5) hay accounting. Transfer activities are employed to transfer commodities in the feed-accounting rows to livestock feed supplies. However, before any of the commodities in these accounting rows can be used for livestock feed, it is necessary to meet predetermined regional demands for wheat, feed grain, soybean meal, and cottonseed meal for human consumption, industrial uses, and foreign exports, and hay used for making alfalfa meal. These requirements are treated as negative supplies, as explained earlier. Each crop activity has a cost coefficient which enters the objective function. These coefficients differ among regions according to the technology used and the natural conditions surrounding production.

FEED TRANSFER ACTIVITIES

Feed requirements are expressed in terms of feed units, protein, and harvested roughage. Feed transfer activities move the various types of feedstuffs from the regional accounting rows mentioned above to the livestock feed supply rows for the same regions. These transfer activities, five in each livestock region, convert (1) wheat to feed units and protein, (2) feed grain to feed units and protein, (3) soybean meal to feed units and protein, (4) cottonseed meal to feed units and protein, and (5) hay to roughage. For example, the transfer activity of soybean meal to feed takes one feed unit from the soybean accounting row and places one feed unit into the feed unit row and 0.273 pound of protein into the protein row.[4] Similarly, other feed transfer activities move feed units from the accounting rows to the joint components of concentrate feed for livestock feed units and

4. Soybean meal was assumed to be 45 percent protein. One feed unit of soybean meal is $1/1.65 = 0.606$ pounds of soybean meal. Pounds of protein per feed unit are soybean meal, 0.273; cottonseed meal, 0.304; wheat, 0.110; corn, 0.086; oats, 0.139; barley, 0.116; and grain sorghum, 0.112.

protein. Silage output is moved directly from the crop activity producing it into the roughage row in hay-equivalent units.

In addition, five other transfer activities were employed in each region. Transfer activities were used to move feed from four national concentrate supplies, exogenous to the model, to feed units and protein of the regions. These concentrates, moving from exogenous national supplies, are E_1, oil meals excluding soybean oil meal and cottonseed oil meal; E_2, animal proteins; E_3, grain proteins; and E_4,[5] other by-product feeds including wheat and rice millfeeds, and miscellaneous grains. A transfer activity was also employed to move regional supplies of harvested roughages exogenous to the model (beet silage and pulp, citrus pulp, peanut hay, and others) to the roughage supply row. Estimated in hay equivalents, these regional supplies of exogenous roughages were forced into the roughage supply row at regional hay prices. Concentrates and roughages transferred to the regional livestock feed equations could not be used for the regional livestock activities in the model until feed requirements for livestock (horses, mules, sheep, goats, and poultry) exogenous to the model had been met. As explained previously, these predetermined quantities were treated as negative supplies of harvested roughages, feed units, and protein.

LIVESTOCK ACTIVITIES

Twelve livestock-producing alternatives were defined for each of the 20 livestock-producing regions. These include milk cows, beef cows, hogs, yearling feeder calves, and the following eight beef-fattening activities: eastern deferred calves; extended silage calves; calves fed on silage; calves fed no silage; southern deferred calves; short-fed yearlings; yearlings fed on silage; and yearlings fed no silage. The eight designated types of cattle-feeding activities are indicative of the feeding systems considered. Variations were made for regional differences within these eight general feeding systems. Table 5.2 indicates the general nature of resource requirements and outputs of these activities.

Nongrain-fattened beef (grade 2) is supplied from (1) animals culled from beef cow and dairy herds and from vealed dairy calves, (2) slaughter of yearling feeder calves, and (3) slaughter of feeder calves. Slaughter activities for yearlings and calves represent alternatives to their use as inputs for grain-fed beef and provide the requirements of grade 2 beef in excess of that available from culled stock of dairy and beef cow herds.

TRANSPORTATION ACTIVITIES

Transportation activities among regions are defined for each final and intermediate product. Production processes in each of the 157 crop areas and the 20 livestock regions thus can compete with processes in the other areas and regions for the various commodity markets. Commodities for which transportation activities are defined include wheat, feed grain, soybean meal, cottonseed meal,

---

5. Pounds of protein per feed unit for the exogenous concentrates are E_1, 0.224; E_2, 0.550; E_3, 0.193; and E_4, 0.144.

hay, feeder calves, yearling feeder calves, grade 1 beef, grade 2 beef, fluid milk, manufactured milk products, and pork.

Transportation activities exist only among the 20 livestock-producing regions, which are identical with the 20 consuming regions. The crop products from the 157 crop-producing areas are aggregated, through the accounting rows, into regional supplies conforming to the 20 livestock (consuming) regions. However, this procedure still allows each of the crop-producing areas to compete with the other 156 areas, the supplies of each crop within each area being determined within the model. Potentially, there are $20 \times 19 = 380$ transportation activities for each intermediate or final product; or, since there are 12 products, there are 4,560 $(380 \times 12 = 4,560)$ potential transportation activities in all (each region can ship commodities to each of the other 19 regions). Of course, some potential transport activities are not operable (e.g., cottonseed meal is not produced in the Dakotas).

MATHEMATICAL STRUCTURE OF THE MODEL

As mentioned previously, the basic structure is the same for the three specific models expressing differences in constraints and technical coefficients. Most of the basic notations are also similar to the ones used in the previous chapters. In view of considerably increased number of activities, crops, and livestock production included in the model, a complete set of notations will be presented below.

Let n be a superscript or subscript denoting the type of products:

$$
\begin{aligned}
n &= \ \ 1 \text{ for wheat} \\
n &= \ \ 2 \text{ for feed grain} \\
n &= \ \ 3 \text{ for soybeans} \\
n &= \ \ 4 \text{ for cottonseed} \\
n &= \ \ 5 \text{ for hay} \\
n &= \ \ 6 \text{ for beef, grade 1 (grain fed)} \\
n &= \ \ 7 \text{ for beef, grade 2 (nongrain fed)} \\
n &= \ \ 8 \text{ for pork} \\
n &= \ \ 9 \text{ for fluid milk} \\
n &= 10 \text{ for manufactured milk} \\
n &= 11 \text{ for cotton lint}
\end{aligned}
$$

j subscript or superscript denoting the consuming regions (also livestock-producing regions), $j = 1, \ldots, \ldots 20$

v^j number of crop-producing areas located in consuming region j

k subscript denoting the crop-producing area, $k = 1, \ldots, \ldots, v^j$

m subscript denoting the land-quality class, $m = 1, \ldots, \ldots 4$

q subscript denoting the type of crop activity:

$$
\begin{aligned}
q &= 1 \text{ for cotton} \\
q &= 2 \text{ for wheat} \\
q &= 3 \text{ for feed grain} \\
q &= 4 \text{ for feed-grain–soybean rotations} \\
q &= 5 \text{ for feed-grain–soybean–silage rotations}
\end{aligned}
$$

$q = 6$ for feed-grain–silage rotations
$q = 7$ for tame hay–silage rotations
$q = 8$ for tame hay
$q = 9$ for wild hay

p subscript denoting the livestock activity:

$p = $ 1 for hog
$p = $ 2 for milk cow
$p = $ 3 for beef cow
$p = $ 4 for yearling production
$p = $ 5 for calves, eastern deferred feeding plan
$p = $ 6 for calves, southern deferred feeding plan
$p = $ 7 for calves, extended silage feeding plan
$p = $ 8 for calves, silage feeding plan
$p = $ 9 for calves, no-silage feeding plan
$p = 10$ for yearlings, short-fed feeding plan
$p = 11$ for yearlings, silage feeding plan
$p = 12$ for yearlings, no-silage feeding plan

e subscript denoting the type of exogenous concentrates:

$e = 1$ for oil meal, excluding soybean meal and cottonseed activity
$e = 2$ for animal protein
$e = 3$ for grain proteins
$e = 4$ for other by-product feeds, including wheat and rice millfeeds
and miscellaneous grains

h type of feeder cattle:

$h = 1$ for 400-pound calves
$h = 2$ for 700-pound yearlings

t type of livestock feed:

$t = 1$ for TDN
$t = 2$ for protein
$t = 3$ for harvested roughage

v categories of livestock capacity restraints:

$v = 1$ for milk cows
$v = 2$ for beef cows
$v = 3$ for feeder cattle placements
$v = 4$ for hogs

x subscript for the type of grain:

$x = 1$ for wheat
$x = 2$ for feed grain
$x = 3$ for soybean
$x = 4$ for cottonseed

C_{qkj} acres of crop activity q produced by farms in kth area of region j

L_{pj} livestock activity p on farms of region j

M_j amount of fluid milk transferred to manufactured milk

S_j^h number of feeder cattle slaughtered in consuming region j

E_{ekj} amount of exogenous concentrate of type e used in area k of region j

Q national cotton lint requirements

F_j^t type of livestock feed t required for exogenous livestock produced in area j

G_{xkj} amount of grain of type x transferred to the concentrate feed supply of area k in region j

G_{kj}^1 amount of hay transferred to the harvested roughage supply of area k in region j

G_j supply of exogenous roughage in region j

V_j quantity of exogenous roughage transferred to livestock feed in region j

R_{nj} quantity of nth product required for human consumption, industrial uses, and exports in jth region

$T_{njj'},T_{nj'j}$ level of transportation activities transporting nth product between regions j and j'

$B_{hjj'},B_{hj'j}$ level of feeder calf transportation activities transporting the h-type product between regions j and j'

AUM animal unit months of pasture available in the jth region

A_k^m cropland and hay land of quality class m available in area k

c_j^v capacity limit of the vth class of livestock in the jth region

c_{qkj}^1 cost of producing one acre of crop activity q in area k of region j

c_{ej}^2 cost of one unit of exogenous concentrate in consuming region j

c_j^3 cost of transfer of one unit of exogenous roughage to livestock feed in the jth region

c_{pj}^4 cost of producing one unit of livestock activity p in region j

$c_{njj'}^5,c_{nj'j}^6$ cost of transporting product n from consuming region j to consuming region j'

$c_{hjj'}^7,c_{hj'j}^8$ cost of transportation per unit of feeder calves of h type between regions j and j'

r_{qkj}^n output of product n per acre of crop activity q in area k of region j

o_{pj}^n output of product n per unit of livestock activity in region j

z^1 grade 2 beef produced per feeder calf slaughtered

z^2 grade 2 beef produced per feeder yearling slaughtered

h_{qkj} amount of aftermath pasture made available by per acre of crop activity q in area k of region j

λ_j^t quantity of t-th category of livestock feed supplied per unit of the exogenous roughage transfer activity in region j

f_{pj}^t amount of feed of type t required per unit of livestock activity p produced in region j

g_e^2 protein content of exogenous concentrate e

Z total production cost, transportation cost, and transfer cost

w_{pj}^v amount of vth livestock capacity constraint required per unit of the pth livestock activity in jth region

The objective is to

$$\min Z = \sum_{j=1}^{20} \sum_{k=1}^{v^j} \sum_{q=1}^{9} c_{qkj}^1 \, C_{qkj} + \sum_{j=1}^{20} \sum_{k=1}^{v^j} \sum_{e=1}^{4} c_{ej}^2 \, E_{ekj} + \sum_{j=1}^{20} c_j^3 \, V_j$$

$$+ \sum_{j=1}^{20} \sum_{k=1}^{v^j} \sum_{x=1}^{4} (0) G_{xkj} + \sum_{j=1}^{20} \sum_{k=1}^{v^j} (0) \, G_{kj}^1 + \sum_{j=1}^{20} (0) \, M_j$$

$$+ \sum_{j=1}^{20} \sum_{p=1}^{12} c_{pj}^4 \, L_{pj} + \sum_{j=1}^{20} \sum_{\substack{j'=1 \\ j' \neq j}}^{20} \left[\sum_{n=1}^{11} c_{njj'}^5 \, T_{njj'} + \sum_{n=1}^{11} c_{nj'j}^6 \, T_{nj'j} \right]$$

$$+ \sum_{j=1}^{20} \sum_{h=1}^{2} (0) \, S_j^h + \sum_{j=1}^{20} \sum_{\substack{j'=1 \\ j' \neq j}}^{20} \left[\sum_{h=1}^{2} c_{hjj'}^7 \, B_{hjj'} + \sum_{h=1}^{2} c_{hj'j}^8 \, B_{hj'j} \right] \quad (5.1)$$

subject to following restraints:
    (1) national cotton lint requirements

$$\sum_{j=1}^{20} \sum_{k=1}^{v^j} r_{1kj} \, C_{1kj} \geq Q \quad (5.2)$$

    (2) national exogenous concentrate restraints

$$\sum_{j=1}^{20} \sum_{k=1}^{v^j} \sum_{e=1}^{4} E_{ekj} = E \quad (5.3)$$

    (3) requirements for food processing, industrial uses, and exports of crop products in region j

$$- \sum_{k=1}^{v^j} \sum_{q=2}^{8} r_{qkj}^n \, C_{qkj} + \sum_{\substack{j'=1 \\ j' \neq j}}^{20} T_{njj'} - \sum_{\substack{j=1 \\ j' \neq j}}^{20} T_{nj'j} + \sum_{x=1}^{4} \sum_{k=1}^{v^j} G_{xkj} + G_{kj}^1 \leq - R_{nj}$$

$$n = 1, \ldots, 5 \quad (5.4)$$

(4) feeder calf account

$$-\sum_{p=2}^{3} O_{pj} L_{pj} + \sum_{p=4}^{9} L_{pj} + S_{j}^{1} - \sum_{\substack{j=1 \\ j' \neq j}}^{20} B_{1j'j} + \sum_{\substack{j'=1 \\ j' \neq j}}^{20} B_{1jj'} \leqslant 0 \qquad (5.5)$$

(5) yearlings account

$$- O_{4j} L_{4j} + \sum_{p=10}^{12} L_{pj} + S_{j}^{2} - \sum_{\substack{j'=1 \\ j' \neq j}}^{20} B_{2j'j} + \sum_{\substack{j'=1 \\ j' \neq j}}^{20} B_{2jj'} \leqslant 0 \qquad (5.6)$$

(6) grain-fed beef (grade 1) requirements of region j

$$\sum_{p=5}^{12} O_{pj}^{6} L_{pj} - \sum_{\substack{j'=1 \\ j' \neq j}}^{20} T_{6jj'} + \sum_{\substack{j'=1 \\ j' \neq j}}^{20} T_{6j'j} \geqslant R_{6j} \qquad (5.7)$$

(7) other beef (grade 2) requirements of region j

$$\sum_{p=2}^{3} O_{pj}^{7} L_{pj} - \sum_{\substack{j'=1 \\ j' \neq j}}^{20} T_{7jj'} + \sum_{\substack{j'=1 \\ j' \neq j}}^{20} T_{7j'j} + \sum_{h=1}^{2} S_{j}^{h} \geqslant R_{7j} \qquad (5.8)$$

(8) pork requirements of region j

$$O_{1j}^{8} L_{1j} - \sum_{\substack{j'=1 \\ j' \neq j}}^{20} T_{8jj'} + \sum_{\substack{j'=1 \\ j' \neq j}}^{20} T_{8j'j} \geqslant R_{8j} \qquad (5.9)$$

(9) fluid milk requirements of region j

$$O_{2j}^{9} L_{2j} - M_{j} - \sum_{\substack{j'=1 \\ j' \neq j}}^{20} T_{9jj'} + \sum_{\substack{j'=1 \\ j' \neq j}}^{20} T_{9j'j} \geqslant R_{9j} \qquad (5.10)$$

(10) manufactured milk requirements of region j

$$-\sum_{\substack{j'=1 \\ j' \neq j}}^{20} T_{10jj'} + \sum_{\substack{j'=1 \\ j' \neq j}}^{20} T_{10j'j} + M_{j} \geqslant R_{10j} \qquad (5.11)$$

(11) pasture restraints in region j

$$\sum_{k=1}^{v^{j}} \sum_{q=1}^{8} h_{qkj} C_{qkj} + \sum_{p=1}^{12} f_{pj}^{4} L_{pj} \leqslant A U M_{j} \qquad (5.12)$$

(12) upper limit on livestock production

$$\sum_{p=1}^{12} w_{pj}^v L_{pj} \leqslant c_j^v \tag{5.13}$$

(13) supply of exogenous roughage in region j

$$V_j = G_j \tag{5.14}$$

(14) livestock feed restraints in region j

$$\sum_{p=1}^{12} f_{pj}^t L_{pj} - \sum_{x=1}^{4} \sum_{k=1}^{v^j} G_{xkj} - \sum_{k=1}^{v^j} G_{kj}^1 + \sum_{e=1}^{4} g_e^2 E_{ekj} - \lambda_j^t V_j$$

$$- \sum_{q=5}^{7} \sum_{k=1}^{v^j} r_{qkj} C_{qkj} \leqslant F_j^t \tag{5.15}$$

(15) land restraints in area k

$$\sum_{q=1}^{9} C_{qk} \leqslant A_k^m \tag{5.16}$$

(16) The above land restraints are structured as follows:
    Land 1

$$C_{1k} \leqslant A_k^1 \tag{5.17}$$

(17) *Land 2*

$$\sum_{q=1}^{7} C_{qk} \leqslant A_k^2 \tag{5.18}$$

(18) *Land 3*

$$\sum_{q=1}^{8} C_{qk} \leqslant A_k^3 \tag{5.19}$$

(19) *Land 4*

$$C_{qk} \leqslant A_k^4 \tag{5.20}$$

(20) The nonnegativity restraints

$$C_{qkj}, V_j, E_{ekj}, T_{nj'j}, T_{njj'}, M_j, S_j^h, G_{xkj}, G_{kj}^1, B_{hjj'} \geqslant 0 \tag{5.21}$$

SPECIFIC MODELS AND SOLUTIONS

Three empirical models were constructed within the overall mathematical structure outlined above. Solutions were obtained for two levels of technology, and output requirements were estimated for two models, the 1954 and the 1965. The third specific model uses the same level of crop technology as the 1965 model but uses a level of livestock technology for all producers equal to that of the more efficient livestock producers in each region. The third model is designated the EM (efficient management model).

The two study periods were chosen so that the net effects of changes in technology, consumer income, population growth, and relative shifts in population density on the optimal allocation of farm production could be ascertained. Thus 1954, a year of no surplus stocks for the commodities studied, was selected for comparison with 1965, when surplus capacity and stocks were relatively large and output was restrained by various programs. For this purpose the optimal regional allocation of production was estimated for both periods within the model framework previously outlined.

Several solutions were obtained for each model corresponding to variations in different levels of livestock capacity constraints and demand in each region. The solutions are coded as follows: solutions numbered 1 through 26 are for the 1965 model; 31 through 56^6 are for the EM model; and 71 through 75 are for the 1954 model. Indices of the level of demand constraints, I_d^{54} and I_d^{65}, and the livestock capacity constraints, I_c^{54} and I_c^{65}, for each solution of the 1965 and 1954 models are outlined below. Each solution has a unique combination of capacity and demand (constraints). A summary of the combinations of the various solutions follows:[7]

A. 1965 model
    1. Solutions 1 through 19;[8] demand held constant at the level I_d^{65} = 1.0 and capacity at the 19 levels where I_c^{65} = 1.0, 1.1, 1.2, . . . 2.9, 3.0.
    2. Solutions 20 through 24; capacity held constant at the level I_d^{65} = 3.0 and demand at the five levels I_c^{65} = 1.05, 1.10, 1.15, 1.20, 1.22.
B. EM model
    1. Solutions 31 through 50; demand held constant at the level I_d^{65} = 1.0 and capacity at the 20 levels I_c^{65} = 1.0, 1.1, 1.2, . . . 2.9, 3.0.
    2. Solutions 51 through 54; capacity held constant at the level I_d^{65} = 3.0 and demand at the four levels I_d^{65} = 1.01, 1.10, 1.15, 1.2.
    3. Solutions 55 and 56; capacity at the level I_c^{65} = 1.0 and at the two levels I_d^{65} = 1.05, 1.08.
C. 1954 model
    1. Solution 71; I_d^{54} and I_c^{54} = 1.0.
    2. Solution 72; I_d^{54} = 1.0 and I_c^{54} = 1.4.
    3. Solutions 73, 74, and 75; I_d^{54} = 1.0 and I_c^{54} = 1.45, 1.50, 1.56.

The index, I_d, defines the level of the minimum output constraints on final commodities in relation to the first solution of each model. As noted below,

6. Because of the magnitude of the study and the large volume of results generated, results of the EM model are not presented in this report.
7. The indices are the same for each of the 20 regions for all solutions.
8. Parametric programming was employed with solutions printed at approximately 10 percent changes in regional livestock capacity constraints and at 5 percent changes in the regional demand constraints.

I_d^{65} = 1.0 refers to demand at 1965 levels; thus I_c^{65} = 1.1 would refer to solutions made for 1965 technical and restraint conditions, but demand levels 10 percent higher than 1965 actual conditions. A similar interpretation holds for the index of livestock capacity constraints I_c. For example, demand and capacity indices for solution 2 are I_d^{65} = 1.0 and I_c^{65} = 1.1. Thus, for solution 2, the demand constraints are the same as for solution 1, at the 1965 level, while the livestock capacity constraints are 110 percent of their levels in solution 1. For solution 24 (I_d^{65} = 1.22, I_c^{65} = 3.0) the demand constraints are 122 percent of their levels in solution 1 or solution 19, while the capacity constraints are 300 percent of their levels in solution 1 but the same as in solution 19. Regional demand levels, constraints 5.2, 5.4, 5.10, and 5.15, were varied simultaneously and in the same proportions over all regions and categories of final commodities.

In review, final commodities included in these constraints are grade 1 beef, grade 2 beef, fluid milk, manufactured milk products, pork, and cotton lint, as well as requirements for domestic human consumption, industrial uses, and export of wheat, feed grain, soybean meal, and cottonseed meal. A portion of the output requirements of these latter crop products is treated as intermediate resources for livestock production. Initial demand levels for solution 1, I_c^{65} = 1.0, for commodities represented in Equations 5.2, 5.4, and 5.7 through 5.11 are estimated to reflect requirements for domestic human consumption, exports, and industrial uses in 1965, based on trends observed through 1963.[9] Feed requirements for livestock and poultry exogenous to the model, Equation 5.3, are based on trends in feed requirements and trends in the number of units of each type of livestock and each type of poultry over a similar period. For solution 71 of the 1954 model, demand or minimum input requirements, I_d^{54} = 1.0, are set at observed 1954 levels of domestic human, export, and industrial utilization of the various commodities represented in Equations 5.2, 5.4, and 5.7 through 5.11. Solution 71 feed requirements for animals exogenous to the models—Equation 5.3—are based on observed 1954 feeding rates and number of animals.

The index, I_c^{54}, or I_c^{65}, defines the livestock capacity constraints for each solution in relation to the levels of these constraints used in the first solution of each model. These capacity constraints, Equation 5.13, also were varied simultaneously and in the same proportions for each region and class of livestock. Initial livestock capacity levels for the 1954 model, I_c^{54} = 1.0, were based on the maximum number of each class of livestock produced in any year through 1963. The year in which the maximum number occurred in most regions was 1945 for hogs and 1954 for milk cows. The maximum numbers for both cattle on feed and beef cows occurred in 1962 or 1963 for most regions.

For the 1965 model, these capacity constraints were based on the maximum number of livestock ever produced. The level I_c^{65} = 1.0 was based on observed inventory levels through January 1, 1965, for beef cows and milk cows.[10] For numbers of cattle placed in feedlots and for beef cows, capacity constraints

9. This procedure somewhat underestimated export demand for grains. It was used to estimate 1965 demand or consumption levels since formulation of the model and data were started before 1965.

10. For hogs and milk cows, the capacity constraints used for the 1954 model applied in most regions to the 1965 model.

$I_c^{65} = 1.0$ were based on observations through 1965. To have some slack for regional adjustments in the beef sector, the latest observed numbers for beef cows and cattle on feed were multiplied by 1.1 in each region.

DATA USED

A large amount of analysis was required to estimate production coefficients for the many commodities of each model. Coefficients had to be estimated for each commodity, region, and model. Each activity required estimates of labor, land, capital requirements, and yield or output. Coefficients for feed grain, wheat, cotton, and soybeans were largely available from studies in collaboration with Heady by Egbert,[11] Skold,[12] and Whittlesey.[13] Approximately nine man-years were required to develop and assemble the additional data for the three models used in this study. A different set of data was developed for each of the three models. Coefficients were estimated to represent average regional production input-output relations in crop and livestock production for 1954 and 1965. The third set of coefficients involved new estimates for only the livestock activities. They represent input-output relations achieved by the more efficient producers of livestock in each region.

The average regional cost coefficients include charges for depreciation, maintenance, and interest on all items of machinery, equipment, buildings, and other facilities involved in production. They also include charges for labor, fertilizer, fuel, lubricants, insecticides, herbicides, seeds, prepared feeds, veterinary charges, breeding fees, and other direct costs incurred in production. No charge is made for land, however. Land costs are not included in the cost coefficients. If land has no major alternative uses except those included in the model, exclusion of land costs has no logical or theoretical shortcomings with respect to the solution vector and imputed product prices. Few other land-use alternatives are important over the wide expanse of the Corn Belt and northern Great Plains. However, in some areas, excluded crops are of major importance in determining opportunity costs for land.

A rather complete collection of recent studies containing input-output coefficients for farm enterprises was secured from all states. This collection included the publications listed in *Publications Containing Farm Enterprise Input-Output Data* by Marlowe M. Taylor.[14] Other publications also were reviewed, many being supplied by individuals at the various state agricultural colleges. All state agricultural experiment station bulletins and agricultural extension circulars from 1950 to the present were included.

Even with this large collection of data, considerable difficulty was encountered in developing cost coefficients for hay and livestock activities. Since hay is usually of minor importance relative to other farm enterprises, costs for

11. See Chapter 1.
12. See Chapter 4.
13. See Chapter 2.
14. Marlowe M. Taylor, *Publications Containing Recent Farm Enterprise Input-Output Data*, USDA, ERS, 1963.

hay are seldom studied in detail. Production costs for any particular livestock enterprise vary widely even within regions, and similar procedures are not always used in aggregating their unit costs. Because of space limitations and the larger amount of material involved, it is not possible to detail the estimation procedures, data sources, and data used in preparing this study. Only a resumé of the general nature of the various coefficients is given here.

CROP COEFFICIENTS

Crop costs include those for machine use, buildings, labor, and direct input items such as seed, fertilizer, etc. Estimates of 1954 costs for crops other than hay were secured by first determining the machines used, the times over for each machine, and the time required per once-over for each machine operation. Production practices were separated into preharvest and harvest operations. Components of machine costs included depreciation, interest, taxes, insurance, grease, repairs, fuel, and oil. These components of costs were estimated for each machine. Estimates of labor use were developed at the same time by determining the labor hours by machine operations. In addition, estimates were secured for costs per acre of seed, lime, insecticides, herbicides, and irrigation. These estimates were developed by Egbert[15] for crop-producing areas 1 through 137. For areas 138 through 157, these coefficients were estimated in the same manner by the authors.

For the 1965 model, costs for nonroughage crops were developed by Whittlesey and Skold. Recent data on crop production practices were obtained for only a few areas. To secure up-to-date estimates for crop production costs, an index of operating expenses per acre for each crop was developed for each state by years from 1949 to 1961. These indices were then projected linearly to provide costs for 1965, starting from the basic estimates for 1954. The projected 1965 index of costs per acre was then related to the 1954 index of per-acre costs. The ratio so formed was then multiplied by the 1954 costs per acre estimated by Egbert as follows:

$$C_{nk}^{65} = (I_{65}/I_{54})_{nj} \, C_{nk}^{54} \tag{5.22}$$

where $(I_{65}/I_{54})_{nj}$ denotes the ratio of the projected 1965 index of costs per acre in the 1965 trend value of the index of costs per acre for the nth crop activity in the jth state, C_{nk}^{54} denotes the per-acre cost estimates for 1954 by Egbert for the nth crop in kth area in jth state, and thus C_{nk}^{65} denotes the estimated per-acre costs for 1965 for the nth crop in the kth area. These coefficients were then checked with data on cost of production in the area for which up-to-date estimates were available.

To eliminate stochastic weather results, nonforage crop yields for the 1954 model were estimated from the 1949–54 trend value for each crop in each crop-producing area, with the 1954 points taken as the value. When the trend was negative, the average yield over the period 1949–54 was used as the 1954 yield.

15. See Chapter 1.

For the 1965 and EM models, the yields for these crops were estimated as follows:

$$\hat{y}_{nk} = (\overline{y}_{nk} / \hat{Y}_{nj})\, \overline{Y}_{nj} \tag{5.23}$$

where $\hat{y}_{nk}$ denotes the projected 1965 yield for the nth crop in area k, $\overline{y}_{nk}$ denotes the average yield of the nth crop in the kth area within the jth state, $\hat{Y}_{nj}$ denotes the linearly projected value of the 1954–62 trend in yield in the nth crop in the jth state (this yield was not allowed to exceed the highest historic yield of any particular crop in each state), and $\overline{Y}_{nj}$ denotes the average yield of nth crop in the jth state for the two years 1954 and 1959.

Cost coefficients for the tame hay, wild hay, and silage (corn and sorghum silage were combined) activities of the three models were developed in a manner similar to that outlined for the 1954 nonforage crops. Preharvest costs were broken down into the following components: machinery, labor, spraying and dusting, fertilizer and lime, seed or sprigs, and irrigation. Costs were estimated for each type of hay produced, with adjustments for years of stand and for the portion attributable to companion crops. The costs for the various tame hay crops were weighted by the proportion of total tame hay planted to each crop in each area. Harvest costs were estimated for each hay crop for each of the three methods of harvesting: baled, loose, and chopped. Cost estimates for mowing and raking were made on a per-time-over basis, then weighted by the number of estimated cuttings per year for each crop. Tame hay harvest costs for each method of harvesting were then weighted by the frequency of each harvesting method. Wild hay was assumed to incur no preharvest costs. For the silages, preharvest costs for corn were used. All silage was assumed to be harvested by field forage harvesters. For the 1965 model, preharvest costs for hay and silage were estimated in a manner similar to that used by Skold and Whittlesey for non-roughage crops. Methods for estimating 1965 harvest costs for hay and silage were the same as the procedure outlined for 1954. Area yields for the forage crops were developed as in Equation 5.23.

LIVESTOCK COEFFICIENTS

All livestock coefficients had to be estimated anew for this study. Only crop coefficients were included in the previous interregional programming analyses. The general procedures developed for estimating programming data for the 1954 set of livestock and transportation activities, demand requirements, livestock capacity constraints, and supplies of exogenous feeds were used also for estimating these data for the 1965 model. Hence, the following discussion of these data applies in general to both time periods.

MILK COWS

Input-output coefficients for the milk cow activities include nonfeed costs, pasture, harvested roughage, feed units, protein, milk, meat, and feeder calves. Each of these coefficients forms an element in the activity vector for milk cows in each region. Cost coefficients for milk cows were developed from data from a large number of state publications in conjunction with information on the distribution of methods of milking by size of herds and by states. Feed requirements and meat output per cow were estimated mostly from unpublished data from the USDA. Estimates of milk output per cow were taken from *Dairy Statistics*[16] for the 1954 model. For the 1965 model estimates were based on trends indicated from data in *Dairy Statistics* and from *Milk Production and Dairy Products*[17] through 1964. Output of feeder calves per dairy cow was estimated to be 70 percent of the calves not kept for dairy herd replacements. Input coefficients for milk cow activities included both requirements for milk cows and requirements for herd replacements per milk cow.

BEEF COWS

Input-output coefficients for beef cows include all nonfeed costs, pasture, harvested roughage, feed units, protein, calves, and meat. Nonfeed costs were estimated from various state publications. Feed requirements were estimated from unpublished data and from the work by R. D. Jennings.[18] Meat output was estimated from unpublished data on inventory weights, multiplied by estimated replacement rates adjusted for death losses. Estimates of calf output per cow were 5-year averages of calving rates adjusted for death losses. Beef calves were assumed to be weaned at 400 pounds in all regions.

CATTLE ON FEED

Eight different general systems were used for cattle-feeding activities. Yearling feeders and calves could be fed varying combinations of forages and concentrates. Each of these general systems was varied according to general feeding practices of each region. Data from various state studies on cattle feeding were used to estimate nonfeed costs. Feed requirements were estimated by first developing a detailed outline by regions of the typical feeding phases and rates of gain within each feeding phase. Rations that would achieve the rates of gain estimated were then developed on the basis of experimental and survey information. Rates of gain for the various feeding systems were estimated from published surveys or from farm record studies.

YEARLINGS

The yearling activities represent an operation whereby a 400-pound calf grows to 700 pounds on a ration of mostly hay and pasture. Coefficients for the

---

16. USDA, *Dairy Statistics through 1960*, Stat. Bull. 303, 1962.

17. USDA, *Milk Production and Dairy Products*, Annual Summaries, Crop Rptg. Bd., 1960–64.

18. R. D. Jennings, *Consumption of Feed by Livestock, 1909–56: Relation between Feed, Livestock and Food at the National Level*, USDA Prod. Res. Report 21, 1958; *Feed Consumed by Livestock, Supply and Disposition of Feeds, 1949–50, by States*, USDA Stat. Bull. 145, 1955; *Relative Use of Feeds for Livestock Including Pasture, by States*, USDA Stat. Bull. 153, 1955.

yearling feeder–producing activities were estimated in a manner similar to that used for cattle-fattening activities.

HOGS

Feed requirements for hogs were estimated from unpublished data. Total feed fed to hogs was allocated to each state by using unpublished estimates of the number of grain-consuming animal units of hogs, multiplied by the feed units of concentrates fed per grain-consuming animal unit of hogs. These estimates were then divided by estimates of state liveweight production of hogs. Cost coefficients for hogs were estimated from various state studies and surveys of hog production costs and returns.

TRANSPORTATION COSTS

Cost coefficients among regions were developed for transportation activities by the authors and others, mainly from waybill sample statistics. Milk transportation costs were taken from work by Snodgrass and French.[19] Commodities for which transportation costs were estimated include feed grain, wheat, cottonseed meal, soybean meal, fluid milk, manufactured milk products, pork, beef, yearling feeders, feeder calves, and hay.

QUANTITATIVE RESULTS

As mentioned previously, results from only two of the 57 solutions are presented in detail because of the large amount of results involved and space limitations. The two solutions are 71 of the 1954 model and 1 of the 1965 model. Solutions 19 and 24, which represent the terminal solutions for parametric operations in the livestock capacity restraints and demand restraints respectively, are compared with the solution 1 for 1965.

Tables 5.3 through 5.10 show actual production for 1954 and 1965 and the production resulting from solutions 1, 19, 24, and 71 for each of several different crops and types of livestock. Solution 71 is the basic solution of the 1954 model. It features levels of technology and utilization of final commodities observed for 1954. Solution 1, the basic solution for the 1965 model, features levels of technology and utilization of final commodities estimated for 1965. Demand levels for solution 19 are the same as for solution 1 but the livestock capacity constraints for solution 19 are 300 percent of their levels in solution 1 (i.e., $I_d^{65} = 1.0$ and $I_c^{65} = 3.0$). Thus solution 19 represents a situation with virtually no limitation on the number of livestock produced in any one region except for considerations of site and cost. For solution 24, demand levels for final commodities are 22.39 percent greater than for solution 1 or solution 19, and livestock capacity constraints are the same as in solution 19 (i.e., $I_d^{65} = 1.22$ and $I_c^{65} = 3.0$). Thus in

19. Milton M. Snodgrass and Charles E. French, *Linear Programming Approach to the Study of Interregional Competition in Dairying*, Ind. Agr. Exp. Sta. Bull. 637, 1958.

Tables 3 through 10, 1954 actual production is compared with solution 71, and 1965 actual production is compared with solution 1. Differences between solutions 1 and 19 are due only to changes in the livestock capacity constraints, and differences between solutions 19 and 24 are due only to changes in specified levels of demand. It is not expected that the actual production for 1954 and 1965 will be the same as the programmed production for these years. Actual patterns of production are not expected to be optimal, whereas, against the objective function and constraints employed, programmed results are optimal patterns.

1954 MODEL, SOLUTION 71

Solution 71 represents optimal patterns of production and product distribution under regional average input-output relations estimated for 1954. The restraints for the 20 demand regions represent domestic and export requirements for each final commodity. Livestock capacity restraints for the 20 regions represent the historical maximum production of each type of livestock through 1963. Restraints for each of the 157 crop-producing areas represent the acreages planted to the various crops in 1953.

Figure 5.3 shows the area and geographic production patterns for wheat,

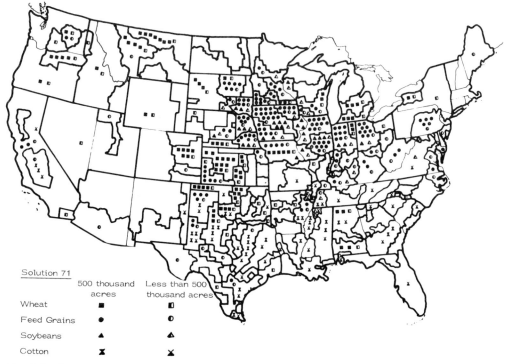

Fig. 5.3. Geographic locations and acreage of grain and cotton production for 1954 model, solution 71.

Fig. 5.4. Geographic locations and acreage of harvested roughage production for 1954 model, solution 71.

feed grain, soybeans, and cotton resulting from solution 71. Production patterns for harvested roughages are shown in Figure 5.4. Under solution 71, a total of 31.4 million acres of cotton and grainland is diverted to hay and pasture production and 28.0 million acres are diverted to uses other than those specified by the model. An additional 32.8 million acres of hay land and pastureland are diverted as surplus land to idle capacity. A total of 51 million acres of land devoted to pasture and crops of the base period 1953 are not needed for these uses in 1954 under the conditions of solution 71.

If allocated on an interregional optimum basis as specified by the model, crop and livestock products used in 1954 could have been produced with significantly fewer acres. The gain is posed as a possibility in restricting the production of that period in a manner which better utilized the comparative advantage of the many producing regions. Also, some gain went into storage as publicly financed surplus; a use not incorporated into the activities of the model. Patterns of regional specialization in crop production specified by the model follow generally the patterns expected. Hence, interregional shifts to improve efficiency in crop production appear feasible.

COTTON

Cotton production shows a westward shift as compared with actual 1954 patterns of cotton production (Table 5.6). Region 3 (West Virginia, Virginia, and North Carolina), region 4 (South Carolina, Georgia, and Alabama), region 5 (Florida), and region 17 (Arizona and New Mexico) show reductions in cotton acreage. Increases in cotton acreage are shown for Tennessee, Missouri, region 11 (Mississippi, Arkansas, and Louisiana), region 12 (Oklahoma and Texas), and region 20 (California).

GRAIN

Solution 71 proposes a total wheat acreage of 3 million acres less than was actually planted in 1954. Approximately 2.4 million tons of wheat are fed to livestock in three regions: 1.3 million tons in region 15 (Montana and Idaho), 1.0 million tons in region 16 (Wyoming and Colorado), and 0.1 million tons in region 18 (Utah and Nevada). Wheat production is concentrated in the traditional wheat-growing regions of the Great Plains, northern Montana, and eastern Washington and Oregon. Some wheat acreage also appears in Missouri, Illinois, Wisconsin, Michigan, Ohio, Indiana, New York, Alabama, and Arkansas.

Feed-grain and soybean production is concentrated in the Corn Belt and on its fringes, as shown in Figure 5.3. On the larger regional basis, regions 4, 5, and 8 show no feed-grain production under solution 71. Region 7 (Ohio and Indiana) is the only region that shows a larger acreage of feed grain than was actually planted in 1954. The remaining 16 regions all show a smaller acreage. Total feed-grain acreage is 61.8 million acres less under solution 71 than was actually planted in 1954. Soybean acreage is approximately 3.2 million acres greater than was planted in 1954 (Table 5.5).

DIVERTED LAND

Table 5.11 shows the amount of land (by consuming regions) in the various categories not needed for wheat, feed grain, soybeans, cotton, hay, silage, and pasture. For the conditions and the formulation of specific models, the amount of land so indicated could be considered as "surplus land." This land is located primarily in the Appalachian area and in the Great Plains.

The total surplus figures shown in Table 5.11 represent total acreage not needed to meet national demand restraints under the models and solutions.[20] The pasture portion of this total is measured in open permanent pasture equivalents. The pasture figures represent the acres of unused or idle pastureland measured in open permanent pasture equivalent acres (land restraint 5, minus land restraint 3, minus pasture used). Hay figures represent the amount of original hay land not diverted to pasture and used for hay (land restraint 3, plus land restraint 4, minus land restraint 2, minus land used to produce tame hay and wild hay). The cotton land and grainland figures represent this land not diverted to hay or pasture and not planted to cotton, feed grain, wheat, soybeans, or corn-sorghum silage (land restraint 2, land diverted to hay and pasture, minus land used to produce cotton, feed grain, wheat, soybeans, and corn or sorghum silage).

20. National demand restraints did not allow for movement of surplus production into storage, an operation which did take place to an extent in 1954.

Eight of the 20 livestock-producing regions have no surplus land. Two additional regions (regions 1 and 19) use all available grainland for grain and silage production but have some surplus land for hay and pasture production. Total land use for the various crops in solution 71 is wheat, 51,311,400 acres; feed grain, 84,004,100 acres; soybeans, 20,169,200 acres; cotton, 21,079,400 acres; silage, 7,945,300 acres; and hay, 66,197,000 acres.

LIVESTOCK

Table 5.12 shows the geographic distribution of milk cows and beef cows for solution 71. Milk cows appear in every region except regions 11 (Arkansas, Mississippi, and Louisiana) and 12 (Oklahoma and Texas). Milk cow capacity constraints are limiting in only six of the 20 regions (5, 7, 8, 9, 13, and 20). Shadow prices on these constraints vary from $8.59 per head in region 13 to $63.79 in region 20; that is, an increase of one cow in the milk cow capacity constraint in region 13 would reduce total costs by $8.59, and in region 20 an additional milk cow would reduce total costs by $63.79.

Beef cows appear in all regions except four (1, 2, 3, and 8). Beef cow capacity constraints are not limiting in these regions or in regions 7 and 20. In the remaining regions, shadow prices on the capacity constraints range from $2.14 in region 9 to $38.25 in region 12. Shadow prices on beef cow capacity constraints are above $20 per head in eight regions (4, 11, 12, 13, 14, 15, 16, and 17).

The geographic patterns of cattle on feed, yearling feeder calves, and hogs for solution 71 are also shown in Table 5.12. Region 20 (California) has 197,400 head of excess capacity for feeding cattle. All other regions are limited by the beef-feeding capacity constraints in solution 71. Shadow prices on the beef-feeding capacity constraints in these regions vary from $3.08 per head in region 17 (Arizona and New Mexico) to $39.21 per head in region 12 (Oklahoma and Texas). Regions 1, 6, 11, 12, 13, and 14 have shadow prices in excess of $30 per head on cattle-feeding capacity constraints. Hogs are produced in only 5 of the 20 regions (7, 9, 10, 13, and 14). Only regions 7, 13, and 14 have exhausted their hog production capacity constraints. Shadow prices on hog production in these regions are $0.15, $0.24, and $0.53 per cwt, respectively.

LAND RENTS

Table 5.13 lists the imputed equilibrium rents or shadow prices for all land categories in each of the 157 crop areas. These shadow prices indicate the amount by which total national cost could be reduced if one more unit of a particular land resource were available. The composition of these equilibrium rents can be illustrated as follows: the corn-equivalent yield of wheat in area 106 in eastern Colorado is 4.40 cwt per acre for 1954. The equilibrium price of wheat in consuming region 16 is $1.54 per cwt of feed units ($0.97 per bushel of wheat). Multiplying yield times price (4.40 × $1.54), a revenue of $6.78 per acre is indicated for area 106. Subtracting the nonland costs for the wheat activity in area 106 ($6.78 - 5.50 = $1.28) gives the land rent for the area.

The difference of $0.01 per acre as shown in Table 5.13 for land rent on land 2 for area 106 is due to rounding. In an area where some, but not all, of the available land is used, the equilibrium rent is zero. The equilibrium price of wheat in a particular region may include two components: (1) the costs per unit of the highest cost-producing area within a consuming region, and (2) the cost of transporting the product from one region to another.

In a wheat-deficit region, the equilibrium price of wheat is derived from its highest cost source and includes both production and transportation costs. In a region that neither exports nor imports wheat, the equilibrium wheat price is equal to production costs in the highest cost-producing area within that region. In a region that exports wheat, the equilibrium price of wheat is equal to the price of wheat in the region to which it exports, minus transportation costs.

Equilibrium commodity prices are shown in Tables 5.14 and 5.15. The commodity prices and land rents seem low. Some of the reasons for the low prices are explained in the section on limitations of the model and data. In addition, the cost coefficients used include no returns to management and only average reported wage rates for farm labor. Upward adjustments in the cost coefficients to reflect higher returns to labor and management would result in higher shadow prices. However, the derived prices are expected to be lower than observed prices, since no supply control or price subsidy programs are included in the model.

INTERREGIONAL AND COMMODITY FLOWS

Interregional commodity flows for solution 71 are shown in Figures 5.5 through 5.11. Some flows of cottonseed meal, soybean meal, and grain seem unrealistic. The deficiencies are explained as follows: (1) The exogenous concentrates, which are largely high protein concentrates, are allocated to only 11 of the 20 regions. Livestock feed in regions 1 and 19 consists entirely of these exogenous concentrates. Regions 4, 11, and 17 feed only soybean meal or cottonseed meal. Regions 15 and 18 feed only wheat and no high protein feeds. (2) Data on consumption of high protein feeds from which protein requirements were estimated seem to have a downward bias, particularly for milk cows and hogs. (3) The level of hog production, as explained in the limitations section, is low. (4) The beef activities selected by the model require relatively less concentrates and more roughage than the average of existing or observed cattle-feeding systems. These deficiencies can be eliminated by the suggested modifications discussed in the section on limitations of the model and data. For the current phase of this continuing project, a much more detailed model has been developed which incorporates the suggested modifications. Problems encountered with solution 71 also apply to other solutions. Hence, conclusions drawn are based largely on differences from one solution to another. The discussion that follows deals mainly with differences from one solution to another.

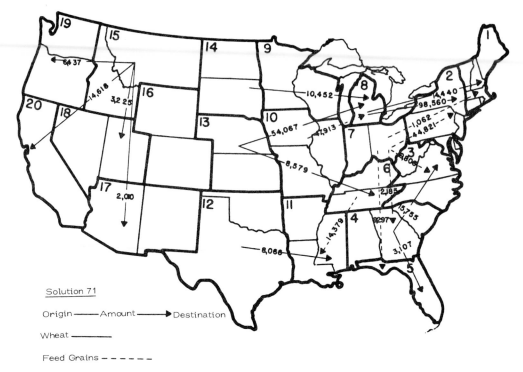

Fig. 5.5. Interregional flows of wheat and feed grain for 1954 model, solution 1 (1,000 cwt of feed units).

Fig. 5.6. Interregional flows of soybean meal and cottonseed meal for 1954 model, solution 71 (1,000 cwt of feed units).

182

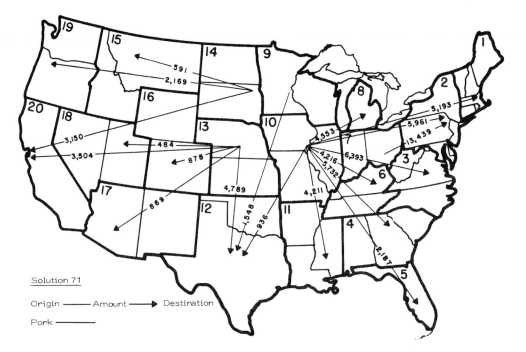

Fig. 5.7. Interregional flows of pork for 1954 model, solution 71 (1,000 cwt).

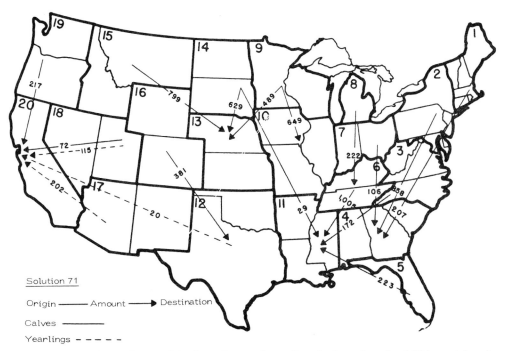

Fig. 5.8. Interregional flows of feeder calves and yearling feeder calves for 1954 model, solution 71 (1,000 head).

Fig. 5.9. Interregional flows of manufactured milk products and whole fluid milk for 1954 model, solution 71 (1,000 cwt).

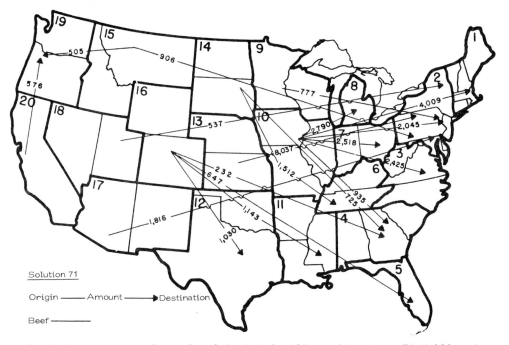

Fig. 5.10. Interregional flows of beef, Grade 1, for 1954 model, solution 71 (1,000 cwt).

Fig. 5.11. Interregional flows of beef, Grade 2, for 1954 model, solution 71 (1,000 cwt).

1965 MODEL, SOLUTION 1

Solution 1 presents optimal patterns of production and product distribution under regional average crop and livestock input-output relations estimated for 1965. Regional demand constraints represent domestic and export requirements for each final commodity. Livestock capacity constraints limit production of each type of livestock to its historical maximum production in each region.[21]

Figure 5.12 shows the area and geographic production pattern for wheat, feed grain, soybeans, and cotton resulting from this solution. Geographic patterns of crop specialization under solution 1 are very similar to those specified in the basic models of Heady and Skold[22] and Heady and Whittlesey.[23] Table 5.16 shows comparisons of solution 1 of the 1965 model with solution 33, model I, of Whittlesey's model.[24] Solution 33 of Whittlesey's models most nearly resembles solution 1 in the structuring of land constraints. However, important differences in the structuring of the land constraints between the two models still exist. Also, Whittlesey's models featured 31 consuming regions and 144 crop-producing regions (areas) as against 20 consuming regions and 157 crop-producing areas.

21. The historical maximum limitation on number of fed cattle was insufficient to meet the specified demands for grade 1 beef. About 0.3 percent more total capacity was required. The constraints on fed-cattle capacity were then multiplied by 1.1.
22. See Chapter 4.
23. See Chapter 2.
24. Ibid.

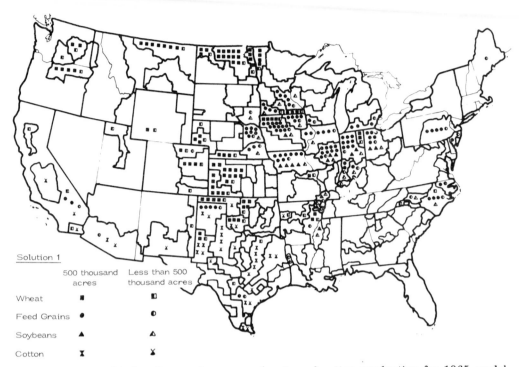

Fig. 5.12. Geographic locations and acreage of grain and cotton production for 1965 model, solution 1.

Whittlesey's model is dealt with only crudely by aggregating the production of above crops in 31 regions into the 20 regions featured in the current study. Since the total acreages are substantially different for some crops, general production patterns for the two models are shown in terms of the percentages of total acreages by regions for each crop. Reasons for the discrepancies in total acreages are presented later.

Solution 1 indicates no cotton production for areas east of Texas, except for area 137 in west central Arkansas. Wheat production is located mainly in the northern Great Plains, northeastern Colorado, northeastern Montana, eastern Washington, northeastern Oregon, and western Kansas. A substantial amount of the wheat produced in these areas is used as feed grain. Approximately 14.5 million tons or roughly 34 percent of total wheat production is used as livestock feed under solution 1. Figure 5.12 also indicates some scattered wheat production in California, Utah, Wyoming, western Colorado, the Corn Belt, the Delta states, and North Carolina.

In addition to the heavy concentration of feed-grain production in the Corn Belt and Lake states, solution 1 shows production of feed grain for California, Arizona, Texas, Nebraska, North Carolina, Pennsylvania, Maryland, and the New England states. Soybean production is located mainly in the Corn Belt, with additional production in eastern Nebraska, southeastern South Dakota, Minnesota, Wisconsin, Arkansas, Louisiana, and North Carolina.

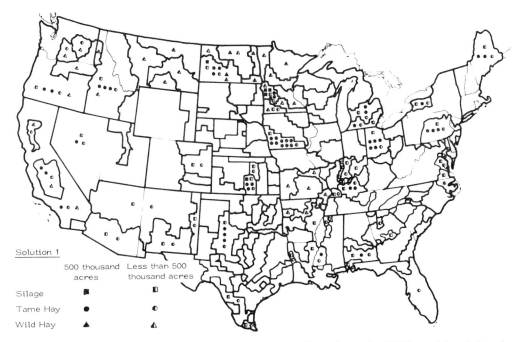

Fig. 5.13. Geographic locations and acreage of harvested roughages for 1965 model, solution 1.

The geographic distribution of harvested roughages for solution 1 is shown in Figure 5.13 by crop-producing areas. Harvested roughages tend to be concentrated in only one or a few crop-producing areas within each livestock-producing region. These results, due to the lack of geographic coincidence in livestock-producing regions and crop-producing areas, provide a distribution which is unrealistic in terms of transport costs and intrafarm use of resources.

The shadow prices of hay-producing activities are low in many of the areas where the solution specifies a zero hay output. Hence, the solution is nearly indifferent between the pattern of hay production exhibited in Figure 5.13 and a pattern which exhibits hay production distributed more widely over each region. Shadow prices on hay activities not in solution 1 are distributed as follows: 15 areas have shadow prices of $1 per acre or less;[25] 34 areas have hay-producing activities with shadow prices of $2 per acre or less; and 118 areas have hay-producing activities with shadow prices of $5 per acre or less. By distributing the hay among additional areas within livestock-producing regions, the reduction of hay production in one area would be compensated for by surplus hay land or pastureland, or by pasture usage, in other areas.

The hay land constraint explained earlier could be used only for hay or pasture activities. However, the land constraint for cotton and grains could also produce hay. Thus as the solutions divert cotton land or grainland to hay, pro-

25. A shadow price of $1 on a hay-producing activity would mean that total cost would increase by $1 for every acre that was substituted for the present source of hay. Likewise, if the per-acre costs were $1 lower, the activity would replace one of the existing hay activities.

duction in a rather small area results in sufficient hay supplies to support all livestock in rather large regions. A greater dispersion of hay production within regions would have only a small effect on total costs, but might result in a different geographic pattern of livestock and crop production.

In solution 71, hay and silage production are widely dispersed (Figure 5.4). The basic models for solutions 1 and 71 are the same. They differ only in demand levels and technical coefficients. However, solution 71 for the 1954 model, having lower yield coefficient, exhibits much less excess production capacity than solution 1. Hence, specified demands for solution 1 allow greater use of excess capacity in grain and cotton production than in hay production by individual areas within regions. The extreme specialization in hay production, sometimes specified by the solutions, would not occur if crop-producing and livestock-producing regions coincided. However, the number of equations required for such a model exceeded available computational capabilities.

Table 5.17 presents the amount of land in the various categories not needed for wheat, feed grain, soybeans, cotton, hay, silage, or pasture. For the conditions and the formulation of the specific model, the amount of land so indicated could be considered "surplus land" which can be diverted to noncrop uses. This land is located primarily in the Appalachian area of the East, in the Great Plains, and in the fringes of the Corn Belt. All regions, except California and Florida, have some surplus land under solution 1. In region 4 (South Carolina, Georgia, and Alabama) about 9 million acres are specified as surplus or to be diverted from cotton and grain. Since no production of cotton, wheat, feed grain, or soybeans appears in region 4, about 2.4 million of the 11.4 million acres of cotton and grainland are diverted to hay and pasture production. In region 10 (Iowa, Illinois, and Missouri) about 12 million acres of land are specified to be diverted from grain to the surplus category. Unused grainland also appears in regions 2, 3, 6, 7, 8, 9, 13, 14, and 15 (Table 5.17). Cottonland and/or grainland was used entirely for cotton, feed grain, wheat, soybeans, and silage, or diverted to hay and pasture, in regions 1, 4, 5, 11, 16, 17, 18, 19, and 20 (Table 5.17). Hence no land was left idle in the latter set of regions. Total surplus land for solution 1 is 102.7 million acres. Of this total, 9.9 million acres are pasture measured in acres of open permanent pasture equivalents. Surplus hay land is 19.0 million acres, and surplus cottonland and grainland make up 73.7 million acres. Total acreages for the various crops in solution 1 are wheat, 54.2 million acres; feed grain, 55.7 million acres; soybeans, 11.3 million acres; cotton, 12 million acres; silage, 7.4 million acres; hay, 33.7 million acres; and wild hay, 4.1 million acres.

This larger acreage of surplus land for 1965 compared with the parallel 1954 solution is due to the fact that the growth in agricultural technology, or yields, over the 11-year period was greater than the growth in food requirements, or demand, as reflected in the constraints for the 2 years. Hence, the two sets of trends (except for some large "abnormal" increments such as greater international food aid or effective supply control programs) suggest that surplus capacity in American agriculture will continue to exist.

Table 5.18 shows the geographic distribution of milk cows and beef cows for solution 1. Milk cows appear in every region but region 6 (Kentucky and Tennessee). However, the shadow price for the milk cow activity of region 6 for solution 1 is only $0.076 per head. Hence, milk production could take place in gion 6, with only negligible effects on production efficiency and national costs for the "bill of goods" prescribed in the demand constraints. Solution 1 proposes beef cows in all regions except region 1 (New England), region 2 (New York, New Jersey, Pennsylvania, Maryland, and Delaware), and region 8 (Michigan). Shadow prices for beef cow activities not in the basis are $36.52, $11.52, and $4.15 per head, in regions 1, 2, and 8, respectively. Regions that use all "available capacity" for milk cows are 5, 7, 8, 9, 16, 17, and 20. Beef cows are limited by the beef cow capacity constraints in 12 regions (3, 4, 5, 10, 11, 12, 13, 14, 15, 16, 17, and 18). The shadow prices on milk cow capacity constraints for solution 1 range from $123.53 to $28.67 per head in regions that exhaust these constraints. For beef cows the corresponding range in shadow prices is $32.77 to $0.04 per head.

The geographic patterns for the production of cattle on feed, yearling feeder calves, and hogs in solution 1 are shown in Table 5.18. Region 17 (Arizona and New Mexico) and region 20 (California) have 302,300 and 132,900 head, respectively, or excess capacity for feeding cattle. All other regions are limited by the beef-feeding capacity constraints of solution 1. Regions with the highest shadow prices on beef-feeding capacity are regions 3, 15, and 16. Solution 1 produces a total of 8.9 million head of yearlings of which only 1.8 million head are placed in feedlots. The remaining 7.1 million head are slaughtered for grade 2 beef. Of the 19.4 million head of cattle fed, approximately 17.6 million head are placed in feedlots as calves rather than as yearlings.

The model tends to select beef-feeding activities that use relatively large amounts of forage and produce relatively heavy animals. In the Midwest and southern and eastern regions, these activities are the deferred feeding systems. In the Great Plains and northern Rocky Mountain states the extended silage system is specified by the model. Calves on silage and yearlings are the two cattle-feeding activities selected by the model in the western states. The extended silage and the deferred feeding systems start with calves which are fed over a relatively long period of time on high roughage rations before being finished on high concentrate rations. These systems provide only a small portion of the finished beef actually produced. However, under the conditions of perfect knowledge and single-valued expectations implied in the models, these systems would become more universally employed.

Hogs are produced in only 9 of the 20 regions. Regions with the highest shadow prices on hog capacity are 13 (Kansas and Nebraska), 14 (North Dakota and South Dakota), and 15 (Montana and Idaho). These regions also have relatively high shadow prices on the fed-cattle capacity constraints.

Table 5.19 lists the imputed equilibrium rents or shadow prices for all land categories in each of the 157 crop areas. Equilibrium commodity prices for solution 1 are shown in Tables 5.20 and 5.21. The commodity prices and land rents are, for reasons presented earlier, somewhat low.

Many changes have taken place in circumstances affecting spatial equilibrium among commodity sectors between 1954 and 1965. These changes are the basis for the differences between solution 71 and solution 1. Technological changes have taken place at different rates among regions producing a particular commodity, as well as among commodities produced in a particular region. Changes in aggregate demands for the various products have also taken place at varying rates. In addition, relative changes in population among regions have affected the site advantage or disadvantage of the various regions. Since transportation costs from points of production to points of consumption are relatively more significant for some commodities than for others, relative shifts in population among regions might be very influential in affecting the geographic configuration of production among commodities. The interregional product flows for solution 1 are in conformity with the changes in production locations and regional demand (Figure 5.14 through Figure 5.20). To determine the net effect of these changes, the differences between solution 71 of the 1954 model and solution 1 of the 1965 model are examined.

CHANGES FROM SOLUTION 71 TO SOLUTION 1

Crop output per acre and livestock output per unit of feed are generally higher in the 1965 model than in the 1954 model. Costs per acre excluding land costs for the various crops are higher in the 1965 model but are offset by higher yields. Costs per unit of livestock product are lower in the 1965 model than in the 1954 model, due to increased feeding efficiency and lower feed costs. Total

Fig. 5.14. Interregional flows of wheat and feed grain for 1965 model, solution 1 (1,000 cwt of feed units).

Fig. 5.15. Interregional flows of soybean meal and cottonseed meal for 1965 model, solution 1 (1,000 cwt of feed units).

Fig. 5.16. Interregional flows of manufactured milk products and whole fluid milk for 1965 model, solution 1 (1,000 cwt).

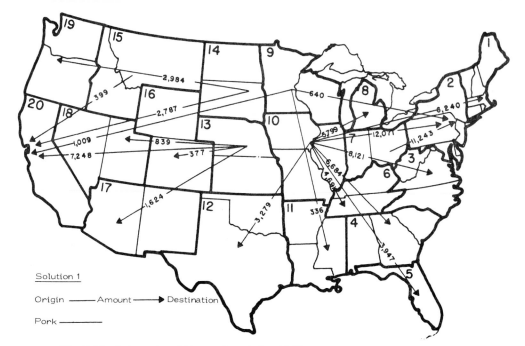

Fig. 5.17. Interregional flows of pork for 1965 model, solution 1 (1,000 cwt).

Fig. 5.18. Interregional flows of feeder calves and yearling feeder calves for 1965 model, solution 1 (1,000 head).

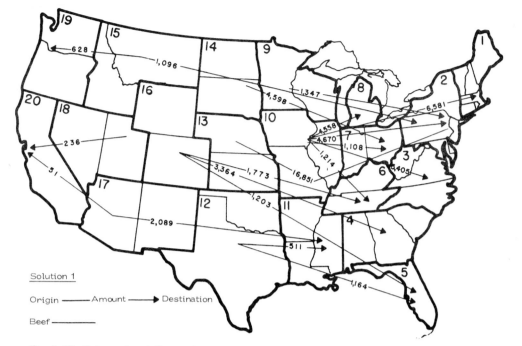

Fig. 5.19. Interregional flows of beef, Grade 1, for 1965 model, solution 1 (1,000 cwt).

Fig. 5.20. Interregional flows of beef, Grade 2, for 1965 model, solution 1 (1,000 cwt).

costs for solution 1 are higher than for solution 71, as considerably higher output is required for solution 1. However, the increased crop yields and improved livestock feed conversion more than offset the effect of the higher output requirements on commodity prices (hogs and soybeans excepted).

SHADOW PRICES

The percentage changes in national shadow prices from solution 71 to solution 1 are wheat, -1.03; feed grain, -5.6; soybeans, $+1.5$; fed cattle, -21.0; hogs, $+5.5$; and milk, -36.3. Changes in product shadow prices from solution 71 to solution 1 by regions are given in Table 5.22. As detailed earlier, this change results because of a growth in production technology which exceeds population and demand growth during the 11-year period. Several factors are involved in the relative price changes among the various products. The large decrease in milk prices between solution 71 and solution 1 is related to the following factors: (1) milk output per cow increased much more between 1954 and 1965 than feed inputs and nonfeed costs per cow; (2) the price of feed is lower for solution 1 than for solution 71; (3) while total demand for milk increased, this increase was relatively small compared to the increased output requirements for other commodities; and (4) in relation to total milk consumption, less fluid milk is transported between regions in solution 1 than in solution 71.

SURPLUS LAND

As shown in Tables 5.11 and 5.17, regional patterns of idle land for these two solutions are quite different. In solution 71 no idle land appears in regions 2, 5, 7, 8, 10, 11, 18, and 20. However, some cotton land and/or grainland has been diverted to hay or pasture in all these regions. Regions 1 and 19 have some surplus pastureland and hay land, but no surplus grainland. The 10 remaining regions all have surplus cropland but 5 of them show no surplus pastureland or hay land. In contrast, only two regions show no surplus land in solution 1 (regions 5 and 20) and have diverted some cropland to hay and pasture. Regions 3, 12, 14, 16, and 17 show less surplus land in solution 1 than in solution 71. Regions 5 and 20 show no change, having used all available land in both solutions. Again, these results stem from differential interregional changes in technology and/or demand over the 11-year period.

CROPS

The geographic patterns of crop production are shown in Figures 5.3 and 5.4 for solution 71, and in Figures 5.12 and 5.13 for solution 1. Table 5.23 shows percentage production allocations of wheat, feed grain, soybeans, and cotton among regions for solutions 71 and 1. Feed-grain acreage in areas on the fringe of the Corn Belt is substantially reduced under solution 1 compared with solution 71. Many of these areas showing feed-grain acreage for solution 71 have zero acreage in solution 1. The acreage of feed grain is decreased in the Corn Belt itself, but feed-grain output is higher there compared with solution 71. In comparing feed-grain production of solution 1 with that of solution 71 the most significant fact is that acreage decreases and output increases. Total feed-grain acreage is reduced from 84.0 million acres to 55.7 million acres, yet feed-grain output is increased by 13.2 percent.

Wheat acreage increases relatively little, from 51.3 million acres to 54.2 million acres, between solutions 71 and 1. Yet wheat output increases 48.8 percent between the two solutions. An increase also occurs in the amount of wheat fed to livestock. In solution 71, the 2.4 million tons of wheat comprise 3.3 percent of the grain fed to livestock while the 16.1 million tons of wheat in solution 1 account for 17.9 percent of the livestock grain. Thus 58.8 percent of the increased wheat production was used for feed. Regional changes include the following: the wheat acreage of regions 2, 4, and 8 drops to zero; in regions 7, 15, and 18, wheat output increases despite lower total acreages; wheat acreage increases in 11 of the remaining 14 regions; regions 1, 5, and 6 have no wheat production in either solution (Table 5.22); South Dakota drops a substantial amount of wheat acreage in solution 1, while North Dakota adds 10.1 million acres (Figure 5.12).

Total cotton acreage is 9.1 million acres (43 percent) lower in solution 1 than in solution 71, but total lint output is 9.2 percent greater. Cotton acreage east of the Great Plains (area 137 in west central Arkansas excepted), totaling 9.8 million acres in solution 71, is reduced to zero in solution 1. Area 137 in Arkansas, producing no cotton in solution 71, shows 3,900 acres in solution 1. Other changes in cotton include increases in acreage in Texas, 115,000 acres; New Mexico and Arizona, 477,200 acres; and California, 116,400 acres.

Total harvested roughage measured in hay equivalent is 18.6 percent lower in solution 1. The decrease in roughage output is mostly attributable to the substitution of grain for roughage in the feeding of milk cows and a 3.0 percent reduction in the number of milk cows. Another contributing factor is the relative shift in the milk cow population from the northern regions to the southern regions, where lower quantities of harvested roughages per cow are fed. In addition, there are lower roughage requirements for animals exogenous to the model in 1965 than in 1954.

The pattern of hay production also changes significantly. Hay is produced in only 67 areas in solution 1 (Figure 5.13) compared to 148 areas in solution 71 (Figure 5.4). Regions 20, 11, and 12 show the greatest increases in harvested roughages, with 56.5, 45.0, and 34.2 percent increases, respectively. Regions 7, 14, 15, 17, and 19 show only small increases. Decreased roughage output occurs in regions 13, 16, 18, and all regions east of the Great Plains (except regions 7 and 11). The decreases in acreage from solution 71 to solution 1 within each category of roughage are 6, 37, and 67 percent, for regions 13, 16, and 18, respectively. This trend toward a greater regional concentration of grains and forage is one which has been taking place despite government programs.

LIVESTOCK

The significant changes in total livestock production can be summarized as follows: milk cows, -14.77 percent; beef cows, +38.66 percent; fed cattle, +84.14 percent; yearlings for grade 2 beef, -37.39 percent; hogs, +28.83 percent. Table

5.24 shows the percentage production allocation of milk cows, beef cows, cattle on feed, and hogs among regions for solutions 71 and 1.

Cattle feeding is limited by the fed-cattle capacity constraints in all regions except region 20 (California) in solution 71. Hence, if the capacity constraint is increased by one unit in any of these regions, cattle feeding in California would decrease by one unit. In solution 1 all regions except two, 17 (New Mexico and Arizona) and 20 (California), are limited by the fed-cattle capacity constraints. These two regions have shown the greatest gains in beef-feeding efficiency in terms of feed conversion but are not in a better competitive position than in 1954. Lower grain prices tend to offset the importance of their gains in feeding efficiency.

RESUMÉ OF CHANGES FROM SOLUTION 1 TO SOLUTION 19

Solution 19, along with other solutions from 1 through 18, was obtained by parametric programming on the livestock capacity constraints. These constraints were relaxed by intervals of approximately 10 percentage points from 100 percent up to 300 percent of the initial levels. Thus for solution 19, $I_d^{65} = 1.0$ and $I_c^{65} = 3.0$. A large number of changes in the equilibrium basis takes place as a result of changes in regional livestock capacity constraints. However, total national costs, the magnitude of the objective function, are only 2.5 percent lower for solution 19 than for solution 1. Shadow prices for livestock products are considerably lower. Fed-cattle prices decrease by 23.6 percent, and hog and milk shadow prices decrease by 15.9 and 8.6 percent, respectively. The shadow prices of wheat and feed grain increase. The wheat shadow price is 2.7 percent higher in solution 19 than in solution 1 and feed-grain price is 0.8 percent higher. The total transportation bill for product distribution is also higher in solution 19. Thus the price decreases in livestock products are partially offset by higher grain prices and greater total transportation costs.

Total surplus land increases from 102.7 million acres in solution 1 to 163.4 million acres in solution 19. Much more of the diverted land in solution 19 is surplus pasture (90.8 million acres vs. 9.9 million acres) since more cropland is diverted to hay and pasture. Total wheat production increases in region 12 (Texas and Oklahoma), region 9 (Minnesota and Wisconsin), and all six regions west of the Great Plains. Total feed-grain production decreases, but regions 2, 10, 12, and 14 show increased feed-grain production. The major decreases in feed-grain production are in the eastern Corn Belt and in Nebraska and Kansas.

Fed-cattle production decreases in the New England states, the western Corn Belt, and the Far West. Increases in fed-cattle production take place in the Great Plains, the northern Rocky Mountain states, the East, and the South. The total number of milk cows decreases by about 1 million head as milk cows are shifted to regions with higher average milk production per cow. The total number of beef cows increases to offset the reduction in both calves and grade 2 beef from the dairy sector. Increases in beef cow numbers occur mainly in the South and Southeast (regions 4 and 11), in the northern Great Plains, and in Montana, Idaho, Wyoming, and Colorado. Beef cow numbers decrease in the southern Great

Plains, the West, and Southwest (regions 17, 18, 19, and 20), the Corn Belt, and Lake states. Hog production increases in region 10 (Iowa, Minnesota, and Missouri) and region 15 (Montana and Idaho). All regions, except Florida, have excess capacity for milk cows in solution 19. For beef cows, excess capacity appears in all regions. Excess capacity for hogs appears in all regions except region 15. Capacity for fed cattle is exhausted in regions 2, 3, 4, 5, and 15.

RÉSUMÉ OF CHANGES FROM SOLUTION 19 TO SOLUTION 24

Starting with the level of livestock capacity constraints at solution 19, the specified levels of demand for all commodities are increased simultaneously, and in the same proportion, with solutions printed out at approximately 5 percent demand increments up to a 22.39 percent increase. Thus in solution 24, the index level of the livestock capacity constraints is the same as for solution 19 (I_c^{65} = 3.00), while the index level of demand constraints is 22.39 percent greater than in solution 19 (I_d^{65} = 1.2239 in solution 24). The increased demand results in a 24.9 percent increase in total costs under solution 24 as compared to solution 19. Surplus land decreases from 163.4 million acres to 44.4 million acres with only 4.9 million idle acres of cottonland and grainland.

Many of the regional adjustments under solution 24 are characterized by expanded production of the commodities which were produced in the same region under solution 19. However, in some regions the output of certain products is reduced while production of others is expanded. Because few broad adjustment patterns are observable, the nature of these changes is best summarized by regions. These changes are summarized for crop and livestock production in Table 5.25. Certain interactions among commodity groups are evident from the positive and negative changes in production. For example, in regions 1 and 2 feed-grain production is decreased; grain imports and roughage production are increased to support increased numbers of milk cows. In region 4 no changes take place. Regions 7, 8, 10, and 15 increase the output of all products, while region 9 decreases soybean production but increases the output of grain, roughage, and milk cows.

Other regions exhibit positive changes in the output of some products and negative changes in the output of others. These changes are accompanied by changes in interregional flows of the various commodities. For example, region 11 increases the output of wheat and feed grain to compensate for reduced inshipments of these commodities from regions 10 and 12. Region 12 shifts land from wheat, much of which had been fed to livestock, to feed grain. A change in relative prices of wheat and feed grain induces the shift away from wheat production to the higher-yielding feed grain in region 12. A similar shift takes place in region 13. Region 12 increases feed-grain production and also reduces exports of wheat and feed grain, using the increased supplies to increase production of fed cattle and hogs. In regions 17, 18, and 19, the production of harvested roughages is increased as more milk cows are brought into production. In region 17 the number of beef cows and fed cattle is decreased. The production of wheat and fed beef is increased in region 20, while the production of feed grain and milk cows is decreased.

SIGNIFICANCE AND LIMITATIONS OF THE STUDY

A major objective of this study was to formulate and test mathematical models that are more realistic in accounting for regional and commodity interdependence than those used in previous studies which considered the wheat, feedgrain, soybean, and cotton sectors. The number of commodity sectors was expanded to include forage, hog, beef, and dairy production. This study also shows a continued existence of surplus land even when the constraints on livestock production are relaxed uniformly (solution 19).

Although this study marked a considerable improvement over previous studies, there are a number of model and data limitations. The lack of geographic coincidence in crop-producing areas and livestock-producing regions results in excessive area specialization in the production of harvested roughages. In the specification of the models, cottonland and grainland in each area can be used for hay or pasture. By shifting cotton land and/or grainland to hay production, it is possible for one or a few areas in a region to specialize in hay production and supply sufficient roughage for all the livestock in a rather large region. The effect of the programming model, then, is to shift all land from grain to pasture in areas not required for grain production. However, shadow prices on many of the producing activities not in the basis are low. Hence, hay costs would not be greatly affected by reallocating hay acreage among areas within a livestock-producing region.

As indicated in Table 5.10, there is a considerable discrepancy between actual liveweight hog production and the hog production resulting from the programmed solutions. Total liveweight hog production for solution 71 should be nearly identical to the actual 1954 hog production. The same is true for actual 1964 production compared with solutions 1 and 19. Analysis of the estimation procedures revealed an inconsistency between the dressing coefficient used in the input-output matrix and that used to estimate pork consumption requirements. In the absence of this inconsistency, approximately 25 percent more hogs requiring about 8 percent more grain for the livestock and poultry sectors would have been required to satisfy the levels of pork consumption specified.

Three possible sources of bias exist for crop yield coefficients. Two result from the structuring of the model; the third results from the method of estimating feed-grain rotations. First, outputs of feed grain, soybeans, wheat, and cottonseed from areas within each of the larger regions were placed in regional accounting rows corresponding to each of these commodities. Transportation activities could transfer each commodity to a corresponding accounting row in another region. Feed transfer activities then could place each of these crops, as a joint product, into the "feed unit" row and the "protein" row in each region as appropriate feed for livestock. The composition of feed grain in a particular region depends on the crop areas brought into production by the program. But feed unit–protein combinations were calculated on the basis of all producing areas in a region. Further, the implied ratios of feed units and protein in feed grain produced in a given region would change when feed grain was transported to another region, as the composition of the feed-grain aggregate differs from one region to another. Thus, if a particular feed-surplus region, which produces predominantly corn, ships feed grain to a feed-deficit region which produces predominantly barley, the receiving region would transfer the in-shipped corn to the livestock feed rows as barley. Since barley has a higher protein content than corn, this construction of the model causes an upward bias in the total protein contributed by feed grain. This bias may cause too much land to be allocated to feed grain and too little to soybeans in the solutions. To prevent the bias, separate accounting rows for each type of feed grain are needed—an additional 60 equations and several hundred additional transportation activities.

However, a second source of bias in yields has the opposite effect on allocation of land to feed grain and soybeans. This second source of bias relates to the choice of feed units and various concentrates. The feed unit factor is influenced by the protein in feed. Thus soybean meal and cottonseed meal are given rather large feed unit weights (1.65 and 1.35, respectively). This bias results in one region feeding only soybean meal and cottonseed meal as concentrates. Four other regions also feed relatively high proportions of high protein feeds. The price ratios generated by the various solutions indicate that such a result would be prevented by the use of TDN (total digestible nutrients) or net energy rather than feed units.

The TDN weights for soybean meal and cottonseed meal are 0.789 and 0.784, respectively, while the TDN weight for corn is 0.801. This problem was anticipated and calculations were made prior to accepting the feed unit measures in feeding. Existing corn-soybean price ratios indicate that, on a cost basis for "energy," soybean meal would not have been used in excess of minimum protein requirements in the solutions. However, the derived prices for soybean meal are lower relative to observed prices than are the feed-grain prices.

As a third source of bias, feed-grain yields are calculated on the basis of a 10-year average of the proportions of the various feed-grain crops (corn, oats, barley, and grain sorghum). Recent downward trends in the proportion of oats in the feed-grain rotation have resulted in a substantial increase in per-acre yield of feed grain, even without yield trends by individual crops. The measure used results in an upward bias in acreage required for feed grain.

The total numbers of milk cows, beef cows, and cattle placed on feed are quite consistent with 1954 and 1965 requirements (Tables 5.7, 5.8, and 5.9). This result indicates that output coefficients are consistent, on the average, with actual occurrences. Difficulties can arise in reflecting the quantity of a commodity, such as grade 1 beef, back through the weight of the animals slaughtered, dressing percentages, calving percentages, and death losses, to derive the appropriate number of beef cows.

Such difficulties are apparent in the feed-grain–soybean sectors (Tables 5.4 and 5.5). Table 5.4 shows a substantial difference between the 1965 acreage of feed grain and that resulting from solution 1 of the 1965 model. A small part of this difference is accounted for by the use of wheat for feed grain (about one-third of the wheat produced in solution 1 was used for livestock feed). One would also expect the acreage of feed grain generated by solution 1 to be smaller than the actual 1965 acreage, as feed-grain production is more concentrated in regions with higher yields. The fact that the solutions show some substantial geographic shifts in livestock production also accounts for some savings in feed-grain requirements. Such savings are rather significant in the dairy sector. The average grain requirement per unit of milk is substantially reduced in the solutions, compared with the actual figures for 1954 and 1965. This difference results because regions with relatively high milk output per cow account for a greater proportion of total milk production in the programmed solutions.

Estimated 1965 requirements of wheat, feed grain, and soybeans for export are also low relative to actual export of these commodities. Estimated export requirements for solution 1 of the 1965 model are low in relation to actual 1965 exports; the ratio of the estimates used in the model to the preliminary estimates for actual 1965 exports is 0.62 for wheat, 0.46 for feed grain, and 0.60 for soybeans. Correction for these requirements would have required 17.9 percent more wheat production, 12.5 percent more feed-grain production, and 34.3 percent more soybean production in solution 1. Specified output requirements in solution 24 are 22.39 percent greater than in solution 1.

The solutions show cattle-feeding activities of the Corn Belt and other regions east of the Great Plains to be "deferred feeding systems." These systems involve purchasing of calves in the fall, light winter feeding, and summer grazing, followed by grain feeding for an additional gain of approximately 250 pounds. The widespread occurrence of these systems in the solutions implies a large substitution of hay and pasture for grain in the production of grade 1 beef. If the deferred feeding systems were excluded from the model, considerably more grain and soybean production would have been required for the fed-cattle sector. Shadow prices indicate that fed-yearling activities would have been selected if the deferred systems were excluded. Substituting the yearling feeding system for deferred systems would have required about 3.5 percent more total concentrates for livestock and poultry (about 25 percent more for the grade 1 beef sector).

In Table 5.5, soybean acreage shown for solution 1 is only 37 percent of the actual 1965 acreage. Factors explaining the difference between total feed-grain acreage for solution 1 and actual 1965 acreage also apply to the differences in soybean acreage. In addition, errors in protein requirement coefficients may exist, especially for milk cows and hogs. Indicated average protein content in nonforage feeds fed to hogs and milk cows nationally are 10 and 11.5 percent, respectively.

This downward bias in grain production also results in downward biases in the equilibrium prices derived from the solutions. However, feed-grain prices increase by only $0.07 per bushel to $0.78 per bushel (corn equivalent) between solutions 19 ($I_d^{65} = 1.0$) and 24 ($I_d^{65} = 1.2239$), even though specified output is increased by 22.39 percent. Evidently, surplus capacity to meet 1965 demands is sufficiently high so that a much larger output is possible with only a 10 percent increase in programmed equilibrium prices. While correction of some of the biases mentioned would result in slightly higher shadow prices, adjustment for other biases would result in lower shadow prices. Substantially refinements are made in subsequent chapters to overcome the limitations of the data and specific models.

Chapter 6: A Model Incorporating Farm Size and Land Classes

ROGER K. EYVINDSON, EARL O. HEADY,
and UMA K. SRIVASTAVA

The studies reported in previous chapters have assumed that a regional producing unit (representative farm) can represent a collection of farm firms in an inter-regional programming model. Thus the optimal product mix for an area was assumed to be optimal for all farms in that area, and the estimated proportion of available resources to be withdrawn from agricultural production was assumed to be the same for all farms in an area. The simplifying assumption about a single regional producing unit was necessitated because of the computer capacity limitations and lack of data at the time. This assumption is now relaxed in this study.

To partially account for the differences in production efficiencies existing among farms located in the same area, the economic classes of farms defined by the *United States Census of Agriculture*[1] are used to divide the farms in each producing area among three "farm size groups." These farm size groups are the producing units of the current model and a full set of crop and livestock activities is defined for each of these groups. Production by each of the farm size groups included in the current model is limited by land, pasture, labor, and capital constraints. This set of constraints should restrict production more realistically than land constraint alone (used in earlier studies). In addition, the inclusion of these constraints allows the direct determination of the amounts of resources used and left idle by the farms of each size group in the optimal production pattern.

The land constraints used in the current model are similar to those used in the Brokken-Heady model in that (1) these constraints allow the intensive crops (wheat, feed grain, soybeans, cotton, and silage) to be produced only on the land used for those crops in 1965 and on the land idled by government programs in that year, and (2) these constraints allow hay to be produced on the land not used for intensive crop production. However, for the current model, the cropland and

NOTE: For details, see Roger K. Eyvindson, Earl O. Heady, and Uma K. Srivastava, *A Model of Interregional Competition in U.S. Agriculture Incorporating Consuming Regions, Producing Areas, Farm Size Groups and Land Classes*, being published by Iowa State University Press, Ames.

1. U.S. Bureau of Census, *United States Census of Agriculture: 1959*, vol. 1, Counties, parts 1 through 48, 1961.

hay land available to each farm size group are divided among three land-quality classes. Thus three sets of land constraints and three sets of crop production activities are defined for each farm size group. In addition, the model allows the cropland and hay land of each quality class that are not used for crop production to be used for pasture.

In all earlier studies, transportation of products between the producing areas within a single region was implicitly assumed to be costless. This assumption of costless transportation within regions led to somewhat unrealistic results because frequently all the harvested roughage required in a consuming region was produced in a few of the producing areas of that region. To provide a more realistic transportation scheme, the current model includes activities to transport (1) final products (wheat, feed grain, soybeans, cottonseed, grain-fattened beef, nongrain-fattened beef, pork, fluid milk, and manufactured milk) between consuming regions, (2) intermediate products (wheat, feed grain, soybeans, cottonseed, hay, feeder calves, and feeder yearlings)[2] between producing areas located in the same consuming region, and (3) intermediate products between each consuming region and producing areas located outside the boundaries of that region.

The primary objectives of the present study are (1) to determine the optimal regional production pattern for the major crop and livestock of American agriculture (with 1965 as the base year), and (2) to determine from this optimal production pattern those resources which should have been shifted to nonagricultural occupations if the excess capacity problems of the industry were to be overcome. A secondary objective of the study is to determine the effect of the elimination of cotton lint exports on the optimal production pattern for agriculture in 1965. The determination of this second optimal production pattern is useful because cotton lint exports have been declining in recent years, and because this determination illustrates the importance of having a model which allows us to determine how the optimal production pattern will change in response to changes in economic conditions.

NATURE OF THE MODEL

The model used in the present study is an extension of that used by Brokken and Heady. There are a number of similarities between the models used by Brokken and Heady and the present study: (1) both use the same 157 producing areas, (2) both use basically the same consuming regions (one of Brokken and Heady's regions was divided into two regions for the present study), (3) the crop and livestock products are the same for both studies, and (4) both studies define the optimal production pattern as that pattern which minimizes total production and transportation cost. There are, however, some significant differences between the two models: (1) the current model incorporates various farm size groups and land-quality classes as producing units, (2) the current model makes the livestock-

---

2. Wheat, feed grain, soybeans, and cottonseed serve both as final and intermediate products.

producing regions correspond to the crop-producing areas, (3) the current model also minimizes the transportation cost from producing areas within a consuming region to the region center, and (4) the current model also includes the labor and capital constraints in addition to land and pasture constraints. These additions make the current model more realistic as compared to the previous studies.

MATHEMATICAL STRUCTURE OF THE MODEL

To formally identify the interrelations of the activities and constraints, the mathematical model is now presented. It can be seen that the basic notations are the same as used in previous chapters but the subscripts and superscripts have been increased to include the additions mentioned above. The activities which had no cost associated with them in the Brokken-Heady model have been deleted from the objective function and their purpose is served by the accounting rows. To somewhat simplify the notation, once again the producing areas within each consuming region are assumed to be numbered consecutively beginning with one. The notations used are as follows:

Let n be a subscript or superscript denoting the type of product:

$$n = \quad 1 \text{ for wheat}$$
$$n = \quad 2 \text{ for feed grain}$$
$$n = \quad 3 \text{ for soybeans}$$
$$n = \quad 4 \text{ for cottonseed}$$
$$n = \quad 5 \text{ for hay}$$
$$n = \quad 6 \text{ for feeder calves}$$
$$n = \quad 7 \text{ for feeder yearlings}$$
$$n = \quad 8 \text{ for grain-fed beef}$$
$$n = \quad 9 \text{ for other beef}$$
$$n = 10 \text{ for pork}$$
$$n = 11 \text{ for fluid milk}$$
$$n = 12 \text{ for manufactured milk}$$
$$n = 13 \text{ for silage}$$
$$n = 14 \text{ for cotton lint}$$

j subscript or superscript denoting the consuming region, $j = 1, 2, \ldots, 21$
v^j number of producing areas located in consuming region j
k subscript denoting the producing area, $k = 1, 2, \ldots, v^j$
i subscript denoting the farm size group, $i = 1, 2, 3$
m subscript denoting the land-quality class, $m = 1, 2, 3$
q subscript denoting the type of crop activity:[3]

$$q = 1 \text{ for cotton activity}$$
$$q = 2 \text{ for wheat activity}$$

3. Since wild hay activities do not use cropland and hay land, they are considered separately and are not included in this classification.

$q = 3$ for feed-grain activity
$q = 4$ for feed-grain–soybean rotation
$q = 5$ for feed-grain–soybean–silage rotation
$q = 6$ for feed-grain–silage rotation
$q = 7$ for tame hay–silage rotation
$q = 8$ for tame hay activity

p subscript denoting the type of livestock activity:

$p =$ 1 for hog activity
$p =$ 2 for milk cow activity
$p =$ 3 for beef cow activity
$p =$ 4 for yearling production activity
$p =$ 5 for activity in which calves are fattened on the deferred feeding plan
$p =$ 6 for activity in which calves are fattened on the extended silage-feeding plan
$p =$ 7 for activity in which calves are fattened on the silage-feeding plan
$p =$ 8 for activity in which calves are fattened on the no-silage-feeding plan
$p =$ 9 for activity in which yearlings are fattened on the short-fed–feeding plan
$p = 10$ for activity in which yearlings are fattened on the silage-feeding plan
$p = 11$ for activity in which yearlings are fattened on the no-silage–feeding plan

s subscript or superscript denoting the season of the year:

$s = 1$ for crop season
$s = 2$ for noncrop season

e subscript denoting the type of exogenous concentrate, $e = 1, 2, 3, 4$

C_{qmikj} acres of crop activity q produced on farms of size group i in the kth area of region j

W_{ikj} acres of wild hay produced on farms of size group i in the kth area of region j

L_{pikj} production of livestock activity p on farms of size group i in the kth area of region j

$T^{1j}_{nj'k}$ amount of product n transported from consuming region j' to the kth producing area of consuming region j, $n = 1, 2, \ldots, 7$

$T^{2j}_{nkk'}$ amount of product n transported from the kth producing area of region j to the k'th producing area of region j, $n = 1, 2, \ldots, 7$

$T^{3}_{njj'}$ amount of product n transported from consuming region j to consuming region j', $n = 1, 2, 3, 4, 8, 9, \ldots, 12$

B_j amount of grain-fed beef transferred to other beef in consuming region j

M_j amount of fluid milk transferred to manufactured milk in consuming region j

S_j^1 number of feeder calves slaughtered in consuming region j

S_j^2 number of feeder yearlings slaughtered in consuming region j

G_{xkj} amount of grain (oilseed) of type x transferred to the concentrate feed supply of the kth area of region j:

$$x = 1 \text{ for wheat}$$
$$x = 2 \text{ for feed grain}$$
$$x = 3 \text{ for soybeans}$$
$$x = 4 \text{ for cottonseed}$$

G_{kj}^1 amount of hay transferred to the harvested roughage supply of the kth area of region j

E_{ekj} amount of exogenous concentrate of type e used in the kth area of region j

P_{mikj} amount of class m cropland and hay land used for pasture on farms of size group i in the kth area of region j

H_{ikj}^s amount of labor hired during season s by farms of size group i in the kth area of region j

U_{ikj} amount of pasture not on farms rented by farms of size group i in the kth area of region j

X_{nkj} amount of product n transferred from the kth producing area of region j to region j, $n = 1, 2, \ldots, 7$

c_{qmikj}^1 cost of producing one acre of crop activity q on land of quality class m on farms of size group i in the kth area of region j

c_{ikj}^2 cost of producing one acre of wild hay on farms of size group i in the kth area of region j

c_{pikj}^3 cost of producing one unit of livestock activity p on farms of size group i in the kth area of region j

$c_{nj'k}^{4j}$ cost of transporting product n from consuming region j' to the kth producing area of region j

$c_{nkk'}^{5j}$ cost of transporting product n from the kth producing area of region j to the k'th area of region j

$c_{njj'}^6$ cost of transporting product n from consuming region j to consuming region j'

c_{ej}^7 cost of one unit of exogenous concentrate e in consuming region j

c_{mikj}^8 cost of converting one unit of class m cropland and hay land to pasture on farms of size group i in the kth area of consuming region j

c_{skj}^9 cost of hiring one hour of labor during season s in the kth area of region j

c_j^{10} cost of renting one unit of pasture not on farms in consuming region j

r_{qmikj}^n output of product n per acre of crop activity q on land of class m on farms of size group i in the kth area of region j, $n = 1, 2, \ldots, 5, 13, 14$

w_{ikj} hay production per acre of wild hay on farms of size group i in the kth area of region j

o^n_{pikj} output of product n per unit of livestock activity p produced by farms of size group i in the kth area of region j, $n = 6, 7, \ldots, 12$

z^1 other beef produced per feeder calf slaughtered

z^2 other beef produced per feeder yearling slaughtered

g^1_{xkj} protein content per TDN unit of grain (oilseed) x in the kth area of region j:

$$x = 1 \text{ for wheat}$$
$$x = 2 \text{ for feed grain}$$
$$x = 3 \text{ for soybeans}$$
$$x = 4 \text{ for cottonseed}$$

g^2_e protein content of exogenous concentrate e

f^t_{pikj} amount of feed of type t required per unit of livestock activity p produced by farms of size group i in the kth area of region j:

$$t = 1 \text{ for TDN}$$
$$t = 2 \text{ for protein}$$
$$t = 3 \text{ for harvested roughage}$$
$$t = 4 \text{ for pasture}$$

h^1_{qmikj} amount of aftermath pasture made available per acre of crop activity q harvested from land of class m by farms of size group i in the kth area of region j

h^8_{mikj} amount of pasture made available by converting one acre of cropland and hay land of class m to pasture on farms of size group i in the kth area of region j

a_{7mikj} amount of cropland required by one acre of the tame hay–silage activity on land of class m on farms of size group i in the kth area of region j

d^1_{qmikj} crop season labor required per acre of crop activity q produced on class m land by farms of size group i in the kth area of region j

d^2_{ikj} crop season labor required per acre of wild hay produced by farms of size group i in the kth area of region j

d^3_{pikj} crop season labor required per unit of livestock activity p produced by farms of size group i in the kth area of region j

d^8_{mikj} crop season labor required to convert one acre of class m cropland and hay land to pasture on farms of size group i in the kth area of region j

b_{pikj} noncrop season labor required per unit of livestock activity p produced on farms of size group i in the kth area of region j

y^1_{qmikj} capital required per acre of crop activity q produced on class m land by farms of size group i in the kth area of region j

y^2_{ikj} capital required per acre of wild hay produced by farms of size group i in the kth area of region j

y^3_{pikj} capital required per unit of livestock activity p produced by farms of size group i in the kth area of region j

y^8_{mikj} capital required to convert one acre of class m cropland and hay land to pasture on farms of size group i in the kth area of region j

y^9_{sikj} capital required for farms of size group i in the kth area of region j to hire one hour of labor during season s

y^{10}_{ikj} capital required for farms of size group i in the kth area of region j to rent one unit of pasture not on farms

Q national cotton lint requirement

K_e national supply of exogenous concentrate e

R_{nj} export and domestic consumption requirements of product n in consuming region j, $n = 1, 2, \ldots, 5, 8, 9, \ldots, 12$

N_j pasture not on farms available in consuming region j

F^1_{kj} total digestible nutrients (TDN) required for the exogenous livestock product in the kth area of region j

F^2_{kj} protein required for the exogenous livestock produced in the kth area of region j

F^3_{kj} net harvested roughage required for the exogenous livestock produced in the kth area of region j (i.e., the total roughage required for exogenous livestock less the production of harvested roughage not included in the model)

A^1_{mikj} cropland and hay land of quality class m available on farms of size group i in the kth area of region j

A^2_{mikj} cropland of quality class m available on farms of size group i in the kth area of region j

A^3_{ikj} cotton land available on farms of size group i in the kth area of region j

A^4_{ikj} wild hay land available on farms of size group i in the kth area of region j

V_{ikj} amount of pasture available on farms of size group i in the kth area of region j

D^s_{ikj} family labor available to farms of size group i in the kth area of region j during season s

Y_{ikj} capital available to farms of size group i in the kth area of region j

Z Total production cost, transfer cost, transportation cost, and purchase cost

Given the notations just defined, our objective is to find the combination of production, transportation, and transfer activities that will minimize the total cost (national cost of production and interregional transportation). More specifically the objective function is

$$\min Z = \sum_{j=1}^{21} \sum_{k=1}^{v^j} \sum_{i=1}^{3} \sum_{m=1}^{3} \sum_{q=1}^{8} c^1_{qmikj} C_{qmikj}$$

$$+ \sum_{j=1}^{21} \sum_{k=1}^{v^j} \sum_{i=1}^{3} c^2_{ikj} W_{ikj} + \sum_{j=1}^{21} \sum_{k=1}^{v^j} \sum_{i=1}^{3} \sum_{p=1}^{11} c^3_{pikj} L_{pikj}$$

$$+ \sum_{j=1}^{21} \sum_{k=1}^{v^j} \sum_{\substack{k'=1 \\ k' \neq k}}^{v^j} \sum_{n=1}^{7} c_{nkk'}^{5j} \, T_{nkk'}^{2j}$$

$$+ \sum_{j=1}^{21} \sum_{\substack{j'=1 \\ j' \neq j}}^{21} \left[\sum_{n=1}^{4} c_{njj'}^{6} \, T_{njj'}^{3} + \sum_{n=8}^{12} c_{njj'}^{6} \, T_{njj'}^{3} \right]$$

$$+ \sum_{j=1}^{21} \sum_{k=1}^{v^j} \sum_{e=1}^{4} c_{ej}^{7} \, E_{ekj} + \sum_{j=1}^{21} \sum_{k=1}^{v^j} \sum_{i=1}^{3} \sum_{m=1}^{3} c_{mikj}^{8} \, P_{mikj}$$

$$+ \sum_{j=1}^{21} \sum_{k=1}^{v^j} \sum_{i=1}^{3} \sum_{s=1}^{2} c_{skj}^{9} \, H_{ikj}^{s} + \sum_{j=1}^{21} \sum_{k=1}^{v^j} \sum_{i=1}^{3} c_{j}^{10} \, U_{ikj} \qquad (6.1)$$

subject to the following restraints:

(1) national cotton lint requirements

$$\sum_{j=1}^{21} \sum_{k=1}^{v^j} \sum_{i=1}^{3} \sum_{m=1}^{3} r_{1mikj}^{14} \, C_{1mikj} \geqslant Q \qquad (6.2)$$

(2) national exogenous concentrate restraints

$$\sum_{j=1}^{21} \sum_{k=1}^{v^j} E_{ekj} = K_e \qquad (6.3)$$

(3) region j wheat requirements

$$\sum_{k=1}^{v^j} X_{1kj} - \sum_{\substack{j'=1 \\ j' \neq j}}^{21} \sum_{k=1}^{v^j} T_{1jk}^{1j'} - \sum_{\substack{j'=1 \\ j' \neq j}}^{21} T_{1jj'}^{3} + \sum_{\substack{j'=1 \\ j' \neq j}}^{21} T_{1j'j}^{3} \geqslant R_{1j} \qquad (6.4)$$

(4) region j feed-grain requirements

$$\sum_{k=1}^{v^j} X_{2kj} - \sum_{\substack{j'=1 \\ j' \neq j}}^{21} \sum_{k=1}^{v^j} T_{2jk}^{1j'} - \sum_{\substack{j'=1 \\ j' \neq j}}^{21} T_{2jj'}^{3} + \sum_{\substack{j'=1 \\ j' \neq j}}^{21} T_{2j'j}^{3} \geqslant R_{2j} \qquad (6.5)$$

(5) region j soybean requirements

$$\sum_{k=1}^{v^j} X_{3kj} - \sum_{\substack{j'=1 \\ j' \neq j}}^{21} \sum_{k=1}^{v^j} T_{3jk}^{1j'} - \sum_{\substack{j'=1 \\ j' \neq j}}^{21} T_{3jj'}^{3} + \sum_{\substack{j'=1 \\ j' \neq j}}^{21} T_{3j'j}^{3} \geqslant R_{3j} \qquad (6.6)$$

(6) region j cottonseed requirements

$$\sum_{k=1}^{v^j} X_{4kj} - \sum_{\substack{j'=1 \\ j' \neq j}}^{21} \sum_{k=1}^{v^j} T_{4jk}^{1j'} - \sum_{\substack{j'=1 \\ j' \neq j}}^{21} T_{4jj'}^{3} + \sum_{\substack{j'=1 \\ j' \neq j}}^{21} T_{4j'j}^{3} \geqslant R_{4j} \qquad (6.7)$$

(7) region j hay requirements

$$-\sum_{k=1}^{v^j} X_{5kj} + \sum_{\substack{j'=1 \\ j' \neq j}}^{21} \sum_{k=1}^{v^j} T^{1j'}_{5jk} \leqslant -R_{5j} \tag{6.8}$$

(8) region j feeder-calf account

$$-\sum_{k=1}^{v^j} X_{6kj} + \sum_{\substack{j'=1 \\ j' \neq j}}^{21} \sum_{k=1}^{v^j} T^{1j'}_{6jk} + S^1_j \leqslant 0 \tag{6.9}$$

(9) region j feeder-yearling account

$$\sum_{k=1}^{v^j} X_{7kj} + \sum_{\substack{j'=1 \\ j' \neq j}}^{21} \sum_{k=1}^{v^j} T^{1j'}_{7jk} + S^2_j \leqslant 0 \tag{6.10}$$

(10) region j grain-fed beef requirements

$$\sum_{k=1}^{v^j} \sum_{i=1}^{3} \sum_{p=5}^{11} o^8_{pikj} L_{pikj} - \sum_{\substack{j'=1 \\ j' \neq j}}^{21} T^3_{8jj'} + \sum_{\substack{j'=1 \\ j' \neq j}}^{21} T^3_{8j'j} - B_j \geqslant R_{8j} \tag{6.11}$$

(11) region j other beef requirements

$$\sum_{k=1}^{v^j} \sum_{i=1}^{3} \sum_{p=2}^{3} o^9_{pikj} L_{pikj} - \sum_{\substack{j'=1 \\ j' \neq j}}^{21} T^3_{9jj'} + \sum_{\substack{j'=1 \\ j' \neq j}}^{21} T^3_{9j'j} + B_j + \sum_{u=1}^{2} z^u S^u_j \geqslant R_{9j} \tag{6.12}$$

(12) region j pork requirements

$$\sum_{k=1}^{v^j} \sum_{i=1}^{3} o^{10}_{1ikj} L_{1ikj} - \sum_{\substack{j'=1 \\ j' \neq j}}^{21} T^3_{10jj'} + \sum_{\substack{j'=1 \\ j' \neq j}}^{21} T^3_{10j'j} \geqslant R_{10j} \tag{6.13}$$

(13) region j fluid milk requirements

$$\sum_{k=1}^{v^j} \sum_{i=1}^{3} o^{11}_{2ikj} L_{2ikj} - \sum_{\substack{j'=1 \\ j' \neq j}}^{21} T^3_{11jj'} + \sum_{\substack{j'=1 \\ j' \neq j}}^{21} T^3_{11j'j} - M_j \geqslant R_{11j} \tag{6.14}$$

(14) region j manufactured milk requirements

$$-\sum_{\substack{j'\neq 1 \\ j' \neq j}}^{21} T^3_{12jj'} + \sum_{\substack{j'=1 \\ j' \neq j}}^{21} T^3_{12j'j} + M_j \geqslant R_{12j} \tag{6.15}$$

(15) region j pasture not on farms constraint

$$\sum_{k=1}^{v^j} \sum_{i=1}^{3} U_{ikj} \leqslant N_j \tag{6.16}$$

(16) wheat account for the kth area of region j

$$-\sum_{i=1}^{3} \sum_{m=1}^{3} r^1_{2mikj} C_{2mikj} + G_{1kj} + X_{1kj} + \sum_{\substack{k'=1 \\ k' \neq k}}^{v^j} T^{2j}_{1kk'} - \sum_{\substack{k'=1 \\ k' \neq k}}^{v^j} T^{2j}_{1k'k} - \sum_{\substack{j'=1 \\ j' \neq j}}^{21} T^{1j}_{1j'k} \leqslant 0$$
$$\tag{6.17}$$

(17) feed-grain account for the kth area of region j

$$-\sum_{i=1}^{3} \sum_{m=1}^{3} \sum_{q=3}^{6} r^2_{qmikj} C_{qmikj} + G_{2kj} + X_{2kj} + \sum_{\substack{k'=1 \\ k' \neq k}}^{v^j} T^{2j}_{2kk'} - \sum_{\substack{k'=1 \\ k' \neq k}}^{v^j} T^{2j}_{2k'k} - \sum_{\substack{j'=1 \\ j' \neq j}}^{21} T^{1j}_{2j'k} \leqslant 0$$
$$\tag{6.18}$$

(18) soybean account for the kth area of region j

$$-\sum_{i=1}^{3} \sum_{m=1}^{3} \sum_{q=4}^{5} r^3_{qmikj} C_{qmikj} + G_{3kj} + X_{3kj} \sum_{\substack{k'=1 \\ k' \neq k}}^{v^j} T^{2j}_{3kk'} - \sum_{\substack{k'=1 \\ k' \neq k}}^{v^j} T^{2j}_{3k'k} - \sum_{\substack{j'=1 \\ j' \neq j}}^{21} T^{1j}_{3j'k} \leqslant 0$$
$$\tag{6.19}$$

(19) cottonseed account for the kth area of region j

$$-\sum_{i=1}^{3} \sum_{m=1}^{3} r^4_{1mikj} C_{1mikj} + G_{4kj} + X_{4kj} + \sum_{\substack{k'=1 \\ k' \neq k}}^{v^j} T^{2j}_{4kk'} - \sum_{\substack{k'=1 \\ k' \neq k}}^{v^j} T^{2j}_{4k'k} - \sum_{\substack{j'=1 \\ j' \neq j}}^{21} T^{1j}_{4j'k} \leqslant 0$$
$$\tag{6.20}$$

(20) hay account for the kth area of region j

$$-\sum_{i=1}^{3} \sum_{m=1}^{3} \sum_{q=7}^{8} r^5_{qmikj} C_{qmikj} - \sum_{i=1}^{3} w_{ikj} W_{ikj} + G^1_{kj} + X_{5kj}$$

$$+ \sum_{\substack{k'=1 \\ k' \neq k}}^{v^j} T^{2j}_{5kk'} - \sum_{\substack{k'=1 \\ k' \neq k}}^{v^j} T^{2j}_{5k'k} - \sum_{\substack{j'=1 \\ j' \neq j}}^{21} T^{1j}_{5j'k} \leqslant 0 \tag{6.21}$$

(21) feeder-calf account for the kth area of region j

$$-\sum_{i=1}^{3} \sum_{p=2}^{3} o^6_{pikj} L_{pikj} + \sum_{i=1}^{3} \sum_{p=4}^{8} L_{pikj} + X_{6kj}$$

$$+ \sum_{\substack{k'=1 \\ k'\neq k}}^{v^j} T^{2j}_{6kk'} - \sum_{\substack{k'=1 \\ k'\neq k}}^{v^j} T^{2j}_{6k'k} - \sum_{\substack{j'=1 \\ j'\neq j}}^{21} T^{1j}_{6j'k} \leqslant 0 \qquad (6.22)$$

(22) yearling-feeder account for the kth area of region j

$$- \sum_{i=1}^{3} o^7_{4ikj} L_{4ikj} + \sum_{i=1}^{3} \sum_{p=9}^{11} L_{pikj} + X_{7kj} + \sum_{\substack{k'=1 \\ k'\neq k}}^{v^j} T^{2j}_{7kk'} - \sum_{\substack{k'=1 \\ k'\neq k}}^{v^j} T^{2j}_{7k'k} - \sum_{\substack{j'=1 \\ j'\neq j}}^{21} T^{1j}_{7j'k} \leqslant 0$$

$$(6.23)$$

(23) TDN restraint for the kth area of region j

$$- \sum_{i=1}^{3} \sum_{p=1}^{11} f^1_{pikj} L_{pikj} + \sum_{x=1}^{4} G_{xkj} + \sum_{e=1}^{4} E_{ekj} \geqslant F^1_{kj} \qquad (6.24)$$

(24) protein restraint for the kth area of region j

$$- \sum_{i=1}^{3} \sum_{p=1}^{11} f^2_{pikj} L_{pikj} + \sum_{x=1}^{4} g^1_{xkj} G_{xkj} + \sum_{e=1}^{4} g^2_e E_{ekj} \geqslant F^2_{kj} \qquad (6.25)$$

(25) roughage restraint for the kth area of region j

$$\sum_{i=1}^{3} \sum_{m=1}^{3} \sum_{q=5}^{7} r^{13}_{qmikj} C_{qmikj} - \sum_{i=1}^{3} \sum_{p=2}^{11} f^3_{pikj} L_{pikj} + G^1_{kj} \geqslant F^3_{kj} \qquad (6.26)$$

(26) cropland and hay land restraint for class m land on farms of size group i in the kth area of region j

$$\sum_{q=1}^{8} C_{qmikj} + P_{mikj} \leqslant A^1_{mikj} \qquad (6.27)$$

(27) cropland restraint for class m land on farms of size group i in the kth area of region j

$$\sum_{q=1}^{6} C_{qmikj} + a_{7mikj} \leqslant A^2_{mikj} \qquad (6.28)$$

(28) pasture restraint for farms of size group i in the kth area of region j

$$- \sum_{m=1}^{3} \sum_{q=1}^{8} h^1_{qmikj} C_{qmikj} - \sum_{m=1}^{3} h^8_{mikj} P_{mikj} - U_{ikj} + \sum_{p=1}^{11} f^4_{pikj} L_{pikj} \leqslant V_{ikj} \qquad (6.29)$$

(29) cotton land restraint for farms of size group i in the kth area of region j

$$\sum_{m=1}^{3} C_{1mikj} \leqslant A^3_{ikj} \qquad (6.30)$$

(30) wild hay land restraint for farms of size group i in the kth area of region j

$$W_{ikj} \leqslant A^4_{ikj} \tag{6.31}$$

(31) crop season labor restraint for farms of size group i in the kth area of region j

$$\sum_{m=1}^{3} \sum_{q=1}^{8} d^1_{qmikj} C_{qmikj} + d^2_{ikj} W_{ikj} + \sum_{p=1}^{11} d^3_{pikj} L_{pikj} + \sum_{m=1}^{3} d^8_{mikj} P_{mikj} - H^1_{ikj} \leqslant D^1_{ikj} \tag{6.32}$$

(32) noncrop season labor restraint for farms of size group i in the kth area of region j

$$\sum_{p=1}^{11} b_{pikj} L_{pikj} - H^2_{ikj} \leqslant D^2_{ikj} \tag{6.33}$$

(33) capital restraint for farms of size group i in the kth area of region j

$$\sum_{m=1}^{3} \sum_{q=1}^{8} y^1_{qmikj} C_{qmikj} + y^2_{ikj} W_{ikj} + \sum_{p=1}^{11} y^3_{pikj} L_{pikj} + \sum_{m=1}^{3} y^8_{mikj} P_{mikj}$$

$$+ \sum_{s=1}^{2} y^9_{sikj} H^s_{ikj} + y^{10}_{ikj} U_{ikj} \leqslant Y_{ikj} \tag{6.34}$$

(34) the nonnegativity restraints

$$C_{qmikj},\ W_{ikj},\ L_{pikj},\ T^{1j}_{nj'k},\ T^{2j}_{nkk'},\ T^3_{njj'},\ B_j,\ M_j,\ S^1_j,\ S^2_j,\ G_{xkj},\ G^1_{kj},$$

$$E_{ekj},\ P_{mikj},\ H^s_{ikj},\ U_{ikj},\ X_{nkj} \geqslant 0 \tag{6.35}$$

PARAMETERS OF THE MODEL AND THEIR DETERMINATION

The mathematical model presented above involves the linear programming matrix of the dimension of 6,838 by 41,677 elements. Although a large number of matrix elements are equal to zero, estimates were required for nearly 204,000 nonzero input-output coefficients and about 5,700 nonzero restraint levels. A great deal of human effort and a substantial amount of computer time were expended in the data collection process to generate the required coefficients and constraint levels for the model. The data collection process was complicated not only by the volume of the data required but also by the fact that many of the data required were not readily available. Also, the data that were available were often not in the form required for this study. Thus it was not possible to directly use the published data. Therefore, new methods and procedures had to be developed to estimate the necessary data from the data that were available. Considerable use was made of data generated and procedures devised by the studies reported in earlier chapters.

Fig. 6.1. Geographic location of the consuming regions.

PRODUCING AREAS AND CONSUMING REGIONS

This study uses the crop-producing areas delineated by Brokken and Heady (Figure 5.1). These crop-producing areas are also the livestock-producing regions. Also, this study uses the 20 consuming regions defined by Brokken and Heady (Figure 5.2), except for the consuming region 12. The number of producing areas in Brokken's region 12 exceeded the maximum allowable by the computer program used. Therefore, Brokken's consuming region 12 was divided into two regions: region 12 (Texas) and region 21 (Oklahoma). The boundaries of these consuming regions are shown in Figure 6.1.

DEFINITION OF FARM SIZE GROUPS

Land area is normally used as a measure of farm size, but this unit is not satisfactory for identifying the size of many types of farms. A farm size grouping based on land area can result in the combination of relatively small cash-grain farms with farms which have relatively large livestock operations. To overcome this difficulty, the farm size classification used in this study is based on the economic classes of farms defined by the U.S. Bureau of the Census. This classification is based on gross sales as given below.

1. Farm size group 1 includes all farms of economic class I (those with gross sales of $40,000 or more).

2. Farm size group 2 includes all farms of economic classes II and III (those with gross sales of $10,000 to $39,999).
3. Farm size group 3 includes all farms of economic classes IV and V (those with gross sales of $2,500 to $9,999).

Four economic classes of farms defined by the census are not included in the farm size group definitions: (1) class VI (commercial farms with gross sales of less than $2,500), (2) part-retirement (these farms also have gross sales of less than $2,500), (3) part-time (again farms with gross sales of less than $2,500), and (4) abnormal (institutional farms and Indian reservations). One or more additional farm size group could have been defined for these farms, although the addition of even one size group would have increased the number of rows in the problem by 25 percent.[4] However, the usefulness of the model would not be greatly increased by including these farms. These farms accounted for only 3.7 percent of the total value of the farm products sold in 1964 so that any change in their production levels would have little effect on the rest of agriculture.[5] Also, production costs on the very small farms (which make up 99.8 percent of the farms excluded) are relatively high, so it is unlikely that any solution of the model would attribute any significant production to a size group composed of these farms.

INPUT-OUTPUT COEFFICIENTS FOR CROP ACTIVITIES

For each crop activity, estimates were needed of the production cost, labor requirements, crop yield, and amount of aftermath pasture made available. The capital requirements for crop activities are equal to the cost of production so that separate estimates of the capital coefficients were not needed. Input-output coefficients were estimated for each of the seven crops (i.e., cotton, wheat, feed grain, soybeans, tame hay, silage, and wild hay) considered in the study. Crop activities are based on a harvested acre rather than on a planted acre because the yield estimates published by the USDA are on a harvested acre basis.

For every crop that could be produced in an area, activities were included for each class of land on each farm size group. In estimating the coefficients for the feed-grain activity, coefficient estimates were first made for each of the feed-grain crops—corn, oats, barley, and grain sorghum. Feed-grain acre proportions were assumed to be the same for all farm size groups and land classes in an area. These proportions were then used as weights in obtaining the coefficients for the feed-grain activity from the coefficients for the individual feed-grain crops. The coefficients for the silage activity were estimated from coefficients for corn and sorghum silage. The coefficients for the rotation activities (e.g., the feed-grain–soybean rotations) were obtained by weighting the coefficients for the crops included in the rotation by the rotation weights. The rotation weight for a crop is defined as the proportion of total harvested acres of a given rotation that is made up by that crop.

4. The number of rows is the size factor which is most significant in determining the feasibility, difficulty, and time requirements of computations for linear programming problems.
5. U.S. Bureau of Census, *United States Census of Agriculture: 1964*, vol. 2, General Report, 1968.

PRODUCTION COSTS FOR CROP ACTIVITIES

Crop production cost estimates were made for each of the farm size groups defined for each area. Production cost for a crop activity includes machinery and equipment, fertilizer, pesticides, irrigation water, and miscellaneous costs. For all crops except hay and silage, the seed requirements are subtracted from the yield coefficients so that the cost of seed is not included in the estimates of cost of these crops. Since the acreage on a typical farm in all the three farm size groups was used in all the calculations of per-acre costs, the procedure to estimate cropland per farm is described first.

CROPLAND PER FARM

Estimates were made of the acres of cropland available on the typical farm of each size group in each area. These estimates were used in determining the size and type of machines used on these typical farms and in specifying cropland use for these farms. The number of farms in each size group was then obtained from the census,[6] and the acres of cropland per farm were calculated for each size group.

The *United States Census of Agriculture* classifies the commercial farm in each state into twelve farm types, i.e., cash-grain farms, tobacco farms, poultry farms, etc. In many states, the farms included in a few of these type classifications produce a large proportion of the state production of the crops included in this study. In areas located in states where this is true, the procedure illustrated by Equation 6.36 was used to estimate the amount of cropland available on the typical farm of each size group in state j:

$$C_{ik} = V_{ik} \cdot \frac{W_{ij}^I}{W_{ij}^T} \tag{6.36}$$

$$i = 1, \ldots, \ldots 3$$
$$k = 1, \ldots, \ldots h$$

where h denotes the number of producing areas in state j

       C_{ik} denotes the acres of cropland on the typical farm of size group i in area k (area k is located in state j)

       V_{ik} denotes the acres of cropland per farm of size group i in the area k

       W_{ij}^I denotes the acres of cropland per farm for farms in state j that are of size group i and that are classified as one of the types of farms that produce important amounts of the crops included in the present study

       W_{ij}^T denotes the acres of cropland per farm for farms of size group i in state j

In areas where the associated state data showed that the adjustment illustrated

6. U.S. Bureau of Census, *United States Census of Agriculture: 1959*, vol. 1, Counties, parts 1-48, 1961.

by Equation 6.36 was not necessary, the acres of cropland on the typical farm of each size group were assumed to equal the acres available on the average farm of that group (i.e., $C_{ik} = V_{ik}$).

MACHINERY AND EQUIPMENT COSTS

In making estimates of machine costs for the crop activities, a sequence of harvest and preharvest field operations was first established for each crop grown by each farm size group. Next, the complement of machinery and equipment available on the typical farm of each size group was specified, and the cost per unit of use was estimated for each machine. The cost of using a given machine on a particular crop is then equal to the cost per unit of use for that machine multiplied by the units of use on that crop. The costs of machines used in preharvest operations were summed to obtain the preharvest machine cost per planted acre. Similarly, the costs of machines used in harvest operations were summed to determine the harvest machine cost per harvested acre. Finally, Equation 6.37 was used to estimate total machinery and equipment costs per acre. In Equation 6.37 the preharvest machine costs are converted from a planted acre basis to a harvested acre basis.

$$M_{nik} = \frac{M^P_{nik}}{P_k} + M^H_{nik} \tag{6.37}$$

$$n = 1, \ldots, \ldots 7$$
$$i = 1, \ldots, \ldots 3$$
$$k = 1, \ldots, \ldots 157$$

where M_{nik} denotes the total machinery and equipment cost per harvested acre for crop n on farms of size group i in area k

M^P_{nik} denotes the preharvest machine cost per planted acre for crop n on farms of size group i in area k

M^H_{nik} denotes the harvest machine cost per harvested acre for crop n on farms of size group i in-area k

P_k denotes the proportion of planted acres in area k that are harvested

The sequence of field operations for a crop grown on irrigated land is quite different from the sequence of operations needed for the same crop grown on dryland. Therefore, in areas where irrigation is used, separate machine cost estimates were made for production on irrigated land and on dryland. The data from the *United States Census of Agriculture*[7] were used to calculate the proportion of total acreage of each crop grown in an area that was irrigated. These proportions were then used to obtain a weighted average of the machine costs on dryland and on irrigated land. For this weighting, the proportions calculated for an area were assumed to be applicable to all farm size groups in that area. Estimates of the machine cost per acre of cultivated summer fallow were made for farm size groups in areas where this practice is used.

7. Ibid.

The machine cost per unit of use includes the cost of depreciation, interest, shelter, insurance, taxes, repairs, lubrication, and, for powered machines, the cost of fuel and oil. Equations 6.38 through 6.42 were used in estimating these elements of machine cost per unit of use:

$$D_{mik} = \frac{P_{mj} - 0.1\, P_{mj}}{L_m} \cdot \frac{1}{U_{mik}} \tag{6.38}$$

$$I_{mik} = \frac{P_{mj} + 0.1\, P_{mj}}{2} \cdot R_e \cdot \frac{1}{U_{mik}} \tag{6.39}$$

$$S_{mik} = \frac{0.025\, P_{mj}}{U_{mik}} \tag{6.40}$$

$$G_{mik} = \frac{P_{mj}\, H_m}{U_{mik}} \tag{6.41}$$

$$F_{mik} = (f_m\, c_j)\, 1.15 \tag{6.42}$$

$$m = 1, \ldots, \ldots M$$
$$i = 1, \ldots, \ldots 3$$
$$k = 1, \ldots, \ldots h$$

where D_{mik} denotes the depreciation cost per unit of use of machine m on the typical farm of size group i in area k

P_{mj} 1965 purchase price of machine m in state j (area k is located in state j)

L_m total life of machine m in years

U_{mik} annual use of machine m on the typical farm of size group i in area k

I_{mik} interest cost per unit of use of machine m on the typical farm of size group i in area k

R_e rate of interest on farm machinery loans in USDA region e (area k is located in region e)[8]

S_{mik} cost of shelter, insurance, and taxes per unit of use of machine m on the typical farm of size group i in area k

0.025   proportion of total purchase price of a machine that must be spent annually for shelter, insurance, and taxes

G_{mik} cost of repairs and lubrication per unit of use of machine m on the typical farm of size group i in area k

H_m proportion of the purchase price of machine m that must be expended annually for repairs and lubrication

F_{mik} cost of fuel and oil per unit of use of machine m on the typical farm of size group i in area k

f_m amount of fuel required per unit of use of machine m

8. The ten regions defined by the USDA are the Northeast, Appalachian, Southeast, Lake states, Corn Belt, Delta states, Northern Plains, Southern Plains, Mountain, and Pacific regions.

c_j price of fuel used by machine m in state j

h number of producing areas in state j

1.15   assumed relationship between total fuel and oil cost and the cost of fuel

In some cases the estimated annual use of a machine was so small that per-unit cost was unrealistically high. For these machines the cost of custom hiring was substituted for the cost per unit of use. If a farm size group supplies custom service it must also provide the labor required to operate the machine, and in addition, the cost per unit of use of a machine will be lowered if it is used in custom operations. Therefore, it is important to determine which farm size groups provide custom service. In reality, the custom service required by the typical farm of a size group could be supplied by any of the farm size groups in the area. A completely realistic treatment of custom operation would, therefore, greatly complicate and enlarge the model. Thus the following simplifying assumptions were used: (1) if the typical farm of a size group required custom service, it would be supplied by a farm of the same size group, and (2) the annual utilization of machines used in custom operations would be such that the cost per unit of use was just equal to the normal custom charge. Under these assumptions, the labor required for custom operations would be charged to the size group on which the operation was performed.

Special procedures were needed to estimate the annual machine cost associated with the establishment of tame hay stands. In areas where part of the hay acreage is irrigated, estimates were made of the machine cost required for establishing tame hay both on dryland and on irrigated land. The establishment costs for dryland and irrigated hay were then added to the other machine costs of hay production on dryland and irrigated land, respectively. After estimating establishment costs for each type of hay, Equation 6.43 was used to determine the annual cost of establishing tame hay stands on the typical farm of each size group in state j.

$$e_{ik} = \sum_{m=1}^{7} \frac{e'_{mik}\, v_{mk}}{Y_{mj}} \tag{6.43}$$

$i = 1, \ldots, \ldots 3$

$k = 1, \ldots, \ldots h$

$m = 1$ for alfalfa, 2 for clover-timothy, 3 for lespedeza, 4 for grain hay, 5 for soybean hay, 6 for cowpea hay, 7 for other hay

where h denotes the number of producing regions in state j

e_{ik} machine cost of establishing tame hay stands on the typical farm of size group i in area k

e'_{mik} machine cost of establishing hay of type m on the typical farm of size group i in area k

v_{mk} proportion of total hay acres in area k that is made up by hay of type m[9]

9. Ray F. Brokken, Dept. of Economics, Iowa State Univ., Ames, "Percentage distribution of types of hay within producing areas," private communication, 1967.

Y_{mj} years of stand for hay of type m in state j (area k is located in state j)[10]

The per-acre cost of using a particular machine on a given crop was found by multiplying the cost per unit of use for that machine on that crop. The units of use are hours for tractors, miles for trucks, and acres for all other machines. The preharvest (harvest) machine cost for each crop was then calculated by adding the cost of all machines used in the preharvest (harvest) operations required for that crop. Next, Equation 6.37 was used to combine harvest and preharvest machine costs for each crop. In Equation 6.37, the proportion of planted acres that are harvested is equal to 1.0 for irrigated crops and is equal to p_k for dryland crops.

COSTS OF FERTILIZER, PESTICIDE, AND IRRIGATION WATER

Ibach and Adams[11] report 1964 fertilizer applications for each crop grown in state parts[12] of each of 99 agricultural subregions. A correspondence was established between the producing areas defined for the present study and these state parts. Fertilizer prices were assumed to be the same in all producing areas within each of these ten regions, and fertilizer cost for each crop grown in an area was then calculated directly from estimated prices and application rates. To maintain consistency with yield estimates, fertilizer costs were assumed to be the same for all farm size groups located in the same area. In addition, the same fertilizer costs were used for all three land classes.

Per-acre pesticide costs were estimated for each relevant crop in each state from unpublished data collected for the 1964 pesticide uses survey conducted by the USDA.[13] The pesticide cost estimates for each state were then assumed to be applicable to all areas located in that state. In the absence of necessary data, pesticide costs also were assumed to be the same on all farm size groups and on all classes of land located in the same producing area.

Irrigation water costs per acre for each crop in an area were derived from Brokken's estimates,[14] and water costs were assumed to be the same on all farm size groups and on all classes of land in an area. In estimating water costs for individual crops, it was assumed that these costs were proportional to the amount of water used. This assumption is supported by information obtained from Hughes et al.[15] Hence, data from various state bulletins were used to develop a judgment estimate of the ratio of per acre of water requirements to per acre of cropland irrigated. This ratio was estimated to be (1) 1.0 for corn grain, corn

10. Ibid.
11. D. B. Ibach and J. R. Adams, *Fertilizer Use in the United States, by Crops and Areas, 1964 Estimates*, USDA, ERS and SRS Stat. Bull. 408, 1967.
12. A state part of an agricultural subregion is that part of the region located in a particular state.
13. USDA, ERS, and SRS data collected for the 1964 pesticide user survey, private communication, 1967.
14. Ray F. Brokken, "Interregional Competition in Livestock and Crop Production in the United States: An Application of Spatial Linear Programming," Ph.D. diss., Iowa State Univ. Library, Ames, 1965.
15. William F. Hughes, A. C. Magee, Don Jones, and Earnest L. Thaxton, Jr., *Economics of Water Management for Cotton and Grain Sorghum Production, High Plains*, Tex. Agr. Exp. Sta. Bull. 931, 1959.

silage, cotton, and soybeans; (2) 0.8 for grain sorghum and sorghum silage; (3) 0.7 for wheat, oats, and barley; (4) 1.4 for tame hay; and (5) 0.5 for wild hay. Next, Brokken's estimate of the water cost per acre of cropland irrigated in an area was multiplied by these ratios to determine the water cost per irrigated acre for each crop grown in the area. The cost per irrigated acre for each crop was then multiplied by the proportion of harvested acres of that crop in the area that is irrigated to obtain the water cost per harvested acre.

MISCELLANEOUS COSTS

Miscellaneous costs for crops include the cost of lime, of seed for tame hay and silage, of ginning cotton, of shelling corn, and of drying corn and grain sorghum. Drying costs for crops other than corn and grain sorghum were not estimated because only very small proportions of these crops are dried. Data limitations made it necessary to assume that all miscellaneous costs would be the same on all farm size groups of an area. Since separate yield estimates were made for each class of land, separate estimates of those miscellaneous costs dependent on yield could have been made for each land class. However, the same miscellaneous costs were used for all classes of land in an area because (1) data were not available to estimate differences in other cost components—some of which would be expected to offset differences in those miscellaneous costs dependent on yield; and (2) the cost of those factors for which separate estimates could be made is small relative to total costs.

CROP YIELDS

For all crops except wild hay, yields were estimated for each land class in each area. Since wild hay can be produced only on wild hay land, yields by land class were not needed for this crop. The yields to be estimated were normal yields for 1965, that is, the yields that would have been attained in that year if average weather conditions had prevailed. In estimating crop yields, normal yields in 1965 were first estimated for each state, and normal yields in each producing area were then determined from the yield estimates for the state in which the area is located. Finally, for crops other than wild hay, yields for each land-quality class were estimated from the area yields. Crop yields on a given land class were assumed to be the same for all farm size groups in a producing area. This assumption was necessary because of two reasons: (1) lack of complete data of production and acreage by economic class of farm for all the included crops in each state; and (2) the observed differences in crop yields between farm size groups located in the same state are probably due, at least in part, to differences in the average quality of land available. Also, factors other than land quality will cause yield differences between farm size groups. However, it was not possible to determine the effects of these factors. The effects of two important yield factors were eliminated by assuming the same fertilizer use and the same pesticide use on all farm size groups in an area.

Normal 1965 crop yields in each state were estimated from the 1948-65 yield trends. State crop yields were related to the area crop yields. The area crop yields were calculated in the form of gross yields. Net yields were then calculated for all crops except hay and silage by subtracting seed requirements from gross yields. In determining gross area yields, estimates were first obtained for

R_{nk} which denotes the ratio of the yield of crop n in area k to the yield of crop n in the state in which area k is located

Estimates of R_{nk} for crops other than hay and silage were obtained from Whittlesey.[16] The procedure used by Whittlesey in estimating values for R_{nk} for area k located in state j is illustrated by Equation 6.44:

$$R_{nk} = \overline{Y}_{nk} / \overline{Y}_{nj} \tag{6.44}$$

$$n = 1, \ldots, \ldots 7$$
$$k = 1, \ldots, \ldots h$$

where R_{nk} is as just defined

$\overline{Y}_{nk}$ average yield for crop n in area k during the period 1950–60

$\overline{Y}_{nj}$ average yield for crop n in state j during the period 1950–60 (area k is located in state j)

h number of producing areas in state j

The estimates of R_{nk} used for hay and silage were obtained from work done by Brokken.[17] Brokken's procedure for estimating R_{nk} was identical to that used by Whittlesey except that Brokken used a 1949–54 rather than a 1950–60 time period. Equation 6.45 was then used to estimate gross crop yields in each producing area:

$$\hat{Y}_{nk} = R_{nk} \ \hat{Y}_{nj}^{1965} \tag{6.45}$$

$$n = 1, \ldots, \ldots 7$$
$$k = 1, \ldots, \ldots 157$$

where $\hat{Y}_{nk}$ is normal gross yield for crop n in area k in 1965

R_{nk} as previously defined

$\hat{Y}_{nj}^{t}$ estimated yield of crop n in state j for year t

Since cotton yield includes both cotton lint and cottonseed, special procedures were needed to estimate yields for this crop. Area yields for cotton lint were estimated using the procedure just described, and cottonseed yields were then derived from the yields for cotton lint using a procedure developed by Whittlesey. For each state in which cotton is grown, Whittlesey[18] used Equation 6.46 to calculate the ratio R_j^c:

---

16. Norman K. Whittlesey, Dept. of Economics, Iowa State Univ., Ames, "Ratios of area yields to state yields for crops other than hay and silage," private communication, 1967.

17. Ray F. Brokken, Dept. of Economics, Iowa State Univ., Ames, "Ratios of area yields to state yields for hay and silage," private communication, 1967.

18. Norman K. Whittlesey, Dept. of Economics, Iowa State Univ., Ames, "Ratio of cottonseed yield to cotton lint yield in each state," private communication, 1967.

$$R_j^c = C_j^S / C_j^L \qquad (6.46)$$

$$j = 1, \ldots, \ldots z$$

where R_j^c denotes the ratio of cottonseed yield to cotton lint yield in state j

       C_j^S 1956–60 average yield of cottonseed in state j

       C_j^L 1956–60 average yield of cotton lint in state j

       z number of states where cotton is grown

The cottonseed yield for an area located in state j was then determined by multiplying the cotton lint yield by R_j^c.

CROP YIELDS BY LAND CLASS

The procedure used in estimating crop yields for each land-quality class from the area yields was taken from Whittlesey.[19] Whittlesey developed equations in 6.47 that relate yields by land classes to the distribution of land between quality classes. The definition of cropland used in Equation 6.47 is adapted from the *Conservation Needs Inventory*[20] and includes cropland used for hay and pasture as well as cropland used for intensive crops.

$$I_{1k} = 121.95 - 0.217S_{1k}$$

$$I_{2k} = 84.01 + 0.227S_{2k} \qquad (6.47)$$

$$I_{3k} = 58.75 + 0.564S_{3k}$$

$$k = 1, \ldots, \ldots 157$$

where I_{mk} denotes the index of crop yield on the mth class of land to the mean yield for area k

      S_{mk} percent of total cropland in area k that is represented by land class m

The acres of cropland of each land class in each area were obtained by summing our county data from the *Conservation Needs Inventory*, and values for S_{mk} were then calculated for each producing area from these average data.

YIELD UNITS IN THE LINEAR PROGRAM

The final step necessary in the estimation of crop yields was the conversion of yields to the units used in the linear programming model. The yields of wheat, all feed grains, cottonseed, and soybeans were converted to hundredweight of total digestible nutrients (TDN). The TDN content of each of these crops is given in Table 6.1. Silage yields were expressed in tons of hay equivalent. Brokken[21] es-

19. Norman K. Whittlesey, "Linear Programming Models Applied to Interregional Competition and Policy Choices for U.S. Agriculture," Ph.D. diss., Iowa State Univ. Library, Ames, 1964.

20. USDA, Conservation Needs Inventory Committee, *Basic Statistics of the National Inventory of Soil and Water Conservation Needs*, Stat. Bull. 317, 1962.

21. Brokken, "Interregional Competition in Livestock and Crop Production."

timated that a ton of silage is equivalent to 0.36 tons of hay. We have adapted this estimate. Hay yields were expressed in tons, and cotton lint yields were expressed in hundredweight.

AFTERMATH PASTURE

After a crop has been harvested, some pasture is available from the crop residue. This pasture and the winter grazing possible on winter grains were defined as aftermath pasture. The only aftermath pasture data that could be obtained were Jennings's estimates[22] of the total amount of this type of pasture available by state in 1950. Jennings's estimates were expressed in cropland pasture acre equivalents—the amount of pasture available on one acre of cropland pasture. Equation 6.48 was used to estimate the animal unit months (AUM) of aftermath pasture available per acre of cropland harvested in each area located in state *j*. Since no other aftermath pasture data were obtainable, the amount of aftermath pasture available from all crops grown on all land classes in an area was assumed to be the same as estimated from Equation 6.48.

$$A_k = \frac{P_j}{H_j} Y_{1k}$$ (6.48)

$$k = 1, \ldots, \ldots h$$

where A_k denotes the AUM of aftermath pasture available per acre of cropland harvested in area *k*

       P_j Jennings's estimate of the cropland pasture acre equivalents of aftermath pasture available in state *j*, 1950

       H_j acres of corn, wheat, oats, barley, sorghum, soybeans, cotton, and tame hay harvested in state *j*, 1950

       Y_{1k} 1965 cropland pasture yield (AUM) for area *k*

       h   number of producing areas in state *j*

INPUT-OUTPUT COEFFICIENTS FOR LIVESTOCK ACTIVITIES

Dairy, beef-cow–calf, hog, yearling, and feeder-cattle activities were defined for each farm size group in each producing area. Seven types of feeder-cattle activities were set up for the study—four feeding plans for calves and three feeding plans for yearlings. The calves needed for the feeder-cattle activities were produced by the beef-cow–calf and dairy activities. The feeder animals needed for the yearling-feeding plans were supplied by yearling-producing activities in which a calf (400 pounds) is raised to a yearling (675 pounds) on a high roughage ration. The dairy, beef-cow–calf, and hog activities used in the study were defined to include the raising of all necessary replacement livestock. For the hog activities, replacement livestock includes not only replacement breeding animals but also replacement feeder pigs. The separate activities were not included for feeder-

22. R. D. Jennings, *Relative Use of Feeds for Livestock Including Pasture by States*, USDA, ARS, Stat. Bull. 153, 1955.

pig production and for hog finishing. Hogs were raised from birth to market weight in the one hog activity defined for each farm size group.

By definition, the replacement livestock necessary for the dairy, beef-cow–calf, and hog activities are raised on the farms of the size group on which the activity is carried out. Feeder calves and yearlings can be transferred between farm size groups located in the same area and, through transportation activities, between farm size groups located in different areas.

For each livestock activity it was necessary to determine output coefficients, the cost of production, capital requirements, feed requirements, and labor requirements. Some livestock activities produce only one type of output while others produce both primary and secondary outputs. Milk is the primary output of dairy activities, but these activities also produce feeder calves, veal calves, and culled animals. The veal calves and culled animals are used for other beef (nongrain-fed beef). The output from beef-cow–calf activities includes feeder calves and other beef from culled animals. Pork is, of course, produced by the hog activities, and yearling feeders are produced by the yearling activities. The grain-fed beef requirements specified for the model are satisfied by the feeder-cattle activities. The cost of production for a livestock activity includes (1) depreciation, interest, insurance, and taxes on buildings and equipment; (2) interest, insurance, taxes, and, where applicable, depreciation on the investment in livestock; (3) the cost of veterinarian and medicine; (4) the cost of salt and minerals; (5) the cost of supplies; (6) breeding expense; (7) the cost of power and fuel; (8) marketing cost; and (9) the cost of pasture fertilization.

The cost of production for livestock activities does not include the cost of feed since the cost of endogenous feed is included in the costs of crop production, and the cost of exogenous feed is included in the cost coefficients for the exogenous feed purchase activities. The capital requirements for a livestock activity were defined to equal the cost of production for that activity plus the value of the feed used by that activity.

Three types of feed requirements were specified for each livestock activity: (1) concentrate requirements, (2) harvested roughage requirements, and (3) pasture requirements. Concentrate requirements are represented by requirements for TDN and by protein requirements. Harvested roughage requirements are expressed in tons of hay equivalents, and pasture requirements are expressed in animal unit months (AUM).

Annual labor requirements were first estimated for each livestock activity. These annual requirements were then divided between labor requirements in the crop season and labor requirements in the noncrop season. Labor requirements for livestock activities should have included, as did those for crop activities, both direct and indirect labor requirements. The labor coefficients for livestock activities were developed from labor requirement estimates published by Hecht.[23] Since Hecht's estimates include only direct labor requirements, the labor requirements for livestock are somewhat underestimated. Indirect labor requirements for livestock activities include the time spent on buildings and fence maintenance, on

23. Reuben W. Hecht, *Labor Used to Produce Livestock, Estimates by States, 1959*, USDA, ERS, Stat. Bull. 336, 1963.

repairing the machines and equipment used in livestock enterprises, etc. The amount of labor used in these tasks is likely to be small relative to the total labor requirements for livestock so that labor requirements for livestock activities were not seriously underestimated.

The types of livestock activities included in the present study are identical to those defined for the study done by Brokken.[24] Since Brokken's estimates were the best set of livestock input-output coefficients available, many of the livestock coefficients used in this study were derived from his estimates. Most of the procedures used in estimating additional coefficients were also derived from Brokken. A few important additional procedures are described below. These are the procedures used to (1) estimate the value of feed used, (2) divide labor requirements between the crop season and the noncrop season, and (3) estimate the cost of pasture fertilization. These three estimation procedures were used for all types of livestock activities.

VALUE OF THE FEED USED BY LIVESTOCK ACTIVITIES

The value of the feed required for each livestock activity was estimated from the concentrate and roughage requirements defined for that activity. For this estimation, the concentrate requirements were expressed in hundredweight of TDN and protein. The roughage requirements were expressed in tons of hay equivalent. In estimating the value of the feed used by livestock activities, concentrate requirements were assumed to be satisfied by feed grain, soybean oil meal, and cottonseed oil meal. The most commonly fed feed grain and the most commonly fed oil meal in each area were determined by examining total production data for that area. Then, the amounts of feed grain and oil meal used by each livestock activity defined for a farm size group were determined by solving Equation set 6.49 for X_1 and X_2:

$$a_{11} X_1 + a_{12} X_2 = b_1$$
$$a_{21} X_1 + a_{22} X_2 = b_2$$

(6.49)

where X_1 denotes the bushels of feed grain used by the activity

         X_2 hundredweight of oil meal used by the activity

         a_{11} hundredweight of TDN in a bushel of the feed grain most commonly fed in the area in which the farm size group is located

         a_{21} hundredweight of protein in a bushel of the feed grain most commonly fed in the area in which the farm size group is located

         a_{12} hundredweight of TDN in a hundredweight of the oil meal most commonly fed in the area in which the farm size group is located

         a_{22} hundredweight of protein in a hundredweight of the oil meal most commonly fed in the area

         b_1 hundredweight of TDN required by the livestock activity

         b_2 hundredweight of protein required by the livestock activity

24. Brokken, "Interregional Competition in Livestock and Crop Production."

Occasionally, the solution to Equation set 6.49 resulted in a negative value for X_2. This means that requirements of protein are so low relative to TDN requirements that protein requirements will be exceeded even when only feed grain is fed. Since feed grain is a cheaper source of TDN than oil meal, X_2 was set equal to zero and X_1 was set equal to b_1/a_{11} whenever the solution to Equation set 6.49 included a negative value for X_2. Feed prices were assumed to be the same for all farm size groups in a state, and the total value of the feed used by a livestock activity was calculated as

$$V = X_1 P_F + X_2 P_0 + RP_R \tag{6.50}$$

where V denotes the value of the feed used by the livestock activity

X_1 and X_2 are defined as for Equation set 6.49

P_F price of a bushel of the appropriate feed grain in the state in which the farm size group is located

P_0 price of a hundredweight of the appropriate oil meal in the state in which the farm size group is located

R roughage requirement for the livestock activity, expressed in tons of hay equivalent

P_R price of a ton of hay in the state in which the farm size group is located

DIVISION OF LABOR REQUIREMENTS BETWEEN SEASONS

The total labor requirements for each livestock activity had to be divided into crop and noncrop season labor requirements. The distribution of labor requirements by months was obtained for each of five types of livestock production: (1) dairy cattle, (2) beef cows, (3) hogs, (4) yearlings, and (5) feeder cattle. There was sufficient data available to allow the definition of a percentage distribution of labor requirements by months for each of these five types of livestock in each of four regions of the United States: (1) the Northeast, (2) the Midwest, (3) the South, and (4) the West. To differentiate these regions from consuming regions they will be referred to as "labor regions." The dates on which the crop season begins and ends in each producing area were selected by examining the usual planting and harvesting dates for crops. These dates were obtained from Burkhead et al.[25]   Equation 6.51 was used to determine the percentage of crop season labor requirements to total labor requirements for each type of livestock in each area located in state j:

$$p_{nk}^c = \left[\frac{D_B - (A - 1)}{D_B}\right] P_{Bnj} + \sum_{m=B}^{E-1} P_{mnj} + \left[\frac{Y}{D_E} P_{Enj}\right] \tag{6.51}$$

25. C. E. Burkhead, J. W. Kirkbride, and L. A. Losleben, *Field and Seed Crops, Usual Planting and Harvesting Dates, by States, in Principal Producing Areas*, USDA, SRS, Crop Rptg. Bd. Agr. Handbook 283, Mar. 1965.

$n = 1, \ldots, \ldots 5$
$k = 1, \ldots, \ldots h$
$m = 1$ for January, 2 for February, . . ., 12 for December
$B = 1$ for January, 2 for February, . . ., 12 for December
$E = 1$ for January, 2 for February, . . ., 12 for December

where P_{nk}^c denotes the percent of total labor required for livestock of type n in area k that is required in the crop season

       D_m number of days in month m

       B month in which the crop season begins in area k

       A day of month B on which the crop season begins in area k

       P_{mnj} percent of total labor requirements for livestock of type n in labor region j that are required during month m (area k is located in labor region j)

       E month in which the crop season ends in area k

       Y day of month E on which the crop season ends in area k

       h total number of producing areas located in state j

Finally, the equations in 6.52 were used to divide the total labor requirements for livestock activities between the crop season and the noncrop season:

$$C_{nik} = T_{nik} \, P_{nk}^c \qquad\qquad (6.52)$$

$$N_{nik} = T_{nik} \, (1.0 - P_{nk}^c)$$

$$n = 1, \ldots, \ldots 5$$
$$i = 1, \ldots, \ldots 3$$
$$k = 1, \ldots, \ldots 157$$

where C_{nik} denotes the crop season labor requirements for a livestock activity of type n on farm size group i farms in area k

       N_{nik} noncrop season labor requirement for a livestock activity of type n on farm size group i farms in area k

       T_{nik} total labor requirements for a livestock activity of type n on farm size group i farms in area k

       P_{nk}^c is as defined for Equation 6.51

COST OF PASTURE FERTILIZATION

The cost of fertilizing the pasture used by a livestock activity is included in the cost of production for that activity. The fertilizer cost per animal unit month (AUM) of pasture in each area was calculated as follows:

$$C_k = \frac{M_k + (A_k P_k)}{Y_{3k}} \qquad\qquad (6.53)$$

$$k = 1, \ldots, \ldots 157$$

where C_k denotes the pasture fertilization cost per AUM in area k

M_k per-acre cost of the fertilizer materials applied to permanent pasture in area k

A_k per-acre cost of custom fertilizer application in area k

P_k percent of total permanent pasture in area k that was fertilized in 1964

Y_{3k} 1965 yield of unimproved permanent pasture in area k

The per-acre cost of fertilizer materials in each area was estimated from the data and the procedures used in the studies of Ibach and Adams.[26] The per-acre cost of custom fertilizer application in each area was taken from the studies of Brown and Hagen,[27] Caton et al.,[28] Hedges,[29] Jeffrey et al.,[30] and McCutcheon and Burlingame.[31] The yield of permanent pasture in each area was determined in the estimation of pasture restraints. Equation 6.54 was next used to estimate the pasture fertilization cost for each livestock activity defined for a farm size group:

$$F_{nik} = R_{nik} \, C_k \tag{6.54}$$

$$n = 1, \ldots, \ldots 5$$
$$i = 1, \ldots, \ldots 3$$
$$k = 1, \ldots, \ldots 157$$

where F_{nik} denotes the pasture fertilization cost for livestock activity n on farms of size group i in area k

R_{nik} AUM of pasture required by livestock activity n on farms of size group i in area k

C_k is as defined for Equation 6.53

26. D. B. Ibach, *Fertilizer Use in the United States, Its Economic Position and Outlook*, USDA, ERS, Agr. Econ. Report 92, 1966; D. B. Ibach and J. R. Adams, *Fertilizer Use in the United States, by Crops and Areas, 1964 Estimates*, USDA, ERS, SRS, Stat. Bull. 408, 1967.

27. Thomas G. Brown and Albert R. Hagen, *1960 Missouri Custom Rates*, Univ. College of Agr. Ext. Serv. Folder 92, 1961.

28. Douglas D. Caton, Trimble R. Hedges, and Neill W. Schaller, "Inputs and Costs for Producing Field Crops" (a Statistical Supplement to "Farm Adjustments and Earnings under 1955 Cotton Acreage Allotments"), San Joaquin Valley Eastside Cotton Farms, 1953–55, Calif. Agr. Exp. Sta., Giannini Foundation of Agri. Econ. Mimeographed Report 203, 1958; "Inputs and Costs for Producing Field Crops" (a Statistical Supplement to "Farm Adjustments and Earnings under 1955 Cotton Acreage Allotments"), Central San Joaquin Valley Cotton Farms, 1953–55, Calif. Agr. Exp. Sta., Giannini Foundation of Agr. Econ. Mimeographed Report 209, 1958; "Inputs and Costs for Producing Field Crops" (a Statistical Supplement to "Farm Adjustments and Earnings under 1955 Cotton Acreage Allotments"), San Joaquin Valley Westside Cotton Farms, 1953–55, Calif. Agr. Exp. Sta., Giannini Foundation of Agri. Econ. Mimeographed Report 212, 1958.

29. Trimble R. Hedges, "Inputs and Costs for Producing Field Crops" (a Statistical Supplement to "Farm Adjustments and Earnings under 1955 Cotton Acreage Allotments"), Upper San Joaquin Valley Cotton Farms, 1953–55, Calif. Agr. Exp. Sta., Giannini Foundation of Agr. Econ. Mimeographed Report 192, 1956.

30. D. B. Jeffrey, Cecil D. Maynard, and Odell L. Walker, "Oklahoma Custom Rates, 1960," Okla. State Univ. Ext. Serv. Leaflet L-50, 1960.

31. O. D. McCutcheon and Burt B. Burlingame, "Sample Costs per Acre to Produce Cotton—Solid Planting, Univ. Calif. Agr. Ext. Serv., Kings County Cost Analysis Work Sheet, 1965.

TRANSPORTATION COSTS

Activities are included in the model to transport products from each producing area to areas located in the same consuming region, from each consuming region to areas located outside the boundaries of that region, and from region to region. The procedures used to estimate transportation costs for a particular product was identical for all three types of transportation activities. For all products, transportation costs were determined from regression equations relating cost and distance. Regression techniques were used to fit several forms of equations relating transportation cost and distance to the data obtained from the Interstate Commerce Commission publication *Carload Waybill Statistics.*[32] The following form gave the best fit and was therefore selected for the estimation of transportation costs.[33]

$$C = aD^b \qquad (6.55)$$

where C denotes the transportation cost in cents per ton-mile
$\quad D$ short line rail miles
$\quad a$ and b are the regression coefficients

Whenever an activity was needed to transport feed grain between two points, the costs of transporting corn, oats, barley, and grain sorghum were first calculated. Then the transportation cost for feed grain was determined by weighting the costs for these four crops by the proportions of total feed-grain production in the exporting region (area) that was made up by each crop. The region proportions were calculated from state acreage data and the 1965 state yield estimates. Similarly, the area weights were derived from acreage data and the 1965 area yield estimates. The transportation costs for meat, feeder cattle, fluid milk, and manufactured milk were directly taken from Brokken.[34]

INPUT-OUTPUT COEFFICIENTS FOR THE TRANSFER, PURCHASE, AND HIRE ACTIVITIES

Activities were included in the model to transfer wheat, feed grain, soybeans, and cottonseed to the concentrate feed supply of each producing area. An activity to transfer crop g from area k' to the feed supply of area k reduces the supply of crop g in area k' by one TDN unit, increases the TDN supply of area k by one unit, and increases the protein supply of area k by the amount of protein in one TDN unit of crop g. The protein content of each of the grains and oilseeds used as concentrate feed was derived from Brokken's estimates.[35]

32. Interstate Commerce Commission, *Carload Waybill Statistics, 1963, Mileage Block Distribution, Traffic and Revenue by Commodity Class, Territorial Movement, and Type of Rate, Products of Agriculture*, Interstate Commerce Comm., Bur. of Econ. Statement MB-1, 1966.

33. The following equation was used to estimate transportation cost for hay:

$$C_R = 15.0 + 0.1D$$

where C_R denotes the cost of transporting hay in cents per cwt, and
$\quad D$ denotes the short line rail miles.

For details, see Irvine F. Fellows, *Forage Procurement and Use by the California Dairy Industry and Selected Dairy Farms*, Calif. Agr. Exp. Sta. Res. Report 262, 1963.

34. Brokken, "Interregional Competition in Livestock and Crop Production."

35. Ibid.

The model included activities which allowed the feed supply of each area to be augmented through the purchase of exogenous concentrates. Four types of exogenous feeds could be purchased: (1) oil meals other than soybean oil meal and cottonseed oil meal (F_1), (2) animal proteins (F_2), (3) grain proteins (F_3), and (4) other exogenous concentrates (F_4). Each unit of exogenous feed purchased increases the TDN supply of the purchasing area by one unit and increases the protein supply of that area by the amount of protein contained in a TDN unit of the feed.

Activities were included which allowed nongrain fattened beef to be obtained by slaughtering feeder calves and feeder yearlings. A calf slaughter and a yearling slaughter activity were defined for each consuming region. Each calf slaughtered yielded 221.6 pounds of beef, and 368.2 pounds of beef were produced from each yearling slaughtered.[36]

Pasture-renting activities were included so that the farms of each farm size group in a consuming region could use the off-farm pasture available in that region. An estimate of the cost of renting pasture not on farms was obtained for each consuming region, and pasture rent was then assumed to be the same for all farm size groups in a region. The capital requirements for pasture-renting activities are equal to the amount of rent paid.

The model allows each farm size group to use land of each quality class for pasture. For each of the land-to-pasture transfer activities, estimates were needed of the cost, labor, and pasture yield coefficients. Capital coefficients for the land-to-pasture transfer activities were equal to the cost coefficients. We assumed, as we did for crop activities, that on a given farm size group the cost and labor coefficients would be the same for all land-quality classes and that pasture yield on a given land-quality class would be the same for all farm size groups in an area. The cost of transferring an acre of land to pasture was set equal to the annual cost of establishing a stand of tame hay.

The model was set up so that the labor supply of each farm size group could be increased by hiring crop season labor, noncrop season labor, or both. Cost and capital coefficients for the labor-hiring activities of each size group were set equal to the wage rate for hired labor in the state in which the farm size group is located. Average hourly wage rates in 1965 for crop season and noncrop season hired workers in each state were obtained from the Crop Reporting Board publication.[37]

FARM SIZE GROUP RESTRAINTS

Production of each farm size group was constrained by the amount of resources available in 1965 to the farms of that group. Farm size group restraints were defined for seven types of resources: (1) cropland, (2) cropland and hay land, (3) cotton land, (4) wild hay land, (5) pasture, (6) labor, and (7) capital. The procedures used in setting up of labor and capital restraints are briefly described below.

36. Ray F. Brokken, Dept. of Economics, Iowa State Univ., Ames, "Data on beef obtained by slaughtering calves and yearlings," private communication, 1968.
37. USDA, SRS, Crop Rptg. Bd., *Farm Labor*, Publication La (1-65-12-65), 1965.

FAMILY LABOR

For each farm size group, family labor restraints were first estimated for 1959. Family labor restraints were then determined by assuming that, for each group of farms, the amount of family labor available per farm would be the same in 1965 as in 1959. Equation 6.56 was used to determine the family labor restraints (net family labor available) for each farm size group in area k in 1959.

$$L_{mik}^{1959} = O_{ik}^m + U_{ik}^m - W_{ik}^m \tag{6.56}$$

$m = 1$ for the crop season, and 2 for the noncrop season
$i = 1, \ldots, \ldots 3$

where L_{mik}^{1959} denotes the season m family labor restraint in 1959 for farm size group i in area k

O_{ik}^m hours of operator labor available for farm work on farms of size group i in area k during season m

U_{ik}^m hours of family labor other than operator labor available to farms of size group i in area k during season m

W_{ik}^m amount of family labor required for exogenous crops and livestock on farms of size group i in area k during the season m

CAPITAL RESTRAINTS

The capital restraint for each farm size group was defined as the expenditures incurred in 1965 by the farms of that group for the production of the crops and livestock considered in the study. These expenditures include not only outlays for inputs that were consumed in 1965 but also the depreciation and interest for inputs (other than land) which had a life of more than one year. Specifically, the capital restraints include

1. Current farm operating expenses including expenditures for (a) feed, (b) seed, (c) fertilizer and lime, (d) repairs and operation (including fuel and lubrication) of machinery, equipment, and buildings, (e) hired labor, and (f) miscellaneous items (including interest on nonreal-estate debt).
2. Depreciation and other consumption of the investment in buildings, machinery, and equipment.
3. The value of the feed used on the farm on which it was grown.
4. Expenditures for the purchase of hogs and cattle (other than feeder cattle).
5. Interest charges on the investment in farm service buildings.
6. Interest on the equity in nonreal-estate investment.

PRODUCTION AREA CONSTRAINTS

Minimum feed requirements and feeder-cattle imports were included in the model. Although hired labor restraints were not defined for the model, the amount of hired labor availability in each producing area was calculated so that these amounts could be compared with the hired labor use specified in the optimal solution. Feed requirements for each type of exogenous livestock produced in an area were determined by multiplying estimates of the feed required per unit by the amount of production in 1965. Feed requirements per unit of production were estimated for each type of exogenous livestock in each state. The estimates for a state were then used for all producing areas located in that state.

All feeder cattle imported to the United States originate either in Mexico or in Canada. But it was not possible to identify the actual ports of entry. We have assumed that (1) all feeder cattle imported from Mexico would be shipped through area 130 in southern Texas, and (2) all feeder cattle imported from Canada would be shipped through area 61 in eastern North Dakota. Feeder-cattle imports in all other producing areas were, therefore, set equal to zero. Since the available data did not differentiate feeder-cattle imports from cattle imported for immediate slaughter, it was assumed that all imported cattle weighing between 200 and 700 pounds that were not to be used for breeding would be used for feeder cattle. The normal U.S. imports of feeder cattle in 1965 were assumed to equal the average imports in the years 1961 to 1965.

In making estimates, the amount of hired labor available in each area in 1959 was first determined, and estimates for 1965 were then obtained by adjusting the 1959 estimates for changes in the number of hired workers. This is expressed as follows:

$$L_{mk}^{1965} = L_{mk}^{1959} \ (V_{mj}^{1965}/V_{mj}^{1959}) \tag{6.57}$$

$$m = 1 \text{ for the crop season,}$$
$$2 \text{ for the noncrop season}$$
$$k = 1, \ldots, \ldots h$$

where L_{mk}^{t} denotes the hired labor available in area k during season m of year t

V_{mj}^{t} average number of hired workers employed in state j (in which area k is located) during season m of year t

h number of producing areas in state j

In using Equation 6.57 we have assumed that any change in the amount of hired labor available in the 1959–65 period is due to changes in the total number of hired workers. Thus we have implicitly assumed that (1) the distribution of total workers between regular and seasonal workers was unchanged in the 1959–65 period, and (2) the hours of labor supplied per worker were unchanged in this period. These last two assumptions are supported by data in USDA bulletins.[38]

CONSUMING REGION CONSTRAINTS

Two types of restraints had to be estimated for each consuming region: the supply of pasture not on farms had to be determined, and minimum consumption requirements had to be specified for (1) grain-fed beef, (2) other beef, (3) pork, (4) fluid milk, (5) manufactured milk, (6) wheat, (7) feed grain, (8) soybeans, (9) cottonseed, and (10) hay. Consumption requirements for each product were defined to include the amount of that product used for food, the amount used by industry, and the net foreign exports.

38. USDA, ERS, *The Hired Farm Working Force of 1959*, Agr. Info. Bull. 238, 1961; *The Hired Farm Working Force of 1966*, Agr. Eco. 120, 1967; USDA, *Farm Labor*, SRS, Publication La 1 (3-63), 1963, and La 1 (1-65-12-65), 1965.

NATIONAL RESTRAINTS

National restraints include minimum requirements of cotton lint and maximum supplies of exogenous concentrate feeds. Cotton lint requirements were set equal to the actual disappearance in 1965. The cotton lint restraint for solution 1 includes both domestic and net export requirements while the cotton lint restraints for solution 2 include only domestic requirements. These requirements were equal to 12.3 million bales for solution 1 and 9.5 million bales for solution 2. Estimates of the supply of each of these feeds were obtained from Brokken.[39]

EMPIRICAL RESULTS

Two optimal solutions were obtained for the model set up in this study. The models and data used for the two solutions are identical except that for the first solution (solution 1) cotton lint requirements include both domestic and export requirements while for the second solution (solution 2) cotton lint requirements include only domestic requirements. These solutions to the model provide production plans for each of the 471 farm size groups. This involves a large amount of numeric results from each of the two solutions. In view of the space limitations, we will present only aggregate results and some broader geographic aspects of these results.

AGGREGATE RESULTS

In this section, national totals for the crop and livestock production and resource use specified in solution 1 are presented. Also, the distribution of national totals among farm size groups is given. Wherever it was possible these figures are compared with the actual figures for 1965 (the base year for the study).

TOTAL CROP ACREAGE

For each crop considered in the study, the acreage produced in solution 1 and the actual acreage in 1965 are given in Table 6.2. The solution 1 and 1965 acreages are not, however, exactly comparable because the solution 1 acreages are based on the feed requirements for the 1965 calendar year plus the consumption requirements for the crop year beginning in 1965, while the production obtained from the acreage harvested in 1965 is equal to the amount used for feed in the crop year beginning in 1965 plus the consumption requirements in that crop year plus the increase in stocks that occurred in that crop year. In addition, the wheat and feed-grain export requirements in solution 1 are equal to the estimated normal exports for that year rather than the actual exports. The relationships between the solution 1 and 1965 acreages for wheat, feed grain, soybeans, and silage are approximately what would be expected, given the differences in the use of crops for feed. Feed-grain, soybean, and silage acreages in solution 1 are sub-

39. Brokken, "Interregional Competition in Livestock and Crop Production."

stantially below those for 1965, and wheat acreage is higher in solution 1 than in 1965.

The small difference between the amount of hay used in solution 1 and the amount used in 1965 does not warrant the large difference between the hay acreages for these two situations. This large difference occurs because most tame hay production in solution 1 takes place on high quality land (65 percent on class 1 land and 31 percent on class 2 land), and as a result the average tame hay yield in solution 1 is 2.43 tons per acre while the average yield in 1965 was only 2.01 tons per acre.[40]

The difference between the cotton acreage for solution 1 and the actual acreage in 1965 is explained by two factors: (1) nearly all cotton production in solution 1 takes place on class 1 land (the average cotton lint yield for solution 1 is 664 pounds per acre versus an average yield of 527 pounds per acre in 1965)[41] and (2) the cotton lint carry-over increased by 2.6 million bales during the 1965 crop year.[42] Solution 1 production is equal to consumption in the 1965 crop year.

TOTAL LIVESTOCK PRODUCTION

The production of livestock specified for the United States in solution 1 and the actual 1965 production of livestock are presented in Table 6.3. The number of milk cows specified in solution 1 is considerably less than the actual number in 1965. This occurs because in solution 1 milk cow production is concentrated more on large farms than it is in reality (Table 6.4). Since milk production per cow is greater on large farms than on small farms, this shift means that the same amount of milk can be obtained with a smaller number of cows.

The feeder-cattle production specified in solution 1 is higher than the actual production in 1965. This difference is apparently a result of allowing grain-fed beef to be transferred to other beef if sufficient nongrain-fattened beef is not available as a by-product to the production of beef and milk cows. In solution 1, 29.36 million hundredweight of beef is so transferred. Since the feeder cattle produced in solution 1 (calves fed on the deferred plan and calves fed on the silage plan) produce about 6.15 hundredweight of beef per animal, the beef from approximately 4.77 million feeder cattle was transferred to the other beef supply. Thus about 19.11 million feeder cattle were used for grain-fed beef in solution 1, and this figure is very close to the actual number of cattle fattened in 1965.

The relatively small number of beef cows produced in solution 1 is apparently also a result of the transfer of grain-fed beef to other beef. In explaining this relationship, we first note that in 1965 about 32.16 million calves, heifers, and steers were slaughtered in the United States, of which perhaps 1.02 million were culled replacement heifers (assuming a 20 percent replacement rate for cows and a 10 percent culling rate for replacement heifers). Thus approximately 11.83 million calves, heifers, and steers were slaughtered in 1965 that were neither grain-

40. USDA, *Agricultural Statistics, 1967.*
41. Ibid.
42. Ibid.

fattened nor culled replacement heifers. The only comparable cattle slaughtered in solution 1 are the approximately 2.26 million veal calves produced by milk cows (each of the milk cows produced in solution 1 a yield of about 0.15 veal calf) and the 4.77 million feeder cattle used for other beef. The numbers of cattle used to supplement the nongrain-fed beef requirements are low in solution 1 relative to the actual numbers in 1965 because the weight per animal is higher (i.e., 7.79 million of the 11.83 million animals slaughtered in 1965 were calves[43] and these calves produced only 131 pounds of beef per animal).[44] To complete the explanation, we note that the smaller numbers of cattle slaughtered for other beef means that fewer beef cows will be required to produce these cattle. About 7.4 million beef cows would be required to produce 4.8 million calves since each cow produces approximately 0.65 calf. Note that the model did allow the slaughter of feeder calves and yearlings for other beef so that the sources of other beef in solution 1 could have been approximately the same as in 1965. Costs, however, are apparently lower if these feeder animals are fattened before slaughter.

DISTRIBUTION OF PRODUCTION BETWEEN FARM SIZE GROUPS

The distribution between farm size groups of the solution 1 production of each of the crops and of each of the types of livestock considered in the study is presented in Table 6.5. The farms of size group 1 produce nearly 96 percent of the feeder cattle and 50 percent of the milk cows produced in solution 1. This specialization leaves relatively few resources available for the production of beef cows and hogs on these farms so that much of the hog and beef cow production is carried out on farms of size groups 2 and 3.

Although feed and labor requirements for hogs were estimated to increase as farm size decreases, costs (excluding feed and labor costs) were estimated to decrease as farm size decreases. This combination of coefficients apparently resulted in a comparative advantage in hog production for size group 3 farms since the percentage of total hog production found on size group 3 farms is higher than the analogous percentages for the other types of livestock.

A comparison of the percentage distribution of crops between farm size groups and the percentage distribution of land between groups indicates the comparative advantages of different sizes in crop production. Suppose that x percent of total cropland and hay land available in the United States is available on farms of size group i. If the farms of size group i produced more than x percent of the total production of the crop, this would indicate a comparative advantage in production of that crop by the farms of size group i. However, the comparative advantages and disadvantages indicated between farm size groups at the national level may at least partially be due to the geographic distribution of farms of different sizes.

Twenty percent of the cropland and hay land and 28 percent of the wild hay land available in the United States are found on the farms of size group 1. Thus,

43. Ibid.
44. USDA, ERS, *Livestock and Meat Statistics, Supplement for 1966*, Stat. Bull. 333, 1966 Supplement, 1967.

using the criterion just described and the data in Table 6.5, we conclude, that farms of size group 1 have a decided comparative advantage in cotton production, a slight comparative advantage in the production of soybeans and wild hay, and a slight comparative disadvantage in wheat production.

Farms of size group 3 control 29 percent of the cropland and hay land in the United States and 30 percent of the wild hay land. From the data in Table 6.5, we conclude that farms of size group 3 have a comparative advantage in tame hay production and a comparative disadvantage in the production of all other crops. The advantage of size group 3 farms in tame hay production likely occurs because these farms frequently custom hire part or all of the operations necessary for hay harvest. Except for harvest operations, most of the field operations for crops other than hay are performed with owned machines on farms of size group 3, and the small acreages on these farms often result in relatively high costs for these operations. Thus production costs for crops other than hay are frequently significantly higher on farms of size group 3 than on the larger farms of size groups 1 and 2.

In view of the argument presented in the preceding paragraph, it may seem inconsistent for farms of size group 3 to have a comparative advantage in tame hay production and a comparative disadvantage in wild hay production. However, an examination of the figures for producing areas in which significant amounts of wild hay are produced shows that in many of these areas size 3 farms have a decided comparative disadvantage in both tame and wild hay production. Thus this apparent inconsistency is a result of geographical differences in the comparative advantages and disadvantages of farms of size group 3.

Fifty-one percent of the cropland and hay land and 42 percent of the wild hay land in the United States are found on farms of size group 2. Thus the figures in Table 6.5 suggest that size group 2 farms have a comparative disadvantage in cotton and tame hay production, and a comparative advantage in the production of the other crops considered in the study. The comparative advantages and disadvantages of farms of size group 2 are to be expected in view of the advantages and disadvantages of the farms of the other two size groups.

CROP AND HAY LAND USE

In addition to the effect of geographical location, land use is affected by the quality of the land and by the size of farm on which the land is located. The solution 1 land use for each farm size group is presented by land-quality class in Tables 6.6 through 6.8. For each farm size group, the distribution of land between the crops considered in the study is approximately what would be expected from the preceding discussion of comparative advantages and disadvantages. For example, a comparison of the land-use distribution for farm size group 1 with the average distribution shows that the farms of this size group devote a higher than average proportion of the cropland available to the production of cotton and soybeans, a lower than average proportion of the cropland available to the production of wheat, and about an average proportion to the production of feed grain, silage, and hay. A comparison of the land-use distributions for farm size groups 2 and 3 with the average distribution shows that these distributions are also consistent with the conclusions drawn in the previous section.

Farms of size group 1 transfer a large amount of cropland and a large amount of hay land to pasture. This pasture is needed because (1) milk cow production on these farms is much higher in solution 1 than in reality, and (2) these farms fatten a large number of feeder cattle on the deferred calf-feeding plan.

For a given farm size group, land is more likely to be used for pasture or left idle and less likely to be used for crops as the land quality declines. Similarly, the land of a given quality is more likely to be left idle as farm size decreases. The data presented in Tables 6.6 through 6.8 also identify the combined effects of farm size and land quality on land use. At the two extremes, for example, only 0.2 percent of the class 1 cropland and hay land available to farms of size group 1 is left idle while 83.2 percent of the class 3 cropland and hay land available to farms of size group 3 is left idle.

USE OF RESOURCES OTHER THAN CROP AND HAY LAND

The use of family labor, capital, pasture, and wild hay land in solution 1 is summarized by farm size groups in Tables 6.9 through 6.14. The farms of size group 1 have considerable idle capital and some idle wild hay land, but nearly all the family labor and pasture available to these farms is used. On the farms of size group 2, a relatively small amount of each of these resources (8 to 18 percent of the amount available) is left idle. The farms of size group 3 use most of the capital available to them but have substantial unused supplies of family labor, pasture, and wild hay land.

In Tables 6.9 through 6.14, the percentage distribution between farm size groups is given for the amount of each resource available, the amount of each resource used, and the amount of each resource left idle. The proportion of the total amount of a resource available to the resources available with a particular farm size group can be defined as the share of that resource for that farm size group. Using this definition, farms of size group 3 use less than their share of the available family labor, wild hay land, and pasture, while farms of size groups 1 and 2 use more than their share of these resources. On the other hand, farms of size group 1 use less than their share of the available capital, and the farms of both size group 2 and size group 3 use more than their share of the capital available.

Table 6.15 summarizes the use of cotton land by farm size groups. The cotton-land restraint for each farm size group limits cotton acreage to a historical maximum. The large amounts of cotton land left idle by the farms of each size group show that these restraints were not binding. In fact, cotton-land restraints were defined for the farm size groups in 64 producing areas but the available cotton-land supply was exhausted on only 11 of the size 1 groups, 8 of the size 2 groups, and 13 of the size 3 groups.

There is one further interesting aspect of the resource use specified in solution 1: none of the 471 farm size groups included in the model had the entire stock of all resources left idle. This is in contrast to the earlier studies reported in previous chapters in that the solutions obtained in these earlier studies specified that all the resources available in some regions of the United States should be left idle. The additional detail included in the model for the current study has, therefore, resulted in the specification of a more realistic resource use pattern.

GRAPHICAL ASPECTS OF SOLUTION 1

In this section the results of solution 1 are summarized geographically. The large volume of data available from solution 1 necessitates limiting the discussion in this section to the broader geographic aspects of these results. However, we will indicate the geographic distribution of production and resource use according to farm size groups and land-quality classes.

GEOGRAPHIC DISTRIBUTION OF GRAIN AND COTTON ACREAGES

A map showing the geographic distribution of the land used for wheat, feed grain, soybeans, and cotton in solution 1 is presented in Figure 6.2. Similar maps are presented for each of the three farm size groups in Figures 6.3 through 6.5.

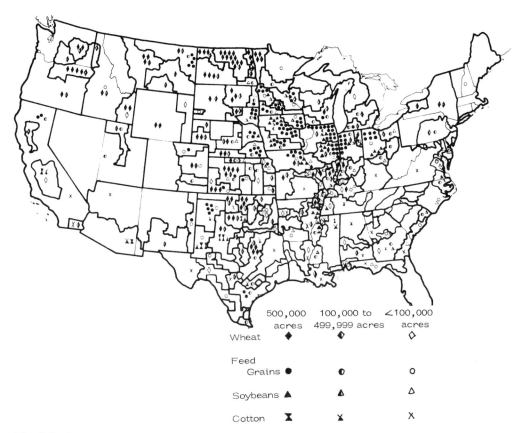

Fig. 6.2. Geographic distribution of land used for wheat, feed grain, soybeans, and cotton in solution 1.

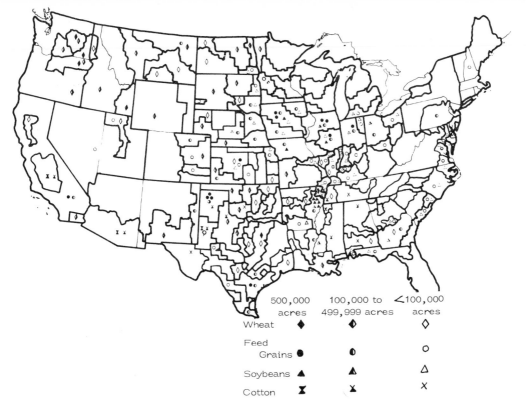

Fig. 6.3. Geographic distribution of the land on farms of size group 1 used for wheat, feed grain, soybeans, and cotton in solution 1.

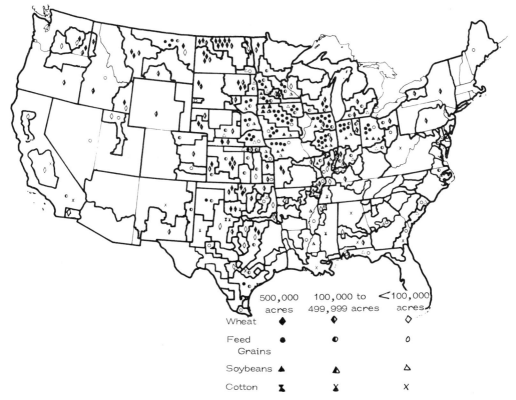

Fig. 6.4. Geographic distribution of the land on farms of size group 2 used for wheat, feed grain, soybeans, and cotton in solution 1.

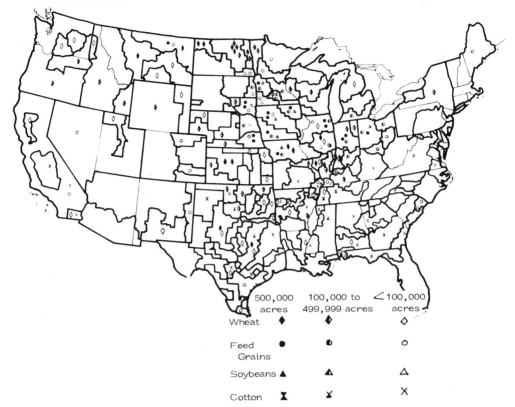

Fig. 6.5. Geographic distribution of the land on farms of size group 3 used for wheat, feed grain, soybeans, and cotton in solution 1.

The map presented in Figure 6.2 shows that the geographic distributions of wheat, feed-grain, soybean, and cotton acreages in solution 1 are quite similar to the historical distributions. Feed-grain and soybean acreages are concentrated in the Corn Belt and eastern Arkansas and northwestern Mississippi. Most wheat acreage is found either in the Great Plains or Pacific Northwest areas, and there is some concentration of cotton acreage in the Southwest, with cotton acreage otherwise quite evenly distributed throughout the South.

The farm size group maps (Figures 6.3 through 6.5) in general exhibit the same geographic distributions as were noted in Figure 6.2. However, in some cases the acreage concentrations shown in Figure 6.2 can be traced to a single farm size group. For example, the concentration of soybeans in eastern Arkansas and northwestern Mississippi is due almost entirely to soybean production on size group 1 farms, and the wheat acreage shown on Figure 6.2 for southwestern North Dakota is produced almost entirely on farms of size group 2.

The approximate distribution of grain and cotton acreages between the farm size groups of each area can be determined by comparing Figures 6.3 through 6.5. This distribution is, of course, influenced by the distribution of cropland between the farm size groups. Thus, for example, the farms of size group 2 control the largest share of the cropland in most areas and these farms also have the largest share of the wheat, feed-grain, and soybean acreages. The distribution of cotton acreage appears, however, to be somewhat more independent of the distribution of cropland since more than half the cotton acreage is produced by size group 1 farms even though these farms control only 37 percent of the cropland in the South. The geographic distribution of the land class 1 used for grain and cotton is very similar to the geographic distribution of all land used for these crops. A considerable acreage of class 2 land is used for wheat production, relatively small amounts of this land are used for feed grain and soybeans, and virtually no class 2 land is used for cotton production. This distribution is at least partly explained by the fact that in many of the western areas, which have a comparative advantage in wheat production, the cropland is of relatively low quality. Except for some wheat production in western areas of the United States, class 3 land is not used for the production of grain and cotton. The use of class 3 land for wheat in the West is again at least partly explained by the low average quality of the cropland in this area.

A comparison of the solution 1 and 1964 distribution of feed-grain acreage between farm size groups shows that both at the national level and in most consuming regions the share of that feed-grain acreage is (1) less in solution 1 than in 1964 for farm size group 3, and (2) greater in solution 1 than in 1964 for farm

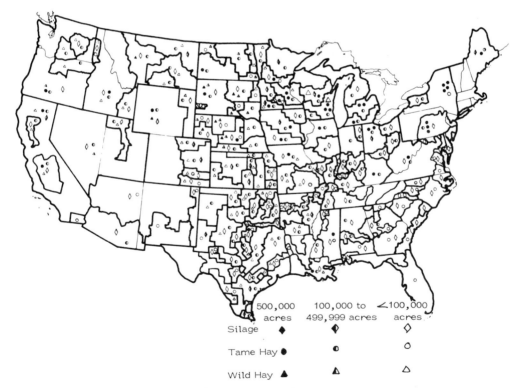

Fig. 6.6. Geographic distribution of the land used for silage, tame hay, and wild hay in solution 1.

size group 1, farm size group 2, or both these farm size groups. This proportional shift from small to large farms is to be expected with a decreased total acreage because the acreage reduction will be attributed to the least efficient producers.

GEOGRAPHIC DISTRIBUTION OF HARVESTED ROUGHAGE ACREAGES

The geographic distributions of the acreages of silage, tame hay, and wild hay produced in solutions are shown on the map presented in Figure 6.6. Maps showing the geographical distribution of the land used for harvested roughage by the farms of each size group are presented in Figures 6.7 through 6.9. Figure 6.7 shows that the land used for tame hay and silage is quite evenly distributed throughout the United States, and the land used for wild hay is uniformly distributed over the western half of the United States (wild hay is not grown in the East). The solution 1 harvested roughage production by the farms of each of the three farm size groups is also widely distributed over the United States. The dispersion of harvested roughage production is probably explained by the relatively high transportation cost for hay. These high shipping costs are avoided and total cost minimized if the farms of each producing area are required to produce the roughage necessary for the livestock production in that area.

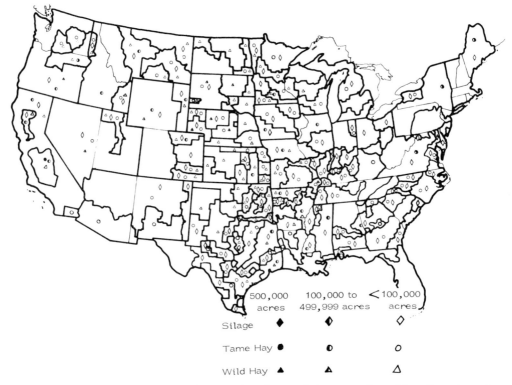

Fig. 6.7. Geographic distribution of the land on farms of size group 1 used for silage, tame hay, and wild hay in solution 1.

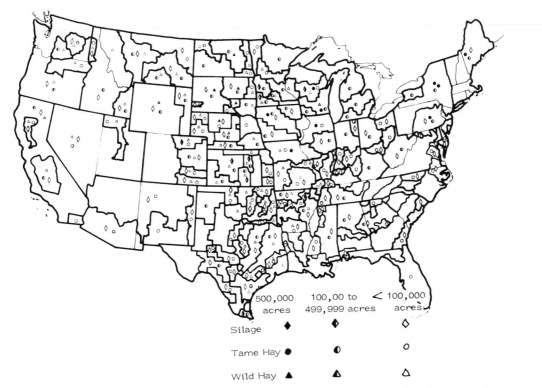

Fig. 6.8. Geographic distribution of the land on farms of size group 2 used for silage, tame hay, and wild hay in solution 1.

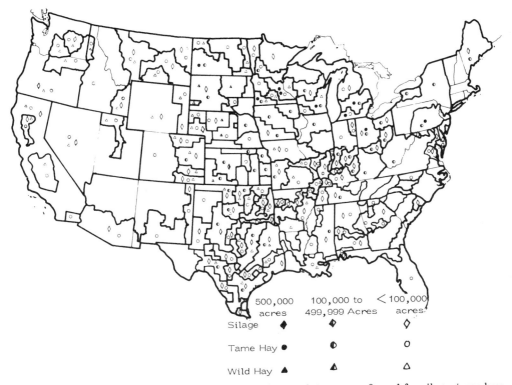

Fig. 6.9. Geographic distribution of the land on farms of size group 3 used for silage, tame hay, and wild hay in solution 1.

GEOGRAPHIC DISTRIBUTION OF MILK COWS AND HOGS

The geographic distribution of the milk cow and hog production specified in solution 1 is shown in Figure 6.10, and the geographic distribution of the production on each farm size group is shown in Figures 6.11 through 6.13. In solution 1 milk cow numbers are concentrated in the Lake states, the Northeast (including Ohio), Florida, and California. These same geographical concentrations exist for the milk cow production by farms of size group 1 (see Figure 6.11), but geographical concentrations of milk cow production by farms of size group 2 are confined to the Lake states and the Northeast (see Figure 6.12). Virtually no milk cows are produced by size group 3 farms in solution 1 (see Figure 6.13).

There are no significant differences between the regional distribution of milk cow numbers in solution 1 and the distribution in 1964. However, there are substantial differences between the farm size group distributions for solution 1 and the actual distributions for 1964. At the national level, the farms of size group 1 have a much larger share of milk cow production in solution 1 than they did in 1964, the farms of size group 2 have a slightly smaller share, and the share of size group 3 farms is even smaller. Large farms have lower production costs and labor requirements per milk cow than smaller farms.

Total hog production is concentrated (as it is in reality) in the Corn Belt. From Figures 6.11 through 6.13 we see that this concentration of hog production in the Corn Belt is due mainly to production on farms of size groups 1 and 2.

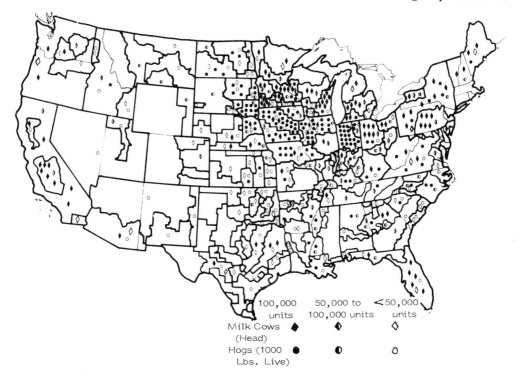

Fig. 6.10. Geographic distribution of the solution 1 milk cow and hog production.

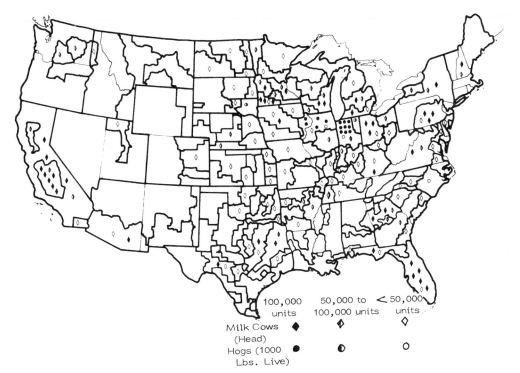

Fig. 6.11. Geographic distribution of the solution 1 milk cow and hog production by farms of size group 1.

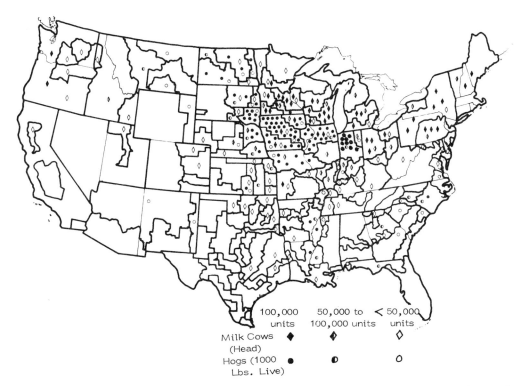

Fig. 6.12. Geographic distribution of the solution 1 milk cow and hog production by farms of size group 2.

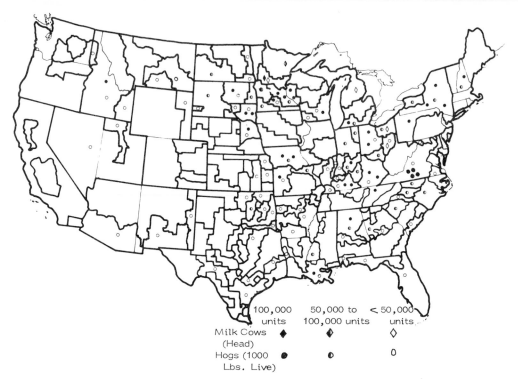

Fig. 6.13. Geographic distribution of the solution 1 milk cow and hog production by farms of size group 3.

These figures also show that although there is relatively little hog production on the size group 3 farms in the Corn Belt, these small farms account for much of the hog production that occurs outside the Corn Belt. The difference between the solution 1 and 1964 distribution of hog production between farm size groups indicates a shift of this production from larger to smaller farms. The apparent comparative advantage in hog production for small farms is caused by two factors: hog production costs (excluding feed and labor costs) were assumed to decrease as farm size decreases, and resources have been withdrawn from hog production on size group 1 farms to fully exploit the advantage these farms have in dairy-cattle and feeder-cattle production.

GEOGRAPHIC DISTRIBUTION OF BEEF-COW AND FEEDER-CATTLE PRODUCTION

The geographic distribution of total beef-cow and feeder-cattle production in solution 1 is shown in Figure 6.14, and the geographic distribution of beef-cow and feeder-cattle production by each farm size group is presented in Figures 6.15 through 6.17. Total beef-cow production in solution 1 is quite widely dispersed over the West and Midwest, but there are few beef cows produced in the East. Beef-cow production on the farms of size group 1 is confined for the most part of the Far West (including west Texas), although the size group 1 farms of

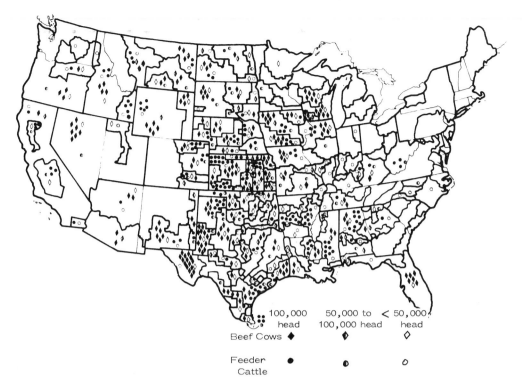

Fig. 6.14. Geographic distribution of the solution 1 beef-cow and feeder-cattle production.

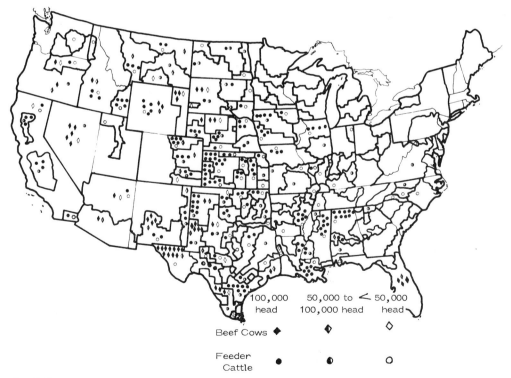

Fig. 6.15. Geographic distribution of the solution 1 beef-cow and feeder-cattle production by farms of size group 1.

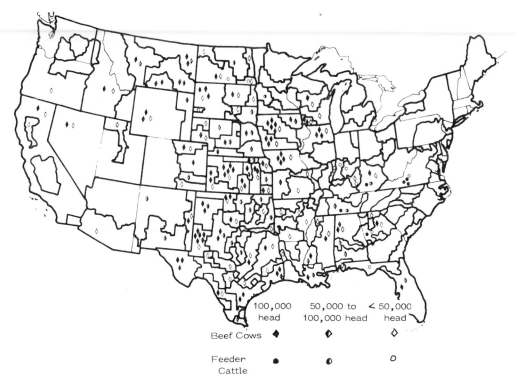

Fig. 6.16. Geographic distribution of the solution 1 beef-cow and feeder-cattle production by farms of size group 2.

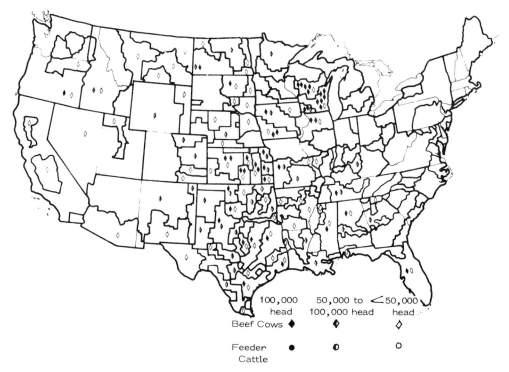

Fig. 6.17. Geographic distribution of the solution 1 beef-cow and feeder-cattle production by farms of size group 3.

southern Florida produce a considerable number of beef cows (see Figure 6.15). Beef-cow production on farms of size groups 2 and 3 is, as is total production, widely distributed over the West and Midwest (see Figures 6.16 and 6.17).

Since nearly all feeder cattle produced in solution 1 are produced on farms of size group 1, the geographical distributions shown in Figures 6.14 and 6.15 are almost identical. These figures show considerable feeder-cattle production in the western half of the United States with additional concentrations in the western Corn Belt, the Delta states, and Northern Alabama. The most extensive concentrations of feeder-cattle production in the west are found in California, Colorado, Kansas, and Oklahoma, and in parts of Texas, Nebraska, and Idaho. The shift of feeder-cattle production to large farms does not represent a radical change in comparative advantages in feeder-cattle production between farm size groups but rather represents an intensification of the comparative advantages evident in the production of 1964. A strong comparative advantage in feeder-cattle production of size group 1 is indicated in the actual production pattern because in 1964 these farms produced 70 percent of the feeder-cattle production in the United States but only 23 percent of the beef cows, 19 percent of the hogs, and 16 percent of the milk cows.

GEOGRAPHIC DISTRIBUTION OF YEARLING PRODUCTION

Only 123.2 thousand yearlings were produced in solution 1. Of these 121.1 thousand were produced by size group 3 farms in area 157, 1.6 thousand were produced by size group 2 farms in area 136, and the remaining 0.5 thousand were produced by size group 3 farms in area 136 (areas 136 and 157 are both located in California). These yearlings were than fattened on the yearlings no-silage feeding plan by the farms of size group 1 in areas 136 and 157. Yearling production in solution 1 cannot be compared with actual production since actual production figures are not available.

TRANSPORTATION ACTIVITIES INCLUDED IN SOLUTION 1

In this section a brief description of the producing area to producing area, consuming region to producing area, and consuming region to consuming region transportation activities included in solution 1 is presented. The levels of these activities indicate the direction of interregional flows of commodities included in the model.

AREA TO AREA TRANSPORTATION ACTIVITIES

The area to area transportation activities included in the model transport intermediate products between producing areas located in the same consuming region. Although 8,650 of these activities were included in the model, only 75 were used in solution 1. The optimal solution should, however, be expected to include only a small number of interarea transportation activities since the costs of loading and unloading make the short hauls involved relatively expensive and since production costs for most products are not likely to differ greatly between neighboring areas. Most of the area to area transportation activities included in solution 1 involve the shipment of feed grain or the shipment of feeder calves.

REGION TO AREA TRANSPORTATION ACTIVITIES

Region to area transportation activities were included in the model so that each area could obtain wheat, feed grain, soybeans, cottonseed, hay, feeder calves, and feeder yearlings from outside the region in which the area is located.

The general directions of region to area shipments of wheat, feed grain, soybeans, cottonseed, and feeder calves are indicated in Tables 6.16 through 6.20. No region to area transportation of hay or feeder yearlings was specified in solution 1. To simplify these tables, the destinations of the shipments are identified only by consuming regions. Thus a single entry was made for shipments from a given region to two or more producing areas located in the same consuming region.

The transportation patterns for wheat, feed grain, soybeans, and cottonseed in solution 1 are not greatly different from what would be expected with the traditional production patterns. However, the geographical distribution of feeder-cattle production in solution 1 has resulted in a transportation pattern quite different from the traditional movement of feeder cattle. Traditionally, feeder cattle have been shipped from the West to the Corn Belt, but in solution 1 the Corn Belt is a net exporter of feeder cattle while some western regions (e.g., the Montana-Idaho and Colorado-Wyoming consuming regions) are net importers of feeder cattle. The other major differences between the feeder-cattle transportation pattern specified in solution 1 and the traditional transportation pattern are that in solution 1 the Lake states and the Northeast regions export large numbers of feeder calves and that in solution 1 the Delta states and Southeast regions import considerable numbers of feeder calves.

REGION TO REGION TRANSPORTATION ACTIVITIES

The directions of movement for the region to region shipments specified in solution 1 for grain-fed beef, other beef, pork, and manufactured milk are indicated in Tables 6.21 through 6.24, respectively. In addition, solution 1 specifies region to region shipments of (1) wheat from North Dakota–South Dakota to New England and to Nevada-Utah, (2) feed grain from Texas to New England, and (3) fluid milk from the Northeast (excluding New England) and from the Mid-Atlantic states (North Carolina, Virginia, and West Virginia) to New England. As noted in the previous section, wheat, feed grain, soybeans, and cottonseed also move between consuming regions via the region to area transportation activities.

The transportation patterns specified for meat and milk in solution 1 are, of course, determined by the geographical distribution of livestock production. The rather significant differences between the solution 1 and actual geographic distributions of feeder-cattle production are evident in the solution 1 transportation

pattern for grain-fed beef. Further, since 43 percent of the other beef requirements in solution 1 were obtained by transferring grain-fed beef to other beef,
these differences in the distribution of feeder-cattle production are also evident in
the solution 1 transportation pattern for other beef. For example, the Corn Belt
is, unexpectedly, a net importer of both grain-fed beef and other beef (the
western Corn Belt is self-sufficient in grain-fed beef). Similarly, the wide geographic distribution of hog production in solution 1 relative to the actual distribution is reflected in the transportation pattern for pork. Thus pork exports from
the western Corn Belt and the Minnesota-Wisconsin regions are relatively low in
solution 1, and many of the other regions either have relatively low imports in
solution 1 (e.g., the Delta states have become self-sufficient in pork) or have
relatively high exports (e.g., the North Dakota–South Dakota region).

TRANSFER ACTIVITIES INCLUDED IN SOLUTION 1

TRANSFER OF COMMODITIES FROM AREAS TO REGIONS

The model included activities to transport wheat, feed grain, soybeans,
cottonseed, hay, feeder calves, and feeder yearlings from each producing area to
the consuming region in which that area is located. These activities imply spatial
movement but were classified as transfer rather than transportation activities
because no charge was made for this movement. The level of each of the area to
region transfer activities included in solution 1 is presented in Tables 6.25 and
6.26. From these levels the source of the commodities used for consumption in
and exporting from each consuming region can be determined.

TRANSFER OF FLUID MILK TO MANUFACTURED MILK

The manufactured milk required in each consuming region can be obtained
either by importing manufactured milk or by transferring fluid milk to the
manufactured milk supply. The amounts of fluid milk so transferred in each
consuming region are given in Table 6.27. Although some fluid milk is transferred
to manufactured milk in 14 of the 21 consuming regions, 75 percent of the total
amount transferred in solution 1 is transferred in the Lake states, the eastern
Corn Belt, and California. Much of the fluid milk transferred to the manufactured
milk supply in the Lake states is exported to other consuming regions.

TRANSFER OF GRAIN-FED BEEF TO OTHER BEEF

Grain-fed beef was assumed to be a perfect substitute for other beef although
the inverse relationship was not assumed. Thus each consuming region was
allowed to augment its other beef supply by transferring grain-fed beef to other
beef. The amounts of grain-fed beef used for other beef in each consuming
region are given in Table 6.28. In total, 2.94 billion pounds of grain-fed beef were
transferred to other beef. This total is distributed among 12 consuming regions,
but 41 percent of the total is transferred in region 11 (the Delta states) and region

16 (Colorado-Wyoming). Much of beef transferred to the other beef supply in these two regions is then exported to other regions.

In addition to the above results on transfer activities, solution 1 also provided the data on (1) the types of grain and oilseeds used for concentrate feed in an area, (2) the use of exogenous feed in producing areas, (3) the total amount of pasture rented, and (4) the distribution of hired labor. In view of space restraints, these results are not presented in detail but the main points are reported in the summary.

GEOGRAPHIC DISTRIBUTION OF IDLE CROPLAND AND HAY LAND

The amount of cropland and hay land left idle in solution 1 is fairly uniformly distributed throughout the United States, although there are areas of concentration in the Southeast and the Great Plains (see Figure 6.18). However, this uniformity of distribution does not apply to all sizes of farms or to all qualities of land. Figures 6.19 through 6.21 show that (1) nearly all idle land on farms of size group 1 is found in a belt running from eastern Texas through the Delta states and the Southeast to the Appalachian region; (2) the idle land on farms of size group 2 is more widely distributed than that on size 1 farms, but this land is somewhat concentrated in the southeastern part of the United States (e.i., the area in which idle land on size group 1 farms is concentrated) and in the

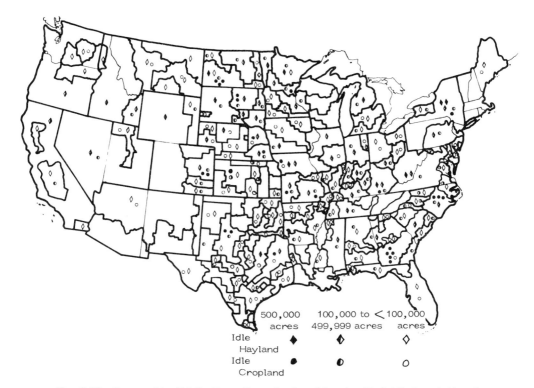

Fig. 6.18. Geographic distribution of cropland and hay land left idle in solution 1.

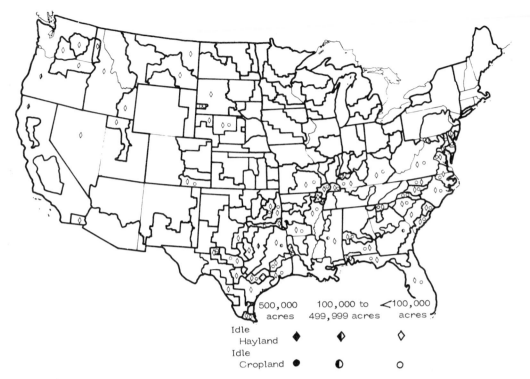

Fig. 6.19. Geographic distribution of the cropland and hay land left idle in solution 1 by the farms of size group 1.

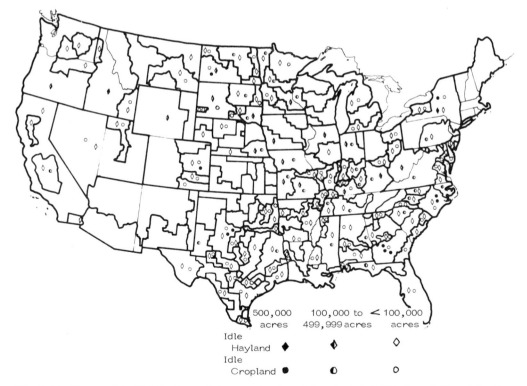

Fig. 6.20. Geographic distribution of the cropland and hay land left idle in solution 1 by the farms of size group 2.

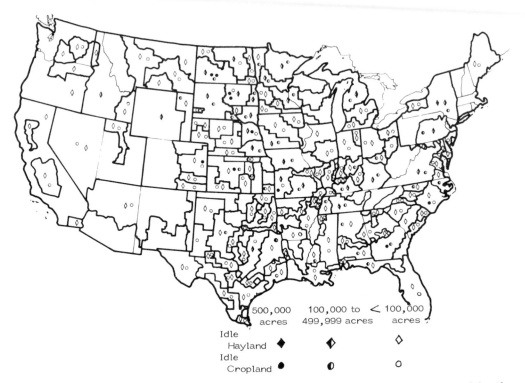

Idle Hayland

	500,000 acres	100,000 to 499,999 acres	< 100,000 acres
Idle Hayland	◆	◈	◇
Idle Cropland	●	◖	○

Fig. 6.21. Geographic distribution of the cropland and hay land left idle in solution 1 by the farms of size group 3.

Northern Plains; and (3) the idle land on size group 3 farms is quite widely distributed, although there is a significant concentration of this land in the Northern Plains. Figures 6.22 through 6.24 show that in solution 1 (1) there is little quality class 1 land left idle except in the extreme Southeast, (2) some idle land of quality class 2 is found in many producing areas but the largest acreages are located in the southeastern part of the United States and in the Northern Plains, and (3) idle land of quality class 3 is quite uniformly distributed throughout the United States.

SHADOW PRICES GENERATED IN SOLUTION 1

To facilitate the presentation of the shadow prices generated in solution 1, these prices have been divided into four groups: (1) national, (2) consuming region, (3) producing area, and (4) farm size group. In this section the interpretation of mainly a national and consuming region shadow price will be given, and the magnitude of the prices obtained will be discussed.

NATIONAL SHADOW PRICES

Five national restraints were included in the model. The shadow prices generated in solution 1 for these restraints are presented in Table 6.29. The shadow

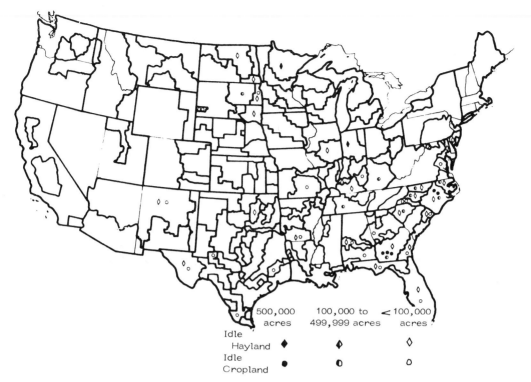

Fig. 6.22. Geographic distribution of the cropland and hay land of quality class 1 left idle in solution 1.

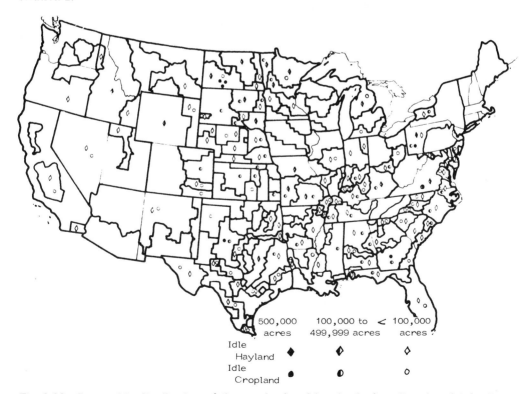

Fig. 6.23. Geographic distribution of the cropland and hay land of quality class 2 left idle in solution 1.

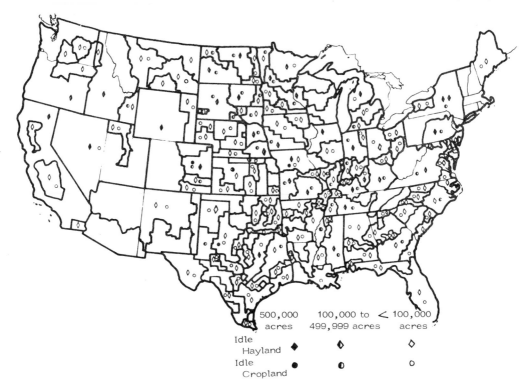

Fig. 6.24. Geographic distribution of the cropland and hay land of quality class 3 left idle in solution 1.

price generated in solution 1 for cotton lint is equal to the amount by which total production cost would decrease if cotton lint requirements were reduced by one unit. The actual price of cotton lint in 1965 was equal to $28.14 per hundred-weight so that the shadow price generated in solution 1 is considerably below the actual price. The inclusion of charges for land and family labor in the objective function would, of course, result in a higher shadow price for cotton lint. How-ever, three other factors cause the solution 1 shadow price for cotton lint to be lower: (1) nearly all the cotton produced in solution 1 is produced on class 1 land, (2) a higher proportion of total cotton production in solution 1 was produced by size group 1 farms than was the case in 1964, and (3) less cotton lint was pro-duced in solution 1 than in 1965 (because cotton lint carry-over was increased in 1965). The cost of exogenous concentrates is included in the objective function so that the shadow price for each of these feeds is equal to the difference between the cost of one unit of that feed and the cost of the grain and oil meal required to replace that unit. However, since the model insures that the entire supply of each of these feeds will be exhausted in any feasible solution, these shadow prices could represent either the amount by which the cost of replacement exceeds the cost of the feed or the amount by which the cost of the feed exceeds the cost of replacement. At the margin, each of these feeds proves to be more expensive than the grain and oilseed required to replace it. Thus, for example, if the marginal unit of exogenous concentrate 1 were replaced by the concentrate feeds endogenous to the model, total cost would be reduced by $1.24.

CONSUMING REGION SHADOW PRICES

The range of the consuming region shadow prices generated in solution 1 for each of the final and intermediate products included in the model and national average prices for each of these products in 1965 are presented in Table 6.30. The interpretation of the consuming region shadow prices for final and intermediate products is similar to the interpretation of the cotton lint shadow price except that the consuming region prices also reflect transportation costs. The consuming region shadow price for a final or intermediate commodity is equal to the production and transportation cost of that commodity unit which has the highest total (transportation and production) cost of all those units used to satisfy the requirements for that product in that region.

The consuming region shadow prices are lower than the actual prices in 1965, but as with the cotton lint prices, these shadow prices would be higher if charges for family labor and land were included in production costs. Further, the greatest differences between the shadow prices and actual prices are found (1) when production in solution 1 is considerably less than in 1965 (e.g., soybeans, cottonseed, and yearlings) and (2) when the proportion of total production that is produced by large farms is higher in solution 1 than in 1964 (e.g., grain-fed beef and milk).

It may seem contradictory that the shadow prices for pork are considerably lower than the actual price even though production in solution 1 is virtually identical to that in 1965 and the proportion of production on small farms to total production is higher in solution 1 than in 1964. However, as pointed out earlier, production costs for hogs decrease as farm size decreases so that a shift of hog production from large to small farms is equivalent to a shift of other types of production from small to large farms.

In addition to the shadow prices just described, a shadow price for pasture not on farms was generated for each consuming region. Since the cost of renting pasture not on farms is included in the objective function, the shadow price for a pasture not on farms restraint represents the net cost increase (the increase in costs other than pasture renting cost less the cost of the pasture) that would result if the supply of this pasture were reduced by one unit. The shadow prices for pasture not on farms range up to $6.78 per animal unit month with the highest shadow prices being those for the eastern consuming regions.

FARM SIZE GROUP SHADOW PRICES

The shadow price for each resource available to a farm size group is equal to the amount by which total cost would increase if one unit of that resource were withdrawn from production. The relatively high production costs on small farms lead us to expect shadow prices for resources to decrease as farm size decreases. This expectation is generally fulfilled but there are exceptions because the shadow price for each resource available to a farm size group depends on the total resource situation for that size group. For example, shadow prices for capital are frequently higher on small farms than on large farms because the large farms either have excess capital or have exhausted not only the available capital but also the available supplies of other resources while the small farms have exhausted the available capital but have unused supplies of all other resources.

A RESUME OF CHANGES FROM SOLUTION 1 TO SOLUTION 2

The total cost of producing and transporting the products required in solution 1 equaled $13.37 billion while this cost equaled $13.12 billion in solution 2. The total amount of this cost reduction is not directly attributable to the reduced cotton lint requirements but is in part due to the resultant redistribution of crop and livestock production among geographical regions and among farms of different sizes.

Since the consumption requirements for all products except cotton lint are identical in solution 1 and solution 2, any change in the national production of crops other than cotton must be due to changes in the use of those crops for feed. In part, the changes in the use of crops for feed are a direct result of the smaller amount of cottonseed available for feed, and in part, these changes result from the differences between the production plans specified in solution 1 and solution 2.

In addition to the expected substitution of soybeans for cottonseed, wheat is substituted both for cottonseed and for feed grain, and hay is substituted for silage. Much of the substitution of wheat for feed grain in solution 2 is accounted for by the substitution of wheat production on farms in regions 11 and 12 for feed-grain production in regions 7, 10, and 14. Apparently, costs are reduced if at least part of the resources released for cotton production in these regions is used to produce wheat to substitute for the feed grain produced in solution 1 by the farms of regions 7, 10, and 14. A factor contributing to this substitution may be that the relatively high protein content of wheat makes it a more desirable concentrate feed when the amount of cottonseed (a high protein feed) available is reduced. Feed-grain production on farms of size groups 1 and 3 is higher in solution 2 than in solution 1 because the decrease in feed-grain production between the two solutions is concentrated on size group 2 farms in areas 38 (northern Indiana) and 45 (northern Illinois and eastern Iowa). The decrease in feed-grain production on these farms was offset by increased soybean production. The shift of tame hay production from farms of size group 3 to the larger farms was not confined to a single area or region. Apparently, the less restrictive conditions of solution 2 cause these small farms to lose some of the comparative advantage in hay production that they exhibited in solution 1.

The solution 1 to solution 2 changes in the distribution of livestock between farm size groups at the national level show an intensification of the solution 1 concentration of feeder cattle on size group 1 farms and of the solution 1 concentration of hog production on the size group 3 farms. In addition, these national figures show a shift of milk cows and beef cows from the farms of size group 1 to the farms of size groups 2 and 3. However, milk cow numbers are higher in solution 1 than in solution 2 for size group 1 farms in regions 12 and 17—regions in which the solution 2 cotton production for size 1 farms is considerably below the solution 1 level. Although the solution 1 to solution 2 changes in the livestock and crop activities have caused numerous quantitative changes in the transportation activity levels and some changes in the transportation activities included in the solution, the transportation pattern for solution 2 is basically the same as that for solution 1. As for the transportation activities, there are numerous small quantitative differences between the solution 1 and solution 2 area to region transfer activity levels and a limited number of differences in the activities included, but the basic pattern of the area to region transfer activities is the same for both solutions.

GENERAL IMPLICATIONS

A unique feature of the model used in this study is that it delineates the producing units in each area on the basis of various farm size groups and land-quality classes. Therefore, the results of this study provide us with information about the interarea adjustments in production patterns as well as information about the interfarm adjustments within an area to obtain agricultural output in the most efficient manner. The additional information about the interfarm adjustments within producing areas permits us to explain the observed trends in farm size and scale in U.S. agriculture.[45]

The total production required of agriculture is divided into 471 farm size groups in such a way that the total cost of obtaining this production is minimized. The production specified for a group of farms differs from the actual production for that group of farms in two ways: (1) the types of production specified in the results of this study are different from the actual types and (2) the production levels specified are different from the actual levels.

If the types of production specified for a group of farms in our results are different from the types usually produced, these farms will have to replace buildings and equipment no longer needed for the optimal production patterns. The amount of production facility replacement will depend on the type of product substitution specified; that is, the substitution of one crop for another will usually require little replacement of buildings and equipment, but the substitution of (1) one type of livestock production for another, (2) crop production for livestock production, or (3) livestock production for crop production will usually necessitate considerable changes in the production facilities.

The results of this study show a marked comparative advantage on large over small farms in crop production, and milk-cow, beef-cow, and feeder-cattle production. Small farms have, however, a comparative advantage over large farms in hog

---

45. There has been a marked tendency toward the fewer and larger farms in U.S. agriculture. Farm numbers declined by 37.6 percent between 1940 and 1960 and by 50.9 percent between 1950 and 1970. See A. Gordon Ball and Earl O. Heady, "Trends in Farm and Enterprise Size and Scale," in A. Gordon Ball and Earl O. Heady, eds., *Size, Structure, and Future of Farms*, Iowa State Univ. Press, Ames, 1972, pp. 43-44.

production. In the model used for this study, any necessary replacement of production facilities is assumed to take place without difficulty, but in reality these replacements are not so easily accomplished. Frequently there is no market for the resources that must be disposed of to implement the required change. Thus some of the changes in types of production specified for farm size groups in our results could only be accomplished over an extended period of time or would have to be assisted by public policy measures in some way.[46] Extensive product substitution in a geographic area would also necessitate adjustments by the businesses serving agriculture in that area. For example, an extensive substitution of feeder-cattle or hog production for crop production in an area would make it necessary to expand the meat-packing facilities in that area.

If the optimal production pattern for a farm size group is of the same type as in reality, but the levels are higher, then the farms of that group will have to expand their production facilities and will, perhaps, have to hire additional labor. Conversely, if the types of production specified for a group of farms in our results are the same as those currently produced but the levels are lower, some of the resources available to the farms of that group will have to be shifted out of agricultural production. This aspect will be taken up later while discussing the implications of idle resources.

The types of adjustment in production facilities implied in our results for a particular farm size group can be determined by comparing the optimal production levels and actual production figures for that group of farms. Some idea of the types of adjustments necessary can be obtained by comparing the actual and optimal production figures reported by farm size groups for each consuming region and for the United States. For example, the farms of size group 1 in the United States produce more feeder-cattle and milk cows and fewer hogs in our results than in 1964 so that in adjusting to the optimal production pattern these farms must increase the capacity of their feeder-cattle and milk-cow production facilities and dispose of some of the hog-production facilities they currently possess. As with changes in the types of production, extensive changes in the levels of production by the farms in an area will necessitate adjustments by the business serving agriculture in that area.

IMPLICATIONS OF IDLE RESOURCES

The amounts of resources that should have been withdrawn from agriculture if the excess capacity problems of that industry were to be overcome in 1965 are directly identified in the results of solution 1. These results indicate that 13 percent of the cropland, 34 percent of the hay land, 16 percent of the pasture, 28 percent of the wild hay land, 30 percent of the family labor, 29 percent of the hired labor, and 26 percent of the capital used in agriculture in 1965 would have to be withdrawn from production if the overcapacity problems of agriculture were to be solved in that year.

---

46. For a discussion on some public policy means and alternatives for preventing a further increase in farm size and increasing the competing power of small farms, see Earl O. Heady and A. Gordon Ball, "Public Policy Means and Alternatives," in A. Gordon Ball and Earl O. Heady eds., *Size, Structure, and Future of Farms*, Iowa State Univ. Press, Ames, 1972, pp. 373-98.

The proportion of the resources available to a farm size group that are designated as idle in solution 1 is a good indicator of the adjustment problems facing the farms of that group; that is, if a high proportion of the resources available to a group of farms is designated as idle in solution 1, the operators of the farms in that group will have serious adjustment problems. Further, the adjustment problems of the rural nonfarm population will be greatest in those areas in which a high proportion of the resources available to all farms is designated as idle in solution 1.

In solution 1 a very high proportion of the resources available to the farms of size group 3 is designated as idle. Furthermore, if a charge for family labor would have been included in the model, the magnitude of idle resources would have been even larger on these farms. The adjustment problems of the operators of small farms can, therefore, be expected to be very severe. The problems of these farm families are further complicated by the fact that the family members usually have few skills suited to nonagricultural occupations and the fact that there are few markets for their meager supplies of capital resources. The large number of size group 3 farms in the United States (949 thousand in 1964) make the solution of the problems of these farm operators difficult for society.

The solution 1 results further suggest that many of those presently employed in agriculture as hired workers also face serious adjustment problems. The results indicate that many of these workers will have to seek nonfarm employment and many others should be shifted to regions other than those in which they are presently employed. The problems of these hired workers, like those of the operators of size group 3 farms, are complicated by the fact that the individuals involved have few skills that are useful in nonagricultural occupations and have only a very small amount of capital.

The farms classified by the *United States Census of Agriculture* as economic class VI (part-time or part-retirement) were excluded from the study so that no definite statements can be made about the adjustment problems resulting from idle resources on these farms. The problems of families operating class VI farms seem likely, however, to be similar, but perhaps even more severe than those of families operating size group 3 farms. Many of the operators of part-retirement farms also have severe problems, but the adjustments these farm operators can make are limited because their age prohibits them from shifting to nonagricultural employment. The production of part-time farmers is not needed to satisfy the requirements of agricultural products, but since these farms are not entirely dependent on agriculture for their income, the problems of part-time farmers are likely to be less severe than those of the other small farms.

The resources specified as idle in solution 1 are not concentrated in any geographic area. In fact, contrary to the results of the earlier studies of this series, some resources are used in all of the 157 producing areas defined for this study. Thus the adjustment problems indicated in solution 1 are not confined to specific geographic areas of the United States. The proportion of the resources available that are left idle is, however, generally higher in the southeastern part of the United States than in other areas of the country,[47] so that the adjustment prob-

47. The proportion of crop season family labor left idle is lower in the southeastern part of the United States than in other areas, but as pointed out earlier, this is due to limitations of the model and the data collection procedures.

lems for both the farm and the rural nonfarm population in this area will be more severe than in other geographic areas. Further, a large number of the small farms excluded from the study are located in southeastern United States.[48] The problems of these farms will add to the general problems of the area.

48. In 1964, 59 percent of the farms in the Southeast, Appalachian, and Delta states regions were of economic class VI, part-time or part-retirement.

Chapter 7:   Trade-Offs in Farm Policy

HOWARD C. MADSEN, EARL O. HEADY,
and KENNETH J. NICOL

The primary objective of this study is to estimate the trade-offs among net farm incomes, government costs, amount and distribution of land retired, and regional distributions of government payments with alternative government programs and price levels. Trade-offs among these variables are analyzed for the year 1975 based on projection of yields, demands, and other basic parameters to that date. Three different price levels are used in the analysis. One set of prices is called *lower* prices, another is labeled *medium* prices, while the third is called *higher* prices. The medium level of prices essentially provides for prices at existing support levels for major field crops. The following basic set of government program alternatives is studied for each price level:

1. A long-term land rental program with no restrictions on the concentration of land diversion (*unlimited diversion*) in the regions.
2. A long-term rental program with a restriction that *no more than 75 percent* of the cropland in any region can be retired by the government.
3. A long-term rental program with a restriction that *no more than 50 percent* of the cropland in any region can be retired by the government.
4. A long-term program with a restriction that *no more than 25 percent* of the cropland in any region can be retired by the government.

The three price levels and land-retirement alternatives result in 12 different program combinations. For each of these combinations, we estimate the level of farm income, level of treasury costs, amount of land retired, location of diverted land, and the regional distribution of government payments to farmers. These quantities show the amount of change or sacrifices in one item (e.g., the total cost of programs) as another item (e.g., the price level or regional concentration of land retirement) is changed or achieved. The farm and general public must, in the end, determine the weights or values which should be attached to each item and the optimal combination of the various items or effects of different programs.

ASSUMPTIONS FOR PRICES AND RELATED PARAMETERS

THREE ALTERNATIVE PRICE LEVELS STUDIED

Each of the price levels used has a set of per capita consumptions and exports of wheat, feed grain, oil meal, and cotton associated with it. Production of crops meets prespecified levels of domestic and export demand estimated for each alternative price level. Carry-over stocks of major commodities are assumed constant for all three price levels. The study further assumes the land base to remain constant between 1965 and 1975.

Farm level prices of major commodities used in the study are presented in Table 7.1. With each set of 1975 projected prices (i.e., lower, medium, and higher), the levels of production consistent with each price level and the prespecified domestic and export demand were determined. With lower prices in 1975, the average price of corn received by farmers is $0.85 per bushel while wheat and soybeans are $1.00 per bushel and $1.50 per bushel, respectively. The price of cotton, $0.26 per pound of lint, is assumed constant at all three price levels. The average price of all cattle and calves at the lower price level is $0.185 per pound of liveweight while the hog price is $0.150 per pound. Broiler price is $0.135 per pound, a level near that of 1967. Medium prices are near both the 1967 actual prices received by farmers and the present support rates for wheat, feed grains, and soybeans. With this set of prices in 1975, corn would be $1.05 per bushel, wheat $1.25 per bushel, and soybeans $2.15 per bushel. The medium level price for all cattle and calves is $0.225 per pound of liveweight while hogs and broilers are $0.182 and $0.153 per pound, respectively. A third 1975 price level, higher prices, is above the other two sets and has individual prices of $1.25 per bushel of corn, $1.50 per bushel for wheat, and $2.75 per bushel of soybeans. Livestock prices include cattle and calves at $0.27 per pound liveweight and hogs and broilers at $0.21 and $0.17 per pound, respectively.

PER CAPITA CONSUMPTION AND EXPORT LEVELS ASSUMED

Per capita consumption estimates for beef and veal, pork, and broilers for each price level studied are summarized in Figure 7.1. With lower prices in 1975, per capita consumption of beef and veal is estimated at 143 pounds (carcass weight equivalent), compared with 113 pounds in 1968. Consumption of pork is estimated at 65 pounds per person (carcass weight equivalent) versus 66 pounds in 1968. Consumption of broilers is estimated at 38 pounds (ready-to-cook weight), slightly higher than the 1968 level of 37 pounds per person. Under medium level prices in 1975, per capita consumption of beef and veal is estimated at 127 pounds, compared to 113 pounds actually consumed in 1968. Pork consumption is estimated at 60 pounds per person versus 66 pounds in 1968, while broiler consumption is estimated at 41 pounds or 4 pounds higher than actual 1968. With higher crop and livestock prices in 1975, per capita consumption of beef and veal is projected at 113 pounds or the same as 1968. Pork consumption is projected at 57 pounds per person, 9 pounds less than actual 1968. Broiler consumption is estimated to increase to 44 pounds per person, 7 pounds more than actual consumption in 1968.

Figures 7.2, 7.3, and 7.4 summarize export levels of wheat, feed grain, and oil meal used for each price level included in the study. Wheat exports are assumed to be the same at all three price levels. With the new International Wheat Agreement, wheat exports will be restricted by institutional factors and the price of wheat will not be the primary determinant of exports. Hence, wheat exports

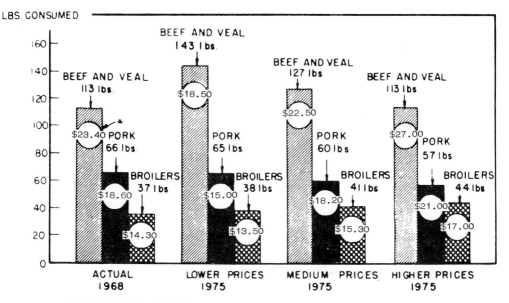

Fig. 7.1. Per capita consumption: projected 1975 and actual 1968.

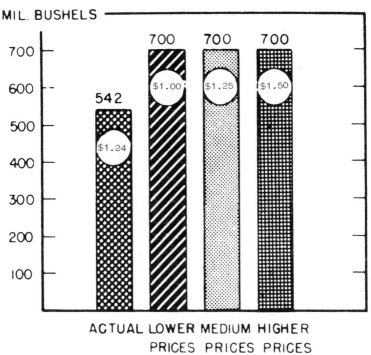

Fig. 7.2. Wheat exports.

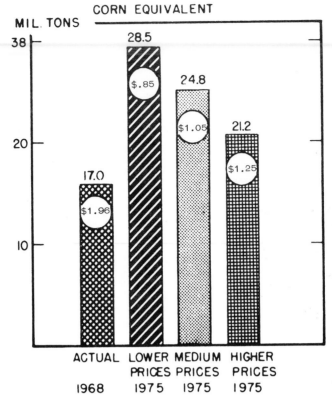

Fig. 7.3. Feed-grain exports.

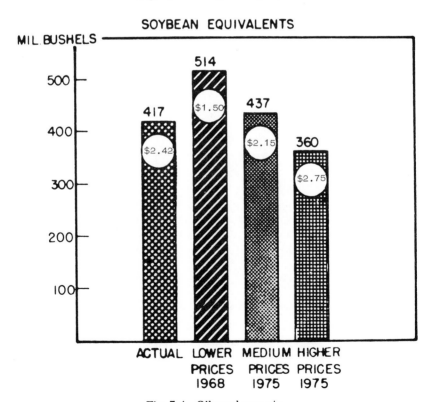

Fig. 7.4. Oil-meal exports.

of 700 million bushels are used for all price levels in 1975. Actual exports were 542 million bushels in 1968 (Figure 7.2).

Exports of both feed grain and oil meal are assumed to be more responsive to price changes. With lower prices in 1975 ($0.85 corn), feed-grain exports are estimated at 28.5 million tons (corn equivalent). Feed-grain exports are estimated at 24.8 million tons with medium prices ($1.05 corn) and 21.2 million tons for higher prices ($1.25 corn). Actual feed-grain exports were 17 million tons in 1968 (Figure 7.3). Soybean exports are projected at 514 million bushels (soybean equivalent) under lower prices ($1.50 soybeans), 437 million bushels at medium prices ($2.15 soybeans), and 360 million bushels at higher prices ($2.75 soybeans) in 1975 (Figure 7.4). Cotton lint exports are estimated at 5 million bales for all price levels studied. The price of cotton lint is held constant for all the alternatives reported.

METHOD AND TERMINOLOGY

The analysis which follows is based on results from a 150-region linear programming model.[1] For each price level studied, a set of projected per-acre yields and costs was computed for each crop in each producing area. Total demand levels for wheat, feed grain, oil meal, and cotton were projected for 31 consuming regions of the nation (as shown in Chapter 2). The programming model was applied within the land restraints and demand levels specified for each producing and consuming region. The model then maximized the net return from production of wheat, feed grain, soybeans, and cotton, given the costs of producing these crops, their selling prices, and the costs of transportation between the various producing and consuming regions.

The following terms are used throughout the analysis:

Major crops are wheat, feed grain, soybeans, and cotton.

Minor crops include flax, rye, buckwheat, and tame hay.

Unlimited diversion allows entire regions to be retired from crop production in a voluntary rental program on a long-term basis. For the lower price set in 1975, this program is designated by L_u. For medium prices and higher prices, the designation is M_u and H_u, respectively.

75 percent maximum diversion allows a maximum of 75 percent of the cropland in any region to be retired from crop production under a voluntary rental pro-

---

1. Mathematical structure of the programming model is the same as used by Skold and Heady (Chapter 4), except for the additional quota restraints. The additional restraints simulate a farm economy with farm programs that restrict production by restraints on acreage of individual crops. The additional restraints can be shown as

$$C_{kq} \leqslant Q_{kq}$$

$k = 1, \ldots, \ldots, 150$
$q = 1$ for wheat, 2 for feed grain, 4 for soybeans, and 5 for cotton

where Q_{kq} denotes the acres of allotment or quota in the kth producing area of qth crop
       C_{kq} denotes the acres of crop activity q in kth producing area

gram. For the three price levels studied, this program is designated by L_{75}, M_{75}, and H_{75}.

50 *percent maximum diversion* (L_{50}, M_{50}, and H_{50}) allows a maximum of one-half of any region to be retired from crop production under a voluntary rental program.

25 *percent maximum diversion* (L_{25}, M_{25}, and H_{25}) allows a maximum of one-fourth of any region to be retired from crop production under a voluntary rental program.

PAYMENT LEVEL

The payment necessary for farmer participation is assumed to equal the estimated profit margin per acre now being realized for major crops in the regions analyzed. Under a given program, the farmer could simply "rent" his land to the government and receive a payment equal to the return now realized from farming. Actually, he could receive a higher return than at present, since through whole-farm participation he could eliminate certain overhead costs such as those related to machinery and equipment, and investment in these capital items would be freed for use elsewhere. Also, his labor would be freed for employment in other alternatives.

This above method provides a yardstick to compare the four retirement programs analyzed. In the short run, some farmers would not want to stop farming at the computed level of payment. On the other hand, some farmers would participate even at a lower payment rate since this level of compensation plus employment of labor and capital elsewhere would give them a greater net income. Many farmers approaching or reaching retirement would participate at a payment rate lower than one made competitive under farm operation, since their alternative would be to rent the farm. Under each of the price levels analyzed, a minimum per-acre payment is provided and a payment of $5 per acre is added for weed control and related costs. The computed payments are levels estimated to achieve farmer participation for land retirement only. They do not include additional income supplements as in the case of current wheat, feed-grain, and cotton programs.

TRADE-OFFS AMONG ACRES RETIRED, GOVERNMENT PROGRAM COSTS, AND NET FARM INCOME WITH ALTERNATIVE GOVERNMENT PROGRAMS AND PRICE LEVELS

This section summarizes the results of the 12 alternative land-retirement programs studied for 1975. These results assume that land not needed for crop production remains idle and is not used for other purposes such as grass for beef production or trees.[2] Tables 7.2, 7.3, and 7.4 show the estimated acreages, production, and yields by program of the major crops for the three levels studied (i.e., lower, medium, and higher prices in 1975).

2. For an analysis of the effects when excess cropland is grazed for additional beef production, see *An Analysis of Some Farm Program Alternatives for the Future*, (CAED Report 34, Center for Agriculture and Economic Development, Iowa State Univ., Apr. 1969.)

LOWER PRICES IN 1975

With lower prices in 1975, total wheat acres vary from 48.2 million with 75 percent maximum diversion (L_{75}) up to 57.4 million with 25 percent maximum diversion (L_{25}) in a region (Table 7.2). Wheat production varies from a low of 1.5 billion bushels with 75 percent maximum diversion (L_{75}) in a region to a high of 1.7 billion bushels under program L_{25}. More wheat is used for feed purposes under program L_{25} and, consequently, total wheat production is higher.[3] Wheat yield is estimated at 30.7 bushels per acre with program L_u versus 29.6 bushels per acre under L_{25}. With lower prices and 25 percent maximum diversion in any given region (L_{25}), more marginal land is brought into production and the resulting yield is lower while acres are higher.

Total feed-grain acres are lowest, 96.2 million, with unlimited diversion (L_u), and reach a high of 99.5 million acres with program L_{75}. Total feed-grain production is also highest (184 million tons) under program L_{75} but lowest (177 million tons) with program L_{25}. As is the case with wheat, variations in feed-grain production can be explained by the amount of wheat used for feed (i.e., wheat is a substitute for feed grain). Feed-grain yields follow a pattern similar to wheat. Fewer acres of feed grain are required with unlimited diversion since feed grain becomes concentrated in areas which are both the most profitable and have the highest yields. Yields are highest (1.90 tons corn equivalent per acre) with program L_u and lowest (1.78 tons) with program L_{25} as more marginal land is farmed.

Acreages and production of soybeans and cotton are essentially constant for all programs with lower prices in 1975. Yields of soybeans and cotton follow the same pattern as wheat and feed grain. Yields are highest with unlimited diversion (L_u) and lowest under program L_{25}. In general, as restrictions are placed on the location of retired cropland, more marginal land is farmed, acres of crops harvested increase, and yields decrease.

MEDIUM PRICES IN 1975

Acreages, production, and yields of the major crops under medium prices are reported in Table 7.3. Since the demand for wheat, feed grain, and soybeans is less under medium prices than under lower prices, the amount of production cleared through the market is less. (Wheat exports and total cotton production are held constant for all three price levels studied.) Total wheat acres range from 43 million with 75 percent maximum diversion (M_{75}) to 56.2 million with 25 percent maximum diversion (M_{25}) in a region. Wheat production ranges between 1.4 billion bushels under program M_{75} and 1.7 billion bushels with program M_{25}. Again, this variation is due to the increased use of wheat for feed purposes under program M_{25}. With unlimited diversion (M_u), wheat yields are estimated at 32.8 bushels per acre versus 30.4 bushels per acre under program M_{25}. With program M_{25}, more marginal land is farmed and the resulting wheat yield is lower.

---

3. Under 25 percent maximum diversion, farmers find it more profitable to use wheat rather than feed grain for feed purposes.

Total feed-grain acres vary from 79.1 million under program M_u up to 82.7 million with 50 percent maximum diversion (M_{50}). Feed-grain production is highest (174 million tons) with program M_{75} and reaches a low of 163 million tons under program M_{25}. This variation in feed-grain production is due to the use of wheat for feed purposes. As feed-grain production declines under a particular program, wheat production rises accordingly. The lowest yield of feed grain is 1.97 tons per acre under program M_{25} and highest (2.17 tons) with program M_u. Acreages and production of soybeans and cotton with medium prices in 1975 are essentially constant for all programs studied. Yields of soybeans and cotton follow the same pattern as wheat and feed-grain yields. Yields are highest with unlimited diversion (M_u) and lowest with the most restrictive diversion program M_{25}, as under lower prices when restrictions are placed on the location of retired cropland, more marginal land is farmed, acres of crops harvested increase, and yields decrease.

HIGHER PRICES IN 1975

Acreage, production, and yield patterns with higher prices in 1975 are presented in Table 7.4. Demand for wheat, feed grain, and soybeans is less under higher prices than either lower or medium prices. As a result, the amount of production cleared through the market under higher prices is the lowest of all price levels studied. Total wheat acres are 40.2 million with unlimited diversion (H_u) versus 56.0 million with 25 percent maximum diversion (H_{25}). Wheat production varies from a low of 1.4 billion bushels under program H_{75} to a high of 1.7 billion bushels under program H_{25}. This difference in wheat production is due to variations in the amounts of wheat used for feed purposes. Yields of wheat are estimated at 34.5 bushels per acre with program H_u versus 31.2 bushels under program H_{25}.

Total feed-grain acres vary from a low of 72.1 million with program H_u to a high of 80.5 million acres under program H_{25}. Feed-grain production is lowest (152 million tons) with program H_{25} and highest (164 million tons) under program H_{75}. Variations in total feed-grain production also are due to the use of different quantities of wheat for feed purposes under the various programs and price levels. Soybean acres show greater variation under higher prices than under the other two price levels. Total soybean acres vary from a low of 29.7 million with program H_u to a high of 31.9 million under program H_{25}. Soybean production is constant for all programs and price levels, but yields range from 31.3 bushels per acre with program H_u to 29.3 bushels under program H_{25}. Cotton production is constant under all programs and price levels, and acreage varies only slightly. Cotton yields are highest (523 pounds of lint per acre) under program H_u and lowest (495 pounds) with program H_{25}. Once again as locational restrictions are placed on retired cropland, more marginal land is farmed, acres of cropland harvested increase, and yields decrease.

ACRES RETIRED WITH ALTERNATIVE GOVERNMENT PROGRAMS AND PRICE LEVELS

Acres retired by programs for each price level are summarized in Figure 7.5. Total acres retired vary from a low of 40.3 million with lower prices and 25 per-

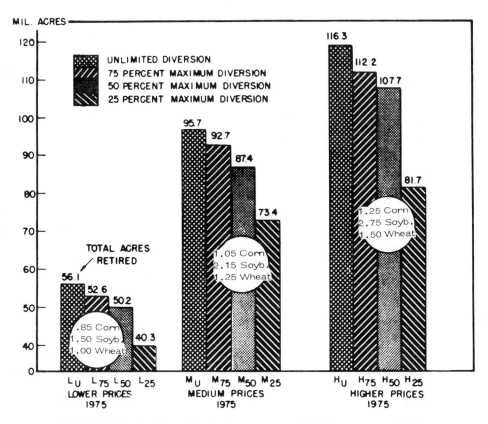

Fig. 7.5. Total major and minor crop acres retired by program, 1975.

cent maximum diversion up to 116.3 million acres with higher prices and unlimited diversion in a region. Earlier estimates have shown similarly that excess capacity will prevail in 1980.[4] The type of retirement program used determines the extent of adjustments posed in different rural communities. The price level generally affects the total acres that must be idled to attain the resulting production of crops. The demand for wheat, feed grain, and soybeans declines as the price level rises. At the same time, the supply or amount offered for sale in the market increases as the price level rises. Therefore, to balance supply and demand, more cropland acres must be diverted from crop production as the price level rises.

A land-retirement program with unlimited diversion in any region would have a different effect on rural communities than would a program limiting diversion to 25 percent. Programs limiting land retirement to a maximum of 75 percent, or only 50 percent, in each region would have still different effects on communities. The Soil Bank program of the 1950s was not popular because it allowed fairly

4. Rex Daly and Alvin C. Egbert, "A Look Ahead for Food and Agriculture," *Agr. Econ. Res.*, Jan. 1966; Earl O. Heady and Leo V. Mayer, *Food Needs and U.S. Agriculture in 1980*, volume 1, Technical Papers, National Advisory Commission of Food and Fiber, *Washington*, D.C., Aug. 1967; Martin Abel and Anthony S. Rojko, *World Food Situation: Prospects for World Grain Production, Consumption and Trade*, FAER No. 35, USDA, Sept. 1967.

concentrated land retirement (whole-farm) in many rural communities. It provided measures for income improvement only for farmers and farm owners and neglected to offset the effects of such programs on local businesses and institutions. A land-retirement program with unlimited regional concentration would have effects even more severe than those of the Soil Bank program of the 1950s. If diversion is unlimited, smaller farm communities of the country must absorb the major portion of the adjustment effects created by land diversion.[5] However, when land retirement is limited to a maximum of 25 percent of the cropland in a given region, all areas of the country must absorb some of the adjustment effects.

LOWER PRICES IN 1975

With lower prices in 1975, total crop acres retired range from 40.3 to 56.1 million, depending on the type of program selected. With unlimited diversion (L_u), 56.1 million acres must be retired to balance supply and demand. With the program modified to allow a maximum 75 percent diversion (L_{75}), a total of 52.6 million acres are diverted, while under program L_{25} total diverted acres decline to 40.3 million.

MEDIUM PRICES IN 1975

This same kind of comparison can be made between alternative programs for the medium and higher price levels. With medium prices in 1975 and unlimited diversion (M_u), 95.7 million acres are retired. Program M_{25} has 73.4 million acres diverted. Between these two extremes, program M_{75} has 92.7 million acres diverted and program M_{50} has 87.4 million acres retired.

HIGHER PRICES IN 1975

With higher prices in 1975, acres retired vary from a high of 116.3 million with program H_u to a low of 81.7 million under program H_{25}. Under program H_{75}, 112.2 million acres are diverted. With program H_{50}, 107.7 million acres are retired. For all programs studied, land would be placed in the programs on a bid basis with whole-farm–cropland participation. Rental contracts on the retired excess cropland could run for 10 or more years.

ADDITIONAL TRADE-OFFS

Additional trade-offs exist between acres retired and alternative price levels. If a program with unlimited diversion were desired by the public and its policy-makers, L_u, M_u, or H_u could be selected. If L_u (unlimited diversion with lower prices) were selected, 56.1 million acres would be diverted. If medium prices were desired (M_u), then 95.7 million acres would be retired. If higher prices were selected (H_u) a further sacrifice (i.e., the adjustment impacts on particular rural

5. See Figures 7.11 through 7.15 for a comparison of the locational effects of different land diversion programs in 1975. These adjustment effects are analyzed in the next chapter.

communities) must be made in the number of acres (116.3 million) diverted. If the goal were to retire around 80 million acres, either program M_{50} with 87.4 million acres retired or program M_{25} with 73.4 million acres would approach this level at a medium price level. Program H_{25} with 81.7 million acres diverted is very near the 80-million–acre level.

Four alternative programs can support prices at the medium level. More land must be retired with unlimited diversion because it emphasizes the retirement of low-yield land. On the other hand, the cost of programs will increase as more restraints are placed on land retirement by individual regions and larger per-acre payments must be made to retire better land over more regions. These types of effects must be considered, along with the impact of each program on community adjustments and public acceptance of the program costs involved.

GOVERNMENT COSTS PER ACRE WITH ALTERNATIVE GOVERNMENT PROGRAMS AND PRICE LEVELS

LOWER PRICES IN 1975

Under lower prices in 1975, average government costs per acre vary between $8.67 and $9.72 (Figure 7.6).[6] Much of the excess cropland is retired at the mini-

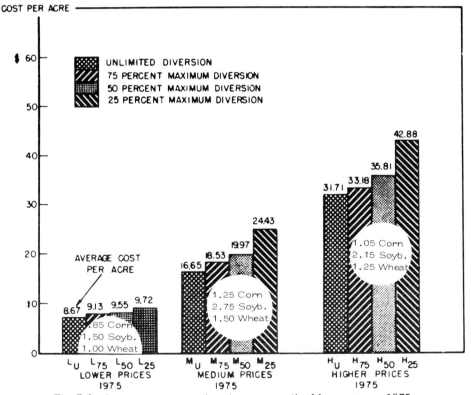

Fig. 7.6. Average government cost per acre retired by program, 1975.

6. See Tables 7A-1, 7A-2, and 7A-3 for the calculation of the average government costs.

mum payment and the resulting averages are relatively close. Under lower prices, many farmers in each region would not cover all costs of production for wheat, feed grain, and soybeans, and others would have only a small positive return. For the programs studied, the payment for diversion land equals the alternative return if the land were used in crop production. Since, under lower prices, not all production costs would be covered in some regions, a minimum payment of $1.50 per acre is assumed to cover land taxes and other fixed costs. When $5.00 is added for weed control, the minimum per-acre payment for the lower price program is $6.50.[7]

Under lower prices in 1975, returns are negative on much of the excess cropland, and the government payment necessary to hold this land from production and redirect its uses also would be low. As the price level rises, the return on cropland increases, and the government payment (both average and total) necessary to enroll cropland to balance supply and demand also rises.

MEDIUM PRICES IN 1975

Under medium prices in 1975, the average government cost per acre varies more than for lower prices (Figure 7.6). With unlimited diversion (M_u), the average government payment is $16.65 per acre versus $24.43 with 25 percent maximum diversion (M_{25}). The remaining medium price programs fall between these two extremes. With program M_{75} the average government payment is $18.53 while under program M_{50} the average cost is $19.97. In other words, the per-acre cost rises as more restraints are placed on the proportion of land diverted in each region.

HIGHER PRICES IN 1975

The average government cost per acre with higher prices and unlimited diversion (H_u) is almost twice as high as for the medium price program of the same type (Figure 7.6). The average cost is $31.71 per acre under program H_u. With program H_{75}, average cost is $33.18 per acre, while under program H_{50} the average cost is $35.81 per acre. With 25 percent maximum diversion (H_{25}), the average government cost is $42.88 per acre.

TOTAL GOVERNMENT COSTS WITH ALTERNATIVE GOVERNMENT PROGRAMS
AND PRICE LEVELS

Total government costs for the various programs and price levels studied are presented in Figure 7.7. For the three price levels analyzed (i.e., lower, medium, and higher) total government costs vary from a low of $0.8 billion up to $4.2 billion.

7. The minimum assumed for medium price programs is $11 per acre and for higher price programs $15 per acre.

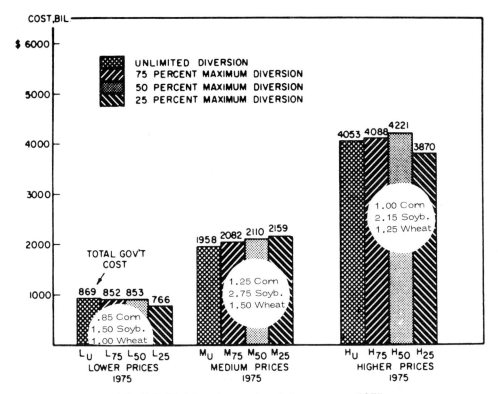

Fig. 7.7. Total government costs by program, 1975.

LOWER PRICES IN 1975

Under lower prices in 1975 and unlimited diversion (L_u), total government costs for diversion are estimated at $869 million. Under program L_{75}, total costs are $852 million, and with program L_{50} total government costs only increase to $853 million. Under program L_{25}, total government costs decline to $766 million. With program L_{25}, the average cost per acre retired is higher than for other lower price programs (Figure 7.6) but total acres retired are fewer since a much greater amount of less productive land is used for crop production (Figure 7.5). As a result, total government costs are lower for program L_{25} than for any other lower price program.

MEDIUM PRICES IN 1975

With medium prices in 1975, total farm program costs range from $2 billion up to $2.2 billion. With program M_u, total costs are projected at $2 billion, while under both programs M_{75} and M_{50}, total government costs are estimated at $2.1 billion. Under program M_{25}, total costs rise to $2.2 billion.

HIGHER PRICES IN 1975

With higher prices in 1975 and unlimited diversion (H_u), total government costs are $4.1 billion. Under program H_{75}, total government costs remain near

$4.1 billion, while under program H_{50}, total costs rise to $4.2 billion. With program H_{25}, government costs fall to $3.9 billion. With program H_{25}, a much greater amount of less productive land is used for crop production. As a result, total government costs are lower for program H_{25} than for any other higher price program (even though average cost per acre is higher).

ADDITIONAL TRADE-OFFS

Comparisons also can be made of land-retirement costs among the three price levels. With unlimited diversion and lower prices in 1975 (L_u), total government costs are $869 million. Under program M_u total costs are $2 billion while with program H_u they are $4.1 billion. If higher levels of farm prices were the goal, without respect to government costs, a higher level of prices could be attained with any of the programs H_u, H_{75}, H_{50}, and H_{25}. However, these programs have a total government cost for diversion about twice as great as the costs for the same programs at the medium price level. Also, the higher level of prices requires diversion of up to 116 million acres, about 20 percent more than the largest diversion under medium prices. Program costs for land retirement would be halved again, as compared to medium price costs, if the lower level of prices were attained in 1975. Under lower prices, land diversion would range between 40.3 and 56.1 million acres (Figure 7.5).

These trade-offs emphasize that a number of goals and criteria must be considered before a particular farm policy or farm policy combination is selected. Especially important is the level of income and the optimum distribution of payments and retired cropland across the United States. In the next section we discuss the level of income associated with each price level.

NET FARM INCOMES WITH ALTERNATIVE GOVERNMENT PROGRAMS AND PRICE LEVELS

The level of farm income and farm program cost associated with each program and price level studied is given in Figure 7.8. For the 12 programs analyzed, net farm income[8] ranges from $12.2 billion to $18.5 billion. In general, net farm income increases with the amount of land retired and the level of prices attained under the various programs.

Under lower prices, net farm income ranges from $12.2 billion to $13.3 billion. With program L_u, net farm income is estimated at $13.3 billion. Under program L_{75}, net income declines to $13.1 billion, while with program L_{50}, net farm income is $12.8 billion. With 25 percent maximum diversion (L_{25}), net income would be even lower, $12.2 billion. The lower net income under L_{25} is due mainly to higher cash expenses associated with this program (see Table 7A-4). The medium price programs follow a similar pattern. Net farm income is $16.6 billion under medium prices and unlimited diversion (M_u). Under program M_{75}, net farm income is $16.4 billion, while under M_{50}, it is $16 billion. Net farm income is only $14.6 billion under program M_{25}, due mainly to higher cash ex-

---

8. See Tables 7A-4, 7A-5, and 7A-6 for a breakdown of the items which enter into the calculation of net farm income.

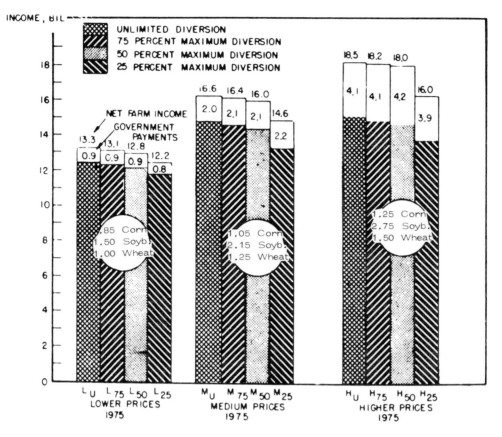

Fig. 7.8. Net farm income by program, 1975.

penses associated with this program. For the higher price level, net farm income is lowest under program H_{25} ($16 billion) and highest with program H_u ($18.5 billion). The variation in level of income is small for programs which retire 50, 75, and an unlimited percentage of land by regions.

ADDITIONAL TRADE-OFFS

A large number of trade-offs (i.e., sacrifices in one direction for increases in another item or direction) are possible for the 12 programs in Figure 7.8. For example, estimated net farm income in 1975 is $13.3 billion under program L_u. With program L_{25} net farm income is $12.2 billion, more than $1 billion less. Government payments for these two programs are essentially the same ($0.9 billion and $0.8 billion). On the other hand, the location of retired cropland and distribution of government payments are greatly different. The lower net farm income under L_{25} is due mainly to higher cash expenses associated with this program (see Appendix Table 7A-4). More marginal land must be farmed under program L_{25} and fertilizer costs and power and machinery costs are generally higher on the marginal land.

With the price level constant, all programs analyzed have essentially the same cash receipts from farm marketings. As a result, differences in net farm incomes are due to regional changes in the distribution of production and to corresponding changes in expenses and government payments. Changes in expenses cause most of the variations in net farm incomes when government payments are relatively constant. Under a given set of prices, these changes reflect the cost of inefficiency associated with alternative programs as production is allocated to different regions and soils.

Under L_u and L_{25}, regional changes cause a difference in net farm incomes of $1 billion. With medium prices, net farm incomes differ by $2 billion between unlimited diversion and 25 percent maximum diversion programs. Government payments under program M_{25} are only $0.2 billion higher than for program M_u, but expenses under program M_{25} are $2.2 billion higher (see Table 7A-5). With higher prices in 1975 and unlimited diversion (H_u), net farm income is $2.5 billion more than under H_{25}. Again inefficiencies due to restrictions on retired cropland cause net farm income to decline. More marginal land must be farmed under the more restrictive diversion programs, and fertilizer costs as well as machinery costs are usually higher on the marginal land.

It is the responsibility of farm groups, the public, and policymakers to determine whether the inefficiencies caused by more restrictive diversion programs and the associated lower net farm incomes merit the reduced pressures for adjust-

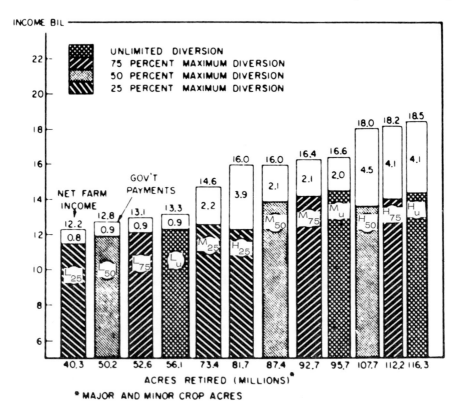

Fig. 7.9. Net farm income and acres retired by program, 1975.

ment on the rural communities. While net farm income is greater under the less restrictive programs, it has a different distribution among farming regions with respect to both farm marketings and government payments. These facets also are important in farm program selection. Policymakers and the public also have the option of long-term programs used alone or annual programs such as those of the present continued at higher costs. They also can select a combination of such programs, with different mixes of the two selected over time.

NET FARM INCOMES AND ACRES RETIRED WITH ALTERNATIVE GOVERNMENT PROGRAMS AND PRICE LEVELS

Results presented in Figures 7.5, 7.8, and 7.9 are summarized in Figure 7.9. For 11 of the 12 program alternatives, net farm income rises as the number of acres retired increases. Net farm income ranges from $12.2 billion with 40.3 million acres retired (L_{25}) up to $18.5 billion with program H_u and 116.3 million acres retired. Government costs are $0.8 billion under program L_{25} versus $4.1 billion with program H_u. Many other trade-offs and comparisons are possible but many of these have been discussed earlier. Each of the programs evaluated for 1975 has a particular regional distribution of acres retired and government payments associated with it. In the following sections we discuss these distributional aspects and the effects of alternative price levels on selected farm types and land values.

PATTERNS OF LAND RETIREMENT—SOME ADDITIONAL TRADE-OFFS

Location of retired cropland under four levels of regional concentration for medium price programs is shown in Figures 7.10 through 7.14. Only the regional distributions under medium price programs are shown since the patterns of land retirement under different degrees of regional concentration for lower and higher price programs are similar to those for the medium price level. (Only the total amount of retired acres changes materially.) Tables 7.5 through 7.10 include a regional breakdown of retired cropland for all programs studied, as well as the regional distribution of government payments.

UNLIMITED DIVERSION

Location of retired cropland with unlimited diversion and medium prices in 1975 is shown in Figure 7.10. Areas of heaviest concentration include the Northern Plains, an area extending from the Panhandle of Oklahoma through eastern Kansas and western Missouri and a belt extending through the Southeast. With unlimited diversion there are no restrictions on the amount of cropland retired in a given area. Government costs are minimized since land retirement is concentrated in those areas which have the lowest comparative advantage in producing the major crops.

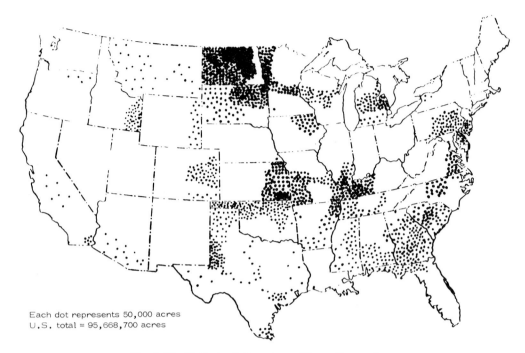

Each dot represents 50,000 acres
U.S. total = 95,668,700 acres

Fig. 7.10. Unlimited diversion with medium prices.

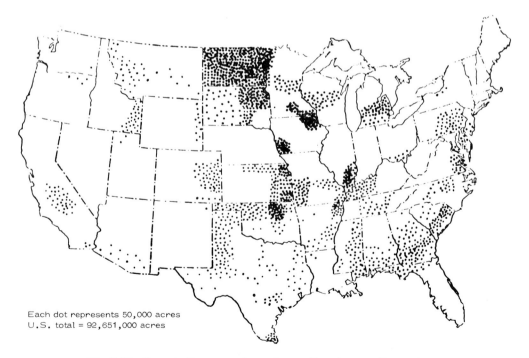

Each dot represents 50,000 acres
U.S. total = 92,651,000 acres

Fig. 7.11. Seventy-five percent maximum diversion, medium prices.

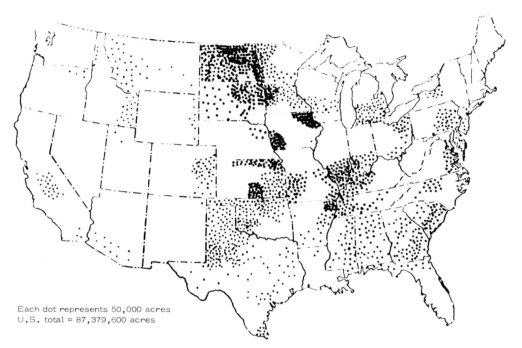

Each dot represents 50,000 acres
U.S. total = 87,379,600 acres

Fig. 7.12. Fifty percent maximum diversion, medium prices.

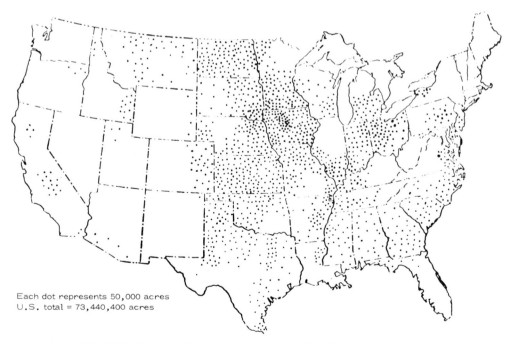

Each dot represents 50,000 acres
U.S. total = 73,440,400 acres

Fig. 7.13. Twenty-five percent maximum diversion, medium prices.

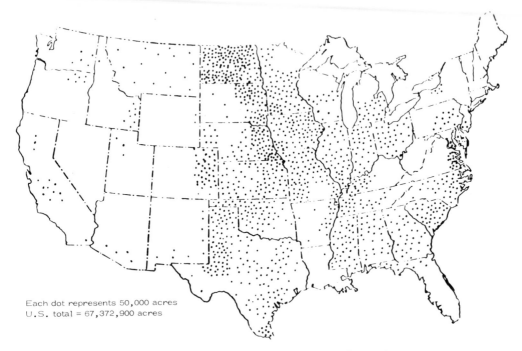

Each dot represents 50,000 acres
U.S. total = 67,372,900 acres

Fig. 7.14. Present programs continued, medium prices.

75 PERCENT MAXIMUM DIVERSION

Location of retired cropland under a 75 percent maximum diversion program and medium prices in 1975 is shown in Figure 7.11. Land retirement is less concentrated than under unlimited diversion but the general pattern of retirement is the same. Land retirement is still concentrated in the Northern Plains. With this program in 1975, a maximum of three-fourths of an area can be retired.

50 PERCENT MAXIMUM DIVERSION

Under this program in 1975 a maximum of one-half a region can be diverted from major or minor crop production. Location of retired cropland with medium prices and 50 percent maximum diversion is shown in Figure 7.12. Concentration of retired land is less with this program than with either unlimited diversion or 75 percent maximum diversion. Total acres retired are also less—87.5 million. Many regions that did not have land retired under the unlimited diversion program now have some cropland diverted. The areas of land retirement include a belt running from North Dakota through Michigan, a belt starting in central Texas and running through the southern part of the Corn Belt, and a broad belt extending through the Southeast.

25 PERCENT MAXIMUM DIVERSION

Location of retired cropland with medium prices and 25 percent maximum diversion in 1975 is shown in Figure 7.13. With this program land retirement is the least concentrated of many medium price programs studied. Retired cropland is dispersed over nearly all areas of the United States. This allocation of retired cropland has a more "dampening effect" on forces for change in the rural community than do the above programs. However, it also results in somewhat reduced efficiency of agricultural production and a somewhat lower total net farm income. The lower net farm income leads to a somewhat lower total national income, but income is distributed more evenly among regions. The pattern of land retirement under a 25 percent limit in concentration is quite similar to the pattern under current programs.

PRESENT PROGRAMS CONTINUED

With present programs continued in 1975 and medium prices, the location of retired cropland would be that shown in Figure 7.14. Under this program the concentration of retired cropland falls between 50 percent maximum diversion and 25 percent maximum diversion programs (Figures 7.12 and 7.13). Total acres retired, 67.4 million, are less under this program than under any of the other programs studied for the medium price levels. All cropping regions of the United States have some diverted cropland.

DISTRIBUTION OF RETIRED CROPLAND AND GOVERNMENT PAYMENTS FOR PRICE LEVELS STUDIED

The regional distributions of diverted acres and government payments for all programs analyzed are summarized in Tables 7.5 through 7.10. These tables provide the same general information as Figures 7.10 through 7.14 and supply additional information on other farm program alternatives studied.

LOWER PRICES IN 1975

The regional distributions of retired cropland at lower prices are summarized in Table 7.5 with four program alternatives. Under lower prices and unlimited diversion in 1975 (L_u), 24.2 million acres (42.5 percent of the total) are retired in the Northern Plains. Another 10.5 million acres (18.4 percent of the total) are retired in the Southern Plains. The Corn Belt has 4.4 million acres or 7.8 percent of the total retired acres. A total of 57 million acres are retired for the United States. With lower prices and 75 percent maximum diversion (L_{75}), a total of 53.4 million acres are retired in the United States. Of this total, 21.3 million acres (39.8 percent) are retired in the Northern Plains and 11 million acres (20.6 percent) are retired in the Southern Plains. Of the total, the Corn Belt retires 4.3 million acres (8.1 percent). With program L_{50} a total of 51.1 million acres are retired. The Northern Plains retires 17.5 million acres (34.4 percent) while the Southern Plains diverts 11.5 million acres (22.5 percent of the total). The Corn Belt retires 3.9 million acres (7.7 percent of the total). Under program L_{25} a total of 41.2 million acres are retired. The Northern Plains again has the highest number of acres retired with 14.3 million (34.5 percent of the total). The Southern Plains has 8 million acres retired (19.4 percent) and the Corn Belt 4.7 million acres (11.4 percent). In general, for programs at lower prices, the amount of cropland diverted in more productive areas increases as more restrictions are placed on the regional concentration of retired cropland. In contrast, the amount of crop-land diverted in the more marginal areas decreases as the program becomes more restrictive (e.g., compare the Corn Belt and Northern Plains).

The distribution of government payments for programs under the lower price level is given in Table 7.6. The payment distributions follow a pattern similar to the land-retirement patterns described above. With unlimited diversion and lower prices in 1975 (L_u), government payments total $494 million. Payments in the Northern Plains are $161 million (32.5 percent of the total) while the Southern Plains receives $112 million (22.8 percent of the total). This payment pattern compares with the land-retirement pattern of 42.5 percent in the Northern Plains and 18.4 percent in the Southern Plains for the same program. With lower prices and 75 percent maximum diversion (L_{75}), government diversion payments total $487 million. The largest payment is in the Northern Plains ($151 million or 31 percent of the total) while the Southern Plains is second ($125 million or 25.6 percent of the total). The Corn Belt receives only $28 million (5.8 percent of the total). With lower prices and 50 percent maximum diversion (L_{50}), government payments total $488 million. Payments in the Northern Plains are $123 million (25.2 percent of the total) while payments in the Southern Plains total $131 million (26.9 percent). The Corn Belt ranks fifth in total payments with $33 million (6.7 percent of the total). With a limit of 25 percent maximum diversion (L_{25}), the Northern Plains ranks first with $109 million (27 percent of the total). The Southern Plains is second with $93 million (23.1 percent), the Delta is third with $54 million (14 percent), and the Corn Belt is fourth with $48 million (12 percent of the total). Estimated payments to farmers are lower under program L_{25} than for other alternatives. Although the average payment per acre is highest for L_{25} (see Figure 7.6), total acres retired are less (Figure 7.5) and total payments are lower. As explained in an earlier section, net farm income under program L_{25}, $12.2 billion, is lower than for any other program.

MEDIUM PRICES IN 1975

The results in Table 7.7 are summarized in Figures 7.10 through 7.14. The largest amount of retired cropland under program M_u in the Northern Plains— 29.2 million acres or 30.4 percent of the total. The Southern Plains ranks second with 12.4 million acres (13 percent), while the Corn Belt retires 7.7 million acres (8 percent of the total). A total of 95.7 million acres are retired under program M_u. With medium prices and 75 percent maximum diversion (M_{75}), a total of 92.6 million acres are idled. The Northern Plains retires 26.8 million acres (28.9 percent) while the Southern Plains retires 13.1 million acres or 14.2 percent of the total retired. The Corn Belt ranks fourth with 9.6 million acres (10.3 percent) retired. The Northern Plains, with 20.9 million acres (23.9 percent) retired, again has the most idled land under program M_{50}. The Southern Plains is second with 15.4 million acres (17.6 percent), while the Corn Belt is third with 13.6 million acres retired (15.6 percent of the total). A total of 87.4 million acres are retired for the United States. With program M_{25} a total of 73.4 million acres are retired. The distribution includes 18.9 million acres (25.8 percent) in the Northern Plains,

17 million acres retired (23.1 percent) in the Corn Belt, and 9.9 million acres (13.5 percent) in the Southern Plains. Of all medium price programs, this program has the lowest net farm income ($14.6 billion; Figure 7.8). In general, as the retirement program becomes more restrictive, the more productive regions retire more cropland and the marginal regions retire less.

With present wheat, feed-grain, and cotton programs continued in 1975, a total of 67.4 million acres are diverted. The Northern Plains ranks first with 18 million acres (26.7 percent of total) and the Corn Belt is second with 13.1 million acres retired—19.5 percent of the total. The Southern Plains is third again with 10.9 million acres retired or 16.1 percent of the total. The regional distributions of government payments for the medium price programs are summarized in Table 7.8. The payment distributions follow a pattern similar to the acreage distributions discussed above. Total government payments are $1.6 billion under medium prices and unlimited diversion in 1975 (M_u). The rank of regions in payment receipts is in this order: Northern Plains, Southern Plains, Southeast, Corn Belt, Lake states, Mountain, Delta, Pacific, and Northeast. A considerable shift takes place, however, as concentration is restricted to 25 percent. With medium prices and 25 percent maximum diversion (M_{25}), government payments total $1.8 billion. The Corn Belt receives $564 million (31.4 percent), while the Northern Plains receives $367 million or 20.4 percent of total payments. The share of payments to the Southeast declines from 11.9 percent under M_u to 4.1 percent under M_{25}. Although total government payments under M_{25} are highest among all programs under medium prices, net farm income is the lowest—$14.6 billion. The more inefficient interregional pattern of production associated with this program causes farm expenses to be considerably higher than for other programs (see Table 7A-5). However, the smaller income is distributed more evenly among all regions.

HIGHER PRICES IN 1975

The distribution of diverted acres for programs under the higher price level is summarized in Table 7.9. Under higher prices and unlimited diversion in 1975 (H_u), retired cropland of 116.3 million acres is the highest of any of the programs analyzed. The Northern Plains ranks first with 33.1 million acres (28.5 percent) retired, the Southern Plains is second with 14.3 million acres (12.3 percent) retired, the Lake states third with 13.4 million acres (11.5 percent) retired, and the Corn Belt fourth with 13.0 million acres diverted (11.2 percent of the total). With program H_{75} a total of 112.2 million acres are retired and are distributed 27.9 percent to the Northern Plains, 15.1 percent to the Corn Belt, 12.8 percent to the Great Lakes, 12.6 percent to the Southern Plains, and 8.9 percent to the Southeast. With higher prices and 50 percent maximum diversion (H_{50}), the total of 107.7 million acres retired includes 23.6 percent in the Northern Plains and 19 percent in the Corn Belt. Under program H_{25}, 81.7 million acres are idled and the Corn Belt ranks first with 22.6 million acres or 27.7 percent of the total. The Northern Plains is second with 19.5 million acres or 23.8 percent of the total, and the Southern Plains is third with 12.2 percent. Program H_{25} has the lowest net farm income and least cropland retired of all programs under the higher price level.

The distributions of government payments for the four higher price programs are given in Table 7.10. These distributions are similar to the cropland retirement patterns discussed above. With program H_u, government payments to farmers total $3.7 billion. The Northern Plains receives $749 million (20.3 percent of the total), while Corn Belt payments are $489 million—13.3 percent of the total. The Southern Plains ranks third with payments of $423 million (11.5 percent of total payments). Under H_{25}, as compared to H_u, the Corn Belt moves up sharply in percentage of payments, while the Southeast declines by a relatively large amount. Under higher prices and 75 percent maximum diversion (H_{75}), government payments total over $3.7 billion with 20.6 percent going to the Northern Plains and 19 percent to the Corn Belt. Under program H_{50}, payments to farmers are $3.9 billion and the Corn Belt ranks first with payments of $942 million (24.3 percent of the total). The Northern Plains is second with 18.2 percent, and the Southern Plains third with 13.5 percent of the total. The Corn Belt also ranks first (38.8 percent) under program H_{25} which has total government payments of $3.5 billion. The Northern Plains is second with 18.3 percent, and the Southern Plains third with 8.4 percent of the total. As mentioned above, this program has the lowest net farm income of the several programs under the higher price level.

EFFECT OF ALTERNATIVE PRICE LEVELS ON SELECTED FARMS IN 1975

Aggregate results for regions and the United States were discussed in previous sections. We now relate the analysis to conditions of selected individual farms. The effect of the three price levels on the value of farmland also is analyzed. Finally, the response of selected Iowa farms to lower prices in 1975 is evaluated.

COSTS OF PRODUCTION FOR SELECTED FARMS

For each price level studied, a set of projected yields and costs per acre was computed for each crop in each of the 150 producing areas. The results indicate that with lower prices in 1975 ($0.85 corn, $1.00 wheat, etc.) many farmers could not cover their costs of production.[9] Production costs of selected farms in the Northeast, Corn Belt, and Southern Plains are summarized in Table 7.11. Variable costs on these farms range from $14.91 per acre for wheat in the Southern Plains up to $57.45 per acre for corn in the Northeast. Total production costs are $28.34 per acre for wheat on the Southern Plains farm, $66.10 per acre for corn on the Corn Belt farm, and $90.82 per acre for corn on the Northeast area farm.

---

9. For computational purposes, with the lower price programs only variable costs of production were used in the linear programming model. When total production costs were used in the model, many farms did not earn a positive return on their crop enterprises (farmers lost money). This indicates that lower prices ($0.85 corn, $1.00 wheat, etc.) are below long-run equilibrium prices for the costs and yields projected.

Given the production costs and the yields specified in Table 7.11, the average variable and total cost per bushel can be calculated.

The average variable cost per bushel of corn on the Northeast farm is $0.77. If the short-run market price of corn is above $0.77, this farmer may continue to grow corn (except where he has more profitable alternative uses of his resources). In the short run he can consume his capital equipment and avoid paying depreciation since it is not a cash expense. However, in the longer run he must earn a positive return on his labor and pay fixed costs such as land taxes. He must replace his equipment or go out of business. However, without alternative economic opportunities, this farmer might have to take a lower return on his labor than is indicated ($10.93 per acre).

Including all resources and fixed costs, the average total cost per bushel of corn is $1.21 for the Northeast farmer. This price includes return on labor but does not include an interest charge for investment in land. In the long run the price of corn in the Northeast must be at least $1.21 for this farmer to continue growing corn.[10] Under lower prices in 1975 ($0.85 corn, $1.00 wheat, etc.), the average price of corn per bushel in the Northeast is $1.17. In the short run this farmer could continue to grow corn. In the longer run the price is not high enough to cover all costs of production. The same situation exists for the two other farms characterized in Table 7.11.

The average variable cost of corn per bushel on the Corn Belt farm is $0.56. The average total cost per bushel is $0.89. With lower prices in 1975, the price of corn in the Corn Belt is $0.87. In the short run this farmer could cover his variable costs of $0.56 per bushel. In the longer run, however, he would have to discontinue farming, change to a farming operation that is competitive at these lower prices, or take lower returns for his labor. The average variable cost of wheat per bushel on the Southern Plains farm is $0.62 and the average total cost (excluding interest on land investment) is $1.18. Under lower prices in 1975, the price of wheat in the Southern Plains is $1.17 per bushel. As is the case for the other farms above, this farmer must also discontinue farming, reorganize his operation, or accept submarginal returns on his labor and capital resources.

COMPARISON OF MARGINAL WITH PRODUCTIVE FARMS FOR ALTERNATIVE PRICE LEVELS IN 1975

The costs and returns on four selected farms are shown in Table 7.12 for the three price levels included in the study. Two farms are in the Corn Belt—one marginal and one productive farm. Two farms are in the Northern Plains. The marginal farms are so named because the regions in which they are located always have the maximum amount of cropland retired for the program and price level studied.[11] The productive farms are in regions that always have (under all programs analyzed) crop production (wheat or corn) at the three price levels of the study.

---

10. The rental or investment value of land takes on a residual character.
11. In the linear programming model used, these regions always have the maximum amount of cropland idled that is allowed by the program restrictions.

LOWER PRICES IN 1975

Under lower prices in 1975, the marginal farm in the Corn Belt has total production costs of $66.54 while the productive farm has costs of $55.81 per acre for corn. Given the yields in Table 7.12, the average production costs are $0.98 and $0.56 per bushel, respectively. The net return above costs is - $10.79 for the marginal farm and $21.19 for the productive farm. The latter farm would have a positive return while the marginal farm would suffer a deficit in return to land investment and management or labor.

The marginal farm in the Northern Plains has total production costs of $21.01 while the productive farm has costs totaling $22.53 per acre for wheat. Given the yields in Table 7.12, the average cost per bushel produced is $1.05 for the marginal farm and $0.86 for the productive farm. (Interest on land investment is excluded.) The net returns above costs are - $0.41 and $4.25 per acre, respectively. With lower prices in 1975, both marginal farms incur losses while the productive farms have a small positive return at prices even lower than those studied. The margin above costs represents the return which could be a residual return to land investment and management.

MEDIUM PRICES IN 1975

Under medium prices in 1975, none of the four farms incurs losses relative to the cost items included. The marginal farm in the Corn Belt has total production costs of $68.55 while the productive farm has costs of $56.72. Given the projected yields, average costs per bushel are $0.97 on the marginal farm and $0.54 on the productive farm. The net returns above costs are $3.85 and $43.03, respectively. The profit margin of $3.85 would represent a small return on the investment value of land.

The marginal farm in the Northern Plains has total production costs of $21.11 per acre. The productive farm has costs totaling $22.60. With the yields of Table 7.12, the average costs per bushel produced are $1.01 and $0.84, respectively. The marginal farm has a net return above cost, an amount which could be a return to land investment of $5.77 per acre while the productive farm's net return is $11.96 per acre. The relative profitability of the productive farms in the Corn Belt and the Northern Plains gives them a comparative advantage, respectively, in corn and wheat production. To get the farmers with marginal land to retire their cropland, the government would have to pay them at least $3.85 in the Corn Belt and $5.77 in the Southern Plains. The government costs discussed earlier (see Figure 7.7) are based on the net return above costs for the marginal areas (see also Tables 7A-1 through 7A-4).

HIGHER PRICES IN 1975

With higher prices in 1975, the marginal farm in the Corn Belt has total production costs of $71.59. The productive farm has total costs of $58.81. Given the projected yields, the average cost per bushel produced is $0.95 for the marginal farm and $0.53 for the productive farm. The net returns above the costs cited are $19.16 and $64.39 per acre, respectively. These are the amounts which could be a residual return on land investment and management.

Total production costs on the marginal farm in the Northern Plains are $21.24 per acre, while the productive farm has total costs per acre of $22.76. Given the yields in Table 7.12, the average costs per bushel produced are $0.97 and $0.81, respectively. The net return above costs is $12.64 for the marginal farm and $20.36 for the productive farm. With higher prices, the government would have to pay the marginal farmers at least $19.16 in the Corn Belt (versus $3.85 under medium prices) and $12.64 in the Northern Plains (versus $5.77 under medium prices) to get this land into a retirement program.

ALTERNATIVE PRICE LEVELS AND VALUE OF FARMLAND

Given the costs and returns in Table 7.12, it is possible to evaluate the effect of alternative price levels on the value of land. Land values in Table 7.13 are derived for the four selected farms discussed in the previous sections—two farms in the Corn Belt and two in the Northern Plains.

LOWER PRICES IN 1975

With lower prices in 1975, the return to land and labor on the marginal farm in the Corn Belt is - $5.47. Subtracting a charge for labor and taxes gives a return to land of - $12.79. This farmer could not achieve a positive return on his land investment even if he accepted a low return on his labor. The derived or capitalized value of land on this farm would be zero. The land would have a positive value in the market only if land buyers anticipated some positive return from land ownership in the future (such as the expectation of higher prices) or an alternative use for it. The return to land and labor on the productive farm in the Corn Belt is $24.39. Subtracting out a charge for operator labor leaves a return to land of $17.19. The capitalized value of land on this productive farm, using a 7 percent interest rate, is $246 per acre.[12] The capitalized value of land for the marginal farm in the Northern Plains also is zero. The productive farm in the Northern Plains has a return to labor and land of $6.49. Subtracting a charge for operator labor leaves a return to land of $3.25 per acre. The capitalized value of this land using a 7 percent interest rate if $46 per acre.

MEDIUM PRICES IN 1975

With medium prices in 1975, the capitalized value of land on all the selected farms is positive. The marginal farm in the Corn Belt has a return to labor and land of $9.17 per acre. Subtracting a charge for operator labor leaves a return to

12. This price is considerably lower than the going market value of $642 per acre of productive central Iowa farmland as reported by William G. Murray and Daniel E. Porter, "Rise in Land Values Slows to 2 Percent in 1969," *Iowa Farm Sci.* 24 (Feb. 1970): 7.

land of only $1.85 and a capitalized price of land of $26 per acre. If the farm operator were willing to accept a lower return on his labor, the return to and value of land could be higher. The return to land and labor on the productive farm is $46.23 per acre. The return to land is $39.03 and the resulting capitalized land value is $558 per acre. The marginal farm in the Northern Plains has a return to labor and land of $8.01 per acre. The return above operator labor leaves a residual return to land of $4.77 and gives a capitalized land value of $68 per acre. The return to labor and land on the productive farm is $14.20 and a return to land alone is $10.96 per acre. The capitalized value of this land is $157 per acre.

HIGHER PRICES IN 1975

Under higher prices in 1975, the capitalized value of land increases further. Computed as above, the marginal farm in the Corn Belt has a capitalized land value of $245 per acre. The productive Corn Belt farm has a capitalized value of $863 per acre. The marginal farm in the Northern Plains has a return to land of $11.64 per acre and a capitalized value of $166 per acre. The productive farm has a return to land of $19.36 and a capitalized land value of $277 per acre. The capitalized value of land for the marginal farm in the Corn Belt ranges, depending on the price level, from zero to $245 per acre. The productive Corn Belt farm has a capitalized land value ranging between $246 and $863 per acre. For the marginal farm in the Northern Plains, the capitalized value ranges from zero to $166 per acre. For the productive farm in the same area, the capitalized value of land is estimated at $46 per acre under lower prices and $277 per acre under higher prices.

IOWA FARMS AND LOWER PRICES IN 1975

To evaluate the effects of lower prices in 1975 on Iowa farms, three regions of Iowa were arbitrarily selected for study. These three areas are shown in Figure

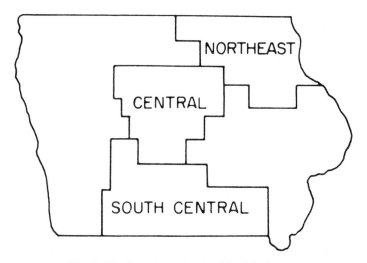

Fig. 7.15. Location of retired land in Iowa.

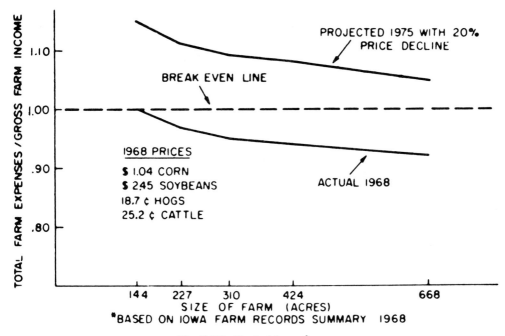

Fig. 7.16. Central Iowa farms.

7.15. Data from farms included in the Iowa Farm Business Associations are used for analysis of the effects of different price levels on profit margins and resource returns.

CENTRAL IOWA FARMS

The profitability of selected central Iowa farms in 1968 is shown in Figure 7.16. The curves (actual 1968 and projected 1975) represent all costs required to produce $1 of gross farm income for farms of different sizes.[13] Farms with sizes lying on the curve below the break-even line have a positive return to management.[14] The average size of the smaller farms included in the *Farm Records Summary* was 144 acres. In 1968 the ratio of total farm expenses to gross farm income was unity for these smaller farms. For the largest size farms in the *Records Summary*, the ratio was 0.89. Farms in this group received $1 of gross farm income for every $0.89 of expenditure and the return to management was $0.11 for every dollar of gross income.

13. Farm expenses include feed and livestock purchases, power and machinery costs, crop and other livestock expenses, hired labor, taxes, depreciation, interest paid, rent, operator and family labor, and a charge for operator equity in the farming operation. Gross income includes crop and livestock sales, government payments, value of home consumption, and inventory change. Any difference between total farm expenses and gross farm income is a residual return to management.

14. In the case of these farms, a return on land investment has been subtracted and is included in the cost curve. Hence, the difference between this curve and the break-even line is profit or return to management.

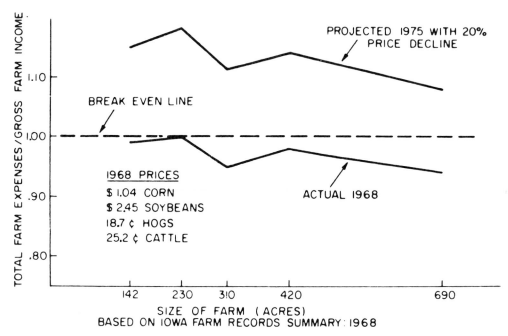

Fig. 7.17. Northeastern Iowa farms.

The higher curve in Figure 7.16 shows the cost of producing a dollar of gross farm income for farms of the same sizes (i.e., at the bottom of the graph) if prices in 1975 were 20 percent lower than prices in 1968. This second curve assumes that the farms maintain the same structure in 1975 as in 1968 (i.e., the same number of corn acres, soybean acres, cattle numbers, etc. as in 1968).[15] With a 20 percent price decline, all farms have a cost level lying above the break-even line. With 20 percent lower prices, farms of all sizes would lose money when charges for operator labor and equity capital are included in the cost curve. Several sizes of farms would still incur losses even if the operator were willing to accept a low or no return on his labor and/or equity capital.

NORTHEASTERN IOWA FARMS

Farms in the smallest size group for northeastern Iowa (Figure 7.17) averaged 142 acres in 1968. Farms in the larger size group averaged 690 acres. Farms in the smallest size group received $1 of gross income for every $0.99 of total farm expenses—a return to management of $0.01 for every dollar of gross income.

15. The actual 1968 structure of two of these groups of farms is given in Table 7.14. If prices of crops and livestock decline, that part of total expenses due to feed and livestock purchases will also decline. The projected 1975 line shown in Figure 7.17 is the net movement of the actual gross farm income for a 20 percent price decline.

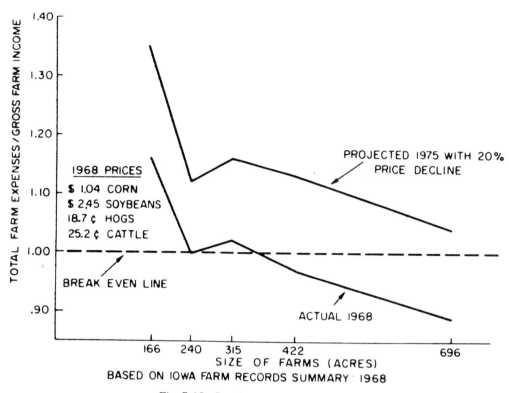

Fig. 7.18. South central Iowa farms.

Those in the larger size group received $1 of gross farm income for every $0.94 of total farm expenses.[16]

With 1975 prices 20 percent lower than in 1968, farms of all sizes would incur losses. The projected 1975 profitability curve (cost per $1 of gross income) is above the break-even line at all points. With 20 percent lower prices in 1975, these farms would have to discontinue operations, be reorganized on a more competitive basis, accept lower imputed land value, or suffer labor returns below market levels.

SOUTH CENTRAL IOWA FARMS

Farms in the smallest size group for south central Iowa averaged 166 acres while those in the largest size group averaged 696 in 1968 (Figure 7.18). The smallest size group received $1 of gross farm income for every $1.16 of total farm expenses—a negative return to management of - $0.16 per dollar of gross farm income. Farms in the largest size group received $1 of gross farm income for every

16. The profitability line for the sample of farms in northeastern Iowa slopes upward in two areas. This could be due to poor management on these specific size farms, indivisibility of certain farm inputs, or goals in farming other than profit maximization.

$0.89 of farm expenses—a return to management of $0.11 per dollar of gross farm income.

Assuming a constant structure, all farms in the south central Iowa group also would incur losses at prices 20 percent below 1968 levels. The projected 1975 cost or profitability curve lies above the break-even line for all sizes of farms included in the analysis. Under lower prices land owners would have to accept a greatly reduced land value unless farm operators were willing to take lower returns on their labor.

A POSSIBLE REORGANIZATION OF CENTRAL IOWA FARMS

None of the farms in the central Iowa group could cover costs with a 20 percent price decline under the 1968 farm structure (Figure 7.16). Two farm size groups are examined in depth in Table 7.14 to determine whether these farms could be profitably reorganized at the lower price level. A structure is projected for each of the two size groups which provides a return to management equal to actual management returns in 1968 under a price level 20 percent lower. A single structure is projected for the smaller size group. For the larger size group, two alternative structures are projected. Farm size is assumed constant between 1968 and 1975 for both groups.

The reorganized structure for the 300-acre size group in 1975 would increase corn acres from 133 to 184 and soybeans to 100 acres. The number of pigs weaned would increase from 316 up to 1,250 and the number of cattle sold would fall to zero. Total labor months required would increase from 14 months to over 21 months (essentially a two-man operation). Total gross income in 1975 is projected at $65.6 thousand compared to $63.1 thousand in 1968. With the new structure, net income would be slightly higher in 1975—$20.8 thousand compared to $17.9 thousand in 1968. These changes would represent a large increase in the physical volume of production and require a sizable increase in operating capital.

Of the two alternative structures for the 600-acre farms, Structure I emphasizes specialization in hog production while Structure II emphasizes specialization in cattle production. Under Structure I corn acres would increase from 275 acres to 393 acres and soybeans to 200 acres. Pigs weaned would increase from 330 to 1,800. Total labor requirements would increase from 24 months in 1968 to more than 33 months in 1975 (essentially a three-man operation). With Structure I, total gross income is projected at $111.5 thousand in 1975 compared with $129.9 thousand in 1968. Projected net income in 1975 is $37 thousand—slightly higher than 1968.

With Structure II in 1975, total corn and soybean acres are the same as under Structure I. However, number of pigs weaned falls to zero, while the number of cattle sold would increase from 204 in 1968 to 1,550 in 1975. Total labor required would be 48 months (essentially a four-man operation). Total gross income is nearly tripled, or $344.2 thousand compared with $129.9 thousand in 1968. Net income is projected at $44.3 thousand in 1975 versus $35.8 in 1968. While management return is approximately at the 1968 level, the considerably greater volume of this structure would entail greater uncertainties, especially if the additional capital were borrowed.

The projected structures in Table 7.14 are only a few of numerous alternatives. However, the data of Figures 7.16, 7.17, and 7.18 and Table 7.14 indicate that at lower levels of prices many of the farmers represented would be forced out of business over the long run, have to take very low returns on their labor and capital resources, or profitably reorganize their operations. Even under reorganization, volume per farm would have to be greater if management return were maintained. Consequently, fewer farmers could exist. The reorganizations examined involve only a greater volume of crop and livestock output on a given acreage. Another alternative, and one prospective in terms of a tentative analysis and the slope of the cost functions in Figures 7.16, 7.17, and 7.18, would be larger farms in terms of acreage. The pressure indeed would be toward larger farms, in terms of both livestock volume and acreage, under prices as much as 20 percent lower than the 1968 level.

SUMMARY OF POLICY CONSIDERATIONS

Several alternatives in land retirement, directed toward controlling supply to attain a specified price level, have been analyzed in this study. Any of the alternative land-retirement programs allow attainment of the three price levels considered. Several different land-retirement programs would allow attainment of a given price level. However, the effects of the alternative programs would be different in the amount of land retired to attain the price level, the location of land retired, total government costs and net farm income, the geographic distribution of payments, and the regional location of agricultural adjustments. The data for each program of the study can be used to determine the trade-offs among these items—the amount of one item which must be sacrificed to attain more of another item.

These types of information should be useful to farm groups, the general public, and policy administrators in decisions relating to future farm policies. Of course, the set of policy alternatives analyzed in this study involve only a few of the many possible. Other possibilities include marketing quotas, free market prices, direct payments without production controls, subsidization of inputs and outputs, or others. This study has been concerned only with some alternatives in land retirement as a means of attaining given levels of supply control and price levels. Other alternatives will be analyzed in subsequent studies.

The many alternatives in land retirement as a mechanism of supply control can be combined in various manners. Under present methods, retirement is on a partial-farm basis dispersed over all major producing regions. At the other extreme, land retirement could be on a whole-farm basis concentrated by marginal crop-producing regions as under alternatives L_u, M_u, and H_u of this study. Retirement programs also can be on an annual or a long-term basis. Current programs are on an annual basis with contracts being initiated or renewed each year.

Each type of program has particular advantages and disadvantages. Programs vary in their effect on long-term solutions of overcapacity problems depending on their short-run or long-run nature. They vary in their costs of attaining a given level of supply control and price supports; an annual program based on partial-farm retirement over more regions has higher costs than long-term programs on a whole-farm basis concentrated by marginal producing regions. The programs have differential impacts on the interregional distribution of government payments and the social costs of adjustment. Annual programs on a partial-farm basis are dispersed over all regions, bringing a lower regional concentration of government payments and social costs of adjustment than a long-term program on a whole-farm basis allowed to concentrate land retirement in marginal regions. Finally, a partial-farm land-retirement system is more beneficial to tenant farmers since the unit is not withdrawn from the rental market.

The people involved with policy decisions and selections are the relevant groups which must decide the relative importance or weights to be attached to the levels of prices, government payments, and farm income. Similarly, they must determine the weights to be attached to various degrees of regional concentration of retirement, distribution in government payments, and secondary or social costs of adjustment. An optimal policy can be prescribed or selected only in light of these weights and trade-offs—the amount of one item gained or sacrificed (long-term solution, government costs, farm income, secondary social or adjustment costs, regional distribution or retirement, or payments, etc.) for a sacrifice or gain of another item in the same set. Of course, different land-retirement schemes are not "black or white" or "either or" choices. It is possible to combine them in many ways. A partial-farm method spread over regions can be combined with another program such as whole-farm retirement on a regional and long-term basis. The proportions can be 80, 50, or 20 percent of the first combined with 20, 50, or 80 percent of the second—or any other combination that might be selected. For example, the feed-grain program has been carried on simultaneously with the Conservation Reserve and Cropland Adjustment programs during the last several years. This arrangement represents a combination of annual and long-term programs, whole-farm and partial-farm participation, and interregional dispersion with regional concentration characteristics. Also, the most desired type of program can be phased in as the primary mechanism over a 5-, 10-, 20-, or 40-year time span.

DECISIONS BY POLICYMAKERS

This study has provided information relating to trade-offs among variables for several land-retirement alternatives. Policymakers and the relevant public must decide on the weights to apply to each of the major variables involved in different policy alternatives. Whether the relevant public accepts a long-term regionally concentrated land-retirement program will depend on whether all sectors of the rural community are adequately compensated for the adjustments involved. Both a social and economic policy should be developed for rural communities which are part and parcel of the adjustment problems stemming from the technological transformation of agriculture. A policy for commercial agriculture alone is insufficient. A shift to a long-term land-retirement program would reduce government costs, along with other effects mentioned previously. Savings so generated could be used along with additional funds to guarantee improved education, training, and career guidance in rural areas so that more people are afforded positive economic opportunity. Funds also are needed as retraining grants or for minimum income assistance of nonfarm rural people with a declining employment outlook as farm numbers and population decline. In addition, funds for rural communities could well be invested in establishing Area Development Districts and for rebuilding and reorganizing rural areas. Finally, some funds should be available for research on the desirable structures for rural communities in the future and for planning generally. The differences in government costs for different types of land-retirement programs are large enough that funds could be provided for functions and activities directed toward the rural community as a whole. Hence, an important policy question for the future is, What combination of policies for commercial agriculture and programs in rural communities and important and desirable in solving the total of problems which emerge under the further technological transformation of agriculture?

Chapter 8: Farm Policy and Rural Income and Employment Models

STEVEN T. SONKA and EARL O. HEADY

The nation's agriculture has made rapid advances in productivity over the past three decades. Reflecting this growth in productivity, output per farm worker increased by 237 percent between 1947 and 1970. The growth in labor productivity, along with favorable prices of machine capital relative to labor, not only has directly reduced the farm work force but also has done so indirectly as it brought about pressure for larger and fewer farms. Reduced labor requirements in agriculture (Table 8.1) have required that farm family workers look elsewhere for employment. Since employment alternatives have been absent in many rural communities, persons replaced from agriculture have migrated to other locations with growing industry and employment opportunities. With this exodus of farm workers and families, rural towns and businesses have been faced with declining demand for the goods and services which they supply in rural areas. The majority of rural communities experiencing a rapid growth in farm productivity and decline in agricultural labor force have had a great decline in nonfarm economic activity, employment, and capital value of business establishment. Consequently, rural communities that are primarily dependent on agriculture have been losing population from these towns at a rate paralleling the decline in the farm labor force.

Under the realization that rapid farm technological advance, which caused food production to increase more rapidly than demand, could increase welfare of consumers at the expense of income to farmers, the nation initiated supply control and price support programs during the 1930s. Except during periods of war-inflated demand, the United States has had some type of supply control, price support, and export subsidy in effect over the last three decades. To an important extent, the public has been successful in its attempt to protect farm income while allowing consumer gains in reduced real prices for food in recent decades. Similar protection has not been provided, however, to the nonfarm strata of rural communities generally. The higher farm income under government programs, of course, brings more employment and business to rural towns as farmers invest more in producers goods and have higher family expenditures for

NOTE: For further details, see Steve T. Sonka and Earl O. Heady, *Income and Employment Generation in Rural Areas in Relation to Alternative Farm Programs*, North Central Regional Center for Rural Development, Iowa State Univ., Dec. 1973.

consumer goods and services. However, indirect support of these rural business transactions, through government programs which increase farm income, does not offset the decline in rural employment brought about by increased size of farms and a reduction in the farm population and labor force. Even with the support of farm income through the government programs of the last two decades, employment opportunities in towns of many rural communities have declined under the rapid reduction in the number of farm families. Further, rural business owners have experienced a decline in capital assets as business opportunities were eroded by the reduction in the farm work force, and stores, buildings, and other facilities have come to have little value. This decline in capital values for rural business owners contrasts with the outcome for farmers. Advancing technology in combination with governmentally supported prices and direct payments for land retirement have caused the value of farmland to rise rather continuously over the last two decades. Even the owners of smaller farms, impelled to leave agriculture because of growing capital requirements and a cost-price squeeze for low volumes, have been able to realize an increased value for their assets. In contrast, many rural businessmen not only have had to cease operations because of declining demand but also have been able to salvage little of previous investments in buildings and facilities.

While the rural nonfarm sector would be worse off in the absence of government programs of the conventional kind, these effects do not compensate rural businesses which have suffered a decline in economic opportunity and asset values caused by the widespread substitution of capital technology for farm labor. While not all farmers have realized benefits from farm programs of recent decades, their loss induced by technological change in agriculture has not been as great as their neighbors in small country towns. Society has been much more effective in compensating the farm sector than it has in redressing income and capital losses of the nonfarm sector in rural areas.

In recent years, the public has become increasingly concerned with the plight of rural communities. This concern stems partly from the continuous migration of families from rural areas and the growing social congestion and environmental degradation of large urban centers. However, concern over the welfare of rural nonfarm families per se has been growing more intense. Several federal programs have been initiated in attempts to improve economic opportunity and retard deterioration of living conditions in rural areas. These programs emphasize tax relief, rural industrialization, and improvement of services such as water and sewer systems. Some rural communities do have prospects of a turnabout in their economic opportunities through rural industrialization. More, however, cannot expect to have previous reductions in employment and economic opportunity restored through this means. They lack the proper endowment in location, transportation facilities, capital supplies, augmenting industries already in place, and other characteristics which attract plant locations by foreign firms. It is possible that their welfare will be affected almost entirely by the prosperity of their surrounding farm industry in combination with public service reorganizations or subsidies which lessen tax burdens and improve quality of health, recreation, and other consumer services.

This study has been made accordingly. It investigates the economic impact of different types of farm programs on income generation in rural communities and agriculturally related industries. The study is made not as a suggestion that the foundation of programs to rescue rural communities be through programs for commercial farmers. It has been completed to evaluate the manner in which income and employment in sectors other than farming are affected by farm programs. These effects may be equally as important as those for farming in choice among farm programs of the future. While the farm population is now only 9.7 million, the population of nonmetropolitan areas in total is 63.8 million.

OBJECTIVES

The major objective of this study is to measure the economic impact of several types of farm programs on the income and employment generated in rural areas and agriculturally related industries. The study's main focus is on this objective because of passage of the Rural Development Act of 1972 and preparation of the nation to initiate various programs to promote greater employment and improved living conditions in rural communities. Farm programs represent one means of generating employment and income in the nonfarm sectors of rural communities. Choices and decisions on the best means to improve income and quality of life in rural areas could be best facilitated if information were available on the amount of income and employment generated by both private and public investment in rural industrialization, farm programs, public services, and other alternatives. This study concerns itself with only one of these alternatives, namely, the income and employment generated by four different farm programs.

However, since income and employment generation through farm programs is affected directly by the amount and distribution of crop production and the resulting levels of farm profits, an auxiliary but also major objective of the study is to analyze the impact of four alternative farm programs on the acreage and production of major field crops and on net farm income.

The order of presentation is as follows: first, the methodology employed in the study is summarized; next, the effects of the four program alternatives are explained by major farm production regions of the nation. These data on the level and distribution of acreage and production of crops and net farm income provide a basis for understanding the magnitude and distribution of farm income and employment as secondary effects in rural areas and agriculturally related industries. Next, the secondary or multiplier effects of the farm programs in generating income and employment are presented and explained. Finally, some policy implications of the analysis are presented.

METHODOLOGY

The quantitative results of this study were provided through application of a linear programming model to the major field crops of the United States. This model, constructed to recognize the land restraints of the important agricultural-producing regions and demand or food requirements in consumer markets, is detailed in nature and allows specification of acreage, crop production, and income by 150 rural areas. Incorporating a transportation network or submodel, the overall model also reflects interregional competition among the agricultural supply and food market areas of the United States.[1] Each of the farm program alternatives is analyzed by means of this model. To determine the employment and income generation effects of alternative farm programs, the linear programming solutions are linked with the secondary impact variables as explained below.

POLICY ALTERNATIVES CONSIDERED

Four alternative government farm policies are analyzed to determine their effects on both (1) farm income and (2) employment and income generation in rural areas. These policies were not selected as recommended solutions to the farm problem but are programs currently under discussion. Also, they vary widely in their nature and impact on agriculture. By examining these particular alternatives, we hope to provide a quantitative understanding of the trade-offs and secondary effects which various types of farm policies can have on different sectors of the rural economy.

The first solution estimates patterns of production and income effects which might prevail if agriculture operated in an unrestrained market environment. The forces of supply and demand and market equilibrium alone would determine prices farmers receive for their goods. Direct government intervention in the market through price supports and direct payments to farmers for retiring part of their cropland would not exist. This model will be referred to as the *Free Market Alternative* in this chapter.

The second solution or policy alternative is a land-retirement program. The program is similar to the type of program in effect in the late 1960s (and in the early 1970s, except for the set-aside modification). This program requires government price supports for feed grain, wheat, cotton, and other selected commodities. It also includes payments to farmers to divert part of their cropland from the production of specified commodities. Per-acre payments to farmers for land diversion are projected at levels consistent with payments existing in the late 1960s and early 1970s. The program is referred to later as the *Land-Retirement Alternative* or the *base alternative*.

The third and fourth solutions simulate conditions of production, resource use, income, and employment if farmers effectively unite to exercise market control over the supplies and market prices of the commodities they produce. The implementation of these program alternatives (referred to as *Bargaining Power Alternative A* and *Bargaining Power Alternative B*) might take the form of national legislation which would allow the formation of national commissions with appropriate powers. These commissions would need to determine price levels for farm products and the production quotas necessary to equate farm

---

1. The mathematical structure of the model is the same as used in Chapter 7. The model includes 244 equations and 2,226 real variables. Land in each of the 150 rural areas and demands of each of the 31 markets or consuming regions serve as constraints.

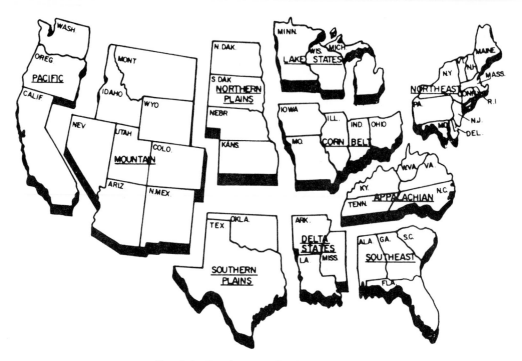

Fig. 8.1. Ten farm production regions.

product supplies with demand at the specified price levels.[2]   The need for direct government intervention would be eliminated under these programs if farmers could effectively control supply. The Bargaining Power Alternatives in this study use production quotas based on historic production patterns. The two models differ only in the level of farm prices (see Table 8.2).

REGIONS USED IN ANALYSIS

Both the linear programming model and the impact analysis are based on various regional or area concepts. Rural areas are for the continental United States and define homogeneous areas of farm commodity production. These 150 rural areas are the same as the 150 producing areas presented in Chapter 7. Production from areas not included in the 150 rural areas is handled outside the programming model.   (Allowance is made for this production in estimating demands for the major farm commodities.)

Consumption of wheat, feed grain, and oil meal is defined for 31 consuming regions delineated by Whittlesey (Figure 2.1). Cotton lint demand is determined on a national basis. Certain results from the study are summarized by farm production regions, the third regional concept used in the study. These regions

2. For a more extensive discussion of the concept of bargaining power and proposals for national legislation in this area, see Howard C. Madsen and Earl O. Heady; *Bargaining Power Programs: Estimated Effects of Production Net Farm Incomes and Food Costs for Specified Price Levels*, CARD Report 39, Center for Agricultural and Rural Development, Iowa State Univ., 1971.

(Figure 8.1) coincide with the ten types of farm production regions used by the ERS, USDA.

SECONDARY IMPACT VARIABLES

The effects of the four farm policies on the income and employment levels of agriculturally related communities and industries were estimated through factors related to the value of output determined in the linear programming solutions for the crops endogenous to this study.[3] For purposes of determining these employment and income generation effects, the following two variables are linked with the linear programming model.

Income generation factor is the amount by which the total income in the U.S. economy will increase due to the production of an additional $1 million worth of output in a sector (the sector of relevance is a specific farm commodity produced in a specific farm production region). This increase in income has three components: (1) the income received by the producers of the additional $1 million worth of farm output, (2) the income resulting from the increased activity in agribusiness industries (through increased sales of productive inputs to farmers and the additional sales of industries that process farm products), and (3) the income resulting from increased sales of consumer goods to farmers and workers in agribusiness industries. For example, the production of an additional $1 million worth of wheat in the Northeast region would result in an additional $1.35 million of income being generated throughout the economy of the United States.

Labor generation factor is the number of additional workers required in the U.S. economy due to the production of an additional $1 million worth of output in a sector (the sector of relevance is a specific farm production region). This increase in employment also has three components: (1) the additional farm workers needed to produce the additional $1 million worth of farm output, (2) the additional workers required by agribusiness industries which sell more inputs to farmers and have more farm output to process because of the additional $1 million worth of farm output, and (3) the additional workers required by industries that produce consumer goods demanded by farm workers and workers in agribusiness industries. For example, a $1 million reduction in wheat production in the Northeast region will eliminate the need for the employment of 228 workers throughout the U.S. economy.

These factors (Table 8.2) were developed from data for the ten farm production regions. Hence, they also are based on and relate to the ten farm production regions. As might be expected, cotton generally has the greatest impact on the economy per dollar of output for both the employment and income generation factors. (Since cotton is not produced in the Northeast, Lake states, or Northern Plains, no entries are made for cotton in these regions in Table 8.2.) The relative importance of the other three commodities varies with the factor and the region

---

3. The crop commodities endogenous to this study are wheat, feed grain, soybeans, and cotton. The basic coefficients used in developing these variables were reported by Schluter (Schluter, Gerald Emil, "An Estimation of Agricultural Employment through an Input-Output Study," Ph.D. diss., Iowa State Univ., 1971). For a discussion of the methods used to calculate the income and employment variables of this study, see Appendix A at the end of this chapter.

being considered. Feed grain has a consistently larger income generation factor than wheat or oil meal in all the regions. The size of the labor generation factor or the income generation factor varies by regions according to the nature of the crop and the technology generally prevailing in the various regions. Of course, the total amount of income and the total amount of employment generated by the production of a crop are functions of the acreage and output of that crop in each of the regions.

DEVELOPMENT OF INDICES

To measure the impact of the different farm programs on producers and on rural communities, indices were developed which compared outcomes under the Land-Retirement Alternative with those for the other three policy alternatives. These indices indicate how the following variables are affected under each of the farm program alternatives: the amount of employment generated, the amount of income generated, and the value of cropland. The amount of employment generated refers to the number of workers required not only in agriculture but also in agriculturally related sectors of the rural areas and regions for which the data are summarized. The amount of income generated includes not only income in agriculture but also in other sectors of rural areas or regions for which data are summarized. The value of cropland, as summarized by regions or rural areas, reflects the manner in which different farm programs may affect the economic base of rural areas.

These indices were computed by first converting the projected value of each variable (i.e., the amount of employment generated, the amount of income generated, and the value of cropland) in the Land-Retirement Alternative to an index value of 100.0 for the individual regions and producing areas. The estimated values of the three variables were then computed for the other farm program alternatives. These values then were weighted by the same factors used in the Land-Retirement Alternative. All variables are then expressed as percentages of the values for the Land-Retirement Alternative. For example, an index value of 250.0 for cropland value under Bargaining Power Alternative A has this meaning: the estimated value of cropland for the particular solution or program alternative is 2.5 times the value of cropland under the Land-Retirement Alternative. A value of 50 means that cropland value under Bargaining Power Alternative A is half as large as it would be under the Land-Retirement Alternative (also referred to as the base alternative). The index value for each region thus is 100.0 under the Land-Retirement Alternative.

An index value of 250.0 for the amount of income generated under Bargaining Power Alternative A has this meaning: the amount of income generated by the production of the crops endogenous to this study is 2.5 times what it would be under the Land-Retirement Alternative.[4] It should be noted that this does not imply that the total income in a region will be 2.5 times larger under Bargaining Power Alternative A than under the Land-Retirement Alternative. The degree to which the total income of any region is affected by changes in government farm policies depends upon the relative importance of the endogenous crops in that

4. The crops endogenous to this study are wheat, feed grain, soybeans, and cotton.

region. The same meaning is applicable to the indices relating to the amount of employment generated.

The income and employment generation factors are assumed constant for all policy alternatives included in this study. In other words, for the commodities studied, the mix of items purchased per dollar of output is assumed to remain constant for all policy alternatives. In actuality, the mix of items purchased would change as the price of commodities varied. Linking the income and employment generation factors directly to the value of output, as done in this study, therefore, does not reflect "real-world" conditions. Ideally, the secondary impact factors should be recalculated for each policy alternative to reflect changes in the mix of items purchased as the farmer's income position changes. However, this could not be accomplished because of the unavailability of the required data. Therefore, we would caution the reader of the limitations of this method used in the study and would stress the need for additional data relating to expenditure patterns in rural America.

Because we relate value of output to secondary income and employment generation, supply control programs are estimated to have positive secondary effects even though farm output would be reduced. This reduction in farm output would probably not have positive effects on the small rural community whose main source of employment is processing farm output or supplying farm inputs. However, the additional farm income associated with a supply control program will generate economic activity in larger rural towns serving as trade centers for the farm community. The income and employment indices developed here relate to this multicounty, trade center concept and should be viewed in this manner. Indeed, supply control programs may have negative rather than positive effects for the small rural village which is more dependent on the quantity of farm output produced than the value of that output.

PARAMETERS AND ASSUMPTIONS

Use of the linear programming model to determine the impact of the alternative commercial farm policies requires estimates for a large number of parameters representing capital and labor coefficients for each crop in each rural area, consumption per capita for different foods in the various market regions, transportation costs for each commodity between each pair of regions, and related data on land restraints and yields in each rural area. These parameters were estimated by using the procedures described in Chapters 6 and 7. The cropland base for each producing area is held constant at the 1965 level. Carry-over stocks for major commodities are considered to be the same for the four policy alternatives. Population, per capita disposable income, and yield coefficients for the major crop commodities were projected to 1975. Hence, all results of the study refer to 1975.

PRICES

Prices received by farmers either had to be prescribed for each model, with the analysis designed to provide this level of prices, or were generated by the results of the model. In case of the Bargaining Power Alternatives, the price levels were established beforehand as a goal of the program, then the degree of supply restraint necessary to generate these price levels was incorporated in the model. In the case of Free Market and Land-Retirement Alternatives, the prices were not prescribed but were generated by the model. Farm prices for the four alternative farm policies are presented in Table 8.3. Prices in the Land-Retirement Alternative generally are similar to the prices actually received by farmers in 1969. However, for broilers, wheat, and cotton lint, actual 1969 prices were nearer the lower prices estimated for the Free Market Alternative. The projected price levels in both the Bargaining Power Alternatives are higher than the actual 1969 prices.

EXPORT LEVELS

Eighteen percent of the total harvested acreage of crops in 1969 produced commodities for export. Hence, export levels for each of the policy alternatives had to be estimated as a component of total demand. The quantities of the major crop commodities exported in 1969 as well as the 1975 projected export levels are presented in Table 8.4.

Due to international trade agreements in effect for wheat, the same level of wheat exports is used for all four policy alternatives. However, the quantity of feed grain exported varies inversely with the price level for the four policy alternatives. The greatest quantity of exports (25 million tons, corn equivalent) is projected for the lowest price level of feed grain resulting under the Free Market Alternative. The quantity of feed grain actually exported in 1969 was nearly equal to the projected 20.5 million tons (corn equivalent) of feed-grain exports projected under the Land-Retirement Alternative.

Due to the upward trend in soybean exports, oil-meal exports greater than the actual 1969 amount are projected for all policy alternatives except Bargaining Power Alternative B. The highest cotton exports are projected for the Free Market Alternative and the lowest for Bargaining Power Alternative B. The 1969 actual export levels approximate those projected for the Land-Retirement Alternative.

PER CAPITA CONSUMPTION OF MEAT

Per capita consumption of the major livestock commodities also had to be estimated in determining the demand for feed grain and oil meal. Per capita quantities at each price level are based on existing estimates of the price elasticity of demand and projected income. These estimated quantities for each of the policy alternatives and the 1969 actual per capita consumption of these commodities are presented in Table 8.5.

Reflecting the growing consumer preference for beef, the estimated quantity of beef and veal is lower than in 1969 only for the higher price levels of the Bargaining Power Alternatives. Per capita consumption of broilers is greater in all the policy solutions than in 1969 due to its low price relative to pork, beef, and lamb.

PRODUCER AND FARM INCOME EFFECTS

Implementation of any government farm policy has direct impacts on the quantity of farm commodities produced and on the income derived from farming. The amount and pattern of production, as well as the levels of prices and direct payments to farmers, not only determine the magnitude of net farm income under each program alternative but also have widespread impact throughout rural areas. The pattern and amount of production determine the amount of inputs used and thus the amount of employment and income generated by the service sectors supplying them. The level of farm income is reflected in consumption expenditures of farm families and thus is reflected in income and employment generated in rural businesses which supply consumer goods and services. For this reason, we summarize the levels of production and farm income generated under each of the policy alternatives. While the models provide these quantities at the level of individual producing areas and farm production regions, the data are presented only at the national level for purposes of brevity. Table 8.6 includes projected levels of production, per-acre yields, and acreages of the major crop commodities for each of the alternative government policies considered and allows comparisons with actual 1969 values of these variables.

WHEAT PRODUCTION

With an estimated 1.66 billion bushels, wheat production is largest under the Free Market Alternative. Wheat production under the Land-Retirement Alternative is nearly equal to the 1.46 billion bushels actually produced in 1969 but is 121 million bushels less than under Bargaining Power Alternative A. Greater wheat production under Bargaining Power Alternative A is due to an increased use of wheat for feed under the set of prices existing. Cropland devoted to wheat production varies somewhat directly with the projected levels of production. The largest wheat acreage is 54.7 million acres under the Free Market Alternative. Bargaining Power Alternative B has the smallest acreage, 44.9 million acres, of the four policy alternatives. Projected wheat yields vary directly with the price of wheat and indirectly with acreage under the policy alternatives. The Free Market Alternative has the lowest projected yield of 30.3 bushels per acre (Table 8.6) while 31.9 bushels under Bargaining Power Alternative B is highest.

FEED-GRAIN PRODUCTION

The highest level of feed-grain production, 181.9 million tons of feed units, is under the Free Market Alternative. The high feed-grain yield under this alternative results because market forces concentrate production on land best suited for these crops. As in the case of wheat, estimated feed-grain production under the Land-Retirement Alternative is similar to 1969 actual production. Due to the relatively large amount of wheat used for feed in Bargaining Power Alternative A, feed-grain production in that alternative would be 16 million tons of feed units less than in the Land-Retirement Alternative and only 8 million tons more than in Bargaining Power Alternative B (Table 8.6).

SOYBEAN PRODUCTION

Soybean production and acreage are largest for the Free Market Alternative even though this policy alternative has the lowest estimated yield per acre. The lower yield results because feed grain would be produced on a greater proportion of the high quality cropland under free market conditions than in the other policy alternatives. Hence, while acreage is largest under the Free Market Alternative, soybeans are pushed out onto less productive land by feed grain. Production, yield, and acreage under the Land-Retirement Alternative are slightly higher than the actual 1969 values for these variables. Both Bargaining Power Models have projected levels of production and acreages used for soybeans which are lower than in 1969. However, projected yields are higher than 1969 actual yields.

COTTON PRODUCTION

Cotton yield under each policy alternative is higher than the 1969 actual yield. In the Free Market Alternative this is due to the concentration of cotton production on high-yielding cotton land. For other solutions, it is due to a cotton price level higher than in 1969, which induces higher fertilizer rates and other improved technology. Estimated cotton production ranges from a high of 11.9 million bales under the Free Market Alternative to a low of 10.1 million bales under Bargaining Power Alternative B (Table 8.6).

INCOME FROM FARMING

Table 8.7 summarizes income for the farming sector under each of the policy alternatives. Estimated net farm income ranges from $9.4 billion in the Free Market Alternative to $25.0 billion in Bargaining Power Alternative B. The projected net return from farming under the Land-Retirement Alternative is $2.9 billion less than under Bargaining Power Alternative A. However, the higher prices are more than offset by government payments to the farming sector in the Land-Retirement Alternative. (No government payments are assumed under the Bargaining Power Alternatives.) Therefore, net farm income under the Land-Retirement Alternative is slightly higher than under Bargaining Power Alternative A.

CONSUMER FOOD COSTS

Each set of prices and production levels also is associated with a level of consumer food expenditures. Table 8.8 shows estimated total consumer food expenditures for each of the four policy alternatives analyzed.[5] Estimated total consumer expenditures for food are greater than 1969 actual food expenditures

5. See Appendix B at the end of this Chapter for methods used to calculate consumer food costs.

under all four policy alternatives. Part of this increase is due to growth in population between 1969 and 1975. Under alternatives with higher farm prices than in 1969, part of the increase also is due to higher costs for the farm commodities going into food. Growing consumer preference for higher quality and more expensive, convenience-oriented food products also adds to costs between 1969 and 1975.

Projected total food expenditures are lowest under the Free Market Alternative and highest under Bargaining Power Alternative B. The range is slightly over $10.7 billion between these two solutions. While projected net farm income is higher under the Land-Retirement Alternative than under Bargaining Power Alternative A, estimated total food expenditures are $3.37 billion smaller under the Land-Retirement Alternative. The higher net farm income under the Land-Retirement Alternative is due to government payments for cropland retirement. These payments under the Land-Retirement Alternative more than offset higher commodity prices under Bargaining Power Alternative A.

Total consumer food expenditures in Table 8.8 were calculated as the product of the retail prices for each solution multiplied by the quantity of food to be purchased at these prices. Hence, the $3.37 billion increases in food expenditures of the Bargaining Power Alternative A over the Land-Retirement Alternative does not completely reflect the difference in consumer well-being between the two policy alternatives because different amounts of food would be consumed. For example, the expenditure for food would be the same if a consumer bought ten apples at a dime apiece or one apple for a dollar. Obviously, he would not consider himself equally well-off in the two situations.

In an attempt to account for this welfare phenomenon, consumer food expenditures were recalculated using the price level computed for each policy alternative with the quantity of food consumption held constant at the level of the Land-Retirement Alternative (Table 8.9). When calculated in this manner, total consumer food expenditures increase by $18.8 billion between the Free Market Alternative and Bargaining Power Alternative B. Total consumer food expenditures increase by $5.8 billion between the Land-Retirement Alternative and Bargaining Power Alternative A when the constant quantity restriction is imposed. The values in Table 8.8 are important as estimates of what food expenditures would be under each of the policy alternatives; the constant quantity estimates of Table 8.9 reflect another aspect of consumer welfare under the several policy alternatives.

SECONDARY EFFECTS IN RURAL AREAS

The summary of yields, production, prices, and income above suggests national outcomes for food producers and consumers. The largest proportion of food consumers is in metropolitan centers which include 69 percent of the nation's population. Another 31 percent of the population resides in rural or nonmetropolitan areas. Income of this portion of the nation's population is dependent especially on the structure of agriculture (as expressed in number and size of farms, capital used, or substitutes for labor, etc.) and income from farming. It is also dependent on industries located in nonmetropolitan areas. A major purpose of this study has been to measure the impact of alternative farm policies on employment and income in rural areas. Many rural communities lack natural endowments, historic economic development, and other attributes which attract industry. Hence, the welfare of their nonfarm population will depend especially on the structure and income of farming as these variables are reflected throughout the community in generating off-farm income and employment. How do different alternatives in farm programs affect income and employment elsewhere in the rural community?

The amount of farm income generated at regional, state, and national levels is only one of the outcomes or variables affected by farm programs. The pattern of agriculture and the level of income related to a particular farm program affect the employment and income of other groups in rural communities who are associated with supplying inputs and processing outputs of agriculture. In other words, production of farm crops generates economic activity beyond that involved directly in the planting and harvesting of crops. This added or related economic activity is reflected in the industries which manufacture and distribute farm inputs such as implements, fertilizers, insecticides, seeds, feed, and other items. It is also reflected in the businesses of rural areas which handle and process agricultural products and in those which develop to service agriculture and other closely related groups in the community through the supply of consumer goods and financial and other services.

Individual farm programs can have entirely different impacts in the various farming areas of the nation. For example, the early land-retirement programs of the 1950s, represented by the Soil Bank or Conservation Reserve, allowed land withdrawal to be concentrated by farming areas. On a semibid basis, farmers were able to select whether or not to idle their land in terms of its productivity and payment rates available. In general, this program caused land retirement to be concentrated in areas where soil productivity and yields were low relative to payment rates (see Figure 8.2). Because land retirement tended to be concentrated in certain regions of the Great Plains, Southeast, and southern Corn Belt, it greatly reduced farmers' purchases of materials of production. Also, since farmers could put their entire farm in the Soil Bank and still receive the payments accordingly, many moved out of the community to take employment at another location. Consequently, their purchases of consumer goods and agriculturally related services in the original community also ceased.

This reduction in the business of rural communities where land retirement became concentrated caused vigorous protests by rural business leaders. Their pressure on congressmen eventually caused land-retirement programs to be reshaped in a manner that did not concentrate idle land by specific regions.

This section indicates how the employment and income generated in rural communities and agriculturally related industries, as well as in agriculture, would be affected by the four farm programs analyzed. Income and employment generated outside agriculture are affected by both (1) the acreages of crops and levels of production and (2) the level of farm income associated with a particular

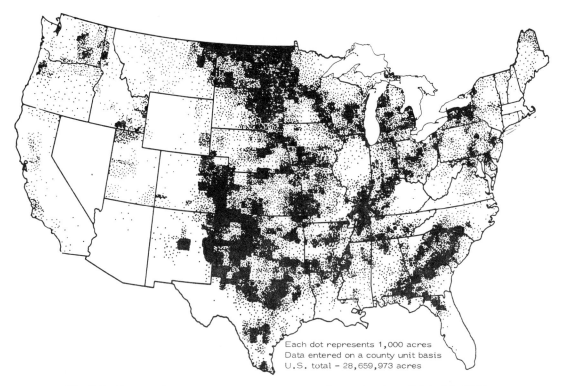

Each dot represents 1,000 acres
Data entered on a county unit basis
U.S. total – 28,659,973 acres

Fig. 8.2. Conservation reserve program acreage under contract as of July 15, 1960.

type of farm policy. The crop acreage and pattern of production have direct effects especially in the amount of production materials used. If the farm policy causes a reduction in crop acreage and production, it also will reduce the amount of tractor fuel, fertilizer, seed, repairs, and equipment moving from processing plants and through the service sector of the rural community. Reduction of income in a rural area will directly affect the amount of consumer goods purchased by farm families. But these reductions in both producer and consumer goods also will have indirect or secondary effects in the rural community business sector. As the fertilizer distributor's volume and income are reduced, his demand for consumer goods and financial services also will decline. As the volume and income of the retailer fall off, he may postpone or eliminate store improvements, thus reducing demand for the products of the rural lumberyard or machine shop.

EFFECTS OF POLICY ALTERNATIVES ON INCOME GENERATED

To allow a direct comparison of how the four program alternatives affect the amount of income generated in rural areas and agriculturally related industries, the income generated by each program has been expressed as an index value. The level of income associated with the Land-Retirement Alternative (the base alternative) has been set at 100 and the results for all other programs are expressed accordingly. These indices for each of the four policy alternatives are presented in Table 8.10 for the United States and for the ten farm production regions.

The figures in Table 8.10 indicate that the type of farm programs can have a very great effect on the amount of income generated in rural areas and agriculturally related industries. It is true, of course, that if the funds and resources required to support and implement a particular type of program were used elsewhere in the economy, income and employment also would be generated in these other sectors and locations—as a national offset of farm programs in rural communities and agriculturally related industries. However, the same can be said of a rural industry. If it were not located in the rural community it also could be located in an urban center where it could equally generate income and employment. Since an important goal of the nation is that of rural community development and a greater spatial dispersion of economic activity and employment, the effects of different farm programs are interesting and important in these respects.

For the nation as a whole, production of the crops endogenous to this study generates about 14 percent less income under the Free Market Alternative than under the base alternative (the Land-Retirement Alternative). The smaller index of income generated under the Free Market Alternative results because of the lower farm income associated with this policy alternative. Income generated under the Free Market Alternative is less than under the Land-Retirement Alternative for all production regions except the Southern Plains. Under the Free Market Alternative, the latter region would have an increased acreage of wheat and cotton to take fullest advantage of its soil and water resources. To supply its growing fed-cattle industry, which is favored by this location, population growth, and market environment, feed grain would be transported to it from other regions and more wheat would be used for feed in the Southern Plains region itself. The Corn Belt and Lake states regions have levels of income generated under the Free Market Alternative which are only 10 percent less than under the base alternative. There is, however, a considerable difference within these regions. Some rural areas in the Corn Belt and Lake states have higher levels under the Free Market Alternative because market forces concentrate grain production in the areas of favorable yields and comparative advantage. Other rural areas of the region have a lower income index under the Free Market Alternative because a national allocation of crops relative to comparative advantage, reflected in natural and market conditions, would cause them to shift out of grain production and into less intensive land uses such as grazing.

Overall, even though some rural areas would suffer very adverse outcomes under the Free Market Alternative, the Corn Belt and Lake states would fare much better than most other regions because a greater proportion of the nation's agricultural production would be concentrated in the central United States. Under the Free Market Alternative, crop acreage in the Southern Plains, Corn Belt, and Lake states regions is 20 percent greater than under the Land-Retirement Alternative. Land also would be shifted from annual crops under the Free Market Alternative, but the shift would concentrate in regions of lowest comparative advantage. Under the Land-Retirement Alternative, land held from production through the inducement of government payments to farmers is scattered throughout all regions on a partial farm basis. It thus tends to hold labor and equipment on the farm as a means of operating the remainder of the unit. Under the Free Market Alternative, entire farms would be shifted from annual crop production and the need for the equipment to handle them would be eliminated. Also, less intensive land use would release labor as farms were consolidated to allow competitive incomes under lower farm prices and the absence of direct payments to farmers. The three regions mentioned previously would increase their crop acreage by a percentage twice as great as for the nation as a whole under the Free Market Alternative. The national crop acreage under the Free Market Alternative is projected to increase by 10 percent over the base alternative in the absence of land-retirement mechanisms.

The Appalachian, Mountain, and Pacific regions would all have a greater acreage devoted to crops under the Free Market Alternative, but all would have a lower index of income generated than under the Land-Retirement Alternative. The Northeast, Southeast, Northern Plains, and Delta states would have both a smaller crop acreage and a reduction in income generated under the Free Market Alternative. Compared to the Land-Retirement Alternative, the reduction in income for rural areas and agriculturally related industries would be severe in these regions.

In contrast, the higher farm income and the spatial distribution of supply restraints associated with the Bargaining Power Alternatives have a large effect in boosting the amount of income generated by production of the endogenous crops for the United States and most of the major producing regions. The index for income generation under Bargaining Power Alternative A is 19 percent higher than under the Land-Retirement Alternative and 138 percent higher than under the Free Market Alternative. Extreme differences prevail for the Northeast region, where income generated under Bargaining Power Alternative A is 31 percent greater than under the Land-Retirement Alternative and 448 percent greater than under the Free Market Alternative. Since the Bargaining Power Alternatives do not include payments to farmers as a means of reducing supply, Bargaining Power Alternative A provides only modest gains in the amount of income generated throughout rural areas and agriculturally related industries for the Southern Plains, Pacific, and Northern Plains regions. In income generation, only the Southern Plains would be better off under the Free Market Alternative than under Bargaining Power Alternative A. The Southern Plains would have a much larger cotton acreage under the Free Market Alternative than under either the Land-Retirement Alternative or Bargaining Power Alternative A. Cotton acreage in the Southern Plains region is 55 percent smaller under the latter than under the Free Market Alternative.

With its much higher prices, Bargaining Power Alternative B would bring large increases in the amount of income generated for all regions, as well as the United States, as compared to the Land-Retirement Alternative. Under Bargaining Power Alternative B the amount of income generated in the Northeast, Appalachian, and Delta states regions increases by more than 40 percent over the amount of income generated in these regions under the Land-Retirement Alternative. Compared to the Land-Retirement Alternative, the Northeast region increases its production of feed grain while the Appalachian and Delta states regions increase their production of cotton under Bargaining Power Alternative B. All the farm production regions except the Southern Plains region have their highest level of income generation under Bargaining Power Alternative B. Under this policy alternative, cotton acreage in the Southern Plains region would be 61 percent less than it is in the Free Market Alternative.

Each of the ten farm production regions we have been discussing is comprised of several rural areas. The effect of a policy alternative upon some of the rural areas within a farm production region may be significantly different from the effect of that policy alternative on the farm production region as a whole. For example, a policy alternative that would increase the amount of income generated in a farm production region may cause the amount of income generated to increase in some rural areas, decrease in others, and remain constant in still others. The following discussion will highlight those rural areas that experience income generation effects which are significantly different from the income generation effect for the entire farm production region. For all the policy alternatives, Table 8.11 presents the indices of income generated for each of the 150 rural areas in our model. In this section we will present only a general discussion of the income generation effects that occur in the rural areas.

Under the Free Market Alternative, the income generated in the Northeast region decreases by 70 percent from its level under the Land-Retirement Alternative. However, in western New York, the income generated under the Free Market Alternative is 34 percent higher than under the Land-Retirement Alternative (see rural area 1). When the production restraints associated with the Land-Retirement Alternative are withdrawn, this rural area concentrates on wheat production which leads to the increase in the amount of income generated under the Free Market Alternative for this rural area. The acreage devoted to wheat in this rural area increases by 65 percent under the Free Market Alternative. In the Appalachian region as a whole, the income generated under the Free Market Alternative is 20 percent lower than under the Land-Retirement Alternative. However, in eastern North Carolina and western Kentucky, the amount of income generated under the Free Market Alternative is much higher than under the Land-Retirement Alternative due to increases in crop production in these rural areas (see rural areas 7, 10, 33, 34, 35, 41). In western Kentucky the acreage in crops increases by 50 percent under the Free Market Alternative while in eastern North Carolina the acreage in crops under this policy alternative is 35 percent greater than under the Land-Retirement Alternative.

Under the Free Market Alternative the production of feed grain in southern Georgia increases by almost 40 percent from its level under the Land-Retirement Alternative (see rural areas 13, 14). This increase in production causes the income generated in these rural areas to be greater under the Free Market Alternative than under the Land-Retirement Alternative. Similarly, in western Louisiana, a threefold increase in the production of cotton causes the income generated in this area to be 176 percent larger under the Free Market Alternative than under the Land-Retirement Alternative (see rural area 120).

The Southern Plains region is the only farm production region for which the amount of income generated under the Free Market Alternative is greater than it would be under the Land-Retirement Alternative. However, this increase in income generated is not distributed evenly throughout the Southern Plains region. Of the 23 rural areas in this region, only 8 have higher levels of income generation under the Free Market Alternative than under the Land-Retirement Alternative (see rural areas 111, 112, 114, 115, 116, 122, 124, 126). These rural areas, which are located in southwestern Oklahoma, northwestern Texas, and south central Texas, experience sizable increases in the number of acres devoted to the production of cotton under the Free Market Alternative. This implies that although the merchants and rural citizens in these 8 rural areas would benefit from a shift from the Land-Retirement Alternative to the Free Market Alternative, the citizens in the remaining 15 rural areas of this region would have less income generated under the Free Market Alternative.

Without the land diversion restraints associated with the base solution, the production of feed grain in the Mountain region shifts from rural areas with primarily dryland production methods to rural areas where irrigation can be used to best advantage. Therefore, while the income generated in the Mountain region as a whole decreases by 34 percent under the Free Market Alternative, the income generated in 3 of the rural areas in this region will increase under this policy alternative. Under the Free Market Alternative the production of feed grain is twice as large as it would be under the Land-Retirement Alternative in eastern New Mexico, east central Colorado, and northeastern Colorado (see rural areas 129, 132, 134).

In central California and central Washington, the income generated under the Free Market Alternative is significantly less than it would be under the Land-Retirement Alternative (see rural areas 144, 150). Both of these rural areas become dependent on the production of wheat under the Free Market Alternative rather than on the production of feed grain and cotton on which they are primarily dependent under the Land-Retirement Alternative. This shift in the commodity mix in these rural areas causes an 81 percent decrease in the amount of income generated in central California and a 53 percent decrease in the amount of income generated in central Washington under the Free Market Alternative. However, in southern California the production of cotton under the Free Market Alternative is three times as large as it would be under the Land-Retirement Alternative (see rural area 143). Therefore, the income generated in this rural area increases by 119 percent under the Free Market Alternative as compared to the base alternative.

While the Corn Belt region as a whole suffers a 10 percent decrease in the amount of income generated under the Free Market Alternative, the rural areas in southern Ohio and central Indiana have more income generated under the Free Market Alternative than they do under the Land-Retirement Alternative (see rural areas 36, 37, 40, 53). These rural areas are allowed to concentrate on the production of feed grain under the Free Market Alternative which causes the amount of income generated to increase in this policy alternative as compared to the base alternative.

Under the Free Market Alternative, production of each of the crops included in our model is concentrated in those rural areas that are best suited for the production of these crops. Thus it was possible that the demands associated with this policy alternative could be satisfied even though many rural areas would not produce any of the crops endogenous to this study under the Free Market Alternative. Therefore, our analysis shows that the amount of income generated by the production of these crops would fall to zero under the Free Market Alternative. Rural areas in which the amount of income generated is at or near the zero level under the Free Market Alternative are in eastern Pennsylvania, southwestern Missouri, northern Wisconsin, central Minnesota, eastern Virginia, western North Carolina, central Tennessee, central Alabama, central Texas, the western areas of the Dakotas, southeastern Montana, eastern Wyoming, east central Colorado, and southern Arizona (see rural areas 2, 64, 47, 78, 5, 6, 16, 28, 22, 23, 121, 123, 128, 82, 83, 85, 86, 136, 135, 131, 142).

Under Bargaining Power Alternative A, the income generated in the Appalachian and Southeast regions is greater than it would be under the Land-Retirement Alternative. The amount of income generated in the Appalachian region increases by 32 percent while in the Southeast region it increases by 24 percent. However, some of the rural areas which are in these regions would experience decreases in the amount of income generated under Bargaining Power Alternative A (see rural areas 9, 16, 17, 18, 21, 22, 23, 24, 26). These rural areas are located in western North and South Carolina, northern Georgia, and central Alabama, and as a group would have over 50 percent fewer acres in crops under Bargaining Power Alternative A than they do under the Land-Retirement Alternative. This decrease in production is due to the lower demands associated with Bargaining Power Alternative A which can be satisfied in rural areas that possess either higher quality land or more advantageous transportation factors. This shift in relative production means that the higher farm commodity prices associated with Bargaining Power Alternative A will not benefit farmers and other citizens in these rural areas (when compared to the base alternative).

In the Delta states region as a whole, the amount of income generated under Bargaining Power Alternative A is 23 percent greater than it would be under the Land-Retirement Alternative. However, in western Louisiana and southern Arkansas, the income generated under Bargaining Power Alternative A is slightly less than it would be under the base alternative (see rural areas 59, 120). And in north central Louisiana, there would be 40 percent less income generated under Bargaining Power Alternative A than under the Land-Retirement Alternative (see rural area 58). This sizable decrease in the amount of income generated in north central Louisiana is the result of a major reduction in the amount of cropland used in this rural area under Bargaining Power Alternative A. Under this policy alternative, there would be 70 percent fewer acres in production in this rural area than under the Land-Retirement Alternative.

Under Bargaining Power Alternative A, the amount of income generated in the Southern Plains region is only 4 percent greater than under the Land-Retirement Alternative and is 17 percent less than it would be under the Free Market Alternative. However, the income generated under Bargaining Power Alternative A is distributed much more widely throughout the Southern Plains region than it is under the Free Market Alternative. Under Bargaining Power Alternative A, 15 of the region's 23 rural areas have increases in the amount of income generated when compared to base alternative. The rural areas that do not have increases in income generated under Bargaining Power Alternative A are located in southern Oklahoma, east central Texas, and southwestern Texas (see rural areas 105, 110, 111, 115, 118, 119, 121, 127). Under this policy alternative, these 8 rural areas would have 25 percent fewer cropland acres in production than they do under the Land-Retirement Alternative.

The Mountain region has 20 percent more income generated under Bargaining Power Alternative A than under the Land-Retirement Alternative. This increase in the amount of income generated occurs throughout the region as only one rural area in east central Colorado would have a sizable decrease in the amount of income generated under Bargaining Power Alternative A (see rural area 132). While this rural area concentrates on the production of feed grain under both policy alternatives, the number of acres in production decreases by 30 percent under Bargaining Power Alternative A which leads to a 15 percent decrease in the amount of income generated in this rural area.

In the Pacific region, only rural area 143 in southeastern California would have a marked decrease in the amount of income generated under Bargaining Power Alternative A. This rural area maintains almost the same level of cotton production under Bargaining Power Alternative A as it did under the Land-Retirement Alternative. However, the production of wheat, which accounts for two-thirds of this area's cropland acreage under the Land-Retirement Alternative, shifts almost entirely out of this rural area under Bargaining Power Alternative A. Due to this drastic reduction in wheat production, the income generated in this rural area under Bargaining Power Alternative A is 20 percent less than it is under the Land-Retirement Alternative.

Under Bargaining Power Alternative A, the increase in the amount of income generated in the Corn Belt and Lake states regions would be distributed throughout the rural areas of these two regions. Only in southern Ohio does the amount of income generated under Bargaining Power Alternative A decrease by more than 10 percent from what it would be under the Land-Retirement Alternative (see rural areas 36, 37). However, in the Northern Plains region, rural areas in southwestern North Dakota, central South Dakota, and southwestern Kansas experience significant decreases in the number of acres in production and in the amount of income generated under Bargaining Power Alternative A (see rural areas 83, 86, 88, 104). Rural area 83 in southwestern South Dakota is the only rural area in the model which does not have any production of the crops endogenous to this study under Bargaining Power Alternative A. Therefore, the amount of income generated in this rural area would fall to zero under Bargaining Power Alternative A.

Nationally, the amount of income generated under Bargaining Power Alternative B is 30 percent greater than under the Land-Retirement Alternative. This increase in the amount of income generated is experienced throughout most of the rural areas delineated for this study. Only 23 of these rural areas have less income generated under Bargaining Power Alternative B than under the Land-Retirement Alternative. These are areas which would have drastic reductions in the amount of farm commodities they produce under Bargaining Power Alternative B. Therefore, even with the high farm prices associated with this policy alternative, the amount of income generated in these areas would be less than under the Land-Retirement Alternative.

In western North Carolina, northern Georgia, and southern Alabama, the amount of income generated under Bargaining Power Alternative B decreases by more than 19 percent from what it is under the Land-Retirement Alternative (see rural areas 16, 18, 21, 24). Under Bargaining Power Alternative B, 70 percent fewer acres are in production in these rural areas than under the Land-Retirement Alternative. While the production of feed grain and cotton in these areas remains almost constant between the two policy alternatives, the production of soybeans is 90 percent lower in Bargaining Power Alternative B.

While the income generated in the Delta states region is 44 percent greater under Bargaining Power Alternative B than under the Land-Retirement Alternative, the amount of income generated in north central Louisiana under this policy alternative is 40 percent less than it would be under the Land-Retirement Alternative (see rural area 58). The total number of acres in crops in this rural area under Bargaining Power Alternative B decreases by 72 percent from what it is under the Land-Retirement Alternative. This decrease in production is concentrated in soybean production which would be 90 percent lower under Bargaining Power Alternative B than under the Land-Retirement Alternative.

While the amount of income generated in the Southern Plains region as a whole is only 10 percent greater under Bargaining Power Alternative B than under the Land-Retirement Alternative, only 4 of this region's 23 rural areas would experience sizable decreases in the amount of income generated under this policy alternative. These 4 rural areas are located in southeastern Oklahoma and northeastern Texas (see rural areas 110, 115, 118, 119). Under Bargaining Power Alternative B, these rural areas have 64 percent fewer acres in production than under the Land-Retirement Alternative. This decrease in the number of acres used for crops is accompanied by a shift from cotton and soybean production to primarily wheat production under Bargaining Power Alternative B which contributes to the decrease in income generated in these 4 rural areas.

The only rural area in the Pacific region which would have less income generated under Bargaining Power Alternative B than under the Land-Retirement Alternative is located in southeastern California (see rural area 143). This rural area, which has 74 percent fewer acres in production under Bargaining Power Alternative B, would have a 19 percent decrease in the amount of income generated under this policy alternative when compared to the Land-Retirement Alternative.

In the North Central region, the only rural areas which have less income generated under Bargaining Power Alternative B than under the Land-Retirement Alternative are in central South Dakota and southwestern Kansas (see rural areas 88, 104). Rural area 88 in central South Dakota has 81 percent fewer acres in production under Bargaining Power Alternative B. Rural area 104 in southwestern Kansas shifts from a production pattern dominated by the production of feed grain under the Land-Retirement Alternative to one in which 70 percent of the cropland acres are used to produce wheat under Bargaining Power Alternative B.

EFFECTS OF THE POLICY ALTERNATIVES ON EMPLOYMENT GENERATED

To show the differential impacts which the four policy alternatives have on the amounts of employment generated in different areas, we have computed indices which compare the amount of employment generated under the Land-Retirement Alternative with the amount of employment generated under each of the other policy alternatives. These indices are presented in Table 8.12 for the United States and for each of the ten farm production regions.

Nationally, the amount of employment that is generated by the production of the crops endogenous to this model would be 14 percent less under the Free Market Alternative than it is under the Land-Retirement Alternative. While the quantity produced increases under the Free Market Alternative, the price received by farmers decreases by a proportionally greater factor. The resulting reduction in the value of farm output leads to a decrease in net farm income and a reduction in the amount of employment generated under the Free Market Alternative.

However, the amount of employment generated in the Southern Plains region increases by 30 percent under the Free Market Alternative. Under this policy alternative, the production of cotton almost doubles in the Southern Plains region. Since the labor generation factor of cotton is high relative to the other crops, this shift to cotton production induces the increase in employment in this region. However, the Appalachian, Southeast, Delta states, Mountain, and Pacific regions all experience sizable reductions in the amount of cotton produced. This reduction in cotton production contributes substantially to the decrease in the amount of employment generated in these regions under the Free Market Alternative.

The Northeast region has a 63 percent decrease in the amount of employment generated under the Free Market Alternative. The amount of cropland in production decreases by 58 percent in this region under the Free Market Alternative. This means that employment in the Northeast region is adversely affected due to two factors: the low farm prices that are associated with the Free Market Alternative and the decrease in production that occurs when acreage restraints are removed. However, the acreage in crops increases under the Free Market Alternative in the Corn Belt and the Lake states regions. This increase in production partially offsets the low farm prices associated with the Free Market Alternative so that the amount of employment generated under this policy alternative decreases by only 10 percent in these two regions.

Under Bargaining Power Alternative A, the amount of employment generated in each of the farm production regions is higher than it would be under the Land-Retirement Alternative and is 20 percent higher for the nation as a whole under Bargaining Power Alternative A. In the Appalachian and the Southeast regions, cotton production increases by more than 30 percent under Bargaining Power Alternative A. This increase in cotton production contributes to the 32 percent increase in employment generated in the Appalachian region and the 29 percent increase in employment generated in the Southeast region.

The amount of employment generated under Bargaining Power Alternative A increases by only 4 percent in the Southern Plains region. Under this policy alternative, the Southern Plains region has fewer acres devoted to producing cotton and soybeans and more acres devoted to producing feed grain and wheat than under the Land-Retirement Alternative. While the total number of acres in production decreases only slightly under Bargaining Power Alternative A, the shift in the production mix under this policy alternative leads to only a slight increase in the amount of employment generated in the Southern Plains region. In the Northern Plains region, the number of acres in production decreases by 11 percent under Bargaining Power Alternative A. However, the acreage devoted to feed grain under this policy alternative is only slightly less than under the Land-Retirement Alternative. Since in this region feed grain has the highest labor generation factor, the maintenance of feed-grain production coupled with the higher prices of Bargaining Power Alternative A induces a 9 percent increase in the amount of employment generated in the Northern Plains region.

Nationally the amount of employment generated by the production of the crops endogenous to this study increases by 31 percent under Bargaining Power Alternative B. While the total number of acres in production under Bargaining Power Alternative B is 12 percent less than under the Land-Retirement Alternative, the high prices associated with Bargaining Power Alternative B more than offset this decrease in production. A sizable increase in the amount of employment generated is experienced in all but the Southern Plains region. The Southern Plains region has only a 9 percent increase in employment under Bargaining Power Alternative B. This relatively small increase in employment is due to a 28 percent decrease in cotton production and an 85 percent decrease in soybean production in the Southern Plains region under this policy alternative.

Since both the income and employment variables are related to the value of output of the endogenous crops under each of the policy alternatives, their index values in any region or rural area vary in the same direction when compared to the Land-Retirement Alternative. Because we have previously presented a detailed description by rural areas of the income effects of the alternative farm policies, we will now present only a general discussion of the employment effects that the alternative policies have on individual rural areas. Table 8.13 presents the indices of employment generated for each of the 150 rural areas in our model.

The decrease in the amount of employment generated under the Free Market Alternative occurs widely throughout the rural areas of the nation. Only those rural areas which have large increases in crop production would have significant gains in the amount of employment generated under the Free Market Alternative. In western New York and northwestern Nebraska, wheat production almost doubles under the Free Market Alternative, which causes the increased employment generated in these rural areas (see rural areas 1, 91). Due to increases in the dryland production of feed grain, the amount of employment rises in southern Ohio and Indiana, western Kentucky, eastern North Carolina, and southeastern Georgia (see rural areas 36, 37, 40, 43, 33, 34, 35, 41, 7, 10, 13). The irrigated production of feed grain increases in eastern New Mexico, east central Colorado, and northeastern Colorado, which induces the greater amounts of employment generated in these rural areas under the Free Market Alternative (see rural areas 129, 132, 134). Cotton production, which has a large labor generation factor, increases in west central Louisiana, southwestern Texas, northwestern and south central Texas, and southeastern California (see rural areas 120, 111, 112, 114,

115, 116, 122, 124, 143). This increased cotton production leads to the large increases in the amount of employment generated under the Free Market Alternative in these rural areas.

In contrast to those rural areas which have gains in the amount of employment generated under the Free Market Alternative, there are numerous rural areas that do not produce any of the endogenous crops under this policy alternative. In rural areas where this occurs, the amount of employment generated by the crops endogenous to this study falls to zero. Rural areas in which the amount of employment generated is at or near the zero level under the Free Market Alternative are in eastern Pennsylvania, southwestern Missouri, northern Wisconsin, central Minnesota, eastern Virginia, western North Carolina, central Tennessee, eastern Alabama, central Texas, and the western areas of the Dakotas, southeastern Montana, eastern Wyoming, east central Colorado, and southern Arizona (see rural areas 2, 64, 47, 78, 5, 6, 16, 28, 22, 23, 121, 123, 128, 82, 83, 85, 86, 136, 135, 131, 142).

As was mentioned previously, the amount of employment generated for the entire nation increases by 20 percent under Bargaining Power Alternative A. In each of the farm production regions, more employment is generated under this policy alternative than is generated under the Land-Retirement Alternative. However, numerous rural areas have less employment generated under Bargaining Power Alternative A than under the base alternative. While for the entire nation the number of acres in production under Bargaining Power Alternative A is only 2 percent less than under the Land-Retirement Alternative, there is a 46 percent decrease in the number of acres in production in the rural areas which have significantly less employment generated under Bargaining Power Alternative A.

In western South Dakota, northeastern Oklahoma, and southeastern California, the production of wheat is markedly lower under Bargaining Power Alternative A than it is under the Land-Retirement Alternative (see rural areas 85, 86, 88, 105, 143). This decrease in wheat production is the primary cause of the reduced amount of employment generated in these rural areas under Bargaining Power Alternative A. Decreased soybean production is the primary reason for less employment being generated under this policy alternative in western North Carolina, northern Georgia, southern Alabama, north central Louisiana, and in northeastern and western Texas (see rural areas 16, 18, 24, 21, 58, 110, 115, 118, 119, 127). The production of both feed grain and soybeans decreases in southern Ohio, west central Wisconsin, central North Carolina, southwestern Kansas, and central Nebraska (see rural areas 36, 37, 76, 9, 93, 104). The reduced production of these two crops leads to decreases in the amount of economic activity and employment that occurs in these rural areas. In central Washington, south central Colorado, and southwestern North Dakota, decreased production of feed grain leads to reductions in the amount of employment generated in these rural areas under Bargaining Power Alternative A (see rural areas 132, 150, 83). The rural area in southwestern North Dakota is the only rural area in our model which would not have any production of the endogenous crops under Bargaining Power Alternative A. Therefore, the amount of employment generated falls to zero under Bargaining Power Alternative A in this rural area.

Only 13 of the model's 150 rural areas would have significantly less employment generated under Bargaining Power Alternative B than they would have under the Land-Retirement Alternative. (All of these 13 were among the 24 rural areas which had less employment generated under Bargaining Power Alternative A.) While the acreage in production under Bargaining Power Alternative B decreases by 12 percent for the entire nation, the acreage in production decreases by 47 percent in the 13 rural areas that have less employment generated under this policy alternative. These rural areas are located in western North Carolina, northern Georgia, southern Alabama, northern Louisiana, southeastern Oklahoma, northeastern Texas, central South Dakota, southwestern Kansas, south central Colorado, and southeastern California (see rural areas 16, 18, 24, 21, 58, 110, 115, 118, 119, 88, 104, 132, 143).

EFFECTS OF THE POLICY ALTERNATIVES ON THE VALUE OF CROPLAND

In the United States the property tax has traditionally served as one of the primary methods of financing local and state governments. In 1969, $0.24 out of every $1.00 of local and state government revenue was from taxes on property. In states that are not heavily industrialized, agricultural land and buildings constitute the major portion of real property upon which property taxes can be levied. For example, in Iowa 40 percent of the state taxes levied on real property in 1970 was levied on agricultural land and buildings.

Therefore, government farm policies that affect the value of farmland will also have an impact on the ability of local and state governments in agriculturally oriented states to generate tax revenues. If the value of farmland were to drop significantly, the rate of taxation per dollar of real property would have to increase for all types of real property in the rural community so that the revenues of state and local governments would not decrease. As the rate of taxation increases, it becomes increasingly more difficult for local governments to finance the services they already provide and to justify the implementation of any new services. In addition to raising the rate of taxation, decreases in the value of farmland would shift the relative burden of property taxes from owners of farmland to owners of nonfarm real property.

While changes in the value of farmland have secondary effects on the economic base of rural communities, they have immediate effects on those individuals who have invested in farmland as a means of accumulating savings. Government farm policies that increase the value of farmland will benefit the present owners of farmland (and their heirs) at the expense of future purchasers of farmland, and farm policies that decrease the value of farmland would have the opposite effect. In addition to the equity aspects of changes in the value of farmland, the asset position of the farming sector is highly dependent on the value of farmland. In 1969, farm real estate comprised over two-thirds of the total value of assets of the farming industry in the United States. This means that changes in the value of farmland can have significant effects on the asset value of the farming industry and the ability of the farming industry to finance capital investments.

Since changes in the value of cropland are extremely important to farmers and to the citizens of rural communities, we have developed indices which compare the value of cropland under the Land-Retirement Alternative to the value of cropland under each of the other policy alternatives analyzed in this study. The capitalized value of cropland under each of the four policy alternatives was computed by summing the annual net return to land from producing each of the crops included in the model (plus government payments in the Land-Retirement Alternative) and then dividing this sum by a capitalization rate.[6] The cropland value under each of the other policy alternatives was then expressed as a percentage of the cropland value under the Land-Retirement Alternative for each region.

Under the Land-Retirement Alternative and under both Bargaining Power Alternatives, the value of cropland we have calculated includes a return due to the quotas associated with those policy alternatives. For example, an owner-operator may have 160 acres on which he could produce the crops endogenous to this study, but under the Land-Retirement Alternative, he might produce these crops on only 140 of the 160 acres. He leaves the other 20 acres idle in order to receive government payments for diverting those 20 acres. Under Bargaining Power Alternative B, he may be able to fulfill his production quota while using only 120 of the 160 acres; therefore, he would leave 40 acres idle under this policy alternative. However, the net return to land under the Land-Retirement Alternative and under both Bargaining Power Alternatives is imputed to the entire 160 acres because the producer is required to maintain idle land in order to receive the benefits of the quotas associated with these policy alternatives.

Under the Free Market Alternative, however, if the owner-operator produces the crops endogenous to this study on only 140 of this 160 acres, he could use the remaining 20 acres for other activities. Therefore, in rural areas that have idle land under the Free Market Alternative, the cropland values calculated in this study may be undervalued, as they do not allow for the net return that could result from production of crops not endogenous to this study. Since this idle land would be used primarily for more extensive agricultural activities and since the general level of farm commodity prices would be lower under the Free Market Alternative, this undervaluation is not expected to be very severe. Therefore, the net return to land from the production of the crops endogenous to this study is imputed to the entire 160 acres under the Free Market Alternative, also.

For each policy alternative, Table 8.14 presents the indices of cropland value for the United States and the ten farm production regions. Under the Free Market Alternative, the value of cropland, nationally, is 77 percent lower than it would be under the Land-Retirement Alternative. Under the Land-Retirement Alternative, net farm income is bolstered by $3.96 billion in government payments. The elimination of government payments for retiring cropland and the low prices for farm commodities under the Free Market Alternative induce the drastic decrease in cropland value under this policy alternative.

Cropland value decreases by more than 64 percent in each of the farm production regions under the Free Market Alternative due to the nationwide impact of eliminating government payments. The farm production region which has the

---

6. The annual net return to land was computed as a residual payment after the costs of the other factors of production had been accounted for. The other factors of production are labor (both hired and operator), power and machinery, fertilizer, lime, seed, pesticides, irrigation, interest and insurance, drying costs, and property taxes.

smallest decrease in cropland value is the Corn Belt region where the cropland value under the Free Market Alternative is 36 percent of what it would be under the Land-Retirement Alternative. Without the restraints imposed under the Land-Retirement Alternative, this region increases its acreage in production by 10 million acres under the Free Market Alternative. However, this increase in the number of acres in production only partially offsets the elimination of government payments under the Free Market Alternative.

In the Northeast region, the value of cropland decreases by 97 percent under the Free Market Alternative. In addition to the loss of government payments, the number of acres in production in this region under the Free Market Alternative is 58 percent less than under the Land-Retirement Alternative. In contrast, the number of acres in production in the Southern Plains region increased by 6 million acres under this policy alternative as compared to the Land-Retirement Alternative, but cropland values are only 9 percent of what they are in the Land-Retirement Alternative. The increase in production does not offset the loss of government payments in this region because this region has historically received a relatively large share of the payments for diverting cropland. The two states in the Southern Plains region received over 15 percent of the government payments for diverting cropland under the feed-grain, wheat, and cotton programs in 1969.

Under Bargaining Power Alternative A, the national cropland value is only 5 percent lower than under the Land-Retirement Alternative. In the Northeast region, the value of cropland under Bargaining Power Alternative A is 53 percent higher than under the Land-Retirement Alternative. There are almost as many acres in production in this region under Bargaining Power Alternative A as under the Land-Retirement Alternative, which means the higher prices associated with Bargaining Power Alternative A can offset the loss of government payments in this region. As was cited previously, the Southern Plains region benefits heavily from the government payments associated with the Land-Retirement Alternative, and their elimination under Bargaining Power Alternative A leads to a 41 percent decrease in the value of cropland in this region under this policy alternative. The Southeast and the Northern Plains regions both experience sizable decreases in cropland value under Bargaining Power Alternative A due to significant reductions in the number of acres in production in these two regions.

Nationally, cropland value would increase by 26 percent under Bargaining Power Alternative B due to the high farm prices associated with this policy alternative. While there are no government payments and fewer acres are in production under Bargaining Power Alternative B, the net return from each acre that is in production is much higher than it would be under the Land-Retirement Alternative. This means that those rural areas which retain relatively more acres in production under this policy alternative have greater gains in cropland value than those rural areas which have relatively fewer acres in production.

Only the Southern Plains and the Mountain regions have decreases in the value of cropland under Bargaining Power Alternative B. While these two regions have fewer acres in production under Bargaining Power Alternative B than under the Land-Retirement Alternative, the proportional decrease in cropland acreage is not greater in these regions than in the other farm production regions. These two regions have decreases in cropland value under this policy alternative due to the elimination of the relatively large government payments that these regions receive under land-retirement–type payments. In 1969 these two regions received 23 percent of the government payments paid under the feed grain, wheat, and cotton programs.

While the eight remaining farm production regions have higher cropland values under Bargaining Power Alternative B than under the Land-Retirement Alternative, the value of cropland in the Southeast and the Northern Plains regions increases only slightly under Bargaining Power Alternative B. The number of acres in production in these two regions under Bargaining Power Alternative B is 19 percent less than it is under the Land-Retirement Alternative. Nationally there is only a 12 percent decrease in the number of acres in production between the two policy alternatives. Since these two regions have a relatively greater reduction in cropland acreage under Bargaining Power Alternative B, they would not experience significant increases in the value of cropland under this policy alternative.

Table 8.15 presents indices of cropland value for each of the 150 rural areas in the model. These indices show that the effect of a policy alternative upon an entire farm production region may be drastically different from the effect of that policy alternative on a specific rural area within the farm production region. The following discussion focuses on those rural areas that experience changes in cropland value which are different from the change in cropland value that occurs for the farm production region as a whole.

The value of cropland falls to zero in 42 of the model's 150 rural areas under the Free Market Alternative. The value of cropland can fall to zero in a rural area for two reasons. Either there is not any production of the crops endogenous to this study in a rural area or the net return from producing these crops is not sufficient to offset the cost of producing them. As was stated earlier, we would expect that more extensive uses of cropland would be undertaken in the rural areas where there is no production of the endogenous crops. but that these activities would only slightly increase the value of cropland in the rural areas affected. In those rural areas where negative returns are occurring, farmers are using equity previously accumulated to offset their production deficits. They would continue to do this only for the short run. In the long run, of course, these farmers would be forced either to increase their income from farming or to give up their farming careers.

The rural areas that have cropland values which decrease to zero under the Free Market Alternative are spread throughout the nation and are present in all the farm production regions.[7] In addition, the value of cropland in the remaining rural areas is much lower under the Free Market Alternative than under the Land-Retirement Alternative. The smallest decrease in cropland values occurs in eastern New Mexico where the value of cropland under the Free Market Alternative is only 65 percent as high as it is under the Land-Retirement Alternative (see rural

7. Those rural areas that have no production under the Free Market Alternative are 5, 6, 16, 22, 23, 28, 47, 64, 78, 82, 83, 85, 86, 121, 123, 128, 131, 135, 136. Those rural acres that have negative returns under the Free Market Alternative are 1, 2, 9, 12, 19, 24, 45, 46, 52, 53, 63, 76, 79, 81, 87, 105, 107, 133, 140, 142, 143, 144, 145.

area 129). This rural area doubles the number of irrigated acres used for the production of feed grain under the Free Market Alternative.

Under Bargaining Power Alternative A, the value of cropland in western New York is 29 percent lower than under the Land-Retirement Alternative (see rural area 1). This occurs even though the value of cropland increases by 53 percent in the Northeast region as a whole. The total number of acres in production in this rural area is almost the same under Bargaining Power Alternative A as it is under the Land-Retirement Alternative. However, under the Land-Retirement Alternative, this rural area primarily produces wheat, while, under Bargaining Power Alternative A, two-thirds of its acres in production are devoted to the production of feed grain. The elimination of government payments, plus the reduction in wheat production under Bargaining Power Alternative A, induces the decrease in cropland value in this rural area.

While the value of cropland in the entire Appalachian region is slightly higher under Bargaining Power Alternative A than under the Land-Retirement Alternative, the value of cropland in 4 of the rural areas of this region decreases by more than 30 percent under Bargaining Power Alternative A. These rural areas are located in northeastern Virginia, western North Carolina, and western Tennessee (see rural areas 5, 9, 16, 28). The acreage in production in these 4 rural areas decreases by 32 percent under Bargaining Power Alternative A, which means that these rural areas do not benefit from the higher prices associated with this policy alternative to the extent that the other rural areas in the Appalachian region do.

The value of cropland in southern Georgia, southwestern Alabama, and northern Florida is higher under Bargaining Power Alternative A than under the Land-Retirement Alternative even though the value of cropland in the Southeast region as a whole is 29 percent lower under Bargaining Power Alternative A (see rural areas 13, 14, 19, 20). The number of acres in production in these 4 rural areas remains almost constant under both policy alternatives, but in the Southeast region as a whole, the cropland acreage decreases by 15 percent under Bargaining Power Alternative A.

In the Delta states region as a whole, the value of cropland under Bargaining Power Alternative A is within 2 percent of what it would be under the Land-Retirement Alternative. However, the value of cropland increases in the central section of this region under Bargaining Power Alternative A (see rural areas 31, 56, 57, 60, 61). These rural areas in eastern Louisiana, northwestern Mississippi, and eastern Arkansas have a 5 percent increase in the total number of acres used for crops, including a 20 percent increase in the number of acres used for soybeans under Bargaining Power Alternative A. This occurs even though the total number of acres used for crops in the entire region decreases slightly under this policy alternative. Therefore, the higher prices associated with Bargaining Power Alternative A can overcome the elimination of government payments in these 5 rural areas, but not for the entire Delta states region.

While the value of cropland in the Pacific region as a whole is slightly lower under Bargaining Power Alternative A than under the Land-Retirement Alternative, the value of cropland increases in northeastern Oregon and southeastern Washington under Bargaining Power Alternative A (see rural areas 147, 148, 149,

150). The number of acres in production increases by 7 percent in these 4 rural areas under Bargaining Power Alternative A, while the number of acres in production in the entire region remains almost constant between the two policy alternatives. This means that the 4 rural areas with increased production derive proportionally greater benefits from the higher prices associated with Bargaining Power Alternative A.

In the entire Corn Belt region and in the rural areas of the southern Lake states region, the value of cropland would be higher under Bargaining Power Alternative A than under the Land-Retirement Alternative. However, in central Minnesota and Wisconsin, the value of cropland under Bargaining Power Alternative A would be significantly lower than under the Land-Retirement Alternative (see rural areas 47, 78, 79). While the Lake states region as a whole has more land in production under Bargaining Power Alternative A, the number of acres in production in these 3 rural areas does not increase under this policy alternative. As was stated previously, the value of cropland in the Northern Plains region decreases by 24 percent under Bargaining Power Alternative A due to the elimination of government payments and the 11 percent decrease in the number of acres in production in this region under Bargaining Power Alternative A. The only rural area in which the value of cropland falls to zero under Bargaining Power Alternative A is in southwestern North Dakota (see rural area 83). The demands for the crops endogenous to this study are satisfied without any of the cropland in this rural area coming into production.

Under Bargaining Power Alternative B, the value of cropland in the Southeast region as a whole is slightly higher than it is under the Land-Retirement Alternative. However, the value of cropland decreases significantly in western South Carolina and in all but the southwestern tip of Alabama under Bargaining Power Alternative B (see rural areas 17, 18, 21, 22, 23, 25). While the number of acres in production in the entire Southeast region decreases by 25 percent under this policy alternative, there would be a 37 percent decrease in cropland acreage in these 6 rural areas. This means that the high farm prices associated with Bargaining Power Alternative B generate proportionally greater net returns in the other rural areas of the Southeast region at the expense of the net return (and thus the value of cropland) in the 6 rural areas which have relatively less production under this policy alternative.

The value of cropland in the Delta states region increases by 37 percent under Bargaining Power Alternative B as compared to the Land-Retirement Alternative. However, in eastern Mississippi, northwestern Louisiana, and southwestern Arkansas, the value of cropland decreases significantly under this policy alternative (see rural areas 27, 58, 59, 62, 120). The total acreage used for crops in these 5 rural areas under Bargaining Power Alternative B is 43 percent less than the acreage used for crops under the Land-Retirement Alternative. Soybean acreage under Bargaining Power Alternative B declines by 88 percent in these 5 rural areas but declines by only 17 percent in the entire Delta states region. This explains the drastic decrease in cropland value that occurs in the 5 rural areas at the same time the value of cropland increases in the entire Delta states region.

In 20 of the Southern Plains regions' 23 rural areas, the value of cropland would be highest under the Land-Retirement Alternative. Only in central Oklahoma, northwestern Texas, and the southern tip of Texas does the value of cropland under Bargaining Power Alternative B exceed the level attained under the Land-Retirement Alternative (see rural areas 106, 112, 125). As has been mentioned previously, the Southern Plains region receives relatively large payments for idling cropland under land-retirement–type programs. Thus under the Land-Retirement Alternative, the value of cropland is high relative to the value of cropland under the other policy alternatives in this region. The two states in this region received over $552 million in government payments under the feed-grain, wheat, and cotton programs in 1969.

While the total number of acres in production under Bargaining Power Alternative B decreases by only 7 percent in the Mountain region, the number of acres devoted to feed grain decreases by 45 percent. This decrease in the production of feed grain, coupled with the elimination of government payments, causes the 16 percent decrease in the value of cropland in this region under Bargaining Power Alternative B. However, in southeastern and northeastern Colorado, northwestern Idaho, and central Montana, the value of cropland is higher under Bargaining Power Alternative B than under the Land-Retirement Alternative (see rural areas 131, 134, 138, 139, 146). The acreage devoted to feed grain in these 5 rural areas almost doubles under Bargaining Power Alternative B which induces higher cropland values under Bargaining Power Alternative B in these rural areas than under the Land-Retirement Alternative.

In central California the value of cropland under Bargaining Power Alternative B is 49 percent lower than under the Land-Retirement Alternative (see rural area 144). In this rural area, cotton acreage declines by 27 percent under Bargaining Power Alternative B and the total acreage in production declines by 20 percent. However, the value of cropland in the entire Pacific region increases by 27 percent under Bargaining Power Alternative B since the total number of acres in production in this region declines by only 10 percent from its level under the Land-Retirement Alternative.

The value of cropland increases in almost all the rural areas of the Corn Belt and the Lake states regions under Bargaining Power Alternative B. Only in southwestern Missouri and central Minnesota does the value of cropland decrease under this policy alternative (see rural areas 64, 78). However, in the Northern Plains region, the value of cropland in western North and South Dakota, western Nebraska, and southwestern Kansas decreases significantly under Bargaining Power Alternative B (see rural areas 82, 83, 85, 88, 91, 92, 104). These rural areas do not benefit from the high farm prices associated with Bargaining Power Alternative B because of the relatively large decreases in production that occur in these rural areas.

POLICY IMPLICATIONS

In this study we attempt to quantitatively examine the potential effects of four government farm policies on selected key economic variables. While some of these variables relate directly to farmers and the quantity of output they produce,

tween the production of major crops and indicators of economic well-being are determined. The theoretical tool used for this assessment is input-output analysis.[8]

A transactions table serves as a double-entry ledger and provides the basis of input-output analysis. Table 8A-1 presents a hypothetical transactions table which is used in the following discussion as an example of the methods used in this study. To construct the transactions table, each producing sector of the economy (sectors A, B, C, and H in Table 8A-1) is assigned a row and a column in the table. The row assigned to each sector describes the distribution of that sector's output throughout the economy. The column assigned to each sector shows from what sectors in the economy that sector purchases its inputs. This means that every element of the transaction table can be viewed in two ways. For example, the $16 million transaction between sectors A and B (first row, second column, Table 8A-1) can be looked upon either as the sale of part of sector A's output to sector B or as a purchase of inputs by sector B from sector A for use in the production of sector B's output.

Sector H represents the household sector of the hypothetical economy. In input-output analysis the household sector can be included either as one of the producing sectors or as a part of final demands. In Table 8A-1, households are included as a producing sector; therefore, consumption purchases are regarded as inputs to the household sector's production process and the sale of labor is considered an output of the household sector.

The final demand sector in Table 8A-1 corresponds to an autonomous demand for the output of the producing sectors including such things as inventory accumulation, exports from the economy, government purchases, and other exogenous demands. The final payments sector in Table 8A-1 introduces the value of the inputs purchased from outside the economy's producing sectors, including such items as imports, purchases from existing inventory stocks, or depreciation allowances. The final column of Table 8A-1, the total output column, is the summation of each sector's value of output sold throughout the economy, and the final row of the table (total outlay) is the total purchases of inputs by each sector. Total output and total outlay must be equal for each of the producing sectors.

The direct requirements table (Table 8A-2) is constructed from the transactions table and simultaneously presents each transaction in the economy as a proportion of total output and as a proportion of total outlay for each sector of the economy. Each row entry represents the proportion of a million dollars worth of output sold to that column sector by that row industry. In the example, sector C sells $94.6 thousand worth of its output to sector A and $216.7 thousand worth of its output to sector H for every million dollars worth of output it sells. Each column entry in Table 8A-2 represents the proportion of each million dollars worth of inputs that column sector purchases from the row sector. In the example, every million dollars worth of inputs purchased by sector A contains $202.7 thousand worth of the output of sector H. The direct requirements table is cal-

8. Further discussion of these methods can be found in William H. Miernyk, *The Elements of Input-Output Analysis,* Random House, New York, 1965; William E. Martin and Harold O. Carter, *A California Interindustry Analysis Emphasizing Agriculture, Parts 1 and 2,* Calif. Agr. Exp. Sta., Giannini Foundation Res. Report 250, 1962.

culated by dividing each column element by the total output of that column sector after the total output is adjusted for inventory depletion.

Each entry of Table 8A-3, the interdependence table, measures the increase in output of that row sector generated by an increase of a million dollars of sales to final demand by the related column sector. These entries reflect not only the direct and indirect effects of the increased sales to final demand but also the induced effects of the increased consumer spending by the household sector.[9] For example, the value of the output of sector A would increase by $982.9 thousand for every million dollar increase of deliveries to final demand by sector B. Table 8A-3 is formed by first subtracting from an identity matrix the direct requirements table (Table 8A-2) and then inverting the resulting matrix.

The interdependence coefficients in Table 8A-3 measure the additional output forthcoming from every row sector generated by the production of an additional million dollars worth of output delivered to final demand by the respective column sector. To determine the effect of producing an additional million dollars worth of output by any sector, the coefficients in the column of that sector in Table 8A-3 must be adjusted. Table 8A-4 presents the adjusted interdependence matrix which is computed by dividing every element in each column by the diagonal element of that column. The coefficients in Table 8A-4 then represent the additional output of each row sector generated by the production of an additional million dollars worth of output by the column sector. For example, sector B produces $377.6 thousand worth of output for each million dollars worth of output from sector A. The income generation factor of a million dollars worth of output from any sector can be read directly from the household row of that column sector in Table 8A-4.[10]

To calculate the impact of alternative policies on employment, the direct labor requirement for each sector must first be determined. The direct labor requirements of a producing sector are defined as the number of workers needed in that sector to produce a million dollars of output by that sector. To determine the number of workers needed per million dollars of output in a sector, the average yearly employment for that sector is divided by that sector's gross domestic output. Table 8A-5 presents direct labor requirements for the hypothetical economy as the diagonal elements of a matrix with zeroes as the off-diagonal elements (household sector deleted).

The labor generation factor of each sector is determined using the direct labor requirements for each sector (Table 8A-5) and the adjusted interdependence matrix (Table 8A-4). Premultiplying the adjusted interdependence matrix by the matrix containing the direct labor requirements as diagonal elements determines the hypothetical employment matrix shown in Table 8A-6. Each element of the

9. The direct effects of an economy are given by the direct requirements table (Table 8A-2 in the example). The indirect effects are those increases in output that are due to the additional spending of all the producing sectors in the economy, but not allowing increased consumer expenditures. The induced effects reflect the increased output of each sector caused by increased consumer spending.

10. The income generation factors developed in this study are related to, but not equivalent to, the type II income multipliers developed in other input-output studies. The type II income multiplier for a sector is equal to the income generation factor (the household row of that sector's column of Table 8A-4) divided by the direct income effect (the household row of that sector's column of Table 8A-2).

employment matrix represents the number of workers in that row sector required to produce a million dollars of output from that column sector. In the hypothetical economy, 6.4018 workers are required from sector A and 6.2567 workers from sector B to produce one million dollars worth of output from sector C (Table 8A-6). To determine the total number of workers needed to produce an additional million dollars worth of output from a given sector (the labor generation factor of that sector), it is necessary to sum the column of the employment matrix representing that sector. For example, the labor generation factor of sector A is 22.9382 workers per million dollars worth of output.[11]

The previous discussion can be presented mathematically by the following set of equations. Assume the system under discussion has n processing sectors, m final demand sectors, and d final payments sectors. Let X_i be the output of each of the n processing sectors, x_{ij} be the amount of output of sector i used by sector j, and Y_{ik} be the demand for output of sector i by the kth final demand sector. Let the following system of equations (8A-1) represent this system:

$$
\begin{aligned}
X_1 &= x_{11} + x_{12} + \cdots + x_{1n} + Y_{11} + \cdots + Y_{1m} \\
X_2 &= x_{21} + x_{22} + \cdots + x_{2n} + Y_{21} + \cdots + Y_{2m} \\
&\ \ \vdots \\
X_n &= x_{n1} + x_{n2} + \cdots + x_{nn} + Y_{n1} + \cdots + Y_{nm} \\
&\ \ \vdots \\
X_{n+d} &= x_{n+d,1} + x_{n+d,2} + \cdots + x_{n+d,n} + Y_{n+d,1} + \cdots + Y_{n+d,m}
\end{aligned}
$$

(8A-1)

Assuming constant technical coefficients for the n processing sectors, new terms can be calculated as in Equation 8A-2.

$$a_{ij} = x_{ij}/X_j \qquad (8A\text{-}2)$$
$$i, j = 1, \ldots n$$

Deleting the final payments sector, the producing sectors can now be summarized as in Equation 8A-3 for all n producing sectors.

$$X_i - \sum_{j=1}^{n} a_{ij} X_j = \sum_{k=1}^{m} Y_{ik} \qquad (8A\text{-}3)$$
$$i = 1, \ldots n$$

---

11. As in the case of type II income multiplier, the type II employment multiplier for a sector is equal to the labor generation factor of that sector divided by the direct labor requirement of that sector.

The system defined by Equation 8A-3 can be expressed equivalently in matrix form as in Equations 8A-4 or 8A-5.

$$
\begin{pmatrix}
(1 - a_{11}) & - a_{12} & \cdots & - a_{1n} \\
- a_{21} & (1 - a_{22}) & \cdots & - a_{2n} \\
\cdot & \cdot & & \\
\cdot & \cdot & & \\
\cdot & \cdot & & \\
\cdot & \cdot & & \\
- a_{n1} & - a_{n2} & \cdots & (1 - a_{nn})
\end{pmatrix}
\begin{pmatrix}
X_1 \\ X_2 \\ \cdot \\ \cdot \\ \cdot \\ \cdot \\ X_n
\end{pmatrix}
=
\begin{pmatrix}
Y_1 \\ Y_2 \\ \cdot \\ \cdot \\ \cdot \\ \cdot \\ Y_n
\end{pmatrix}
\tag{8A-4}
$$

or

$$(I - A) X = Y \tag{8A-5}$$

where A is an $n \times n$ matrix of technical coefficients, I is an identity matrix of the same dimension as A, X is an $n \times 1$ column vector of outputs, and Y is an $n \times 1$ column vector of final demands. To solve this system for the X vector, the $(I - A)$ matrix is inverted to form an interdependency table (such as Table 8A-3). Define a new matrix R, where $R = (I - A)^{-1}$, which when expanded appears as in Equation 8A-6.

$$
R =
\begin{pmatrix}
r_{11} & r_{12} & \cdots & r_{1n} \\
r_{21} & r_{22} & \cdots & r_{2n} \\
\cdot & \cdot & & \cdot \\
\cdot & \cdot & & \cdot \\
\cdot & \cdot & & \cdot \\
r_{n1} & r_{n2} & \cdots & r_{nn}
\end{pmatrix}
\tag{8A-6}
$$

where r_{ij} is the amount of output of sector i required to deliver one unit of output of sector j to final demand. Define a further relationship:

$$s_{ij} = r_{ij}/r_{ii}$$

for all i and j to form a new matrix S in Equation 8A-7.

$$
S =
\begin{pmatrix}
s_{11} & s_{12} & \cdots & s_{1n} \\
s_{21} & s_{22} & \cdots & s_{2n} \\
\cdot & \cdot & & \cdot \\
\cdot & \cdot & & \cdot \\
\cdot & \cdot & & \cdot \\
s_{n1} & s_{n2} & \cdots & s_{nn}
\end{pmatrix}
\tag{8A-7}
$$

where each s_{ij} represents the amount of output of sector i required to produce one unit of output of sector j. Matrix S corresponds to Table 8A-4.

APPENDIX B. CONSUMER FOOD COSTS

Total consumer expenditures for food are estimated in this study by summing the projected consumer expenditures in 1975 for the following commodities: beef and veal, pork, lamb and mutton, edible offal, broilers, turkeys, eggs, dairy products, bakery products, fruits and vegetables, grain mill products, and miscellaneous items. Projections of consumer expenditures for each of these categories are estimated for each of the policy solutions.

Consumer expenditures in 1975 for beef and veal, pork, lamb and mutton, broilers, turkeys, eggs, and dairy products are estimated with Equation 8B-1.

$$E_{i75} = (P_{iR75})(C_{i75})(N_{75}); i = 1, \ldots 7 \qquad (8B-1)$$

where E_{i75} = consumer expenditures for the ith commodity in 1975

C_{i75} = per capita consumption of the ith commodity in 1975 (retail equivalent weight basis for meat and poultry products)

P_{iR75} = retail price of the ith commodity in 1975 (in 1966 equivalent dollars)

N_{75} = population estimate for 1975

Consumer expenditures for edible offal in 1975 are estimated from Equation 8B-2.

$$E_{et} = -1074.174 + 2.0602E_{et-1} + 56.67T \qquad (8B-2)$$

where E_{et} = consumer expenditure for edible offal in year t

T = time; $1951 = 1, 1952 = 2, 1975 = 25$

Consumer expenditures for fruits and vegetables, bakery products, and miscellaneous items for 1975 are estimated using the relationships given by Equation 8B-3.

$$E_{it} = b_{0i} + b_{1i} E_{it-1} + b_{2i} I_t \qquad (8B-3)$$

where E_{it} = consumer expenditures for the ith commodity in year t

I_t = per capita income in year t (in 1954 constant dollars)

The estimates for b_0, b_1, and b_2 for each of the commodities are given in Equations 8B-4, 8B-5, and 8B-6.

$$E_{fv,t} = -1484.46 + 0.8633E_{fv,t-1} + 2.1775I_t \qquad (8B-4)$$

$$E_{bt} = -707.226 + 0.8672E_{bt-1} + 0.9971I_t \qquad (8B-5)$$

$$E_{mt} = -545.50 + 1.0003_{mt-1} + 0.3611I_t \qquad (8B-6)$$

where $E_{fv,t}$ = consumer expenditure for fruits and vegetables in year t

E_{bt} = consumer expenditures on bakery products in year t

E_{mt} = consumer expenditures on miscellaneous items in year t

Consumer expenditures for grain mill products in 1975 are estimated in Equation 8B-7.

$$E_{gt} = 814.68 + 0.5419E_{gt-1} + 51.29T \qquad (8\text{B-7})$$

where E_{gt} = consumer expenditure for grain mill products in year t

T = time; 1951 = 1, 1952 = 2, 1975 = 25

Chapter 9: Water Demand, Land Use, and Farm Policy Models

EARL O. HEADY, HOWARD C. MADSEN, KENNETH J. NICOL, and STANLEY H. HARGROVE

The water demand-allocation models reported in this study were developed and applied at the request of the National Water Commission. They incorporate all major agricultural commodities into a supply-demand and resource use interaction reflecting restraints in land resources for 223 agricultural-producing regions, water resources for 51 water supply regions in the 17 western states, and 27 consumer markets. The models, which incorporate a transportation submodel for commodities and water and product transfer activities, allow selection of optimal resource use patterns for the nation in future time periods. They also reflect comparative advantage in the allocation of land and water to competing alternatives as represented in relative yields, technologies, production costs, and transport costs. They allow substitution of land at one location for water at another location a thousand miles away (or vice versa). Finally, they allow evaluation of various policy alternatives in use of land and water resources, in interaction with commercial agricultural policies.

BACKGROUND

Over most of the last 40 years, the nation has used land-retirement programs to reduce supply and bolster farm prices and income. Land retirement distributed over the entire nation has been attained through voluntary programs financed from the U.S. Treasury. Recent estimates indicate that the total annual costs of these land-retirement and supply control programs approximate $5 billion.[1]

NOTE: For further details, see Earl O. Heady, Howard C. Madsen, Kenneth J. Nicol, and Stanely H. Hargrove, *Agricultural and Water Policies and the Environment: An Analysis of National Alternatives in Natural Resource Use, Food Supply and Environment Quality*, CARD Report No. 40T, Center for Agricultural and Rural Development, Iowa State Univ., June 1972; Howard C. Madsen, "Future Water and Land Supply-Demand Balances for U.S. Agriculture: A Spatial Analysis Incorporating Producing Areas, Consuming Regions and Water Supply Regions," Ph.D. diss., Iowa State Univ., Ames, 1972.

1. G. E. Brandow, "Cost of Farm Programs," in *Benefits and Burdens of Rural Development*, Center for Agricultural and Economic Development, Iowa State University Press, Ames, 1970.

During this same period, the nation also has continued to invest in public irrigation projects which increase the supply capacity of agriculture. As more irrigation is developed, an increased amount of land must be retired under commercial farm programs to maintain farm price and income goals. The public programs which develop more irrigated land, on the one hand, and finance land retirement as a supply control means, on the other hand, have two basic effects: (1) they cause water in the 17 western states to be substituted for land in the rest of the nation. This substitution results as added land is irrigated in the 17 western states and land is withdrawn from production under public subsidy in other regions; (2) the public has a double cost in first investing in increased supply capacity through irrigation and second in investing in land retirement to reduce supply.

The outlook for supply capacity of U.S. agriculture and the potential amount of water available for irrigation may, however, change with the future. Continued population growth, especially in the 17 western states, will greatly increase the demand for water for urban and manufacturing uses. Too, increased concern over water quality and pollution of streams through modern agricultural technology has encouraged proposals for reduced use of inputs such as insecticides, chemical fertilizers, and fragile lands. Questions thus arise whether future population, food demands, environmental considerations, and nonfarm uses of water will change the supply capacity of American agriculture.

One possibility would be that the diversion of water from irrigation to urban uses and restraints on insecticide and land fertilizer use might greatly reduce food supply capacity. If so, can the nation meet its future domestic and export demands for food at reasonable real costs? Will the supply of water be large enough to meet both the urban and farm requirements in the future? Would return to production of land now retired under government supply control programs allow the nation to meet future food demands with either no further development of irrigated agriculture from surface water supplies or some diversion of water from agriculture to urban, municipal, and manufacturing uses? How would these possibilities be altered by reduced use of certain insecticides and fragile lands? Would diversion of water to nonfarm uses and restriction on use of inputs with pollution potential cause food supplies to be extremely limited relative to demand? Or, would these diversions and restrictions only reduce food supplies to a better balance with demand, so that farm prices and income can rise with reduced treasury outlays for supply control and income supports?

This study has been made to appraise supply potentials in the year 2000. It evaluates the nation's needs for land and water in agriculture and its food supply potentials under various levels of population, farm programs, water prices, agricultural exports, technological advances, and environmental controls. It also estimates levels of farm prices projected to prevail under various combinations of these several variables affecting the supply of and demand for food.

SUBSTITUTABILITY OF TECHNOLOGIES AND INPUTS

The various capital technologies developed for agriculture serve as substitutes for both land and labor. Over the period 1940 to 1970, U.S. agriculture added

$63.6 billion in nonland capital while output increased by 73 percent and the farm labor force fell from 11.0 million to 4.2 million workers—a decline of 62 percent. While total crop output increased 31.6 percent between 1950 and 1970, total crop acreage declined by 41 million acres during the same period. This decline over 1950–70 in total cropland was accompanied by a $37.4 billion increase in nonland capital, an increase of 11.3 million acres in irrigated land, and a decline of 5.7 million (58 percent) in farm workers.

The substitutability of capital technology for land and labor is obvious. If new varieties, pest control, and fertilizers increase crop yields from 60 to 100 bushels per acre, the substitution potential is this: prior to the added technologies, 1,200 bushels could be produced on 20 acres; after the technologies are added, the same output can be produced on 12 acres. If an acre with a yield of 60 bushels requires 5 hours of labor before the added technologies, but requires 6 hours for servicing the larger inputs and greater output after the yield-increasing technologies, the following labor quantities are involved: to produce 1,200 bushels, 100 hours before and 72 hours after the added technologies.

It is technological change of this type that has been important in increasing the productive capacity of U.S. agriculture and allowing a greater output to be produced with smaller labor and land inputs. Of course, in addition to effects of biological innovations and a smaller crop acreage, farm employment also has been reduced by mechanical innovations which are direct labor substitutes. These capital technologies used for crops grown under rainfed conditions and improved livestock practices also serve as substitutes for irrigation water. A given level of output can be attained through use of more capital technologies under rainfed conditions and less streamwater or groundwater used for irrigation, or vice versa.

Water for crop irrigation serves similarly in substituting for nonirrigated land, total cropland, and farm labor. Since it greatly increases yields, greater farm use of water has large land-substituting effects. For example, if corn yields are 20 bushels before and 120 bushels after development of irrigated farming, these are the substitution effects: prior to irrigation, 1,200 bushels could be produced with 60 acres of land and 300 hours of labor when per-acre labor requirements are 5 hours. However, if per-acre labor requirements are 8 hours after irrigation development, the 1,200 bushels can be produced with 10 acres of land and 80 hours of labor.

Water and capital technologies also serve as substitutes for each other. Typically, water used on newly irrigated land in western locations has, through the mechanisms of government programs and supply control, been substituted for land in other regions. In the above illustration, for example, if we suppose 2,400 bushels have been produced by 20 acres of nonirrigated land producing 60 bushels per acre plus 60 acres of land producing 20 bushels per acre, then this substitution is possible: the entire 2,400 bushels can be produced on 20 acres of newly irrigated land where the yield is increased from 60 to 120 bushels. The 60 acres of nonirrigated land (producing 20 bushels per acre) then can be displaced (or idled) while production remains at 2,400 bushels.

The substitutability of water and other technical inputs can be illustrated more formally through technical examples based on experimental data. The water-fertilizer response or production function in Equation 9.1 has been estimated for corn on Nunn clay loam in Colorado where $G*$ is pounds of corn (grain) per acre, W is irrigation water applied in inches, and N is pounds of elemental nitrogen applied per acre.[2]

$$G* = 4,579.50 + 549.20W + 10.90N - 29.96W^2 - 0.03N^2 + 0.06WN \qquad (9.1)$$

From this response function, it is possible to derive a "substitution (yield isoquant) equation" between water and nitrogen by representing quantity of water "required" as a function of the yield levels.

$$W = 0.15 + 0.00107N - [(9.15 + 0.00107N)^2 - 2.00G* + 0.06186N^2$$
$$- 0.18260N - 76.43]^{.5} \qquad (9.2)$$

Using Equation 9.2, combinations of irrigation water (inches applied per acre) and nitrogen (pounds per acre) which will produce two yield levels have been derived in Table 9.1. As expected, a declining marginal rate of substitution of nitrogen for water is indicated and vice versa. Clearly, water is a substitute for fertilizer in attaining a given output level and vice versa.

The substitutability of water for land also can be illustrated from the response function in Equation 9.1. To illustrate the effects for water alone, first set the level of nitrogen fertilizer at 100 pounds per acre. Next, since Equation 9.1 refers to per-acre rates, multiply the right-hand side of the equation by A (acres). The resulting Equation 9.3 expresses grain production as a function of irrigation water and acreage (fertilized at 100 pounds per acre).

$$G = 5,369.50A + 555.20W - 29.962W^2 A^{-1} \qquad (9.3)$$

For this land and year, yield alone for an acre fertilized at 100 pounds of nitrogen is high. Hence, the marginal rates of substitution of land for water (and vice versa) are lower than normally would be the case for land of low rainfall. However, the equation expressing the marginal rate of substitution of applied irrigation water for the Nunn clay loam to which it is applied becomes

$$\frac{\partial A}{\partial W} = \frac{59.92W - 555.20}{5369.5A + 29.96W^2 A^{-2}} \qquad (9.4)$$

These relationships, although restricted to a specific soil type, capital input, year, and crop, indicate the direct nature of substitution possibilities between water and other resources. Actually, the rates of substitution will be even larger if we compare (1) the combined inputs of water and capital technologies on newly irrigated land as replacement resources for (2) nonirrigated land and complementary inputs on other land at the same or a different location. However, the formal relations indicated above systematically illustrate that society does have technical substitution possibilities in capital technologies for both land and irrigation water (and vice versa) in meeting food demand.

2. These data result from a set of studies conducted cooperatively by the Center for Agricultural and Rural Development of Iowa State University, the Bureau of Reclamation of the U.S. Department of Interior, and Colorado State University. For details on experimental design and statistical analysis, see Alan P. Kleinman, "The Production Function and the Imputation of Economic Value of Irrigation Water," Ph.D. diss., Iowa State Univ., Ames, 1969.

United States
Total
33,162,978

1 Dot – 10,000 Acres

Fig. 9.1. Acreage of irrigated land in farms, 1959.

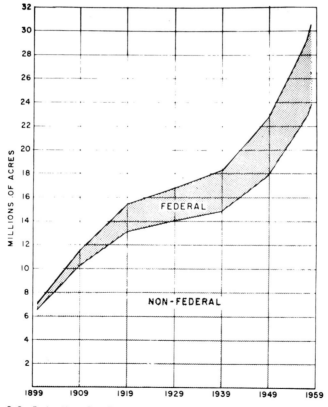

Fig. 9.2. Irrigation development in the 17 Western states, 1899–1959.

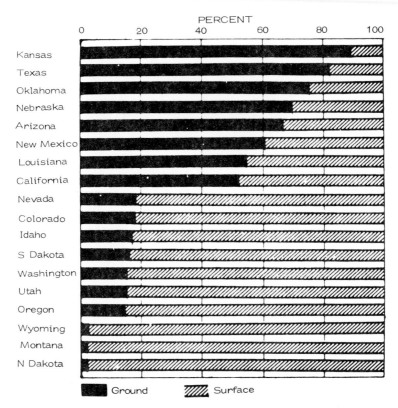

Fig. 9.3. Source of water in irrigation development in 17 Western states, 1899-1959.

DEVELOPMENT, DISTRIBUTION, AND OUTPUT OF IRRIGATED AGRICULTURE

Expanded use of water in agriculture has come from both private and public investment. Total U.S. irrigated acreage increased from 14.6 million acres in 1929 to 25.8 million acres in 1949 and 43.3 million acres in 1969. While the increase over the period 1949-69 is considerably greater than that for 1929-49, the rate of increase evidently has been fairly steady at somewhat more than 800,000 acres per annum since 1949. The ERS estimates that 20 percent of the total value of crops produced in the United States comes from irrigated land.[3] In 1959, the most recent census year for which published data are available, 92.5 percent of the irrigated land was in the 17 western states (Figure 9.1). Data from the 1959 *Census of Agriculture* (Figure 9.2) show that of a total of 30.5 million irrigated acres in these 17 states, only 6.6 million were under federal projects while 23.9 million were nonfederal (districts, individual farm, etc.). Nonfederal developments dominate in acreage for water from both natural flows and groundwater.

3. George A. Pavelis, "Irrigation Policy and Long-Term Growth Functions," *Agr. Econ. Res.* 17 (Apr. 1965): 50-60.

Acreage under federal projects represents the majority source for land irrigated from storage sources (Figure 9.4). Figure 9.3 shows the distribution of irrigation water from groundwater and surface sources for the 17 western states. In recent years, the dominant increase in irrigated acreage has been from private investment of farmers in pump irrigation from groundwater sources (Figure 9.4). Land irrigated from federal storage projects increased by 131 percent from 1939 to 1959. However, the acreage irrigated from groundwater supplies, which are almost entirely developed and financed by individual farmers, increased by about 306 percent and dominated increased water use and additional land irrigated during the period. Irrigation from flowing water, under both federal and non-federal development, has been nearly static since 1919.

As Figure 9.5 indicates, irrigated acreage bears the highest proportion to total crop acreage in the 17 western states. Because water is the main limiting resource in crop production, the proportion of the value of the crops produced on irrigated land in the 17 western states is much greater than the proportion of the total crop acreage grown under irrigation. However, pasture and hay dominate all other crops in the use of irrigated land even in these states (Figure 9.6).

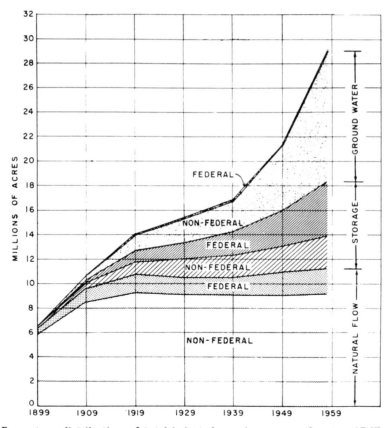

Fig. 9.4. Percentage distribution of total irrigated area by source of water, 17 Western states, 1959.

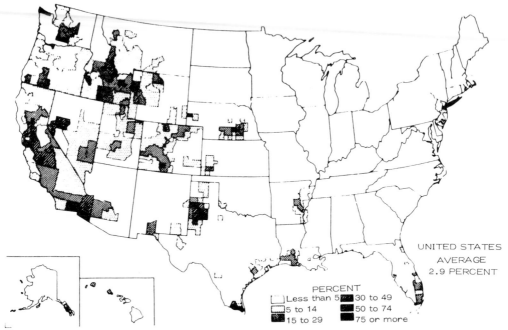

UNITED STATES
AVERAGE
2.9 PERCENT

PERCENT
Less than 5   30 to 49
5 to 14   50 to 74
15 to 29   75 or more

Fig. 9.5. Irrigated land as a percent of all land in farms, 1959.

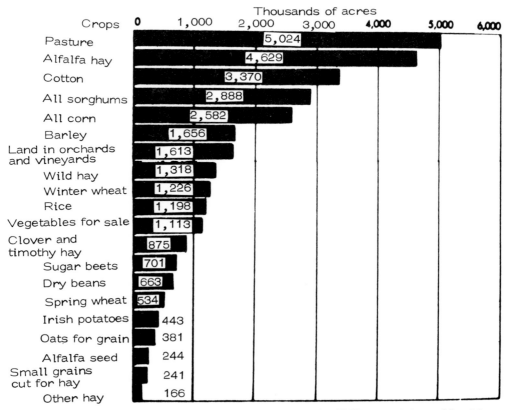

Fig. 9.6. Irrigated acreage of specified crops and pasture in the 17 Western states and Louisiana, 1959.

IRRIGATED FARMING AND AGRICULTURAL POLICY

For those unacquainted with the data, a belief prevails that the dominant source of investment and the large increment in investment in recent decades has been by the public through the government Bureau of Reclamation. This is not true, however, since only 609,471 acres were added through public development while 6,449,313 acres were added through private development between 1939 and 1959.[4] The respective amounts between 1919 and 1959 were 4,920,086 and 7,225,143. Hence, far more of the large increment in output due to higher yields on irrigated land is attributable to private investment than to public investment. To an extent, individual farmers who invest in tapping groundwater supplies to produce higher yields and increase output are not unlike farmers elsewhere in the nation who invest in more fertilizer to boost yields and supply. Both invest in a category of inputs which is profitable to them because of yield increments under favorable costs and prices. True, further investment in water supplies and distribution by irrigation farmers has been profitable because prices have been supported through the various federal programs. Too, some public subsidy has gone into the development of private irrigation systems by means of technical help by technicians of the Soil Conservation Service (SCS) and cost-sharing under Agricultural Stabilization and Conservation Service (ASCS) payments. Other farmers of the nation, however, have received exactly these same public benefits for the crops they produce and the inputs they emphasize. Farmers in the Corn Belt and Southeast, for example, use more fertilizer inputs because they are highly profitable under the price levels maintained by federal programs. SCS technicians have helped them attain higher yields through plans for drainage and for moisture conservation and greater soil productivity by means of contouring, terracing, and other mechanical practices. Similarly, these and other yield-increasing practices and inputs have been extended over the Corn Belt, Southeast, and agriculture generally through cost-sharing ASCS payments. Irrigation farming is not unique in the extent that its output has been furthered by favorable prices of outputs and inputs of federal programs.

The problem of prices and returns imputable to large supplies of agricultural products and highly inelastic demands for foods is not caused by farmers who invest in irrigation systems any more than it is caused by farmers who invest in other practices and inputs because it is profitable to them. The basic problem of all farmers, those depending on rainfall and (or) irrigation water, is the competitive structure of the market for farm products. Under these market conditions, it is profitable for the individual farmers, before the masses have done so, to invest in water, new varieties, more fertilizer, and in other practices. However, when the masses of farmers follow a similar development, as they eventually do, the aggregative effect is a decline in total market revenue due to the inelastic demand for food. It has been the objective of federal programs to control or reduce supply to offset this aggregative effect when the mass of farmers use output-increasing practices and resources more rapidly than demand allows their absorption at

4. U.S. Dept. Commerce, *U.S. Census of Agriculture, 1950*, vol. 3, "Irrigation of Agricultural Lands," Washington, D.C., Dec. 1952; *U.S. Census of Agriculture, 1959*, vol. 3, "Irrigation of Agricultural Lands," Washington, D.C., Oct. 1972.

favorable prices in the market. The need for such programs must be attributed to the actions of farmers who produce under rainfed conditions as much or more than to those who employ irrigation water. The latter account for only 20 percent of the total value of crops produced and emphasize fruits and vegetables which generally have higher price elasticities of demand than commodities such as pork, feed grain, and wheat.

Hence, the important questions of water use are not those of needs and expenditures related to agricultural supply and pricing policy alone. Rather, the questions of future water use are those of allocations of this resource among the most urgent and highly productive alternatives as the nation's population and economic activity grow. The basic question analyzed in this study is, Can the United States meet future food demands without unreasonable real costs of food to consumers—considering the total natural resources available to agriculture, the prevalence of farm policies that have immobilized around 56 million acres of cropland, and the potential need to reallocate some water from agriculture to municipal and industrial uses?

INSTITUTIONAL RIGHTS, PRICING, AND COMPENSATION

The allocation of water among competing crop and locational uses of agriculture is based, of course, upon a complex and deeply imbedded system of historical and legal rights. The distribution of water rights and uses among crop and locational alternatives generally bears little relationship to the marginal productivity of water in either physical or value terms. Hence, if required, it is possible that given water supplies could be allocated among crops and locations to allow (1) the same waters to produce a greater output or (2) the same output from a smaller amount of water. The lack of effective market and pricing mechanisms and the institutionalization of water rights prevents reallocation of water in terms of its marginal productivity to allow either of these accomplishments. It is possible, however, that a pricing structure and compensation methods can be established for both water and water rights to encourage these reallocations and benefit both producers acquiring larger water supplies and those releasing or selling water rights and supplies. These possibilities are outlined in later sections. The output from models such as the one applied in this study provides a quantitative basis (or set of imputed values) for examining such pricing structures.

PREVIOUS STUDIES OF WATER SUPPLY-DEMAND BALANCES

A number of studies have been made of current and future demands for water. The Water Resources Policy Commission, appointed in 1950, made recommendations for a comprehensive policy of water resources development. In its report, *A Water Policy for the American People*, the commission stated that midway through the twentieth century two facets became compellingly clear:[5]

5. U.S. President's Water Resources Policy Commission, *A Water Policy for the American People*, vol. 1, USGPO, Washington, D.C., Dec. 11, 1950, p. 2.

The first is that water is limited in relation to the many and varied needs for its use. These needs will grow in size and complexity as the population grows and as industry develops. The second ... is that the management, conservation, and use of our resources are inextricably bound up with the management, conservation, and use of our land and that both are essential to our expansion as a Nation.

The commission also recognized the interregional relationships between land and water use:[6]

Irrigation and drainage, navigation and flood control, the maintenance of underground water levels, the control of stream pollution resulting from human, animal and industrial wastes, the generation of electric power, the protection of salmon and other fish resources, the provision of ample domestic water supply—all these purposes have legitimate claims within any one basin; but if one is developed without regard for its effect on the others, conflicts and losses will result.

A Presidential Advisory Committee on Water Resources Policy was appointed in 1954. In its report, *Water Resources Policy*, the committee stated the need for a sound water policy.[7]

A sound water policy ... must look toward an adequate supply of water for our people, prevent waste, reduce water pollution to its lowest practicable level, provide means for the best and most effective distribution of water, improve navigation, and take steps to check the destructive forces of water which destroy land, property and life. There are many different problems in different areas. It is neither practicable nor desirable to have only Federal responsibility. There is no single "national" water problem.

The U.S. Senate Select Committee on National Water Resources was established in 1959. The chairman of the committee was Senator Kerr and the committee's report is commonly known as the *Kerr Report*. In its summary report, the select committee concludes:[8]

... the task confronting the Nation in the water field is one of meeting the growing demands on water resources in the most efficient manner consistent with accepted public aims.

The select committee recognized that if demands such as waste dilution, irrigation, outdoor recreation, and fish and wildlife conservation are to be met, the first and most important step toward getting the job done is:[9]

... development of increased public awareness and understanding of the Nation's water resources problems; of their effects on the Nation's economy; and of possible ways of solving them.

Facilitating this step was one of the primary objectives of the select committee.

As a direct result of the select committee's recommendations, a Water Resources Planning Act (S.2246) was proposed in 1961 by President Kennedy.[10] During the following years, a number of changes were made in the proposed bill,

6. Ibid., p. 6.
7. Presidential Advisory Committee on Water Resources Policy, *Water Resources Policy*, the report by the committee, USGPO, Washington, D.C., Jan. 17, 1956.
8. U.S. Senate Report of the Select Committee on National Water Resources, Part I, Summary Report, USGPO, Washington, D.C., Jan. 30, 1961, p. 15.
9. Ibid., p. 2.
10. Sandor C. Csallany, "Planning Water for 2000 A.D.," *Proceedings of the Fourth American Water Resource Conference*, sponsored by the American Water Resources Association, Proc. Series No. 6, Nov. 1968, p. 160.

and the bill was not enacted until 1965 as the Water Resources Planning Act (PL 89-90). The bill consisted of three major provisions: (1) establishment of the Water Resources Council, (2) establishment of River Basin Commissions and (3) grants to states for water resource planning and for pursuit of an active role in the comprehensive planning program of the federal government. One of the first tasks of the Water Resources Council was to make an assessment of the nation's water resources. The Nation's Water Resources was completed and submitted to Congress in November 1968. The report describes the nation's water and related land resources and their use and management problems.

Projections were made of water and related land use for 1980, 2000, and 2020. Water supplies and projected water withdrawals and consumptive uses were obtained for 19 river basins in the conterminous United States. In its findings, the council does not report any basins as being water deficient by 2020. There are a number of basins, however, particularly the Upper Colorado and Lower Colorado river basins, where the consumptive use is more than 70 percent of the total available supply by 2020.[11]

In a more recent study, Wollman and Bonem calculated the total required flows (consumption) plus waste dilution and water available in 1960 and 2000 for 15 river basins in the United States.[12] Their results are summarized in Table 9.2. Although the Water Resources Council did not report any water-deficit areas for either 2000 or 2020, Wollman and Bonem project water deficits in four river basins for 2000. The river basins are the Texas-Gulf, Rio Grande, Colorado, and Great Basin. According to their study, the last three river basins also had a water deficit in 1960 along with the lower Mississippi and California–South Pacific basins. In summary, research and work on water over the past two decades have stressed the importance of a coordinated land and water use policy determined on an interregional basis with emphasis in the most recent studies on the future water demand-supply situation.

In 1965 agriculture (irrigation and livestock water requirements) used 92.5 percent of all the water consumed in the 17 western states and 85.3 percent of all the water used in the nation. For 2000, the Water Resources Council estimates that agriculture will use 82.2 percent and 72.6 percent, respectively.[13] Since agriculture is and will continue to be the largest user of water, a study of future water requirements in agriculture is of primary importance, especially if a reallocation of water among alternative uses becomes necessary in the future. A study of future water needs in agriculture is also needed in light of recent presentations to Congress of broad proposals for water developments in the western states.[14] The study should include an interregional analysis and consider both land and water use alternatives.

11. U.S. Water Resources Council, *The Nation's Water Resources*, USGPO, Washington, D.C., Nov. 1968.

12. Nathaniel Wollman and Gilbert W. Bonem, *Outlook for Water: Quality, Quantity and National Growth*, Resources for the Future, Inc., Johns Hopkins Press, Baltimore, 1971, Table 82.

13. U.S. Water Resources Council, *The Nation's Water Resources*.

14. National Water Commission, *The National Water Commission Annual Report for 1969*, Interim Report No. 1, USGPO, Washington, D.C., Dec. 1969.

OBJECTIVES OF THE QUANTITATIVE ANALYSIS

This study includes the application of a large-scale mathematical programming model to estimate demand or need for land and water used in agriculture. Projections are made for the year 2000. The analysis is made in the context of water needs and irrigation development as an integral part of overall land use, agricultural policy, and food policy. We are concerned with the efficient use of water and agricultural resources generally when policy alternatives are used both for commercial farming and irrigated agriculture. Hence, we examine the demand for water in irrigation should current types of supply control programs be eliminated and all land currently retired be returned to production. We also examine the potential of meeting future food demands under alternative rates of population growth, economic development, and farm exports under both (1) the absence of farm programs of current types and (2) the continuation of these programs. In the case where other restraints on agricultural supply are removed, the analysis suggests the amount of land which might be diverted from irrigation and, hence, the amount of water that might be made available to meet future nonfarm demands. Since water and other improved farm technologies can serve as substitutes for each other in attaining a given food output, examination is made of total acreage and irrigated production needed if the rate of technological advance in agriculture is accentuated beyond trend levels by public or other means. For these purposes, accentuated rates of technological advances for (1) crop production in the Southeast and (2) feed conversion rates for all U.S. livestock production are introduced into the programming model. Examination is made of the potential effects of alternative pricing policies for water on agricultural output and future water requirements. Finally, supply potentials are examined under conditions wherein restraints on the use of insecticides and fragile lands might be exercised.

In general, the study is an analysis of the interregional distribution of agricultural production, land use, and farm water demand or requirements under alternative futures with respect to commercial agricultural policy, technological advance, export levels of farm products, magnitude of the U.S. population, and the pricing and public investment policies for agricultural water uses. Commodities included in the analysis are corn, sorghum, wheat, barley, oats, soybeans, cotton, sugar beets, hay, pasture, fruits, nuts, rice, vegetables, milk, pork, beef, broilers, turkeys, eggs, and lamb and mutton. All projections are for the year 2000.

BASIC MODEL USED IN THE ANALYSIS

The quantitative analysis has been made by means of a mathematical programming model. Since time limits did not allow incorporation of demand functions and formulation of a nonlinear objective function, the programming model is of purely linear construction. The linear model includes 5,426 real variables or activities and 3,220 equations including 1,650 limits or bounds on individual activities. The activities include those for crop production, livestock production, water distribution, commodity transformation, final domestic demands, net export demands, and commodity transportation.[15] Bounds on specific activities serve as restraints on land available for wild hay and pasture, domestic and net export demands, and regional concentration of production. Other restraints are provided by equations for land, crop and livestock commodities, water, and certain intermediate products. The construction of the programming model is given below.

REGIONS AND THEIR DELINEATION

This programming model of interregional competition determines the location of crop and livestock production and water use, given resource availability and commodity demands in the year 2000. To reflect the interregional nature of the analysis, the United States was partitioned into sets of areas and regions appropriate for various restraints and demands.

PRODUCING AREAS

Producing areas are delineated such that (1) a single activity can be legitimately defined to represent production of a crop in that area and (2) the set of producing areas can be used as the elements of sets of market and water supply regions. The United States is partitioned into 223 producing areas, each of which is an aggregation of contiguous counties (Figure 9.7). The producing areas are composed of subsets of the counties within water resources subregions defined by the Water Resources Council.[16]

WATER SUPPLY REGIONS

Since the supplies and uses of water are basic to the programming model, water supply regions are defined such that each approximately represents a physical region in which a water supply can be said to exist. In the western states, 51 water supply regions were constructed. Each is an aggregate of contiguous producing areas and is wholly contained within one of the river basins shown in Figure 9.8. The water supply regions closely approximate those defined by the Water Resources Council.[17]

CONSUMING REGIONS

Consuming regions are defined to represent regions in which a market can be said to exist. Based on "central place" theory, 27 consuming regions are deline-

15. A set of land-retirement activities was defined for certain solutions as described in a later section.

16. U.S. Water Resources Council, *Water Resources Regions and Subregions for the National Assessment of Water and Related Land Resources*, USGPO, Washington, D.C., July 1970.

17. U.S. Water Resources Council, *The Nation's Water Resources*.

Fig. 9.7. The 223 producing areas.

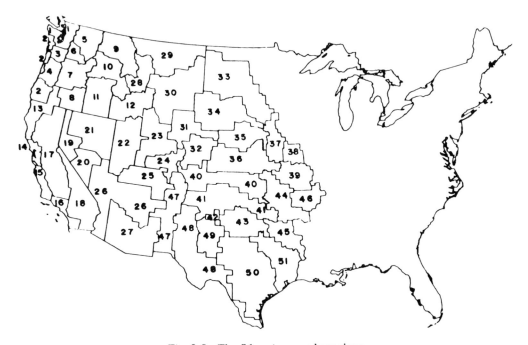

Fig. 9.8. The 51 water supply regions.

Fig. 9.9. The 27 consuming regions.

ated around major United States metropolitan areas and/or transportation centers. Each region is an aggregate of contiguous producing areas (Figure 9.9).

ACTIVITIES

Over 5,000 activities are employed to represent production, purchase, transformation, transportation, and consumption of agricultural resources and intermediate and final products. Each activity level is allowed to vary such that $L_i \leqslant X_i \leqslant B_i$. Where X_i is the level of the ith activity, L_i is the minimum level of X_i allowed and B_i is the maximum level of X_i allowed, i.e., L_i is the lower bound and B_i is the upper bound on the ith activity. Generally, L_i is set at 0 and B_i is set at $+\infty$, but under certain circumstances L_i and/or B_i is set at a specified finite real number as described below.

FINAL DEMAND

1. A "population and industry" activity is defined for each of the 223 producing areas and, for each, L_i is set at the projected level of population of that PA. Coefficients are entered into the programming model for each such activity so that the following commodity and water supplies are depleted:
   (a) beef, pork, and milk products based on demand relations
   (b) water (when the producing area is in the water supply region) based on quantities of water consumed for municipal, industrial, recreational, and thermal electric power purposes

(c) corn and sorghum, oats and barley, and wheat based on quantities used for milling, brewing, etc.

(d) cotton lint and sugar beets based on quantities used for all purposes.

All coefficients in these activities are on a per capita basis.

2. One activity is defined for the national production of each of broilers, turkeys, sheep and lambs, eggs, and other animals such as horses and mules. The level of each activity is bounded so that L_i is equal to the national demand. Coefficients are defined to deplete the supplies of water, corn and sorghum, oats and barley, wheat, hay, and oil meal.

3. An activity is defined for the production of fruits, nuts, rice, and vegetables, and another is defined for onsight water uses in each water supply region. The level of each of these activities is bounded so that L_i is equal to the estimated water consumed by each kind of activity in the appropriate region. One coefficient is defined for each so that the water supplies in the regions are depleted by the amount of the activities.

4. One water export activity is defined for each water supply region from which international export is made. Each is bounded so that L_i is equal to the legal requirement for export of water. One coefficient is defined to deplete the water supplies in those regions accordingly.

5. One national net export activity is defined for each of corn and sorghum, oats and barley, wheat, oil meal, beef, pork, milk products, and cotton lint. The level of each is set at the assumed net export level (always positive). Coefficients in each of these activities are defined to change the regional supplies of commodities—negative for exports and positive for imports.

PRODUCTION

Production of the commodities demanded is determined as follows:

1. Crop production activities are defined for each producing area. To reflect agronomic or institutional constraints the B_i's are set at finite levels in some cases (e.g., one-half the total cropland in the case of soybeans). Since wild hay and pasture activities are not constrained by available cropland or hay land, B_i is equal to the land historically available for each of these activities. In the West, both dryland and irrigated activities are defined, and the programming model can choose between them during optimization. Coefficients are defined to indicate the use of land, consumption of water, and the yield of the crop activities (Table 9.3).

2. Livestock production activities are defined for each producing area. For dairy and beef cow production, B_i is set at infinity while for beef feeding and pork production B_i is set at a finite level to represent institutional and/or physical limits of geographic concentration of these activities. Coefficients are defined to indicate the use of feed nutrients, consumption of water, and the outputs of each activity (Table 9.4).

The protein, TDN, and roughage requirements for each of the four kinds of livestock are separated to prevent nutrient sharing. To accomplish this, activities are defined by consuming region for each kind of livestock that transforms commodities into nutrients; e.g., the "transfer of hay for beef cows" activity depletes the regional supply of hay and augments the regional supplies of "beef-cow protein," "beef-cow TDN," and "beef-cow roughage."

WATER PURCHASE AND TRANSFER

1. For each water supply region, one activity is defined to simulate the purchase of water. The level of each activity is bounded so that B_i is equal to the quantity of net surface runoff available in the water supply region. A coefficient is defined to augment the usable water supply in the water supply region.
2. Activities are defined for the flow of water between pairs of water supply regions. These flows represent both natural and man-made water transfers. The activity levels are bounded so that B_i represents the capacity of the system, river, or stream to carry water between the regions.

TRANSPORTATION

Transportation activities are defined to permit specialization of production by geographic advantage and to account for the associated cost of transportation. Transportation is allowed between each pair[18] of adjacent consuming regions for each of eight commodities.[19] For each activity a positive coefficient is defined to represent augmentation of the commodity supply in the importing region, and a negative coefficient is defined to represent depletion of the commodity in the exporting region.

RESTRAINTS

In addition to the activity bounds already described, two general kinds of restraint equations are employed. First, land restraint equations allocate available land supplies among competing uses. Second, commodity equations assure that water, intermediate productions, and final products are produced as they are used.

LAND AND WATER RESTRAINTS

Land equations of four types are defined by producing areas: (1) total cropland and hay land, (2) cropland, a subset of total land; (3) irrigated total land, a subset of total land, and (4) irrigated cropland, a subset of both cropland and irrigated total land. The restraint of type 1 is that the land used by the annual crops[20] and tame hay[21] in a producing area must not be greater than the total

18. Additional activities are defined for certain well-established long-haul routes.
19. The eight commodities are wheat, corn and sorghum, oats and barley, oil meal, milk, beef, pork, and feeders.
20. The annual crops are corn grain, corn silage, grain sorghum, sorghum silage, oats, barley, wheat, soybeans, cotton, and sugar beets.
21. Tame hay includes alfalfa and alfalfa mixtures, clover and timothy, lespedeza, small grains for hay, and other hay.

land available in the area. The restraint of type 2 is that the land used by the annual crops must not be greater than the cropland available. The restraint of type 3 is that the irrigated land used by the irrigated annual crops and tame hay must not be greater than the irrigated total land available. This restraint of type 3 is only defined for producing areas that are within a water supply region. The restraint of type 4 is that the irrigated cropland used by the irrigated annual crops must not be greater than the irrigated cropland available.

One water restraint is defined for each water supply region so that the amount of water supplied through surface runoff and transfer from other water supply regions must at least equal the consumption by irrigated crop production, livestock production, exports from the water supply region, and on-site uses.

COMMODITY RESTRAINTS

Crop commodity restraints are defined for each of 8 commodities. For sugar beets and cotton lint the restraints are national, while for the other 6 commodities the restraints are by consuming region. The restraint is that the availability of the commodity (other than sugar beets and cotton) in a consuming region must at least equal the quantity used in livestock feed, milling and brewing, plus net exports from the consuming region. The national restraints for sugar beets and cotton are formulated such that production must equal or exceed use.

Livestock commodity restraints are defined in each consuming region for each of the four commodities beef, milk, feeders, and pork. The restriction is that the commodity must equal or exceed the sum of the use as an intermediate product (feeders only), consumption, and net export from the region.

NUTRIENT RESTRAINTS

One restraint is defined for each type of nutrient used by each type of livestock activity by consuming region. The TDN, protein, and roughage restraints for a livestock type in a consuming region require that the nutrients may be used only in the amounts produced by the transportation activities.

THE OBJECTIVE FUNCTION

The objective in obtaining a solution for the programming model is to minimize the cost of meeting food and fiber demands, given land and water resources. For each activity, a unit cost of production is defined. This unit cost excludes the cost of inputs provided by the other activities in the programming model (including land), but includes all other relevant costs. For example, the cost of the beef-feeding activity includes labor, capital, and veterinary costs but excludes the cost of feeders, feed, and water which are generated within the programming model.

MATHEMATICAL STRUCTURE OF THE MODEL

Before the programming model is formally described, the variables and parameters comprising the model are defined. The subscripts and symbols used to describe the model areas follow:

k subscript denoting the producing area, $k = 1, 2, \ldots 223$
i subscript denoting the type of endogenous crop or livestock activity:

  $i = 1$ for dryland corn grain–oats–corn silage activity
  $i = 2$ for dryland sorghum grain–silage activity
  $i = 3$ for dryland soybean activity
  $i = 4$ for dryland wheat activity
  $i = 5$ for dryland barley activity
  $i = 6$ for dryland cotton activity
  $i = 7$ for dryland sugar beet activity
  $i = 8$ for irrigated corn grain–oats–corn silage activity
  $i = 9$ for irrigated sorghum grain–silage activity
  $i = 10$ for irrigated soybean activity
  $i = 11$ for irrigated wheat activity
  $i = 12$ for irrigated barley activity
  $i = 13$ for irrigated cotton activity
  $i = 14$ for irrigated sugar beet activity
  $i = 15$ for irrigated tame hay activity
  $i = 16$ for dryland tame hay activity
  $i = 17$ for dryland cropland–improved pasture activity
  $i = 18$ for irrigated cropland–improved pasture activity
  $i = 19$ for dryland unimproved permanent pasture–woodland pasture–
    public grazing lands activity
  $i = 20$ for dryland wild hay activity
  $i = 21$ for irrigated wild hay activity
  $i = 22$ for dairy cow production activity
  $i = 23$ for beef-feeding activity
  $i = 24$ for beef-cow production activity
  $i = 25$ for pork production (hog) activity

j subscript denoting the consuming regions, $j = 1, 2, \ldots 27$
m subscript denoting the water supply region, $m = 1, 2, \ldots 51$
p subscript denoting the type of exogenous livestock activity:

    $p = 1$ for turkeys
    $p = 2$ for eggs
    $p = 3$ for lamb and mutton
    $p = 4$ for broilers
    $p = 5$ for other livestock

n subscript denoting the type of commodity:

   $n = 1$ for corn (includes sorghum in corn equivalent)
   $n = 2$ for barley (includes oats in barley equivalent)
   $n = 3$ for wheat
   $n = 4$ for soybean oil meal (includes cottonseed meal)
   $n = 5$ for hay (includes all pasture)

$n = 6$ for silage (includes corn and sorghum)
$n = 7$ for milk (includes all dairy products)
$n = 8$ for beef
$n = 9$ for pork
$n = 10$ for feeders
$n = 11$ for cotton lint
$n = 12$ for sugar beets

Z total costs—crops and livestock production, transportation, and certain water transfer costs to meet domestic and export demands

c_{ki}^1 cost per unit of ith crop or livestock activity in the kth producing area (livestock costs do not include certain feed costs determined internally to the programming model)

X_{ki} level of ith activity in the kth producing area

c_m^2 cost of water per acre-foot consumed in the mth water supply region

w_m^B acre-feet of water bought for consumption in mth water supply region

$c_{m'm}^3$ difference between cost of water per acre-foot consumed in the m'th and mth water supply region

$W_{m'm}^T$ acre-feet of water transferred by natural flows from m'th water supply region to the mth water supply region

$c_{nj'j}^4$ cost of transporting a unit of nth type commodity from jth consuming region to j'th consuming region (where j and j' regions are contiguous except for certain long-haul routes)

$T_{nj'j}$ amount transported of nth type of commodity from jth consuming region to j'th consuming region (where j and j' must be contiguous except for certain long hauls)

a_{ki} amount of land used by ith crop activity in kth producing area (since crop activities are in acre basis, $a_{ki} = 1$ for these activities)

b_{kn} per capita consumption of nth commodity in kth producing area

e_{jn} proportion of exports of nth type commodity exported historically from jth consuming region

f_{ki}^1 amount of total digestible nutrients (TDN) consumed per unit of ith type livestock in kth producing area

f_{ki}^2 amount of protein consumed per unit of ith type livestock in kth producing area

f_{ki}^3 amount of roughage consumed per unit of ith type livestock in kth producing area

f_{npj} amount of nth crop commodity consumed by pth type exogenous livestock in jth consuming region

r_{ki} amount of acreage quota, Q_i, used by ith type of crop activity in kth producing area

t_{nij}^1 amount of total digestible nutrients (TDN) per unit of nth type of commodity transformed into feed to be used by ith type of livestock activity in jth consuming region

t^2_{nij}	amount of protein per unit of nth type commodity transformed into feed to be used by ith type of livestock activity in jth consuming region
t^3_{nij}	amount of roughage per unit of nth crop product transformed into feed to be used by ith type livestock activity in jth consuming region
w_{ki}	amount of water consumed per unit of ith crop or livestock activity in kth producing area
w_{mp}	amount of water consumed by pth exogenous livestock activity in mth water supply region
wn_k	per capita consumption of water for municipal, industrial, recreational, and thermal electric power uses in kth producing area
y_{ki}	yield per acre or per unit of ith crop or livestock activity in kth producing area
E_n	national export activity for nth type of commodity
N_{jn}	proportion of imports of nth type commodity historically imported into the jth consuming region
$\overline{E}_n$	national level of exports (lower bound) of nth product
g_{nij}	amount of nth commodity transformed into feed (TDN, protein, and roughage) for use by ith type livestock in jth consuming region
g_p	national activity for pth type of exogenous livestock
$\overline{g}_p$	national level (lower bound) of pth type of exogenous livestock
I_n	national import activity for nth commodity
$\overline{I}_n$	national level of imports (upper bound) of nth commodity
N_k	population-industry activity in kth producing area
$\overline{N}_k$	lower bound of population in kth producing area
$W^I_{m'm}$	acre-feet of water transferred by interbasin networks from m'th water supply region to mth water supply region
$W^T_{m'm}$	acre-feet of water transferred by natural flows from m'th water supply region to mth water supply region
w^0_m	acre-feet of water consumed by other uses, including fish and wildlife, wetlands, and swamps in mth water supply region
w^X_m	acre-feet of water exported to regions outside 17 western states from mth water supply region
A_{kC}	acres of cropland available for annual crop production in kth producing area
A_{kT}	acres of the total land (cropland and hay land) available for annual crops and tame hay production in kth producing area
A^I_{kC}	acres of irrigated cropland available for irrigated crops in kth producing area
A^I_{kT}	acres of irrigated total land available for irrigated crops and tame hay in kth producing area
A^D_{kCD}	acres of land available for dryland cropland improved pasture production in kth producing area

A^I_{kCP} acres of land available for irrigated cropland improved pasture production in kth producing area

A_{k0} acres of land available for dryland unimproved pasture, woodland pasture, and public grazing lands pasture in kth producing area

A^D_{kW} acres of land available for dryland wild hay in kth producing area

A^I_{kW} acres of land available for irrigated wild hay production in kth producing area

W^F_m acre-feet of water consumed by fruits, nuts, rice, and vegetables in mth water supply region

Q_k acres of acreage quota available, in annual land-retirement policy for annual crops (wheat and feed grain only) in kth producing area

C_k harvested acreage of cotton in 1964 in the kth producing area

S_k harvested acreage sugar beets in 1964 in kth producing area multiplied by two

R_k acres retired in annual land-retirement policy model in kth producing area

R_{kL} minimum (lower limit) of acreage retired in annual land-retirement policy model in kth producing area

The objective function is

$$\min Z = \sum_{i=1}^{25} \sum_{k=1}^{223} c^1_{ki} X_{ki} + \sum_{m=1}^{51} \left(c^2_m W^B_m + \sum_{m'=1}^{51} c^3_{m'm} W^T_{m'm} + c^3_{m'm} W^I_{m'm} \right)$$

$$+ \sum_{j=1}^{27} \sum_{j'=1}^{27} \sum_{n=1}^{8} c^4_{nj'j} T_{nj'j} \qquad (9.5)$$

The total cost (Z) is to be minimized subject to
   (1) cropland restraint in producing area k:

$$\sum_{i=1}^{14} a_{ki} X_{ki} \leqslant A_{kC} \qquad (9.6)$$

   (2) total land restraint in producing area k:

$$\sum_{i=1}^{16} a_{ki} X_{ki} \leqslant A_{kT} \qquad (9.7)$$

   (3) irrigated cropland in producing area k:

$$\sum_{i=8}^{14} a_{ki} X_{ki} \leqslant A^I_{kC} \qquad (9.8)$$

   (4) irrigated total land in producing area k:

$$\sum_{i=8}^{15} a_{ki} X_{ki} \leqslant A^I_{kT} \qquad (9.9)$$

(5) dryland wild hay land in producing area k:

$$a_{k20} X_{k20} \leqslant A_{kW}^D \qquad (9.10)$$

(6) irrigated wild hay land in producing area k:

$$a_{k21} X_{k21} \leqslant A_{kW}^I \qquad (9.11)$$

(7) dryland crops and improved pasture in producing area k:

$$a_{k17} X_{k17} \leqslant A_{kCP}^D \qquad (9.12)$$

(8) irrigated crops and improved pasture in producing area k:

$$a_{k18} X_{k18} \leqslant A_{kCP}^I \qquad (9.13)$$

(9) dryland unimproved pasture in producing area k:

$$a_{k19} X_{k19} \leqslant A_{k0} \qquad (9.14)$$

(10) agronomic restraint, soybeans, in producing area k:

$$X_{k3} \leqslant 0.5 \, A_{kC}$$
$$X_{k10} \leqslant 0.5 \, A_{kC}^I \qquad (9.15)$$

(11) population restraint in each area:

$$N_k \geqslant \bar{N}_k \qquad (9.16)$$

(12) acreage quota restraint in each area:

$$\sum_{i=1}^{12} r_{ki} X_{ki} \leqslant Q_k \qquad (9.17)$$

$$i \neq 3, 6, 7, 10$$

(13) acreage restraint, cotton, in each area:

$$X_{k6} + X_{k13} \leqslant C_k \qquad (9.18)$$

(14) acreage restraint, sugar beets, in each area:

$$X_{k7} + X_{k14} \leqslant S_k \qquad (9.19)$$

(15) land retirement min and max, in each area:

$$R_k \geqslant R_{kL}$$
$$R_k \leqslant 0.5 \, A_{kT} \qquad (9.20)$$

(16) water restraint water supply in region m:

$$W_m^B + \sum_{m'=1}^{51} [w_{m'm}^T - w_{mm'}^T + w_{m'm}^I - w_{mm'}^I] - w_m^X - w_m^0 - w_m^F$$

$$- \sum_{k \in m} \left[\sum_{i=8}^{25} w_{ki} X_{ki} + w n_k N_k \right] - \sum_{p=1}^{4} w_{mp} g_p \geqslant 0 \qquad (9.21)$$

$$i \neq 16, 17, 19, 20$$

(17) demand for nth crop commodity in each consuming region:

$$\sum_{k \in j} \left[\sum_{i=1}^{21} y_{ki} X_{ki} - b_{ki} N_k \right] - \sum_{i=22}^{25} g_{nij} - e_{jn} E_n - \sum_{p=1}^{5} f_{npj} g_p$$

$$+ \sum_{j'=1}^{27} [T_{nj'j} - T_{njj'}] \geq 0 \qquad (9.22)$$

$$n = 1, \ldots, \ldots 6$$

(18) demand for nth livestock commodity in each consuming region:

$$\sum_{k \in j} \left[\sum_{i=22}^{25} y_{ki} X_{ki} - b_{ki} N_k \right] + N_{jn} I_n + \sum_{j'=1}^{27} [T_{nj'j} - T_{njj'}] \geq 0 \qquad (9.23)$$

(19) requirement of TDN for ith livestock type:

$$\sum_{n=1}^{6} t^1_{nij} g_{nij} - \sum_{k \in j} f^1_{ki} X_{ki} \geq 0 \qquad (9.24)$$

(20) requirement of protein for ith livestock product:

$$\sum_{n=1}^{6} t^2_{nij} g_{nij} - \sum_{k \in j} f^2_{ki} X_{ki} \geq 0 \qquad (9.25)$$

(21) requirement of roughage for beef cows:

$$\sum_{n=5}^{6} t^3_{n24j} g_{n24j} - \sum_{k \in j} f^3_{k24} X_{k24} \geq 0 \qquad (9.26)$$

(22) requirement of roughage for dairy ($i = 22$) and beef feeding ($i = 23$):

$$\sum_{n=5}^{6} t^3_{nij} - \sum_{k \in j} f^3_{ki} X_{ki} \leq 0 \qquad (9.27)$$

(23) national restraint for cotton:

$$\sum_{k=1}^{223} y_{k6} X_{k6} + y_{k13} X_{k14} - b_{k11} N_k \geq 0 \qquad (9.28)$$

(24) national restraint for sugar beets:

$$\sum_{k=1}^{223} [y_{k7} X_{k7} + y_{k14} X_{k14} - b_{k12} N_k] \geq 0 \qquad (9.29)$$

(25) imports of pth exogenous type livestock:

$$g_p \geq \overline{g}_p \qquad (9.30)$$

(26) exports of nth commodity:

$$E_n \geqslant \overline{E}_n \tag{9.31}$$

(27) imports of nth commodity:

$$I_n \leqslant \overline{I}_n \tag{9.32}$$

(28) nonnegativity restraints:

$$g_{nij}, X_{ki}, I_{nj'j}, W^B_m\ W^I_{m'm} \geqslant 0 \tag{9.33}$$

EMPIRICAL MODELS

To attain the objectives of this study, nine alternative policy models are analyzed in the following sections. Six basic policy models are referred to as: model A, model B, model C, model D, model E, and model F. Model A and model B are free market policy models with population levels of 300 million and 280 million, respectively. Model C, with a population level of 280 million, simulates an annual land-retirement program similar to the wheat, feed-grain, and cotton programs used during the 1961–71 decade. Model D uses an advanced level of technology in 2000 and has a population of 325 million and increased level of exports. Model E incorporates a population of 280 million with elimination of insecticides in corn and cotton production but with no restrictions on land use. Model E also uses a population of 280 million but has fragile lands removed from any type of crop production.[22] These six basic policy models assume present prices for water in 2000.

In addition to the basic policy models, three policy models (A1, A2, and A3) are formulated as free market policy models with population at the 300 million level but each assumes an alternative price for water in the year 2000. Under model A1, farmers in the 51 water supply regions pay at least $15.00 per acre-foot for water (from surface runoff); under model A2, at least $22.50 per acre-foot; and under model A3, at least $30.00 per acre-foot. The nine policy models analyzed are summarized in Table 9.5.

MODEL PARAMETERS AND THEIR DETERMINATION

Many coefficients used in this study are derived directly from regional programming models reported in previous chapters.[23] However, the addition of water supplies and water-using activities to the programming model necessitated new methods and procedures to generate coefficients in the areas and regions

---

22. Fragile lands include land classes V through VIII across the nation and land class IV in certain areas of the Great Plains where wind erosion has been severe in the past. On the class IV lands defined as fragile, only pasture production is included in the analysis.

23. Particularly the models reported in Chapters 5 and 6. Some coefficients are also taken from Earl O. Heady and Leo V. Mayer, "Food Needs and U.S. Agriculture in 1980," Technical Papers, vol. 1, National Advisory Commission on Food and Fiber, Washington, D.C., Aug. 1967.

where water use is considered. The procedures used to estimate coefficients relating to water supplies, prices, and transfers are presented below. The details of various other coefficients are presented in our report to the National Water Commission.[24]

WATER SUPPLIES AND DETAIL

The water supply in each water supply region is a function of the total reservoir storage and the mean annual runoff in the region.[25] First, the total storage capacities of reservoirs in each of the water supply regions were determined by adding the active conservation and joint use capacities for storage dams in the region as obtained from the Bureau of Reclamation, the Army Corps of Engineers, and a survey of reservoirs in the United States.[26] Active conservation capacity is water storage available for irrigation, municipal and industrial uses, power, fish and wildlife, or other direct uses. The joint use capacity includes that storage area of the dam allocated for flood control during part of the year and to active conservation for the remainder of the year. Second, the mean annual runoffs reported were determined from *The Nation's Water Resources.*[27] Then using the relationships between storage and mean annual flow developed by Lof and Hardison,[28] the net water supply as a proportion of the mean annual runoff was determined.

Water supplies were first calculated for all water supply regions. Gross water supplies then were adjusted for reservoir evaporation, giving a net water supply in each water supply region. Mining of underground water supplies was not allowed in any of the water supply regions. We assume that most closed underground water supplies will be depleted by the year 2000.

WATER USE COEFFICIENTS

Water use coefficients for each crop activity in the model reflect the net diversion requirement to provide the crop with the amount of water needed for growth in addition to that provided by precipitation. Withdrawal coefficients are also calculated to indicate the diversion requirements needed to supply the water consumed. Gross delivery requirements in area k for crop i are

$$GDR_{ki} = \frac{CU_{ki} - EP_k}{(IE_i)(CE_k)} \qquad (9.34)$$

24. See Earl O. Heady, Howard C. Madsen, Kenneth J. Nicol, and Stanley H. Hargrove, *Agricultural Water Demands; Future Water and Land Use: Effects of Selected Public Agricultural and Water Policies on Water Demand and Land Use,* Natl. Tech. Info. Serv., Springfield, Va., Report No. PB 206-790 (NWC-EES-71-003), Nov. 1971.

25. Ibid., Table 3.3.

26. R. O. R. Martin and Ronald L. Hansen, "Reservoirs in the United States," Water Supply Paper 1838, Geological Survey, U.S. Dept. Interior, Washington, D.C., 1966.

27. U.S. Water Resources Council, *Water Resources Regions and Subregions.*

28. George O. G. Lof and Clayton H. Hardison, "Storage Requirements for Water Supply in the United States," *Water Resources Research* 2 (1966): 323-54.

where CU_{ki} is the amount of water required by crop i in producing area k as determined from regional publications on consumptive use of water by crops; EP_k is the effective precipitation in producing area k representing water available after evaporation and deep percolation are subtracted from the rainfall; IE_i is the irrigation efficiency or the efficiency of the crops in using the water applied (as affected by the surface of the land exposed between plants and the ability of the plants to hold the water in the ground for use); and CE_k is the canal efficiency or efficiency of the delivery system between the diversion point and the farm delivery gate (calculated for each region from data on Bureau of Reclamation projects).

The net diversion requirements, NDR_{ki}, or the consumptive water coefficients for each of the activities are calculated as

$$NDR_{ki} = CU_{ki} - EP_k + (1 - RF)\,[GDR_{ki} - (CU_{ki} - EP_k)]$$
$$= CIR_i + (1 - RF)\,[GDR_{ki} - CIR_{ki}] \qquad (9.35)$$

where GDR_{ki}, CU_{ki}, and EP_k are defined above, CIR_{ki} is the crop irrigation requirement of the ith crop in the kth producing area; RF is percent of the water used by the plant which is returned for reuse in the region. This return flow is assumed to be 55 percent for all river basins except the Columbia–North Pacific where 60 percent is used; and $GDR_{ki} - (CU_{ki} - EP_k)$ is water diverted but not directly used by the crops.

CURRENT WATER PRICES

The price presently paid by farmers for water in water supply region m, P_m, was determined by using a weighted average of present water costs in the Bureau of Reclamation irrigation projects or

$$P_m = \sum_{q \in m} (CA_q / AF_q)\,(WD_q) / \sum_{q \in m} WD_q \qquad (9.36)$$

where CA_q is the cost per acre to farmers in project q; AF_q is the acre-feet of water applied per acre in project q; and WD_q is the total acre-feet of water delivered to the farms in project q. For regions in which Bureau of Reclamation data are not available, the water price in the most immediate upstream region is used. These water prices were then increased to account for farm waste and deep percolation and are measured as cost per acre of water consumed. No correction is required for canal losses since the deliveries, WD_q, are measured at the farm.

WATER TRANSFERS

Water transfer activities are defined to allow water in upstream regions to flow along the natural slopes to downstream water regions. Each of these activities is limited to a maximum level equal to 70 percent of the upstream water supply due to losses occurring from evaporation, removal by natural vegetation, and some deep percolation. The costs associated with these transfers are set at a level such that the upstream water price plus the transfer cost is greater than the price of water in the receiving region.

Existing interbasin transfers are simulated by transfer activities. Due to the fixed nature of the facilities and, since present water prices reflect their variable cost, no cost is associated directly with these transfers. An upper bound on each activity is set at the projected capacity of the project to transfer water in the year 2000.

One water export activity is defined to transfer water (1.5 million acre-feet) in accordance with the Mexican Treaty of 1944. Another activity allows for the transfer of 1.1 million acre-feet from water supply region 33 (the Dakotas) to the Souris-Red-Rainy river basin as is projected with the completion of the Garrison diversion project. A depletion activity is defined for water supply region 29 (northern Montana) to account for the expected increased depletion of the Milk River by Canada in the year 2000.

Unbounded desaltation activities are defined for all sea coast water supply regions to allow for augmentation of the water supply. The price of $100 per acre-foot placed on these activities approximates the best estimates available of the cost of large-scale desalting schemes under present technologies. A water-augmenting activity is placed in water supply region 26 (the Lower Colorado basin) with a high cost in the event of a water shortage to satisfy the exogenous water requirements projected for that region in 2000.

EMPIRICAL RESULTS

In this section, results are presented on the land and water use under the nine alternative policy models. Results are summarized and reported for the 18 river basins shown in Figure 9.10. The New England and Middle Atlantic basins are joined as the North Atlantic, thus only 17 river basins are shown in Figure 9.10. Maps showing the locations of crop production are provided for selected crops and policy models. For the price variation policy models, A, A1, A2, and A3, demand functions for water in the West and land in the East are presented. The substitutions of land in the East for water in the West and dryland production in the West for water (irrigated land) in the West are also analyzed.

FULL COMPARATIVE ADVANTAGE AND SIMULATED FREE MARKET POLICY MODELS WITH 300 MILLION POPULATION

Four of the nine policy models analyzed are intended to simulate conditions of full comparative advantage and a free market in American agriculture with 300 million people in 2000. Full comparative advantage is allowed in this manner: crop production can be allocated and land and water can be used among areas and regions so that the national production pattern is most efficient. Land in the East can be substituted for land in the West or vice versa to attain the economically most efficient national pattern. No policy restraints, such as land retirement, are placed on geographic and land-water substitutions. The four policy models evaluated in this sector differ only with respect to the price of water. These four policy models, then, provide estimates of data needed for an analysis of the trade-

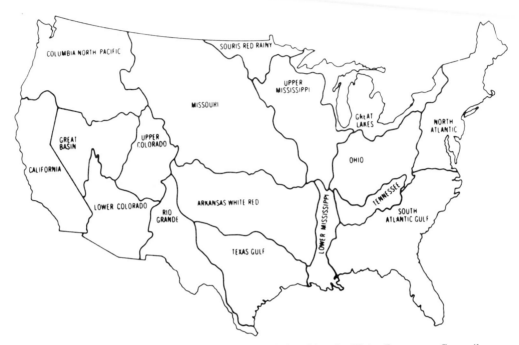

Fig. 9.10. River basins in the United States as defined by the Water Resources Council.

offs between alternative futures in the United States. Model A will be used as a benchmark in the analysis.

MODEL A: FREE MARKET, 300 MILLION POPULATION, PRESENT
WATER PRICES, AND TREND TECHNOLOGY IN 2000

The results of this policy model indicate that, for a 300 million population and the conditions of management, technology, and exports projected, the nation will have no problems in meeting its aggregate demands in 2000. With currently retired land allowed to return to production, irrigated acreage and water used in agriculture could be reduced accordingly. Thus water is available to transfer to other uses. Water and land are allowed to substitute for each other, and surplus capacity in both land and water is projected to prevail for 2000. The total food-producing capacity of the nation would still tend to be large relative to demand, and the tendency toward depressed farm prices, in the absence of supply control programs, would still prevail in the year 2000. Even with reduced water use for agriculture and a substitution of land over the nation for water in the West, some land still could go unused for field crops.

Total acreage and distribution of dryland and irrigated crops. Figures 9.11 through 9.13 show the distribution of both irrigated and dryland wheat, feed grain, and soybeans under optimizations of the objective function of model A. Maps are available for other crops and livestock but are not shown.

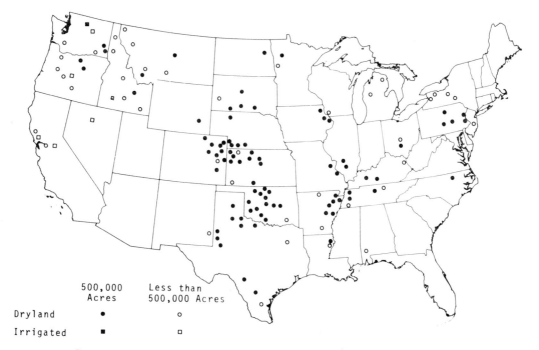

Fig. 9.11. Location of dryland and irrigated wheat under model A in 2000.

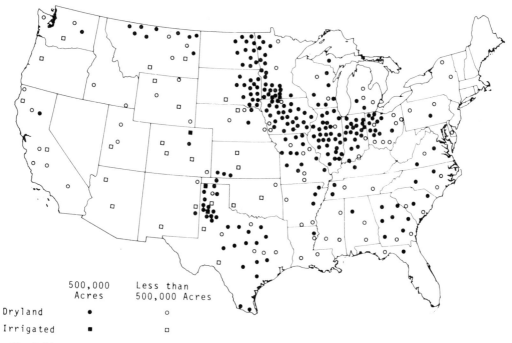

Fig. 9.12. Location of dryland and irrigated feed grain and soybeans under model A in 2000.

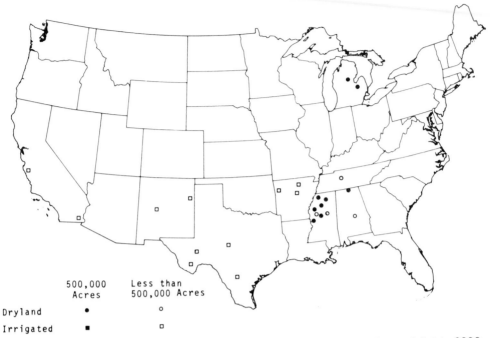

Fig. 9.13. Location of dryland and irrigated cotton and sugar beets under model A in 2000.

Under the assumptions of model A, total acreage of dryland crops in 2000 is 13.1 million higher than in 1964 (Table 9.6). Acreages of corn for grain and cotton are significantly lower while wheat, grain sorghum, and soybean acres are higher than at present. Based on total dryland acres, the rank of river basins generally is the same as in 1964, except the Texas-Gulf basin increases feed-grain acreage by 6.9 million acres as grain sorghum expands to satisfy the beef demand for an increased population in the Houston-Dallas area. Also, the dryland production of grain sorghum substitutes for some currently irrigated grain production. This substitution is especially important in water supply region 49 where groundwater is projected to be depleted by 2000. Dryland acres of cotton decrease in 2000 due to the continued decline in average cotton yield. Cotton production also moves into the lower Mississippi basin (southeastern United States, Figure 9.13) in response to increased competition for water from nonagricultural water requirements and increased forage production in the West. Compared with 1964, the total acres harvested (dryland and irrigated) of major field crops is 7.2 million higher due to the greater food and fiber demand in 2000 and the substitution of dryland acres for some currently irrigated land. Since dryland yields are less than irrigated yields, especially in the West, more land is used for food and fiber production.

Total dryland acres of tame hay and silages are projected to increase 41.9 million acres over 1964. This large increase in dryland forage production is necessary (1) for the increased cattle fed in 2000, (2) for the increased beef-cow herd to provide feeder cattle for the increased fed-beef production, and (3) because

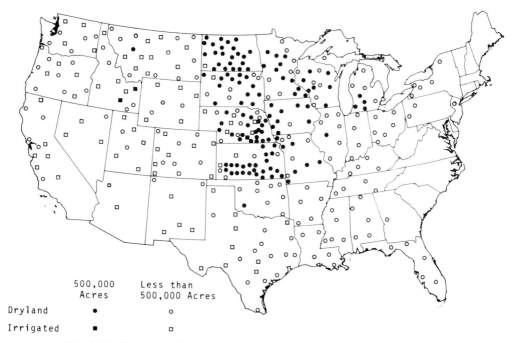

Fig. 9.14. Location of dryland and irrigated hay under model A in 2000.

dryland production is substituted for irrigated production. Figures 9.14 and 9.15 show the distribution of dryland and irrigated pasture and hay as determined by the model. Pasture and hay are large users of water. Considerable adjustment would be made in these uses of water. Some regions would reduce greatly the use of water for hay and pasture, but because of the large demand for beef, some would increase use.

In terms of the objective function of the model, irrigated acreage of annual crops in 2000 declines by 5.1 million acres from the 1964 level. The supply of both land and water is large enough to allow this shift while attaining a greater total output. It should be remembered that this model allows land now held out of production under government supply programs to be returned to cropping. The use of less irrigated land and the return to production of land now idled by supply control programs would allow the nation's overall agriculture to be optimized by this pattern and shift. Agriculture could either produce the nation's food needs at a lower total factor cost or produce a given amount at a greater national farm profit by this pattern. However, the shift to a smaller dependence on irrigated acreage would have important effects on the interregional distribution of incomes.

Even with the higher food and fiber requirements in 2000, 16.4 million acres of land could remain unused as shown by location in Figure 9.16. The term *unused* refers to the amount of land not needed to meet the domestic and export food demands at the numerical levels specified in the restraint equations of the programming model. Of course, in a completely free market, we would expect

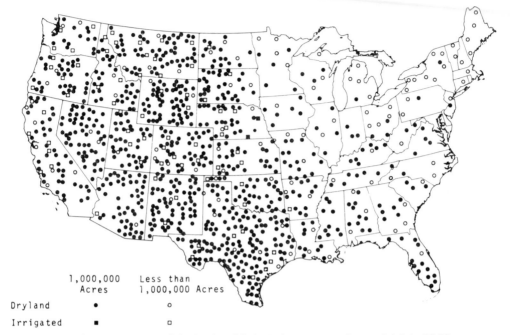

	1,000,000 Acres	Less than 1,000,000 Acres
Dryland	•	o
Irrigated	▪	▫

Fig. 9.15. Location of dryland and irrigated pasture under model A in 2000.

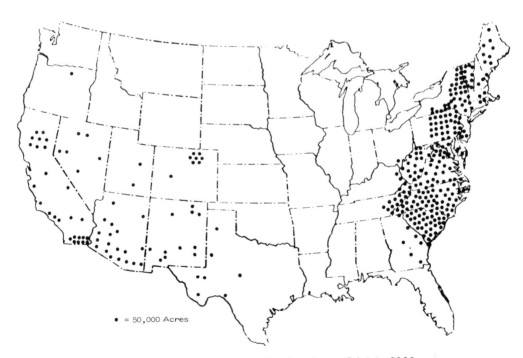

• = 50,000 Acres

Fig. 9.16. Location of unused land under model A in 2000.

the acreage denoted as unused to be absorbed into agricultural or urban uses. Also it could provide a supply of land to be used for public purposes such as parks and recreation. The greatest proportion of land designated as not needed for agricultural production (in terms of the specific demand restraints of the programming model) is in the Appalachian, Smokey, and other mountainous areas of the East. Another large proportion of the unused land is along the heavily populated area of the eastern seaboard, where the demand for recreational lands will be large over the next three decades. Most of the remaining unused land occurs in the 17 western states either as land is reduced from irrigation or as supply controls are relaxed and more productive soil in the Corn Belt or elsewhere is substituted.

MODEL A1: FREE MARKET, 300 MILLION POPULATION, $15 WATER PRICE, AND TREND TECHNOLOGY IN 2000

This policy model is the same as model A except that the price of water is higher and farmers in the 17 western states pay at least $15 per acre-foot for water (from surface runoff) used for crop irrigation or livestock production. The higher price on water affects its allocation in terms of the programming model's objective function.

Total acreage and distribution of dryland and irrigated crops. Compared with those in model A, dryland acreages of the annual crops, hays, and pastures would increase by 4.6 million, while irrigated acreages of these same crops would decrease by 4.6 million. The dryland acreage of annual crops, however, would be 1.0 million acres smaller than that under model A. Under model A1, the dryland acreage of annual crops would increase 0.2 million acres in the South Atlantic-Gulf basin and decrease 0.6 million acres in the Arkansas-White-Red basin, 0.4 million acres in the Lower Mississippi basin, 0.2 million acres in the Upper Mississippi basin, 0.1 million acres in the Missouri basin, and 0.1 million acres in the Great Lakes basin. The dryland acreage of wheat would decline 2.1 million acres, and dryland acreages of corn for grain, grain sorghum, soybeans, and cotton would increase slightly. Compared with that in model A, the irrigated acreage of annual crops would increase by 0.3 million acres under model A1, including 0.5 million acres more irrigated wheat in the Columbia–North Pacific basin.

Under model A1, the dryland acreage of tame hay and silages would be 5.5 million acres higher than that under model A. The following river basins show most of the projected increase (and amounts): Missouri (1.4 million acres), Columbia–North Pacific (1.4 million acres), and Arkansas-White-Red (0.8 million acres). The irrigated acreage of tame hay and silages would decrease by 3.5 million from model A. The following river basins show most of the projected decrease (and amounts): Upper Colorado (0.4 million acres), Columbia–North Pacific (1.8 million acres), Missouri (0.9 million acres), and Great Basin (0.4 million acres).

Dryland acreages of wild hay and pasture would be nearly the same as those under model A. However, the projected irrigated acreage of wild hay and pasture is 1.3 million acres fewer than that under model A. Most of the decrease would be in the following river basins (and amounts): Upper Colorado (0.4 million acres), Columbia–North Pacific (0.3 million acres), California–South Pacific (0.2 million acres), Missouri (0.2 million acres), and Rio Grande (0.2 million acres).

In summary, the price of water is assumed to increase to $15 under model A1, and in conformance with the national objective function, the projected mix of crops within the annual crop category changes and the proportion of annual crops and hay and pasture changes. For example, compared with that in model A, the total dryland acreage of all crops would be 4.6 million acres higher and the total irrigated acreage would be 4.6 million acres lower under model A1. Under A1, compared with that in model A, projected dryland production of all crops in both the West and the East is substituted for irrigated production in the West.

Total unused land under model A1 would be 1.3 million acres fewer than that under Model A. In addition, 3.3 million acres more irrigable land would be switched to dryland production compared with that in model A, and 0.5 million acres more cropland would be shifted to tame hay production. These changes are a result of the projected 5.5 million acres increase in dryland tame hay and silages under model A1.

MODEL A2: FREE MARKET, 300 MILLION POPULATION, $22.50 WATER
PRICE, AND TREND TECHNOLOGY IN 2000

This policy model is the same as model A1 except that the water price is even higher than under that in model A1. Farmers in the 17 western states would pay at least $22.50 per acre-foot for surface runoff used for irrigation or livestock production.

Total acreage and distribution of dryland and irrigated crops. The dryland acreage of annual crops would be 0.6 million acres more under model A2 than that under model A. The dryland acreage of wheat would decrease under model A2. Dryland acreages of all other crops would increase as compared with those in model A. The dryland acreage of annual crops in the following river basins would not change from that in model A: Upper Colorado, Lower Colorado, and Rio Grande. Compared with that in model A, the following river basins would show a decrease in the dryland acreage of annual crops: Middle Atlantic, Great Lakes, Upper Mississippi, Missouri, and Lower Mississippi (which would have the largest decrease, 1.1 million acres). All other river basins would show an increase compared with model A. In the East, the largest projected increases in the dryland acreage of annual crops are in the South Atlantic–Gulf (0.7 million acres) and the Souris-Red-Rainy (0.8 million acres) basins. In the West, the California–South Pacific basin would have the largest increase, 1.3 million acres.

River basins with the largest increases in the projected dryland acreage of tame hay and silages include most of those with decreases in the dryland acreage of annual crops: South Atlantic–Gulf, Great Lakes, Upper Mississippi, Lower Mississippi, Missouri, Arkansas-White-Red, and Columbia–North Pacific. The largest projected increase is 2.6 million acres in the Missouri basin. Compared with that in model A, only the Souris-Red-Rainy basin would show a decrease, while the

Tennessee and Rio Grande basins would show no change in the dryland acreage of annual crops. The dryland acreage of tame hay and silages under model A2 would exceed that of model A by 10.3 million acres and that of model A1 by 4.8 million acres. The dryland acreage of wild hay and pasture under model A2 would change very little from that of model A. Under model A2, the effect of the increase in water price on the substitution of dryland production for irrigated production would be evident.

Compared with that in model A, the irrigated acreage of annual crops would be 1.1 million acres fewer under model A2, since, at the higher water price, land would be substituted for water. This decrease would be shared by all annual crops except soybeans and all river basins except the California–South Pacific basin. Compared with that of model A, dryland production would be substituted for irrigated production. Also the projected crop mix would change, with dryland and irrigated acreages of wheat and dryland acreage of tame hay and silages declining relatively. A reduction of 6.4 million acres of tame hay and silages is projected under model A2, compared with that in model A. Including wild hay and pasture, irrigated forage acreage would decline by 9.0 million acres under model A2. In other words, when the price of water is raised from the implied level of model A to $22.50 per acre-foot under model A2, projected acreage of irrigated land in the 17 western states would decrease by 10.1 million acres. Over 90 percent of this total decrease would take place in the irrigated acreage of forage crops. Considering all irrigated forage crops, the following river basins (acres in parentheses) would show the largest decreases: Missouri (2.5 million), California–South Pacific (1.9 million), and Upper Colorado (1.0 million). The irrigated acreage of fruits, nuts, rice, and vegetables under model A2 would be the same as under model A. The amount of cropland available for annual crops but shifted to tame hay production under model A2 would be about the same as that under model A. Irrigated land would decrease by 10.1 million acres. Again, with the national objective function of model A2, land without irrigation would be substituted for water and irrigated land as the water price is increased to $22.50 per acre-foot. With the projected decline in yield on formerly irrigated land, as compared with that in model A, a larger national acreage of crops is required to meet the restraints of the regional food demand equations. Consequently, the unused land category would be smaller under model A2 than under either model A1 or model A.

MODEL A3: FREE MARKET, 300 MILLION POPULATION, $30 WATER PRICE, AND TREND TECHNOLOGY IN 2000

Model A3 with a water price of $30 represents the final water price variation of model A. Model A3 and the three previous policy models provide points on a demand curve for agricultural water in the West. Also, the projected substitution rates between water in the West and land employed for rainfed crops in the East and the West can be evaluated.

Total acreage and distribution of dryland and irrigated crops. Compared with that in model A, the dryland acreage of wheat would decline 6.5 million acres under model A3. Projected dryland acreage is the same for sugar beets and de-creases 1.4 million acres for grain sorghum. Dryland acreages of all other crops would be higher than those projected under model A. A substitution of dryland production for irrigated production again would occur. Compared with that in model A, the following river basins would have a larger dryland acreage of annual crops under model A3: New England, South Atlantic–Gulf, Ohio, Tennessee, Souris-Red-Rainy, Arkansas-White-Red, Great Basin, Columbia–North Pacific, and the California–South Pacific. The Rio Grande, Upper Colorado, and Lower Colorado river basins show no projected change. The following river basins would have decreases: Middle Atlantic, Great Lakes, Upper Mississippi, Lower Mississippi, and Texas-Gulf. The California–South Pacific basin has the largest projected in-crease in dryland acreage of annual crops, 1.8 million acres, and the Texas-Gulf basin has the largest projected decrease, 4.3 million acres.

In general, the locations of both dryland and irrigated wheat would be the same as those under model A, except that irrigated acreage would be less. The change between model A3 and model A is more apparent for feed grain and soy-beans. Not only is the projected irrigated acreage of feed grain and soybeans less, but the projected dryland acreage is even more concentrated in the East, especially in the U-shaped belt running through the Corn Belt and Great Lakes, and in Texas. Also, the dryland acreage of annual crops would increase significantly over a broad area stretching from the Corn Belt to Texas. Projected locations of dryland and irrigated acreages of cotton and sugar beets are nearly identical with those of model A. As for the previous policy models, the optimal solution under model A3 indicates a shift of cotton acreage from the Southwest to the Southeast. With a water price of $30 per acre-foot, the shift would be augmented as compared with the water price levels of models A, A1, and A2. As noted for model A, however, an optimal land and water use pattern at the national level in the year 2000 under assumptions of a free market also would specify a shift of cotton acreage from the Southwest to the Southeast. This shift conforms with a projected reduced use of irrigation for cotton production as it would move back into the Southeast. This pattern would be the most efficient national use of land and water under the as-sumptions of model A3, which specify attainment of the nation's food and fiber needs at minimum factor cost (or, from a national standpoint, the most profitable production pattern in meeting a specific set of demands).

The solution is most evident for dryland acreage of tame hay and silages, which would increase by 16.4 million acres over that in model A. Both the Souris-Red-Rainy and Arkansas-White-Red basins would have a reduced dryland acreage of tame hay and silages under model A3, but both of these basins would have a higher dryland acreage of annual crops under model A3. The Rio Grande and Lower Colorado basins would show no change from model A. All remaining river basins would have larger dryland acreages of tame hay and silages under model A3. The river basins with major increases in projected dryland acreages of tame hay and silages (and amounts in acres) are Texas-Gulf (4.4 million), Missouri (3.9 million), Columbia–North Pacific (2.5 million), Middle Atlantic (1.0 million), and the Great Lakes (1.0 million). Compared with that in model A, there would be a significant shift of hay acreage from the states west of the Northern Plains to the Northern

Plains and western Corn Belt states.   Irrigated acreage of hay would be significantly lower under the higher water price of model A3.

As compared with that in model A, the irrigated acreage of annual crops would
decline by 2.1 million acres and the irrigation acreage of tame hay and silages
would decline by 8.6 million acres under model A3.   Irrigated acreages of wild hay
and pasture would decline by 4.2 million acres under model A3.   The projected
location of irrigated pasture under model A3 is mainly in California, Idaho, Utah,
Nebraska, and Kansas, essentially the same as that under model A.   The projected
irrigated acreage of fruits, nuts, rice, and vegetables is the same as for model A.
The largest reductions in acreages of irrigated annual crops would occur in the
Missouri, Arkansas-White-Red, and Columbia–North Pacific river basins.   For all
irrigated hays, silages, and pasture, the largest projected acreage reductions are in
the following river basins (amounts in acres): Columbia–North Pacific (3.9 million), Missouri (3.8 million), and California–South Pacific (2.4 million).

With an assumed water price of $30 per acre-foot under model A3, total irri-
gated land in the West would decline by 14.9 million acres and the national dryland acreage of all crops would increase by 14.9 million acres, compared with
those in model A.   Considering only the crops that use cropland and hay land (excluding wild hay and pasture), 14.6 million acres of dryland crops would substitute for 10.7 million acres of irrigated land and 26.8 million acre-feet of water as
compared to those in model A.

Total unused land would decline by 3.9 million acres between model A and
model A3 because a further substitution of land for water would occur over the

= 50,000 Acres

Fig. 9.17. Location of unused land under model A3 in 2000.

nation. Under model A, over 7 million acres of irrigable cropland and irrigable hay land would switch to dryland production. Also, 49.3 million acres of cropland either currently in land-retirement programs or currently used for annual crops production would be shifted to tame hay production. Under model A3, compared with those in model A, an additional 9.7 million acres of irrigable land would be switched to dryland production, and an additional 2.9 million acres of cropland would be shifted to tame hay production. The Middle Atlantic and South Atlantic–Gulf basins would account for more than three-fourths of increased dryland acreage of all crops. The Missouri basin has almost a third of the projected decrease in irrigated land (4.2 million acres) under model A3. The projected location of unused land under model A3 is shown in Figure 9.17. Compared with that in model A, unused land would be more dispersed throughout southwestern United States.

DEMAND FOR WATER: SUMMARY

Figures 9.18 and 9.19 and Tables 9.7 and 9.8 summarize projected land and water use for agricultural purposes under the four policy models of the preceding sections (model A, model A1, model A2, and model A3). The results from model A and the three price variation policy models provide information on (1) the projected demand curve for water in the 17 western states and (2) the possible substitutions between land used for rainfed crops in the East for water (irrigated production) in the West and rainfed production in the West for irrigated production in the West. A third possible substitution, irrigated production in the East for irrigated production in the West, is not evaluated in the present study.

The projected demand curve for water in the 17 western states is shown in

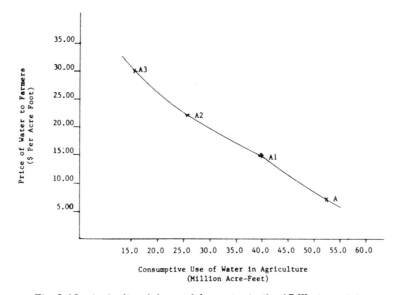

Fig. 9.18. Agricultural demand for water in the 17 Western states.

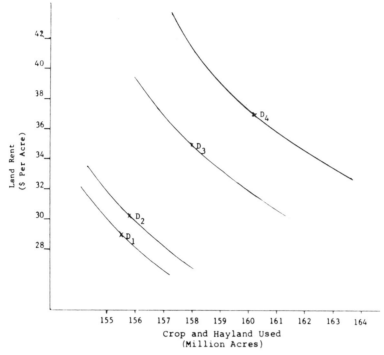

Fig. 9.19. Agricultural demand for land in the 31 Eastern states.

Figure 9.18.[29]   Given the points on the curve and the formulation of the programming model which underlie them, the arc price elasticities of demand for water can be calculated and are shown in Table 9.9.[30]

These elasticities have the following interpretation: on the lower portion of the demand curve ($A1$-A) in Figure 9.18, a 1.0 percent increase in the water price is associated with a decrease of 0.329 percent in the quantity of water used in agriculture. On the higher portion of the demand curve (above $A1$), a 1.0 percent increase in the water price results in a decrease of more than 1.0 percent in the quantity of water purchased or used. The segment of the curve below point A1 (Figure 9.18) is inelastic and the portion above is elastic. The curve in Figure 9.18

29. The curve in Figure 9.18 is drawn as a smooth curve although there are only four points shown on this curve. It is not entirely valid to join point A with the other three points because the assumptions behind model A are not entirely consistent with the three price variation policy models. Recall that under the price variation policy models, farmers must pay at least a certain amount for surface runoff water (i.e., $15.00, $22.50, and $30.00). Under model A, present prices for water in 2000 are assumed. To make model A completely consistent with the price variation policy models, and make the demand curve more correct, farmers should have been required to pay at least $7.50 per acre-foot for water in every water supply region. Additional points below point A could then have been derived by assuming farmers pay at least $2.50 or $1.50, etc.

30. The demand curve in Figure 9.18 expresses the projected relationship between water price and water used in the West for livestock, annual crops, tame hay and silages, wild hay, and pasture. Water for fruits, nuts, rice, and vegetables and nonagricultural water requirements are not reported in Figure 9.18 as water used, since the amount for these purposes does not vary between the policy models under consideration.

is a normative demand function expressing the response of agriculture to an increase in the price of water used for irrigation and livestock production. For a water-scarce area, a similar curve could be derived to suggest the level of water price required to release water for higher priority uses. In the optimizing sense of the programming model employed, the curve suggests the rate of appropriate water-pricing policies in potential reallocations of water use in the 17 western states and the reallocation of land use both within these states and between them and the rest of the nation.

As the water price is increased (i.e., model A1, model A2, and model A3), land and its production in the East would be substituted for water and its production in the West. Also, the same type of land-water substitution in the West would occur. These two types of substitutions are shown clearly in Figure 9.19 and Tables 9.7 and 9.8. Movement from right to left along the demand curve in Figure 9.18 (i.e., points A, $A1$, $A2$, and $A3$) conforms with movement between the points on the different demand curves in Figure 9.19 (i.e., points D_1, D_2, D_3, and D_4). In other words, as the water price in the West rises, the demand curve for land used in annual crop and tame hay production in the East shifts to the right.[31] Nationally, dryland production in the East would be substituted for irrigated production in the West as the water price rises. The second projected substitution, dryland production in the West for irrigated production in the West, is shown in Tables 9.7 and 9.8. As the price of water rises, total dryland acreage of annual crops and tame hay and silages in the West would increase by 10.5 million acres. Total irrigated acreage of annual crops, tame hay and silages, wild hay, and pasture would decrease by 14.9 million acres. Excluding wild hay and pasture, total irrigated acreage would decrease by 10.7 million acres in the West.

In summary, when the price of water increases to $30 per acre-foot, total irrigated land in the West would decrease 14.9 million acres; total irrigated acreage of annual crops and tame hay and silages would decrease by 10.7 million acres. At the same time, total dryland acreage of annual crops and tame hay would increase by 4.0 million acres in the East and by 10.5 million acres in the West. When 1 acre is removed from irrigated production in the West, on the average, 1 acre dryland production would replace it. The replacement acre would be composed of about one-third of an acre in the East and two-thirds of an acre in the West. This projected one-to-one substitution is possible because the mix of annual crops would change (e.g., wheat would decrease relative to corn for grain) and the relative mix of hays to grain would change.

ALTERNATIVE POLICY MODELS WITH 280 MILLION POPULATION

Four alternative policy models, all using 280 million population, are analyzed in this section. The first policy model analyzed, model B, is the same as model A

---

31. Only points D_1, D_2, D_3, and D_4 in Figure 9.19 are generated from the programming model. Smooth curves have been drawn through each point for illustrative purposes only. In actuality, the demand curves may be more inelastic than those shown, but given time and resources available, additional points on these curves were not estimated.

except that a lower level of population is used. The second policy model, model E, incorporates the lower population and full comparative advantages of free market condition with the elimination of insecticides in corn and cotton production. The third policy model, Model F, assumes that all fragile lands would be removed from crop production, and the final policy model, model C, simulates an annual land-retirement program similar to the wheat, feed-grain, and cotton programs used during the period 1961–71.

MODEL B: FREE MARKET, 280 MILLION POPULATION, PRESENT WATER PRICES, AND TREND TECHNOLOGY IN 2000

This is the fifth full comparative advantage and free market policy model analyzed using a given set of technologies. It is the same as model A except a lower population of 280 million people (D level) is used.

Total acreage and distribution of dryland and irrigated crops. With a lower population in 2000 (280 million as compared to 300 million under model A and its variants), the projected dryland acreage of annual crops would decrease by 12.2 million acres or by 6.4 percent. The dryland acreage of wheat, however, would increase by 4.9 million acres and the dryland acreage of oats would decrease by 9.0 million acres. The dryland acreage of corn for grain would decrease by 3.6 million acres, soybeans by 3.1 million acres, and grain sorghum by 1.7 million acres, as compared with model A. More wheat would be used for livestock feed under model B than under model A. Thus the dryland acreage of wheat would increase and dryland acreages of other grains would decrease. The following river basins have the largest projected decrease in dryland acreage of annual crops: Missouri, Upper Mississippi, Middle Atlantic, South Atlantic–Gulf, Ohio, and Arkansas-White-Red. The Souris-Red-Rainy basin has a projected increase in the dryland acreage of annual crops. The New England, Lower Mississippi, Rio Grande, Upper Colorado, Lower Colorado, Columbia–North Pacific, Great Basin, Tennessee, Great Lakes, and California–South Pacific basins would have little or no change compared with model A.

Under model B compared with model A, the acreage of wheat would increase in North Dakota and Minnesota and the acreage of feed grain would decrease in these same areas. Under model B, as under model A, there would be a shift of cotton acreage to the Southeast. Under model B, projected dryland acreage of tame hay and silages is 22.5 million acres or 20.8 percent below that projected in model A. The Missouri basin would have a decrease of 13.3 million acres, the Ohio basin a decrease of 3.1 million acres, the Arkansas-White-Red a decrease of 1.8 million acres, and the Great Lakes a decrease of 1.6 million acres. The South Atlantic–Gulf, the Souris-Red-Rainy, and Arkansas-White-Red basins each would have a decrease of 0.6 million acres, compared with model A. The Upper Mississippi basin would have an increase of 1.0 million acres. The remaining river basins would show little or no change from model A. Compared with model A, there would be much less hay production in the Missouri river basin.

The projected irrigated acreage of annual crops under model B would be nearly the same as under model A. This projected constancy in irrigated acreage is possible because of the lower population used in model B and a conforming reduction in water needed for municipal and industrial uses. At the same time that more water would be available for agricultural uses, the relative availability of land under rainfed production would be increased in both the East and the West.

The projected irrigated acreage of tame hay and silages would be 1.1 million acres lower and the decrease would be spread uniformly over the 9 western river basins. Irrigated acreages of wild hay and pasture would be nearly the same as under model A. The irrigated acreage of fruits, nuts, rice, and vegetables would decline slightly because of the smaller population. The large projected decrease in cropland and hay land requirements (and thus a large increase in unused land) under model B indicates the sensitivity of farm output to livestock feed requirements and total food needs as related to population. Under model B, the projected number of beef cows is 5.6 million less than under model A. Production of other livestock also would be lower, as would food and industry requirements generally. In total, 34.6 million fewer acres of cropland and hay land would be utilized for the smaller population projected under model B.

Fifty-one million acres of cropland and hay land would be unused with the 280 million population of model B. Of the total projected unused land, 25.6 million acres would be available for annual crop or tame hay production and an additional 25.3 million acres would be available for tame hay production only. The greatest projected change is in the Missouri basin where 17.1 million acres of cropland and hay land would be unused under model B compared with 0.4 million acres unused under model A. Compared with model A, 0.3 million acres more of irrigable land would be switched to dryland production but 6.5 million acres less land currently used for annual crop production would be shifted to tame hay production.

Compared with model A, much more unused land would be located along the eastern seaboard and in southwestern United States. In addition, there would be a concentration of unused land in a belt extending from Texas to North Dakota and South Dakota as the acreage of unused cropland and hay land would increase to 51.0 million acres under the smaller projected food and fiber requirements of model B.

With a population of only 280 million in the year 2000, the projected surplus capacity of agriculture promises to approach that of the 1961–70 period, when an annual average of 56.0 million acres of cropland were idle under federal supply control programs. While a reduced population growth rate is posed by some as a necessary future means to retain environmental quality, the projected lower food demand would pose a long-run continuation of price and income problems for the agricultural sector. With the projected 51.0 million acres of land not used to meet food demand for the 280 million population in 2000, capacity would exist to alter land and water use for agriculture so that this sector would not add to environmental deterioration even under a population considerably greater than at the present.

MODEL E: FREE MARKET, INSECTICIDE LIMITATION, 280 MILLION
POPULATION, PRESENT WATER PRICES, AND TREND TECHNOLOGY
IN 2000

Model E is the same as model B except that insecticides are eliminated in corn
grain, corn silage, and cotton production. Using available data on application
rates and costs of insecticides, acreages treated with insecticides, and crop damage
in the absence of insecticides, new cost and yield coefficients were developed and
used in the programming model. Thus model E measures the projected impact on
land and water use and farm prices should insecticides be eliminated in corn and
cotton production in attempts to improve the quality of the environment.

Total acreage and distribution of dryland and irrigated crops. Nationally, compared with model B, the dryland acreage of annual crops would increase 2.2
million acres under model E. The dryland acreage of corn would increase 1.0
million acres and the dryland acreage of oats would increase 0.6 million acres, in
response to the insecticide limitation. The dryland acreage of soybeans would
decrease 0.9 million acres, the dryland acreage of grain sorghum would decrease
0.7 million acres, and the dryland acreages of cotton and sugar beets would
decrease only slightly compared with model B. Regionally, under model E, the
dryland acreage of annual crops would increase 1.3 million acres in the Upper
Mississippi and 0.4 million acres in the Missouri river basins. The projected dryland acreage of annual crops in remaining river basins shows only relatively small
changes compared with model B.

Compared with model B, there would be an increase in the acreages of corn
grain and silage in Iowa, Illinois, Indiana, and Ohio (Corn Belt states) in response
to the insecticide limitation. Even with projected lower yields due to increased
crop damage from insects, the Corn Belt still would be the primary source of U.S.
corn production. Under model E, there would be a small increase in the irrigated
acreage of cotton in the West. The largest part of the projected U.S. cotton
acreage, however, still would be in the Southeast even with the insecticide
limitation.

Nationally, under model E, the dryland acreage of tame hay and silages would
be only slightly higher than that of model B. Regionally, the largest projected
increase in the dryland acreage of tame hay and silages would be in the Missouri
river basin, 1.4 million acres. With model E, the largest decrease in the dryland
acreage of tame hay and silages would be in the Upper Mississippi river basin, 1.3
million acres, which also would have an increase in the dryland acreage of annual
crops of 1.3 million acres. The projected dryland acreage of tame hay and silages
in the remaining river basins show little or no change compared with model B.
The dryland acreages of wild hay and pasture under model E would be slightly
higher than under model B.

With insecticides eliminated in corn and cotton production, the irrigated
acreage of annual crops would increase 0.4 million acres. Compared with model
B, the irrigated acreages of wheat, grain sorghum, and cotton would be higher
under model E. The projected irrigated acreage of corn grain would be lower.
Regionally, under model E, the projected irrigated acreage of annual crops would

increase slightly in the following river basins: Missouri, Arkansas-White-Red, and Great Basin. The irrigated acreage of cotton would be higher in the Texas-Gulf and California–South Pacific river basins under model E.

The projected irrigated acreages of tame hay and silages, wild hay, and pasture under model E show little or no change compared with model B. Under model E, the irrigated acreage of tame hay and silages would be 0.2 million acres higher in the California–South Pacific river basin and 0.1 million acres lower in the Great Basin river basin.

When insecticides are eliminated in corn and cotton production, the projected acreage of annual crops increases. Thus, under model E, unused cropland and hay land would be 2.9 million acres less than under model B. Regionally, the largest change in unused land would occur in the Missouri River basin which would have 2.0 million acres less unused cropland and hay land. Even with the insecticide ban, there still would be large amounts of unused cropland and hay land along the eastern seaboard and in the northern part of the Northern Plains.

Compared with model B, the amount of land switched from irrigated to dry land production would be 0.2 million acres fewer under model E. And land shifted (i.e., land either currently in land-retirement programs or currently used for annual crop production) would be 0.4 million acres fewer under model E.

MODEL F: FREE MARKET, FRAGILE LANDS REMOVED, 280 MILLION POPULATION, PRESENT WATER PRICES, AND TREND TECHNOLOGY IN 2000

Model F is the same as model B except that fragile lands (i.e., blow lands, wash lands, and wetlands) or lands that would have detrimental effects on the environment (quality of water and air, vegetative cover, wildlife, etc.), if subjected to agricultural uses, are removed from the potential land base. In total, over 656 million acres of land are removed from the "normal" land base under model F. Nearly 97 percent of this land currently is used for dryland pasture production. Generally, this land is low yielding. Since projected aggregate demand for farm products is the same under model F and model B, adjustments would take place in both the crop mix and location of production to maintain output.

Total acreage and distribution of dryland and irrigated crops. Compared with model B, the dryland acreage of annual crops would be 6.8 million acres fewer under model F. The largest projected change is the dryland acreage of wheat, which would be 13.6 million acres less under model F. The dryland acreage of grain sorghum would be 2.5 million acres less, the dryland acreage of barley would be 1.6 million acres less, and the dryland acreages of cotton and sugar beets would be only slightly lower under model F. The dryland acreages of oats, corn grain, and soybeans under model F would increase by 7.8 million acres, 2.6 million acres, and 0.7 million acres, respectively.

Regionally, the largest projected decreases in dryland acreages (and amounts) of annual crops under model F would be in the following river basins: Missouri (2.6 million acres), Texas-Gulf (2.4 million acres), Arkansas-White-Red (1.4 million acres), and Souris-Red-Rainy (1.3 million acres). Compared with model B, the dryland acreages of annual crops would be higher in the Middle Atlantic, Ohio, and South Atlantic–Gulf river basins.

The most notable change in the projected location of the acreage of annual crops between model F and model B is the large decrease in wheat acreage and corresponding increase in feed-grain acreage (oats and corn grain) in western North Dakota and northern Minnesota. Under model F, the U.S. cotton acreage still would be concentrated in the Southeast but there would be a shift in the acreage of sugar beets to Nevada and Idaho from Michigan.

With the removal from production of a large amount of pasturelands, the dryland acreage of tame hay and silages would increase by 18.2 million acres (primarily tame hay). Under model F, the dryland acreage of wild hay would be 0.4 million acres less and the dryland acreage of pasture would be 580.2 million acres fewer than under model B. Regionally, under model F, the largest projected increase in the dryland acreage of tame hay and silages would be in the Missouri river basin (8.5 million acres). No river basin would have a decrease in the dryland acreage of tame hay and silages under model F. There would be substantial increases in the acreages of hay in the Missouri, Ohio, and Texas-Gulf river basins under model F. All river basins would have a decrease in the acreage of pasture under model F.

With the removal of fragile lands from crop production (primarily forage), there are small projected increases in the irrigated acreages of annual crops and tame hay and silages. The irrigated acreages of wild hay and pasture would be less than under model B. Thus there would be no net change in the total irrigated acreage of annual crops, hay, and pasture under model F.

Compared with model B, unused cropland and hay land would be 30.9 million acres fewer. The amount of land switched from irrigated to dryland production would be nearly the same as under model B. But an additional 7.3 million acres of land would be shifted from annual crops production to tame hay production under model F in response to the large amount of fragile lands removed from pasture production. (Of the more than 656 million acres removed from crop production, nearly 97 percent currently would be used for pasture.)

In areas with large amounts of fragile lands, there would be a corresponding decrease in the amount of unused cropland and hay land under model F. Thus, under model F, there would be less unused cropland and hay land in the northern part of the Northern Plains (i.e., North Dakota and South Dakota), the Great Basin river basin, the Texas-Gulf river basin, the western part of the Arkansas-White-Red river basin, the southern part of the Upper Mississippi river basin, the western part of the Ohio river basin, the South Atlantic–Gulf river basin and the eastern seaboard. These are the same areas with large amounts of fragile lands.

MODEL C: 45-MILLION-ACRE ANNUAL LAND-RETIREMENT PROGRAM, 280 MILLION POPULATION, PRESENT WATER PRICES, AND TREND TECHNOLOGY IN 2000

This is the fourth and final policy model analyzed with 280 million population. It assumes that 45 million acres are retired in 2000 on a partial-farm basis with most areas of the nation sharing in supply control. The program simulated is like the annual wheat, feed-grain, and cotton programs used during the 1961–71 decade and does not allow land uses and crop production to be fully allocated among regions on a comparative advantage basis. The policy model forces some land retirement in all regions of the nation, but aside from this restraint, crop production can be allocated interregionally on a comparative advantage basis.

A land-retirement program that controls supply effectively is a means of substituting water in the 17 western states for land in states east of the Missouri River (but with some substitution also of water in the West for land used under rainfed conditions in the West). Previous policy models allow land, especially in the East, to be substituted for water in the West in meeting food demands in the sense of a national economic optimal pattern. Model B, with the lower population, indicates considerable surplus food capacity and a surplus of 147.4 million acre-feet of water for other uses. As compared to current water and land-use programs and patterns, it allows land in the East to be substituted for water in the West. Model C forces the substitution of water in the West for rainfed production in the East (and also for some dryland production in the West) in meeting projected food needs for the 280 million population. Of course, this is the outcome of the agricultural and water policies of the 1960s: they reduce the supply of land for crops by payments which divert it from the food-producing framework and use public investments to increase the supply of water for food production.

The pattern of crop production under this policy model would be substantially different than that under any previous policy model. With the lower population, aggregate food demand is less than under model A but is the same as under model B. Under model C, however, farmers are limited in the amount or acreage of certain crops they can harvest. In this specific policy model, crop acreages are tied to their 1964 base for wheat, feed grain, and cotton. Thus the pattern of production should compare favorably with 1964 and the spatial distribution of unused or retired land should parallel that of the 1961–71 decade.

The primary purpose of a land-retirement program of the type simulated is price support through supply control. In a later section we analyze the expected farm prices under each of the nine policy models included in this study. But our general conclusion thus far has been that the outlook in 2000 is for continued large or even surplus capacity of American agriculture and continued "low" prices, especially under model B. With a land-retirement program of the type simulated, farm prices could be raised substantially and commodity stocks could be effectively controlled. We wish to analyze how a program of this type might affect the agricultural demand for water in the year 2000 and the manner and extent it would alter the supply of water available for municipal and industrial uses.

Total acreage and distribution of dryland and irrigated crops. Compared with model B, the dryland acreage of annual crops would decline by 10.7 million acres (Table 9.10). The dryland acreage of both wheat and barley would decline substantially, 21.6 million and 4.0 million, respectively. On the other hand, dryland acreages of grain sorghum and soybeans would increase substantially, by 10.5 million acres and 13.1 million acres, respectively. Compared with model B, the dryland acreage of annual crops would increase 12.5 million acres in the Missouri river basin, 3.9 million acres in the Arkansas-White-Red river basin, and 2.3 million acres in the Upper Mississippi river basin. Dryland acreages of grain sorghum and soybeans would increase substantially in the Missouri and Arkansas-White-Red river basins. The acreage of soybeans also would increase in the Upper Mississippi river basin, and the acreage of grain sorghum would increase in the South Atlantic–Gulf river basin. Under model C, farmers would feed less wheat, more of the other grains, more oil meal and less forage than under either model A or model B. In tying crop production to a historic crop and geographic base by supply control through land retirement, dispersed spatially over many regions and farms, a substantial change in the crop mix would result. Projected locations of acreages of annual crops under model C are shown in Figures 9.20 through 9.22. The production of each type of annual crop would be much more dispersed than that under any of the free-market policy models discussed previously.

The dryland acreage of tame hay and silages would be 7.7 million acres fewer than under model B. Compared with model B, large decreases in the dryland acreage of tame hay and silages would occur in the Missouri, Arkansas-White-Red and Upper Mississippi river basins. Under model C, large increases in the dryland acreage of tame hay and silages would occur in the Middle Atlantic, South Atlantic–Gulf, and Ohio river basins.

With an annual land-retirement program, the irrigated acreage of annual crops would be 2.8 million acres higher than that projected under model B. Only the irrigated acreage of barley would be less than under model B. Both the Missouri and California–South Pacific river basins would have increases of over a million

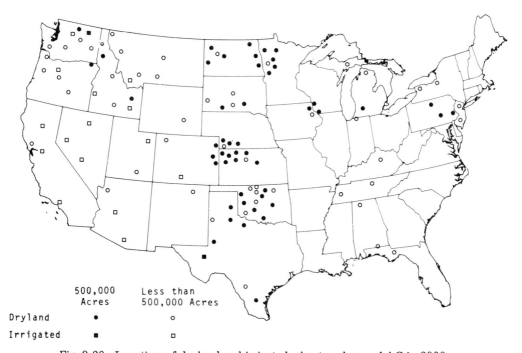

Fig. 9.20. Location of dryland and irrigated wheat under model C in 2000.

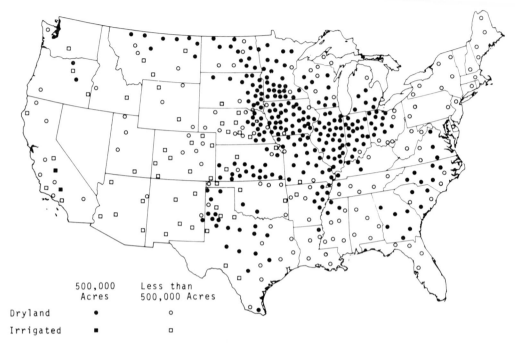

	500,000 Acres	Less than 500,000 Acres
Dryland	●	○
Irrigated	■	□

Fig. 9.21. Location of dryland and irrigated feed grain and soybeans under model C in 2000.

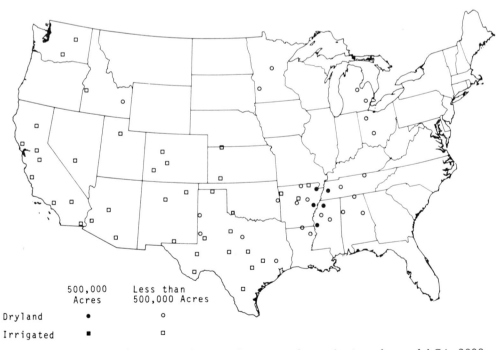

	500,000 Acres	Less than 500,000 Acres
Dryland	●	○
Irrigated	■	□

Fig. 9.22. Location of dryland and irrigated cotton and sugar beets under model C in 2000.

acres in the irrigated acreage of annual crops compared with model B. The irrigated acreage of annual crops in the Arkansas-White-Red basin would decrease by 0.4 million acres. (See Figures 9.20 through 9.22 for the locations of the irrigated acreages of annual crops under model C.) Under model C, irrigated acreages of tame hay and silages, wild hay, and pasture would be nearly the same as under model B.

In summary, under model C, the dryland acreage of annual crops would be less than under model A, but 10.7 million acres more than under model B. The dryland acreage of wheat would decline substantially under model C and dryland acreages of grain sorghum and soybeans would increase substantially as farmers switch from feeding as much wheat and are required to plant within their historic base. The dryland acreage of tame hay and silages would decrease by 9.9 percent from model B. Under model C, the irrigated acreages of hays, silages, and pasture would increase only slightly but the irrigated acreage of annual crops would increase by 2.8 million acres, compared with model B. The projected location of dryland and irrigated acreages and annual crops under model C compares favorably with 1964.

As is expected, under model C all areas of the nation would have unused cropland. Since farmers would be required to "set aside" part of their historic base under the supply control programs simulated, areas with large acreages of annual crops in the past would have the largest amounts of unused or idle land (primarily cropland). Since the irrigated acreage of annual crops would be higher under model C than under any other policy model included in this study, 4.4 million acres less irrigable cropland and hay land would be switched to dryland produc-

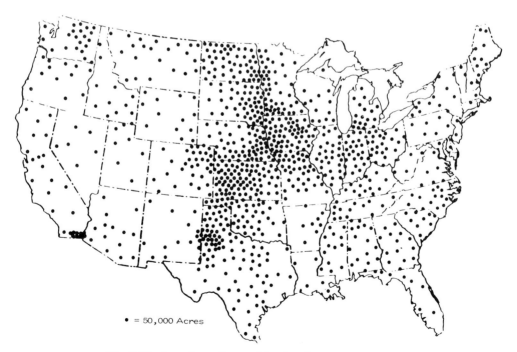

• = 50,000 Acres

Fig. 9.23. Location of unused land under model C in 2000.

tion as compared with model B. Also, under model C only 2.1 million acres of land available for annual crops would be shifted to tame hay production compared with 42.8 million acres under model B. The projected location of unused land under model C is shown in Figure 9.23 and is widely dispersed over the nation compared with the comparative advantage and free market policy models discussed earlier (models A, A1, A2, A3, and B).

A FREE MARKET POLICY MODEL WITH 325 MILLION POPULATION AND ADVANCED TECHNOLOGY

MODEL D: FREE MARKET, 325 MILLION POPULATION, PRESENT WATER PRICES, AND ADVANCED TECHNOLOGY IN 2000

Model D is the ninth and final policy model included in this study. It differs from model A in three respects. First, the population in 2000 is assumed to be 325 million (B level) rather than the 300 million (C level) used for model A. Second, advanced technology is assumed for crops and livestock in the Southeast and for livestock across the entire nation. In general, agriculture in the Southeast is assumed to "catch up" to agriculture in the Corn Belt by 2000. For livestock in the nation, average feed conversion rates are assumed to approach levels now attained under research conditions and the calving rate is assumed to increase considerably. Third, under model D, the level of exports of farm products is assumed to be nearly twice as high as the 1967–69 average level incorporated into model A. Compared with model A, exports of feed grain and wheat would be 83.0 percent higher and exports of oil meals 120.0 percent higher. Thus the combination of a higher population and higher exports under model D would increase total demand for agricultural products to a maximum foreseeable level.

Total acreage and distribution of dryland and irrigated crops. The large increase in demand under model D would result in sharply higher farm prices compared with model A. In general, model D prices of crop commodities would be about 50 percent higher and livestock prices about 12 percent higher. With the higher projected demands, especially all export demand, the dryland acreage of annual crops would increase by 29.7 million acres or 25.2 percent more than under model A. The dryland acreage of soybeans would increase by 22.2 million acres, corn for grain by 12.8 million acres, and grain sorghum by 1.4 million acres. Dryland acreage of barley would decrease by 4.2 million acres, oats by 1.1 million acres, and wheat by 0.9 million acres. The river basins (and amounts in acres) with large projected increases in the dryland acreage of annual crops would be: Missouri (17.7 million), Upper Mississippi (5.1 million), Arkansas-White-Red (4.8 million), Souris-Red-Rainy (3.3 million), and South Atlantic–Gulf (2.6 million). The largest projected decrease in total dryland acreage of annual crops would be in the Texas-Gulf river basin, 5.1 million acres.

With the higher calving rate assumed under model D, the number of beef cows would be 12.0 million head (39.0 percent) less than under model A. Although the numbers of dairy cows and fed beef would increase due to the higher domestic demands, the total demand for forages would decrease somewhat. As a result, the dryland acreage of tame hay and silages would be 18.9 million acres or 19.1 percent less than under model A. (The dryland acreage of tame hay decreases 20.1 million acres.) Compared with model A, the following river basins (and amounts in acres) show large projected increases in dryland acreage of tame hay and silages: Texas-Gulf (5.4 million), Middle Atlantic (4.4 million), and South Atlantic–Gulf (1.8 million). The following river basins (and amounts in acres) show large projected decreases: Missouri (18.2 million), Arkansas-White-Red (5.9 million), Upper Mississippi (5.1 million), and Souris-Red-Rainy (3.2 million). Remaining river basins show relatively small changes from model A. The dryland acreages of wild hay and pasture would be nearly the same as under model A. In summary, under model D the dryland acreage of annual crops would increase substantially and the dryland acreage of tame hay and silage would decrease substantially. The increased food and fiber demands and advanced technology in the Southeast would result in an increase of over 5 million acres of dryland annual crops and tame hay and silage in the Southeast (South Atlantic–Gulf and Tennessee river basins).

The irrigated acreage of annual crops under model D would be 2.0 million acres higher than under model A. The irrigated acreages of grain sorghum, oats, and corn grain would decline, while the irrigated acreages of all other annual crops would increase over model A. The largest increases would be for irrigated wheat (0.9 million acres) and irrigated cotton (0.8 million acres). All river basins except the Texas-Gulf and Lower Colorado basins would have a larger irrigated acreage of annual crops under model D. The largest increase in irrigated acreage of annual crops would be in the Great Basin river basin (1.8 million acres).

The irrigated acreage of tame hay and silages under model D would decline only slightly from model A (0.8 million acres). The irrigated acreage of tame hay and silages would increase the most in the Missouri river basin (0.3 million acres) and decrease the most in the Columbia–North Pacific river basin (0.7 million acres). The irrigated acreages of wild hay and pasture under model D would be nearly the same as under model A.

Under model D only 4.5 million acres of cropland hay land would remain unused. Nearly 50 percent of the total unused land would be in the Great Lakes river basin and northeastern United States. Thus nearly 12 million acres more would be used for annual crops and tame hay under model D compared with model A. Also, under model D 28.3 million acres less of cropland would be shifted to tame hay production. And 0.5 million acres less of irrigable land would be switched to dryland production under model D. Thus the increased domestic and export demands under model D would leave only a small amount of unused land.

SUMMARY OF LAND AND WATER USE, LIVESTOCK PRODUCTION, AND COMMODITY PRICES UNDER ALTERNATIVE POLICY MODELS

Projected land and water use under the nine alternative policy models are summarized in Tables 9.11 and 9.12. Three things are evident from the results: (1) land would not be a physically or economically scarce resource in 2000, although under model D only 4.5 million acres of cropland and hay land remain unused; (2) with a national objective function of economic optimum in food production and water and land use, such as the one employed in the policy models of this study, land irrigated in the West would be less than at present; (3) relative to this objective function, water would be in surplus supply in the West under all policy models for the year 2000.

LAND USE

For the nine policy models analyzed, total land used for all crops would be highest under model D and lowest under model F (Table 9.11). Total unused cropland and hay land would be lowest under model D and highest under model B. Under model D a high level of domestic and export demands for farm products is specified and only 4.5 million acres of cropland and hay land would remain unused. However, other researchers have estimated that from 50 to 150 million acres of new land could be brought into production if needed. The higher price levels resulting from model D could encourage reclamation of these new lands. Total land used for all crops would be lowest under model F because nearly 656 million acres of fragile lands are taken out of production. Under model B a low level of domestic and export demands for farm products is specified. Thus 51 million acres of cropland and hay land would remain unused, and surplus capacity would approach levels of the 1961–71 decade. Projected farm prices also are low. Model C, the annual land-retirement policy model, places part of the land base in retirement and farm prices would rise accordingly. With 300 million people in 2000 (models A, A1, A2, and A3), 12.5 to 16.4 million acres of cropland and hay land would remain unused.

Compared with that in 1964, land irrigated in 2000 under the nine alternative policy models would range from 2.1 to 18.9 million acres less. Total irrigated acreage would be higher under model C, the annual land-retirement policy model, and lowest under model A3, the $30 water price policy model. From 2.7 million to 15.0 million acres of land either currently irrigated or in authorized reclamation projects would be switched to dryland crop production in 2000. Some of this irrigable land also would be unused in 2000, mostly because of projected scarcity of water in some regions.

A large amount of cropland either currently in land-retirement programs or currently used for annual crop production would shift to tame hay production in 2000. Under model C, only 2.7 million acres would be shifted because of the nearly 45 million acres of cropland in the annual land-retirement programs. Under model A3, however, nearly 52.1 million acres of cropland would be shifted to tame hay production in 2000. Thus a clear conclusion appears. Present land surpluses could substitute for future water and irrigated land development projects in agriculture.

The large projected increase in forage production and the resulting shifts of cropland to tame hay production are results of the large increases in projected numbers of beef cows and fed beef. In general, compared with current levels, beef-cow numbers would more than double and fed-beef numbers would nearly triple by the year 2000 (Table 9.13). The relationship between projected forage requirements and land surpluses can be illustrated by comparing model A with model B. Under model A, with a population of 300 million, 16.4 million acres of cropland and hay land would remain unused. Under model B, with a population of 280 million, 51.0 million acres of cropland and hay land would remain unused. About one-third of the unused land under model B would be located in the Missouri river basin, which includes part of the Northern Plains, and this land would be used mostly for tame hay production under model A. Thus projected land needs are highly sensitive to future food and fiber requirements, especially forage requirements for beef production.

Two environmental control policy models are analyzed in this study (model E and model F). Model E measures the projected impacts on land and water use and farm prices when insecticides are eliminated in corn and cotton production. Model F measures these same projected impacts when fragile lands are removed from crop production in attempts to improve the quality of air and water, vegetative cover, wildlife, etc.

As expected, when insecticides are banned in corn and cotton production (model E), there is a smaller projected land (and water) surplus. But the reductions in land and water surpluses would be very small at the implied population and demand level. Even with the removal of nearly 656 million acres of fragile lands in 2000 (model F), over 20 million acres of cropland and hay land would remain unused (Table 9.11). Since the fragile land removed is low yielding (primarily pasture), it could be replaced with a much smaller increased use of higher-yielding cropland and hay land.

WATER USE

Relative to the objective function employed, there would be surplus water in the West under all nine alternative policy models in 2000 (Table 9.12). However, the distribution of water supplies still could be a problem in 2000. The Lower Colorado, Great Basin, and Rio Grande river basins most frequently appear as regions of projected water scarcity (Figures 9.24 and 9.25). Under the 325-million-population and the 300-million-population policy models, the Texas-Gulf river basin would be water deficient. The deficit, however, could be solved through additional reservoir construction, since rainfall is plentiful in the region.

Agriculture was the biggest consumer of water in 1965 and our projections indicate that it will continue to be, even in 2000. But projected nonagricultural water requirements in 2000 are nearly four times larger than the 1965 level. Thus there would be a relative shift of water consumption toward municipal, industrial, and other uses by 2000. If nonagricultural water requirements projected for 2000 are underestimated, agriculture could release additional water for these other uses. With a $15 water price (model A1), more than 11 million acre-feet of water per year would be released from agriculture. Thus adoption of a pricing system for agricultural water use would release water from agriculture for other uses if needed.

Under the alternative policy models, total consumption of water in 2000

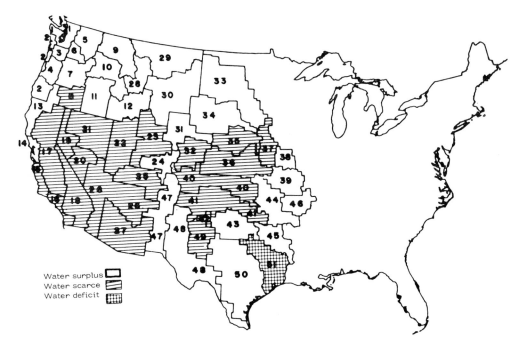

Fig. 9.24. Water supply-demand balances under model A in 2000.

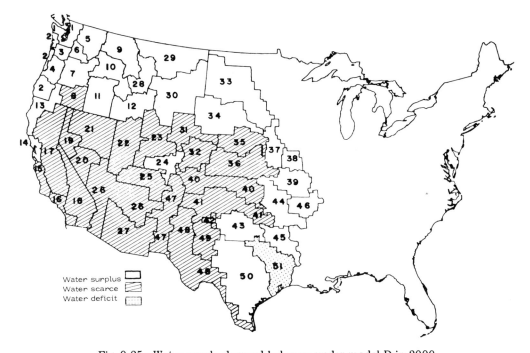

Fig. 9.25. Water supply-demand balances under model D in 2000.

would be highest under model D, with high domestic and export food and fiber demands, and lowest under model A3, the $30 water price policy model. Under model D, 42.0 percent of the total water supply would be consumed, while under model A3, only 27.3 percent of the total water supply would be consumed. Thus a large proportion of the water supply would be surplus, even with a maximum foreseeable level of food and fiber demand in 2000. With either a ban on insecticides in corn and cotton production (model E) or removal of fragile lands from crop production (model F), total water consumed would increase only slightly. Under all the policy models analyzed, the Columbia–North Pacific river basin always has the largest projected water surplus.

In summary, even with little further development of present water supplies, there does not seem to be an absolute water shortage in 2000. The distribution of the water supply, however, still could be a problem. In general, present land surpluses could substitute for future irrigated land developments, reduce pressures on water supplies, and hence, release plenty of water for increased nonagricultural uses in 2000.

LIVESTOCK AND POULTRY PRODUCTION IN 2000

Projected livestock and poultry production for three alternative policy models are reported in Table 9.13. Figures are not reported for models A1, A2, and A3, since they are nearly the same as for model A. Likewise, projected livestock and poultry production under models C, E, and F are nearly the same as for model B.

The production of a specific kind of livestock or poultry is dependent on the level of population, per capita consumption, level of imports or exports, and the rate of technological advance. Thus, aside from beef cows, livestock and poultry production would be highest under model D, with 325 million population and advanced technology, and lowest under model B, with 280 million population and trend technology. The number of beef cows would be less under model D because of the higher calving rate used under the advanced technology assumption.

The most significant change in projected livestock output under the policy models analyzed is the large increase in beef production. Of course, this increased production is a result of higher per capita consumption of beef and veal in 2000. With higher levels of both per capita consumption and population in 2000, beef cow numbers would more than double over the 1969 level. Fed beef would nearly triple in number by 2000 under model D with a 325 million population. Both beef cows and fed beef use large quantities of forage. As a result, the increased land which would be needed for concentrates and forages and the much larger exports under model D would leave only 4.5 million acres of cropland and hay land unused in 2000.

Under model A (300 million population), 16.4 million acres of cropland and hay land would remain unused. Model B, with 280 million population, would require about 10 million acres less land for forages as compared with model A. As much as 51.0 million acres of cropland and hay land would be left unused, however, under model B. Thus the projected level of future forage requirements can have an important role in need for or the formulation of water and land policies, especially since a large percentage of irrigated land would be used for forage production (about 40 percent in 1959).

CROP AND LIVESTOCK PRICES IN 2000

Farm commodity prices projected under the nine policy models are summarized in Table 9.14.[32]   In general, prices would be lowest under model B because of its smaller population and highest under model D because of its large food and fiber demands.   Both model B and model D are free market policy models, and production would be allowed to concentrate in areas of greatest comparative advantage.   Some prices under model C would be higher than those under model D.   Model C incorporates supply control features to disperse production throughout the United States to restrain output and increase prices (and also force a substitution of water in the 17 western states for land in the East).   More marginal and lower-yielding areas would be brought into production under both model C and model D, and prices would rise accordingly.

Farm prices under model A would be nearly the same as 1969 actual prices for corn grain, soybeans, and hay.   They would be higher for cattle and calves and barley and oats, but lower for hogs, milk, and cotton.   The higher projected prices for livestock and livestock feeds can be explained by increased demand for livestock, especially beef and veal.   Although the average price received for sugar beets is not available for 1969, the price under model A would be only 40 to 50 percent of current levels in some states.   Thus those products that have "tight" controls over production (sugar beets, cotton, and milk) could have lower prices in the future (as well as the present) in the absence of production controls or marketing quotas.   Even with the large increase in food and fiber demands under model D, prices of these "controlled" products would not exceed current levels in 2000. These are products for which competitive substitutes may be more widely used. Imports and domestic cane are substitutes for sugar beets.   Synthetic fibers have already captured a large part of the market for cotton.   Dry milk, soybean milk, margarine, and dairy imports already have an adverse effect on the market for fluid milk.   (The impact of soy substitutes on future meat consumption is not evaluated in this study.)

Results from model A3 indicate that 36.2 million acre-feet of water could be released from agriculture annually for other uses in 2000, if the minimum water price were increased from present levels to $30 per acre-foot.   Generally, if such a policy were adopted, farm prices would rise by about 10 percent.   But cotton, sugar beets, and milk prices would still stay below current levels.   However, under model B, a free market and the 280 million population level, farm commodity prices generally would be even lower than in 1969.   Except for cattle and calves, most commodity prices would be around 18 percent lower than under model A

32. The commodity prices reported in Table 9.14 are the shadow prices for commodities determined by the programming model.   These shadow prices are available for each of the 27 consuming regions, but only national averages are reported here.   The lower prices for hogs indicate that hog production costs may be underestimated in the programming model.

and about 18 percent below the 1969 level. Thus policymakers might consider a price support program to increase farm prices. Under model C, a geographically dispersed land-retirement program, farm prices generally would be more than a third higher than in 1969 and over 50 percent higher than under model B.

With a ban on insecticides in corn and cotton production (model E), projected prices do not increase significantly from model B. Thus the costs to society in terms of food costs and resource use would not increase substantially under model E. But the detrimental effects of some insecticides on the environment could be reduced. The quality of the environment also could be improved with removal of fragile lands from crop production. Under model F, the fragile land policy model, prices would be about 12 percent higher than under model B, with the same population and aggregate levels of domestic and export demands. In general, under the higher demands of model D, prices of crop commodities would be about 50 percent higher and livestock prices about 12 percent higher than those under model A.

In summary, farm prices under model A would not be significantly higher than at the present. Under model B, they would be substantially lower and under model C and model D, they would be substantially higher than in 1969. Thus consumer food costs would not rise significantly under any of the policy models based on a C population level. They would decline under the D population level of model B, but would rise substantially under the supply control features of model C or the high level of domestic and foreign demands under model D.

Differences in projected net farm income among the policy models and the present, including the free market of model B, would parallel those of prices and food costs. Net farm income in 2000 would be lowest under model B and highest under either model C or model D, depending upon the level of government payments under model C. In addition to the higher food costs under model C, government payments also would be required to insure farmer participation. Thus not only would consumers pay more for food but also taxpayers would contribute to farm income through price support and land diversion payments. Prices about 12 percent higher than model B could be obtained with relatively low levels of government payments by removal of nearly 656 million acres of fragile land (model F). Most fragile land in the nation already is owned by the government (Bureau of Land Management permit and lease lands and Forest Service lands). Government payments to take other fragile lands out of production would not be substantial.

A number of studies have indicated the effect on farm prices and incomes of removing all production controls.[33] In general, conclusions are that aggregate net farm income initially would drop by as much as 40 percent in the sudden turn to a free market. After a period of adjustment, farm prices would rise again, but aggregate net farm income still would remain from $4 to $5 billion below comparable levels under land-retirement programs of the type in effect.

33. See Leo V. Mayer, Earl O. Heady, and Howard C. Madsen, *Future Programs for the 1970's*, Center for Agricultural and Economic Development, Iowa State Univ., CAED Report No. 32, Oct. 1968.

POLICY IMPLICATIONS

The results of this study, based on conservative yield trends, indicate that U.S. agriculture should not be faced with aggregative strains on food-producing capacity and water supplies relative to needs in the year 2000. Rather, the projections suggest that, even by 2000, U.S. farmers still could be faced with a large supply capacity relative to food demands. Farmers in specific locations and operating under particular agro-climatic conditions will continue to be faced with depressed yields due to limited rainfall and groundwater or stream flows. Relative to projected demand and food supplies, however, there should not be an aggregative food supply problem for the nation.

The study indicates that even if the irrigated area is not increased over the next 30 years, capacity of American agriculture will be sufficiently large to extend potential depressed prices and incomes to the year 2000. The term "depressed" refers to real prices compared to levels being realized through the supply control and price support programs financed from the U.S. Treasury. If the full supply capacity projected for the year 2000 were used in the absence of government programs, real prices would be lower than those realized by farmers in recent years. The level of farm income in 2000 under any level of prices also will depend on the number of farms existing at that time and the prices paid for farmland (and hence, on the number of acres farmers with given investment funds can operate, the amount of interest paid on credit for land investment, etc.).

The study results also indicate that projected food demands in 2000 could be met by returning land now idled under government programs to production and by using less irrigated land than at the present. If the United States had a 300 million population in the year 2000 (model A), projected food demand could be met with 11.3 million acres less irrigated land than in 1969, with 5.3 million acres of cropland (including that now withheld from production by government supply control programs) remaining out of production, with 7.3 million acres of irrigable land switched to dryland production, and with 49.3 million acres of cropland shifted to less intensive uses such as pasture and hay. Under a 280 million population (model B), 12.5 million acres less of irrigated land would be needed than in 1969, 25.6 million acres of present cropland could remain idle, 7.6 million acres of irrigable land would be switched to dryland production, and 42.8 million acres of cropland could be shifted to less intensive uses. With a 325 million population in 2000 (model D), but also with higher levels of exports and advanced technology, food and fiber demands could be satisfied with 9.9 million acres less of irrigated land than in 1969, with 1.4 million acres of present cropland idled, with 6.8 million acres of irrigable land switched to dryland production, and with 21.0 million acres of cropland shifted to less intensive uses. (These are the aggregative patterns which optimize national food production for the demand and implied price levels of this study.)

Hence, in the case of future water scarcities, especially in the West, agriculture need not use more but actually could release a fairly large supply of water for industrial and urban uses. As study results indicate, if the price of water were increased to $30 per acre-foot as a minimum for the 17 western states, this would allow release of an additional 36.2 million acre-feet per year from agriculture compared with model A (with crops reallocated among producing areas of the nation in a manner consistent with the objective function of the programming model employed at the 300 million population level). Clearly then, if the value of water in nonfarm uses specifies it, water could be released from agriculture to uses in other sectors and locations. This transfer of water from agriculture to other uses would not put pressure on the nation's food supplies or export possibilities. Neither would it have other minimal effects on the cost of food to the nation's consumers.

ALTERNATIVES AND OPTIONS IN POLICY

If the major objective of public agricultural policies were to attain specified national minimum farm price levels and income at minimum treasury cost, the present policy mix of supply control measures and continued investment in irrigation would be highly inconsistent. Each increment in public irrigation investment and improved water use is effectively linked with a parallel increment of public expenditure to control supply and lessen output. In other words, the increase in yields and production forthcoming from further irrigation development requires expenditures to induce farmers at other locations to retire land to offset the increased output in the newly irrigated area. To the extent that these increases and decreases in output at different locations cancel each other, the public must pay twice to hold supply at a given level; once to increase production in the newly irrigated area and once to reduce it in nonirrigated areas.

If the public employed a criterion of minimum public costs to maintain given nationwide levels of farm prices and income, a recommendation of minimal water development and use would prevail; further public investment should not be made in irrigation development. Under this restraint, farmers on potentially irrigable land would make no absolute or actual sacrifice in income and capital values. Also, the public would not be faced, as it has been in the past, with expenditures for supply control on both irrigated and nonirrigated land to offset the added production forthcoming from newly developed irrigated land.

INTERACTIONS OF WATER AND AGRICULTURAL POLICIES

As indicated earlier, the dominant increase in water use and irrigated acreage over the last 30 years has been through private investment, especially by individual farmers in wells and irrigation systems based on groundwater supplies. Individual farmers have made these investments because they have been profitable. In this sense their decisions and actions have been exactly the same as for farmers producing under rain-fed conditions who have added more fertilizer, pesticides, improved varieties, and better livestock rations. In terms of proportion of total farm output, the latter group is even more responsible than the former group for the large supplies which press heavily on prices in a market environment of very low price elasticities of demand. Federal supply control and price support programs which offset supply increments, due to use of more inputs and improved practices, encourage the farmer with profitable water supplies available to him to develop them. Similarly, these programs make it profitable for farmers in the Corn Belt, Southeast, and elsewhere to use more fertilizer, pesticides, and improved strains and rations. Because of the greater cropland acreage involved, even the subsidization of inputs through SCS technical aid and ASCS payments increases output as much or more for rain-fed agriculture than for irrigated farming. In both cases, the individual farmer makes investments and uses public aids because it is profitable for him to do so. When the majority of farmers do so, the inelastic demand causes market revenue to decline because prices fall by a greater percentage than output increases. Federal supply control, price support, and international food aid programs have been initiated to offset these mass market effects of actions of individual farmers as the agricultural sector develops further. It is no more appropriate to claim that these federal programs are needed to offset the effects of farmers who increase output through their own irrigation investments than it is to claim that they are needed for farmers depending on rainfall who use more fertilizer, pesticides, machines, high-yielding varieties, and improved additives for livestock rations. Neither is it any more appropriate to suggest that profitable development or irrigation by individuals should be restrained than it is to suggest that fertilizer and similar input restraints should be imposed on farmers who depend on rainfall. True, farmers do invest in irrigation which produces more, then receive direct government payments to leave land idle so that supply will be reduced. But on an even broader geographic and volume basis, farmers apply added fertilizer and other modern inputs so that each acre produces more, then idle part of their land upon receipt of public payments.

Some land idled under government supply control programs is irrigated land served through federal projects. Howe and Easter suggest that the total cost of land retirement and price support for publicly served irrigated land could have been as high as $350 million in 1964.[34] It is in this sense that two public investments that cancel each other arise; one to develop irrigation which increases output, then supply control programs which reduce output. However, even considering public funds involved per se for agriculture over the past 40 years, these investments for irrigation may be less important than other public investments which initially result in augmented farm output which then necessitates direct payments to farmers to idle land to reduce output by a corresponding amount. For example, the public invests heavily in research and education to promote improved practices and greater input use in the 31 states east of the Mississippi River which depend mainly on rainfall. Then, to offset successful effects in increased productivity, it implements the complex of supply control, price support, and demand-augmenting programs previously mentioned. Data are not available to show how much the public must pay through commercial farm policies to offset the increased output resulting from a dollar of public investment in irrigation projects on the one hand and general agricultural development (research, education, credit facilities, subsidized nonwater inputs, etc.) on the other. Through programs that increase

34. Charles W. Howe and William K. Easter, *Interbasin Transfers of Water: Economic Issues and Evaluations*, Resources for the Future, Inc., Johns Hopkins Press, Baltimore, 1971, pp. v-14–v-20.

productivity in the one case and that restrain supply and bolster prices in the other case, farmers have been able to improve efficiency, reduce the real cost of food to consumers, and simultaneously retain some of the benefits through their contribution to technological and economic development.

Public investments in irrigation and general agricultural development thus relate similarly where both have a positive net benefit/cost ratio or marginal payoff to society. There is no logical basis for sorting one out more than the other for restraint. More important for this study are the prospective demands for water in nonfarm uses relative to future food demand and the real price of food. This study indicates clearly that the availability and productivity of natural resources for agriculture are sufficiently large that by 2000 some water could be shifted to municipal and industrial uses, should economic development and water demand in western states specify it. Land now immobilized through federal supply control programs can be substituted for water so diverted and the productivity and supply capacity of American agriculture will remain high. In fact, from the results of this study, even with some reduced water use for agriculture, the supply capacity still could be so great relative to domestic demand in 2000 that problems of food more nearly will revolve around low prices and incomes of farm producers rather than around high real prices and strained budget outlays for consumers. Currently, American families spend only 17 percent of their disposable income for food. Since the greatest proportion of this expenditure is for the packaging, processing, freezing, and other services incorporated with food after it leaves the farm, the food product in the farm form leaving the agricultural producer absorbs less than 7 percent of the American consumer's disposable income. The percentage could be considerably lower by the year 2000 as per capita incomes increase and the large agricultural capacity identified in this study is attained even with some diversion of water from agriculture.

The discussion above has been of federal irrigation projects which have positive net benefit/cost ratios or marginal payoffs. Given the total supply or productive capacity projected for agriculture in this study, the implementation of federal irrigation projects that do not have positive net payoffs, or that have high opportunity costs in the returns foregone in other uses, should not be implemented in behalf of national agriculture. The potential water supplies so implemented could more readily be economically justified for municipal and industrial uses with population and economic growth at particular locations than in agriculture, which is part of a national supply complex with the prospect that large production capacity in 2000 is more likely to cause surplus potential than domestic food shortages.

DISTRIBUTION AND COMPENSATION

Should population and economic activity grow beyond projected levels for 2000 at particular locations, causing nonfarm uses of water to have a greater value productivity than farm uses, diversion of water supplies from agriculture for these purposes would have distributive impacts on income and employment of rural communities using water from publicly developed projects or through water rights of historic origin. Incomes of farmers and communities from which these water supplies and rights were withdrawn would suffer economic losses, and communities and urban centers, realizing a larger water supply for municipal and industrial uses, would gain in economic activity and employment generated. In terms of equity, the diversion of income and capital values from one location and economic group to another, or the potential diversion of water from agricultural to municipal and industrial uses, is of the same sort as a revision of public irrigation and commercial farm policies, as outlined previously, that benefit one group at the expense of another.

In areas of long-established water rights and publicly developed irrigation projects, these water supplies made available to farmers have become property with capitalized values based on greater streams of income over time. Also, the greater volume of trade and employment generated in these communities from water inputs and increased agricultural output serves as the base of definite capital values in the nonfarm sector of the rural communities involved. The value placed on these property rights and the nonfarm capital values are economic quantities justified in terms of public laws and investments and the economic outlook and forecast information available in past periods to farm and nonfarm investors in the particular water supply regions. To erode these income streams and capital values through a transfer of water to other locations and uses would not per se guarantee an increase in aggregative social welfare due to the income loss required for one sector to bring gain to another sector. Inability to make quantitative comparisons of the relative magnitude of utility and welfare gains and losses prohibits any such simple arithmetic.

However, means do exist for transfers which guarantee that the sector from which water supplies are diverted does not sacrifice for the gains of the recipient sector. Various forms of compensation can be used to guarantee a positive-sum outcome over both the losses of the farm and nonfarm enterprises in regions from which water is diverted and the gains in the other locations and uses to which it is transferred. This compensation would need to cover the discounted value of future income which erodes as water supplies and rights are withdrawn. A basic amount involved is the expected decline in asset values associated with reduced availability of water and withdrawal of rights in irrigated regions. But other social values and losses also are implied. These include social costs attached to reduced employment, population thinning, and the decay of community facilities as the economic base resting on water is withdrawn.

PRICING AND QUALITY OF WATER

This study provides quantitative results which can serve as a partial basis for farm compensation associated with reduced water use. The shadow prices attached to water and land under different variants of the programming model serve in this manner. With further analysis, the reduction in shadow prices associated with a shift from the current structure of water uses and returns in agriculture could be compared, area by area and region by region, with that resulting from a pattern needed to provide future municipal and industrial transfers. Capitalized, these decrements in shadow prices approximate the capital values for which farmers, now benefiting from water supplies and rights supplied through public investments and legal institutions, should be compensated. The magnitudes so represented do not, however, reflect compensation appropriate for the nonfarm sector of rural communities where economic activity is reduced or population shifts and decay of local institutions induce social costs.

Supposing implementation of appropriate compensation means to safeguard against welfare reductions in these communities, alternatives also exist through which water can be diverted from agriculture and increased in supply to municipal and industrial uses at indicated locations of water scarcity in 2000. An abrupt procedure, of course, would be that of legislating outright withdrawal of water rights from farmers in the water supply region of relevance. Another procedure with greater economic justification is a pricing system orienting water use toward the highest value alternatives in municipal, industrial, and farm uses. This pricing mechanism also could allow the public to recover fully its investment in water supply development so that both those who benefit from its value productivity eventually pay the associated costs and the public capital so restored can be invested repeatedly in further augmentations of water quality and quantity where they have positive net benefit/cost ratios exceeding other public alternatives.

Assuming a 300 million population without government program restraints, instituting a water-pricing system and increasing the price from $15 to $22.50 per acre-foot of irrigation water would reduce total irrigated land (and hence water use) in the 17 western states by 5.5 million acres. Concurrently, 3.1 million additional acres of annual crops (including corn and sorghum silages) would be grown on nonirrigated land. Also, 3.5 million additional acres of all hays and pasture would be grown on nonirrigated land. Increasing the water price further, from $22.50 to $30 would reduce total irrigated acreage by an additional 4.8 million acres and increase all crops grown on nonirrigated land by 3.7 million acres. In comparisons between the lowest price, $15, and the highest price, $30, for water, the acreage of annual crops (including corn and sorghum silages) grown on irrigated land would decline by 72.4 percent. Hence, the pricing of water not only would alter its allocation among agricultural, municipal, and industrial uses but also would bring about reallocations within agriculture. Water could still be used for irrigation but its concentration would be on high value crops. Much less would be employed for lower return uses such as pasture and hay production. For example, of the total water consumed by all crops with a water price of $15, about 70 percent is consumed by hay and pasture. With a water price of $30, hay and pasture consume about 50 percent of the total. As identified by this study, water supplies not only are large enough to allow ready attainment of projected food demand at reasonable real costs but also to allow some diversion of water to municipal and industrial uses at the scattered scarcity locations based on projections for 2000. Pricing and compensation means prevail whereby these reallocations can be attained with gains to some population and locational groups without sacrifice to others.

AGRICULTURAL POLICIES AND THE ENVIRONMENT

With 280 million population in 2000, attempts to improve the quality of the environment would not place undue stress or strain on the productive capacity of agriculture. With a ban on the use of insecticides in corn and cotton production (model E), the use of cropland and hay land would increase by about 3 million acres. Land irrigated and, hence, total water consumed also would increase slightly. Farm prices would rise only slightly.

With nearly 656 million acres of fragile lands removed from crop production (model F), cropland and hay land used would increase by about 30 million acres. Total irrigated acreage would remain unchanged but total water consumed would increase slightly. In general, with fragile lands removed, farm prices would rise about 12 percent over the comparable prices with fragile lands still in production. Government costs of removing these fragile lands from production would not be great, since a large amount of this land already is owned by the government.

Thus policies adopted to improve the quality of the environment would lead to higher farm incomes. Not all areas of the country, however, would gain from such policies. With a ban on insecticides in corn and cotton production, farmers in areas of the nation susceptible to severe damage from insects would be forced out of production. In areas of the nation where the insect population was very low or nonexistent, production of either corn or cotton or substitutes for these crops would increase. Businesses in rural communities would be similarly affected. It would decline in areas that cease or reduce production and increase in areas with higher levels of agricultural production.

Removal of fragile lands from crop production would have a bigger impact on agricultural land, water use, and farm prices than a ban on insecticides in corn and cotton production. Currently, most of the fragile lands in this nation are used for extensive types of crops such as dryland pasture and dryland wild hay. Thus those areas with agriculture structured around these crops would face the most severe adjustment problems with these lands removed from production, especially farmers in areas of the nation depending on grazing from public lands. Other areas of the nation would gain as additional cropland and hay land were brought into production to replace the output from these fragile lands. Some areas of the nation would reduce acreages of annual crops and increase acreages of forage or more extensive crops.

The negative effects, however, of such a program both nationwide and in those areas that suffer losses are potentially less than under alternative types of programs. A program to remove fragile lands from crop production would reduce wind and water erosion and have other positive effects on the environment. Siltation of streams and reservoirs could be reduced, the air would be cleaner, etc. Those areas with large amounts of fragile lands already are structured around an extensive agriculture, and adjustments would be less than if these same areas were structured around an intensive agriculture. Conceptually some of this fragile land could be devoted to recreation, trees, or other uses. Hence, certain areas would not be faced with elimination of all economic activity and certain areas might even experience a gain.

The supply capacity of agriculture would be reduced by such a program, but a considerable slack still would exist. With such a program, however, farm prices and incomes would be higher than if these lands were to remain in production at the implied demand level. And since the government already owns a large amount of the fragile lands in the nation, the government costs of the program would be less than for alternative types of price support and supply control programs.

Chapter 10: Environmental Quality and Land and Water Use

EARL O. HEADY, KENNETH J. NICOL and HOWARD C. MADSEN

This chapter reports results from the first of a sequence of resource use and environmental models being solved. The model set investigates restraints on nitrogen, phosphates, pesticides, animal wastes, and soil loss for 223 producing regions, 51 water supply regions, and 30 market regions. The delineation of these regions is the same as outlined in Chapter 9. (See Figures 9.7, 9.8, and 9.9. For the model of this chapter, three more market regions were added to those in Figure 9.9.)

Land use and environmentally related models can range from the micro or site-specific analysis of a particular urban fringe or small watershed to macro or national models. Detailed computer land-use and environmental models have emphasized site-specific or spatially localized problems and resource areas. Several factors contribute to this tendency: particular problems do relate to specific locations and must be solved at this level of disaggregation; research workers frequently do not have planning horizons allowing them to consider spatially extended models; and the time required and the intense data needs restrict analysts to localized problems and prevent extension to larger models and broader problems.

The set of models under way incorporates both (1) national or macro dimensions and (2) local areas (regions) and their agroclimatic and economic dimensions. These models currently emphasize land and water use, technological and environmental impacts, food supplies, farm costs and income, and employment effects as they relate to the nation's agricultural sector. However, they have great promise for analyzing the nation's total land and water use potentials as these relate to spatial distributions of population and economic activity, environmental standards, and related problems. The models have the capacity to evaluate simultaneously variables and outcomes in (1) national markets, prices, incomes and employment, and (2) production patterns, resource use, and economic structure of rather small resource regions under the posed imposition of alternative policies or futures. Models with these characteristics and capabilities are extremely important for the future as national, state, and local entities evaluate and consider implementation of environmental, land-use, water, and other resource and technological restraints related to problems emerging under the nation's advanced state of economic development. Otherwise, the programs and policies imposed by states, municipalities, and regional planning bodies will encounter unexpected economic effects, causing them to be nullified because they give inequitable distributions of the costs and benefits of the goals attained. For example, initial solutions of these models pose the certainty that individual states which impose restrained patterns of land use, water runoff, sedimentation, and technologies will find that, through market impacts, producers and resource owners of other states and locations will realize economic gains while those of the imposing state will bear the costs in lower incomes and reduced resource prices. Even for certain quality controls imposed at the national level, relative returns can be positive in some regions and negative in other regions.

While the models under construction emphasize land use, water technology, and environmental quality as they relate to the agricultural sector, with some modifications to accommodate sedimentation generated by highway and urban construction, they can be adapted eventually to incorporate a major share of society's aggregate land-use planning problems at the national level. They can, given various national objective functions and with planning restrained to conform with local goals in land use and technology, trace the impacts back to individual land and water resource regions. Or, conversely, the models also can trace the impacts of plans imposed independently at region or area levels to other regions and to the aggregate national level. Optimal patterns of land, water, and technology (fertilizer, insecticides, livestock scale and dispersion, etc.) use can be evaluated whether they relate to discrete regulations or pricing mechanisms imposed by the public. The models under construction also allow examination of the effect of different environmental and land-use programs on employment and income generation in rural areas and the potential reflection of these impacts through various agricultural structures as represented by different farm size and employment patterns.

Models which specify possibilities and outcomes at both the national and local levels can prove extremely important in future years and decades as the nation and states come to explore and require particular environmental quality and land-use controls. Not only can a range of problems at the national level be analyzed through them but also detailed land-use plans and potentials of localized areas can be inserted in them to allow estimation of economic interactions through national markets and interrelationships with other areas.

ROLE AND NATURE OF LAND-USE STUDIES

Studies relating to the use and planning of land and environmental quality fall into four major categories: (1) inventory and descriptive studies which quantify the physical amount and characteristics of land or its subclasses. Largely, the inventory-descriptive activities suggest the restraints on use in terms of upper limits on availability or physical suitability to various uses. Mapping of land according to potentials in use through physical limits and characteristics also falls in the inventory-descriptive category. (2) Predictive (usually statistical) studies which explain behavior in the use of land as it relates to economic, social, policy, and climatic and other variables. (3) Normative, optimizing or allocation models which explain how land ought to and could be used relative to variables and parameters which relate its potential use to physical, economic, and institutional restraints while considering the various goals or objectives (objective functions) of society, regional or other particular groups. (4) Simulation models which portray outcomes when variables surrounding land use take on various values. Both the normative programming and more conventional simulation models can be used to indicate outcomes when different policies or futures are to be examined or posed. Of course, other combinations of the above categories also can prevail. For example, descriptive studies of land indicate the quantity of each productivity group to serve as supply equations or restraints in a programming or allocative model. The predictive or statistical study can supply demand functions for the objective function of a nonlinear land or water allocation or normative study; or it can provide behavioral equations for a statistically based simulation model. Even a normative allocation model is an attempt to predict or estimate potentials in land use and environmental attainment relative to limits in land supply, food demand, exports, publicly improved limits, and other bounds. It incorporates both (1) physical features in terms of land characteristics, climatic variables, water supplies, and technology, and (2) economic and social features in terms of demand relations, resource costs, and public policies and goals.

The model summarized in this chapter largely is of the third category and indicates optimal spatial allocation of agricultural production and technology and land-use patterns relative to restraints in markets, natural resource supplies and locations, environmental quality controls, alternatives in domestic and export policies, etc. It can be used to simulate outcomes under various economic, policy technology, and natural endowment parameters and possibilities (or can be linked with other types of simulation models). Largely, however, models of this type specify optimal and potential land and water use and environmental possibilities relative to amounts and qualities of land classes, the distribution of population and economic activity, per capita income and food demand, transportation costs and facilities, capital and labor costs, and other relevant conditions which can be quantified.

The models reviewed in this chapter encompass the whole of U.S. agriculture and the land and water use relating thereto. These demand-allocation models incorporate all major agricultural commodities into a supply-demand, resource use, and environmental quality interaction reflecting restraints in resources for 223 agricultural producing regions, soil characteristics in 1,891 land resource groups, water resources for 51 water supply regions in the 17 western states, and demand or commodity balances in 30 consumer market regions. The models, which incorporate a transportation submodel for commodities and water and product transfer activities, allow selection of optimal resource use patterns and environmental quality impacts for the nation in future time periods. They also reflect comparative advantage in the allocation of land and water to competing alternatives as represented in relative yields, general technologies, environmentally restrained technologies, production costs, transport costs, and imposed environmental restraints. They allow substitution of land at one location for water at another location a thousand miles away (or vice versa). Similarly, they allow and analyze these substitutions when environmental restraints are applied to restrain the technologies used in any one resource region. Finally, they allow evaluation of various policy alternatives in use of land and water resources, and environmental quality controls in interaction with commercial agricultural policies, export goals, and domestic demands in both regional and national markets.

OBJECTIVES

The overall objectives in building these models are to determine (1) whether the nation has enough land and water resources to meet domestic and export food needs when various environmental quality restraints are imposed, (2) the optimum spatial allocation, for the nation and internally for each individual producing land and water region, of these resources accordingly, (3) the extent to which sacrifices must be made in environmental quality goals as other goals (food prices, exports, treasury costs, farm income, energy use, resource values, income distribution, etc.) are attained—or vice versa, (4) the cost to regions and the nation as various land-use patterns and environmental quality goals are attained, (5) the optimal selection among alternative producing technologies and land-use patterns, for each region and for the nation, as various environmental quality restraints are imposed, and (6) miscellaneous impacts including those relating to farm size and income, the distribution of the costs and benefits of these patterns or allocations, employment, and income generation in rural areas.

The models in the process of quantification incorporate variables relating to sediment loss, livestock wastes, irrigated and dryland farming, alternatives in farm and enterprise sizes, technologies using various levels of chemical fertilizers and pesticides—as well as all major crop and livestock commodities produced in each of 223 producing regions, 1,891 land resource groups, and 51 water supply regions in the western states. These models grow to very large size and can soon mount to thousands of equations and variables. A model of modest size is summarized and emphasizes land-use selection. It includes 3,800 equations and 30,000 real variables, including transportation.

Because of regional interdependencies, it is impossible to plan nationally efficient uses of land and environmental quality controls on a region-by-region or regionally independent basis. The models used for analysis and planning need to incorporate these interdependencies among the hundreds of land resource regions and allow for both direct and indirect impacts among regions whether they are contiguous or distant from each other. Not only do they need to incorporate these interdependencies among land resource regions, water regions, and market regions but also they need to allow them among resources and commodities. They need to allow substitution of land at one location for water at a different and distant location, since a policy restraint which limits the use of capital technology on land at one location can be offset by a reallocation or extended use of water at another location, or vice versa. Great flexibility prevails in the national livestock

ration, the major demand determinant in national land use, and shifts in or restraints on land use can allow or cause limits on grain production in one location
to be replaced by soybean, forage, or a substitute feed grain in another location.
An efficient land-use–environmental quality model needs to allow all these interdependencies over the nation with reflection back to optimal land employment for
each land resource region. The model reported allows full range of these substitutions and interrelations not only among the land resources of the many regions of
the nation but also among land, water, and capital technology and among the
many commodities of agriculture.

NATURE OF MODEL

The model projects to the year 2000 for a population of 284 million, free
market conditions with trend levels of agricultural technology in each of 223
agricultural producing regions, 1,891 land resource groups, and 51 water supply
regions. This model emphasizes optimal land-use patterns, agricultural water allocation, agricultural technology, and soil conservation methods under environmentally restrained soil loss. (Subsequent formulations of the model set include
environmental limits on chemical fertilizers, pesticides, and livestock wastes.) The
objective function in Equation 10.1 minimizes the cost of producing and transporting the various crop and livestock commodities among producing and land resource regions of origin, regions of processing, and regions of consumption. The
costs allow the system to consider different technologies (cropping or land-use
systems and mechanical practices) in restraining soil loss to alternative environmental quality levels. The costs of water consumption and transfer also are included in Equation 10.1. The programming prices and costs cover all factor costs
(except land rents which are reflected in shadow prices) and thus allow simulation
of a long-run market equilibrium for each commodity with a national allocation
reflecting the comparative advantage of each of the 223 producing regions, 1,891
land regions, and the 51 water supply regions—subject to environmental restraints
and the level and location of consumer demands. The objective function is to
minimize OF where

$$OF = \sum_i \left[\sum_k \left(\sum_m X_{ikm} \ UC_{ikm} + \sum_n Y_{ikn} \ UC_{ikn} + \sum_m Z_{ikm} \ UC_{ikm} \right) \right.$$

$$+ \sum_p L_{ip} \ UC_{ip} + DPP_i \ UC_i + IPP_i \ UC_i + DWH_i \ UC_i + IWH_i \ UC_i + FLG_i \ UC_i$$

$$\left. + FP_i \ UC_i \right] + \sum_w \left(WB_w \ UC_w + WD_w \ UC_w + WT_w \ UC_w \right)$$

$$+ \sum_t \sum_c T_{tc} \ UC_{tc} \tag{10.1}$$

where the variables, parameters, and other terms are defined in a following section.

RESTRAINTS AND VARIABLES

Each land group has alternative crop management systems producing commodities with associated yields and soil loss subject to the soil types, average weather prevailing, and conservation tillage practices utilized. Data were developed in conjunction with the Soil Conservation Service, USDA, to represent soil loss per acre under various mechanical practices and rotations or land-use systems. The soil loss alternatives are evaluated through a universal soil loss equation (10.2). The equation used for each crop management system is of the form

$$SL = K \cdot L \cdot S \cdot R \cdot C \cdot P \tag{10.2}$$

where SL is the per-acre gross soil loss
K the erodibility factor associated with the soil type
L the computed value relating slope length to soil loss control
S derived from a nonlinear function relating slope gradient to level of soil loss
R an index of erodibility for the rainfall of the area accounting for varying levels of intensity, duration, and measured rainfall
C an adjustment factor giving an index of the relative ability of alternative cropping patterns to reduce soil loss
P an adjustment factor to account for the potential soil loss reduction from adopting conservation practices

Each activity in the model represents an alternative crop management system which incorporates a given rotation, crop tillage method, and a conservation practice for an individual land resource group. The rotation and tillage method combine to give the unique C value and the conservation practice determines the P factor. The K, L, and S factors are dependent on the soil characteristics, and the regional rainfall patterns determine the R factor.

Associated with the alternative crop management systems are specific per-acre crop costs and crop yields. The average regional cost and yield data are adapted from other modeling efforts completed in the Center for Agricultural and Rural Development. The cost data reflect expenditures on machinery, labor, pesticides, nonnitrogen fertilizers (nitrogen is balanced endogenous to the model), and miscellaneous production items. The component costs reflect different efficiencies of farming resulting from working land in straight rows, contours, strip cropping, or with terraces. The alternative costs also reflect the higher pesticide requirements and lower machinery and labor requirements for crops under a reduced tillage cultivation pattern. The costs sum to an aggregate which depends on the particular cropping management system, and when combined with the outputs from the system, reflect the comparative advantage of each system on each land class in each region.

The outputs from the system reflect yields of each crop and the associated quantity of gross soil loss. The interaction within the system also is reflected in a nitrogen balance subsector where the nitrogen flows in the model are examined for each of the 223 producing areas. The nitrogen equations receive inputs from chemical fertilizers, biological processes of plants and soils, and livestock wastes. They provide outputs for crop production for each crop in each region and can be used to restrain chemical nitrogen inputs into crop production of the region, thus forcing nitrogen to be generated more or less within the agricultural system of the area if the decision is invoked at different levels. The entire cost and yield section of the model is interlocked with alternative technologies, levels of resource input, and alternative input uses to meet domestic and export demands. As an example of other interrelationships in the model, consider the nitrogen-fertilizer–crop-yield section. Nitrogen available in an individual region is an independent variable in the crop yield equation but the source of the nitrogen may vary. It can be supplied from chemical fertilizers, livestock wastes, and nitrogen fixation by legumes. For legumes the amount of nitrogen produced is dependent on their yield, which in turn is dependent on the early spring nitrogen availability (through fertilizer) and the nonnitrogen fertilizer availability on the type and quantity of feed available for livestock and the concentration of the animals in the region. Also affecting the yields of the crop is the land class on which it is grown and the conservation and tillage practice associated with the cropping management system.

Each region also has a livestock waste equation which can be used to examine this facet of environmental quality control. By setting restraints on waste levels or dispersion at different levels, the density of livestock and waste production at different quality control levels can be examined. The nitrogen, animal waste, and soil loss restraints will be affected in more complex ways in later models which include other fertilizers and pesticides. Nitrogen is only balanced in this model. Dispersion of livestock and its waste is restrained only to the extent that each of the regions must use wastes produced therein at limited levels. The main emphasis is on soil loss controls.

Both dryland and irrigated crop variables are included for producing regions in the 17 western states which grow irrigated crops, and the model allows selection among dryland or irrigated farming for each region. A range of livestock rations (variables) is allowed in all producing regions since the least-cost feed mix can be drawn from various grain, forage, and pasture crops grown in the region or imported (where allowed) from others. The model includes variables representing various cropping systems and technologies affecting soil loss, livestock production, commodity transportation, water transfers, consumer demand fulfillment, and alternative export levels.

Each of the 223 producing regions has land restraints of the nature indicated in Equations 10.3 to 10.9. Each region has a soil loss restraint as in Equation 10.10, a nitrogen balance as in Equation 10.11, and a pasture restraint as in Equation 10.12. Each water supply region has a water restraint as in Equation 10.13, where variables and parameters are defined subsequently.

Each of the 30 consuming regions has net demand equations for all of the relevant crop and livestock activities as illustrated by Equation 10.14. Regional consumer demand quantities were determined exogenously from geographic and national projections of population, economic activity, per capita incomes, and international exports through the region for 2000. National demands were defined for cotton and sugar beets as indicated in Equation 10.15. Poultry products, sheep, and other livestock were regulated at the consuming region level. International trade was regulated at the regional levels as indicated in Equations 10.16 and 10.17.

Commodities included in the endogenous analysis are soil loss, nitrogen, water, corn, sorghum, wheat, barley, oats, soybeans, cotton, sugar beets, tame hay, wild hay, improved pasture, unimproved and woodland pasture, cropland pasture, public grazing lands, forest lands grazed, all dairy products, pork, and beef. Also accounted for prior to solution of the model are other crops including fruits, nuts, vegetables, rice, flax, broilers, turkeys, egg production, and sheep and other livestock.

Dryland cropland restraint, each region by land class:

$$\sum_m X_{ikm} \, a_{ikm} \leqslant LD_{ik} \qquad (10.3)$$

Irrigated cropland restraint, each region by land class:

$$\sum_n Y_{ikn} \, a_{ikn} + \sum_m Z_{ikm} \, a_{ikm} \leqslant LR_{ik} \qquad (10.4)$$

Dryland wild hay restraint, each region:

$$DWH_i \, a_i \leqslant ADWH_i \qquad (10.5)$$

Irrigated wild hay restraint, each region:

$$IWH_i \, a_i \leqslant AIWH_i \qquad (10.6)$$

Dryland permanent pasture restraint, each region:

$$DPP_i \, a_i \leqslant ADPP_i \qquad (10.7)$$

Irrigated permanent pasture restraint, each region:

$$IPP_i \, a_i \leqslant AIPP_i \qquad (10.8)$$

Forest land grazed restraint, each region:

$$FLG_i \, a_i \leqslant AFLG_i \qquad (10.9)$$

Soil loss restraint, each region, each land class, each activity:

$$SL_{ikm+n} \leqslant ASL_{ikm+n} \qquad (10.10)$$

Nitrogen balance restraint, each region:

$$FP_i + \sum_p L_{ip} \, b_{ip} + EL_i b_i - EC_i f_i -$$

$$\sum_k \left(\sum_m X_{ikm} \, f_{ikm} + \sum_n Y_{ikn} \, f_{ikn} + \sum_m Z_{ikm} \, f_{ikm} \right)$$

$$- DPP_i \, f_i - IPP_i \, f_i - DWH_i \, f_i - IWH_i \, f_i - FLG_i \, f_i = 0 \quad (10.11)$$

Pasture use restraint, each region:

$$\sum_k \left(\sum_m X_{ikm}\ r_{ikm} + \sum_n Y_{ikn}\ r_{ikn} + \sum_m Z_{ikm}\ r_{ikm} \right) + DPP_i\ r_i$$

$$+ IPP_i\ r_i + FLG_i\ r_i - \sum_p L_{ip}\ q_{ip} - EL_i\ q_i \geqslant 0 \quad (10.12)$$

Water use restraint, each water region:

$$WB_w \pm WT_w \pm WI_w - WO_w - WX_w - WE_w + WD_w - \sum_{i \in w} IWH_i\ d_i - \sum_{i \in w} IPP_i\ d_i$$

$$- \sum_{i \in w} \sum_k \left(\sum_m X_{ikm}\ d_{ikm} + \sum_n Y_{ikn}\ d_{ikn} + \sum_m Z_{ikm}\ d_{ikm} \right)$$

$$- \sum_{i \in w} \sum_p L_{ip}\ d_{ip} - \sum_{i \in w} PN_i\ d_i \geqslant 0 \quad (10.13)$$

Commodity balance restraint, each consuming region:

$$\sum_{i \in j} \sum_k \left(\sum_m X_{ikm}\ cy_{ikmc} + \sum_n Y_{ikn}\ cy_{iknc} + \sum_m Z_{ikm}\ cy_{ikmc} \right) \pm \sum_{i \in j} \sum_p L_{ip}\ cy_{ipc}$$

$$\pm \sum_{t \in j} T_{tc} \pm E_{jc} - \sum_{i \in j} PN_i\ cy_{ic} - EL_j\ cy_{jc} \geqslant 0 \quad (10.14)$$

National commodity balance restraints, for cotton, sugar beets, and spring wheat:

$$\sum_i \sum_k \left(\sum_m X_{ikm}\ cy_{ikmg} + \sum_n Y_{ikn}\ cy_{ikng} + \sum_m Z_{ikm}\ cy_{ikmg} \right)$$

$$- \sum_i PN_i\ cy_{ig} - EX_g \geqslant 0 \quad (10.15)$$

National export restraints:

$$\sum_j E_{jc} \geqslant EX_c \quad\quad\quad\quad\quad (10.16)$$

National import restraints:

$$\sum_i E_{ic+e} \leqslant IM_{c+e} \quad\quad\quad\quad (10.17)$$

Nonnegativity restraints:

$$X_{ikm},\ Y_{ikn},\ Z_{ikm},\ L_{ip},\ DWH_i,\ IWH_i,\ DPP_i,\ IPP_i,\ FLG_i,\ FP_i,\ EL_i,\ WB_w,$$

$$WT_w,\ WI_w,\ WD_w,\ WX_w,\ WE_w,\ PN_i,\ T_{tc},\ E_{jc},\ E_{ic+e} \geqslant 0 \quad (10.18)$$

The subscripts and variables for the above equations are defined in the following section.

SUBSCRIPTS AND VARIABLES OF THE MODEL

The subscripts and variables relating to the equations in the text are those which follow:

subscripts

$c = 1, 2, \ldots, 15$ for the endogenous commodities in the model

$e = 1, 2, \ldots, 5$ for the exogenous livestock alternatives considered

$g = 1, 2, 3$ for the commodities balanced at the national level

$i = 1, 2, \ldots, 223$ for the producing areas of the model

$j = 1, 2, \ldots, 30$ for the consuming regions of the model

$k = 1, 2, \ldots, 9$ for the land classes in each producing area

$m = 1, 2, \ldots,$ for the dryland crop management systems on a land class in a producing area

$n = 1, 2, \ldots,$ for the irrigated crop management systems on a land class in a producing area

$p = 1, 2, \ldots,$ for the livestock activities defined in the producing area

$t = 1, 2, \ldots, 458$ for the transportation routes in the model

$w = 1, 2, \ldots, 51$ for the water supply regions in the model

variables

$a,$ amount of land used by the associated activity from the land base as indicated by the subscripts

$AIPP,$ number of acres of irrigated permanent pasture available in the subscripted producing area

$ADWH,$ number of acres of dryland wild (noncropland) hay available in the subscripted producing area

$AFLG,$ number of acres of forest land available for grazing in the subscripted producing area

$ADPP,$ number of acres of dryland permanent pasture available for use in the subscripted producing area

$AIWH,$ number of acres of irrigated wild (noncropland) hay available in the subscripted producing area

$ASL,$ per-acre allowable soil loss subscripted for land class, producing area, and activity

$b,$ units of nitrogen equivalent fertilizer produced by livestock, subscripted for producing area and activity

$cy,$ interaction coefficient (yield or use) of the relevant commodity as regulated by the associated activity and specified by the subscripts

$d,$ per-unit of activity water use coefficient as regulated by the associated activity and specified by the subscripts

$DPP,$ level of use of dryland permanent pasture in the subscripted producing area

$DWH,$ level of use of dryland wild (noncropland) hay in the subscripted producing area

$E,$ level of net export for the associated commodity in the associated region as specified by the subscripts

EC, level of exogenous crop production by subscripted region

EL, level of exogenous livestock production consistent with the subscripted region

EX, level of national net export for the subscripted commodity as determined exogenous to the model

f, units of nitrogen equivalent fertilizer required by the associated activity and specified by subscripts

FLG, level of forest land grazed in the subscripted producing area

FP, number of pounds of nitrogen equivalent fertilizer purchased in the subscripted producing area

IM, level of national net imports for the subscripted commodities as determined exogenous to the model

IPP, level of use of the irrigated permanent pasture in the subscripted region

IWH, level of use of the irrigated wild (noncropland) hay in the subscripted region

L, level of the livestock activity with the type and region dependent on the subscripts

LD, number of areas of dryland cropland available for use as specified by the region and land class subscripts

LR, number of acres of irrigated cropland available for use as specified by the region and land class subscripts

PN, level of population projected to be in the subscripted region

q, units of pasture, in hay equivalents, consumed by the associated livestock activity and specified by the subscripts

r, units of aftermath or regular pasture, in hay equivalents, produced by the associated cropping or pasture activity and identified by the subscripts

SL, level of soil loss associated with any activity over the range $m + n$ in the region and land class designated by the subscripts

T, level of transportation of a unit of the commodity either into or out of the consuming region designated by the subscripts

UC, cost per unit of the associated activity and specified by subscripts

WB, level of water purchase for use in the water balance of the water supply region designated by the subscript

WD, level of desalting of ocean water in the water supply region designated by the subscript

WE, level of water to be exported from the water supply region subscripted

WI, level of movement of water in or out of the water supply region through the interbasin transfer network

WO, level of water requirement for onsite uses such as mining, navigation, and estuary maintenance in the water supply region subscripted

WT, unit of natural flow of water from the region

WX, level of water use for the exogenous agricultural crops and livestock in the water supply region subscripted

      X, level of employment of the dryland crop management system, rotation, in the region and on the land class as designated by the subscripts

      Y, level of employment of the irrigated crop management system, rotation, in the region and on the land class as designated by the subscripts

      Z, level of employment of the dryland crop management system, rotation, on the land class in the region as designated by the subscripts when the land has been designated as available for irrigated cropping patterns

ILLUSTRATION OF RESULTS

Solution of the model provides indication of optimal land use in each producing region and each land resource group at prescribed levels of environmental quality restraints, consumer demand and distribution, export levels and other policy, or market and technology parameters. Our illustration is in the case where the only environmental restraint is soil loss. It also designates the level of production in each region and the optimal flows of commodities to consuming regions and export markets. For purposes of illustration, we refer to solutions where (1) soil loss is not restricted and (2) soil loss is restricted to 5 tons per acre per year for each soil resource group and exports are at a given level. While land use could be mapped or indicated by each of the 1,891 land resource groups, we illustrate on the basis of the 223 producing regions only. The model not only indicates land devoted to each crop use in each region and group but also can indicate technologies for each, such as dryland or irrigated, alternative rotations, conventional or reduced tillage methods, and others which affect land and water use and sedimentation.

Figure 10.1 indicates an optimal distribution of row crop acreage among the 223 producing regions, Figure 10.2 indicates an optimal distribution of the close grown crops, and Figure 10.3 gives the hayland distribution when no restraints are placed on soil loss or chemical nitrogen use. The model allows indication of production of each crop, acreage of each crop and erosion control practice, soil loss, livestock production, shadow prices and resource prices, and commodity prices by the individual regions shown in Figures 9.1 and 9.2. Because of space limitations, these detailed maps are not included here. In a later publication, we will depict distribution of land uses and technologies by land resource groups. The models are able to generate large amounts of data of this type which reflect optimal land use and environmental restraint distributions among individual natural resource regions when goals and markets prevail at the national level. Mapping models can be formulated so that location and extent of use of land in each region by each crop can be indicated automatically when national and environmental goals or policies are imposed and national and regional markets are reflected. These maps, which we do not present here, also can detail by regions the optimum method of soil loss control by individual regions—considering

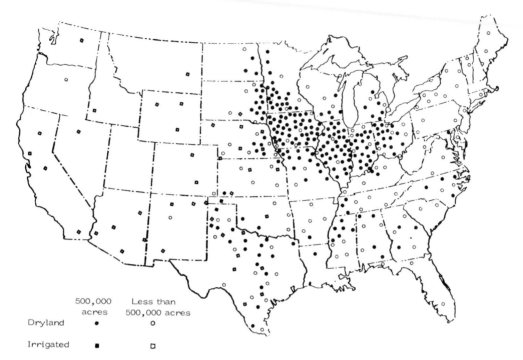

Fig. 10.1. Location of dryland and irrigated row crops with no soil loss restriction in 2000.

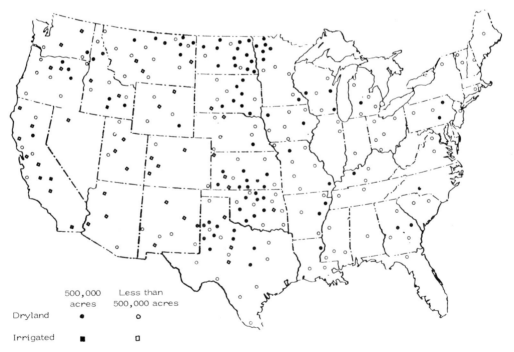

Fig. 10.2. Location of dryland and irrigated close-grown crops with no soil loss restriction in 2000.

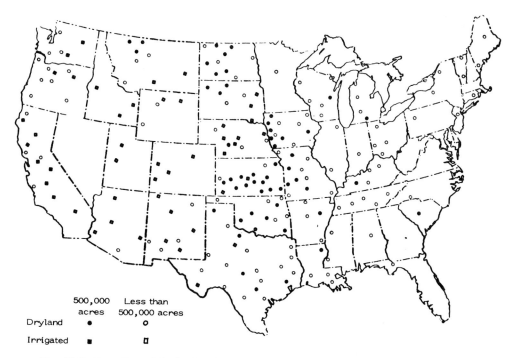

Fig. 10.3. Location of dryland and irrigated hay with no soil loss restriction in 2000.

the physical nature of soil and climatic variables in all regions and the comparative advantage of each in terms of land characteristics, yields, production and transportation costs, and national and regional markets.

SOIL LOSS

While land use, tillage methods, and soil loss are generated in the models by producing regions and land resource groups, we summarize results for only seven major geographic regions of the United States because of time and space restraints. While solutions of the model were made for several soil loss, export, and nitrogen restriction levels, we similarly summarize solutions for only two soil loss levels, one export level, and one unrestrained nitrogen use (except for nitrogen balance within a producing region).

Restricting soil loss per acre to 5 tons would distribute land use and technologies interregionally to reduce national soil loss to 727 million tons. Without the restriction, interregional land use allocations and technologies to meet export demands would generate a national soil loss 3.5 times greater, or 2.68 billion tons. As Table 10.1 indicates, the reduction in average per-acre soil loss, as a source of sedimentation, would be extremely large on land classes V to VIII, which are most erosive. While we do not do so here, our models allow indication of soil loss changes by each individual region.

Regional variation in reduced soil loss per acre is great. Largest reductions take place in the South Atlantic (18.2 tons) and South Central (11.5 tons) regions where land and current land-use methods give rise to serious erosion (Table 10.2). The reduction in soil loss when a 5 ton per acre limit is imposed is attained especially by a switch from conventional tillage–straight-row farming to contour, strip-cropping, and terraces (Table 10.3). There also is a significant shift to reduced tillage farming practices to attain the environmentally attained soil loss of 5 tons per acre. Acres receiving reduced tillage practices increase from around 21 million in the unrestricted solution to near 58 million acres under the 5-ton solution. Conventional tillage practices decline from 248 million acres under the unrestricted soil loss to 201 million acres under the solution for a 5-ton soil loss. Within the conventional tillage group, straight-row farming is nearly halved. Contouring is tripled and strip-cropping–terracing practices are increased 1,000 percent to meet soil loss restrictions (Table 10.3). While reduced tillage nearly triples and very large increases occur in contouring, terracing, and strip cropping, straight-row methods of reduced tillage do not increase importantly.

The shift in acreages (Table 10.4) is partly hidden in the reduction of 16.5 million acres used for grain crops and a corresponding increase of only 5.5 million acres in hay on cultivated lands (Table 10.4). Part of the production required to meet national demands comes from an increase in noncropland roughage production (permanent hay and pasture). More of the reduced acreage required to meet the demand for agricultural products results because of the shift in production to the higher cost and higher-yielding erosion control practices. Also a shift in acreage between land classes puts the grain crops on the higher-yielding and less erosive lands.

Costs of production, in conjunction with the transportation network and the soil loss restrictions imposed, determine the national equilibrium prices for the commodities. Table 10.5 indicates the relative equilibrium prices of the commodities generated by the model under the two levels of soil loss and a single export level. Soil loss restrictions have the largest effect on prices for commodities which concentrate on land with high soil loss potential. Compared to absence of soil loss restrictions, cotton and soybean prices increase over 20 percent while wheat and hay crops increase by less than 10 percent. The increases in grain prices result in corresponding increases in cattle prices. In evaluating the effect of any environmental policy alternative, the effect on the desired parameter and the change in farm price of agricultural products are two easily observed changes in our models.

Changes summarized at the national level do not, of course, reflect the effects in particular regions and on individual enterprises. These, however, are all available from our models. The shift in production from one region to another results in income repercussions on the rural community affected. The effect of such a shift depends on the degree of multiple level resource use. As grain production shifts, livestock activities also may drift away from the region and underemployment of resources may occur in one region as prosperity is promoted in another rural area.

The data in Tables 10.1 to 10.5 indicate that American agriculture has great capacity and flexibility in adapting to certain environmental quality goals. By shifting land use among the many producing regions and land resource groups in terms of their comparative advantage in yields, commodity costs, location, and transportation, national and regional demands can be met without large increases in food prices and costs for consumers at the export level examined. The level of exports per se may have greater impact on consumer food costs than does a relatively wide adaptation of agriculture and land use to environmental quality goals. The quantitative analysis of these possibilities, along with other environmental quality practices, will be analyzed in upcoming models.

FURTHER ANALYSES

The model outlined above is the first in a series which incorporates environmental quality considerations with the planning of water and land use and the analysis of agricultural production potentials on a region-by-region, as well as a national, basis. Models under way also incorporate sediment transport sectors by watersheds and direct restraints on use and distribution of nitrogen, phosphates, insecticides, and animal wastes. They measure the impact of these restraints with various levels of exports, the location of production by region (on both restrained and unrestrained national bases), the distributions of cropping and erosion control practices and soil loss by land classes of individual regions, the region-by-region effects on farm income and resource values, and other interrelated phenomena. These models rather fully incorporate all facets of agricultural, resource, and environmental planning.

Chapter 11: Quadratic Programming of Spatial Equilibrium

HARRY H. HALL, EARL O. HEADY,
ARTHUR L. STOECKER, and VINCENT A. SPOSITO

Linear programming has been used to obtain an optimal solution in all the previous models. Such a solution, if it exists, is theoretically guaranteed by linear programming. However, the use of linear programming requires us to make some rather restrictive assumptions such as given prices or given demand quantities. This tends to limit the empirical usefulness of the results. If such assumptions are to be eliminated, we have to resort either to lengthy and expensive iterative procedures[1] or to nonlinear programming. If the latter is used, we are no more guaranteed the compatibility of the results with theoretic requirements. Thus, for instance, solutions to nonlinear programming problems are not necessarily efficient. Hence, before any particular nonlinear programming model is used to derive empirical information, its relation to accepted theory has to be established.

In this chapter we propose a quadratic programming model for U.S. agriculture. We will show that the results satisfy the usual equilibrium conditions.[2] We also apply the model to U.S. agriculture and compare with Brokken's results.[3] We will begin by discussing briefly (1) the use of the term *efficiency* in the subsequent analysis and (2) the linear case to bring out some characteristics important for the presentation and realization of the potential advantages of our model.

---

1. See, for example, L. F. Schrader and G. A. King, "Regional Location of Beef Cattle Feeding," *J. Farm Econ.* 44 (1962): 64–81.

2. This discussion heavily draws upon Yakir Plessner and Earl O. Heady, "Competitive Equilibrium Solution with Quadratic Programming," *Metroeconomica* 17 (Sept.–Dec. 1965): 117–30; Yakir Plessner, "Quadratic Programming Competitive Equilibrium Models for the U.S. Agricultural Sector," Ph.D. diss., Iowa State Univ. Library, Ames, 1965.

3. See Chapter 5.

EFFICIENCY

Koopmans defines efficiency as follows:

An attainable bundle of activities is called an efficient bundle if there exists no attainable bundle which produces more of some desired commodity and no less of any other desired commodity.[4]

An attainable bundle of activities is a feasible one, i.e., one for which resource use does not exceed the supply.   Dorfman, Samuelson, and Solow give a similar definition of efficiency:

We then describe an input-output pattern $(x_1, \ldots, x_n; r_1, \ldots, r_m)$ as efficient if (1) it is a feasible pattern; and (2) if there is no other feasible pattern $(y_1, \ldots, y_n; s_1, \ldots, s_m)$ which is such that $y_1 \geqslant x_1, \ldots, y_n \geqslant x_n$, with at least one strict inequality, and $s_1 \leqslant r_1, \ldots, s_m \leqslant r_m$.[5]

Dorfman et al. add the observation, "Efficiency is a purely technological concept having to do only with production."[6]   Neither definition mentions prices.

For convenience let $x = (x_1, \ldots, x_n)$, $y = (y_1, \ldots, y_n)$, $r = (r_1, \ldots, r_m)$ and $s = (s_1, \ldots, s_m)$. x and y are vectors in the output space (the space of desired commodities in Koopmans' terminology); r and s are vectors in the input space (the space of primary commodities in Koopmans' terminology).   Intermediate commodities are ignored for simplicity.

It will be useful to distinguish between two aspects of efficiency—output efficiency and input efficiency.   If $r = \bar{r}$ (i.e., the quantities of inputs are fixed), the vector x is output efficient if there does not exist another vector y such that $y_j \geqslant x_j$, $j = 1, \ldots, n$, with strict inequality holding at least once.   Output is maximized in the sense that, if all outputs, except one, are fixed, production will be output efficient if output of the remaining commodity is maximized.   Figure 11.1 illustrates output efficiency for two outputs and three inputs when output is a linear function of inputs. $ABCD$ is the efficiency frontier for all vectors x such that $Ax \leqslant \bar{r}$, where $\bar{r}$ is fixed.   At B, for example, x_1 can increase only if x_2 decreases.   Interior points, such as I, are inefficient because, for any northeastward movement, x_1 and x_2 increase simultaneously.   Clearly, the efficiency frontier may have many efficient points.

If $x = \bar{x}$ (i.e., the quantities of outputs are fixed), the vector r is input efficient if there does not exist another vector s such that $s_i \leqslant r_i$, $i = 1, \ldots, m$, with strict inequality holding at least once.   Inputs are minimized in the sense that, if all inputs, except one, are fixed, production will be input efficient if input of the remaining resource is minimized.   Figure 11.2 illustrates input efficiency for two inputs and three outputs,[7] for the case of linear production again. $EFGH$ is the efficiency frontier for a vector r such that $A\bar{x} \leqslant r$, where $\bar{x}$ is fixed.   At F, r_2 decreases only if r_1 increases.   From I, however, r_1 and r_2 decrease simultaneously for any southwestward movement.

4. Tjalling C. Koopmans, *Three Essays on the State of Economic Science*, McGraw-Hill, New York, 1957, p. 84.
5. Robert Dorfman, Paul A. Samuelson, and Robert M. Solow, *Linear Programming and Economic Analysis*, McGraw-Hill, New York, 1958, p. 392.
6. Ibid.
7. Ibid., p. 24.

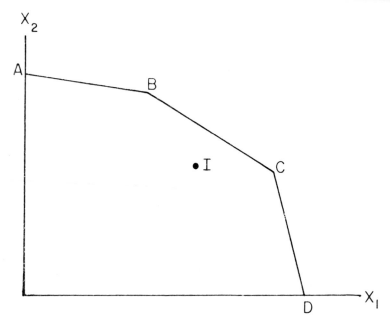

Fig. 11.1. Efficiency frontier in the output space.

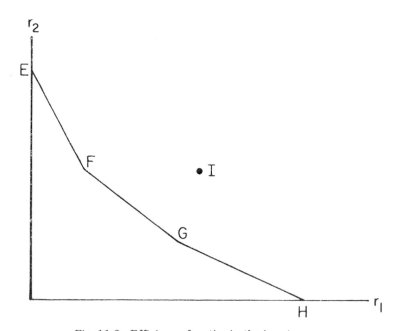

Fig. 11.2. Efficiency frontier in the input space.

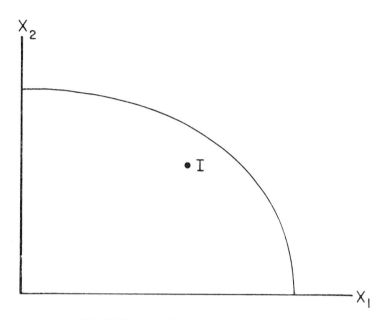

Fig. 11.3. A product transformation curve.

Output efficiency and input efficiency can be regarded as two sides of the same coin—one is impossible without the other. Suppose not. Suppose that (x, r) is an input-output bundle for which x is efficient but r is not. Then there is another input-output bundle (y, s) such that $y \geqslant x$ and $s \leqslant r$, $s_i < r_i$ for at least one i. y need not be greater than x; $y = x$ is sufficient. There is an acceptable s by assumption. By definition, x is not efficient and we have reached a contradiction. Thus x is not efficient unless r is. The argument can be reversed to show that r is not efficient unless x is.

Both Koopmans and Dorfman et al. emphasize output efficiency almost to the exclusion of input efficiency. Both stress the efficiency frontier, as illustrated in Figure 11.1. Koopmans, for example, elaborating on his definition, says, "The definition expresses that within the limitations of technology and resources no opportunity to increase the output of some desired commodity while holding the line on others has been overlooked or passed up."[8] It seems very clear from the definition of Dorfman et al., however, that there is at least one efficient input combination for every output and at least one efficient output combination for every input. Suppose, in Figure 11.1, that $I = (x^I, r^I)$. If there does not exist an s such that $s_i \leqslant r_i^I$, $i = 1, \ldots, m$, with strict inequality holding at least once, then by the Dorfman definition, x^I is efficient. A similar argument can be used to show that r^I can be efficient. If x^I is produced efficiently, not all available resources will be used, it is true. Specifically, $\bar{r} - r^I$ resources will be idle. This is not necessarily inconsistent with the Dorfman definition, however.

Both definitions are couched in the language of activity analysis, but the con-

8. Koopmans, *Three Essays*, p. 84.

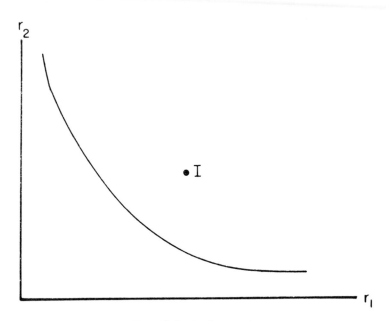

Fig. 11.4. An isoquant.

cept of efficiency also applies in the case of classical production. The product transformation curve in Figure 11.3 results from fixed inputs.[9] It represents an efficiency frontier in the same manner as $ABCD$ in Figure 11.1; an interior point is inefficient in exactly the same sense. The isoquant in Figure 11.4 is for fixed outputs.[10] It represents an efficiency frontier in the same manner as $EFGH$ of Figure 11.2; an interior point is inefficient in exactly the same sense.

Some authors[11] distinguish technological efficiency from economic efficiency. As we have seen, technological efficiency emphasizes only the technical relationships between inputs and outputs. Economic efficiency considers prices (implicitly consumer preferences and the motivations of resource holders) as well as the technological conditions of production. Given a set of prices, however, it is possible to specify which of many technologically efficient points is also economically efficient. In Figure 11.5, for example, k is one of a family of parallel lines of the form $p_1 x_1 + p_2 x_2 = k$, k a constant. For the prices p_1 and p_2, B is the optimal efficient point. Koopmans[12] and Dorfman et al.[13] show that, in the linear case, every efficient point is optimal for at least one set of prices.

To summarize, efficiency is a phenomenon of production; it describes a particular relationship between inputs and outputs. Production of a given output

9. See James M. Henderson and Richard E. Quandt, *Microeconomic Theory*, McGraw-Hill, New York, 1958, p. 68.

10. Ibid., p. 47.

11. See Earl O. Heady, *Economics of Agricultural Production and Resource Use*, Prentice-Hall, Englewood Cliffs, N.J., 1952, p. 98; Tiber Scitovsky, *Welfare and Competition*, Richard D. Irwin, Chicago, 1951, Ch. 8.

12. Koopmans, *Three Essays*, p. 88.

13. Dorfman, Samuelson, and Solow, *Linear Programming*, p. 395.

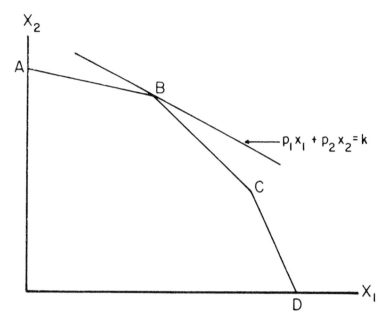

Fig. 11.5. Optimal efficient point for given prices.

is input efficient if no input can be reduced without increasing some other input. Production from given inputs is output efficient if no output can be increased without decreasing some other output. Although this fact has been neglected, nothing in the Dorfman definition precludes efficient interior points; that is, points other than those on the efficiency frontier may be efficient.

LINEAR MODELS

Plessner set out to formulate a model that permits the computation of "efficient points in general, and that efficient point which is associated with market equilibrium in particular."[14] He argues that the solution to such a model must have the following characteristics:[15]

B.1. Be efficient.
B.2. Guarantee maximum gross and net profits for the sector and for each firm in the sector.
B.3. Guarantee nonpositive net profits for any firm in any activity.
B.4. Be brought about by a free market which generates prices so as to equate supply and demand.

He first shows that linear models with these characteristics can be formulated, but he observes that they are impracticable for large problems because they require expensive iterative solution procedures. He then formulates a nonlinear (quadratic) model with these characteristics.

14. Plessner, "Quadratic Programming Competitive Equilibrium Models," p. 27.
15. Ibid., p. 28.

In this and subsequent discussions, lower case letters denote vectors, capital letters denote matrices, and prime (') denotes transposition. (The transposition symbol may be omitted if it is clear that an expression is the scalar product of two vectors.) These symbols are used:

x is an n vector of output levels
p an n vector of output prices
c an n vector of pecuniary costs for the purchased inputs associated with x
b an m vector of limited resources
A an $m \times n$ technology matrix
u an m vector of imputed prices for the limited resources

In addition, the postulates of linear activity analysis are assumed to hold.[16]   In particular, production is represented by a set of reproducible "basic activities" for which the additivity postulate holds. Supply functions for unrestricted inputs are assumed perfectly elastic so that their prices can be regarded as fixed (i.e., c is a vector of constants). Finally, consumer demand is represented by a set of linear demand functions

$$d = d(p) \tag{11.1}$$

These definitions and assumptions will be useful in the search for a model to satisfy B.1 to B.4. The search begins with problem I.

1. PROBLEM I[17]

Suppose that p and c are given (i.e., they are vectors of constants). Problem I maximizes

$$f(x) = (p - c)x \tag{11.2}$$

subject to

$$Ax \leqslant b \tag{11.3}$$

$$x \geqslant 0 \tag{11.4}$$

If $(p - c) \geqslant 0$, the optimal solution, $\bar{x}$, is always efficient.[18]   If for some i $(p_i - c_i) = 0$ and if the constraint set has the form illustrated in Figure 11.6, the solution may not be efficient. In Figure 11.6, $(p_1 - c_1) = 0$ for any point on EF is a possible solution but only F is efficient. For any point between E and F, x_1 can increase without affecting x_2. In this special case, the efficiency frontier consists of only the portion FG. Since this case presents a difficulty only if $p_1 - c_1 = 0$, let us ignore it and assume that the solution to problem I is efficient.[19]

16. Tjalling C. Koopmans and Augustus F. Bausch, "Selected Topics in Economics Involving Mathematical Reasoning," *SIAM Rev.* (July 1959) 1:79–148.
17. Problem I corresponds to Plessner's problem 1. See Plessner, "Quadratic Programming Competitive Equilibrium Models," p. 28.
18. Dorfman, Samuelson, and Solow, *Linear Programming*, pp. 394–95.
19. Efficiency is used here in the sense of output efficiency for all resources represented by *EFG*.

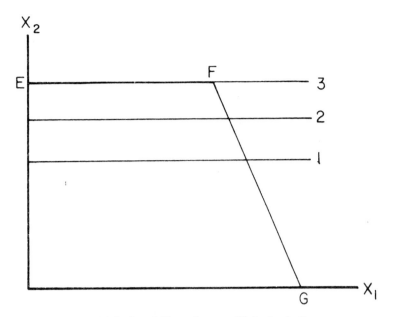

Fig. 11.6. Possibility of a nonefficient solution.

Plessner argues[20] that, if problem I has the decentralization property, it also satisfies B.2. He observes that it is difficult, because of aggregation bias, to ensure that practical problems have this property; but he ignores this difficulty.

The dual to problem I minimizes

$$g(u) = bu \tag{11.5}$$

subject to

$$A'u \geqslant p - c \tag{11.6}$$

$$u \geqslant 0 \tag{11.7}$$

By the duality theorem of linear programming,[21] $g(u) \geqslant f(x)$ and $g(\bar{u}) = f(\bar{x})$, where $\bar{u}$ is the optimal dual solution and $\bar{x}$ is the optimal primal solution.

2. PROBLEM II[22]

Problem I and its dual can be treated as a primal-dual combination. Problem II maximizes

$$F(x, u) = (p - c) x - bu \tag{11.8}$$

subject to 11.3, 11.4, 11.6, and 11.7. Dorfman et al.[23] observe that 11.8 can be

20. Plessner, "Quadratic Programming Competitive Equilibrium Models," p. 31.
21. Saul I. Gass, *Linear Programming*, 2nd ed., McGraw-Hill, New York, 1964.
22. Problem II corresponds to Plessner's problem 2. See Plessner, "Quadratic Programming Competitive Equilibrium Models," p. 28.
23. Dorfman, Samuelson, and Solow, *Linear Programming*, p. 405.

regarded as a net profit function. By the duality theorem, $F(x, u) \leqslant 0$ for all feasible (x, u) and $F(\bar{x}, \bar{u}) = 0$ where $(\bar{x}, \bar{u})$ is the optimal solution.

Since including the primal and dual in the same problem does not affect the optimal solution $(\bar{x}, \bar{u})$, problem II satisfies B.1 and B.2 if problem I does. Constraint 11.6 assures that problem II also satisfies B.3. However, B.4 requires that supply equal demand, i.e., $\bar{x} = d(\bar{p})$ where p is the equilibrium price vector. If it were possible to always choose the correct prices, $\bar{p}$, problem II would satisfy all the requirements, B.1 to B.4. But it is unlikely that a set of prices, selected arbitrarily, will equate supply and demand. The model needs a mechanism for determining market price.

3. PROBLEM III[24]

Problem III is another primal-dual problem. It maximizes

$$G(x, u, w) = \bar{d}w - cx - bu \tag{11.9}$$

subject to

$$Ax \leqslant b \tag{11.10}$$

$$w - A'u \leqslant c \tag{11.11}$$

$$-x \leqslant -\bar{d} \tag{11.12}$$

$$x, u, w \leqslant 0 \tag{11.13}$$

$\bar{d} = d(\bar{p})$ is the quantity demanded in equilibrium and w is a vector of imputed prices for the outputs, $\bar{d}$. Problems II and III are very similar. The constraints on resource use, 11.3 and 11.10, are exactly alike. Both 11.6 and 11.11 require that no activity be profitable; for a given price vector, $w = \bar{p}$, 11.11 can be rewritten exactly like 11.6. Multiplying 11.11 by -1 and moving $w = \bar{p}$ to the right-hand side of the inequality, we have

$$A'u \geqslant \bar{p} - c$$

The objective functions 11.8 and 11.9 differ somewhat, but only constraint 11.12 is completely new. It requires that output be at least as large as the quantity demanded. Multiplying Equation 11.12 by -1, we have

$$x \geqslant \bar{d}$$

Plessner shows that the primal part of problem III can be solved by an iterative procedure, for $\bar{w} = \bar{p}$, the equilibrium price vector.[25]

Thus problem III satisfies condition B.4. It also satisfies conditions B.2 and B.3 under any circumstances that problem II satisfies them. That is, maximum net profits for the sector 11.9, are zero; maximum net profits for any firm in the sector are zero if the decentralization property is satisfied; and 11.11 assures that no process is profitable. Problem III seems to be a linearized version of the model

---

24. Problem III corresponds to Plessner's problem 3. Plessner, "Quadratic Programming Competitive Equilibrium Models," p. 32.
25. Ibid. p. 23.

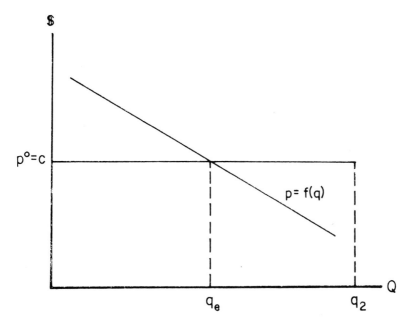

Fig. 11.7. Nonefficient output.

we want. The difficulty is that the solution to problem III, unlike the solution to problem II, may not be efficient, although Plessner thought he proved that it was.

Plessner's proof supposes that $w^0 = p^0$ is the equilibrium price vector. The associated quantities demanded are given by $d^0 = d(w^0) = d(p^0)$. Plessner writes, "we imposed the condition $x^0 = d^0$,"[26] and then he observes that problem III can be reformulated as problem IIIa: maximize

$$(p^0 - c) x - bu \qquad (11.9a)$$

subject to

$$Ax \leqslant b \qquad (11.10a)$$

$$-A'u \leqslant c - p^0 \qquad (11.11a)$$

$$x, u \geqslant 0 \qquad (11.13a)$$

Problem IIIa has the form of problem II and, if $(p^0 - c) > 0$, its solution will be efficient. Suppose, in equilibrium, however, that $(p^0 - c) = 0$. This simply means that price and the cost of purchased inputs are equal, and that imputed resource rents are zero. Such a situation may be unlikely but it is certainly not impossible. In such case, the coefficient of x in 11.9a is zero and the value of x is indeterminate. $(x, u) = (0, 0)$ satisfies all the constraints and gives 11.9a its maximum value. That is, zero supply $(x = 0)$ is feasible for problem IIIa. But demand is greater than zero, i.e., $d^0 = d(p^0) > 0$. Retaining 11.12 in problem IIIa would avoid this difficulty but would not guarantee an efficient solution.

The difficulty for the one-commodity case is illustrated in Figure 11.7. Price

26. Ibid. p. 33.

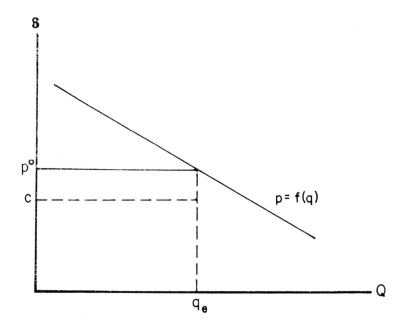

Fig. 11.8. Efficient output.

and cost are measured on the vertical axis; quantity is measured on the horizontal axis. If production must be at least as great as demand, the quantity q_e will be produced and $p^0 = c$, i.e., price equals the cost of purchased inputs. q_2 is potential production from the given inputs so q_e is not output efficient. An efficient one-commodity case is illustrated in Figure 11.8. Equilibrium price is greater than the cost of purchased inputs and the difference $p^0 - c$ is imputed resource rent per unit of output. In this case, q_e is efficient.

Separating problem III into its primal and dual components demonstrates the difficulty for the multicommodity case.

Primal	Dual
max $\bar{d}w - bu$	min cx
$w - A'u \leqslant c$	$Ax \leqslant b$
$w, u \geqslant 0$	$-x \leqslant -\bar{d}$
	$x \geqslant 0$

The dual component of problem III and the linear models in problem I have exactly the same form. Plessner argues[27] that the solutions to such problems are not necessarily efficient. Figure 11.9, which is a reproduction of Plessner's Figure 1,[28] illustrates his argument. ABC is the efficiency frontier defined by expression 11.10. If d_1 and $\bar{d}_2$ are the quantities demanded, the solution occurs at E, at a nonefficient point. The solution illustrated in Figure 11.10 for a similar problem is efficient, however. The question arises, Is a competitive equilibrium always ef-

27. Ibid. p. 16.
28. Ibid. p. 18.

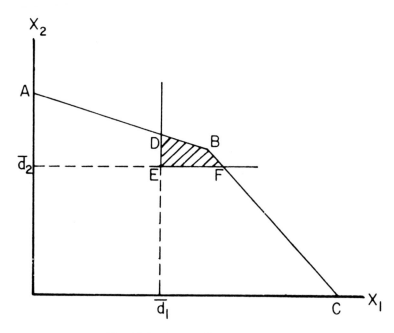

Fig. 11.9. A nonefficient solution.

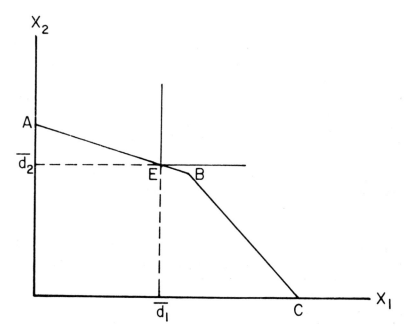

Fig. 11.10. An efficient solution.

ficient? Plessner assumes that it is, as the quotation in the first paragraph of this section indicates. That question will be examined in the next section. But first, a further digression on efficiency will be useful.

A linear function $g(x)$, defined on a compact (closed and bounded) set $X = \{x|Ax \leqslant b, x \geqslant 0\}$, reaches its maximum at a boundary point of X. This fact, apparently, is the basis for the emphasis by Koopmans[29] and Dorfman et al. on efficiency frontiers. It is the basis for Plessner's assertion[30] that problems like the one illustrated in Figure 11.9 are not efficient. But, $DEFB$ in Figure 11.9 is also a compact set, $X^* = \{x|Ax \leqslant b, x \geqslant \overline{d}\}$. A linear function, $f(x) = cx$, defined on X^* reaches its minimum at a boundary point. And, if $c > 0$, the minimum is at E, where it is impossible to decrease inputs and maintain output. E, therefore, is an input-efficient point. The "dual" nature of efficiency tells us that, at E, output cannot be increased without using more resources. It appears that Plessner's assertion about Figure 11.9 is based on too narrow a definition of efficiency.

COMPETITIVE EQUILIBRIUM

The subject of this section is competitive equilibrium, particularly what might be called "partial competitive equilibrium"—an equilibrium for only one market or subsector of an economy. Two characteristics distinguish partial from full competitive equilibrium:

1. Not all prices are variable. Specifically, the prices of those resources represented by the vector c are fixed.
2. Lack of alternative uses for resources. No uses for the resources b, other than as inputs to production processes in the subsector, are defined.

Koopmans defines a competitive equilibrium as follows:

A competitive equilibrium is a balancing bundle of choices satisfying postulates 1–4 and a system of prices, one for each commodity, such that, if all "values" are computed at those prices,

(a) the choice of each consumer is preferred or equivalent to all other choices in his consumption set that are of equal or lesser value,
(b) the choice of each producer yields the maximum value attainable in his production set,
(c) the value of the commodities released by each resource holder is the maximum value attainable to him under postulate 4.[31]

A balancing bundle of choices is one for which supply and demand are equal. Koopmans' postulates 1–4 define the rules by which decision makers—consumers, producers, and resource holders—may make choices:

1. *Consumer choices.* Condition (a) requires that if $\overline{x}_i$ is the choice of goods for the ith consumer and if x_i^* is any other choice in his consumption set such that $\overline{p}\overline{x}_i \geqslant \overline{p}x_i^*$, then $\overline{x}_i$ must be preferred or at least equivalent to x_i^*. This is Samuelson's axiom of revealed preference;[32] it requires "rationality" on the

29. Koopmans, *Three Essays*, p. 15.
30. Plessner, "Quadratic Programming Competitive Equilibrium Models," p. 29a.
31. Koopmans, *Three Essays*, p. 46.
32. See Dorfman, Samuelson, and Solow, *Linear Programming*, p. 368.

part of consumers. Dorfman et al. argue that, because of potential changes in income distribution that may result from price changes, this "rationality" requirement is not necessarily satisfied when demand is represented by market demand functions.[33] "With a changed income distribution, different 'preferences' will be revealed."[34] There is no obvious way around this difficulty except to assume that price changes are such that income distribution is not affected. Admittedly, this is not a very satisfying assumption. Except for this difficulty, problem III satisfies condition (a).

2. *Producer choices.* In the simplest case, a producer is represented by a single activity with only one output. His net profits are given by

$$P_j - c_j - \sum_{i=1}^{m} a_{ij} u_i \tag{11.14}$$

where p_j is the price of his output, c_j is the cost of purchased inputs, a_{ij} is the quantity of the ith resource required per unit of output, and u_i is the imputed price of the ith resource. In the programming problems examined up to now, the maximum value of 11.14 is zero. Expression 11.14 illustrates that efficient resource use may be extremely important for a producer. If $u_i > 0$, only by using the minimum amount (a_{ij}) of the associated resource can profits be maximum. Otherwise, per-unit profits and, consequently, total profits will be negative. If $u_i = 0$, however, there is no particular urgency to economize because the associated resource has no effect on costs, regardless of the amount used.

3. *Resource holders' choices.* In the simplest case, again, a resource holder is responsible for only one resource. He maximizes the value attainable to him by releasing all his resource if the price is positive and none if the price is negative. If the price is zero, it makes no difference how much he releases. There is no reason to suppose, in the absence of information to the contrary, that a resource holder would not permit his resource to be used when its price is zero.

Nothing in this discussion precludes a competitive equilibrium at a nonefficient point. Such an occurrence may be highly unlikely, as a practical matter, but it is not theoretically impossible. If efficiency is necessary for a competitive equilibrium, it is a requirement on the producing sector. If resource prices are positive, producers can avoid negative profits only by using resources efficiently.

Under what conditions might a competitive equilibrium occur at a nonefficient point? Since supply must equal demand in equilibrium, we must examine both supply and demand to find the answer. The demand equations reflect the usual condition that as price falls the quantity demanded rises. If price falls far enough, the quantity demanded may be very large indeed, especially if the assumption of nonsaturation holds. Thus, if prices are freely variable, the quantity demanded will conceivably be large enough that the resulting allocation is efficient even in the most richly endowed economy.

33. Ibid.
34. Ibid.

Expression 11.14 is instructive about what can be expected on the supply side. First, we recall that the producer has no control over c_j; it is fixed. Consequently, he has no incentive to produce if p falls below c, i.e., $(p - c) < 0$, even if $u_i = 0$ for all i. In a completely general equilibrium model, there would be no fixed c because all prices, including those represented in c, would be variable. In a richly endowed economy, many resource prices may be very low; some may even fall to zero. There may be motivation for producers even at such low prices and, because of the low prices, the quantity demanded may be very large. In short, a competitive equilibrium may never occur at a nonefficient point.

What of an isolated sector of an economy, e.g., agriculture? Because of the large quantity of resources purchased from other sectors of the economy, c may be large. In such case, $(p - c) = 0$ may occur for a relatively large p. In this case producer motivation, not consumer preference (nonsaturation), is the deciding factor. If the sectoral resource endowment is large (e.g., land in U.S. agriculture), production may not exhaust resource supply before $(p - c) = 0$ is reached. If not, $u = 0$ and 11.14 becomes

$$(p - c) \leqslant 0 \qquad\qquad (11.14a)$$

There is no motivation for producers if $(p - c) < 0$ so, in equilibrium, we expect strict equality in 11.14a. This is the basis for arguing that the solution to problem III, even if not efficient, represents a partial competitive equilibrium.

Koopmans makes the following statement:

Proposition 7. In the linear activity analysis model (defined by Postulates 6-10) there is associated with each efficient bundle of activities at least one system of prices compatible with the technology, such that every activity in that bundle breaks even, such that desired commodity prices are positive and such that the price of a primary commodity is nonnegative, zero, or nonpositive, according as its available supply is fully used, partly used, or not used at all, respectively.[35]

The efficient points described here satisfy all the requirements for a competitive equilibrium. We might conclude that every competitive equilibrium is an efficient point. Dorfman et al. say almost exactly that:

. . . if firms maximize their profits competitively with respect to any given set of positive prices for goods and factors, the resulting configuration of inputs and outputs will be efficient. Conversely, if we are given an efficient input-output situation, there is a set of nonnegative prices for which this situation is the competitive profit-maximizing equilibrium.[36]

For completely general models, competitive equilibrium solutions will be efficient, i.e., the solution will be on the efficiency frontier. Partial competitive equilibrium solutions, by contrast, may not be on the efficiency frontier. To argue that such solutions are no efficient, however, involves an overly strict definition of efficiency, as discussion in the two preceding sections indicates. It seems likely that such solutions are efficient for the given output, even if not on the efficiency frontier. This argument on efficiency will not be pursued further here. The principal purpose of this section—to show that a partial equilibrium solution is, in fact, an equilibrium, if its assumptions are granted—has been accomplished.

35. Koopmans, *Three Essays*, p. 88.
36. Dorfman, Samuelson, and Solow, *Linear Programming*, p. 414.

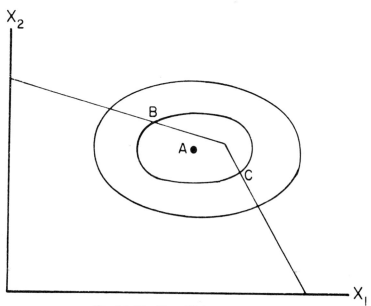

Fig. 11.11. Nonefficient maximum.

NONLINEAR MODELS

Solutions for nonlinear programming problems, unlike those for linear programming problems, are not generally efficient.[37]   They may be efficient for particular problems, of course. The difficulty is illustrated in Figure 11.11. Each concentric ellipse connects the points that give a fixed objective function value. The maximum value of the objective function is associated with A, a nonefficient point. For the efficient points B and C, $f(A) > f(B) = F(C)$. In Figure 11.12, the unconstrained maximum occurs at A, outside the feasible space. The maximum feasible value occurs at $\bar{x}$, an efficient point.

Plessner attempts to formulate a nonlinear model like the one illustrated in Figure 11.12, one that also incorporates many of the characteristics of problem III. Problem III can be rewritten: maximize

$$G(x, u, w) = \bar{d}w - cx - bu \qquad (11.15)$$

subject to

$$\begin{bmatrix} 0 & A & 0 \\ -A' & 0 & I \\ 0 & -I & 0 \end{bmatrix} \begin{bmatrix} u \\ x \\ w \end{bmatrix} \leqslant \begin{bmatrix} b \\ c \\ -\bar{d} \end{bmatrix} \qquad (11.16)$$

$$x, u, w \geqslant 0 \qquad (11.17)$$

The coefficient matrix in 11.16 is skew-symmetric, i.e., it equals the negative of its transpose. This is characteristic of self-dual problems. Moreover, the coeffi-

37. In this section, the term efficiency is used in the limited sense of efficiency on the efficiency frontier.

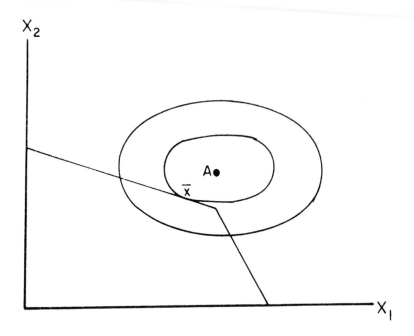

Fig. 11.12. Efficient maximum.

cients of the objective function 11.15 are the negatives of the right-hand side of 11.16. And, in addition, $G(\bar{x}, \bar{u}, \bar{w}) = 0$.

Now, suppose that demand is represented by

$$d = d_0 + Dp \tag{11.18}$$

where d_0 is a vector of constants and D is negative semidefinite. The general form of the nonlinear model, call it problem IV, is to maximize

$$F(x, p, u) = d_0 p + p' Dp - cx - bu \tag{11.19}$$

subject to

$$Ax \leqslant b \tag{11.20}$$

$$p - A'u \leqslant c \tag{11.21}$$

$$Dp - x \leqslant -d_0 \tag{11.22}$$

$$x, p, u \geqslant 0 \tag{11.23}$$

To illustrate the resemblance between problems III and IV, constraints 11.20 to 11.22 can be rewritten

$$\begin{bmatrix} 0 & -A' & I \\ A & 0 & 0 \\ -I & 0 & D \end{bmatrix} \begin{bmatrix} x \\ u \\ p \end{bmatrix} \leqslant \begin{bmatrix} c \\ b \\ -d_0 \end{bmatrix} \tag{11.24}$$

Except for the submatrix D, the coefficient matrix of 11.24 is skew-symmetric. Furthermore, the coefficients of the linear portion of 11.19 are the negatives of the right-hand side of 11.24. The objective function 11.19 is quadratic in prices. It is the sum of a linear form and a negative semidefinite quadratic form. Linear forms are both concave and convex; negative semidefinite quadratic forms are concave.[38]   Consequently, 11.19 is concave and any maximum will be a global one.[39]

To show that a solution to problem IV (Plessner problem 1.1), if it exists, satisfies the conditions of efficiency and competitive equilibrium, Plessner proves two theorems.[40]   Theorem 1 establishes that the maximum value of the objective function is zero, i.e., $F(\bar{x}, \bar{p}, \bar{u}) = 0$. A corollary to theorem 1 shows that, for any commodity with a positive price, supply will exactly equal demand. Theorem 2 establishes that the solution to problem IV is efficient.   These proofs are presented below.   First, Hanson's theorem[41] is used to derive the dual to problem IV and refers to it as problem V:

$$\text{to minimize } G(z, w, y, v) = -d_0 y - zDz + cw + bv \qquad (11.25)$$

subject to

$$-Aw + b \geqslant 0 \qquad (11.26)$$

$$-y + A'v + c \geqslant 0 \qquad (11.27)$$

$$-d_0 - Dz - D'(z - y) + w \geqslant 0 \qquad (11.28)$$

$$w, y, v \geqslant 0 \qquad (11.29)$$

The vector z here represents that part of the vector u in Hanson's theorem, whose elements enter the dual objective function with nonzero coefficients: v, w, and y are the dual variables.

Theorem 1. If problem IV has a solution $(\bar{x}, \bar{p}, \bar{u})$ then $F_1(\bar{x}, \bar{p}, \bar{u}) = 0$.
Proof. First, rewrite 11.19 as

$$F_1(x, p, u) = -[(-d_0 - Dp + x)'p] - [(-p + A'u + c)'x] - [(-Ax + b)'u] \qquad (11.30)$$

Each of the three terms in 11.30 is an inner product of vectors which are restricted to the nonnegative. Hence, over the feasible set for problem IV,

$$F_1(x, p, u) \leqslant 0 \qquad (11.31)$$

From the Kuhn-Tucker[42] necessary and sufficient[43] conditions, letting $(\bar{z}, \bar{w}, \bar{y}, \bar{v})$ be the solution of problem V, we have

38. See G. Handley, *Nonlinear and Dynamic Programming*, Addison-Wesley, Reading, Mass., 1964, p. 85.

39. Ibid., p. 212.

40. See Plessner, "Quadratic Programming Competitive Equilibrium Models," pp. 42–45.

41. M. A. Hanson, "A Duality Theorem in Nonlinear Programming with Nonlinear Constraints," *Australian J. Statist.* (1961) 3:64–71.

42. See H. W. Kuhn and A. W. Tucker, "Nonlinear Programming," *Proceedings of Berkeley Symposium on Mathematical Statistics and Probability* 2(1951): 481–92.

43. Since we assume that the matrix D is negative semidefinite, Equation 11.17 is convex; hence these conditions are also sufficient.

$$- [(-d_0 - D\overline{p} + \overline{x})'\overline{y}] - [(-\overline{p} + A'\overline{u} + c)'\overline{w}] - [(-A\overline{x} + b)'\overline{v}] = 0 \qquad (11.32)$$

from the three inner products of 11.32. From 11.30, 11.31, and 11.32, $x = \overline{w}$, $p = \overline{y}$, and $u = \overline{v}$ is a solution to problem IV if it is feasible. For feasibility, we must have

$$- A\overline{w} + b \geqslant 0, \; -\overline{y} + A'\overline{v} + c \geqslant 0 \text{ and } -d_0 - D\overline{y} + \overline{w} \geqslant 0 \qquad (11.33)$$

But with $\overline{z} = \overline{p}$ by Hanson's theorem and $p = \overline{y}$, these are precisely the dual conditions which are satisfied by $(\overline{w}, \overline{y}, \overline{v})$. Hence, $\overline{x} = \overline{w}$, $\overline{p} = \overline{y}$, and $\overline{u} = \overline{v}$, and $F_1(\overline{x}, \overline{p}, \overline{u}) = 0 \leqslant F_1(x, p, u)$.

Corollary. Whenever $\overline{p} > 0, \overline{x} = d_0 + Dp$, i.e., $\overline{p}$ equates $\overline{x}$ and $d(p)$.

The corollary follows immediately from the first term in 11.32, since $\overline{y} = \overline{p}$.

Theorem 2. If problem IV has a solution $(\overline{x}, \overline{p}, \overline{u})$, then $\overline{x}$ is efficient, i.e., x is a boundary point of the set $X = [x: Ax \leqslant b]$.

Proof. Consider the linear programming problem

$$\text{to maximize } F_1(x, \overline{p}, u) \qquad (11.34)$$

subject to

$$Ax \leqslant b \qquad (11.35)$$

$$- A'u \leqslant -\overline{p} + c \qquad (11.36)$$

$$- x \leqslant -d_0 - D\overline{p} \qquad (11.37)$$

$$x, u \geqslant 0 \qquad (11.38)$$

Clearly, this problem and problem IV have the same solution in x and u. Since $\overline{p} > 0$ because of nonsaturation, we can rewrite the linear problem using the corollary, as problem IV:

$$\text{to maximize } f_1(x, u) = (\overline{p} - c) x - bu \leqslant F_1(\overline{x}, \overline{p}, \overline{u}) \qquad (11.39)$$

subject to

$$Ax \leqslant b \qquad (11.40)$$

$$- A'u \leqslant -\overline{p} + c \qquad (11.41)$$

$$x, u \geqslant 0 \qquad (11.42)$$

Suppose now that $\overline{x}$ is not efficient, i.e., $A\overline{x} < b$. Then from the third term in 11.32, since $\overline{v} = \overline{u}$,

$$\overline{u} = 0 \qquad (11.43)$$

11.41 and 11.43 imply $\overline{p} - c \leqslant 0$. The case $\overline{p} - c = 0$ is trivial, since then $f_1(x, \overline{u}) = 0$ for all x. If $\overline{p} - c < 0$, then $\overline{x} \geqslant 0$ ($\overline{x} = 0$ is, again, trivial) implies

$$f_1(\overline{x}, \overline{u}) = F_1(\overline{x}, \overline{p}, \overline{u}) < 0 \qquad (11.44)$$

which contradicts theorem 1. Hence, $\overline{u} \geqslant 0$ and $\overline{x}$ is efficient.

Corollary. The solution to problem IV possesses the decentralization property, if $\overline{p}$ is universal.

This follows immediately from the fact that problem IV, whose solution in x is the same as for problem III, is a self-dual linear programming problem. Its primal constituent is

$$\text{to maximize } (\overline{p} - c)\, x$$

subject to

$$Ax \leqslant b$$
$$x \geqslant 0,$$

The solution to this problem is always efficient, hence $\overline{x}$ is efficient.[44]

APPLICATION OF QUADRATIC PROGRAMMING MODEL TO U.S. AGRICULTURE

The formulation and results of a spatial quadratic programming model for U.S. agriculture are presented in this section. The model has the same basic characteristics as problem IV. In each region, demand is presented by linear price-dependent demand equations and production by linear activities. Interregional shipping is represented by transportation activities. The problem maximizes aggregate producer profits which, because of the linear demand equations, are quadratic functions of product prices.[45] The analysis is for the year 1965. The choice of year was dictated by our desire to compare the results with those from a study by Brokken and Heady,[46] an application of linear activity analysis to the same "economy." We compare equilibrium price and quantity predictions with Brokken and Heady's predictions and with actual 1965 figures.

PROBLEM SPECIFICATION

Following Koopmans and Bausch,[47] we classify agricultural commodities into three mutually exclusive classes: primary, intermediate, and desired. Primary commodities are inputs flowing into production from outside the system. Intermediate commodities are produced only as inputs for further production. Desired commodities are wanted either for consumption or for other uses outside the productive system.

Table 11.1 lists the commodities in each class. Quantities of desired commodities are in farm-level rather than in retail units. This simplification excludes the processing sector but was essential to keeping the problem manageable. Perhaps the most conspicuous exclusion from Table 11.1 is cotton; its treatment will be discussed later. Horticultural and specialty crops are also excluded.

44. This excludes, of course, some "pathological" cases. See Dorfman, Samuelson, and Solow, *Linear Programming*, pp. 392–404.
45. This formulation is similar to one by Takayama and Judge that maximizes "net consumer surplus." See T. Takayama and G. G. Judge, "Spatial Equilibrium and Quadratic Programming," *J. Farm Econ.* 46(Feb. 1964): 67–93.
46. See Chapter 5.
47. Koopmans and Bausch, "Selected Topics in Economics."

Fig. 11.13. Location of consuming regions.

The 48 contiguous states and the District of Columbia are included in the study. This area is partitioned into 10 markets or consumption regions (Figure 11.13).[48] Demand equations for desired commodities and livestock-producing activities are defined for each market. For the analysis of crop production, each market is further partitioned into a number of crop-producing regions (Figure 11.14); crop-producing activities are defined for each of these smaller regions. Within a market, all production (both crop and livestock) contributes to a central supply. This supply may be consumed (desired commodities), used as inputs for further production (intermediate commodities), or shipped at some positive cost to other markets (either desired or intermediate commodities). Intramarket shipping costs are neglected.[49] Crop and livestock data for this study were adapted from Brokken's study.[50]

Limited computer capacity, or rather limited computer-program capacity, forced several simplifications. We exclude the processing sector, as noted above. In addition, cotton is treated only indirectly. We first determined the quantity of cotton lint used in 1965. Then, using Brokken's production coefficients, we assumed that cotton production was distributed so as to minimize the aggregate cost of producing this quantity of lint. This required 14.056 million acres of cotton. The maximum cotton acreage permitted in any crop-producing region is

48. The 10 markets coincide with the 10 USDA production regions.
49. Eyvindson, Heady, and Srivastava (Chapter 6) include both intermarket and intra-market shipping costs.
50. Brokken (Chapter 5) defines 20 livestock-producing or consuming regions (markets) and 157 crop-producing regions. Computer program limitations forced some aggregation of these regions for the present study.

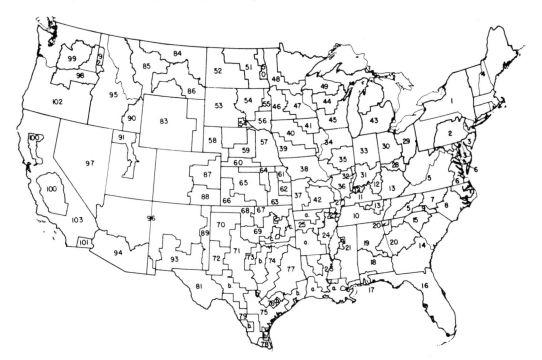

Fig. 11.14. Location of producing areas.

Brokken's Land-1 (cotton land). The estimated acreage devoted to cotton was then deducted from the cropland and hay-land acreages. Thus the acreages of cropland and hay land (Table 11.1) used in this analysis are net of cotton production. Cottonseed oil and cottonseed oil meal produced jointly with the lint are assumed to contribute to supplies in the 10 market areas in proportion to the population. We make no particular defense for this treatment of cotton. With cotton excluded, however, our programming matrix was $m + n = 3,524$, where m is the number of primal constraints and n is the number of primal variables.[51] The computer program we used[52] requires $m + n \leqslant 3,550$.

MATHEMATICAL STRUCTURE OF THE MODEL

Let d be the vector of quantities demanded of desired commodities and let p be the vector of prices received by farmers. National demand for desired commodities is given by

51. Recent independent efforts by Yoran, Takayama, and Judge and Stoecker show that problems of this type can be formulated with only $(m + n)/2$ equations. Nevertheless, computer programs for quadratic programming still have smaller capacities than those for linear programming. See D. Yoran, "Incorporation of Income Effects into Mathematical Models," *Metroeconomica* 19(Dec. 1967): 141–60; T. Takayama and G. G. Judge, "Alternative Spatial Equilibrium Models," *J. Reg. Sci.* 10(Apr. 1970): 1–12; Art Stoecker, "A Quadratic Programming Model of U.S. Agriculture in 1980—Theory and Application," Ph.D. diss., Iowa State Univ., Ames, 1973.

52. D. J. Soults, J. J. Zynbek, and V. A. Sposito, "Zorilla, an Algorithm for the Optimization of a Quadratic Form Subject to Linear Restraints," Iowa State Univ. Statist. Lab. Numerical and Data Processing Series No. 9, May 1969.

$$d = d_0 + Dp + E - O \tag{11.45}$$

The vector E is average annual (1963 to 1965) commercial exports and O is domestic production of cottonseed oil. Demand for desired commodities in the kth market is given by

$$d^k = d_0^k + D^k p^k \tag{11.46}$$
$$k = 1, \ldots, 10$$

where

$$d_0^k = a_k d_0 + E^k - O^k \tag{11.47}$$

and

$$D^k = a_k D \tag{11.48}$$

The scalar, a_k, is the proportion of 1965 U.S. population (48 states and D.C.) in the kth market. E and O in 11.45 are such that $E = \sum_k E^k$ and $O = \sum_k O^k$.

The model maximizes[53]

$$f(p^k, x^{hk}, u^{hk}, s^{jk}) = \sum_{k=1}^{K} \left[(d_0^k + D^k p^k)' p^k - \sum_{h=1}^{H} c^{hk} x^{hk} - \sum_{h=1}^{H} b^{hk} u^{hk} \right]$$

$$- \sum_{j \neq k} t^{jk} s^{jk} \tag{11.49}$$

subject to

$$- (A_p^{hk})' u^{hk} - (A_i^{hk})' w^k - (A_d^{hk})' p^k \leqslant c^{hk} \tag{11.50}$$

$$A_p^{hk} x^{hk} \leqslant b^{hk} \tag{11.51}$$

$$\sum_{h=1}^{H} A_i^{hk} x^{hk} - \sum_{j \neq k} (s_i^{jk} - s_i^{kj}) \leqslant 0 \tag{11.52}$$

$$\sum_{h=1}^{H} A_d^{hk} x^{hk} + D^k p^k - \sum_{j \neq k} (s_d^{jk} - s_d^{kj}) \leqslant -d_0^k \tag{11.53}$$

$$p^k - p^j \leqslant t_d^{jk} \tag{11.54}$$

$$w^k - w^j \leqslant t_i^{jk} \tag{11.55}$$

$$x^{hk}, u^{hk}, w^k, s^{jk}, p^k \geqslant 0 \tag{11.56}$$

where, for producing region h in market k:

53. In the discussion, it should be written as H_k. That is, the number of crop-producing areas is not the same in every market. In the interest of simplicity, the subscript k will be omitted.

c^{hk} a vector of activity costs representing purchases of inputs from other sectors of the economy

x^{hk} a vector of levels for activities other than transportation

b^{hk} a vector of available primary commodities (resources) assumed to be immobile

u^{hk} a vector of imputed prices for the primary commodities, b^{hk}

A^{hk} the technology (input-output) matrix relating b^{hk} to x^{hk}

t^{jk} a vector of transportation costs between markets j and k, $j \neq k$

s^{jk} a vector of transportation-activity levels between markets j and k, $j \neq k$

w^{k} a vector of imputed prices for intermediate commodities

t^{jk} and s^{jk} can be partitioned into "desired" and "intermediate" components as follows:

$$t^{jk} = \begin{bmatrix} t_d^{jk} \\ t_i^{jk} \end{bmatrix} \qquad s^{jk} = \begin{bmatrix} s_d^{jk} \\ s_i^{jk} \end{bmatrix}$$

The technology matrix A^{hk} can also be partitioned to conform with the partitioning of the commodity space as follows:

$$(A^{hk})' = (A_d^{hk} \ A_p^{hk})'$$

Each column, a_j^{hk}, of A^{hk} represents a process that transforms primary and intermediate commodities into intermediate and desired commodities. The elements a_j^{hk} are negative for of outputs, positive for inputs, and zero for commodities not involved in the process. Thus $A_d^{hk} \leqslant [0]$, $A_p^{hk} \geqslant [0]$, and $A_i^{hk} \gtreqless [0]$.[54] That is, desired commodities are never inputs, primary commodities are never outputs, but intermediate commodities may be either inputs or outputs.

The objective function 11.49 is an aggregate net profit function. It is the value of desired commodities minus production costs, imputed resource values, and transportation costs.

Constraints 11.50 require that no production process be profitable. That is, net returns [value of outputs (desired and intermediate commodities) minus value of inputs (primary and intermediate commodities)] per unit of the process must not exceed the per-unit exogenous costs, c^{hk}. Omitting regional superscripts for simplicity, the gth constraint from 11.50 can be written:

$$-\sum_{j=1}^{s} a_{gj} u_j - \sum_{j=s+1}^{t} a_{gj} w_j - \sum_{j=t+1}^{n} a_{gj} p_j \leqslant c_g \qquad (11.57)$$

where $j = 1, \ldots, s$ represents primary commodities
         $j = s + 1, \ldots, t$ intermediate commodities
         $j = t + 1, \ldots, n$ desired commodities

By 11.56, u_j, w_j, and p_j are nonnegative. As noted, $a_{gj} > 0$ for inputs, $a_{gj} < 0$ for outputs, and $a_{gj} = 0$ for commodities not involved in the process. Thus the left-hand side of 11.57 represents net value of the gth process before exogenous costs are deducted.

54. [0] is a null matrix.

Constraints 11.51 merely require that the use of primary commodities not exceed the supply. Constraints 11.52 require that production of intermediate commodities less net inshipments be nonpositive; i.e., the supply of intermediate commodities in market k cannot exceed the demand. Constraints 11.53 require that the supply of desired commodities be at least as great as demand. Rearranging 11.53 makes this requirement clearer:

$$d_0^k + D^k p^k \leqslant - \sum_{h=1}^{H} A_d^{hk} x^{hk} + \sum_{j \neq k} (s_d^{jk} - s_d^{kj}) \qquad (11.53a)$$

Constraints 11.54 and 11.55 are Samuelson's requirements for equilibrium in trade.[55] They require that the difference in prices between any two regions cannot exceed the transportation charge.

Let us define two submatrices, T_i and T_d, and two vectors $t_i = [t_i^{jk}]$, $t_d = [t_d^{jk}]$, such that 11.54 and 11.55 can be rewritten:

$$- T_i' w \leqslant t_i \qquad (11.54a)$$

$$- T_d' p \leqslant t_d \qquad (11.55a)$$

Then, if regional submatrices and vectors are adjoined appropriately, constraints 11.50–11.55 can be written as follows:

$$
\begin{bmatrix}
0 & -A_p' & 0 & 0 & -A_i' & -A_d' \\
A_p & 0 & 0 & 0 & 0 & 0 \\
0 & 0 & 0 & 0 & 0 & -T_d' \\
0 & 0 & 0 & 0 & -T_i' & 0 \\
A_i & 0 & 0 & T_i & 0 & 0 \\
A_d & 0 & T_d & 0 & 0 & D
\end{bmatrix}
\begin{bmatrix}
x \\ u \\ s_d \\ s_i \\ w \\ p
\end{bmatrix}
\leqslant
\begin{bmatrix}
c \\ b \\ t_d \\ t_i \\ 0 \\ -d_0
\end{bmatrix}
\qquad (11.58)
$$

Except for the submatrix D, the coefficient matrix of 11.58 is skew-symetric, i.e., it equals the negative of its transpose. The coefficients of the linear portion of the objective function 11.49 are the negatives of the right-hand side of 11.58. Thus the model is a self-dual problem with an optimal objective function value of zero.[56] It has been shown earlier that problems of this type have the following additional characteristics: (1) if all H producing regions in the kth market face the prices $(\bar{p}^k, \bar{w}^k)$, net profits for each producing region will be maximum and zero; (2) for every product with positive output, marginal cost will equal price; (3) for every product with positive price, supply will equal demand; and (4) the trade equilibrium conditions will be satisfied as strict equalities for any product actually traded.

The objective function 11.49 is the sum of a quadratic and a linear form and

55. Paul A. Samuelson, "Spatial Price Equilibrium and Linear Programming," *Am. Econ. Rev.* 42 (June 1952): 283–303.

56. A. W. Tucker, "Dual System of Homogeneous Linear Relations," *Annals Math. Studies* 38 (1956): 3–18.

the constraints 11.58 are linear. Thus the model is a quadratic programming problem. If the matrix D is at least negative semidefinite, the problem will be convex so that any local maximum will also be a global maximum. The solution is not necessarily unique, however.

DATA

DEMAND DATA

National demand equations for desired commodities 11.45 were derived from Brandow's estimates.[57] Brandow estimated retail price elasticities for farm commodities for the base period 1955–57. He derived farm-level elasticities from the retail elasticities and then derived farm-level demand equations from the farm-level elasticities. His national demand equations have the form[58]

$$d = d_0 + Dp + tT \qquad (11.59)$$

where t is a trend coefficient and T is a measure of time, $T = 0$ for 1956.

Brandow's estimates can be used in either of two ways. First, it can be assumed that a given price change elicited the same change in quantity demand (other things equal) in 1965 as in 1955–57. This is equivalent to assuming that the matrix D is unchanged but that the intercept d_0 shifted. In this case, Brandow's demand equations can simply be updated:

$$d = d_{0T} + Dp \qquad (11.60)$$

where d_{0T} is the new, time-adjusted intercept

Alternatively, it might be assumed that, although the absolute change in quantity demanded associated with a given price change was not the same, the percentage change in quantity demanded was the same. This second assumption is equivalent to assuming that demand elasticities were unchanged between the two periods. Using this assumption, a new demand matrix D^* can be derived.

Let e_{ij} be Brandow's farm-level elasticity reflecting the percentage change in the quantity of the ith commodity when the price of the jth commodity changes by 1%[59]

$\bar{q}_i$ the average annual quantity of the ith commodity for domestic and export use in 1963–65

$\bar{P}_j$ the average price of the jth commodity for 1963–65.

Then

$$d_{ij} = \frac{\bar{q}_i}{\bar{P}_j} e_{ij}, \qquad (11.61)$$

$$i, j = 1, \ldots, 10$$

57. G. E. Brandow, *Interrelations among Demands for Farm Products and Implications for Control of Market Supply*, Pa. Agr. Exp. Sta. Bull. 680, Aug. 1961.

58. Ibid., p. 45.

59. Ibid., Table 12.

and the new demand matrix is

$$D* = [d_{ij}] \qquad (11.62)$$

Since the alternative formulation yielded the smaller sum of squared errors, [actual quantity - predicted quantity]^2, it was chosen.[60] The demand matrix $D*$ is given in Table 11.2.

Demand equations for the kth market were derived from the national demand system according to 11.46 and 11.47. This treatment implicitly assumes that, except for exports, the demand system in area k is proportional to the national demand system. This does not imply that the quantities demanded in area k will be proportional to national quantities; price variations between areas will prevent that. Nevertheless, this treatment ignores regional differences—in preferences and incomes, for example. The alternative is to estimate separate demand systems for each area. Finding data for such estimates would be formidable.

PRODUCTION DATA

Most of the production data, both crop and livestock, were adapted from Brokken's 1965 data.[61] Crop cost estimates include allowances for machine costs (depreciation, interest, taxes, insurance, repairs, fuel, oil, and grease), labor, lime, fertilizer, insecticides, herbicides, seed, and irrigation water. Livestock cost estimates include allowances for nonfeed items: labor, breeding fees, depreciation and repair on buildings and equipment, equipment operating costs (e.g., electricity and fuel), veterinary and other medical costs, charges against the value of animals (interest, taxes, insurance, and depreciation), supplies, and association fees (e.g., DHIA fees). Feed is an intermediate product, produced within the system and is available for livestock production at an internally imputed cost. Therefore, no direct charge was made for feed.

Cost and production coefficients used in this study are weighted averages of Brokken's coefficients. Land constraints were used as weights for crop coefficients and livestock constraints for livestock coefficients. (Recall that Brokken used 20 livestock-producing regions and 157 crop-producing areas, compared with 10 and 103, respectively, here.)

TRANSPORTATION COSTS

A "central city" was designated for each market area. Shipping cost for any route is a function of the mileage between central cities and a mileage charge, which varies from one route to another. Mileages between central cities are rail mileages; mileage rates are rail mileage block rates. Both were estimated by

60. Errors for manufacturing milk and vegetable oils were so large that new 1963–65 elasticities were estimated. Since 1960, the consumption of vegetable oils has increased much more rapidly than in the 1955–57 period. There is no obvious explanation for the large errors for manufacturing milk.

61. Brokken's data collection procedures are discussed in Chapter 5.

Eyvindson et al.[62]   All desired commodities and all intermediate commodities, except roughage (hay and silage), can be shipped between market areas. To conserve computational capacity, improbable transportation routes (e.g., wheat from Iowa to Kansas) were excluded. As noted, all intramarket shipments were ignored.

EMPIRICAL RESULTS

The model described in section 2 is a competitive equilibrium model. Physical capacity is the only constraint on production and there are no government programs to support prices above competitive equilibrium levels. Estimated production costs vary linearly with the quantities produced. Thus, in a sense, the solution to the model is a long-range competitive equilibrium. By contrast, many actual 1965 prices (e.g., milk and wheat) were artificially high because of supply control programs. Thus we should expect estimated prices to be less than actual prices and estimated quantities to exceed actual quantities.

Estimated results will be compared with actual 1965 results and with results from Brokken's Solution 1. Brokken formulated several variations of his basic model, each incorporating different assumptions about constraints, production coefficients, or both. Solution 1 incorporates technology and demand conditions characteristic of 1965.

DESIRED COMMODITIES

Except for the price of calves, all estimated prices are lower than actual prices, substantially lower except the price of cattle (Table 11.3). Estimated quantities exceed actual quantities, however, for only hogs, manufacturing milk, corn, and barley. The inconsistencies for oil and wheat will be discussed later in this section. Those for cattle and calves can better be discussed in the section on livestock numbers. The difference for oats is trivial.

In Table 11.4, commodities whose cross price elasticities are relatively high are combined. Now, all estimated prices are less than actual prices and, except for oils and wheat, estimated quantities exceed actual quantities. The quantity differences (actual - estimated) for oils and wheat, though not trivial, are relatively small.   The fifth column of Table 11.4 reports the direct price elasticities of demand "implied" by the differences between actual and estimated results. These would be the elasticities *if* actual and estimated results were different points on the same demand functions rather than points on different demand functions. For comparison, some of Brandow's direct price elasticities are given in the last column of Table 11.4. Except for the elasticities for oils and wheat, which are meaningless because of the unrealistic signs, the implied elasticities are reasonably consistent with Brandow's results.

The "inconsistency" in the wheat results can be characterized as a shift in the actual demand function for wheat, primarily for export. Average 1963-65 com-

---

62. See Chapter 6.

mercial exports, on which the model is based (Equation 11.47), were 287 million bushels. Actual 1965 commercial exports were 344 million bushels. For the wheat demand equation in Table 11.2, no reasonable price change would induce this much change in demand. A 50 percent reduction in the estimated price to, say, 35 cents, other prices unchanged, would increase the quantity demanded by 2.45 million bushels. According to Brandow's elasticity in Table 11.4, the same price change would increase the quantity demanded by only 8 million bushels. Alternatively, it can be argued that export demand is more elastic than domestic demand and, therefore, should be treated separately. Such treatment is possible, of course, but the added complication has its price.

The inconsistency for oils is simpler. By an error in coding the data, the supply of cottonseed oil in one area was overstated by approximately 7 million hundredweight. Given the treatment of cottonseed oil in the model (Equation 11.47), the production of soybean oil was reduced by roughly the same amount. If this amount is added to the estimated quantity, assuming the same prices, the implied elasticity in Table 11.4 becomes -0.0858. Brandow's estimate is -0.2702.

LIVESTOCK NUMBERS

Total estimated fed-cattle numbers fall short of actual numbers (Table 11.5) even though fed-cattle capacity is exhausted in every area except Area 10. In Area 10, 1,515,000 head capacity is left idle because no transportation activity to export cattle from Area 10 was defined. Even had total fed-cattle capacity (18,007,000) been exhausted, estimated fed-cattle numbers would still be less than the number of cattle and calves marketed in 1965 (18,718,000, revised estimate). Consequently, in many areas, yearling calves (700 lb liveweight), which are usually fed to heavier weights, are slaughtered to satisfy the demand for cattle.

The excessive requirement for yearling calves makes the requirement for beef cows inordinately high. Estimated beef-cow numbers exceed actual numbers and, in every area except Area 1, beef-cow capacity is exhausted (Table 11.5). The high requirement for yearling calves restricts the number of feeder calves that can be slaughtered to satisfy the demand for calves (the desired commodity). That the estimated number of beef cows in Area 1 is zero does not mean that no feeder calves are available there. The milk cow activity supplies some feeder calves. Moreover, both feeder calves and yearling calves can be imported (intermediate commodities).

Fed-cattle capacity was defined as the maximum historical number of cattle placed on feed.[63] When the defined capacity led to infeasibilities in Solution 1, Brokken arbitrarily increased the constraints by 10 percent.[64] The adjusted capacity (19,807,000) exceeds 1965 marketings (18,718,000, revised estimate) but is less than 1966 marketings (20,345,000). Brokken's original capacity estimates were based on preliminary data, which were less than the revised estimates. In retrospect, Brokken's adjusted capacities would have been more reasonable for the present study.

63. See Chapter 5.
64. Ibid.

Estimated milk cow numbers are less than actual numbers (Table 11.5) even though estimated demand for all milk exceeds actual demand. Actual demand in Table 11.3, however, excludes some production: USDA donations of 52 million cwt, 20.61 million cwt fed to calves, and 6.5 million cwt of USDA exports. Estimated average production per cow is 79.295 cwt compared with average 1965 production per cow of 83.04 cwt.[65] Had estimated average production equaled actual average production, total estimated production would be 1,236.06 million cwt, an increase of 55.75 million cwt. If estimated production were 1,236.06, the implied elasticity in Table 11.4, at the same prices, would be -0.1377.

Hog production (Table 11.5) is completely consistent with the results in Tables 11.3 and 11.4. The price elasticity implied by the results in Table 11.3 (hogs only) is -0.521, slightly more than Brandow's estimate of -0.4578.

CROP ACREAGES

Table 11.6 reports U.S. crop acreages and idle cropland. Table 11.7 reports acreage of wheat, feed grain, soybeans, and idle cropland by market area. For the most part, these results are consistent with the results in Table 11.3, although a few results deserve special comment.

Wheat. Average estimated wheat yields exceed average actual yields only slightly (27.15 bu vs. 26.5 bu).[66] Thus most of the differences between estimated and actual acreages are due to differences in quantities supplied. Actual commercial exports exceed estimated exports by 57 million bushels. Noncommercial exports (523.1 million bushels in 1965) are not included in the model at all. On the other hand, estimated use of wheat for feed exceeds actual feed use (257.9 million bu vs. 153.9 million bu). The net effect is that actual disappearance exceeds estimated use by 477.8 million bushels and that actual acreage exceeds estimated acreage:

	Estimated Use	Actual Use
	mil bu	mil bu
Domestic use and commercial exports	800.7	859.4
Noncommercial exports	. . .	523.1
Wheat for feed	257.9	153.9
Total	1,058.6	1,536.4

Feed Grain. Average estimated feed-grain yield is 1.62 tons per acre; average actual yield is 1.64 tons per acre.[67] As with wheat, most of the difference between estimated and actual acreages is due to differences in quantities supplied rather than to differences in yields. Estimated quantities understate actual quantities in two components: exports and feed requirements for exogenous livestock (livestock not included in the model). Average 1963-65 commercial exports are less than 1965 commercial exports (23.216 million tons vs. 25.549

65. USDA, ERS, *Dairy Situation*, DS 314, Mar. 1967.
66. Yield per harvested acre. From USDA, ERS, *Wheat Situation*, Washington, D.C.
67. See USDA, ERS, *Feed Statistics through 1966*, Stat. Bull. 410, Sept. 1967.

million tons). Noncommercial exports (3.551 million tons in 1965)[68] are not included in the model. Feed-grain requirements for exogenous livestock were estimated from Hodges' work[69] to be 18.348 million tons. By a coding error, this requirement was coded as 1.835 million tons. The net effect is that actual disappearance exceeds estimated use by roughly 22.397 million tons:

	Estimated Use	Actual Use
	mil. tons	mil. tons
Commercial exports	23.216	25.549
Noncommercial exports	. . .	3.551
Exogenous livestock	1.835	18.348
Total	25.051	47.448

At 1.62 tons per acre, approximately 13.8 million additional acres would be required to produce this quantity.

Soybeans. Estimated soybean production is 665.65 million bushels with an average yield of 29.2 bushels per acre. Actual 1965 production was 845.61 million bushels and 24.5 bushels per acre average yield. By the coding error, discussed in the section on desired commodities, oil demand was underestimated by 7 million cwt. Noncommercial exports (5.65 million cwt) are not included in the model at all. To produce an additional 12.65 million cwt of oil would require an additional 118.224 million bushels of soybeans (at 0.107 cwt oil per bu soybeans), and an additional 4.05 million acres of cropland (at 29.2 bu soybeans per acre).

Idle Cropland. Idle cropland by market area is reported in Table 11.7. The estimated acreage of idle cropland substantially exceeds the actual acreage in areas 2, 3, 5, and 7 (Appalachian, Southeast, Corn Belt, and Northern Plains areas, respectively). Solution 1 and estimated results are reasonably consistent in direction in this respect, although the exact amounts differ somewhat. In Solution 1, 33.853 million acres of cropland are used for hay or pasture (see Table 11.5) and are not included in idle cropland. In the estimated results, 24.653 million acres of cropland are used to produce tame hay and are not included in idle cropland; some idle cropland may be used to produce pasture but there is no way to determine the amount.

SUMMARY AND CONCLUSIONS

With one exception (calves), estimated national average prices are less than actual prices, as expected. Either the associated quantities exceed actual quantities or there are plausible explanations why they do not. At first glance, estimated prices appear excessively low compared with actual prices. Further investigation, however, indicates that differences between estimated and actual prices,

68. Ibid.
69. Earl F. Hodges, *Consumption of Feed by Livestock 1940–59*, USDA, ERS, Production Res. Report 79, Mar. 1964

and between estimated and actual quantities, are consistent with widely accepted elasticity estimates. Estimated crop acreages and livestock numbers are consistent with the quantities demanded. Although some assumptions of the analysis can be criticized, and despite some unfortunate errors in the data, we think the results, taken as a whole, are reasonable. The model performed up to our expectation.

We should perhaps end on a note of caution. To date, computer programs for quadratic programming have neither the capacity, the flexibility, nor the reliability of, for example, the IBM MPS-360 system. Thus large problems may require excessive computer time, encounter numeric difficulties, or both. As quadratic programming problems go, the original programming matrix for the problem discussed here was large ($m + n = 3,524$). In solving the problem in this form, we encountered both numeric difficulties and excessive computer times (approximately 9,100 iterations). A subsequent solution, using Stoecker's modification of the programming matrix, required only 1,796 iterations (31.56 minutes CPU time). The size of the matrix is not the only factor that affects computer time, however. The density of the matrix and the interrelatedness of the activities are also important. An earlier problem,[70] with $m + n = 2,672$, a more sparse matrix, and no intermediate activities, required only 2,800 iterations.

70. Harry H. Hall, Earl O. Heady, and Yakir Plessner, "Quadratic Programming Solution of Competitive Equilibrium for U.S. Agriculture," Am. J. Agr. Econ. 50 (Aug. 1968): 536–55.

Chapter 12: A National Grain Transportation Model

JERRY A. FEDELER, EARL O. HEADY,
and WON W. KOO

Spatial models are specified as having two or more interdependent points or regions. The economic interdependencies are comprised of consistencies among the regional supplies and demands of commodities on one hand and the transportation between the regions on the other hand. The motivation for constructing spatial models usually has been the supply and demand of goods or resources associated with the various regions. For these models, transportation has merely provided spatial price differentials among the regions. Even the analytical framework commonly referred to as a "transportation problem" is motivated by finding the optimal distribution of commodities at several origins among several destinations.

The transportation industry depends on the location of production and consumption of commodities just as the location of production and consumption depends on transportation. There is no reason why the use of a spatial model cannot be motivated by questions about the transportation network and flow of goods rather than questions about the regional supplies and demands of commodities. Spatial models can simultaneously answer questions of both types and the emphasis placed on any given study may range from ignoring transportation to a heavy emphasis on transportation. For this study, the emphasis or motivation for using a spatial model is the analysis of transportation networks for grain movements among grain producing and consuming regions. Problems of grain transportation can be avoided only if the supply, transportation, and demand sectors of the grain industry are each mutually aware of the interdependencies of the three sectors. This study coordinates these three sectors in one large model by simultaneously determining the optimal location of grain production and grain flows, given quantities demanded at the consuming regions.

Grain transportation is much more than the mere flow of grain between points. Understanding the demand for grain transportation facilities and equipment and effectively organizing their use require information pertaining to the mode, volume, and distance grain is moved. This information is needed at the national and regional levels—to which this study pertains—and the local level. Depending on the quantity transported, a commodity may or may not be important to the transportation industry. Likewise, depending on the physical characteristics and unit value of a commodity, transportation may or may not be important to the locational supply and demand analysis of that commodity. Transportation is relatively more important for commodities that are heavy, bulky, or require special treatment for transit and that have a low unit value.

OBJECTIVES OF THE STUDY

A regional linear programming model is utilized in the search for an efficient national and interregional grain transportation and production network. The grains included in the study are wheat, soybeans, corn, oats, barley, and grain sorghum; the last four are aggregated into one class called feed grain. In addition to these grains, cotton is included because it competes with the grains for cropland and cotton seed is a major substitute for soybeans. The analysis, applied to the 48 contiguous states for 1980, includes finding the least-cost location for producing each grain class, projecting domestic and export demands for each grain class, and analyzing the transportation services required for projected interregional grain movements.

The interdependence of rail, water, truck, and combinations of these modes is analyzed. The effectiveness of alternative methods of grain transportation is determined to avoid an inefficient mix of transportation modes. The study indicates how optimal transportation patterns are related to production and demand as well as how regional grain production is affected by transportation.

Grain production and sales are a large and important sector of agriculture in the United States. Wheat, soybean, and feed-grain sales from farms in 1971 were $9.9 billion, 18.7 percent of cash receipts of all commodities sold from farms.[1] In addition to these farm sales, $3.5 billion of grain was produced but not sold, i.e., it was used on farms where it was grown. The production of the six grains included in the study doubled between 1951 and 1972, attaining a level of 285 million tons in 1972.[2] However, the quantity of these grains sold from farms tripled in the same period. Nearly 200 million tons of the six grains were sold from farms in 1971.[3] The difference in the growth rates of production and farm sales is because grain exports have increased faster than production, the mix of grains has shifted toward those grains more frequently sold from farms, and production among grain and livestock farms has become more specialized. Concurrent with the expansion of grain sales has been an increase in the demand for grain transportation services. Transportation services are important to the grain industry because grain is heavy and bulky vis-à-vis its unit value. There have been periods of excess demand and periods of excess supply of grain transportation services but the occurrences of the excess demands have been the most severe. The most renown disequilibrium in recent years was the excess demand in the

1. USDA, *Agricultural Statistics, 1972*, Washington, D.C., 1972.
2. Ibid.; USDA Statistical Reporting Service, Crop Reporting Board, *Field Crops*, Washington, D.C., various issues.
3. See footnote 1.

last months of 1972 and 1973. Such excess demands distort the normal grain price–space relationships.

The transportation industry is a major sector of the U.S. economy. Grain is one of only a few commodity classes that comprises a significant portion of all freight traffic. Grain constituted 5.2 percent of all railroad revenue carloadings in 1972.[4] The only other commodity categories accounting for more carloadings were coal (17.5 percent), metallic ores (6.6 percent), and chemicals and allied products (5.4 percent). Grain comprised 4.8 percent of all ton-miles of domestic water traffic in 1971.[5] Trucks haul large quantities of grain but, unfortunately, no national statistics are available for all truck shipments. The past trends of grain sales and grain hauled by rail and water indicate that the quantity of grain hauled by truck has grown rapidly since World War II. Clearly the grain industry is important to both the agriculture and transportation sectors.

THE MODEL

A linear programming model with variables that represent regional grain production and interregional grain transportation is used for the spatial model. A solution of the model is obtained by minimizing the objective function (Equation 12.1) specified as the annual cost of grain production and transportation, ACPT.

$$ACPT = \sum_{k=1}^{4} \sum_{i}^{np_k} C_i^k X_i^k + \sum_{k=1}^{2} \sum_{t=1}^{2} \sum_{i}^{np_k} \sum_{j}^{nc_k} P_{tij}^k T_{tij}^k + \sum_{i}^{np_3} \sum_{j}^{nc_3} P_{ij}^3 T_{ij}^3 \qquad (12.1)$$

where k = crop index; 1 = feed grain, 2 = soybeans, 3 = wheat, and 4 = cotton
   i = producing region index
   j = consuming region index
   t = time period index
   np_k = number of producing regions that apply to crop k
   nc_k = number of consuming regions that apply to crop k
   C_i^k = all costs, except land, of producing one acre of crop k in region i
   X_i^k = number of acres of crop k produced in region i
   P_{tij}^k = cost of transporting one ton of crop k in time period t from producing region i to consuming region j
   T_{tij}^k = number of tons of crop k transported in time period t from producing region i to consuming region j
   P_{ij}^k = cost of transporting one ton of crop k from producing region i to consuming region j

    4. Association of American Railroads, *Yearbook of Railroad Facts*, Washington, D.C., various editions.
    5. U.S. Army Corps of Engineers, Army Engineer Div., Lower Mississippi Valley, *Waterborne Commerce of the United States*, Vicksburg, Miss., various editions.

T_{ij}^k = number of tons of crop k transported from producing region i to consuming region j

The objective function was minimized subject to the following constraints:

$$L_i \geqslant \sum_{k=1}^{4} X_i^k, \quad i = 1, \ldots, 152 \tag{12.2}$$

$$FD_{tj} \leqslant \sum_{i}^{np\ 1} T_{tij}^1, \quad t = 1, 2 \text{ and } j = 1, \ldots, 78 \tag{12.3}$$

$$SD_{tj} \leqslant \sum_{i}^{np\ 4} y_{tij}\, X_i^4 + \sum_{i}^{np\ 2} T_{tij}^2, \quad t = 1, 2 \text{ and } j = 1, \ldots, 47 \tag{12.4}$$

$$WD_j \leqslant \sum_{i}^{np\ 3} T_{ij}^3, \quad j = 1, \ldots 78 \tag{12.5}$$

$$CD \leqslant \sum_{i}^{np\ 4} Y_i^4\, X_i \tag{12.6}$$

$$Y_i^k\, X_i^k \geqslant \sum_{t=1}^{2} \sum_{j}^{nc\ k} T_{tij}^k, \quad k = 1, 2 \text{ and } i = 1, \ldots, np_k \tag{12.7}$$

$$Y_i^3\, X_i^3 \geqslant \sum_{j}^{nc\ 3} T_{ij}^3, \quad i = 1, \ldots, np_3 \tag{12.8}$$

$$LB_i^k \leqslant X_i^k \leqslant UB_i^k \tag{12.9}$$

for all combinations of i and k that are defined

$$X_i^k \geqslant 0, \quad T_{tij}^k \geqslant 0, \text{ and } T_{ij}^k \geqslant 0 \tag{12.10}$$

for all combinations of k, i, t, and j that are defined

where L_i = land (acres) available in region i for production of the crops included in the study

FD_{tj} = demand (tons) for feed grain for time period t in consuming region j

SD_{tj} = demand (tons) for soybeans for time period t in consuming region j

y_{tij} = soybean equivalent of the net yield of cottonseed for time period t in producing region i which is allocated to consuming region j

WD_j = annual demand for wheat in consuming region j

CD = national annual demand for cotton lint

Y_i^k = net yield per acre of crop k in producing region i

LB_i^k = lower bound of crop k for producing region i

UB_i^k = upper bound of crop k for producing region i

All other variables were defined previously.

Equation 12.1 does not contain any variables for the transportation of cotton lint because only a national demand and no regional demands are specified for the model. The relationship between cottonseed and soybeans is defined by inequality 12.4. The demand and yields for soybeans are in terms of soybean meal and the cottonseed yields are expressed in soybean-meal–equivalent units. One ton of cottonseed meal is assumed to be equivalent to 0.8182 tons of soybean meal. All crop yields, including cottonseed, are net of the seed required for production. Cottonseed production, net of seed requirements, is distributed among the consuming regions in proportion to the regional demands for soybeans. In other words, it is assumed that the degree of substitution of cottonseed for soybeans is uniform throughout all regions.

Corn, grain sorghum, barley, and oats are aggregated into feed grain by weighting them by their relative feed values. A unit weight of corn is used as the standard unit. Unit weights of grain sorghum, barley, and oats are assigned cornequivalent feed values of 0.95, 0.90, and 0.90, respectively. The demands and yields are expressed in corn-equivalent feed units because of the aggregation of the four grains into feed grain and because the demands for grains by livestock are determined in feed units. Wheat demands and yields are also in terms of cornequivalent feed values. A unit weight of wheat is assigned a value of 1.05 feed units.

The transportation cost coefficients in Equation 12.1, P_{tij}^k and P_{ij}^k, represent transportation costs for unprocessed and unmixed grain. The transportation costs for each of the grains are calculated and then transformed to be consistent with the expression of the yields and demands in terms of corn-equivalent units. The combination of corn, grain sorghum, barley, and oats creates special problems for the development of transportation costs for feed grain. The costs of shipping barley and oats are greater than for the other grains because of their lower density; their constraining characteristic is volume rather than weight. The transportation costs of feed grain thus depend on the mix of the four grains. The cost of shipping feed grain, P_{tij}^2, is calculated by weighting transportation costs of the individual grains by their relative physical weights in the estimated composition of feed grain shipped from each producing region as given by Equation 12.11.

$$P_{tij}^2 = \sum_{m=1}^{4} C_{tij}^m \frac{Y_i^m \, S_s^m}{\sum\limits_{m=1}^{4} Y_i^m \, S_s^m} \tag{12.11}$$

where m = index for the four grains that make up feed grain

C_{tij}^m = cost of transporting a ton of grain m in time period t from producing region i to consuming region j

Y_i^m = tons of grain m produced per acre of the feed-grain rotation in producing region i

S_s^m = 1970–72 average ratio of the quantity sold from farms to the quantity produced for grain m in state s containing producing region i

Inequality 12.2 represents the limits of the total amount of land available in each of the 152 producing regions. The use of land is constrained from exceeding the quantity available. In addition to the regional total land availabilities, the level of production of the individual crops is constrained by the bounds specified by inequality 12.9. The upper and lower limits are specified to permit some choice in the location of production and to prevent total specialization by region that could result from the linear characteristics of the model. The lower limits in each region as a percentage of the 1969 census acreages are 76 percent for wheat, 80 percent for feed grain and soybeans, and 67 percent for cotton. Similarly, the upper limits are 125 percent for wheat, 140 percent for feed grain, and 120 percent for cotton. The upper limit for soybeans is 50 percent of the land in the region or the number of acres harvested in the region in 1969, whichever is larger. Soybean acreages are permitted greater flexibility because soybeans is a relatively new crop and their production location has not yet stabilized.

Inequalities 12.3, 12.4, and 12.5 require the quantities of crops shipped into a consuming region to be at least as large as their demands. The annual demands for feed grain and soybeans are based on two time periods, December through March and April through November. Two time periods are used for feed grain and soybeans because the Missouri River, the Mississippi River above the Illinois Waterway, and the Great Lakes are closed to navigation during the winter months. The annual regional demands for wheat are not divided into periods because these river sections are less important to the domestic transportation of wheat and because the wheat harvest season is sufficiently early to permit wheat to be transported before the winter season. Inequality 12.6 requires the production of cotton lint to be at least as large as its national demand.

The level of production of a crop in a producing region is required by inequalities 12.7 and 12.8 to be at least as large as the quantity of the crop exported from the region. The last set of constraints, inequality 12.10, is the standard requirement that none of the activities is permitted to be negative.

APPLICATIONS OF THE MODEL

TEN OPTIONAL SETS OF PARAMETERS

The model is applied to 10 alternative sets of interregional transportation costs and projected regional grain demands for 1980. The first option is based on a transportation cost structure estimated to be as it existed in 1972 with rail movements in single, covered hopper cars; highway movements in 5-axle, tractor-semitrailer trucks; barge movements in 195' × 35' jumbo covered hopper barges, except on the Columbia and Snake rivers where costs are estimated for 250' × 42' barges; and ship movements on the Great Lakes. The national demands in the first option are for a normal year in 1980 based on projections of the 1980 U.S. population, per capita disposable income, farm and retail prices, past trends of per capita consumption, and foreign trade. After national demands for livestock products, industrial products, and foreign trade are estimated, they are distributed among the consuming regions on the basis of recent historical distributions of livestock production, industrial demands, and export demands among the consuming regions. The demand for livestock products is converted into direct demands for crops on the basis of projected rates of conversion of grain into livestock products. Crop yields are based on historical trends, fertilization, and irrigation. Crop production costs include machinery, fuel, fertilizer, irrigation, labor, and miscellaneous inputs based on the 1980 projected yields and 1972 price levels.

Following is a list of the 10 options. The last 9 are identical to the first one except for the changes indicated by their titles:

Option I. The *base model* that has an estimated 1972 interregional transportation cost structure with demands and yields projected for normal or average conditions for 1980 based on past trends.

Option II. A *50-car rail transport system* is incorporated to represent a network with large volume, multiple-car rail shipments.

Option III. A *10 percent increase in all rail costs.*

Option IV. A *20 percent increase in all rail costs.*

Option V. A *10 percent increase in all barge costs.*

Option VI. A *20 percent increase in all barge costs.*

Option VII. An *alternative single-car rail transport system* that reduces the variable and increases the fixed costs of rail transportation.

Option VIII. A *reassignment of 10 percent of the Gulf export demand for grains to Seattle*. This and the next option are designed to analyze the redistribution of the traditional demands for exports among the ports at the Gulf and the Northwest Coast.

Option IX. A *reassignment of 25 percent of the Gulf export demand for grains to Seattle.*

Option X. A *25 percent increase in grain exports.*

DELINEATION OF REGIONS

PRODUCING REGIONS

The major grain-producing and cotton-producing areas of the 48 contiguous states are divided into 152 producing regions (Figure 12.1). Each producing region is delineated by aggregating counties with relatively homogeneous production characteristics. Not all regions, however, possess the agronomic features required for the production of each of the four individual crops. Cotton, for example, cannot be grown in the northern states. Each of the 152 regions can grow feed grain but only 145, 116, and 65 of them are permitted to grow wheat, soybeans, and cotton, respectively (Figure 12.1). A town or city represents the

Fig. 12.1. Producing regions and their specification for producing wheat, soybeans, and cotton.

origin for shipping grain from each producing region. The towns are the approximate geographical centers of the regions and generally are located on a railroad.[6]

Not all production of the grains included in the model comes from within the 152 producing regions. The 152 regions do not partition the entire 48 states but only the major crop-producing areas. In 1969, 3.2 percent of wheat, 1.2 percent of soybeans, 3.0 percent of feed grain, and 1.0 percent of cotton were produced outside the 152 regions.[7] The absolute production outside the producing regions is assumed to be the same in 1980 as it was in 1969. Consequently, the demands of each consuming region are reduced by the projected production of the area which lies within the consuming region and outside any producing region. Where this procedure results in a negative demand, the excess production is allocated to an adjacent consuming region.

CONSUMING REGIONS

The 48 states are partitioned into 73 regions of domestic demand for grain (Figure 12.2). Each consuming region has a hub that represents the location of its demand (Table 12.1). Consuming regions are delineated to minimize their number

6. The availability of a railroad is based on maps in *Handy Railroad Atlas of the United States*, Rand McNally, Chicago, 1971. The towns for regions 18, 122, and 128 are not on a railroad.

7. U.S. Dept. Commerce, Bureau of Census, *Census of Agriculture, 1969* Washington, D.C., 1970.

Fig. 12.2. Delineation of consuming regions.

yet keep them small enough so their hubs reflect the location of their demands. The hubs generally are centers of transportation and commerce. The boundaries of consuming regions coincide with producing regions and/or state boundaries unless this interferes with other criteria because the crossing of such boundaries complicates the manipulation of the data required for the model. Each of the consuming regions has a demand for feed grain and wheat, but only 42 have a demand for soybeans (Table 12.1). Fourteen regions of export demand are identified. Nine of the 14 regions are already specified as domestic consuming regions; consequently, only 5 regions specified exclusively for export are added to the 73 domestic regions for a total of 78 (Table 12.1).

TRANSPORTATION COSTS

The model requires transportation costs between each producing region and consuming region by crop and time period. The costs of hauling grain by rail, water, highway, and combinations of the three, are developed whenever they are potentially the least cost of all alternative methods. The transportation costs are those as viewed from the transportation industry, not the grain industry. The "cost" of transportation to the grain industry is the price of grain transportation services and is dependent on both the demand and supply of those services.

The boundaries of the producing and consuming regions do not coincide. No transportation costs are applied to movements of grain from a producing region to a consuming region if the former is totally or partially contained within the latter because the exact location of the demand within a consuming region is not identified by the model.

Grain elevator loading and unloading costs are added to transportation costs because these handling costs are dependent on the mode of transportation used. Handling costs, based on replacement costs for the facilities, are selected from *Cost of Storing and Handling Grain and Controlling Dust in Commercial Elevators, 1971–72 and Projections for 1973–74.*[8] The national averages of all facilities for each mode are used except for the following. Water-receiving costs for port terminals on the Gulf, Columbia-Snake, and Great Lakes are used for their respective areas. The national inland terminal average is used for all other water-receiving costs. Water loadout cost for the Great Lakes is the loadout cost used for port terminals on the Great Lakes. The published handling costs are converted from a per-bushel to a per-ton basis.

RAIL

Five alternative rail costs are used: (1) single-car, (2) multiple 50-car units, (3) 10 percent increase in single-car costs, (4) 20 percent increase in single-car costs, and (5) alternate single-car costs. The single-car costs are used in 6 of the 10 options for which the model is applied. The others are each used in only one option designed specifically to analyze the impacts of the change in rail costs. The single-car costs for 1972 are the inflated variable costs extrapolated from *Rail Carload Cost Scales by Territories for the Year 1969.*[9] These scales provide costs per hundredweight by railroad territory, type of car, short-line distance, and load weight. Variable costs are used because the allocation of fixed costs among freight classes is an arbitrary decision. The published, fully allocated cost scales distribute the fixed costs on the basis of ton-miles and it can be argued that this places a relatively large fixed-cost burden on heavy products like grain. For this study, the relationship between cost and distance is more important than the absolute cost because the costs used are the basis for computing other costs, viz., the 10 and 20 percent increases in rail costs, the multiple 50-car costs, and the alternate single-car costs. The variable costs are important for decision making. They are costs that must be covered by the revenue of each individual haul, or the haul should not be undertaken.[10] The rail costs are computed separately for the following four railroad territories: Official (including New England), Southern, Western (excluding Mountain Pacific and Trans-territory), and Mountain Pacific and Trans-territory. Costs for covered hopper cars are used because most grain in 1980 will be moved by these cars rather than boxcars if past trends continue.

The calculation of rail distances between producing and consuming regions is done in two steps. First, a total mileage matrix is calculated from the *Handy Rail-*

8. USDA, ERS, *Cost of Storing and Handling Grain and Controlling Dust in Commercial Elevators, 1971–72 Projections for 1973–74,* Bull. 515, Washington, D.C., Apr. 1973.

9. Interstate Commerce Commission, Bureau of Accounts, *Rail Carload Cost Scales by Territories for the Year 1969,* Statement No. 1C1-69, Washington, D.C., July 1972.

10. William J. Baumol, "The Role of Cost in the Minimum Pricing of Railroad Service," *J. Business* 35 (Oct. 1962): 357–66.

road Atlas of the United States.[11]   Second, the total distance for each route is allocated to the four railroad territories. This allocation is in proportion to the division, among the territories of a linear path between the origin and destination. When a railroad obviously could not travel on an approximate straight line between an origin and destination, the linear path is broken into line segments. This procedure provides accurate territorial mileages when the ratios of the actual mileages to the linear distances are equal for each of the several territories.

The published cost scales are for ten distances that range from less than 100 miles—the average way train miles in the territory—to 2,000 miles. The scales, however, are constructed to be linear. Consequently, equations are readily calculated to enable rail cost estimations to be continuous with respect to mileage. The 1969 costs are increased by 24 percent to adjust for the rise in prices and wages between 1969 and 1972.[12]   These adjusted cost functions are given in Table 12.2.

The constant terms of the rail costs are a reflection of terminal costs. For interterritorial movements, one-half the constant term is used for both the origination and the destination territories. If an origin or destination lies on the border of two territories, the location is assigned to the territory that has nonzero mileage for the particular movement.

The load-weight capacity of a covered hopper car depends on the kind of grain hauled. The estimated capacity for corn, grain sorghum, soybeans, and wheat is 195,000 pounds. The estimated capacity is 117,500 pounds for barley and 118,000 pounds for oats. The cost scales list load weights only in 10,000-pound intervals, therefore, costs for precise capacities are obtained by interpolation.

No published costs are available for multiple-car shipments that are compatible with the single-car costs. The 50-car costs are calculated by adjusting the single-car costs. Single-car and 50-car costs between each of ten origins and six destinations are computed using the railroad cost methodology developed for a Fort Dodge, Iowa, region study.[13]   Costs are regressed on the distances between origins and destinations for 60 routes and the three load-weight classes used—1,950, 1,775, and 1,180 hundredweight. The resulting constant and distance coefficients are given in Table 12.3. The multiple 50-car costs are estimated by multiplying the single-car costs in Table 12.2 by the ratios of the 50-car to single-car costs in Table 12.3. This procedure assumes the relationship between single-car and 50-car costs is the same for all railroad territories.

The alternate single-car costs are computed to alter the relationship between cost and distance. The constant terms in Table 12.2 are increased 50 percent and the mileage coefficients are decreased 10 percent. These alternate costs more nearly reflect the relationship between distance and rail rates, but they are not designed to be accurate estimates of rates.

11. Rand McNally, Chicago, 1971.
12. The increase is calculated as a Laspeyres index with 1970 as the base year. See C. Phillip Baumel, Thomas P. Drinka, Dennis R. Lifferth, and John J. Miller, *An Economic Analysis of Alternative Grain Transportation Systems: A Case Study*, Dept. Transportation, Federal Railroad Admin. Report PB-224819, Nov. 1973.
13. Ibid., Appendix F.

Fig. 12.3. Geographical location of water access points for domestic grain shipments.

WATER

The representative locations selected for shipping grain on the inland water-ways are listed in Table 12.4 and shown in Figure 12.3. Each location that was selected as an access to the waterways is assumed to have facilities for receiving or shipping grain by truck, water, and rail (if the water access point is on a rail line). The criterion for selecting access points is that they provide a ready access to the inland waterways for at least one producing or consuming region.[14]

The cost of barging grain depends on the river sections, the barge, the tow-boat, and kind of grain. Barging costs are partitioned into four basic classes: (1) investment, (2) towing, (3) switching and fleeting, and (4) other. The invest-ment cost is the ownership cost of the barge and depends on the kind of barge used. Towing costs represent the cost of using towboat facilities to move the barge from one water access point to another. Switching cost is the cost of hav-ing a local tugboat (or river towboat when no tugs are available) maneuver the barge from the towboat to the fleet, from the fleet to the elevator, from the ele-vator to the fleet, and again from the fleet to the towboat. The fleeting cost is the

14. Information on the location of grain-handling facilities was obtained from *Schedule of Grain Handling Facilities at Points on the Inland Waterway System*, Waterway Freight Bureau, Washington, D.C., Mar. 1972; *Guide to Published Barge Rates on Bulk Grain Schedule No. 8*, Arrow Transportation Co., Sheffield, Ala., Oct. 1972; *Naming Local Barge Towing, Commodity and Boat Rates in Unscheduled Service over Irregular Routes*, Pacific Inland Tariff Bureau, Freight Tariff No. 93, Portland, Oreg., 1970.

cost of leaving the barge in a fleet, i.e., a "parking lot" for barges. Other costs for barges include insurance, maintenance, repairs, cleaning, taxes, administration, general overhead, and harbor costs not included in fleeting or switching costs.

Domestic grain shipments on the Great Lakes have consisted largely of shipping wheat from Duluth-Superior to Buffalo. On the basis of a preliminary analysis, only producing regions 78 to 84 and 136 to 139 are permitted to ship grain via the Great Lakes to Buffalo, consuming region 7. These shipping costs are estimated at \$0.15 per bushel, the approximate charge negotiated between grain companies and carriers on the Great Lakes.[15]

Barge investment costs. The investment cost is the product of the number of days required to make the trip and the daily barge investment cost. The daily cost is 1/365 of the annual equivalent cost (AEC) given by Equation 12.12.[16]

$$AEC = \frac{i(1 + i)^n}{(1 + i)^n - 1} P - \frac{i}{(1 + i)^n - 1} P_s \qquad (12.12)$$

where P = purchase price
P_s = salvage value
i = interest rate
n = length of life or ownership of the equipment

For barges on the Mississippi River system, the cost of a barge is estimated at \$125,000. The barges are estimated to have a 1,400-ton capacity at a 9-foot draft. The life of a barge is estimated at 23 years with a salvage value of \$1,000. The AEC is \$12,036.08 or \$32.97 per day. The investment cost for barges servicing Tampa, Florida, is estimated to be 85 percent greater because these barges must cross the open Gulf waters and consequently require water-tight, reinforced construction.

The procedure to determine the investment cost for barges on the Columbia-Snake is identical to that for the Mississippi system. But the initial cost is increased to \$425,000 and the salvage value is increased to \$3,400. The investment cost is higher because the barges are larger (a capacity of 2,500 tons), have electrical screw augers that deliver grain to a central sump from which the marine leg of the elevator can readily unload the barge, and have self-trimming devices for loading.

The time required to complete a trip depends on the origin, destination, and route followed. The actual towing time required is determined by dividing the river miles by the average speed for the appropriate river section as given in Table 12.5.[17] In addition to the time required for towing, time is needed for

15. The cost estimates, which include insurance, are based on conversations with representatives of grain companies which are familiar with these shipments.

16. Gerald W. Smith, *Engineering Economy: Analysis of Capital Expenditures*, Iowa State Univ. Press, Ames, 1968, p. 45.

17. Most of the river miles are taken from volume V of the 1969 *Light List, Mississippi River System*, U.S. Coast Guard, USGPO, Washington, D.C., 1969. The speed and mileages for the Tombigbee, Gulf, and Arkansas rivers are estimates from barge operators traveling on those river sections.

switching, normal delays, loading, unloading, and waiting for a towboat. Normal times for loading, unloading, waiting for a towboat, and delays other than those included in Table 12.6 are estimated at 20 days for a round trip between any two water access points.

The barge travel time adjustments listed in Table 12.6 are required when a barge changes river sections and consequently is likely to change towboats. The adjustments are for round trips. It is estimated that a 3-day delay one way (6 days for a round trip) generally results from a change of river sections. A one-way delay of 4 days is estimated for St. Louis because of congestion. One-way delays of 6 days are estimated for the White and Arkansas rivers because of the infrequency of traffic through these junctions. The days gained in Table 12.6 are a result of not requiring barges that move between the Missouri River, Upper Mississippi River, and Illinois Waterway to go all the way to St. Louis to switch. However, the 4-day switching delay is maintained. The 5-day travel time between Morris and Chicago is a result of two-stage switching. Usually barges are switched at Morris and at Lemont. It is estimated that barges wait 2 days at Morris, spend 1 day traveling from Morris to Lemont, and take 2 days for switching at Lemont, i.e., 10 days for a round trip.

Barge towing costs. Towing costs are separated from other barge costs because they are distinct and often performed by different companies. The towing costs are estimated as the reciprocal towing charges that towing companies charge each other. Representatives of the towing industry believe that these towing charges are accurate estimates of towing costs.

The basic towing charges are given in Table 12.5; adjustments to complete the basic costs are in Table 12.7. The first two adjustments in Table 12.7 are included because the Lower Mississippi charges are based on a continuation of the trip below Cairo, Illinois. The Lower Mississippi costs are very low and cannot be used for the short distance between St. Louis to Cairo. These two cost adjustments are based on the assumption that the barges would remain with the same towboats from St. Louis to Cairo as they are with on the Ohio.

The costs of transport on the section of the Mississippi below Greenville, Mississippi, are increased because most southbound tows already have a full complement of barges by the time they are that far south. If they do not, and can pick up additional barges, it means they have had to forego the revenue they could have received by taking on more barges farther upstream. If the higher tow costs are not paid, it would mean that the loaded barges would not be moved for several extra days.

The towing costs for short trips on the Upper Mississippi and Ohio are increased because the towing charges used in Table 12.5 are for long hauls and have a 400-mile minimum distance associated with them. The navigation factors are relatively constant throughout the lengths of these river sections. Lower costs for long distance reflect the efficiency of long hauls with fewer interruptions for adding or dropping barges from the tow.

When routes can be shortened by avoiding backtracking, some of the trip's towing cost can be saved. Recall that travel time is saved by assuming that barges do not go all the way to St. Louis when they move between the Missouri, the Upper Mississippi, and the Illinois Waterway. The reduction in towing cost in Table 12.8 between those river sections is the counterpart of the time saved shown in Table 12.6.

Towing charges are not as readily available for the Columbia-Snake as for the Mississippi River system. Consequently, towing costs on the Columbia-Snake are based on the estimated cost of operating towboats. A full tow on the Columbia River is four barges and on the Snake River it is two. Larger towboats with 3,200 horsepower are used on the Columbia River. Their operating cost is estimated at $100 per hour. The operating cost of smaller towboats that work on the Snake River is estimated at $60 per hour. These costs, the number of barges per tow, the capacity per barge, and the speeds listed in Table 12.5 are used to derive the towing cost. Empty barges are assumed to be towed at a cost of 75 percent of the towing cost for loaded barges.

Barge switching and fleeting costs. A minimum of eight switches are required for a round trip. The barge must be moved from the tow to the fleet, the fleet to the elevator, the elevator to the fleet, and then back again from the fleet to the towboat at both the origin and the destination. Each switch is estimated to cost $30. Hence, switching costs for a trip with a minimum of eight switches are estimated to be $240.

When a barge changes towboats at a junction of two river sections, additional switches are required for a round trip. Again these switching costs are estimated at $30 each for a total of $120 for each switching junction. Additional switches above the minimum eight are estimated to be required for the following passages:

1. Through, but not to or from, St. Louis, New Orleans, and Mobile
2. Through, but not to or from, Baton Rouge on the Port Allen cutoff for the Intracoastal Canal
3. Between the Kanawha and the Ohio
4. Between the Cumberland and the Ohio
5. Between the Tennessee and the Ohio above the mouth of the Tennessee[18]
6. Between the White and the Mississippi
7. Between the White and the Arkansas
8. Between the Arkansas and the Mississippi
9. Between the Missouri and the Mississippi, except for connection with the Illinois Waterway
10. Between the Illinois Waterway and the Mississippi, except for connection with the Missouri
11. Between the Illinois Waterway and the Missouri
12. Between the Columbia and the Snake

There are special switching costs from Morris, Illinois, to Chicago. The switch is made in two stages as discussed above. The round-trip cost of the Morris-Chicago switch is estimated at $700.

18. The towboats that operate on the Tennessee generally service Cairo and/or St. Louis. Consequently, no switching is required when traffic moves through Cairo to the Tennessee.

Fleeting costs occur when a barge is waiting to be moved to an elevator or to a towboat. Fleeting costs are estimated at $6 per day for each day or part thereof. Barges are assumed to be in a fleet the same number of days as there are nontravel days. A minimum of 20 days nontravel time is estimated for each round trip. Additional delays that result in fleeting costs are estimated to be the same as those given in Table 12.6, with the exceptions that the reductions relating to travel times between the Upper Mississippi, Missouri, and Illinois Waterway do not apply, and only 8 of the 10 days for the Morris-Chicago route apply because 2 days are estimated for travel time between Morris and Lemont.

On the Columbia and Snake rivers, the river towboat itself often must pick up and place the barges at their precise desired location. One-half hour of towboat time for each pickup or drop-off is used as the basis to estimate the switching costs.

The fleeting costs for the Columbia-Snake system are estimated at $6 per day for 4 days for each round trip. Because the Columbia and Snake rivers are relatively short river sections, the towboats service each location frequently and barges need wait only a short time for a towboat.

Other barge costs. Insurance, maintenance, repairs, administration, taxes, cleaning, and harbor costs are grouped into other costs. Cleaning costs are estimated at $100 per round trip for each barge. The major Gulf ports have extra-large switching costs as well as other special port fees. The harbor costs for New Orleans and Mobile are estimated at $140 per entry into these ports. The comparable costs for Houston and Corpus Christi are estimated at $160. The remaining other costs are estimated on a per-diem basis as follows: insurance, $1.50; maintenance and repair, $3.50; and administration and taxes, $9.00. These other costs cover the costs of a barge only. They do not include any towboat costs. The estimated number of days used to compute these costs for each trip is identical to those used for the barge investment costs.

The daily "other costs" on the Columbia-Snake are estimated to be the same as for the Mississippi system except that insurance and maintenance and repair costs are increased because of the greater navigational hazards and more valuable equipment. Insurance costs are estimated at $28.88 and maintenance and repair at $5.00 per day per barge.

Cost of barging a ton of grain. The number of tons hauled for a given trip is based on the capacity of the river section with the smallest capacity of all river sections used for the trip and the density of the grain hauled. The capacity constraints for the river sections are given in Table 12.5. For all river sections, the maximum capacities are the effective capacities for wheat, corn, and grain sorghum. But for oats and barley the volume of the barges is more restrictive. On the Mississippi River system, the payloads are estimated at 880 tons for oats and 1,300 tons for barley. On the Columbia-Snake, the payloads estimated are 1,550 tons for oats and 2,325 tons for barley.

For loads above minimum tonnages, the barge towing costs are based on the actual weight of the payload. If the payload tonnage is less than the minimum tonnage, the towing cost is based on the minimum tonnage in Table 12.5. The effect of these capacity constraints and minimum costs is to increase the per-ton transportation cost of low-density grains.

TRUCK

Truck operating costs vary from one locality to another. The Interstate Commerce Commission has indicated this variation by partitioning the 48 contiguous states into eight regions as follows: New England, Middle Atlantic, Central, Southern, Southwestern, Midwestern, Rocky Mountain, and Pacific Coast.[19] Trucking costs are developed for the Midwest; then the costs for the other regions are calculated as the products of the regional factors (Table 12.8) and the Midwest cost as shown by Equation 12.13.

$$TC = \sum_{i=1}^{8} TC_V \, M_i \, RF_i \qquad\qquad (12.13)$$

where TC = total truck costs for a trip
   TC_V = total truck cost unadjusted for regional variation; the cost of trucking if the trip were entirely within region V
   M_i = ratio of the miles traveled in region i to the total miles[20]
   RF_i = regional variation factor for region i

Each of the eight regional factors is computed as the ratio of the line haul cost of the region and the line haul cost of region V for moving 20,000 to 29,999 pounds 100 to 124 miles.[21] The 20,000–29,999-pound class is assumed to be the best approximation of average weight hauled for an entire round trip. The 100–124-mile class, although possibly longer than the average trucking distance, is chosen because the regional variation may reflect substantial travel within cities as a result of movements between relatively large cities which are close together. Such movements would not be representative of grain shipments.

Total trucking costs are separated into costs allocated to distance and costs allocated to time as given by Equation 12.14.

$$TC_V = C_h \, H + C_m \, M \qquad\qquad (12.14)$$

where TC_V = defined previously
   C_h = the cost per hour of truck use
   H = the hours required for the trip
   C_m = the cost per mile of truck use
   M = the distance of the trip in miles

Costs that are allocated to time include the fixed cost of the truck, interest on its

19. Interstate Commerce Commission, Bureau of Accounts, *Cost of Transporting Freight by Class I and Class II Motor Common Carriers of General Commodities by Regions or Territories for the Year 1970*, Statement No. 2C1-70, Washington, D.C., 1972.
20. Mileages are from the *Standard Highway Mileage Guide*, Rand McNally, Chicago, 1966.
21. See footnote 19.

purchase value, license fees, insurance, highway use tax, overhead, and the driver's wages. The costs allocated to distance include fuel, oil, tires, maintenance, and repairs. The hours required for a trip are based on the distance traveled; average speed; and the time required for loading, unloading, and other required stops.

It is assumed that trucks operate 3,000 hours annually, travel 110,000 miles annually, and have an economic life of 4 years. The estimated purchase price of the tractor and semitrailer is $31,300 and their salvage, or resale, value is $8,900. The investment cost of the truck is converted to an annual equivalent cost (AEC) based on an 8 percent interest rate as shown by Equation 12.15.

$$AEC = \$31,300 \left[\frac{0.08\,(1+0.08)^4}{(1+0.08)^4 - 1} \right] - \$8,900 \left[\frac{0.08}{(1+0.08)^4 - 1} \right] = \$7,475 \quad (12.15)$$

Annual state license fees, personal property taxes, and other fees or taxes, except fuel taxes, for a 5-axle tractor-semitrailer are estimated at $1,320, the average for the 8 states in the Midwest region.[22] In addition to the state fees, the federal use tax is estimated at $220 for the truck tractor.[23] Truck insurance and safety costs are estimated at 4.0 percent of total expenses, $1,380. Overhead, including general administration, is estimated at $2,220, 5.8 percent of the total annual expenses. Driver's wages and benefits are estimated at $4.50 per hour. The hourly truck costs allocated to be dependent upon time are summarized as follows:

Annual equivalent cost of 5-axle tractor-semitrailer truck	$7,475/yr
State fees and taxes	1,320/yr
Federal highway use tax	220/yr
Insurance and safety	1,380/yr
Overhead	2,220/yr
Annual total	$12,615
Cost per hour of operation (annual total/3,000 hr)	$4.20
Drivers wage per hour	4.50
Estimated cost allocated per hour of truck operation C_h in Equation 12.14	$8.70

The costs allocated per mile of truck travel are $0.06945 for fuel and oil, $0.02668 for tires and maintenance, and $0.01423 for repairs. Thus the total cost allocated per mile, C_m in Equation 12.14, is estimated to be $0.11035.

The total time required for a trip is calculated as the sum of the travel, loading, and unloading time. Loading and unloading time is estimated at 40 minutes per trip.

The average speed is dependent on the kind of road traveled. It is assumed that trucks average 40 mph on noninterstate highways and 60 mph on interstate highways. A random sample of producing regions and their surrounding consuming regions shows that for distances up to 300 miles, 42 percent of the mileage is

22. Laurence L. Liston and Robert W. Sherrer, *Road-User and Property Taxes on Selected Motor Vehicles, 1970*, U.S. Dept. Transportation, Federal Highway Admin. Bureau of Public Roads, 1972.

23. U.S. Dept. Treasury. *Federal Use Tax Return on Highway Motor Vehicles*, Internal Revenue Service Form 2290, Washington, D.C., 1972.

on interstate highways. All travel beyond the first 300 miles is on interstate highways. In addition to the driving time, travel time is increased for long trips, because a 30-minute driving break is imposed after every 4 hours of continuous driving.

The trucking cost per ton of grain is calculated by dividing the total cost, TC in Equation 12.13, by the number of tons of grain hauled. The payload for 5-axle trucks is estimated to be 24 tons, except when oats are hauled it is estimated to be 16 tons.

REGIONAL DEMANDS [24]

National demands for livestock products and per capita consumption of grains and cotton for food and industrial purposes are estimated with procedures similar to those described for linear models of previous chapters. The allocation of the national demands among consuming regions is more complex than for the other models because of the larger number of consuming regions and the division of the annual demand into two time periods.

The derived demand for grain by livestock is based on the demand for nine livestock classes: (1) dairy, (2) beef, (3) hogs, (4) chickens, (5) broilers, (6) turkeys, (7) sheep, (8) horses and mules, and (9) other livestock. These nine classes are aggregations of the thirteen categories listed in *National and State Livestock-Feed Relationships*.[25] The demands for the first seven classes are converted to a demand for corn-equivalent feed units by Equation 12.16. The coefficient, 1.287, in Equation 12.16 is the 1980 projected number of corn-equivalent feed units per grain-consuming animal unit; it is based on its historical trend. The 1980 feed units required for horses and mules are projected on the basis of the average number of grain-consuming animal units for this class in 1968–70 and the feed units required for other livestock are based on the historical trend.[26]

$$FU_i = 1.287 \, (GCAU_i/Q_i) \, Q_i' \qquad (12.16)$$

where FU_i = the annual number of corn-equivalent feed units required for the 48 states for livestock class i

$GCAU_i$ = average number of grain-consuming animal units of livestock class i fed annually in the 48 states in 1968–70[27]

Q_i = average number of pounds (dozens in the case of eggs, i.e., chickens) of livestock product i produced annually in the years 1968–70[28]

Q_i' = 1980 projected demand, adjusted for foreign trade, of livestock product i

24. This section describes the estimation of regional demands for option I. The demands for the other options are the same except for changes indicated by their titles.
25. USDA, ERS, Supplement for 1972 to Stat. Bull. 446, Washington, D.C., 1972.
26. Ibid.
27. Ibid.
28. USDA, *Food Consumption, Prices, and Expenditures*. Supplement to Agr. Econ. Report 138, Washington, D.C., 1972.

The national estimates of feed units required for each livestock class are distributed to the 48 states by Equation 12.17, with the exception of other livestock, class 9. Class 9 includes livestock such as pets, laboratory animals, circus animals, zoo animals, etc., not included in the *Census of Agriculture*.[29] The state distribution of other livestock is computed with Equation 12.18.

$$FU_i^s = (GCAU_i^s/GCAU_i)\,FU_i \qquad (i = 1, 2, 3, \ldots, 8) \tag{12.17}$$

where FU_i^s = number of feed units required in state s by livestock class i

$GCAU_i^s$ = average number of grain-consuming animal units of livestock class i fed annually in state s in the years 1968–1970[30]

$GCAU_i$ and FU_i = previously defined

$$FU_9^s = (POP_{80}^s/POP_{80})\,FU_9 \tag{12.18}$$

where POP_{80}^s = population of state s in 1980[31]

$$POP_{80} = \sum_s POP_{80}^s \qquad (s = 1, 2, 3, \ldots, 48)$$

FU_9 = previously defined

The demand for grains by livestock is not uniform throughout the year. The result is that the demand requirements in general cannot be divided uniformly over time into the two time periods (December through March, $t = 1$, and April through November, $t = 2$). In addition, the state demands given by Equations 12.17 and 12.18 must be allocated among the consuming regions. Both the seasonal and regional allocations of the demand for feed grain by livestock are based on their historical allocations when data are available.

Equations 12.19 and 12.20 are used to compute the regional and seasonal demands for feed grain by livestock.

$$FU_{jt}^s = \sum_i \sum_c \left(\frac{N_{ic}^{js}}{N_i^s}\right)\left(\frac{A_{it}^s}{A_{iy}^s}\right) FU_i^s \qquad \begin{array}{l}(j = 1, 2, 3, \ldots, 73)\\(i = 1, 2, 3, \ldots, 9)\\(t = 1, 2)\end{array} \tag{12.19}$$

$$FU_{jt} = \sum_{s \in k_j} FU_{jt}^s \qquad \begin{array}{l}(j = 1, 2, 3, \ldots, 73)\\(t = 1, 2)\end{array} \tag{12.20}$$

where FU_{jt}^s = corn-equivalent feed units demanded by livestock in period t in the part of consuming region j which lies within state s

FU_i^s = defined previously

N_{ic}^{js} = number of class i animals in county c of region j in state s

N_i^s = number of class i animals in the state containing county c

29. See footnote 7.
30. See footnote 25.
31. U.S. Dept. Commerce, Bureau of Census, *Population Estimates and Projections*, Current Population Reports Series No. 477, Washington, D.C., 1972.

A_{it}^s = proxy for the quantity of feed grain consumed by class i animals fed in state s in time period t

A_{iy}^s = proxy for the quantity of feed grain consumed by class i animals fed in state s annually

FU_{jt} = tons of corn-equivalent feed units demanded by livestock in consuming region j and time period t

k_j = the set of states in which part or all of region j is contained

The data for N_{ic}^{js} and N_i^s for all classes except other livestock are taken from the 1969 *Census of Agriculture.*[32] For other livestock, N_{ic}^{js} and N_i^s are set equal to the number of people in county c and in the state containing county c, respectively, as reported in the 1970 *Census of Population.*[33] Admittedly, this is a crude means of approximation for the distribution of other livestock, but there are simply no data available for this class.

The A_{it}^s and A_{iy}^s values are calculated by different methods and data sources, depending upon the class of livestock. In all cases, A_{iy}^s equals the sum of A_{i1}^s and A_{i2}^s. Recall the two time periods are December 1 through March 31 ($t = 1$) and April 1 through November 30 ($t = 2$). Seasonal milk production is used as an estimate for the seasonal demand for the part of dairy comprised of milk cows and heifers 2 years old and older.[34] The consumption of feed by heifers and heifer calves kept for milk is uniformly distributed with respect to time. The A_{it}^s values for that part of beef comprised of cattle on feed are based on cattle on feed for the 23 states for which there are seasonal data[35] and the seasonal distribution for the other 25 states is assumed to be uniform with respect to time. The A_{it}^s values for hogs are based on the December 1 and June 1 inventory of hogs by weight classes[36] and the estimated consumption of feed over time for each weight class. Like dairy and beef, the demand for chickens is a combination of two groups, viz., (1) hens and pullets and (2) replacement chickens. The seasonal demand for the first group is based on seasonal egg production and the seasonal demand for feed by the second group is based on seasonal hatchings of egg-type chickens and their estimated feed consumption with respect to age.[37] The seasonal demand for feed by broilers and turkeys is also based on their seasonal hatchings and their feed consumption with respect to age.[38] Turkeys are divided into two groups, light and heavy breeds, and seasonal hatchings are available for only six regions that partition the 48 states. Each state within a region is assumed to have the same seasonal variation as the region. The demand for feed by sheep, horses and mules, and other livestock is assumed to be distributed uniformly with respect to time.

The regional demands for feed grain are reduced by the estimated quantity of

---

32. See footnote 7.

33. U.S. Dept. Commerce, Bureau of Census, *Census of Population, 1970*, Washington, D.C., June 1972.

34. USDA, SRS, Crop Reporting Board, *Milk Production*, Washington, D.C., various issues.

35. USDA, SRS, Crop Reporting Board, *Cattle on Feed*, Washington, D.C., various issues.

36. USDA, SRS, Crop Reporting Board, *Hogs and Pigs*, Washington, D.C., various issues.

37. USDA, SRS, Crop Reporting Board, *Eggs, Chickens, and Turkeys*, Washington, D.C., various issues.

38. Ibid.; USDA, SRS, Crop Reporting Board, *Hatchery Production*, Washington, D.C., various issues.

the demands that are projected to be supplied by the consumption of wheat by livestock. It is projected that 250 million bushels of wheat will be consumed by livestock in 1980. This national quantity is allocated to the consuming regions and time periods on the basis of the projected total number of feed units required by the consuming regions, the average quantity of wheat fed on farms where grown in a state during 1968–70, and the national average quantity of wheat fed in the two time periods.[39] For those 15 states without data on the quantity of wheat fed, the quantity fed is assumed to be proportional to the number of feed units required in a state to the total quantity required for the 15 states.

The national demands for corn and oats for cereal are each distributed to the states in proportion to the state distribution of the employees in the cereal preparations industry.[40] The national demand for corn for dry processing is distributed among the states in proportion to the state distribution of corn mills.[41]

The national demand for wheat for food and industrial uses is allocated among the consuming regions in proportion to the regional distribution of wheat flour milling capacity.[42]

The regional demands for soybeans for crushing are based on the location of crushing plants and their respective capacities. Unknown capacities of plants within a state are assigned a capacity equal to the difference between the total state capacity and the sum of the capacities known for particular sites divided by the number of sites with unknown capacities. Some state capacities are estimated from actual quantities crushed, others by conversations with persons familiar with the industry in that state, and still others as the sum of the capacities of crushing plants within the state.

The seasonal demands for grain for food and industrial needs are assumed to be uniform over time. The total annual demands are divided such that 33 percent are demanded for December–March and 67 percent for April–November.

The 1980 export demands for wheat and soybeans are projected to be 746 million and 1.04 billion bushels, respectively. The 1980 export demand for feed grain is projected to be 982 million corn-equivalent bushels, i.e., if all feed-grain exports were comprised of corn, 982 million bushels would be exported.

The projected national export levels include exports such as unprocessed grain and the equivalent quantities of grain in exports of grain products. For example, the export level of soybeans includes the grain equivalent of soybean meal exports. The percentage of the total exports of each grain exported as grain in 1980 are approximated by their historical averages for recent years. For 1980, 70, 89.4, and 100 percent of all soybean, wheat, and feed-grain exports, respectively, are projected to be exported as grain. The exports of grain as grain are distributed to the export consuming regions and time periods on the basis of historical amounts exported from the regions between December 1969 and November 1972. This distribution among the port regions and time periods is shown in Table 12.9. The

39. USDA, ERS, *Wheat Situation*, Washington, D.C., various issues.
40. U.S. Dept. Commerce, Bureau of Census, *Census of Manufacturers, 1967*, Washington, D.C., 1971.
41. "List of Flour Mills," *Northwestern Miller*, Miller Publ. Co., Minneapolis, Minn., Sept. 1971.
42. Ibid.

export demand for grain exported as grain products is distributed among the consuming regions with the same procedure as the domestic demand for the identical products is distributed.

When all the several demands for each grain are estimated, the demands for corn, oats, barley, and grain sorghum in each region are aggregated into the demand for feed grain for that region. Likewise, the several demands for wheat and soybeans are aggregated into their respective regional demands.

Only the national demand for cotton lint is estimated. The 1980 domestic demand for lint cotton is projected to be 17 pounds per capita. The 1980 export demand for lint cotton in 480-pound bales is projected to be 2.1 million. The summation of the domestic and export demand projections results in a national lint cotton demand of 10.04 million bales.

RESULTS

The 1972 production of the six grains was 285 million tons. Options I through IX, with the basic level of exports, have a projected grain production of 323 million tons for 1980. Option X, with 25 percent more exports than in the first nine options, has a projected grain production level of 344 million tons.

Grain sales from farms were 201 million tons in 1972 (70.8 percent of grain production). Based on past trends, sales are projected to be 233 million tons (72.1 percent of production) in 1980 with the basic level of exports in the first nine options, and 254 million tons (73.7 percent of production) with the greater exports of option X.

The interregional movements reported in the results of the optimization model exclude the grain traffic that occurs within the 78 consuming regions of the model, i.e., grain that satisfies the local demand is not reported in the interregional shipments. Consequently, grain sales from farms are greater than the interregional flows. The reported flows are the sum of the flows via the individual transportation modes; hence, if the same ton is shipped by a combination of modes, it is counted as many times as the number of modes that carry it. This double counting does not occur with the ton-mile measurement of the traffic.

The nonland costs of producing grain are essentially unchanged under the different transportation systems, except that higher rail costs result in increased production costs (Table 12.10). A 25 percent shift of the Gulf exports to Seattle reduces the cost of producing grain by $3 million and the 25 percent increase in all grain exports increases the production costs substantially. The variations in the transportation and handling—loading and unloading—costs are greater than the variations in production costs (Table 12.10).

A TRANSPORT SYSTEM WITH SINGLE-CAR RAIL UNITS (OPTION I)

The single-car rail transport system is the basic option with 1980 projected grain demands, yields, and production costs expected to occur under normal conditions based on past trends and with a rail, truck, and water transportation cost structure estimated to exist in 1972. With the rail conditions of option I, grain water traffic should increase at a lower rate than in the past. Under this transportation cost structure and grain demands, water traffic is only 2.73 million tons more than in 1971. Under the cost structure of option I, 6.98 million tons are carried by truck. However, this quantity reflects only interregional shipments and excludes local shipments within consuming regions. The quantity carried in the past by trucks is not available. All truck movements selected by the model are in conjunction with water shipments.

A TRANSPORT SYSTEM WITH 50-CAR RAIL UNITS (OPTION II)

Use of a rail system based on 50-car shipments reduces transport costs, including handling, by $68 million compared to the single-car rail system (option I). The multiple-car system would require larger volumes for shipment and would increase assembly and gathering costs that are not included in the model. A saving of this magnitude is adequate to cover the added assembly cost of shipping grain several more miles from a farm to an elevator with a capacity for large-volume shipments. In addition to the direct cost savings, multiple-car shipments reduce the rail equipment necessary to haul a given quantity of grain and provide a means of avoiding additional costs of transporting by the nonoptimal mode when a single-car system would result in rail car shortages. These additional savings may be large. For example, the costs of rail car shortages in 1969 for 874 grain elevators in Iowa were estimated at $2,362,947.[43]

Lower rail costs with the 50-car system result in an increase in the ton and ton-mile traffic of grain (Tables 12.11 and 12.12). The increase in rail equipment required because of this additional tonnage would be more than offset by the effective increase in the supply of rail cars resulting from a faster turnaround time for the cars.[44]

A TRANSPORTATION SYSTEM WITH HIGHER RAIL COSTS (OPTIONS III AND IV)

In option III, rail costs are 10 percent greater than in option I, and in option IV they are 20 percent greater than in option I, otherwise the three models are the same. Options III and IV have the largest transportation costs among the 10, except for option X (Table 12.10). Rail transportation costs are greater for option III than option IV because of a disproportionately greater decline in the ton and ton-miles of rail grain traffic in the latter than in the former (Tables 12.11 and 12.12). The cost of grain production and handling also increases with the higher transportation costs of options III and IV. The available land used for production

43. Phillip C. Baumel, W. W. Thompson, and Roy D. Hickman, *Impact of Transportation Equipment Shortages and Substandard Transportation Service in 1969 on Iowa Country Elevators,* Iowa Agr. and Home Econ. Exp. Sta. Special Report 68, Iowa State Univ., Ames, Dec. 1971.

44. The study by Baumel et al. estimates that the turnaround time for 50-car shipments is approximately half that for single-car shipments. The quantity of grain carried by rail, in contrast, increases by only 3.7 percent with the use of the 50-car shipments. See Baumel et al., *An Economic Analysis.*

and its location are unchanged, but the location of the production of particular grains changes, which increases total grain production costs.

A TRANSPORTATION SYSTEM WITH HIGHER BARGE COSTS (OPTIONS V AND VI)

The effects of higher barge costs are analyzed with options V and VI which respectively have barging costs 10 percent and 20 percent higher than in option I. Otherwise the three options are identical. Grain transportation costs are less sensitive to increased barging cost than to increased rail cost even when the relative quantities carried by the two modes are taken into consideration. The total ton-miles of grain traffic among the first six models vary directly with increases in rail-costs (Tables 12.10 and 12.12). In contrast, the total ton-miles of traffic vary inversely with increases in barge costs. The amount of grain carried by truck is highly correlated with that carried by barge.

A TRANSPORTATION SYSTEM WITH ALTERNATE SINGLE-CAR RAIL COSTS (OPTION VII)

The cost structure of option VII has the effect of raising the cost of short rail hauls and lowering the cost of longer hauls. Trucks, exclusive of the other transportation modes, carry 4.04 million tons of grain interregionally under option VII compared to no such movements in option I. The quantity hauled by water increases by 210 thousand tons but water traffic declines from 37.39 billion ton-miles in option I to 34.77 billion ton-miles in option VII. Although railroads carry fewer tons, their share of the total ton-miles increases from 69.8 percent in option I to 71.4 percent with the alternative single-car costs of option VII (Table 12.12).

A SHIFT IN THE DEMAND FOR EXPORTS FROM THE GULF TO THE
NORTHWEST PORTS (OPTIONS VIII AND IX)

Recent attention has focused on shifting exports from the ports on the Gulf to ports on the Northwest coast because of grain traffic congestion at the Gulf ports, the increase in exports to countries across the Pacific Ocean, and the upcoming increase in large ships that cannot pass through the Panama Canal and require deep-water ports. Ten percent of the traditional Gulf export demand is reassigned to Seattle under option VIII and 25 percent is reassigned under option IX. Total costs of production and transportation increase by $13 million when 10 percent of the exports are reassigned and by $42 million when 25 percent of the exports are reassigned (Table 12.10). However, these costs relate only to those experienced within the United States. When ocean shipping costs to Japan from the Gulf and Seattle are compared with the price differentials at the ports of export, 25 percent of the wheat, more than 10 percent of the feed grain, and 10 percent of the soybeans exported from the Gulf may be reassigned to Seattle if ships that carry 80,000 tons are used.[45] If very large ships of 150,000 to 200,000 tons

45. The shift for wheat may be larger than if wheat had been disaggregated into its various types. The Asian demand for wheat may not be sufficiently large to accommodate the large exports from the Northwest.

are developed, the savings in ocean shipping costs would justify reassigning even more of the exports. If multiple rail car shipments are used to haul grain to the Northwest ports, even more grain under a least-cost optimizing system would be exported from Seattle for destinations across the Pacific. The reassignment of exports from the Gulf to Seattle results in a substantial increase in the share of the traffic carried by rail (Tables 12.11 and 12.12). The ton-miles of rail traffic increase 5 percent for a 10 percent export demand shift and 6 percent for a 25 percent shift. The study also shows that such a shift will likely change the production location of the exports that are reassigned. The Northern Plains region vis-à-vis other regions of production east of the Rocky Mountains has a geographical advantage for shipping to the Northwest ports. The Corn Belt does not lose its comparative advantage in production but ships more of its production to satisfy domestic demands.

AN INCREASE IN GRAIN EXPORTS (OPTION X)

The cost and quantities of interregional grain flows are sensitive to the level of exports. A 25 percent increase in exports above those in option I, analyzed by means of option X, generates an 8.3 percent increase in the ton-miles of grain traffic and a 6.7 percent increase in transportation costs. The traditional distribution of exports among the ports is used. The shares of the traffic carried by truck and water increase and the share carried by rail declines compared to the basic level of exports in option I (Tables 12.11 and 12.12).

CONCLUSIONS

The most important findings are:

1. The demand for rail transportation by grain in 1980 under the 1972 estimated transportation cost structure will grow as rapidly as grain sales from farms between 1972 and 1980. Given the shortage of rail equipment in 1972, the effective capacity of rail transportation will need to expand more rapidly than grain sales if the demand and supply of equipment to haul grain is to be in equilibrium by 1980. However, an expansion in use of multiple rail car shipments could alleviate the rail car equipment shortage by, in effect, increasing the supply of cars because of a faster turnaround time.

2. Using a rail system with 50-car units for grain shipments generates a transportation cost savings of $68 million compared to a system with single-car units. The 50-car system would also greatly increase the effective capacity of the existing fleet of rail cars. These advantages would more than compensate for the additional assembly costs wherever there is a concentration of grain movements to support a larger volume assembly system.

3. A 20 percent increase in rail costs results in a $147 million increase in grain transportation and production costs, but a 20 percent increase in barging costs results in only a $19 million increase in transportation and production costs. Before the increases in transportation costs, rail has 70 percent and

barges 30 percent of the ton-mile grain traffic. Hence, rail cost changes produce larger impacts than equal percentage changes in barge costs even when the quantities carried by rail and barge are taken into consideration.

4. The use of trucks for interregional grain shipments depends largely on the quantities shipped by a combination of truck and water. More trucking occurs when rail costs for short distances increase. All in all, trucks are used only for movements shorter than 100 to 125 miles under the cost minimization systems represented by the models.

5. Grain carried by rail to points on the waterways is a significant quantity of all grain that moves via the waterways. Using the 1972 transportation cost structure, 21 percent of the 30.28 million tons moved by water are moved in conjunction with rail under option I.

6. Elevator costs of loading and unloading grain average approximately 20 percent of the estimated interregional grain transportation costs. Consequently, such costs are an important part of the total grain distribution costs.

7. Rail is not competitive with water for moving grain produced in the Corn Belt to the Gulf if the production occurs near the waters of the Mississippi River system. When there is a shortage of rail equipment, the substitution of truck-barge movements to the Gulf should be coordinated so that the combined truck-barge method substitutes for those shipments where rail has the least comparative cost advantage.

8. The location of grain production is affected little by changes in transportation costs of the magnitudes examined in this study.[46] However, many of the quantities and their direction of the flow and mode of transportation change. Under the 1972 estimated cost structure (option I), rail carried 116.74 million tons and water 30.28 million tons. Increasing rail costs 20 percent results in rail shipments of 107.98 million tons and water shipments of 38.77 million tons. In contrast, increasing barge costs 20 percent results in rail shipments of 121.86 million tons and water shipments of 24.26 million tons.

9. The use of larger ships and increased exports to countries in the Orient would increase the grain exports flowing through ports on the Northwest coast. This shift could require the rail transportation system to carry 4 billion ton-miles more of grain traffic (a 5 percent increase) than under the traditional distribution of exports among the ports.

10. Changes in the level of exports cause large variations in needed transportation services. Increasing exports 25 percent above the basic level of 81.12 million tons increases the ton-miles of grain traffic 8.3 percent (from 124.62 to 134.96 billion ton-miles). The increase in exports also increases transportation costs $75,807,000—an increase of 6.7 percent. The higher exports are associated with only a 6.5 percent increase in grain production.

11. For some markets, the price of grain for the winter months when the Upper Mississippi River, Missouri River, and Great Lakes are closed is not the same

---

46. The model constrains production activities with a range, and consequently the model excluded major changes in the location of grain production. However, nearly all production activities in the solutions of the first seven options occur at identical levels.

as the price for the remaining months when the waters are open. Depending on the model, the soybean price (exclusive of storage costs) at New Orleans, the market that receives the largest quantities by water, for December through March ranges from 0.1 cent to 5.9 cents per bushel more than during the remaining months of the year. The price of feed grain at New Orleans is the same for both time periods.

Applying a spatial model for the analysis of grain transportation can provide a large amount of information relating to modes of transportation, demand for transportation services, grain flows, and a comparison of transportation networks. Much of the detail pertaining to transportation is obtained by relating the solutions of the spatial linear programming model to information used in the computation of the objective function transportation coefficients. Further research is needed on developing improved transportation cost functions and in specifying storage and seasonality characteristics of the grain industry. Nevertheless, this study shows that spatial models can be applied to questions and policies of transportation.

Index